IRISH LITERATURE
THE NINETEENTH CENTURY

VOLUME III

A NEW ANNOTATED ANTHOLOGY OF EIGHTEENTH AND NINETEENTH CENTURY IRISH LITERATURE

Major new book series which demonstrates the growth, variety and achievement of Irish writing in the eighteenth and nineteenth centuries. Covering prose, poetry and drama, the volumes not only contain work by major authors but also include less obvious material gleaned from sources such as letters, diaries, court reports, newspapers and journals.

Irish Literature
The Eighteenth Century
An Annotated Anthology
Edited and Introduced by
A. Norman Jeffares and
Peter van de Kamp
Foreword by Brendan Kennelly

Irish Literature in the Eighteenth Century illustrates not only the impressive achievement of the great writers—Swift, Berkeley, Burke, Goldsmith and Sheridan—but also shows the varied accomplishment of others, providing unexpected, entertaining examples from the pens of the less well known. Here are examples of the witty comic dramas so successfully written by Susannah Centlivre, Congreve, Steele, Farquhar and Macklin. There are serious and humorous essayists represented, including Steele, Lord Orrery, Thomas Sheridan and Richard Lovell Edgeworth. Beginning with Gulliver's Travels, fiction includes John Amory's strange imaginings, Sterne's stream of consciousness, Frances Sheridan's insights, Henry Brooke's sentimentalities and Goldsmith's charm. Poetry ranges from the classical to the innovative. Graceful lyrics, anonymous jeux d'esprit, descriptive pieces, savage satires and personal poems are written by very different poets, among them learned witty women, clergymen and drunken ne'er-do-wells. Politicians, notably Grattan and Curran, produced eloquent speeches; effective essays and pamphlets accompanied political activity. Personal letters and diaries—such as the exuberant Dorothea Herbert's Recollections—convey the changing ethos of this century's literature, based on the classics and moving to an increasing interest in the translation of Irish literature. This book conveys its fascinating liveliness and rich variety.

Irish Literature
The Nineteenth Century
Volume I
An Annotated Anthology
Edited and Introduced by
A. Norman Jeffares and
Peter van de Kamp
Foreword by Terence Brown

'This anthology is a superlative achievement and for at least a generation is sure to be the outstanding work in its field. Jeffares and van de Kamp bring to their task a fine blend of scholarship, good judgment and innovation. And they have produced a fascinating collection of Irish writing which scholars, students and general readers will find both inviting and accessible.'

James H. Murphy, President of The Society for the
Study of Nineteenth-Century Ireland

This, the first of three volumes, spans the first third of the nineteenth century. It documents Ireland's significant literary contribution to an age of invention, with Thomas Moore's romantic Melodies, Maria Edgeworth's regional fiction, and Charles Maturin's voyeuristic Gothic stories. It witnesses the rise of a quest for authenticity—mapping and transmuting the Gaelic past (in Hardiman's *Irish Minstrelsy*, Petrie's essay on the round towers, and O'Curry's research into Irish manuscripts) and faithfully depicting the real Ireland (in the first-hand accounts of Mary Leadbeater, William Hamilton Maxwell, Asenath Nicholson, the peasant fiction of William Carleton and the Catholic fiction of the Banim brothers). In Jonah Barrington's Sketches it records the demise of the rollicking squirearchy, while in the stories of Lover it portrays the rise of the stage Irishman. But it also offers a selection from political documents and speeches, and from popular writings which were imprinted on the Irish consciousness. These are contextualised by historical documents, and by Irish forays into European Romanticism.

Irish Literature
The Nineteenth Century
Volume II
An Annotated Anthology
Edited and Introduced by
Peter van de Kamp and
A. Norman Jeffares
Foreword by **Conor Cruise O'Brien**

The second of the three volumes roughly spans the middle decades of the nineteenth century, a period dominated by the enormity of the Great Famine. Its terror is recorded in first-hand accounts and in the powerless yet forceful reactions which this cataclysmic event engendered in such writers as John Mitchel (who in his *Jail Journal* pits the self against the state). This volume documents the rise of cultural nationalism, in the work of the contributors to *The Nation* (Davis, Mangan, Lady Wilde), and the Irishness of Unionist intelligentsia in the *Dublin University Magazine*. It juxtaposes the authentic Gaelic voice in translation (Ferguson and Walsh) against the haunting intensity of Mangan and the non-conformism of his fellow inauthenticator 'Father Prout'. It witnesses the stage Irishman in Lever's fiction being placed on Boucicault's popular podium, in his reworking of Gerald Griffin's account of *The Colleen Bawn*. It records the rise of Fenianism (in such writers as Charles Kickham), and it sees Ireland taking stock (in the work of W.E.H. Lecky). It notes the emergence of a new literary confidence in the works of Sigerson and Todhunter. It extends well beyond examinations of Irish identity, not only in encapsulating popular writing, but also by incorporating writers of Irish descent who investigated different cultures.

Irish Literature
The Nineteenth Century
Volume III
An Annotated Anthology
Edited and Introduced by
Peter van de Kamp and
A. Norman Jeffares
Foreword by **Bruce Arnold**

The last of the three volumes roughly spans the last thirty years of the
nineteenth century, a period which saw the emergence of the Land
League, the dynamiting campaign of the Fenians, and the rise and fall
of Charles Stewart Parnell. It witnessed changes in all literary genres.
Standish James O'Grady conveyed a sense of heroic excitement in his
affirmation of Gaelic Ireland's literary heritage. Douglas Hyde
promoted Irish language and culture through his foundation of the
Gaelic League. Writers affiliated with the Irish Literary Society tried
to re-energise Young Ireland's ideals of cultural nationalism. Under
the aegis of Ireland's literary renaissance a new interest in Celticism
became manifest. The year after the publication of Allingham's
Collected Poems, W. B. Yeats's *The Wanderings of Oisin* marked the
emergence of Irish mythology and legend in an elegant, sensuous and
highly influential manner. With Wilde, Shaw, Martyn and George
Moore he expanded Ireland's aesthetic horizons; as Yeats introduced
French *Symbolisme* in *The Secret Rose* and *The Wind Among the
Reeds*, Oscar Wilde preached the paradoxes of decadence, Shaw
uncovered society's hypocrisies, while Martyn embraced Ibsen's
social realism, and Moore combined Zola's naturalism with the
synaesthesia of Totalkunst. Major writers combined to form Ireland's
National Theatre. Pioneers such as Lafcadio Hearn were exploring
different cultures, which were to influence European literature and
drama. The last decades of the nineteenth century were a powerfully
creative period, rich in its literary collaborations, and profoundly
impressive in its vitality.

IRISH LITERATURE
THE NINETEENTH CENTURY

VOLUME III

To Jeanne Jeffares (1921–2006)

Irish Literature
The Nineteenth Century
Volume III

Editors

PETER VAN DE KAMP
AND
A. NORMAN JEFFARES

IRISH ACADEMIC PRESS
DUBLIN • PORTLAND, OR

First published in 2007 by
IRISH ACADEMIC PRESS
44 Northumberland Road, Dublin 4, Ireland

and in the United States of America by
IRISH ACADEMIC PRESS
ISBS, Suite 300
920 NE 58th Avenue
Portland, Oregon 97213-3786

www.iap.ie

© 2007 Peter van de Kamp

British Library Cataloguing in Publication Data
An entry can be found on request

ISBN 978 0 7165 3357 3 (cloth)
ISBN 978 0 7165 3358 0 (paper)

Library of Congress Cataloging-in-Publication Data
An entry can be found on request

Printed by Creative Print and Design, Gwent, Wales

Contents

Contents

Contents

NOTE ON TEXT

Where possible, original spellings, syntax and punctuation have been retained. The editors have, however, made a very small number of necessary textual corrections which do not impair the authenticity of the original text.

Foreword

Between the time of his proposal that I should write this Foreword and the actual writing of these words Derry Jeffares died. The event was a personal loss. He had been my external examiner in Trinity College where I read English at the end of the 1950s. We later had contact, I as an editor and journalist, he as a writer and scholar. His last letter came just weeks before his death. This, when it happened, was told to me by a mutual friend, a poet, and I thought back with sadness over the missed opportunities. It was an intermittent friendship but one based on knowledge of each other's work and respect for achievement. We met over the years and more recently he supported my membership of the club in London to which he belonged, the Athenaeum. This was an appropriate meeting ground for both of us, its authority a neutral influence in any debate upon the "supreme theme of art and song". The club has a fine library and has always had a literary flavour in its membership. The letter suggested a meeting. Sadly, that last suggested meeting never took place.

I know the encounter, which would in part have been about this project, would have reflected something that was at the heart, both of his scholarship and of my fundamental concern writing books about Irish artists and writers. I refer to the defining of Irish literature and of the other arts, as well as their location within the body of criticism, enjoyment and sharing which was always part of his approach to literature and life and which has reached a high point in the present work and its associated volumes.

It is apposite that Derry collaborated on these anthologies with a Dutchman – and not just because Derry's first post-War lecturing job was in Groningen. Peter van de Kamp and Derry shared a mutual acquaintance with Fred Bachrach, professor at Leiden University, where, in the '70s, Peter assisted Bachrach in his research on the journal of Lodewyck Huijgens' diplomatic journeys to England, which epitomizes the Renaissance humanism that formed a bond between Peter and Derry. When they first met, at University College Dublin in the early '80s, this humanism was a catalyst of their instant friendship, just as it informed their scholarship (besides, they liked each other's sense of humour).

Humanism informs their liberal agenda. They were dealing always with a complex set of relationships within the framework of literature written in English but inspired by Ireland. All of the writers whose works appear here were British by definition. They were born in Ireland. Many of them looked to London mainly for the fulfilment of their careers, for work and employment, for publishers or theatre directors. They wrote mainly but not exclusively about Ireland.

It is natural to write about where we come from. It is unnatural to make this a burdensome creative passport, stamped with authorizations and visa defining where we belong and whether we are citizens or denizens of the magic territory. It is inescapable that we draw for our characters and poetic situations on real people known or encountered through early experience and on the loved locations of early happiness. But it is not automatic nor constraining. Shaw and Wilde, for example, took over the society that they had become part of and turned it brilliantly into works that captivated their sophisticated English audiences. George Moore did the same. W.B. Yeats did the opposite. His Irish roots were tenuous and his English experiences during his early years were in the main unhappy so he sought Irish mythical subject matter and he turned Irish people, including his own friends, into the heroes and heroines of his writing.

The issue of qualification has given birth to a huge academic literature. It is not as liberal nor as uplifting as the approach Peter van de Kamp and Derry Jeffares adopt, which is a significant and welcome characteristic of the present volume.

Much modern teaching has become obsessed with the meaning of Irish meaning as it can be applied, not to the real Ireland, portrayed with such richness and diversity in the pages of this and its related volumes, but in respect of a newly constructed Ireland to which its accepted writers need to conform. This new academic territory seems obsessed with the Irishness of what is written and with the nationalist framework into which the writing is fitted.

One of its earliest exponents was Daniel Corkery, whose blunt approach, the best part of a century ago, began a process of definition by exclusion. Under the guise of protecting "the tender national cultures of Europe" he spent many years re-defining a "self-contained" national culture for Ireland. He did it in *The Hidden Ireland* and then did it again in *Synge and Anglo-Irish Literature*. A seminal part of his argument is a sustained attack on Anglo-Irish or Ascendancy literature with the added discrimination between writers who "came from" the Ascendancy and those who "came from" the people. Among these latter he lists Padraic Colum who, though born in a workhouse, was the son of the Master, and therefore from the lower middle class *bourgeoisie*. The crudeness of Corkery's approach has been further refined by three generations of literary critics, not necessarily themselves Irish, but taking on the burden of settling the limits, setting forth the essence, describing the exact meaning of a free creative spirit, some of whose greatest exponents – Joyce, Beckett, Shaw, Wilde, Moore – transcended the bounds of their origins without seriously considering the purpose or effect of what they did in this context, either to Irish literature, or to literature at all. Writers do not, as a rule think like this; critics do.

The spirit of Irish writing as expressed in these pages is a free spirit. The book's rich cavalcade of writers moves across the physical landscape, the landscape of memory and belonging, and all its members are welcome for the joy they impart with their writing rather than because of qualifications to belong to a club. It begins with the joyful, French-influenced lyricism of Arthur William O'Shaughnessy, whose work I learned to love as a schoolboy in the Cotswolds, long before I knew anything more about Ireland than the fact that the whole of its centre was a bog named after someone called Allen. It touches the lyrical poetry and prose world of George Moore, the parallel but different early magic of Oscar Wilde, the endearing comedy of Percy French, the wit and intelligence of Shaw and then comes to its end with an understandable flourish of work from the greatest name of all, in Irish eyes, that of W.B. Yeats.

It is a wholesome, rounded and rich assembly of poetry, prose and dramatic extracts, letters, memoirs and, yes, even criticism. Shaw on Richard Wagner is an inspired example of this last category and includes what might serve as emblematic of the Irish writer's role as it emerged during the time covered by this anthology: "The most inevitable dramatic conception, then, of the nineteenth century is that of a perfectly naïve hero upsetting religion, law and order in all directions, and establishing in their place the unfettered action of Humanity".

Bruce Arnold

Acknowledgements

These volumes grew out of a suggestion made by Prof. Augustine Martin in 1983 to produce a series of Irish Readers. We should like to acknowledge our indebtedness to Prof. Terence Brown (Trinity College, Dublin), Prof. Andrew Carpenter (University College Dublin), Prof. Jacques Chuto (University of Paris XII), Peter Costello (Dublin), Prof. Gary Crawford (Mississippi State University), Prof. Anne Crookshank (Trinity College, Dublin), Prof. Adèle Crowder (Queen's University, Kingston), Prof. Christopher Crowder (Queen's University, Kingston), Paul de Beer (The Hague), Ad de Knegt (Boskoop), Dermot Foley (Drogheda County Library), Dr Oona Frawley (Trinity College, Dublin), Beata Goleńska (Dublin), Prof. Tom Garvin (University College Dublin), Prof. Warwick Gould (University of London), Dr Ruud Hisgen (The Hague), John Wyse Jackson (Wexford), Prof. Colbert Kearney (University College, Cork), Prof. John Kelly (University of Oxford), Prof. Brendan Kennelly (Trinity College, Dublin), Prof. José Lanters (University of Wisconsin), Prof. Peter Liebregts (University of Leiden), Sarah Mahaffy, Daphne Maxwell, Dr Colin Meir (University of Ulster), Edmund Moriarty (Tralee), Prof. James H. Murphy (de Paul University, Chicago), Prof. Neil Murphy (Nanyang University, Singapore), Dr Ellen Shannon-Mangan (Astoria, Oregon), Dr Tadhg Ó Dúshláine (St Patrick's College, Maynooth), Odile Oomen (Zeist), Anna and Christopher Rush (Fife Ness), Prof. Colin Smythe, Dr Bruce Stewart (University of Ulster), Dr Wim Tigges (University of Leiden), Prof. Loreto Todd (University of Ulster), Deirdre Toomey (University of London), and Colette Trace (Tralee).

The librarians of the Athenaeum, the Bodleian Library, Oxford, the British Library, the Central Catholic Library, Ireland, the Irish Jesuit Archive, the National Library of Ireland, Trinity College, Dublin, Trinity College, Cambridge, the University of Chicago, University College Cork, University College Dublin, the University of St Andrews, the University of Stirling, the University of Wisconsin, Kerry County Library, and the Institute of Technology Tralee were indispensable in making material available to us. We should particularly like to thank Eamon Brown (Kerry County Library), Charlotte de Bút, Gerry Long, Gerry Lyne, Jim O'Shea and Nichola Ralston

(National Library of Ireland), Siobhan O'Callaghan (ITT Library), Roy Stanley (TCD Library), and Siobhan O'Dwyer (UCC Library).

Our indebtedness to Caroline Doody and Jeanne Jeffares is too obvious to mention.

The following have kindly granted us permission to reproduce works: Belfast Central Library (for Anna Margaret [Amanda] McKittrick Ros, extract from *Irene Iddesleigh* [chapters 18 and 19]; Curtis Brown (for Somerville & Ross, from *The Real Charlotte* and *Some Experiences of an Irish R.M.*); trustees of the National Library of Ireland (for extracts from Joseph Holloway's Journal); Oxford University Press (for W. B. Yeats, Letter to Katharine Tynan, 17 or 24 September 1887, Letter to Katharine Tynan, 18 November 1887, extract from Letter to Katharine Tynan, ?22–28 September 1888, Letter to John O'Leary, ?25 November 1891, Letter to George Russell [AE], 22 January 1898), Douglas Sealy (for Douglas Hyde, 'Like a Star in the Night', 'The Red Man's Wife', 'Young Breed of the Tresses', 'I Shall Not Die for Thee', and *The Necessity for De-Anglicising Ireland*); Colin Smythe (for Lady Gregory, 'The Day Draws Near', 'What Have I Gained', 'Wild Words I Write', extracts from Diaries 1892–1902, extract from *The Felons of Our Land*; and for George Russell, 'The Earth Breath', 'Janus', 'The Gre Eros', 'Nationality and Cosmopolitanism in Literature', two letters to W. B. Yeats); the Society of Authors on behalf of the Bernard Shaw Estate (for Bernard Shaw, 2 Letters to Ellen Terry, dated 24 June 1892 and 6 April 1896, *Widower's Houses* [Acts II & III], and extracts from *The Perfect Wagnerite*); A.P. Watt Ltd. (for W.B. Yeats, 'The Stolen Child', extract from The Wanderings of Usheen, 'The Lake Isle of Innisfree', 'The Sorrow of Love', 'Apologia addressed to Ireland in the coming days', 'The Fiddler of Dooney', 'The Hosting of the Sidhe', 'The Valley of the Black Pig', 'The Song of Wandering Aengus', 'To The Secret Rose', 'Aedh wishes for Cloths of Heaven', 'The Crucifixion of the Outcast', 'The Adoration Of The Magi', 'The Autumn of the Flesh', 'Dust Hath Closed Helen's Eye'). We have made every effort to trace the copyright holders of Shan Bullock, George Egerton, John Eglington (W. K. Magee), Alice Furlong and D.P. Moran. For further details, see the acknowledgement of copyright permission in the back.

Introduction

I. DIVERSITY

A quick glance at the contents of this volume will reveal that many of the Irish authors who were published in the last twenty years of the nineteenth century continue to be read widely today, their work part of the international canon of great literature and of popular literature too. Shaw and Yeats, winners of the Nobel Prize for Literature, still receive ample critical attention, as do Oscar Wilde and Douglas Hyde; Bram Stoker's vampire story *Dracula* has never gone out of print; Percy French still delights with his playful humour, as do Somerville and Ross with their ever-popular *Irish R.M.* stories—though these two gifted women could also write in deeply tragic vein.

How varied are all these authors in their subjects and styles; how varied, too, their personalities and purposes. These writers were born between 1840 and 1870: that is to say that many of them grew up in the period of the Great Famine and its aftermath. The Famine, justly described by Máire and Conor Cruise O'Brien as 'the great dividing line in modern Irish history', had the effect of altering aspects of the national character as it was portrayed in literature. The Famine, which reduced Ireland's population from approximately eight to five million, was largely responsible for banishing the rollicking, happy-go-lucky, even exuberant life, portrayed in pre-famine novels, to something more sombre, thoughtful and purposeful, and not without a touch of the puritanical. The shift is noticeable in the works of Carleton, who serialised *The Black Prophet* during the Famine, and of Lever, who was more enagé than has been acknowledged.

After the famine years the social balance of the country was altering. English was now spoken in nearly all of Ireland except for some pockets and for areas on the Western seaboard. Education, of which Ireland had not been deprived, combined with an increase in the reading public (which developed from the shared reading of, say, *The Nation*), was shaping new attitudes: these were influenced, especially since Catholic Emancipation, by the greater control priests exercised over their parishioners, by the effects of the Temperance movement, founded in 1838 by Father Mathew, and by the complex results of large-scale emigration. Farmers were replacing landlords, many of whom sold up under the provisions of the Encumbered Estates Act of 1849. Rural prosperity was, admittedly slowly, beginning to replace poverty, and urbanization was steadily increasing.

Irish emigration to America led to the subsequent financial support many of the emigrants sent back to Irish national movements (something continued up to recently). This arose partially from a tradition widely held, not only in Ireland but especially among the Irish-Americans, that England could have done more to mitigate the disastrous effects of the Famine. This tradition is part of a recurrent strain in Irish literature and politics, bringing the past to bear upon the present, though it emerges in different forms, in different contexts.

While Daniel O'Connell had achieved Catholic Emancipation in 1829, his movement for the Repeal of the Union between England and Ireland suffered a severe setback in 1843 when he, very sensibly, realised the likely tragic outcome if he was not to cancel the monster meeting at Clontarf which the government had prohibited. O'Connell had brought popular politics into being by various means, such as processions, brass bands and, especially, mass meetings, but his Repeal movement was considered outmoded by the younger intellectuals who founded the Young Ireland movement with, as their mouthpiece, *The Nation*, the first number of which was published in 1842. The journal was suppressed in 1848, but continued in a second series from 1849 to 1896. It proved extremely influential, boasting a readership of about a quarter of a million at the height of its popularity.

The Young Irelanders looked back on the past for their inspiration, and by 1846 had split with O'Connell over the issue of employing physical force to achieve political change. They included Thomas Davis, whose ballad 'A Nation Once Again' had a powerful effect on current nationalism, John Blake Dillon and Charles Gavan Duffy. Driven by emotional republican rhetoric which drew upon the traditions of past risings, they were also echoing European Romanticism when they argued in favour of more active resistance to English rule. Davis died in 1845. Three years later came the abortive Young Ireland rising, which led to John Mitchel and William Smith O'Brien being transported, while Gavan Duffy was arrested but released in 1849.

II. FENIANS AND THE LAND LEAGUE

Another facet of the continuing impulse to achieve independence appeared with the emergence of the Fenian movement, a revolutionary oath-bound secret society known as the Irish Republican (or Revolutionary) Brotherhood, which James Stephens established in Dublin in 1858. In the following year John O'Mahoney, like Stephens a participator in the Young Ireland Rising of 1848, founded a parallel organization in the United States, the Fenian Brotherhood. This group exemplified clearly a widespread desire to bring past mythology into the contemporary context, for O'Mahoney compared Irish opposition to English rule with the exploits of the legendary Fianna, a mythological band of warriors loyal to Fionn MacCumhaill, the central hero in the Fionn or Ossianic cycle of tales which had been developed in medieval times in Munster and Leinster by story-tellers portraying the life of warrior bands in early Irish societies.

The main Fenian novelist was Charles James Kickham, the author of *Knocknagow*. A nephew of John O'Mahoney, he was arrested in 1865, sentenced to fourteen years' imprisonment, and released in the amnesty of 1869. Another Fenian represented in this volume is John Boyle O'Reilly, who had enlisted in the British army with the purpose of recruiting for the secret Fenian movement. His success led to his arrest and a subsequent death sentence, commuted to life imprisonment. After escaping from Dartmoor, he was recaptured and transported to Australia, but he escaped again and got to America in 1867. There he edited the influential *Boston Pilot*, in which he published many contributors from Ireland, notably Lady Wilde, Oscar's mother, who, as 'Speranza', had been a leader writer for *The Nation* in 1848 (and had announced that war with England had begun), Douglas Hyde, Katharine Tynan and W.B. Yeats.

Another Fenian, John Keegan Casey (whose 'The Rising of the Moon' is included here—the title was later used in one of Lady Gregory's plays in which the song is a key element in the plot) drew upon more recent mythology, that of the 1798 Rising, as did William McBurney in 'The Croppy Boy'. Despite the effect of two failed invasions of Canada in 1866 and 1870 and an abortive rising in Ireland in 1867, Fenianism continued to exist, a hidden but powerful factor in Irish political life, anti-establishment and anti-British. In time it gave rise to various groups, the Invincibles for one, which indulged in terrorism.

A heightened awareness that the basic political question centred upon the ownership or tenancy of land began to take effect. Though Gladstone had disestablished the protestant Church of Ireland in

1869 and passed two Land Acts for Ireland, the first of them in 1870, there was an ever-increasing desire that Ireland should be in charge of its own affairs. In 1871, for instance, Isaac Butt founded the Home Government Association. He had been one of the founders of the *Dublin University Magazine*, which he edited from 1834 to 1838; it provided an impressive forum for intellectual discussion. Butt appealed, perhaps surprisingly, to a relatively conservative element in the Anglo-Irish establishment, especially members of the professional classes. And fifty-nine MPs supported Home Rule by the 1874 elections.

Those who had grown up in the traditions of Young Ireland, of the Fenians, and of the agrarian secret societies, such as the Whiteboys, the Defenders and the Ribbonmen, were now to support the Land League. This was founded in 1879—a time of agricultural and general economic crisis in Ireland—and its telling slogan was 'The Land for the People'. It drew its strength to some degree from threats; intimidation was implicit in its activities. Fenianism had influenced its policy of ostracizing landlords or their agents. The movement was originally driven by John Devoy in America, and by Michael Davitt, whose *Leaves from a Prison Diary* (1884) arose from a gaol sentence given him for gun running in 1870. The alliance of these two men was called the 'New Departure'.

Davitt had been the League's creator when he returned to Ireland in 1879. But a more powerful figure now entered the political arena, Charles Stewart Parnell. He became President of the Home Rule Confederation of Great Britain in 1877, and three years later he was to take over from Isaac Butt the chairmanship of the Irish Parliamentary Party. But before that he had managed to shift the Land League's policies away from the attitudes of the 'New Departure'. Davitt, and Devoy in America, had not thought that the movement for independence should be merely constitutional. The Land League, however, was officially constitutional and Parnell, a protestant landlord and an establishment figure, who was soon to surprise many of his fellow landlords by his political views, began to lead a popular, largely Catholic, movement; he succeeded in directing Irish opposition into parliamentary channels, and he made the Irish Parliamentary Party a highly effective force in Westminster.

Parnell was not only an extremely skilled politician; he was also a most effective orator. He spoke with an easy natural assumption of authority (this is demonstrated in his speeches where he addresses his audience as 'you': not for him the politically correct 'we' that would probably be expected today) and out of a genuine heartfelt desire to ameliorate the lot of all the people. The Land League developed into an efficient organization, employing measures such as boycotting from 1880 on. Westminster responded positively to the Irish socio-political situation, for in 1881 Gladstone's Second Land Act was to alter land ownership and to lead to the Ashbourne Act of 1885 and the Wyndham Act of 1903—all measures which were, in effect, to create a largely peasant proprietorship of the land. The Land Act of 1887 had given the courts power to revise and fix rents; and a Land Purchase Act of 1891 furthered the process.

When the Land League was suppressed in 1881 it was succeeded by the Irish National League, which acted in the interests of the Irish Parliamentary Party. Its suppression also led to the setting up of the Ladies Land League, which manifested Irish women's active interest in political life. Parnell's sister Fanny, who emigrated to America in 1874, had written for *The Nation*, attacking landlordism and publishing Land League songs. She had founded an American branch of the Land League in 1880, a year before she died, and she had persuaded her sister Anna to establish the Ladies Land League in Ireland, a suggestion which met with a whole-hearted response, Anna creating a more extreme organization than the one which had been suppressed. Her brother, however, distrusting her political judgment, soon suppressed the Ladies Land League. Anna Parnell detailed the frustration of her political aspirations in an impassioned account of the Ladies' Land League, which was eventually published as *The Tale of a Great Sham*.

Charlotte Grace O'Brien was less curbed by male-dominated politics. She had been brought up with Young Ireland attitudes; she accompanied her father William Smith O'Brien into exile (after his sentence of death for his role in the Young Ireland rising in 1848 had been commuted to penal servitude in Tasmania) and subsequently returned to the United Kingdom with him when he was pardoned in 1856. She typified the blending of various nationalist traditions. She supported the Land League and Parnell's policies; she wrote trenchant articles in English journals as well as a novel about the Fenian Rising of 1869. But she was most successful in her attempts to reform the disgraceful conditions on the ships which brought emigrants across the Atlantic to America in steerage accommodation.

Some of Emily Lawless's novels echoed the use of past history made by political leaders. She set these novels in various periods. *With Essex in Ireland* (1890) suggested something of the Gaelic tradition in 1575; *Maelcho* (1894) dealt with the Desmond Rebellion which ran from 1570 to 1582; and *The Race of Castlebar* (1914) focussed upon aspects of the activities of the United Irishmen and the 1798 Rebellion. *Grania* (1892), a tale set on the Aran Islands, had emphasized the bullying inherent in a male-dominated society. Emily Lawless realized the significance of the Land War. In her novel *Hurrish* (1886) she drew a picture of the effects of agrarian crime; she presents the peasants as brutal in the extreme and yet she sentimentalizes them.

George Moore's *A Drama in Muslin. A Realistic Novel* was published in the same year as Emily Lawless's *Hurrish*. That year the Plan of Campaign came into being. It was pronounced unlawful in a matter of months, yet it was effective up to 1890. Its methods of collective bargaining stoked up the temperature of the Land War again, not least so because the withholding of rents on various estates sometimes gave rise to violence. The ensuing evictions and the misery they caused have been evocatively described in Maud Gonne's autobiographical *A Servant of the Queen* (1938).

Turbulence was increasing throughout the country and its presence provided a sinister, threatening background in *A Drama in Muslin*. Moore had laid the foundation of this novel in the winter of 1883–84 on a return visit to Moore Hall, his ancestral home in Co. Mayo, and greatly enjoyed the publicity he engendered by publishing in the *Freeman's Journal* his correspondence with the authorities in Dublin Castle, complaining that he had not been invited to a State dinner party. In the novel he observed the landlords' hypocrisy and the peasants' frustration, contrasting life in wretched cabins and glittering salons. He condemned the plight of girls in the 'marriage market'; he described the tinsel nature of the Viceregal court, presenting in exuberant language the Levee, the Ball and other social events of the Season, paying particular attention to the dresses of the ladies and the activities of the dressmakers. He followed this novel with the sketches of *Parnell and his Island* (1887), and then came his *Confessions of a Young Man* (1888), a flamboyant account of aestheticism in Paris, a book designed to shock the bourgeoisie.

III. GOING FOREIGN

Some Irish writers found their subjects in societies outside Ireland. While the only one of Bram Stoker's novels to be situated in Ireland was *The Snake's Pass* (1891), the action of which was placed in Co. Mayo, six years later he was to draw upon his mother's memories of the spread of cholera in the West of Ireland to heighten the dramatic tensions of his vampire tale *Dracula* (1897), which was set in the remote, mysterious mountainous region of Transylvania. Sheridan Le Fanu, like Maturin before him, had already explored gothic terror along with the supernatural, notably in his play *Carmilla* (1871). He may well have been an inspiration for Stoker, who, in what W.J. McCormack has called 'an ever-shifting discontinuous chronicle of fascination and pursuit', employed a technique of attributing parts of his story to different narrators, adding in telegrams, part of letters and diaries, as he drew contrasts between Count Dracula's haunted countryside, its physical isolation and its stark wildness, with the apparent respectability of Victorian London.

Lafcadio Hearn, on the other hand, considered himself outside the norms of the nineteenth-century Anglo-Saxon world; outside Ireland, he explored and wrote about the French West Indies before finding in Japan material for reverence, his self-abnegation satisfied in a flowing style, fluid in its procession of delicately described detail as he expressed his admiration for a society that seemed to him to have an inclusive culture, uniting the material and the spiritual.

Stoker and Hearn went far afield for subject matter that seemed strange to their readers; others found themselves within the sphere of French attitudes. Arthur O'Shaughnessy, for instance, was influenced by French poetry in his interest in the erotic, notably by the lays of Marie de France, while Chopin's music also attracted him—forces reflected in his 'Ode' of 1874, one year before Walter Pater in *The Renaissance* wrote that 'all art constantly aspires towards the condition of music':

> We are the music makers,
> And we are the dreamers of dreams,
> Wandering by lone sea-breakers,
> And sitting by desolate streams;—
> World-losers and world-forsakers,
> On whom the pale moon gleams:
> Yet we are the movers and shakers
> Of the world for ever, it seems.[1]

This interest in French sensibilities was part and parcel of the 1890s, heralded in Irish writing by George Moore's *Confessions of a Young Man*, while the *Yellow Book* in London was publishing much to shock staid Victorians (among them George Russell, who responded fiercely to the news that Yeats was going to write for the magazine: 'I never see *The Savoy* nor do I intend to touch it. I will wait until your work is

---

1. See pp. 32–04

published in other ways. I don't want to get allied with the currents of people with a sexual mania like [Arthur Symons] or that ruck'). Explicit sensuousness and sexual frankness were features of the fiction of George Egerton (Mary Chavelita Dunne), a New Woman of the times. Like George Moore, she explored the potential of the musical line in her finely crafted stories in *Keynotes* (1893) and *Discords* (1894). Her best novel, *The Wheel of God* (1898), is written with assurance and self-confident panache. The plight of women in a patri-archal society also forms the subject of the New Woman writings of Sarah Grand. Her trilogy, *Ideala* (1888), *The Heavenly Twins* (1893) and the loosely autobiographical *The Beth Book* (1897) caused consid-erable stir in Victorian England. But where Sarah Grand explores the potential of women's self-development within, or despite, the confines of marriage, Egerton radically queries the validity of the institution.

IV. STANDISH O'GRADY

While some writers were assimilating foreign influences, Irish lore was fuelling the literary imagination. In the late eighteenth century, Charlotte Brooke, Joseph Cooper Walker and Edward Bunting had given a new kind of life in English translations, histories and collections of music; now a fresh impetus was given to the study and appreciation of the Gaelic past with all its rich store of mythology and legend.

This began prosaically enough on a rainy afternoon which kept Standish James O'Grady indoors on a visit where by chance he came across Sylvester O'Halloran's *A General History of Ireland* (1874). Reading O'Halloran triggered his interest in the sources of Irish myths and legends, and set him to four years of intense study in preparation for writing his *History of Ireland: The Heroic Period* (1878), which con-tained versions of mythological tales and of the Ulster Red Branch Cycle.

O'Grady followed it with a series of books designed to capture popular attention with their often verbose, sometimes high-flown style, which Yeats was to describe as 'a kind of blazing torch light'. These included *Early Bardic Literature, Ireland* (1879); *History of Ireland: Cuculain and his Contemporaries* (1880); *History of Ireland: Critical and Philosophical* (1881); and *Cuculain: an Epic* (1882). In these he showed the influence of earlier translators, Sir Samuel Ferguson among them, and of Eugene O'Curry's *Manners and Customs of the Ancient Irish* (1873). His novels conveyed something of the excitement he experienced in his discovery of Irish material. They included *Red Hugh's Captivity* (1889), *Finn and his*

Companions (1892), *In the Wake of King James* (1896) and a trilogy about Cuchulain (1894, 1901, 1920). O'Grady treated the Cuchulain material somewhat stiffly and was careful to emasculate much of the original material, giving it more than a touch of Victorian morality.

Some critics have regarded him as the father of the Irish Literary Renaissance, the development which was to shape new attitudes and ambitions in Irish authors. It was, of course, political as well as cultural in its aims, though these aims naturally varied from person to person, as we see when we consider some of those who were associated with this new way of thinking and writing about Ireland.

While O'Grady was busily creating his vision of Ireland's past, stressing the heroism and the nobility of its heroes, especially in the books he had aimed at children, such as *Finn and his Companions*, he was providing the imaginative stimulus which so inspired other Irish writers. He was also arguing in leading articles in the Dublin *Daily Express* and in the journals he edited, the *Kilkenny Moderator* and the *All-Ireland Review*, that the Anglo-Irish had a duty to play their part in bringing a new Ireland into being.

V. WILDE AND SHAW

Some authors followed the route taken since the close of the seventeenth century by Irish dramatists who found their métier in writing for London audiences, holding up mirrors to the social life they found there but often with a decidedly satiric or comic slant. They may have been uneasily pulled between Ireland and England, but they were completely at home in the comedy of manners.

Oscar Wilde was one of these dramatists. He progressed from *Poems* (1881) through the skilful narration of stories originally intended to amuse his children, *The Happy Prince and Other Tales* (1888) to the more sophisticated technique and subject matter of *Lord Arthur Savile's Crime and Other Stories* (1892). *The Picture of Dorian Gray* (1891), with its insistence on cultivating, in Pater's words, 'not the fruit of experience but experience itself', was a novel which provided the first sign of a wide recognition of his genius.

His talents had, of course, been appreciated earlier, when he was an undergraduate at Trinity College, Dublin, and after that at Magdalen College, Oxford, where he won the Newdigate Prize for poetry. At Trinity he came under the influence of Sir John Mahaffy, the classical scholar and celebrated conversationalist. It was he who had advised Oscar to go to Oxford, saying 'You are not clever enough for us here'.

At Oxford, 'the most flower-like time' of his life, Wilde was exposed to the aesthetic theories of Walter Pater and the more moral attitudes to art taken by John Ruskin. While displaying a deep interest in Freemasonry, he also found himself fascinated by Catholicism, and he flirted with ideas of conversion. Like his character Dorian Gray he was attracted by ritual, and his play *Salomé* (1893) was to demonstrate how he could be affected by religion. An expression of the then-predominantly French artistic fascination with the *femme fatale*, *Salome* was to inform Richard Strauss's opera, and Yeats's haunting later plays, *A Full Moon in March* and *The King of the Great Clock-Tower*.

Wilde's plays catapulted him into widespread fame. They were the immensely successful work of four years: *Lady Windermere's Fan* (1891), *A Woman of No Importance* (1893), *An Ideal Husband* (1895) and *The Importance of Being Earnest* (1895). These were comedies of manners, dazzling in coruscating wit, masterly in paradox and brilliant in stagecraft. Wilde's irreverence exposed the contradictions he observed in the social life of the English upper classes in his time.

His own life became a drama, sin and guilt being part of Wilde's continuous journey to self-discovery. Out of this was to come *De Profundis* (published, posthumously, in 1905), written while he was serving two years penal servitude for homosexuality and cast in the form of a letter to his lover Lord Alfred Douglas, offering some explanations, some excuses, some self-defence. But *The Ballad of Reading Gaol*, written in 1897–98 and published anonymously in 1898 under his prison number, demonstrates not only the classical nature of his own reversal of fortune but his ability to empathise with and convey the sufferings of others.

Like Wilde, George Bernard Shaw followed the traditional journey Irish dramatists had long made to London. He too enjoyed portraying the English to themselves. And, again like Wilde, he owed a great deal to the nature of unorthodox parents. Wilde's mother was a creation of immoderation, an extravagant, flamboyant figure, who, as 'Speranza' had moved from Unionism to fervent nationalism; his father, Sir William Wilde, distinguished surgeon and archaeologist, deserved his raffish reputation. In effect, they were a sanction for their son's own eccentric and exotic behaviour. Shaw's father was not distinguished ('We were downstarts', Shaw once said, describing his own family in contrast to its richer relatives) but though a financial failure and an alcoholic, he had a true sense of comedy, an appreciation of anti-climax and the absurd, as well as a delight in the unexpectedness of irony. From his mother Shaw got his deep interest in music, reinforced by her friendship with George Vandeleur Lee, a conductor and creator of the Dublin

Amateur Musical Society. After a brief but successful experience in business, Shaw left Dublin when offered remarkable promotion and advanced on London, living there with his mother and George Vandeleur Lee, who had moved there earlier from Dublin. Shaw became an influential music and theatre critic, writing trenchantly under the name Corno di Bassetto; he tried his hand at novels which were not successful—*Cashel Byron's Profession* was the best of them—and then, despising the current state of the English theatre, began to deploy in his plays his own blend of socialism, hatred of social hypocrisy, and comic wit against the conventional attitudes of London audiences. His essay *The Quintessence of Ibsenism* (1891) had heralded his intentions. His first play was *Widowers' Houses* (1892), which he included in *Plays Pleasant and Unpleasant* (1898). There followed the *Three Plays for Puritans* (1901). They were shaped by his skilful inversion of normal dramatic techniques to illustrate his own socio-economic politics. He was attacking the evils of prostitution, the conditions prevailing in factories and the slums occupied by the workers, puncturing in the process Victorian codes of respectability, romanticism, and heroism—the last the subject of the ever-fresh humour of *Arms and the Man* (1894).

As he wrote, influenced in part by his admiration of Wagner's music, Shaw was developing the theory which was to inform much of his work after the turn of the century. The 'Life Force'—a form of creative evolution—was founded upon a satirical, often sceptically pessimistic, view of human life. This had surfaced in his earlier plays' portrayal of personal relationships to such a degree that Shaw eventually seemed dominated by a desire to indulge his intellectual preoccupations—with philosophical questionings, and social problems—at the expense of human emotion.

VI. THE MATTER OF IRISH FICTION

Irish fiction offered a podium for various creeds. Patrick Augustine Sheehan stressed the need for an assertion of orthodox Catholicism, especially in the Irish rural parishes he knew so well. He was also concerned about the maintenance of Catholic teaching at a high level—something stressed in his *Geoffrey Austin, Student* (1895) and *The Triumph of a Failure* (1899). His later novels were to explore Catholicism in relation to such subjects as trade unionism. He saw the Church as likely to provide the kind of stability that he thought was needed in the Ireland of his day. The serious purpose behind his fiction sometimes makes the novels seem unduly sermonising and over-didactic, the notable exception being *My New Curate* (1900), where he presents a sympathetic depiction of two priests, contrasting the reforming energy of the one with the settled inertia of the other. Throughout his writing he created an impression of gentleness, belying the control that the Catholic Church had begun to exert after the Famine. It was against this Jansenist Puritanism that so many writers were to rebel in the early days of the Irish Free State.

Another type of Irish Catholicism is presented by Rosa Mulholland, whose fiction falls within the ambit of Victorian respectability. She was launched by Charles Dickens, who published her novel *Hester's History* in *All the Year Round*, and brought out his own *No Thoroughfare* alongside her *The Late Miss Hollingford*. Mulholland did not embrace cultural separatism. In *Marcella Grace* (1886), a novel dealing with the Land War, she advocates the replacement of the Protestant Ascendancy by a Catholic gentry. The moral dilemmas faced by the peasantry form a recurrent subject in her later fiction.

Very different indeed from such Catholic fiction was that of Somerville and Ross, reaching back in some respects to the robust comic effects of Charles Lever's early novels, in their stories of Major Yeates, Resident Magistrate, an Englishman set down in the countryside of West Cork and often bewildered by the complexities of its social and commercial life. The authors well understood how to construct effective stories and how to extract the full measure of comedy from the situations they created so skilfully. 'The House of Fahy' is perhaps the finest example of their use of gentle irony.

Their novels were another matter. Just as Charles Lever's later work (unread by those who pilloried him for amusing English readers with his stage-Irishmen) turned to a more tragic, even elegiac portrayal of the decline of the Anglo-Irish, so Somerville and Ross anatomized the crumbling of the ascendancy world in their masterpiece *The Real Charlotte* (1894). Like Lever, they came in for considerable criticism: The *Freeman's Journal* typified their fiction as 'Lever gone mad', but 'too grotesque to be offensive'. *The Real Charlotte* captured the nuances of social life not only through the action of this tragic story but by the convincing nature of the characters' conversations. It delineated the Irish countryside with loving care—Edith Somerville had trained as an artist in London and continued to draw and paint throughout her life—and they applied a fine sense of comic irony to their stories, setting the action in varying backgrounds suitable to the moods they were evoking, from those of gothic gloom in their first novel *An Irish Cousin* (1889) to the cheerful energy which drove their hunting stories.

Edith Somerville continued to write after her cousin Violet Martin ('Martin Ross') died, but while in *The Big House at Inver* (1925) she developed an idea which Violet Martin had adumbrated after visiting Tyrone House, and envisaging the decline of a family over several generations, she did not bring to this novel the same 'knife-edged slice of sarcasm' that she attributed to her cousin (nor to *Mount Music*, which had preceded it in 1919, an assessment of how Ireland changed after the Wyndham Land Act). That particular gift of Violet Martin had invested the complexity of *The Real Charlotte* with its satiric sharpness as it scrutinized the fast-changing world of the 1890s.

Very unlike them was Jane Barlow, another of the authors who brought memories of the past into the present. Her lugubrious novel *Kerrigan's Quality* (1894) looked back at the Famine and evictions from the point of view of an emigrant who returned to Ireland from Australia. This novel came after she had looked, in her *Irish Idylls* (1892), somewhat cursorily at problems in the relationships between tenants and landlords; these stories were followed by other collections, among them *Strangers at Lisconnel* (1895) and *A Creel of Irish Stories* (1897). Barlow brought a sense of tragedy to bear upon her West of Ireland subjects. Her treatment could at times become melodramatic, and her use of Hiberno-English (learnt from Katharine Tynan) now seems strained and overly self-conscious, but she did successfully present the sense and stricture of a local Irish community.

VII. TOWARDS A LITERARY RENAISSANCE

The earliest singers in Ireland's literary renaissance were women who were inspired by the cause of Ireland. Patriotism formed the subject matter for Ethna Carbery's work. She was yet another to be influenced by the past, by the Fenian movement, writing nationalist poetry with ease, and publishing in *The Nation, Young Ireland* and *The Shamrock*. In 1896, in Belfast, she, and her friend Alice Milligan, founded the short-lived monthly, *The Shan Van Vocht*, which they edited and managed. Primarily political in intent, this nationalist journal contained rousing lyrics and ballads, many of them written by Carbery. It featured translations of Irish songs by Douglas Hyde. It ran into resistance from Ulster Unionism. Carbery's work generated excitement beyond its literary merit. She made her poetic facility subservient to the national agenda.

Another writer who never fully exploited her literary talent was Katharine Tynan, who was a member of the Ladies Land League. She wrote poems which convey simply, and at best impressionistically, her love of nature. Her own distinctive character and her devout Catholicism inform many of her poems. She was stoutly encouraged in her writing by her father, a successful cattle farmer and a staunch— financial—supporter of Parnell, whose powerful personality Yeats would depict in his story 'A Knight of the Sheep'. In the 1880s, Andrew Cullen Tynan established a literary salon for his daughter on his farm, Whitehall, Clondalkin. It became a hospitable gathering place for many talented young people, among them Yeats, AE and Douglas Hyde. Katharine Tynan's friendship with Father Matthew Russell, who edited *The Irish Monthly* and *The Irish Fireside*, led to the publication of some of her friends' work. Coaxed by his father, Yeats, reluctantly, seems to have gone down to Whitehall to make a marriage proposal, but she was secretly engaged to Henry Albert Hinkson, whom she married in 1893. Her husband did not obtain steady employment until he became a Resident Magistrate for Mayo in 1914; and she, having to boil the pot, spread her creative energy over a staggering number of novels, stories, articles and poems. She tested her friendship with Yeats by her candid picture of 'Willie' in the first, and the most revealing of her reminiscences, *Twenty-Five Years* (1913), illustrated with substantial chunks from his letters (for which she had not asked his permission). He professed to forgive her, but then she vilified him in print for his depiction in 'The Tragic Generation' of Lionel Johnson as a drunkard. Yeats refused to write the introduction to the Macmillan edition of her *Collected Poems*, which was published in 1930 (AE obliged), and after her death he referred to her in a letter as an ignorant peasant woman.

There was a great deal of varied writing in the 1880s and 1890s. A.P. Graves's *Father O'Flynn and Other Irish Lyrics* appeared in 1889, and the following year came Percy French's *The First Lord Liftinant and Other Tales*. Theirs were portrayals of Irish life irradiated by a joyous delight in the form of lightly satirical humour. Their light-hearted affectionate regard for their subject matter differed in its detachment from many of the other inspired cultural manifestations of the time, such as the Gaelic Athletic Association, which was found-ed in 1892, and the Gaelic League, founded in 1893.

Douglas Hyde was the first President of the Gaelic League. The son of an Irish country rector, he had grown up in an Irish-speaking area at Frenchpark, Co. Roscommon—as an undergraduate at Trinity College, Dublin, he was known to dream in Irish. There he discovered his intense desire to preserve the Irish language; he began to publish his own poems in Irish, under the signature 'An Craoibhín Aoibhinn' (The

Delightful Little Branch), and to write about the need to support Irish as a means of achieving national self-respect. This led to his cogent, outspoken Inaugural Address to the National Literary Society, 'The Necessity for De-Anglicising Ireland', in which he takes a moral stance against popular 'shilling-shockers'. He published a collection of stories, riddles and rhymes which he had gathered from Irish speakers, providing texts and translations in *Leabhar Sgéaluigheachta* (1889). The next year he published *Beside the Fire*, a collection of Gaelic folk lore; then came the *Love Songs of Connacht* (1893) with a scholarly and stimulating commentary and literal translations. He subsequently wrote a magisterial *Literary History of Ireland* (1899). In the twentieth century his career was to include a Professorship of Modern Irish, membership of the Irish Senate (1925–26) and subsequently the position of first President of Ireland in 1938. Brian O'Nolan (Flann O'Brien), as Myles na gCopaleen, questioned his command of the Irish language.

VIII. WILLIAM BUTLER YEATS

While Hyde was firmly establishing the intellectual history and standing of Gaelic culture and drawing attention to the richness of its oral traditions, Yeats, who knew no Irish, was synthesizing Gaelic material into his—symbolist—vision of an Irish intellectual and artistic identity. Like so many others, Yeats was influenced by political history; his mentor was the old Fenian John O'Leary, who had returned to Dublin from exile in 1885. O'Leary offered his protegé a podium, encouraging him to review for John Boyle O'Reilly's Boston *Pilot*, and for *The Gael*, the organ of the Gaelic Athletic Association. O'Leary's *Recollections of Fenians and Fenianism* (1896) conveys something of his dignity and detachment, and explains why Yeats was so influenced by his attitudes. He guided Yeats in his reading; in it he found the exciting material of myth and legend, all new to him, which would allow him to escape from the staid English literary tradition into the vitality of Irish writing. In this he thought he would fuse pagan and Christian thought. His long poem *The Wanderings of Oisin* (1889) showed what he could achieve with 'new' Irish subject matter, matching it with his development of an original beauty of style influenced especially by Pre-Raphaelitism, and tinged with his own dreamy melancholia.

Gaelic mythology and legend as well as local folklore and tradition could, Yeats thought, stimulate and shape Irish writing in English into a distinctive expression of Ireland's spiritual and cultural heritage. He embarked upon a crusade to get his aims into being: writing reviews and articles, making speeches and compiling books such as *Fairy and Folk Tales of the Irish Peasantry* (1888) and *Irish Fairy Tales* (1892); he founded Irish literary societies in London and Dublin. In 'What Then?', a poem written in 1937, he was to describe, rightly, his 20s as 'crammed with toil'.

What distinguished Yeats from his peers was his insistence on universal literary standards. For most Irish writers, literature was a means to a political end, proof of Ireland's 'nationality'; this, for him, amounted to literary exploitation. Few writers could match his fastidious standards—as his *Poems and Ballads of Young Ireland* (1888), and, to a lesser degree, *A Book of Irish Verse Selected from Modern Writers* (1895) demonstrate.

Yeats was not impervious to influence. Standish James O'Grady, Sir Samuel Ferguson, and the learned team whom that fine artist and scholar George Petrie had gathered round him in the days of the Ordnance Survey—among them Eugene O'Curry, John O'Daly, John O'Donovan and James Clarence Mangan—were all useful to him. Among his contemporaries he respected and learned from Douglas Hyde. Eleanor Hull, who founded the Irish Text Society, and later Kuno Meyer, also aided his intellectual progress with Gaelic material. Arthur Symons deepened his insight into French writing, to which O'Leary had introduced him.

Yeats's own poetry, however, remained *sui generis* with its haunting rhythms, its often dragging cadences. An early—and subsequently famous—poem, 'The Lake Isle of Innisfree', is a good example of this originality, set in the Sligo countryside which he loved and where he spent a good deal of his youth. Then there were the many memorably beautiful poems celebrating his hopeless love for (and life-long obsession with) Maud Gonne, whom he first met in 1889. Perhaps the best—and loveliest—of this devoted defeatist love poetry is to be found in 'He Wishes for the Cloths of Heaven'.

Like Maud Gonne, he had been attracted by, and was involved in, revolutionary movements (both were members for a time of the IRB), but after experiencing the Jubilee riots in Dublin in 1897, and becoming disillusioned with the nationalists when he chaired the Centenary Association to commemorate the '98 Rising and Wolfe Tone, he was to dissociate himself from this kind of politics. At school he had already become interested in Indian thought, and immersed himself in occult studies. In his 20s he edited Blake. He was steeped in Swedenborg and Boehme, and in the workings of the Order of the Golden Dawn, a Rosicrucian occult society. All the while he was studying Gaelic literature, and became influenced by the French *Symbolistes,* as mediated by his friend Arthur Symons. Like Wilde before him—by whose writings and studied manner he was impressed—he fell under the spell of Walter Pater, his own prose progressing from the simple transparent narrative style of his first novels, notably *John Sherman* (1891) to the elaborate allusive expression of the stories of *The Secret Rose* (1893). His criticism, too, became esoteric, even extravagant in the fin-de-siècle mood of the 1890s. But he could also write arrestingly dramatic stories in this period, such as 'The Crucifixion of the Outcast', which is imbued by his studies in the occult.

In 1893 he had published *The Celtic Twilight* and the title of this volume gave a name to the romantic, wistful and melancholic style, misty in outline, which he had successfully created and which was soon being copied, deplorably, by others. His poetry, like his prose, became more allusive and more decorative as he made more use of symbolism, drawing upon his extensive and varied reading in many genres. It reached a consummate expression in *The Wind Among the Reeds* (1899). Looking back at his writings in the nineteenth century from the new attitudes he developed in his middle and late period, the poet, who, more than any writer, had radically changed his style time and again (a quality which T.S. Eliot singled out as Yeats's distinctive strength) remarked: 'We all got down off our stilts'.

There were many reasons for this. There was perhaps the basic one to be expected at the end of a century, so neatly expressed by Dryden at the close of the seventeenth century, ''Tis well an old age is out / And Time to begin a new'. But there were other forces at work in Ireland, bringing about change. One arose out of a desire for a new kind of drama. Yeats had written verse plays from his teens and his *The Land of Heart's Desire* was produced as a curtain raiser for Shaw's *Arms and the Man* in 1894. Creating an Irish theatre had seemed a dream, but then his burgeoning friendship with Lady Gregory led to practical progress. He was staying with her at Coole Park in 1897, the second of many visits—for he was to spend most of his summers there, working and enjoying the orderly life of this Big House. Her interest in folklore led her to bring him out gathering folk beliefs and folk tales in the neighbouring countryside. The effect of this exposure to the simple but idiomatic colloquial speech of the Galway country-people was subsequently to show him a way out of the tangled over-involved prose he had been writing.

IX. A NATIONAL THEATRE

It was at a now-famous meeting at the house of Lady Gregory's neighbour, the Count Florimond de Basterot, that the idea of an Irish national theatre was born. Another of Lady Gregory's neighbours was Edward Martyn, a landlord living in Tulira Castle, his ancestral home, an admirer of Ibsen, who shared Yeats's and Lady Gregory's literary zeal. While Lady Gregory set to work on having the law changed so that plays could be performed outside the two Dublin theatres which had previously held the only patents, Martyn acted as guarantor of the Irish Literary Theatre. In effect the Irish dramatic movement was now launched and by 1904 it was to lead to the establishment of the Abbey Theatre.

Martyn involved his cousin George Moore in the venture as its third director. Like Shaw, Moore loathed the conventional English theatre of the time, thought dramatic criticism was in a sorry state, and (unlike Bram Stoker, who had become Henry Irving's business partner and manager) heartily disliked and distrusted the power of the great actors and actor managers. He had been stirred by the formation and ideals of the Gaelic League, and even, briefly, tried to learn Irish. He now enthusiastically supported the ambitions and hopes of Yeats, Martyn and Lady Gregory.

In 1899 Moore directed the productions of the first two plays, Martyn's *The Heather Field* and Yeats's *The Countess Kathleen*. The Irish theatre, Yeats wrote later, could not have been founded without his help, his knowledge of the stage. A few years before, Moore had won wide fame for *Esther Waters* (1894), his naturalist novel about horse-racing (about which he knew a great deal, his father having successfully run a stable) and about the vulnerability of women—and of the poor—in contemporary life. In his period in Paris he laid the foundations for his excellent, perceptive art criticism, collected and published as *Modern Painting* (1893). His 'café education', which had extended from 1877 to 1880, also comprised the methods of the French naturalists, with which he opposed the sentimental school of novelists. So, originally influenced by Balzac and, particularly, Zola, by Degas, Huysmans and Flaubert, he brought to Ireland cosmopolitan concepts of art, literature and music. His self-confidence led him to take over Martyn's patriotic play *The Bending of the Bough*, produced in 1900, and to collaborate with Yeats in *Diarmuid and Grania*, performed the next year.

X. FRIENDSHIPS AND QUARRELS

Moore could be quarrelsome and Yeats obstinate and astute. By 1902

Moore had, in Yeats's phrase, dropped out of the movement. Having moved from London to Dublin in 1901 he was to provide the sharp observation of the Turgenev-like stories of *The Untilled Field* (1903) and *The Lake* (1905), in which he interwove memories in his prose's melodic line, before proceeding to his masterpiece, the three volumes of *Hail and Farewell* (1911, 1912, 1914), in which he provided magnificently mischievous and malicious, yet also appreciative, portraits of his friends and of the literary, artistic and social life of Dublin.

Moore's highly idiosyncratic work illustrated the close and complex relationships of Irish writers. They lived in a closely knit society where authors were fully exposed to the reactions of others: some friendly, some antagonistic, some encouraging, some discouraging. Their personal associations and friendships, their intimacies and often shifting alliances, were a significant factor in the great flowering of Irish writing which was developing at the end of the nineteenth century. 'Great hatred, little room' was Yeats's pithy comment on the Irish scene; George Russell sagely remarked, in more formal fashion, that 'the trouble about literary movements in any country is that there are only two or three writers of genius and they hate each other, because they see different entities'.

The various differences that occurred between authors at this time were not just intense: they could often be entertaining. Yeats, for instance, described Martyn and Moore as bound one to the other by mutual contempt. He told Martyn that Moore had good points but Martyn replied that he knew Moore a good deal longer than Yeats did, and no: he had no good points. Moore thought Martyn the most selfish man alive because he thought Moore was damned and didn't care. Yeats later put their friendship into a play, *The Cat and the Moon* (1924). He had many scores to pay back, for Moore compared him to a cunning rook enticing Martyn, a profound owl, from his belfry, and described him as a huge umbrella left behind by some picnic party. His full revenge came after Moore's death, in *Dramatis Personae* (1936).

Moore had mocked Lady Gregory's friendship with Yeats, jibing at their joint collection of folklore which was to lead into Lady Gregory's Kiltartan English, modelled on the Hiberno-English spoken locally in her area of Co. Galway. She wanted to be a writer; she had already given expression to her capacity for passionate love (for Wilfrid Scawen Blunt) in 'A Woman's Sonnets', which she gave Blunt the morning after their last night together. The affair remained a well-kept secret, the sonnets published ten years later, though not under her name, in Blunt's *Proteus*. She had edited, but she thought editors dull, and found collaboration with Yeats more exciting. She wanted to be seen to support Irish nationalism, deeply respecting Douglas Hyde, agreeing, like Yeats, Moore and George Russell, with the Gaelic League's anti-English views, paralleled by its presenting Ireland as a place where elevated thoughts and a sense of honour held sway. She edited *Ideals in Ireland* (1901), essays based upon hopes that as it developed the literary movement would harbour varied views.

Lady Gregory used the stylized simplicity of her Kiltartan English to promote the esteem of the Gaelic tradition, which she shared with Standish O'Grady. This was to lead to her fine translations, notably in *Cuchulain of Muirthemne* (1902) and *Gods and Fighting Men* (1904), while she built up her collection of folk material to compile the two volumes of *Visions and Beliefs in the West of Ireland*, which were to appear later, in 1920. Before the turn of the century, however, she had applied an emergent dramatic skill, using the idiomatic speech she invented to give Yeats's plays a direct, apparently authentic, folk speech, the collaboration first emerging in the new century in his *Cathleen Ni Houlihan* (1902) and *The Pot of Broth* (1904).

Yeats's friendship with Lady Gregory not only gave him personal stability but her collaboration was vital to the success of the Irish theatre. In addition to providing numerous plays her social self-confidence and standing gave weight to her conscientious administrative skills. As well as the often creative tensions that arose between writers with their ensuing jealousies and negativities, there were many friendships. Yeats and Lady Gregory had many friends.

For years, Katharine Tynan was one of Yeats's close friends. His youthful letters to her convey something of the intensity which shaped his early poetry. But when she called on him in London in 1893, to interview him for *The Sketch* she found the gentle, shy, youthful Willie Yeats she had known in Dublin had changed. Shedding his provincialism, extending the range of his friends in London, who now included Lionel Johnson, Arthur Symons, and Florence Farr, he had acquired a dignified, studied manner, making himself into what he thought a poet should be. Besides, he was now obsessed with Maud Gonne (not even the brief attempt at alleviating his passion for her by his affair with Mrs Shakespear had worked) and under the spell of MacGregor Mathers, the occultist.

Yeats's friendship with Lady Gregory lasted until her death in 1932. His relationship with George Russell was to prove more complex. They had met in the Dublin Metropolitan School of Art and continued to work in the Royal Hibernian Academy. Russell shared Yeats's deepening interest in mysticism; they wrote plays in friendly rivalry. Yeats brought him to see Katharine Tynan, who found him 'extraordinarily interesting. Another William Blake?' Russell had begun to experience waking visions, had joined the Theosophical Society, and painted fluent representations of the images that rose in his imagination, usually of radiant spirit beings. His first published poems, in *Homeward: Songs by the Way* (1894), were irradiated by images of light, ethereal in their evocation of spiritual and visionary states.

By 1897 Russell was involved in linking his idealism with the realities of Irish life, working for the Irish Agricultural Organization Society, and becoming an influential figure in the Cooperative Movement. He had earlier resisted sharing Yeats's enthusiastic desire for a new literary expression of Irish culture, withdrawing into a consciousness of his own will and centre, the need to guide his soul into a literature that would transcend Irish nationalism. Despite this difference in aim, the two young men praised each other's work in generous terms; they were, Yeats was later to remark perceptively, bound together by 'the antagonism that unites dear friends'. After he had gone to London in 1887, Yeats strove to keep their friendship in being, though the two slowly realized how different were their attitudes to spiritual enquiry (like Moore, Russell could often ridicule Yeats's eccentricities). In 1891 Yeats wrote 'An Irish Visionary', an article on Russell; though AE's name is not mentioned in this at his request we have in the article a forerunner of many enthusiastic pieces written by Irish writers about each other, propaganda engendered by the shared excitement about the literary movement—indeed, Yeats did not escape the accusation of log-rolling.

In 1895 his appreciation of Russell seems to have peaked, and he became more critical of his friend. They held differing views about the collective consciousness, and while Russell shrewdly realized that Yeats often mistook symbolism for mysticism, he did not understand the reasons behind Yeats's increasing preoccupation with the occult. They had, in effect, lasting disagreements, though Russell's dedication of *The Earth Breath* (1897) to Yeats, and Yeats's dedication of *The Secret Rose* (1897) to Russell marked something of a reconciliation. It was in 1897 that Yeats had urged Russell to apply for the position in the Irish Agricultural Organization Society, hoping this would defuse some of his theosophical enthusiasm—he was to become the model for Yeats's strange invented character Michael Robartes. By 1903 they were often arguing over the rituals Yeats was devising, in cooperation with Maud Gonne, for a Celtic Order of Mysteries to be located in the empty castle on Lough Key in Co. Roscommon.

A deeper division, however, was caused by their different attitudes to the theatre. Russell (like Maud Gonne later) thought Yeats was devoting energy to it that should have gone into his poetry while Yeats disliked Russell's belief that what was needed was merely the creation of an amateur group, and was to dislike even more Russell's encouragement of lesser (often Celtic Twilight) poets. By 1898 Yeats had himself moved away from supporting a Celtic style of poetry in favour of an Irish one. Russell disapproved strongly of Moore's influence, not least in the rewriting of Yeats's play *The Shadowy Waters*. The friendship between Russell and Yeats thus became cool. Its vicissitudes have been most ably charted by Peter Kuch in *Yeats and AE*.[1]

Tensions within the Theatre Society ran deep. Factions clashed: Arthur Griffith and Maud Gonne, with the republican sufragette group she founded in 1900 (Inghinidhe na hÉireann) promulgated nationalism; Russell, who wanted an amateur theatre, propagated local talent; Yeats and Lady Gregory, supported by the Fay brothers, and later by J.M. Synge, proffered an international perspective and reputation.

The arguments increased, as the movement developed. For instance, W.K. Magee, the librarian who wrote as 'John Eglinton', was dubious about many aspects of the Revival, attacking Yeats's vision of Celtic poets inspired by legend and folklore. He shared Martyn's preference for literature that related to contemporary life. A controversy ensued in the Dublin *Daily Express*, which reveals the differences developing in various writers' attitudes to subjects and style. Yeats, for instance, was changing, moving away from the ideas he had expressed in *The Autumn of the Flesh* (1898), telling Russell in a letter that he now regarded his early poetry and 'the prevailing decadence' as 'sentiment and sentimental sadness, a womanish introspection'.

These arguments were part and parcel of the lively intellectual processes at work in Ireland during the last years of the nineteenth century (and were to continue into the twentieth century with no abating of gusto). It was a period when writers were self-consciously formulating a new Irish culture which drew upon Gaelic material. At the turn of the century Yeats realized that the vague mistiness of the Celtic Twilight had to be replaced by a new clarity. A hard, even harsh, light was needed to illuminate the reality of Irish life, while allowing sufficient scope for variety of expression: poetic drama as well as peasant realism. And then, of course, there was a developing audience ready for the fiction and fantasy of the coming century. It was a time of flux and creation.

---

1 Peter Kuch, Yeats and A.E.: *The Antagonism that Unites Dear Friends* (Gerrards Cross, Bucks. Colin Smythe; Totowa, UJ: Barnes & Noble Books, 1986).

JOHN BOYLE O'REILLY (1844–90)

Born at Dowth Castle, Co. Louth, where his father was the schoolmaster at the national school of Viscount Netterville's institution for widows and orphans, he was educated by his father and apprenticed at the age of 11 to the Drogheda *Argus*, taking the place of his ailing brother. In 1859 he became the compositor of the Preston *Guardian*; he worked there as a journalist, became a member of the Irish Republican Brotherhood, and enlisted, aged 19, in the 10th Huzzars as an agent for the IRB. He converted some eighty of its soldiers to the Irish revolutionary cause. He was arrested in 1866, and sentenced to be shot. The sentence was commuted to twenty years' penal servitude. Two years later, before being transported to West Australia, he escaped from Dartmoor, made his way to America on a whaler, and settled in Boston, where he then worked as a journalist. He became editor and part-owner of the Boston *Pilot*, recruiting contributions from W.B. Yeats*, Douglas Hyde*, Lady Wilde and Katharine Tynan*. His own poetry included odes on the common soldier; he wrote verse commemorations of national celebrations. An honorary degree was conferred on him by the University of Notre Dame, Indiana. O'Reilly died on 10 August 1890, at Boston, from an overdose of chloral.

From *Songs, Legends and Ballads*

(1878)

A Kiss

Love is a plant with double root,
    And of strange, elastic power:
Men's minds are divided in naming the fruit,
    But a kiss is only the flower.

To-Day

Only from day to day
    The life of a wise man runs;
What matter if seasons far away
    Have gloom or have double suns?

To climb the unreal path,
    We stray from the roadway here;
We swim the rivers of wrath
    And tunnel the hills of fear.

Our feet on the torrent's brink,
      Our eyes on the cloud afar,
We fear the things we think,
      Instead of the things that are.

Like a tide our work should rise—
      Each later wave the best;
To-day is a king in disguise,[1]
      To-day is the special test.

Like a sawyer's work is life:
      The present makes the flaw,
And the only field for strife
      Is the inch before the saw.

A Disappointment

Her hair was a waving bronze, and her eyes
      Deep wells that might cover a brooding soul;
And who, till he weighed it, could ever surmise
      That her heart was a cinder instead of a coal?

From *Complete Poems and Speeches*

(1891)

Constancy

'You gave me the key of your heart, my love;
      Then why do you make me knock?'
'Oh, that was yesterday, Saints above!
      And last night—I changed the lock!'

A Message Of Peace

There was once a pirate, greedy and bold,
      Who ravaged for gain, and saved the spoils;
Till his coffers were bursting with bloodstained gold,

---

1 *To-day is a king in disguise*: 'The days are ever divine.... They come and go like muffled and veiled figures, sent from a distant friendly party; but they say nothing; and if we do not use the gifts they bring, they carry them as silently away.'—*Emerson*. [O'Reilly's note.]

And millions of captives bore his toils.
Then fear took hold of him, and he cried:
    'I have gathered enough; now, war should cease!'
And he sent out messengers far and wide
    (To the strong ones only) to ask for peace.

'We are Christian brethren!' thus he spake;
    'Let us seal a contract—never to fight!
Except against rebels who dare to break
    The bonds we have made by the victor's right.'

And the strong ones listen; and some applaud
    The kindly offer and righteous word;
With never a dream of deceit or fraud,
    They would spike the cannon and break the sword.

But others, their elders, listen and smile
    At the sudden convert's unctuous style.
They watch for the peacemaker's change of way;
    But his war-forges roar by night and by day.

Even now, while his godly messengers speak,
    His guns are aflame on his enemies weak.
He has stolen the blade from the hand of his foe,
    And he strikes the unarmed a merciless blow.

To the ends of the earth his oppression runs,
    The rebels are blown from the mouths of his guns.
His war-tax devours his subject's food;
    He taxes them evil and taxes their good;
He taxes their salt till he rots their blood.
    He leaps on the friendless as on a prey,
And slinks, tail-down, from the strong one's way.
    The pharisee's cant goes up for peace,
But the cries of his victims never cease;
    The stifled voices of brave men rise
From a thousand cells; while his rascal spies
    Are spending their blood-money fast and free.

And this is the Christian to oversee
    A world of evil! a saint to preach!

A holy well-doer come to teach!
　　　A prophet to tell us war should cease!
A pious example of Christian peace!

The Infinite

The Infinite always is silent:
　　　It is only the Finite speaks.
Our words are the idle wave-caps
　　　On the deep that never breaks.
We may question with wand of science,
　　　Explain, decide and discuss;
But only in meditation
　　　The Mystery speaks to us.

Heart-Hunger

There is no truth in faces, save in children:
They laugh and frown and weep from nature's keys;
But we who meet the world give out false notes,
The true note dying muffled in the heart.

O, there be woeful prayers and piteous wailing,
That spirits hear, from lives that starve for love!
The body's food is bread; and wretches' cries
Are heard and answered: but the spirit's food
Is love; and hearts that starve may die in agony
And no physician mark the cause of death.

You cannot read the faces; they are masks,—
Like yonder woman, smiling at the lips,
Silk-clad, bejewelled, lapped with luxury,
And beautiful and young—ay, smiling at the lips,
But never in the eyes from inner light:
A gracious temple hung with flowers without—
Within, a naked corpse upon the stones!

O, years and years ago the hunger came—
The desert-thirst for love—she prayed for love—
She cried out in the night-time of her soul for love!

The cup they gave was poison whipped to froth.
For years she drank it, knowing it for death;
She shrieked in soul against it, but must drink:
The skies were dumb—she dared not swoon or scream.
As Indian mothers see babes die for food,
She watched dry-eyed beside her starving heart,
And only sobbed in secret for its gasps,
And only raved one wild hour when it died!

O Pain, have pity! Numb her quivering sense;
O Fame, bring guerdon! Thrice a thousand years
Thy boy-thief with the fox beneath his cloak
Has let it gnaw his side unmoved, and held the word;
And she, a slight woman, smiling at the lips,
With repartee and jest—a corpse-heart in her breast!

ARTHUR WILLIAM EDGAR O'SHAUGHNESSY (1844–81)

Born in London, he was educated privately. He spent his working life in the British Museum, first, from 1861, as a junior assistant in the library, and from 1863 as an assistant in the zoological department, where he became an expert in herpetology. He was a friend of Dante Gabriel Rossetti and Ford Madox Brown, and married the sister of the English poet Philip Bourke Marston. With her he wrote *Toyland* (1875), a book of tales for children. His first collection of poetry, *An Epic of Women and other Poems* (1870), illustrated by J.T. Nettleship, shows the influence of French poetry in its sensuous imagery—he has been compared to Swinburne, whose fascination for the sinful erotic he shared (the 'femme fatale' charms in such poems as 'Daughter of Herodias' and 'Chaitivel'), but also to Chopin, whom he resembled physically as well as in his dreamy evocations. This collection was followed by *Lays of France* (1872), adapted from the medieval verse romances of Marie de France, and *Music and Moonlight* (1874). He was an accomplished writer of French, and an informed admirer of its *belle-lettres*. Shortly before his death, he became the English correspondent for *Le Livre*.

From *An Epic of Women and other Poems*

(1870)

Palm Flowers

In a land of the sun's blessing,
    Where the passion-flower grows,

My heart keeps all worth possessing;
    And the way there no man knows.

—Unknown wonder of new beauty!
    There my Love lives all for me;
To love me is her whole duty,
    Just as I would have it be.

All the perfumes and perfections
    Of that clime have met with grace
In her body, and complexions
    Of its flowers are on her face.

All soft tints of flowers most vernal,
    Tints that make each other fade:
In her eyes they are eternal,
    Set in some mysterious shade.

Full of dreams are the abysses
    Of the night beneath her hair;
But an open dawn of kisses
    Is her mouth: O she is fair.

And she has so sweet a fashion
    With her languid loving eyes,
That she stirs my soul with passion,
    And renews my breath with sighs.

Now she twines her hair in tresses
    With some long red lustrous vine;
Now she weaves strange glossy dresses
    From the leafy fabrics fine:

And upon her neck there mingle
    Corals and quaint serpent charms,
And bright beaded sea-shells jingle
    Set in circlets round her arms.

There—in solitudes sweet smelling,

Arthur William Edgar O'Shaughnessy

Where the mighty Banyan[1] stands,
I and she have found a dwelling
    Shadowed by its giant hands:

All around our banyan bowers
    Shine the reddening palm-tree ranks,
And the wild rare forest flowers
    Crowded on high purple banks.

Through the long enchanted weather
    —Ere the swollen fruits yet fall,
While red love-birds sit together
    In thick green, and voices call

From the hidden forest places,
    And are answered with strange shout
By the folk whose myriad faces
    All day long are peeping out

From shy loopholes all above us
    In the leafy hollows green,
—While all creatures seem to love us,
    And the lofty boughs are seen

Gilded and for ever haunted
    By the far ethereal smiles—
Through the long bright time enchanted,
    In those solitudes for miles.

I and She—at heart possessing
    Rhapsodies of tender thought—
Wander, till our thoughts too pressing
    Into new sweet words are wrought.

And at length, with full hearts sinking
    Back to silence and the maze
Of immeasurable thinking,
    In those inward forest ways,

---

1 *the mighty Banyan*: not a palm tree, but the *ficus bengalensis*, an Indian fig tree with branches that throw out their own roots which in turn become parent trees. A banyan on the banks of the Nerbudda was described by Alexander the Great's admiral as being so immense that it could shelter seven thousand men.

We recline on mossy couches,
    Vanquished by mysterious calms,
All beneath the soothing touches
    Of the feather-leaved fan-palms.

Strangely, with a mighty hushing,
    Falls the sudden hour of noon;
When the flowers droop with blushing,
    And a deep miraculous swoon

Seems subduing the whole forest;
    Or some distant joyous rite
Draws away each bright-hued chorist:
    Then we yield with long delight

Each to each, our souls deep thirsting;
    And no sound at all is nigh,
Save from time to time the bursting
    Of some fire-fed fruit on high.

Then with sudden overshrouding
    Of impenetrable wings,
Comes the darkness and the crowding
    Mysteries of the unseen things.

O how happy are we lovers
    In weak wanderings hand in hand!—
Whom the immense palm forest covers
    In that strange enchanted land;

Whom its thousand sights stupendous
    Hold in breathless charmed suspense;
Whom its hidden sounds tremendous
    And its throbbing hues intense

And the mystery of each glaring
    Flower o'erwhelm with wonder dim;—
We, who see all things preparing
    Some Great Spirit's world for him!

Under pomps and splendid glamour

Of the night skies limitless;
Through the weird and growing clamour
Of the swaying wilderness;

Through each shock of sound that shivers
The serene palms to their height,
By white rolling tongues of rivers
Launched with foam athwart the night;

Lost and safe amid such wonders,
We prolong our human bliss;
Drown the terrors of the thunders
In the rapture of our kiss.

By some moon-haunted savanna,
In thick scented mid-air bowers
Draped about with some liana,
O what passionate nights are ours!

O'er our heads the squadron dances
Of the fire-fly wheel and poise;
And dim phantoms charm our trances,
And link'd dreams prolong our joys—

Till around us creeps the early
Sweet discordance of the dawn,
And the moonlight pales, and pearly
Haloes settle round the morn;

And from remnants of the hoary
Mists, where now the sunshine glows,
Starts at length in crimson glory
Some bright flock of flamingoes.

———————

O that land where the suns linger
And the passion-flowers grow
Is the land for me the Singer:
There I made me, years ago,

Many a golden habitation,
  Full of things most fair to see;
And the fond imagination
  Of my heart dwells there with me.

Now, farewell, all shameful sorrow!
  Farewell, troublous world of men!
I shall meet you on some morrow,
  But forget you quite till then.

From *Music and Moonlight*

(1874)

Ode

We are the music makers,
  And we are the dreamers of dreams,
Wandering by lone sea-breakers,
  And sitting by desolate streams;—
World-losers and world-forsakers,
  On whom the pale moon gleams:
Yet we are the movers and shakers
  Of the world for ever, it seems.

With wonderful deathless ditties
We build up the world's great cities,
  And out of a fabulous story
  We fashion an empire's glory:
One man with a dream, at pleasure,
  Shall go forth and conquer a crown;
And three with a new song's measure
  Can trample a kingdom down.

We, in the ages lying
  In the buried past of the earth,
Built Nineveh with our sighing,
  And Babel itself in our mirth;
And o'erthrew them with prophesying
  To the old of the new world's worth;
For each age is a dream that is dying,
  Or one that is coming to birth.

Arthur William Edgar O'Shaughnessy

A breath of our inspiration
Is the life of each generation;
    A wondrous thing of our dreaming
    Unearthly, impossible seeming—
The soldier, the king, and the peasant
    Are working together in one,
Till our dream shall become their present,
    And their work in the world be done.

They had no vision amazing
Of the goodly house they are raising;
    They had no divine foreshowing
    Of the land to which they are going:
But on one man's soul it hath broken,
    A light that doth not depart;
And his look, or a word he hath spoken,
    Wrought flame in another man's heart.

And therefore to-day is thrilling
With a past day's late fulfilling;
    And the multitudes are enlisted
    In the faith that their fathers resisted,
And, scorning the dream of to-morrow,
    Are bringing to pass, as they may,
In the world, for its joy or its sorrow,
    The dream that was scorned yesterday.

But we, with our dreaming and singing,
    Ceaseless and sorrowless we!
The glory about us clinging
    Of the glorious futures we see,
Our souls with high music ringing:
    O men! it must ever be
That we dwell, in our dreaming and singing,
    A little apart from ye.

For we are afar with the dawning
    And the suns that are not yet high,
And out of the infinite morning
    Intrepid you hear us cry—
How, spite of your human scorning,

Once more God's future draws nigh,
And already goes forth the warning
That ye of the past must die.

Great hail! we cry to the comers
From the dazzling unknown shore;
Bring us hither your sun and your summers,
And renew our world as of yore;
You shall teach us your song's new numbers,
And things that we dreamed not before:
Yea, in spite of a dreamer who slumbers,
And a singer who sings no more.

CHARLOTTE GRACE O'BRIEN (1845–1909)

Born at Cahirmoyle, Co. Limerick, she was the younger daughter of William Smith O'Brien, the nationalist politician. At her father's release from penal servitude in Tasmania, the family lived in Brussels. They returned to Cahirmoyle in 1856, and, after her mother's death in 1861, she was his constant companion until his death in Bangor in 1864. Charlotte returned to Cahirmoyle, looking after her brother's children until his remarriage in 1880. She then moved to Foynes, Co. Limerick, devoting herself fully to her writing. *Light and Shade* (2 vols, 1878) is a tale of the Fenian rising of 1867. The famine of 1879–80 induced her to embrace politics. She became a firm supporter of Parnell and of the Land League, and wrote trenchant essays for the *Nineteenth Century* and the *Pall Mall Gazette*. A reading of J.F. McGuire's *The Irish in America* prompted her to campaign for legislation to improve shipboard conditions for female emigrants. In 1881 she founded a large boarding house at Queenstown. She made several crossings to America as a steerage passenger in order to inspect conditions. *Lyrics* (1886) presents the plight of the emigrants. In later life she converted to Catholicism.

From *Lyrics*

(1886)

Sonnet—Outliving Love

(1870)

The water as I passed was reddened o'er
With tiny sheaths shed from the bright-green beach,

Which gathered into fleets in every reach,
Or hid themselves 'mid young leaves by the shore,
Their weary days remembered now no more.
When, clinging each to each and fold on fold,
They wrapped their tender nurslings from the cold,
And brought them to their joys 'mid trials sore.
Poor things! Forgotten now 'mid flowers and Spring,
You fill me with a shadow of dark fears,
That love may lessen with the growing years,
And that the changing hours that hour may bring,
When death shall seem the only good thing left,
To me, in loneliness, of love bereft.

From *Selections from her Writings and Correspondence*

(1909)

from The Feminine Animal

(c. 1890)

...We have now come to it that through the classes in which life is artificial the term 'old maid' is no longer one of reproach, whereas one daily hears teeming motherhood lamented almost as a scandal. A woman in herself, and by herself alone, is required to be as hard and as well able to combat with the world as man. Half the female world in London society is running a race with old maidhood; the male world, on the other hand, is looking on cheerfully and speculating. They say, 'It's a pity, but it can't be helped.' Now, I believe that to a large extent it can be helped, and will be helped, and that, in the natural course of things, women are being rapidly compelled to see that the chances of marriage are becoming fewer and fewer in society; they are forced to face the necessity of making their own lives, and I believe it is the best thing that could possibly happen to them, and that, instead of making them harder and more manlike, it will restore to them the womanhood they are in danger of losing, in their present time of waiting on the men who do not come and that, as every one knows, shameful though it may be to say, is exactly what all the idle girls in London and elsewhere are doing. How *can* they do it? idling, amusing themselves, with their senses perfect and their youth and their education and strength, and all the work of the world crying to them. It is enough to make the blood flame to think of it, and to see what women are making of this society they create—for it is their creation, this artificial society. A man wants to be well fed and well clothed, and with that most men are content. But women! What will satisfy them?—servants and carriages, silks and satins. The actual thing they possess is nothing, but they must equal or exceed their neighbour in every ridiculous display. They make marriages impossible by their vanity and emulation.

Now, I picture to myself a state of things when a young and strong woman shall be ashamed of a life of idleness and self-indulgence, or even want of definite work as a man is or ought to be—when, instead of the present division between the sexes, both shall be workers, going in and out together—when men shall meet and respect women in professional life, when they shall see women able to live alone and poorly in lodgings or chambers—then, once again, the woman will become, as she is now among the poor, a help-meet for man, not a burden. Then women will go out to lands where men are now brutalised by their absence. Then the balance of the sexes will recover itself as the dangers and hardships of life are shared more equally, for more men are actually born into the world than women, though boys are more hard to rear than girls. Every symptom that I can see of the increasing freedom of a young woman reassures me that we are only in a transition stage. Would to God that with their desire of freedom their sense of responsibility for the gift of life were also increasing! but freedom is the first step to all progress, national or individual.

If my words can carry influence in this Ireland, let me say to every mother—If you wish your girls a happy life and a happy marriage, teach them that they are responsible to God for every power of brain or body they possess; that idleness is shame in man and woman alike, and that a girl may be as beautiful in plain and pure living as she can be decked in every absurd fashion. Let her make herself as charming as she can, so long as it does not interfere with her working life. A pretty picture here comes to my mind of the Italian girls in peasant costume, all sweet and clean, with bunches of real flowers in their hair, and carrying on their heads the lemon baskets of their washing. Take them as examples. Adorn as much as you like, but let the basis be work and cleanliness, truth, modesty, and pure womanhood.

EMILY LAWLESS (1845–1913)

Born at Lyons Castle, Co. Kildare, the daughter of Sir Nicholas Lawless, who later became the third Lord Cloncurry, she was educated in England and the West of Ireland. Hers was a troubled family: her father and two of her sisters committed suicide; another sister became a recluse, and her brothers led dissolute lives. Emily suffered from clinical depression, and was a noted eccentric. But she was also thoroughly independent, and a born rebel who remained a loyalist. She travelled extensively through rural Ireland. Her fiction has a historical dimension. In 1885 she published *Ireland: The Story of the Nations.* Her first novel, *Hurrish* (3 vols, 1886) deals with agrarian crime during the Land War. It was admired by Gladstone. *With Essex in Ireland* (1890) provides glimpses of the old Gaelic order through the eyes of one of Essex's Englishmen during the campaign of 1575. *Grania: The Story of an Island* (2 vols, 1892) is set on the Aran Islands, and tells the struggle of a girl in a domineering, and heartless, male society. *With the Wild Geese* (1902) consists of ballads and lyrics about Irish wars and, in their aftermath, the exploits of the exiled Irish earls on Europe's battle-fields. She wrote the first authoritative study of Maria Edgeworth, in 1904. Trinity College, Dublin conferred a D. Litt. on her. In 1909 she moved to Surrey.

From *With the Wild Geese*[1]

(1902)

After Aughrim[2]

She said, 'They gave me of their best,
They lived, they gave their lives for me;
I tossed them to the howling waste,
And flung them to the foaming sea.'

She said, 'I never gave them aught,
Not mine the power, if mine the will;
I let them starve, I let them bleed,—
They bled and starved, and loved me still.'

She said, 'Ten times they fought for me,

---

1 The 'Wild Geese' was the name for the Irish soldiers who migrated to the Continent before and after the battle of Aughrim, and the surrender of Limerick in 1691. They were the forerunners of a great exodus of Irishmen. Between 1691 and 1745, 150,000 are said to have died in the service of France alone. Others fought for Spain and Austria.
2 The Battle of Aughrim (12 July 1691), in which the Williamite army defeated the Jacobites, was the bloodiest battle ever fought in Ireland. The total losses of the Jacobites exceeded seven thousand.

Ten times they strove with might and main,
Ten times I saw them beaten down,
Ten times they rose, and fought again.'

She said, 'I stayed alone at home,
A dreary woman, grey and cold;
I never asked them how they fared,
Yet still they loved me as of old.'

She said, 'I never called them sons,
I almost ceased to breathe their name,
Then caught it echoing down the wind,
Blown backwards from the lips of Fame.'

She said, 'Not mine, not mine that fame;
Far over sea, far over land,
Cast forth like rubbish from my shores,
They won it yonder, sword in hand.

She said, 'God knows they owe me nought,
I tossed them to the foaming sea,
I tossed them to the howling waste,
Yet still their love comes home to me.'

from The Desmond War[1]

Dirge of the Munster Forest. 1581[2]

Bring out the hemlock! bring the funeral yew!
The faithful ivy that doth all enfold;
Heap high the rocks, the patient brown earth strew,
And cover them against the numbing cold.
Marshal my retinue of bird and beast,

---

1 'The poems on the Desmond War refer to that terrible time … when during the Geraldine Rebellion between 1579 and 1581 the civil war which had broken out between the Butlers and the Fitzgeralds in 1565, one acting with the English and the other with the Irish, was intensified by the great Earl of Desmond joining the Irish. Pelham and Ormonde, the Government commanders, laid the whole of *Munster* under fire and sword, and hunted the peasants like foxes through the woods and hills.' [*from Stopford A. Brooke's Preface to* With the Wild Geese (*London: Ibister, 1902*).]

2 '*The Dirge of the Munster Forest* deals with the fact that when the rebellion was over the destruction of the Munster woods was seriously taken in hand, because of the shelter they afforded to the last but one of the Desmonds and to his starving followers.' [*from Stopford A. Brooke's Preface.*]

Wren, titmouse, robin, birds of every hue;
Let none keep back, no, not the very least,
Nor fox, nor deer, nor tiny nibbling crew,
Only bid one of all my forest clan
Keep far from us on this our funeral day.

On the grey wolf I lay my sovereign ban,
The great grey wolf who scrapes the earth away;
Lest, with hooked claw and furious hunger, he
Lay bare my dead for gloating foes to see—
Lay bare my dead, who died, and died for me.

For I must shortly die as they have died,
And lo! my doom stands yoked and linked with theirs;
The axe is sharpened to cut down my pride:
I pass, I die, and leave no natural heirs.
Soon shall my sylvan coronals be cast;
My hidden sanctuaries, my secret ways,
Naked must stand to the rebellious blast;
No Spring shall quicken what this Autumn slays.
Therefore, while still I keep my russet crown,
I summon all my lieges to the feast.

Hither, ye flutterers! black, or pied, or brown;
Hither, ye furred ones! Hither every beast!
Only to one of all my forest clan
I cry, 'Avaunt! Our mourning revels flee!'
On the grey wolf I lay my sovereign ban,
The great grey wolf with scraping claws, lest he
Lay bare my dead for gloating foes to see—
Lay bare my dead, who died, and died for me.

JOHN KEEGAN CASEY (1846–70)

Casey was born at Milltown, Co. Westmeath, the son of a schoolmaster. In the 1850s the family moved to Gurteen, Co. Longford, where John became a monitor at his father's school. When he was 16, his first poems appeared in *The Nation* under the pseudonym 'Leo'. He became a frequent contributor, and also wrote poetry for the *Irishman*, and *Irish People*. He published his first collection, *A Wreath of Shamrocks*, at the age of 20. It was followed three years later by the popular *The Rising of the Moon, and Other Ballads, Songs and Legends*. A monitor at his father's school in Gurteen, he became a teacher in Cleraune and Kenagh, Co. Longford. He left teaching and became a commercial traveller in Castlerea (where he met Mary Briscoe, his future wife), and a clerk in Dublin (where he joined the Fenians). He was detained under the Habeas Corpus Suspension Act in 1867, and was released eight months later under the proviso that he would leave Ireland. He stayed in Dublin, posing as a Quaker named Harrington. He died on St Patrick's Day from a haemorrhage of the lungs two years after his release. The prison doctor made public the extent of the injuries which Casey had incurred in gaol, and the Government was forced to hold a Commission of Inquiry. His funeral in Dublin was a nationalist demonstration said to have been attended by 50,000 people. He was buried at Glasnevin beside the Young Irelander Terence Bellew M'Manus.

The Rising of the Moon

A.D. 1798

(1864)[1]

Air—'The Wearing of the Green'

I.

'Oh, then, tell me, Shawn O'Ferrall,[2]
    Tell me why you hurry so?'
'Hush! *ma bouchal*,[3] hush, and listen;'
    And his cheeks were all a-glow:
'I bear ordhers from the Captain—
    Get you ready quick and soon,
For the pikes must be together,
    At the risin' of the Moon.'

II.

'Oh, then, tell me, Shawn O'Ferrall
    Where the gath'rin' is to be?'
'In the ould spot by the river,
    Right well known to you and me;
One word more—for signal token,
    Whistle up the marchin' tune,
With your pike upon your shoulder,
    By the risin' of the Moon.'

---

1 Published in *The Nation*, 24 Dec. 1864.
2 'Just outside the borders of old Meath, to the north-west, was the nation of the O'Farrells, namely Upper and Lower Annalee (Aingle), and now corresponding with the diocese of Ardagh'. [*from Flann Fitzgerald's Preface to* The Rising of the Moon; and other ballads, songs and legends (*Dublin: M.H. Gill and son, Ltd., 1933*).]
3 *ma bouchal*: 'my boy'.

III.

Out from many a mud-wall cabin
  Eyes were watching thro' that night;
Many a manly chest was throbbing
  For the blessed warning light.
Murmurs passed along the valleys,
  Like the *banshee*'s lonely croon,
And a thousand blades were flashing
  At the risin' of the Moon.

IV.

There, beside the singing river,
  That dark mass of men were seen—
Far above the shining weapons
  Hung their own beloved 'Green.'
'Death to ev'ry foe and traitor!
  Forward—strike the marchin' tune
And hurrah, my boys, for freedom!
  'Tis the risin' of the Moon.'

V.

Well they fought for poor old Ireland,
  And full bitter was their fate—
(Oh, what glorious pride and sorrow
  Fills the name of Ninety-Eight)
Yet, thank God, e'en still are beating
  Hearts in manhood's burning noon,
Who would follow in their footsteps
  At the risin' of the Moon!

Maire, My Girl!

(1865)[1]

Air—'Margread ni Chealleadb'

I.

Over the dim blue hills
  Strays a wild river,
Over the dim blue hills
  Rests my heart ever—

1 First published in *The Nation*, 17 June 1865.

Dearer and brighter than
    Jewels and pearl,
Dwells she in beauty there,
    Maire, my girl.

II.

Down upon Clare's heath
    Shines the soft berry—
On the brown harvest tree
    Droops the red cherry—
Sweeter thy honey lips,
    Softer the curl
Straying adown thy cheeks,
    Maire, my girl.

III.

'Twas on an April eve
    That I first met her—
Many an eve shall pass
    Ere I forget her;
Since, my young heart has been
    Wrapped in a whirl,
Thinking and dreaming of
    Maire, my girl.

IV.

She is too kind and fond
    Ever to grieve me,
She has too pure a heart
    E'er to deceive me.
Were I Tyrconnel's chief,[1]
    Or Desmond's earl,[2]
Life would be dark, wanting
    Maire, my girl.

---

1 *Tyrconnel 's chief*: Richard Talbort, 1st earl of Tyrconnell (1630–91), prominent Catholic leader, loyal to James II. After the Battle of Aughrim (12 July 1691), he wanted to continue fighting William III, but he died on 14 August.
2 Desmond's earl: the title of earl of Desmond was held by descendants of Thomas fitz Maurice (d. 1213). Their lands covered a substantial part of Munster. They fought against Tudor centralization in the Desmond rebellions (1569–73, 1579–83).

V.

Over the dim blue hills
  Strays a wide river,
Over the dim blue hills
  Rests my heart ever;
Dearer and brighter than
  Jewels or pearls,
Dwells she in beauty there,
  Maire, my girl!

CHARLES STEWART PARNELL (1846–91)

Born at Avondale, Co. Wicklow, the second son of the nationalist John Henry Parnell and Delia Tudor, daughter of Commodore Charles Stewart of the United States navy, he was educated privately in England, and at the University of Cambridge. The hanging of the Manchester Martyrs in 1867 made him turn to politics. He was returned for Meath in 1875; two years later he started his obstructionist policies, with night-long filibustering. He was elected president of the National Land League, established, in 1879, with the aid of the I.R.B. and Clan-na-Gael, to fight rackrents and to promote ownership of the land by the tenants. That year he embarked on an extended tour of America, in order to garner Fenian support. In 1880 he was returned for Meath, Mayo and Cork (and sat for the latter). In September he made a speech at Ennis in which he introduced a method of public intimidation which became known as 'boycotting' (after its first important victim, Captain Boycott of Lough Mask, Co. Galway). Parnell had supported the Liberal Leader, William Gladstone, during the elections, but after the introduction of the Coercion Bill and the Land Act, which fell short of the Irish party's demands, he joined the opposition. As agrarian violence escalated, he was incarcerated in Kilmainham Gaol. From prison he issued a manifesto calling on the tenants to pay no rents until he and his followers were released. The government responded by suppressing the Land League, but the country was in turmoil, and Gladstone had to make a conciliatory compact, known as the 'Kilmainham Treaty', that led to the release of the Land Leaguers. On 6 May, the day that Michael Davitt was released, Lord Frederick Cavendish, the new chief secretary, and Thomas Henry Burke, the permanent undersecretary, were knifed to death in the Phoenix Park. The murder made the Kilmainham Treaty ineffective, and led to the introduction of further coercion legislation. In 1885, Parnell and his party brought down the Gladstone government. During the recess, Parnell deftly played out one party against the other. Eighty-six Parnellites were returned to parliament, and held the balance of power. Gladstone moved to introduce Home Rule, but any bill to that effect was obstructed by Unionist Liberals. In 1889 Parnell was cited as co-respondent in the O'Shea divorce petition. The scandal led Gladstone to dissociate himself from Parnell, who was condemned by the clergy. The Irish Party, and indeed the country, split in two (with Tim Healy's famous question, in Committee Room 15, 'Who is to be the mistress of the party?'). Parnell struggled in vain to regain control of the party. With his death, all hopes of Home Rule vanished. Yeats claimed that Irish literature flourished in the lull that followed Parnell's fall. His tragedy, that of a leader being sacrificed by the people for whom he had fought unceasingly, was of sufficiently messianic proportions to occupy the Irish imagination for several generations.

from Address at Ennis, Co. Clare, 19 September 1880[1]

... Depend upon it that the measure of the Land Bill of next session will be the measure of your activity and energy this Winter (*cheers*)— it will be the measure of your determination not to pay unjust rents— it will be the measure of your determination to keep a firm grip of your homesteads (*cheers*). It will be the measure of your determination not to bid for farms from which others have been evicted, and to use the strong force of public opinion to deter any unjust men amongst your-selves—and there are many such—from bidding for such farms (*hear, hear*). If you refuse to pay unjust rents, if you refuse to take farms from which others have been evicted, the land question must be settled, and settled in a way that will be satisfactory to you. It depends, therefore, upon yourselves, and not upon any commissions or any Government. When you have made this question ripe for settlement, then, and not till then, will it be settled (*cheers*). It is very nearly ripe already in many parts of Ireland. It is ripe in Mayo, Galway, Roscommon, Sligo, and portions of the county Cork (*cheers*). But I regret to say that the ten-ant-farmers of the county Clare have been backward in organisation up to the present time. You must take and band yourselves together in Land Leagues. Every town and village must have its own branch. You must know the circumstances of the holdings, and of the tenures of the district over which the League has jurisdiction—you must see that the principles of the Land League are inculcated, and when you have done this in Clare, then Clare will take her rank with the other active coun-ties, and you will be included in the next Land Bill brought forward by the Government (*cheers*). Now, what are you to do to a tenant who bids for a farm from which another tenant has been evicted?

Several Voices—Shoot him.

Mr. Parnell—I think I heard somebody say shoot him (*cheers*). I wish to point out to you a very much better way—a more Christian and charitable way, which will give the lost man an opportunity of repenting (*laughter, and hear, hear*). When a man takes a farm from

1 From the *Freeman's Journal*, Monday, 20 Sept. 1880.

which another has been evicted you must shun him on the roadside when you meet him—you must shun him in the streets of the town—you must shun him in the shop—you must shun him in the fair-green and in the market place, and even in the place of worship; by leaving him alone, by putting him into a moral Coventry, by isolating him from the rest of his countrymen as if he were the leper of old, you must show him your detestation of the crime he has committed. If you do this you may depend on it there will be no man so full of avarice—so lost to shame—as to dare the public opinion of all the right-thinking men in the county and transgress your unwritten code of laws. People are very much engaged at present in discussing the way in which the land question is to be settled, just the same as when a few years ago Irishmen were at each other's throats as to the sort of Parliament we would have if we got one. I am always thinking it is better first to catch your hare before you decide how you are going to cook him (*laughter*). I would strongly recommend public men not to waste their breath too much in discussing how the land question is to be settled, but rather to help and encourage the people in making it, as I said just now, ripe for settlement (*applause*). When it is ripe for settlement you will probably have your choice as to how it shall be settled, and I said a year ago that the land question would never be settled until the Irish landlords were just as anxious to have it settled as the Irish tenants (*cheers*).

A Voice—They soon will be.

from Speech in Cork, 21 January 1885[1]

... We shall struggle, as we have been struggling, for the great and important interests of the Irish tenant-farmer. We shall ask that his industry shall not be fettered by rent. We shall ask also from the farmer in return that he shall do what in him lies to encourage the struggling manufactures of Ireland, and that he shall not think it too great a sacrifice to be called upon when he wants anything—when he has to purchase anything—to consider how he may get it of Irish material and manufacture (*hear, hear*), even suppose he has to pay a little more for it (*cheers*). I am sorry if the agricultural population has shown itself somewhat deficient in its sense of its duty in this respect up to the present time; but I feel convinced that the matter has only to be put before them to secure the opening up of most important markets in this country for those manufactures which have always

---

1 From *The Nation*, 24 Jan. 1885.

existed, and for those which have been reopened anew, as a consequence of the recent exhibitions, the great exhibition in Dublin, and
the other equally great one in Cork, which have been recently held
(*cheers*).

We shall also endeavour to secure for the labourer some recognition and some right in the land of his country (*applause*). We don't
care whether it be the prejudices of the farmer or of the landlord that
stand in his way (*hear, hear*). We consider that whatever class tries to
obstruct the labourer in the possession of those fair and just rights to
which he is entitled, that class should be put down, and coerced if you
will, into doing justice to the labourer. We have shown our desire to
benefit the labourer by the passage of the Labourers Act,[1] which, if
maimed and mutilated in many of its provisions, undoubtedly is based
upon correct lines and principles, which will undoubtedly do much
good for that class, and undoubtedly will secure for the labouring
classes a portion of what we have been striving to secure for them.

Well, but gentlemen, I go back from the consideration of these
questions to the land question, in which the labourers question is also
involved, and the manufacturers question. I come back, and every
Irish politician must be forcibly driven back, to the consideration of
the great question of national self-government for Ireland (*cheers*). I
do not know how this great question will be eventually settled. I do
not know whether England will be wise in time and concede to constitutional arguments and methods the restitution of that which was
stolen from us towards the close of the last century (*cheers*). It is given
to none of us to forecast the future, and just as it is impossible for us
to say in what way or by what means the national question may be
settled, in what way full justice may be done to Ireland, so it is impossible for us to say to what extent that justice should be done. We cannot ask for less than restitution of Grattan's Parliament (*loud cheers*),
with its important privileges and wide and far-reaching constitution.
We cannot under the British constitution ask for more than the restitution of Grattan's Parliament (*renewed cheers*), but no man has the
right to fix the boundary to the march of a nation (*great cheers*). No
man has a right to say to his country: 'Thus far shalt thou go, and no
further,' and we have never attempted to fix the *ne plus ultra* to the
progress of Ireland's nationhood, and we never shall (*cheers*). But
gentlemen, while we leave those things to time, circumstances, and
the future, we must each one of us resolve in our own hearts that we

---

1 *Labourers Act*: the cumbersome Irish Labourers Act of 1883 was amended in 1885 (and again
  in 1886). Parnell had become a convert to the labourers' cause while in Kilmainham gaol.

shall at all times do everything that within us lies to obtain for Ireland the fullest measure of her rights (*applause*). In this way we shall avoid difficulties and contentions amongst each other. In this way we shall not give up anything which the future may put in favour of our country; and while we struggle to-day for that which may seem possible for us with our combination, we must struggle for it with the proud consciousness that we shall not do anything to hinder or prevent better men who may come after us from gaining better things than those for which we now contend (*prolonged applause*).

RICHARD DOWLING (1846–98)

Born in Clonmel, Co. Tipperary, he was educated locally and in Limerick and Waterford. He worked in the office of his uncle before moving on to a literary career. He was on the staff of *The Nation*, became editor of *Zozimus* (the Irish *Punch*), and afterwards of *Ireland's Eye*. He moved to London in 1874, and contributed to the *Illustrated Sporting and Dramatic News*. He founded and edited the short-lived *Yorick*, a comic paper. His first novel, *The Mystery of Killard*, was eventually published in 1879; it has an exceptional plot of a deaf-mute trying to kill his son because he can hear and speak, and hence disclose the whereabouts of a hidden treasure. Several novels followed, including *Sweet Inisfail* (1882) and *Old Corcoran's Money* (1897), which are set in Ireland. He also wrote plays, poems and essays.

From *The Mystery of Killard*

(1879)

A Sound from the Island

Between the years 1844 and 1854, famine and pestilence visited Ireland. People perished of hunger in the streets, in the fields, in the churches. They crawled from remote villages in the weary hope of obtaining food in the towns and cities, and were found dead by the wayside. Some who reached towns or cities by night, and knew not whither to turn, lay down near bakehouses where bread was being made at midnight, and were taken away stiff and stark before the first woman came to purchase. Men whose business took them abroad early, in the darkness, fell over the bodies of women taking their long rest on door-steps. Haggard, wild-eyed spectres of men haunted the roads and streets, and desperate mothers clutched starving infants to their barren breasts.

Before the Blight, beggars took offence if offered potatoes only, and potatoes rotted in trenches for sheer want of mouths to eat them. The Blight came, and those who had been donors to the poor gnawed cabbage stalks, or strove to allay the agony of starvation with grass and acorns and scraps of leather. In many districts there were for each day more people than loaves or potatoes, and from such places came hideous whispers, too awful for human lips to speak aloud.

In the wake of famine, pestilence crept to the shore of the stricken land to finish the work of ruin. Time mowed with no sickle then, but with a broad and universal wind. There were no fields of men to slay and fields to spare; but, like a storm passing through orchards when the fruit is heavy, all the trees were shaken and each suffered loss. Burying the dead was a monotonous toil; morning, noon, and night, men were digging graves and others were filling them in. Often he who dug at dawn was covered in himself before sun-down.

In towns large wooden sheds were erected for those who fled the lonely fields, that they might die in sight of man. Most of these fugitives from solitude, after a day or perhaps two days, found the sheds and died within the sight of human eyes. It was not a season for tears. People had no time to indulge sentiments. They sat pale and awe-stricken; carefully, heedfully, watching and noting how the plague fluctuated, who fell; guarding themselves and those dear to them against risk, and swiftly burying the dead. Burying by day and by night. Burying the dead calmly and resolutely, as though all reason for living had passed away, and there was only reason to die. Burying the dead in half-envious despair. Burying the dead as though they cried, 'These go to their brethren who are before them; but we remain to see all, all depart from us; our portion is the silent chamber and the deserted field. Are all we love to go before we go? Which of our kinsfolk, shall we break earth for next? Here are our young daughters, our mothers, our wives, our lusty sons, our fathers. Call the roll! Pay no heed to the places vacant already. But which of those that answer now will fall asleep to-morrow?'

'Good-bye, sweetheart! I am going a journey into the country, and shall not be with you for a week.'

'A week! A whole weary week. How long!'

On the fourth day they had buried him, and on the fifth they had forgotten where.

'He is but three days gone,' she cried, 'and I shall be three days gone away forever before he returns. The shadow of night is gathering on my hands. Look! A week seemed long when he was going, and now a week has grown to Never!'

Never! Who said never? The world had conspired to separate them for a week, but in four days heaven marred the conspiracy.

Those were times thick with sombre horrors in Ireland. Let us hope men may never see their like again.

The little village of Killard suffered severely from both the famine and pestilence. One-fourth of its inhabitants had fallen victims. Within seven days of each other, honest John Cantillon and his faithful wife, Bridget, came to the churchyard, never to depart until the general uprising. A month later, the wife of David Lane found there a quieter resting place than that afforded by the lonely hut on the Bishop's Island.

In the cottage of John Cantillon now dwelt Edward Martin and his wife Mary, daughter of Cantillon, with their little child, a fair-haired, blue-eyed girl of six years.

On the Island lived David Lane and his son, the latter being now ten years old. The boy was tall for his age, lank, long-limbed, uncouth. He possessed the hereditary bright eyes, but he showed no indication of the muscular alertness of his father. He was slow to move. Such time as lay at his disposal was spent in the summer time lying on the short moss and looking at the sea; in winter he loved best to sit by the fire, his chief delight being to weave upon the darkness hoops and bows, and other designs, with a spray of glowing faggot. Often he would sit whole hours together gazing into the dull turf fire; at such times, when his father roused him by putting his hand on his son's shoulder, the boy would start and look up half-alarmed, half-displeased, as though he had been awakened out of a pleasant reverie. For some time before David Lane paid his midnight visit to Dillon's shop, there had been a marked change in the conduct of father and son. Since the hour the boy had been delivered into his father's hands by the stranger who brought him from the inland, the elder Lane had treated the boy with the tenderness of a woman. He allowed him to do no rougher work than bait the hooks of the hand-lines. All else he did himself. He went to Killard and sold the fish, and bought the simple necessaries of their narrow home. He kindled the tire, cooked the food, and, when it was very cold, made a fire in the chamber occupied by the boy. Frequently he would take his child fondly in his arms, and hold him softly to his breast, muttering inarticulate sounds over him.

Of late, although he still kept the boy from toil, he seemed to stand in fear of him, and his affectionate embraces grew very few, and became spasmodic. He would catch his son suddenly and press him wildly to him, and then, setting him down, regard him almost fiercely for a moment, cover his eyes, and rush hastily away. All this perplexed the child. Sometimes, after one of those scenes, when the father returned, the boy would go up to him and wind his arms around him, and gaze into his eyes with a sad, questioning look, as though in protest. For a while the love of the parent predominated, and he would kiss the boy; then, when the latter moved his lips, the father concealed his face with one hand, and with the other repelled his son. All this troubled the child, and often as he sat by the fire his hot tears made gleaming rainbows around the turf, and fell slowly on his listless hands.

This singular man, dwelling apart from all the race save his child, separated from mankind by the terrible affliction his father had deliberately sought to place upon him, had centred the whole affection of his dark and stormy nature on his boy. He had watched him day by day as he grew, and had solaced his soul with the thought of their continual intercourse. When he visited Killard his questioning eyes and hands were ever among children, if they were by. He inquired their ages, took them up and weighed them, felt their limbs curiously, and when the balance turned in favor of his own child, set them down with a proud smile. The people all declared, that, whatever the crimes of the Lanes might be, this man loved his boy as few fathers loved theirs.

Now some canker had entered in—some dark suspicion, some half-developed dread. Yet no alteration was visible in the boy. Tom the Fool, who was strangely quick to notice everything connected with his friends, saw the alteration and wondered. But he was reticent in all things concerning the deaf mute and his son, and told nothing about it in the village. People said the Fool was jealous of his friendship with the Lanes, and in his nebulous mind there lay a band of exclusion round the Bishop's, and he would allow no one inside this band. Tom had frequently interrogated Lane, but could get no reply. The father seemed to deny the alteration, and was always angry when the Fool questioned him. Latterly Tom had been seldom a visitor to the Island. Often a whole month passed without his once leaving the mainland.

It was broad daylight when David Lane, carrying the gun, arrived opposite the Bishop's. He had paid Dillon five times the value of the gun, but it was not till next morning the gunsmith discovered that with the gun had disappeared a half pound canister of powder. This canister was now in Lane's pocket.

Lane threw the gun down, and, standing on the edge of the cliff, looked round, as if to make sure no one watched his movements. Not a soul was in sight. At the point where he stood, the distance from the mainland to the island was no more than sixty feet. It seemed almost possible to jump across. Two hundred feet below groaned and churned the never-quiet waters of the Atlantic. In the brightest day the sun never reached the bottom of this chasm, and it was always filled with a dim grey darkness, like the blue bloom under trees in summer. Down the side of the Island, directly opposite where Lane stood, hung a rope with a loop at the end, and from the loop depended a confused tangle of cordage. The villagers knew that this rope formed the bridge. They had often seen him cross from the Island, but none had ever seen him return.

Having satisfied himself that he was unobserved, Lane stooped, and with his hands removed some clay a few feet from the brink. A large iron hook was disclosed. The eye of the hook pointed inland. Two large iron bolts, driven into the ground, held the hook firmly in its place.

So much the villagers knew, and further, that he, when wanting to leave his home, cast that loop over the hook, and crossed under the rope. But they did not know how, when he was once over, and had cast back the rope, he ever re-formed his bridge. How did he get the loop back again? Often, when feeling ran high against the Lanes, the people had talked of coming in the night and tearing up this hook, and so cutting him completely off. But there was an aspect of murder about the idea, and they forebore.

Lane now thrust his hand into his bosom, and drew forth a small bundle of fishing-line. This he quickly unwound. It was twenty yards long, and in the centre lay what fishermen call a stroke-haul, that is, three hooks tied together, so as to resemble a small grapling-iron. From the end of the stroke-haul depended a bullet as sinker. Again he looked suspiciously around. Then, peering into the dim depths of the chasm, he commenced slowly paying out the line.

The face of the cliff was so sheer that, when the line all but about a yard was run out, the stroke-haul hung free of the rock. He looked carefully over the edge. The eye could not discern the line at more than half its length, and even the bullet had disappeared. Holding the line out at arm's-length, he walked a few paces along the very brink. Then suddenly the line tightened. He wound up a few yards of it, and, drawing it in cautiously, returned to the old station.

Then he took in the line hand over hand. Before half of it lay beside him on the cliff, the rope hanging from the Island began to stretch across the rift towards where he stood. With a jerk the stroke-haul came into view, and in one of the hooks rested a loop of fine black cord. Taking this cord in his hand, he pulled vigorously, and in less than a minute the eye of the rope came up.

Thirty feet down the cliff was a fissure, and in this fissure a small bar of iron, and attached to this bar of iron the cord to which the rope was tied. The bar might be placed there by lowering it from the cliff into the fissure. The dimness of the chasm made it impossible to see the black cord.

Having secured the loop to the hook, he pushed the tangle of cords which had hung from it out on the rope until it hung over the brink. It formed a rude network of five meshes, each mesh being about a foot wide.

Into this network he crept head foremost, taking the gun with him, and facing downwards. As soon as he was fully in, he turned, faced the pale blue morning sky, and, seizing the rope with his hands and feet, worked himself across with surprising swiftness and ease. As soon as he had landed, he, by a vigorous shake, communicated an upward serpentine wave to the rope, at the same moment lowering his hand to the ground. The loop spread out of the hook, and the rope fell to its own position. Thus the Island was once more cast loose into isolation.

Lane paused a moment, turned round, and inspected the Island narrowly, apparently to his satisfaction. Then he crossed the summit, and, opening the door of his chamber, entered it.

The yellow sun stood over the level downs. Far out on the sea reached the dark green water in the shadow of the cliffs. Beyond the shadow the ocean lay, a blue sheet of radiance under a cloudless sky. The dews were ascending from the brittle grass.

Beneath the summits of the gigantic rocks, sea-fowl cried as they flew slowly from the land. No object broke the vast expanse of ocean. No sound fell into the vacant vault of heaven, save the cries of the birds. Peace reigned over all the scene, as though no conflict of tempest ever racked the coast; as though the message of peace to man was written in colossal characters on the face of nature.

In the small chamber facing the south, slept the boy. He knew nothing of his father's visit to Clonmore. The man had left the Island without letting his son know of his intention. During the previous day, the manner of the father had been more excited than ever. One of those scenes had occurred between the two. While Lane was preparing the midday meal of potatoes and fish, an accident occurred. The boy was sitting before the fire watching the fish frying. The father, behind him, held an earthen plate in his hand. Suddenly it slipped from his grasp, and was broken into fragments on the hard earthen floor. With an inarticulate cry, the father turned round to claim his son's attention; but his eyes no sooner met the figure of the child than he sprang back with a yell. The boy had already risen, and stood regarding the fragments.

A wild fury sprang into Lane's eyes. He rushed at the boy, and, raising his arm, struck him heavily. In all that had been before, nothing like this had occurred. A blow! a blow, and no blame attributable to him!

For an instant the boy drew himself up, and glared defiance at his father. Then all the anger went out of his face, and, with a loud sob of pain and grief, he threw himself on his father's bed, and covered his head with the clothes....

A Traitor Discovered

When, on that August morning, Lane's son left his sleeping chamber in the hut, he found his father busily engaged preparing breakfast. The spirits of the boy seemed utterly crushed; the father was dull and gloomy, with a lowering danger in his eyes, but his actions were as kind as usual. He helped his son liberally to food, and pressed him to eat more, when the boy appeared satisfied. But he did not kiss him, or fondle him, as was his custom. The boy's eyes were full of tears, and he could hardly swallow the potatoes and fish. He rarely looked at his father, and when their glances chanced to meet, the latter dropped his and frowned.

As soon as breakfast was finished the father cleared the table. Then, turning to the boy, he made signs to him, and the son, taking a basket, went out, crossed the Island, and descended slowly and heedlessly the precipitous path leading to the ledge. Here he drew in the hand-lines, removed the fish, and rebaited the hooks. Having gathered the fish into the basket, he sat down and fixed his eyes wearily on the sea.

Meanwhile, the father had taken the gun out of its hiding place under the bed, examined it carefully at the nipple, and placed it against the inner edge of the door jamb. When this was done, he stood outside the door, so as to command a view of the head of the path leading to the ledge, folded his arms, set his teeth, knit his brow, and waited.

The sky was serene and blue, not a cloud broke the infinite expanse. The light was cool and gracious; the air fresh and invigorating. The sea-fowl had by this time passed out from shore, and their shrill dreary notes no longer floated above the dull low murmur of the swells two hundred and fifty feet below.

The boy was long—much longer than usual, but David Lane never moved a muscle. His attitude and his features remained as fixed as though a withering vapor from the pole had frozen him as he stood. The expression of his countenance was that of one awaiting fate, rather than one expecting a foe; but it was tragic. Tragic with a dire resolution, and far down under the resolution, a wild appalling grief. It was not the face of a man who thought. There was no trace of succession of ideas, but it seemed as though his mind, like his body, was frozen into one unalterable attitude; as though one picture were burned against that path, and nothing could displace it.

At length, above the level of the Island, appeared the boy's head.

No muscle of the father moved. He remained rigid.

The shoulders and bust of the boy rose into view; then the arms and basket he carried.

Still David Lane never stirred.

The figure of the child emerged completely, and he took one pace in the direction of the hut.

Instantly, as though the vitality of a thousand men had been flung upon him, the father sprang into the hut, seized the gun, lifted it to his shoulder, and aiming at the chimney place, fired.

The explosion was terrific, for the charge was large and the chamber small, and, in the calm of the morning, it seemed as though the Bishop's Island had been riven from summit to base.

Upon the instant he fired, quick as the flash itself, the man spun round on his heel and looked at the door. No smoke had reached it. The smoke lay huddled in blue waves near the fireplace.

Then Lane folded his arms swiftly across his breast, knit his brows, and, setting his teeth, stood inside the door confronting fate, as he had awaited it without.

In a second, the boy bounded into the open, pale and awe-stricken. His eyes were wild with terror. He had lost his hat and his basket, and his hair waved hither and thither as if blown by a wind. When he saw his father standing safe beside him, the expression changed electrically, and with a low moan of relief, he stretched forth his arms and sank to the ground.

The father sprang back, as though the nether realms gaped at his feet, and with a wild shrill of despair threw his hands towards Heaven, and, with his upturned eyes and out-stretched arms seemed to clamour for annihilation. While the father remained thus, the boy lay motionless on the ground. His arms were doubled under him, and his knees drawn up; his face deadly pale, his lips blue, his eyes open but rayless.

In a few moments the father's arms dropped, the expression of his face altered, and his eyes fell upon the prostrate form in the doorway. Stepping hastily forward, he sprang over the child, and, having reached the open air, strode several times up and down the island, through the white warm sunshine and fragrant dewy air. Then he returned to the doorway and looked in.

The position of the figure had not changed in the least. Again David Lane turned away, and dashed hither and thither blindly. Once more he paused at the doorway. The boy had not moved. A sudden fear seemed to seize upon the father. He leaped into the hut, stooped near the fireplace, and examined the wall. Presently, with his fingers, he picked something out from between two of the stones. Holding this to the light, he examined it carefully. Yes, it was the chief portion of the leaden bullet. It broke in two as he turned it in his hand, and showed in the interior an old seam. That was the cut through which the hand-line had passed. A look of angry perplexity now passed over his face, and his eyes turned once more to the ground, near the doorway.

Not a muscle had stirred; not a fold of the clothes had been displaced. Frowning heavily, as if he suspected a trick, the father crossed the room, stooped, and catching the child at the waist, lifted him. The head, and arms, and lower limbs hung down limp and nerveless.

A spasm of horror passed over the features of the father, and he shook the child once, twice, thrice, without effect. Then lifting him higher, he carried him across the little chamber, and placed him on the bed where the boy's mother had died. He put a pillow under his son's head, drew down his limbs, and crossed the long arms over the breast. When this was done, he sat down as far off as he could, and regarded the bed with a rigid expressionless air.

In a little while a light shot into his eyes. He rose, kindled a candle, and held the flame opposite the open lips. He had seen this done in Killard during the cholera years. The yellow flame, pale and sickly in the blaze of the August morning, flicked and waved regularly. The child breathed. He flung the candle down, and resumed his old position.

He had seen death and sleep; these were the only forms of human unconsciousness with which he was familiar. But here was something which was more deep than sleep, less profound than death. What could it be? Was the boy ever to wake ? If sleep, which is less powerful than this, lasts a night time, how long will this last? A week or a month?

Death lasts for ever, and sleep for a night; when will this be over, and what is the end to be, deeper or lighter sleep, death or waking?

Whichever it was, doubts that had haunted his mind for a long time were now made certainties. He had seen sea-fowl, which had been invisible, rise and fly away in terror at the firing of a gun, yet, unless he were quite close, and could feel the concussion, he could not tell a gun had been fired.

Tom the Fool had told him it was possible to know, at a great distance that a gun had been fired, and that the knowledge came, not through the eyes or sense of touch, but through the ears. Nothing came to him through the ears. They were like fingers, they possessed feeling; nothing more.

Tom had told him the firing of a gun could be known through the ears farther off than anything else.

Accordingly, to make sure above all doubt, he had bought the gun. He had fired that gun, and his son knew he had fired that gun, although he could not know it by the sense of touch, or by the sight of smoke, for he had fired so that the boy could see no smoke. Therefore the boy got messages through his ears.

But his father had married a wife who got no messages through the ears; he had married a wife like himself in this respect; here was his boy now unlike him. His father had told him the gold could not be kept by anyone who would send or receive news by the ears, hence he had married a wife like him, David, and he himself one like himself.

The women never knew of the gold, and could not tell anyone; his father had told him, and made him promise to marry a wife such as she that had died of the cholera, and to communicate the secret only to a son, and to a son who could neither know nor make known through the ears. Everyone else was to be kept in darkness; for if once the secret of the gold came to be known, it would be useless to them, and they would all perhaps be slain, for his own father did not know the penalty.

Now here was the traitor, come in the person of his own boy. The boy he loved with all his heart and soul. Here was a traitor in his own house; one who, as soon as he knew of the secret, would send it abroad, and betray his own father unto death.

Yes, this son for whom he would freely have died, could not, on account of his accursed ears, help betraying his father. He would do it as a matter of certainty, as soon as he knew. Here, lying before him, was the only being on earth he cared for, and this being would hurl his own father to destruction on the very first opportunity. This boy would turn his own father off the Bishop's, tear up the Island, and give his father to the police, not because of any want of affection, but because he was cursed with ears that felt and could send messages to other ears!

Monster! Hideous, unnatural child! Mysterious curse! Away! Away! Away! There is infinite malignity of terror in your presence!

The boy's eyelids trembled. With a weary sigh he sat up and yawned, and smiled at his father. His eyes looked a little dull. He had forgotten what had passed.

When David Lane saw the boy return to consciousness and smile upon him, the look of angry dread gave place to one of frantic yearning. It seemed as though he strove with his eyes to draw his child back into his own nature. His heart hungered to absorb him; but he made no sign. His arms lay clasped upon his knees; his head was thrust forward, his figure motionless; but the agony of love betrayed was in his eyes.

There was no indignation now against his child. The worst possible certainty had been reached. If by any perversity of nature intelligible to himself he feared betrayal at the hands of his son, there might have been a struggle between indignation and love, and, for a time at least, love might have triumphed. But it was not his boy opposed him, but fate, in a form he could not understand. The son, by no fault of his own, but by the power of some curse, had been endowed by fate with an ability which he could not fail to exert for his father's destruction.

This boy, his own child, the idol of his life, his own flesh and blood, was the vessel of some spirit of wrath with power to work his destruction through mysterious and infallible agencies against which neither he nor the boy could strive with hope of success. His son was the flesh of his flesh, but the spirit of his ruin!

By this time the boy had realised all, and covered his face, and was weeping.

David Lane caught him by the shoulder and led him forth, flung the loop over the hook, and prepared the meshes for crossing the chasm. When this was done he made signs to the boy.

The latter turned pale with terror. The father repeated the signs calmly, without a trace of passion.

The boy appealed to him with outstretched hands.

Lane pointed to the mainland, and made a swift, decided gesture.

The child flung himself down moaning, and seized his father's knees and clasped them, and rested his pale tear-stained cheek against them in piteous supplication.

The deaf mute never moved. His resolution was taken inexorably.

Nothing could shake him. He raised his son gently, set him on his feet, and turning his back on him, went towards the hut. In a few minutes he came back; the boy was gone.

Raising the rope he shook it free of the hook, and the Island was cast off into isolation, and he into the rayless solitude of a life without a single love, a single hope, a single ambition, a single fear, save the one guilty one, not his own, but which seemed part of himself, born with his nature and laid upon him anew when first his father communicated the secret to him, and named the precautions and possible penalties in case of discovery.

When the rope once more hung idly down the dim deep cleft, Lane went into his own sleeping room. Something bright lying on the floor attracted his attention. He stooped and looked. It was his boy's clasp-knife. A sudden fury of sorrow seized him and shook him. His breath came short, his chest heaved, he bellowed aloud like a stricken beast. His blood-shot eyes ran fiercely round the place seeking something. Suddenly they stopped, riveted by the sight of the gun lying in a corner. He clutched it by the barrel, as though he would drive the sides together, and with a hoarse yell dashed into the sunlight, sprang to the brink of the cliff facing the ocean, and swinging the weapon swiftly twice over his head, let it go, sending it far out into the sunlit air. With a sudden plunge it shot downward and disappeared for ever.

He looked awhile as if to give it time to reach the water, then clutching his head in both his hands, tottered to his own chamber and threw himself heavily on the earthen floor, his arms and legs spread wide and his powerful hands digging into the hard ground until they were covered with blood.

MICHAEL DAVITT (1846–1906)

Born in Straide, Co. Mayo, he was the second child of Martin Davitt and his wife Catherine, both of peasant stock. The family were evicted in 1850, an event which left an indelible impression on Michael. They emigrated to Haslingden, where he was put to work in a mill at the age of nine, and lost his right arm in an accident two years later. He then received a good education at a Wesleyan school. In 1861 he took up work as an errand boy for a printer and postmaster, and became a book-keeper and typesetter. He attended evening classes at the Mechanics' Institute, and embraced Chartism.

In 1861 he joined the Irish Republican Brotherhood. He was the chief arms purchaser for the Fenians when, in 1870, he was sentenced to fifteen years' penal servitude for treason-felony (a letter he had written to a fellow IRB member was misinterpreted as evidence of incitement to murder). A letter he wrote from gaol was published in several English and Irish newspapers, and led to an inquiry into the harshness of the prison regime. He was released in 1877, and received a hero's welcome in Ireland. He became the central figure in the land agitation, founding the Mayo Land League, and persuading Charles Stewart Parnell* to set up the National Land League. As Davitt embraced the constitutional policies of the 'New Departure', he grew more distanced from Fenianism; yet he was sent back to prison several times in the '80s under the Coercion Acts (he was elected MP for Meath while in gaol). He denounced Parnell after the divorce case. In 1891 he founded the Irish Democratic Trade and Labour Federation. He was returned for North Meath (1892), but was unseated on petition, for North-East Cork (1893), having to resign on being declared bankrupt, and for East Kerry and South Mayo (1895-1899). With William O'Brien* he co-founded the United Irish League.

From *Leaves from a Prison Diary*

(1885)

Dedication

TO THE
MEMORY OF THE LITTLE CONFIDING FRIEND
WHOSE PLAYFUL MOODS
AND LOVING FAMILIARITY
HELPED TO CHEER THE SOLITUDE OF A CONVICT CELL;
TO MY
PET BLACKBIRD, 'JOE,'
THESE PRISON JOTTINGS
ARE AFFECTIONATELY DEDICATED.

Preface

I was remitted to Portland Prison on the 3rd of February, 1881. Shortly afterwards, through the kindness of the governor, a young blackbird came into my possession. For some months I relieved the tedium of my solitude by efforts to win the confidence of my companion, with the happiest results. He would stand upon my breast as I lay in bed in the morning and awaken me from sleep. He would perch upon the edge of my plate and share my porridge. His familiarity was such that on showing him a small piece of slate pencil, and then placing it in my waistcoat pocket, he would immediately abstract it. He would perch upon the edge of my slate as it was adjusted between my knees, and watching the course of the pencil as I wrote, would make the most amusing efforts to peck the marks from off the slate. He would 'fetch and carry' as faithfully as any well-trained dog. Towards evening he would resort to his perch, the post of the iron bedstead, and there remain, silent and still, till the dawning of another day, when his chirrup would again be heard, like the voice of Nature, before the herald of civilisation, the clang of the prison bell at five o'clock.

One evening as 'Joe' sat upon his perch, it occurred to me to constitute him chairman and audience of a course of lectures; and with him constantly before me as the representative of my fellow creatures, I jotted down what I have substantially reproduced in the following pages.

Lecture XVI.
Criminal Vanity

That weakness or vanity which induces travellers to carve their names upon the Pyramids, rocks, or stones near famous sites, walls of Roman and other historic ruins, religious shrines and birthplaces of poets, is very largely developed in criminal character. I recollect having occupied the half-hour during which the jury was considering whether to believe the evidence of respectable witnesses or accept that of a creature who can be truly designated a salaried perjurer in my respect, in reading the inscriptions which covered the walls of the cell—the waiting-room of Fate—in Newgate Prison, to which I was conducted while my future was being decided in the jury-room overhead. Every available inch of the blackened mortar contained, in few words, the name of the writer, where he belonged to, the crime with which he was charged, the dread certainty of conviction, the palpitating hopes of acquittal, or the language of indifference or despair. What thoughts must have swept through the minds of the thousands who have passed through that cell, during the necessarily brief stay within its walls! Loss of home, friends, reputation, honour, name—to those who had such to lose; and the impending sentence of banishment from the world of pleasure or business for years—perhaps for ever—with the doom of penal degradation, toil, and suffering in addition!

Yet, despite all these feelings that crowd upon the soul in these short, fleeting, terrible moments of criminal life, the vanity—or what shall I term it?—of the individual prompts him to occupy most of them in giving a short record of himself, his crime or imputed offence, scratched upon these blackened walls, for other succeeding unfortunates to read!

Most of these inscriptions were in slang, showing that the majority of those who had written them were of the criminal order, and guilty of some, if not of the particular offence for which they were doomed to await the announcement of their punishment within that chamber of dread expectancy. Not a few, however, consisted of declarations of innocence, invocations of Divine interposition, appeals to Justice, and confidence in the 'laws of my country;' while others denoted the absence of all thoughts except those of wife, children, or sweetheart. Some who were awaiting that most terrible of all sentences—death— could yet think of tracing the outlines of a scaffold amidst the mass of surrounding inscriptions, with a 'Farewell to life' scrawled underneath. Giving way to the seeming inspiration of the place, and picturing jurors' faces round that dismal den—dark and frowning—into which the sun's rays never entered, lit only by a noisy jet of gas which seemed to sing the death-song of the liberty of all who entered the walls which it had blackened—I stood upon the form which extended round the place, and wrote upon a yet uncovered portion of the low sloping roof—

> M. D. expects ten years for the crime of being an Irish Nationalist and the victim of an informer's perjury.
>
> *July*, 1870.

From the ghastly look of the cell, the penalty I was about to undergo, and my own thoughts at the moment, I might have most appropriately added the well-known lines from the *Inferno*, which invite those who enter its portals of despair to abandon hope.[1]

Not only on the walls of that never-to-be-forgotten black hole, but on the cell-walls and doors in all my subsequent wanderings in penal life—in Millbank, Dartmoor, Portsmouth, and Portland—have I spent hours in deciphering the records of 'famous' deeds and particular 'professions,' dates of sentences and the penalties awarded to the strange beings who had preceded me along that slow, weary, and heartsore journey of punishment.

Fuller accounts of the professions and proficiency of the occupants would be sure to be always found upon the cell slate, written by them for the envious admiration of the prisoner who was next to be located there. These histories, invariably written in slang, have afforded me much amusement at times, and have been a means, among others, of aiding me in the mastery of the criminal vocabulary, which I have so frequently used in these sketches.

---

1 Inferno ... *abandon hope*: Passing through the wide gates of hell, Dante and his guide Virgil read the inscription 'Abandon Hope, all ye who enter' (*Inferno*, Canto III. l. 9).

Young thieves would, of course, 'blow their own horn' in narrating their sentences and exploits, by taking credit for imaginary deeds of fame, not 'honestly' acquired; but old hands could be easily traced in the terse expressions which would record—

'A burst[1] in the City. Copped while boning the swag.[2] 7 stretch, 1869. Roll on 1876. Cheer up, pals.'

Another—

'Hook. 7 ys. Roll on time.'

Another—

'Bob White from the Dials. 5 stretch for slugging a copper.'

'Little Dickey from the New Cut. 10 and a ticket. Put away by a moll' (sold by an unfortunate).

And such like information, on through the whole category of crime.

The great majority of convicts hide their real under assumed names, many of them having a fresh 'monicker' (name) each conviction, to be dropped, for obvious reasons, upon release. The giving of names, therefore, in these sketches, reveals nothing that would injure the persons who were the bearers while undergoing their 'laggings.'[3]

A letter, of which the following is an exact copy, was left by a prisoner in one of the cells which I occupied after receiving sentence in Newgate. It afforded much amusement to the officers of that prison, who kept it in that particular cell, and who called my attention to it upon my removal thereto, in order, I believe, to distract my mind from the sentence that had been passed upon me a couple of days previously.

Shor ditch—1870.

Deere Jim

i was in quod,[4] doin 14 days when i heerd you was lagged i blakked Polly S——'s peepers[5] who called me names she was fuddled and hit me fust, when i kolered her nut[6] and giv her a fine slugging and her mug was all over blud the spiteful thing bit me she did, and funked fight, when we were both taken by the Kopper, and the beek[7] only giv me 14 days, and her got 21 for bitten me fust and been fuddled, cheer up Jim i am sorry wot you are lagged, and i wont pal with nobody wile your in quod. good by Jim from your tru luv   SALLY.

---

1 *burst*: 'burglary'.

2 *Copped while boning the swag*: 'Arrested while stealing from the shop' (i.e. in flagranto delicti).

3 *laggings*: 'prison sentences' (of more than two years).

4 *in quod*: 'in prison' (specifically in Newgate).

5 *peepers*: 'eyes'.

6 *her nut*: 'her head'.

7 beek: 'justice of peace', or 'magistrate'.

Whether this is the fair one whom the song of the period described–

> Her fighting weight was thirteen stone,
> And her maiden name was Sarah,

I know not; but her love-letter to poor Jim was the means of eliciting from me the first laugh in which I felt inclined to indulge in that early stage of penal servitude.

Slang—A pickpocket told me the history of his arrest one day in the following language:—

'I was jogging down a blooming slum in the Chapel when I butted a reeler who was sporting a red slang. I broke off his jerry and boned the clock, which was a red one, but I was spotted by a copper who claimed me. I was lugged before the beak, who gave me six doss in the Steel. The week after I was chucked up I did a snatch near St. Paul's, was collared, lagged, and got this bit of seven stretch.'

In English this would read as follows:—

'As I was walking down a narrow alley in Whitechapel I ran up against a drunken man who had a gold watch-guard. I stole his watch, which was gold, but was seen by a policeman, who caught me and took me before the magistrate, who gave me six months in the Bastille [Middlesex House of Detention, so named by thieves]. When I was released I attempted to steal a watch near St. Paul's, but was taken again, convicted, and sentenced to seven years' penal servitude.'

The use of slang in prisons is prevalent only among the lower order of thieves, but is, of course, employed by all habitual criminals when in company, or on the theft path outside. Some of the pickpocket fraternity are so addicted to it that their true character might be inferred from its almost constant presence in their conversation.

Thieves' Latin.—This improvement upon slang is more a special criminal method of speech than the ordinary slang, and is of general use among the professional burglar and 'hook' orders of thief when in pursuit of game. Its chief peculiarity consists in reversing the position of the syllables of a word containing more than one syllable, and making two syllables of all words having only one in ordinary pronunciation by adding a vowel or liquid consonant to the first or second part of such word. By the application of this simple rule to slang words the 'lingo' becomes too complicated for any but the initiated to understand. For instance, if two thieves were prowling for game, and one were to see a policeman, he would shout to his comrade—

'Islema! Ogda the opperca!' which in slang is–'Misle! Dog the copper!' otherwise—'Vanish! See the policeman!'

If a pair of confederates were in company with some 'flat,' or easily-deceived person whom they were about to fleece, the lingo would be used as a means by which they would intercommunicate their impressions of the victim in his hearing, and give directions what was best to do in order to obtain his money—

'A uffma, ill olloswa a alewha. Itchpa the idesna, or utpo the ukedo in the obfa,' would be some of the phrases needed for such an emergency.

In ordinary slang the foregoing would stand as follows—'He is a muff, and will swallow a whale. Pitch the snide, or put your duke in his fob;' and translated into English would read—'He is such a confounded ass that he will stand almost anything. Try the counterfeit coin, or pick his pocket.'

As some words will not admit very well of the necessary transposition of syllables needed to disguise the talk from listening victims or enemies, the first syllables of such words, if immediately following each other, will change places, so that the first syllable, letter, or letters of the second word will become that or those of the first word, and *vice-versâ*. For instance, if Jack had made the discovery that a person whom himself and Bill were following had only a silver watch, the disgusting fact would be told to Jack as follows:—

'I jay, Sack, the okeblo's wack's clite;' which in slang would be—'I say, Jack, the bloke's clock is only a white one;' and in English—'The fellow's watch is only silver.'

The letters 'J' and 's' of the words 'Jack' and 'say' are exchanged; the ordinary lingo rule is followed in reference to the word 'bloke' and the 'cl' of the word 'clock,' and 'w' of ' white' are exchanged as in the case of the letters 'J' and 's.'

STANDISH JAMES O'GRADY (1846–1928)

Born in Castletown Berehaven, Co. Cork, son of the Viscount Guillamore, who was a Church of Ireland rector, he was educated at Tipperary Grammar School and at Trinity College, Dublin. He was called to the Irish bar in 1872, but practised little, doing extensive research on Irish myths and legends, and writing for the Dublin *Daily Express*. In 1878 he published at his own expense the *History of Ireland: The Heroic Period*, infusing the 'rigid and conscientious spirit' of archaeology with the 'sympathy, imagination, creation' of literature. Its imaginative, idealized rendering of Ireland's heroic past was to have a formative influence on the Irish Literary Renaissance. W.B. Yeats wrote that the Celtic legends which had been the domain of 'Professor Dryasdust and his pupils' were given 'an imaginative existence' by O'Grady, and T.W. Rolleston noted that 'the shadowy gods and warriors ceased to be mere names; they ... were filled with passions, terrific and superhuman...' Initially, however, the book came in for considerable criticism. O'Grady himself apologised for his fancy in a monograph entitled *Early Bardic Literature* (1879); he included more scholarly archaeological data in the *History of Ireland: Cuculain and his Contemporaries* (1880), and published a corrective *History of Ireland: Critical and Philosophical* (1881). Yet it was his lofty epic narrative, reminiscent in style of Thomas Carlyle, which would inspire the Renaissance writers. It is presented without the fastidiousness of archaeological accuracy in *Cuculain: An Epic* (1882), which combines the imaginative sections of his earlier histories.

O'Grady's aristocratic Cuchulain became the mythical embodiment of Ireland's destiny. In the trilogy *The Coming of Cuculain* (1894), *In the Gates of the North* (1901) and *The Triumph and Passing of Cuculain* (1920) he reworked *The History of Ireland* as a popular romance. An opponent of Irish nationalism, he espoused aristocratic values; in *The Crisis in Ireland* (1882) and *Toryism and the Tory Democracy* (1886), he urged the Anglo-Irish ascendancy to take on the responsibility of saving the Irish from the excrescences of materialism, a plea he tirelessly rehearsed in his leaders for the *Daily Express*, in the *Kilkenny Moderator*, which he came to own and edit in 1898, and in *The All-Ireland Review* (1900–06)—a journal which was described by the literary historian Ernest Boyd as 'the soil from which some of the best fruits of the literary revival sprung'. He saw the flight of the great earls as a decisive moment in Irish history, and published six books on the Elizabethan reconquest of Ireland, including *Red Hugh's Captivity* (1889), *Ulrick the Ready* (1896), *The Flight of the Eagle* (1897), and a play, *Hugh Roe O'Donnell* (1902)—all of which deal with the plight of the noble Red Hugh O'Donnell.

O'Grady became increasingly concerned with issues of agriculture, industry and politics, formulating an ideology consistent with Robert Owen's utopian socialism. In 1912–13 he contributed a series of articles to Jim Larkin's *Irish Worker* advocating the relocation of the Dublin unemployed to rural centres under cooperative management, modelled on the Greek city-state.

From *History of Ireland: The Heroic Period*

(1878)

Deirdre

'Yea, for her sake, on them the fire gat hold.'

SWINBURNE.[1]

When Concobar Mac Nessa was called to the Ard-Rie-ship of Ulla[2] he celebrated his inauguration by a great banquet at Emain Macha,[3] and all the knights of the Crave Rue were there, and the chiefs and kings of the Clanna Rury, and the kings and ambassadors of the tribes and nations of Erin that were favourable to his succession. There were also there noble ladies, and amongst them the bride of Felim, chief bard of the Ultonians.[4] It was a year of prophecies and portents, and Cathvah, the druid—he who had eaten of the nuts of knowledge—the interpreter of dreams and omens—had announced that an age was then in its inception, which would be renowned to the ends of the earth, and the last age of the world.

That night the Ultonians feasted with more magnificence than had ever before that been used in Erin, and the sounds of revelry arose out of the vast and high Dûn into the night, and the lights glared far and wide, and there was the sound of the harp and of singing voices, for Emain Macha was wholly given over to festivity.

Then about the time that the shrill cry of the cock is first heard, a rapid fear swept like a wind through the whole city, and smote an universal silence, and men held their breaths awaiting some prodigy. Anon there arose upon the night a shrill and agonizing scream, as of an animal pierced, that utters a cry in its agony. And three times the cry shrilled through the city. But simultaneously were heard low thunder-like mutterings, whereat the earth trembled; but this came from the Tayta Brac, wherein was the warlike equipment of all the Red Branch; and aged warriors who had fought under Rury recognised that solemn warning, and they knew what shield it was that announced impending disaster. And, after this, there arose sounds of battle, crash of meeting hosts and shattering spears, the shoutings of warriors, and the war-cries of the Clans of Ulla, and between these

---

1 'Laus Veneris', 187–188: 'Yet for her sake on them the fire gat hold, / And for their sakes on her the fire of hell.'
2 *Ard-Rie-ship of Ulla*: ruler of the men of Ulster.
3 *Emain Macha*: the capital of the Ulstermen—located at Navan Fort, two miles from Armagh.
4 *Ultonians*: Ulstermen (*Obs.*).

noises was heard, far away, the roaring of the sea. Then the prodigy died away, and men saw the reflection of their own fear in the white faces of their comrades.

But in the king's palace the feast was broken up, and the king summoned a council of his great men, and there it was determined that Cathvah the seer should be interrogated concerning the import of the prodigy. Then Cathvah arose with his druidical instruments in his hands, and chanted the chant of divination; and under the power of that chant the veil that hides futurity was rent before his mind, and in a sacred phrenzy he walked towards the Grianan of the women, and the king and his knights followed him reverently. Then he approached the bride of the chief bard of Ulla, singling her out from amongst all the women in the Dûn, and he stood above her and prophesied:

'No common child bearest thou in thy womb, O lady. Beneath thy zone, veiled yet in infancy, I see a woman of wondrous beauty, bright gold her hair, eyes piercing and splendid, tongue full of sweet sounds, her countenance like the colour of snow blended with crimson; but out of her beauty shall arise a sword. It is the destruction of the wide territories of Ulla that thou bearest in thy womb, O lady—wasting wars and conflagrations and blood. I see the Red Branch divided against itself, and the sons of Usna slain, and the son of Duthrect, and I see the son of the High King, and Fergus, and many kings of the tribes of Ulla flying across the boundary into exile, and wars yet greater arising out of that expatriation which shall consume away the children of Iar.'

After this, Concobar convened his council, and he himself desired that the child, when born, should be slain; but it was finally determined that a tower should be built in a remote and inaccessible spot, and that she should be immured there until she died, for they reverenced the interpretations of Cathvah.

The child was born a beautiful blue-eyed babe, and she was called Deirdré, and Concobar selected a prudent and wise woman named Lowrcam, to whom he committed the child, and she was immured according to the resolution of the saba of the kings, at Emain Macha.

The child Deirdré grew up so beautiful, gentle, and tender, that she drew to herself the whole heart's-love of the lady who guarded her, so that her loyalty to the council of the kings, and to Concobar Mac Nessa, was dissolved, and the memory of the portents that attended Deirdré's birth, and the vaticinations of Cathvah, faded away. Therefore she relaxed the severity of that imprisonment, and suffered her to wander in the forest that surrounded the tower, to gather flowers, and listen to the songs of the birds.

There were at this time amongst the knights of the Red Branch three young warriors, the glory of all Ulla for their beauty and their accomplishments, Naysi, and Anly, and Ardan, the three sons of Usna, and they were loved by all who knew them, and chiefly by Fergus Mac Roy, who was the great sheltering tree of all the noblest and best of the young knights. And now that I have likened Fergus to a great sheltering tree, I mind me how afterwards, in the wars of the Tân-bo-Cooalney, one seeing him moving in the fore-front of Queen Meave's host said, 'He seems to me, observing him, to resemble a great tree that stands alone upon the lawn of some noble Dûn.' But to him the children of Usna were dearer than all the rest of the Red Branch. Naysi was the most beautiful of the brothers, black as the raven were his eyebrows and curling hair, and white and ruddy his countenance.

It so happened that, in a great chase, Naysi, the son of Usna, got separated from his companions, and as he wandered through the forest, seeking to recover his way, he came to where was the lonely tower in which Deirdré was immured. But he presented himself to her as she walked among the trees, and the end of that meeting was, that they gave each other their love, and plighted a faithful troth.

Then Naysi took counsel with his brothers, and with the chiefs of his clan, and they were troubled and afraid, and besought him to cease from that upon which he had resolved. But, when they could not persuade him, they resolved to perish along with him before the wrath of the High King, if it were necessary, rather than suffer him to be unbefriended.

So there was a sudden hosting of the clan, and they bore away Deirdré from her tower, and marched rapidly northwards to the Moyle. But at Dûn Kermnah, upon the sea, a fleet was prepared. Thus the Clanna Usna deserted Concobar Mac Nessa, and they passed into Alba,[1] and went into the service of the king of that land.

Then there was great lamentation over all Ulla, for the loss of the children of Usna, and in every Dûn, from Assaroe to Dundalgan, the poets chanted mournful strains about the exile of the sons of Usna, and the wondrous beauty of Deirdré, and the noblest of the youth of Ulla, and of the rest of Eiré, passed into Alba, to see Deirdré, and many of them took service under them, and the Clan Usna grew mightier every day. But Concobar Mac Nessa passed sentence of perpetual banishment and exile against the clan, for he feared the words of the prophet prophesying the Red Branch divided against itself.

---

1 *Alba*: Scotland.

But, from the time of their departure, Fergus Mac Roy had no rest, for he was disconsolate for the perpetual exile of Naysi, Anly, and Ardan, and he was wroth with Concobar Mac Nessa, and uttered bitter gibes and scoffs against the High King and his star-gazers. But, in the end, he procured a reversal of the sentence of perpetual exile, and forthwith, taking his household troops, and his sons, Illan the Fair, and Bewney the Ruthless Red, he passed over into Alba; and when the sons of Usna heard of the reversal of the sentence, they gave three shouts of joy, and shed tears of pleasure; but Deirdré uttered three cries of lamentation, and shed tears of sorrow, for she said that evil was impending over the children of Usna. Then Fergus Mac Roy said that they were under his protection, and that no harm could happen them, for that there was no king in Erin who could break through his protection. But Deirdré would not be comforted, and all the day and night she shed tears, and related dreams and omens, and predicted the treachery of Bewney the Ruthless Red; yet they did not give heed to her, but hastened forward the sailing. But innumerable were the lamentations of Deirdré concerning the children of Usna, and they are preserved in the books of the poets. And, both in Alba, before they set out, and while they sailed across the intervening sea, were they warned by many portents. But beside many other, it was permitted them to hear the mournful chanting of the unhappy children of Lear. For, as they rowed across the cold expanse of the Moyle,[1] they heard the children singing, and it was night. There the hands of all the mariners were relaxed, and every oar suspended. Then the whole host wept together, and the warriors and strong men sobbed aloud, when they heard the children singing, for the cry of them, as they sang, pierced the starry night, and dissolved every heart.

After this, they rowed on in silence, and came to Dûn Kermnah, and the children of Usna hastened onward to Emain Macha, trusting in the High King, that he would not violate the protection of Mac Roy.

Nay-the-less, Concobar Mac Nessa gave no heed to the protection of Fergus, for he saw that his authority and sovereignty were set aside, and that now the wars predicted by Cathvah were about to burst, and that Fergus and the children of Usna were confederate against him. Therefore, he made a swift and sudden excursion into the north, with his bravest and most agile warriors; but Fergus Mac Roy had delayed at Dûn Kermnah, having been detained there by a stratagem, and Bewney the Ruthless Red went over to his side, and betrayed the chil-

---

1 *Moyle*: the sea that divides Scotland and Ireland.

dren of Usna. But Concobar Mac Nessa seized Deirdré and Naysi, Anly and Ardan, and he slew the children of Usna, and Illan the Fair, and many of the Clan Usna, and despised the protection of Fergus Mac Roy.

But, when Fergus Mac Roy heard how his protection had been set at naught, and his son slain, and the sons of Usna, he passed into rebellion, and drew away with him two-thirds of the Red Branch; for wide territories passed into rebellion along with him, and amongst them Cormac Conlingas, the High King's son, and the children of Iar were divided against themselves, and the whole realm was shaken with war, and Emain Macha burned to the ground; but, in the end, Fergus Mac Roy was defeated, and driven over the border into the country of the Olnemacta, west of the Shannon, and all these exiles went into the service of Aileel More and Queen Meave, and Fergus Mac Roy was the greatest of her generals at the breaking out of the wars of the Tan-bo-Cooalney.[1]

The Nuts Of Knowledge

'And a river went out of Eden to water the garden; and from thence it was parted, and became into four heads. The name of the first river is Pison, and the name of the second river is Gihon, and the name of the third river is Hiddekel, and the fourth river is Euphrates.'

MOSES[2]

In the heart of green Banba a fairy garden, and in the garden an ever-springing fountain of pure translucent water. But, unseen of the Gæil, that well leaped and bubbled, and the Tuatha De Danan alone beheld it, themselves unseen, a divine race. There for ages it leaped and sprang, feeding the great streams of Fohla.

Around the well grew hazel-trees, seven in number, with leaves of tender green, and berries of bright crimson, and the nuts that grew on these trees filled with knowledge the mind of any who ate them, so that to him the past and present and future were revealed, and the Tuatha Eireen alone had access to that garden, and ate not of the fruit of those trees, for holy fear and ancient prophecy forbade.

But Sinân, who was of the race of Lear, the marine god, having an evil mind, resolved to eat of the fruit, and she approached the fountain

---

1 *Tan-bo-Cooalney*: the Cattle Raid of Cuailnge (Irish: *Táin Bó Cuailnge*), the principal epic of the Ulster Cycle, to which the story of Deirdre is a fore-tale.
2 Genesis 2:10–14.

by stealth. But the divine fountain arose in wrath with a roaring, with billows and water-spouts and foam, and it caught and surrounded her, and overwhelmed her as she fled, and whirling her along and around, brake forth westward and southward. And, like a dead leaf, it bore her past the Great Ford, and past the city of the hostings and the fairy hills, where Bove Derg had his habitation, and past Limenich,[1] and cast her into the great sea westward. But thenceforward the waters of western Erin flowed along the channel which had been made by the flood which the sacred well-head had cast forth against the grand-daughter of Lear, and after her it has received its name.

Unseen by the Gaeil the fountain still springs, feeding the great stream of Fohia, and the hazels shed their crimson fruit on the mossy ground, and into the clear water, and beneath the ground it sends forth rills feeding the great streams. But at the time of the shedding of fruit, a salmon, the Yeo Feasa appears in that garden in the clear well, and as each divine nut falls upon the surface, he darts upwards and devours it. He is larger and more beautiful than the fishes of his tribe, glittering with crimson stars and bright hues; but for the rest of the year he roams the wide ocean and the great streams of Inis Fail.[2] Now when any of the Gaeil excelled in wisdom, men said he has eaten of the nuts of knowledge, and of Cathvah, too, the Ard-Druid, men said this.

From *The Coming of Cuculain*

(1894)

The Smith's Supper Party

'Bearing on shoulders immense
Atlantean the weight,
Well nigh not to be borne,
Of the too vast orb of her fate.'

MATTHEW ARNOLD[3]

One day, in the forenoon, a man came to Emain Macha.[4] He was grim and swarthy, with great hands and arms. He made no reverence to Concobar or to any of the Ultonians,[5] but standing stark before them,

---

1 *Limenich*: Limerick.
2 *Inis Fail*: 'Island of Destiny', one of the ancient names of Ireland.
3 'Heine's Grave', 7–10.
4 *Emain Macha*: the mythical capital of Ulster, seat of Concobar mac Nessa.
5 *Ultonians*: Ulstermen (*Obs.*).

spake thus, not fluently:—'My master, Culain, high smith of all Ulster, bids thee to supper this night, O Concobar; and he wills thee to know that because he has not wide territories, and flocks, and herds, and tribute-paying peoples, only the implements of his industry, his anvils and hammers and tongs, and the slender profits of his labour, he feareth to feast all the Red Branch, who are by report mighty to eat and to drink; he would not for all Ireland bring famine upon his own industrious youths, his journeymen and his apprentices. Come therefore with a choice selection of thy knights, choosing those who are not great eaters, and drinkers, and you shall all have a fair welcome, a goodly supper, and a proportionate quantity of drink.' That speech was a cause of great mirth to the Ultonians; nevertheless they restrained their laughter, so that the grim ambassador, who seemed withal to be a very angry man, saw nothing but grave countenances. Concobar answered him courteously, saying that he accepted the invitation, and that he would be mindful of the smith's wishes. When the man departed the Red Branch gave a loose rein to their mirth, each man charging the other with being in especial the person whose presence would be a cause of sorrow to the smith.

Culain was a mighty craftsman in those days. It was he who used to make weapons, armour, and chariots for the Ultonians, and there was never in Ireland a better smith than he. In his huge and smoky dun the ringing of hammers and the husky roar of the bellows seldom ceased; even at night the red glare of his furnaces painted far and wide the barren moor where he dwelt. Herdsmen and shepherds who, in quest of estrays, found themselves unawares in this neighbourhood, fled away praying to their gods, and, as they ran, murmured incantations.

In the afternoon Concobar, having made as good a selection as he could of his chief men, set forth to go. As they passed through the lawn he saw Setanta playing with his comrades. He stopped for a while to look, and then called the lad, who came at once and stood erect and silent before the King. He was now full ten years of age, straight and well-made and with sinews as hard as tempered steel. When he saw the company looking at him, he blushed, and his blushing became him well.

'Culain the smith,' said Concobar, 'hath invited us to a feast. If it is pleasing to thee, come too.'

'It is pleasing indeed,' replied the boy, for he ardently desired to see the famous artificer, his people, his furnaces, and his engines. 'But let me first, I pray thee, see this our game brought to an end, for the boys await my return. After that I will follow quickly, nor can I lose my way upon the moor, for the road hence to the smith's dun is well trodden and scored with wheels, and the sky too at night is red above the city.'

Concobar gave him permission, and Setanta hastened back to his playmates, who hailed him gladly in his returning, for they feared that the King might have taken him away from them.

The King and his great men went away eastward after that and they conversed eagerly by the way, talking sometimes of a certain recent great rebellion of the non-Irian kings of Ulla,[1] and of each other's prowess and the prowess of the insurgents, and sometimes of the smith and his strange and unusual invitation.

'Say no word and do no thing,' said Concobar, 'at which even a very angry and suspicious man might take offence, for as to our host and his artificers, their ways are not like ours, or their thoughts like our thoughts, and they are a great and formidable people.'

The Red Branch did not relish that speech, for they thought that under the measureless canopy of the sky there were no people great or formidable but themselves.

Setanta and the Smith's Dog

> 'How he fell
> From heaven, they fabled, thrown by angry Jove
> Sheer o'er the crystal battlements; from morn
> To noon, from noon to dewy eve,
> A Summer's day, he fell; and with the setting sun
> Dropped from the zenith like a falling star,
> On Lemnos.'
>
> MILTON[2]

When Culain saw far away the tall figures of the Ultonians against the sunset, and the flashing of their weapons and armour, he cried out with a loud voice to his people to stop working and slack the furnaces and make themselves ready to receive the Red Branch; and he bade the household thralls prepare the supper, roast, boiled and stewed, which he had previously ordered. Then he himself and his journey-men and apprentices stripped themselves, and in huge keeves of water filled by their slaves they washed from them the smoke and sweat of their labour and put on clean clothes. The mirrors at which they

---

1 *the non-Irian kings of Ulla*: The Ultonians were descended from Ir, son of Milesius. [*O'Grady's note.*]
2 *Paradise Lost*, Book I, 740–6.

dressed themselves were the darkened waters of their enormous tubs.

Culain sent a party of his men and those who were the best dressed and the most comely and who were the boldest and most eloquent in the presence of strangers, to meet the high King of the Ultonians on the moor, but he himself stood huge in the great doorway just beyond the threshold and in front of the bridge over which the Red Branch party was to pass. He had on him over his clothes a clean leathern apron which was not singed or scored. It was fastened at his shoulders and half covered his enormous hairy chest, was girt again at his waist and descended below his knees. He stood with one knee crooked, leaning upon a long ash-handled sledge with a head of glittering bronze. There he gave a friendly and grave welcome to the King and to all the knights one by one. It was dusk when Concobar entered the dun.

'Are all thy people arrived?' said the smith.

'They are,' said Concobar.

Culain bade his people raise the drawbridge which spanned the deep black moat surrounding the city, and after that, with his own hands he unchained his one dog. The dog was of great size and fierceness. It was supposed that there was no man in Ireland whom he could not drag down. He had no other good quality than that he was faithful to his master and guarded his property vigilantly at night. He was quick of sight and hearing and only slept in the daytime. Being let loose he sprang over the moat and three times careered round the city, baying fearfully. Then he stood stiffly on the edge of the moat to watch and listen, and growled at intervals when he heard some noise far away. It was then precisely that Setanta set forth from Emain Macha. Earth quaked to the growling of that ill beast.

In the meantime the smith went into the dun, and when he had commanded his people to light the candles throughout the chamber, he slammed to the vast folding doors with his right hand and his left, and drew forth the massy bar from its place and shot it into the opposing cavity. There was not a knight amongst the Red Branch who could shut one of those doors, using both hands and his whole strength. Of the younger knights, some started to their feet and laid their hands on their sword hilts when they heard the bolt shot.

The smith sat down on his high seat over against Concobar, with his dusky sons and kinsmen around him, and truly they contrasted strangely with the bravery and beauty of the Ultonians. He called for ale, and holding in his hands a huge four-cornered mether[1] of the same, rimmed with silver and furnished with a double silver hand-

---

1 *mether*: square wooden drinking cup frequently mentioned in Irish song.

grip, he pledged the King and bade him and his a kindly welcome. He swore, too, that no generation of the children of Rury, and he had wrought for many, had done more credit to his workmanship than themselves, nor had he ever made the appliances of war for any of the Gael with equal pleasure. Concobar, on the other hand, responded discreetly, and praised the smith-work of Culain, praising chiefly the shield called Ocean,[1] which was one of the wonders of the north-west of Europe. The smith and all his people were well pleased at that speech, and Culain bade his thralls serve supper, which proved to be a very noble repast. There was enough and to spare for all the Ultonians. When supper was ended, the heroes and the artificers pledged each other many times and drank also to the memory of famous men of yore and their fathers who begat them, as was right and customary; and they became very friendly and merry without intoxication, for intoxication was not known in the age of the heroes.

Then said Concobar: 'We have this night toasted many heroes who are gone, and, as it is not right that we should praise ourselves, I propose that we drink now to the heroes that are coming, both those unborn, and those who, still being boys, are under tutors and instructors; and for this toast I name the name of my nephew Setanta, son of Sualtam, who, if any, will one day, O Culain, if I mistake not, illustrate in an unexampled manner thy skill as an artificer of weapons and armour.'

'Is he then a boy of that promise, O Concobar?' said the smith, 'for if he is I am truly rejoiced to hear it.'

'He is all that I say,' answered the King somewhat hotly, 'and of a beauty corresponding. And of that thou shalt be the judge to-night, for he is coming, and indeed I am momentarily expecting to hear the loud clamour of his brazen hurle upon the doors of the dun, after his having leapt at one bound both thy moat and thy rampart.'

The smith started from his high seat uttering a great oath, such as men used then, and sternly chid Concobar because he had said that all his people had arrived. 'If the boy comes now,' he said, 'ere I can chain the dog, verily he will be torn into small pieces.'

Just then they heard the baying of the dog sounding terribly in the hollow night, and every face was blanched throughout the vast chamber. Then without was heard a noise of trampling feet and short furious yells and sibilant gaspings, as of one who exerts all his strength, after which a dull sound at which the earth seemed to shake, mingled

---

1 *the shield called Ocean*: Concobar's shield. When Concobar was in danger the shield roared. The sea, too, roared responsive. [*O'Grady's note.*]

with a noise of breaking bones, and after that silence. Ere the people in the dun could do more than look at each other speechless, they heard a clear but not clamorous knocking at the doors of the dun. Some of the smith's young men back-shot the bolt and opened the doors, and the boy Setanta stepped in out of the night. He was very pale. His scarlet mantle was in rags and trailing, and his linen tunic beneath and his white knees red with blood, which ran down his legs and over his bare feet. He made a reverence, as he had been taught, to the man of the house and to his people, and went backwards to the upper end of the chamber. The Ultonians ran to meet him, but Fergus Mac Roy was the first, and he took Setanta upon his mighty shoulder and bore him along and set him down at the table between himself and the King.

'Did the dog come against thee?' said Culain.

'Truly he came against me,' answered the boy.

'And art thou hurt?' cried the smith.

'No, indeed,' answered Setanta, 'but I think he is.'

At that moment a party of the smith's people entered the dun bearing between them the carcass of the dog from whose mouth and white crooked fangs the blood was gushing in red torrents; and they showed Culain how the skull of the dog and his ribs had been broken in pieces by some mighty blow, and his backbone also in divers places. Also they said: 'One of the great brazen pillars which stand at the bridge head is bent awry, and the clean bronze defiled with blood, and it was at the foot of that pillar we found the dog.' So saying, they laid the body upon the heather in front of Culain's high seat, that it might be full in his eye, and when they did so and again sat down, there was a great silence in the chamber.

Setanta, the Peace-Maker

'The swine-herd[1] of Bove Derg, son of the Dagda,
The feasts to which he came used to end in blood.'

GAELIC BARD

Culain sat silent for a long time looking out before him with eyes like iron, and when at last he spoke his voice was charged with wrath and sorrow.

'O Concobar,' he said, 'and you, the rest, nobles of the children of

---

1 *The swine-herd*: One of the minor gods. He resembles Mars Sylvanus of the Romans to whom swine were sacrificed. [*O'Grady's note.*]

Rury. You are my guests to-night, wherefore it is not lawful that I should take vengeance upon you for the killing of my brave and faithful hound, who was a better keeper of my treasures than a company of hired warriors. Truly he cost me nothing but his daily allowance of meat, and there was not his equal as a watcher and warder in the world. An eric,[1] therefore, I must have. Consult now together concerning its amount and let the eric be great and conspicuous, for, by Orchil[2] and all the gods who rule beneath the earth, a small eric I will not accept.'

Concobar answered straight, 'Thou shalt not get from me or from the Ultonians any eric, small or great. My nephew slew the beast in fair fight, defending his life against an aggressor. But I will say something else, proud smith, and little it recks me whether it is pleasing to thee or not. Had thy wolf slain my nephew not one of you would have left this dun alive, and of your famous city of artificers I would have made a smoking heap.'

The Ultonians fiercely applauded that speech, declaring that the smiths should get no eric, great or small, for the death of their monster. The smiths thereupon armed themselves with their hammers, and tongs, and fire-poles, and great bars of unwrought brass, and Culain himself seized an anvil withal to lay waste the ranks of the Red Branch. The Ultonians on their side ran to the walls and plucked down their spears from the pegs, and they raised their shields and balanced their long spears, and swords flashed and screeched as they rushed to light out of the scabbards, and the vast chamber glittered with shaking bronze and shone with the eyeballs of angry men, and rang with shouts of defiance and quick fierce words of command. For the Red Branch embattled themselves on one side of the chamber and the smiths upon the other, burning with unquenchable wrath, earthborn. The vast and high dome re-echoing rang with the clear terrible cries of the Ultonians and the roar of the children of the gloomy Orchil, and, far away, the magic shield moaned at Emain Macha, and the waves of the ocean sent forth a cry, for the peril of death and of shortness of life were around Concobar in that hour. And, though the doors of thick oak, brass-bound, were shut and barred, there came a man into the assembly, and he was not seen. He was red all over, both flesh and raiment, as if he had been plunged in a bath of blood. His countenance was distraught and his eyes like those of an insane man, and sparks flew from them like sparks from a smith's stithy when he

---

1 *eric*: compensation.
2 *Orchil*: The queen of the infernal regions. [*O'Grady's note.*]

mightily hammers iron plucked white from the furnace. Smoke and fire came from his mouth. He held in his hand a long boar-yard.[1] The likeness of a boar bounded after him. He traversed the vast chamber with the velocity of lightning, and with his boar-yard beat such as were not already drunk with wrath and battle-fury, and shot insane fire into their souls.[2]

Then indeed it wanted little, not the space of time during which a man might count ten, for the beginning of a murder grim and great as any renowned in the world's chronicles, and it is the opinion of the learned that, in spite of all their valour and beautiful weapons, the artificers would then and there have made a bloody end of the Red Branch had the battle gone forward. But at this moment, ere the first missile was hurled on either side, the boy Setanta sprang into the midst, into the middle space which separated the enraged men, and cried aloud, with a clear high voice that rang distinct above the tumult—

'O Culain, forbear to hurl, and restrain thy people, and you the Ultonians, my kinsmen, delay to shoot. To thee, O chief smith, and thy great-hearted artificers I will myself pay no unworthy eric for the death of thy brave and faithful hound. For verily I will myself take thy dog's place, and nightly guard thy property, sleepless as he was, and I will continue to do so till a hound as trusty and valiant as the hound whom I slew is procured for thee to take his place, and to relieve me of that duty. Truly I slew not thy hound in any wantonness of superior strength, but only in the defence of my own life, which is not mine but my King's. Three times he leaped upon me with white fangs bared and eyes red with murder, and three times I cast him off, but when the fourth time he rushed upon me like a storm, and when with great difficulty I had balked him on that occasion also, then I took him by the throat and by his legs and flung him against one of the brazen pillars withal to make him stupid. And truly it was not my intention to kill him and I am sorry that he is dead, seeing that he was so faithful and so brave, and so dear to thee whom I have always honoured, even when I was a child at Dun Dalgan, and whom, with thy marvel-working craftsmen, I have for a long time eagerly desired to see. And I thought that our meeting, whensoever it might be, would be other than this and more friendly.'

As he went on speaking the fierce brows of the smith relaxed, and

---

1 *boar-yard*: stick for controlling boar.
2 *He traversed the vast chamber .... shot insane fire into their souls*: This was the demon referred to in the lines at the head of the chapter. [*O'Grady's note.*]

first he regarded the lad with pity, being so young and fair, and then with admiration for his bravery. Also he thought of his own boyish days, and as he did so a torrent of kindly affection and love poured from his breast towards the boy, yea, though he saw him standing before him with the blood of his faithful hound gilding his linen lena[1] and his white limbs. Yet, indeed, it was not the hound's blood which was on the boy, but his own, so cruelly had the beast torn him with his long and strong and sharp claws.

'That proposal is pleasing to me,' he said, 'and I will accept the eric, which is distinguished and conspicuous and worthy of my greatness and of my name and reputation amongst the Gael. Why should a man be angry for ever when he who did the wrong offers due reparation?' Therewith over his left shoulder he flung the mighty anvil into the dark end of the vast chamber among the furnaces, at the sound of whose falling the solid earth shook. On the other hand Concobar rejoiced at this happy termination of the quarrel, for well he knew the might of those huge children of the gloomy Orchil. He perceived, too, that he could with safety entrust the keeping of the lad to those people, for he saw the smith's countenance when it changed, and he knew that among those artificers there was no guile.

'It is pleasing to me, too,' he said, 'and I will be myself the lad's security for the performance of his promise.'

'Nay, I want no security,' answered the smith. 'The word of a scion of the Red Branch is security enough for me.'

Thereafter all laid aside their weapons and their wrath. The smiths with a mighty clattering cast their tools into the dark end of the chamber, and the Ultonians hanged theirs upon the walls, and the feasting and pledging and making of friendly speeches were resumed. There was no more any anger anywhere, but a more unobstructed flow of mutual good-will and regard, for the Ultonians felt no more a secret inclination to laugh at the dusky artificers, and the smiths no longer regarded with disdain the beauty, bravery, and splendour of the Ultonians.

In the meantime Setanta had returned to his place between the King and Fergus Mac Roy. There a faintness came upon him, and a great horror overshadowed him owing to his battle with the dog, for indeed it was no common dog, and when he would have fallen, owing to the faintness, they pushed him behind them so that he lay at full length upon the couch unseen by the smiths. Concobar nodded to his chief Leech, and he came to him with his instruments and salves and

---

1 *lena*: Irish, *léine*, 'linen garment'.

washes. There unobserved he washed the cruel gashes cut by the hound's claws, and applied salves and stitched the skin over the wounds, and, as he did so, in a low voice he murmured healing songs of power.

'Where is the boy?' said Culain.

'He is reposing a little,' said Concobar, 'after his battle and his conflict.'

After a space they gave Setanta a draught of mighty ale, and his heart revived in him and the colour returned to his cheeks wherein before was the pallor of death, and he sat up again in his place, slender and fair, between Concobar and Fergus Mac Roy. The smiths cried out a friendly welcome to him as he sat up, for they held him now to be their foster-son, and Culain himself stood up in his place holding in both hands a great mether[1] of ale, and he drank to all unborn and immature heroes, naming the name of Setanta, son of Sualtam, now his dear foster-son, and magnified his courage, so that the boy blushed vehemently and his eyelids trembled and drooped; and all the artificers stood up too and drank to their foster-son, wishing him victory and success, and they drained their goblets and dashed them, mouth downwards, upon the brazen tables, so that the clang reverberated over Ulla. Setanta thereupon stood up while the smiths roared a welcome to their foster-son, and he said that it was not he who had gained the victory, for that someone invisible had assisted him and had charged him with a strength not his own. Then he faltered in his speech and said again that he would be a faithful hound in the service of the artificers, and sat down. The smiths at that time would not have yielded him for all the hounds in the world.

After that their harpers harped for them and their story-tellers related true stories, provoking laughter and weeping. There was no story told that was not true in the age of the heroes. Then the smiths sang one of their songs of labour, though it needed the accompaniment of ringing mettle, a song wild and strange, and the Ultonians clear and high sang all together with open mouths a song of battle and triumph and of the marching home to Emain Macha with victory; and so they spent the night, till Concobar said—

'O Culain, feasting and singing are good, but slumber is good also. Dismiss us now to our rest and our slumber, for we, the Red Branch, must rise betimes in the morning, having our own proper work to perform day by day in Emain Macha, as you yours in your industrious city.'

---

1 *mether*: A four-cornered quadrangular cup [*O'Grady's note.*]

With difficulty were the smiths persuaded to yield to that request, for right seldom was there a feast in Dun Culain, and the unusual pleasure and joyful sense of comradeship and social exaltation were very pleasing to their hearts.

The Ultonians slept that night in the smiths' hall upon resplendent couches which had been prepared for them, and early in the morning, having taken a friendly leave of the artificers, they departed, leaving the lad behind them asleep. Setanta remained with the smiths a long time after that, and Culain and his people loved him greatly and taught him many things. It was owing to this adventure and what came of it that Setanta got his second name, viz., the Hound of Culain or Cu-Culain. Under that name he wrought all his marvellous deeds.

From *Toryism and the Tory Democracy*

(1886)

from Ireland And The Hour

... I believe there is no example in history of a lethargic, effete aristocracy such as yours[1] getting reformed from within, and yet as against such a reform I can perceive no very serious obstacle, save the extreme shortness of the time still left you and the strength of the evil habits which you must abandon. He who leaves the right road has little difficulty in returning if he soon discovers his error. A few steps to the right hand or the left, and he is once more upon the way. But you now for some two hundred years have been travelling all awry, travelling like that pilgrim who at the end of his journey on smooth and level ground found himself at length right beneath an impending mountain, from which thunder rolled and fire flashed. You, too, trusted the smooth glozing words of Mr. Carnal Wise-man, declaring that in the town of Morality lived one Mr. Legality, who had much skill in easing men of those burthens to which all flesh is heir. Well, you have long since taken up your abode with that same smooth-spoken gentleman, and know now that Mr. Legality is a quack in spite of his clean brass door-plate and suave demeanour, and the *Mountain,* as once against that noblesse whose skins were tanned at Meudon,[2] comes closer and closer. Do you know anything of Thomas Carlyle,

---

1 *such as yours*: O'Grady is addressing the Irish landed gentry.
2 *that noblesse whose skins were tanned at Meudon*: during the reign of terror of the French Revolution, the skins of the guillotined were tanned at Meudon, near Paris.

'The writing fellow? Was there not something in the newspapers about his wife?'[1] Christ save us all! You read nothing, know nothing. This great modern democratic world rolls on with its thunderings, lightnings, and voices, enough to make the bones of your heroic fathers turn in their graves, and you know nothing about it, care nothing about it. You sit in the easy-chair of Mr. Legality, with your title-deeds on the table, and comfort your souls with the very unfavourable opinion that that cock-sure gentleman has formed of the Mountain. Yet one stood by you not so long since, grim of aspect and strange of speech, though indeed he spake plain English too, and said this: 'Put not your trust in parchments. Though you have parchments enough to thatch the world, these combustible, fallible sheepskins will not save you.'[2] And even if you should now, winged with terror and pricked by sharp conscience, hasten back to the right road—narrow and rough, but the right road for all that—what a way you have to travel, skirting the edge, nay, rather through the bowels of that flaming Mountain!

Of you as a class, as a body of men, I can entertain not the least hope; who, indeed, can? If the times with their words of thunder do not alarm you, do not send you flying like one assailed by murderers from that same snug solicitor's office, parchment-strewn, I know that my words will not, that the words of no man will. These words of mine you will not read, or reading, will not understand. Your enemies will read them, and in the main understand; but you will do neither. For even those of you who have had the grace to remain in the land have grown as earthy and dull as the earth itself. A respectable Dublin

---

1 *Thomas Carlyle.... his wife*: Thomas Carlyle (1795–1881), Scottish essayist and social historian. After a long courtship Jane Baillie Welsh (1801–66) consented to marry him, in 1826. She, 'the flower of Haddington', was renowned for her wit and beauty. They moved to her farm at Craigenputtick, where he wrote his famous *Sartor Resartus*. Theirs was not a happy union; in his *Reminiscences* (1881) Carlyle admitted to his neglect of her.
2 Thomas Carlyle, *Past and Present* (1843) Bk. 3 Chap. 7:
> To the 'Millocracy' so-called, to the Working Aristocracy, steeped too deep in mere ignoble Mammonism, and as yet all unconscious of its noble destinies, as yet but an irrational or semi-rational giant, struggling to awake some soul in itself, – the world will have much to say, reproachfully, reprovingly, admonishingly. But to the Idle Aristocracy, what will the world have to say? Things painful and not pleasant!
>
> '...To the idler, again, never so gracefully going idle, coming forward with never so many parchments, you will not hasten out; you will sit still, and be disinclined to rise. You will say to him: "Not welcome, O complex Anomaly; would thou hadst staid out of doors: for who of mortals knows what to do with thee? Thy parchments: yes, they are old, of venerable yellowness; and we too honour parchment, old-established settlements, and venerable use and wont.... We apprise thee of the world-old fact, becoming sternly disclosed again in these days, That he who cannot work in this Universe cannot get existed in it: had he parchments to thatch the face of the world, these, combustible fallible sheepskin, cannot avail him. Home, thou unfortunate; and let us have at least no noise from thee!"'

publisher informed me recently that he seldom or never received an order from a country gentleman for a new book. 'Such new books as I sell are bought,' he added, 'by Dublin professional men.' You have hunted the fox till, like that old red hunter, you have come to despise your birthright, and all that treats of it, and cultivated crops, till the very clay of the earth is more intelligent than yours. Your serious talk is of bullocks, and in short, 'Quos Deus vult perdere prius dementat.'[1] Your ancestors, who raised the noble classic buildings of Dublin, loved a Latin quotation. The less ignoble Siren of classicism and culture they were not beyond admiring. Of you now I doubt if one in twenty could translate that hackneyed newspaper phrase. For so, by easy stages, aristocracies run or slide downhill. The heroic ardour goes first, culture and intellectual refinement come and depart. Loyalty to even your own class in due time disappears, and personal worth, the simple cardinal virtues of the private citizen, last of all. These, indeed, still remain with you, and while they last Pandora's box is not empty.

Of you, as a collective body of men, even those of you who have still the grace to remain with us and stick to the sinking ship, I entertain not the least hope. It is for individuals here and there I write this book, knowing that even a very few, such as one might count on the fingers of one hand, if of the right mettle and the right calibre, may be able even now to awake you from your slumber, and breathe, which I and men like me cannot, some breath of life into your nostrils. Here and there, such men, I believe, are in Ireland, men who look with shame and dismay upon your astonishing stupidity, men of finer mould, more subtle intelligence, of more patriotic spirit and class spirit, of a conscience not seared, of a soul not altogether dead in your trespasses and sins. To you, here and there over Ireland, or outside Ireland, and though but one, or two, or three, I would now address myself, and especially to the young, whose hearts are not yet hardened by contact with the rest or worn out by that grinding attrition.

ALFRED PERCEVAL GRAVES (1846–1928)

Born in Dublin, the second son of Charles Graves, chaplain to Dublin Castle and afterwards bishop of Limerick, and Selina Cheyne, physician-general to the forces in Ireland, he spent his childhood partly in Parknasilla, Co. Kerry. He was educated in Windermere College, and in Trinity College, Dublin. After six years as a clerk and private secretary in the Home Office, Graves embarked on his long and distinguished

---

1 *Quos Deus vult perdere prius dementat*: 'Whom God wishes to destroy he first drives mad' (attr. Euripides).

career as inspector of schools. While stationed at Taunton, in Devon, he collaborated on *Songs of Old Ireland* (1882) and *Songs of Erin* (1892) with Sir Charles Villiers Stanford, the Irish composer (of church music, oratorios and cantatas) and conductor, noted for his influence on succeeding generations. For these songs Graves wrote and adapted the words to Irish folk tunes, many derived from the collection of George Petrie (he sold the musical rights to his publisher, and used to say that for his ever-popular 'Father O'Flynn' he received nothing but the original fee of £1. 12s. from the *Spectator*). In 1895 Graves was stationed in Southwark, where he became a leading figure in the London Irish Literary Society. He contributed humorous pieces to *Punch*; as editor and anthologist he contributed to the appreciation of the Irish popular verse tradition. His own translations were based on those of others, for he had but a smattering of Gaelic. In 1902, Graves wrote the libretto of *The Post Bag: A Lesson in Irish*, an opera with music by the Dublin-based Michele Esposito. Graves spent his last years in Harlech, Wales, where he wrote the autobiographical *To Return to All That* (1930) in reply to his son Robert's marvellous autobiography, *Goodbye to All That*, to set the family record straight.

From *Irish Songs and Ballads*

(1880)

The Girl I Left Behind Me[1]

The route[2] has come, we march away,
　　Our colours dance before us,
But sorrow's cloud made dark the day
　　That from our sweethearts tore us.
My own dear lass she sobb'd 'adieu,'
　　Her loving arms entwined me,
And oft she pray'd that I'd be true
　　To the girl I left behind me.

Yes! I'll be true; when steel to steel,
　　The ranks of war are rolling,
And round us every cannon peal
　　A funeral knell is tolling;
Then if from out the battle flame
　　A fatal ball should find me,

---

1 There are several well-known versions of this song. I need hardly say, therefore, that my words are original except so far as the situation of the singer and the refrain are concerned. [*Graves' note.*]

2 *route*: pronounced 'rout' by the soldiers = marching orders. [*Graves' note.*]

My dying lips shall bless the name
    Of the girl I left behind me.

But, if in triumph I return
    To tell a soldier's story,
Though proudly on my breast should burn
    The golden cross of glory;
No other maid with magic art
    Shall break the links that bind me
For ever to the faithful heart
    Of the girl I left behind me.

Father O'Flynn

Of priests we can offer a charmin' variety,
Far renowned for larnin' and piety;
Still, I'd advance ye, widout impropriety,
    Father O'Flynn as the flower of them all.

CHORUS.
    Here's a health to you, Father O'Flynn,
    Slainté,[1] and slainté, and slainté agin;
    Powerfulest preacher, and
    Tinderest teacher, and
    Kindliest creature in ould Donegal.

Don't talk of your Provost and Fellows of Trinity,[2]
Famous for ever at Greek and Latinity,
Faix and the divels and all at Divinity,
    Father O'Flynn 'd make hares of them all.[3]
    Come, I vinture to give you my word,
    Never the likes of his logic was heard,
      Down from Mythology
      Into Thayology,
    Troth! and Conchology, if he'd the call.

CHORUS.

---

1 *Slainté*: Your health. [*Graves' note.*]
2 *Trinity*: Dublin University [*Graves' note.*]
3 *make hares of them*: utterly rout and put to flight in argument, a common Irish peasant phrase. [*Graves' note.*]

Och! Father O'Flynn, you've the wonderful way wid you,
All ould sinners are wishful to pray wid you,
All the young childer are wild for to play wid you,
  You've such a way wid you, Father avick![1]
   Still, for all you've so gentle a soul,
    Gad, you've your flock in the grandest control;
     Checking the crazy ones,
     Coaxin' onaisy ones,
   Liftin' the lazy ones on wid the stick.

CHORUS.

And though quite avoidin' all foolish frivolity,
Still at all seasons of innocent jollity,
Where was the play-boy could claim an equality
  At comicality Father, wid you?
   Once the Bishop looked grave at your jest,
   Till this remark set him off wid the rest:
    'Is it lave gaiety
    All to the laity?
  Cannot the clargy be Irishmen too?'

CHORUS.

The Little Red Lark[2]

O swan of slenderness,
Dove of tenderness,
  Jewel of joys, arise!
The little red lark,
Like a rosy spark
  Of song, to his sunburst flies;
But till thou art risen,
Earth is a prison,
  Full of my lonesome sighs;
Then awake and discover,

---

1 *avick*: 'My son,' a palpable bull in the context. [*Graves' note.*]
2 This poem was suggested by the following passage from Miss Brooke's now rare 'Reliques of Irish Poetry,' p.232. 'In another song, a lover, tenderly reproaching his mistress, asks her, why she keeps morning so long indoors? and bids her come out, and bring him the day.' Its title, 'The Little Red Lark,' is given in Hoffmann's collection of Irish music [*Ancient Music of Ireland*, from the Petrie collection, arranged for the pianoforte by F. Hoffmann, 1877] as the name of an old melody. [*Graves' note.*]

To thy fond lover,
> The morn of thy matchless eyes.

The dawn is dark to me,
Hark! oh, hark to me,
> Pulse of my heart, I pray!
And out of thy hiding
With blushes gliding,
> Dazzle me with thy day.
Ah, then once more to thee
Flying I'll pour to thee
> Passion so sweet and gay,
The larks shall listen,
And dew-drops glisten,
> Laughing on every spray.

From *Father O'Flynn and other Irish Lyrics*
(1889)

The Rose of Kenmare

I've been soft in a small way
On the girleens of Galway,
And the Limerick lasses have made me feel quare;
But there's no use denyin'
No girl I've set eye on
Could compare wid Rose Ryan of the town of Kenmare.

> *O, where*
> *Can her like be found?*
> *Nowhere,*
> *The country round,*
> *Spins at her wheel*
> *Daughter as true,*
> *Sets in the reel,*
> *Wid a slide of the shoe*
> *a slinderer,*
> *tinderer,*
> *purtier,*
> *wittier colleen than you,*
> *Rose, aroo!*

Her hair mocks the sunshine,
And the soft, silver moonshine
Neck and arm of the colleen complately eclipse;
Whilst the nose of the jewel
Slants straight as Carn Tual[1]
From the heaven in her eye to her heather-sweet lips.

O, where, etc.

Did your eyes ever follow
The wings of the swallow
Here and there, light as air, o'er the meadow field glance?
For if not you've no notion
Of the exquisite motion
Of her sweet little feet as they dart in the dance.

O, where, etc.

If y'inquire why the nightingale
Still shuns the invitin' gale
That wafts every song-bird but her to the West,
Faix she knows, I suppose,
Ould Kenmare has a Rose
That would sing any Bulbul[2] to sleep in her nest.

O, where, etc.

When her voice gives the warnin'
For the milkin' in the mornin'
Ev'n the cow known for hornin' comes runnin' to her pail;
The lambs play about her
And the small bonneens[3] snout her,
Whilst their parints salute her wid a twisht of the tail.

O, where, etc.

---

1 *Carn Tual*: Carrauntoohill (from Irish *corrán tuathail*, 'left-handed sickle') in the Macgillicuddy Reeks, between Kenmare and Killarney, is the highest mountain in Ireland (1038 metres).
2 *Bulbul*: a thrush, known as 'the nightingale of the East'.
3 *bonneens*: Young pigs. [*Graves' note*.]

Alfred Perceval Graves

When at noon from our labour
We draw neighbour wid neighbour
From the heat of the sun to the shilter of the tree,
 Wid spuds[1] fresh from the bilin'
 And new milk you come smilin',
All the boys' hearts beguilin', alannah machree![2]

> O, where, etc.

But there's one sweeter hour
When the hot day is o'er
And we rest at the door wid the bright moon above,
 And she sittin' in the middle,
 When she's guessed Larry's riddle,
Cries, 'Now for your fiddle, Shiel Dhuv, Shiel Dhuv.'

> O, where
> Can her like be found?
> Nowhere,
> The country round,
> Spins at her wheel
> Daughter as true,
> Sets in the reel,
> Wid a slide of the shoe
> a slinderer,
> tinderer,
> purtier,
> wittier colleen than you,
> Rose, aroo!

---

1 *spuds*: Potatoes. [*Graves' note.*]
2 *alannah machree*: My heart's delight. [*Graves' note.*]

From *The Irish Song Book*
(1895)[1]

The March of the Maguire

My grief, Hugh Maguire,[2]
    That tonight you must go,
To wreak your just ire
    On your murderous, false foe.
For hark! as the blast
    Through the bowed wood raves past,
The great oaks, aghast
    Rock, rend, and crash below.

Uncheered of your spouse,
    Without comfort or care,
All night you must house
    In some lone, shaggy lair;
The lightning your lamp,
    For your sentry, the tramp
Of the thunder round your camp;
    Hark! 'tis there, 'tis there!

But to-morrow your sword
    More terrific shall sweep
On our foe's monstrous horde
    Than this storm o'er the steep,
And his mansions lime-white
    Flame with fearfuller light
Than yon bolts thro' black night
    Hurled blazing down the deep.

BRAM STOKER (1847–1912)

Born in Dublin, the third and sickly child of a clerk in Dublin Castle, he was educated at the Rev. Woods' private school and at Trinity College, Dublin, where he excelled in athletics. He graduated in science in 1870, and followed his father into the

---

1 This is the second edition of Graves' collection.
2 Hugh Maguire suffered many hardships during the winter of 1600–01 on his campaign with Hugh O'Neill, 2nd Earl of Tyrone, in Munster. The definite article before the surname indicates the leader of a clan. Cf. J.C. Mangan's 'O'Hussey's Ode to the Maguire', Volume II, pp. 93–95.

Civil Service. He was called to the Bar in 1890, as a member of the Inner Temple, but never practised. His first book, *The Duties of Clerks of Petty Sessions in Ireland* (1879) became a standard reference work. In college, Stoker had developed a passion for the theatre. From 1871 he was an unpaid drama reviewer for the *Dublin Evening Mail*, and befriended Sir Henry Irving, who, in 1878, asked him to manage the Lyceum theatre in London, which he did for over twenty years, organizing eight tours of the United States (where he met Walt Whitman) and Canada. A year after Irving's death, Stoker published his fulsome and anecdotal *Personal Reminiscences of Henry Irving* (2 vols). Stoker's first novel, the only one set in Ireland, *The Snake's Pass* (1891) deals with gombeenism in Co. Mayo. His fame was assured with *Dracula* (1897), which was an instant success. Stoker seems to have been influenced by Sheridan Le Fanu's *Carmilla* (1871), in which a countess preys on innocent young women; it is unlikely that he was familiar with the legends surrounding Vlad the Impaler (he did note that 'Dracula in Wallachian means devil'—it is actually 'son of the devil' in Rumanian); he quipped that the idea of the vampire came to him in a nightmare after eating crab. *Dracula* was followed by a stream of books and short stories. Stoker suffered a stroke in 1905, but continued his copious output, writing such popular novels as the panoramic *The Lady of the Shroud* (1909) and *The Lair of the White Worm* (1911), about a worm that adopts a human form. At the age of 60, he contributed an interview with Winston Churchill to the *Daily Chronicle*. Stoker was a giant of a man; in middle age he received the bronze medal from the Royal Society for his attempt to rescue a drowning man from the Thames.

From *Dracula*

(1897)

Jonathan Harker's Journal

[*Later: the Morning of 16 May*] ... I suppose I must have fallen asleep; I hope so, but I fear, for all that followed was startlingly real—so real that now, sitting here in the broad, full sunlight of the morning, I cannot in the least believe that it was all sleep.

I was not alone. The room was the same, unchanged in any way since I came into it; I could see along the floor, in the brilliant moonlight, my own footsteps marked where I had disturbed the long accumulation of dust. In the moonlight opposite me were three young women, ladies by their dress and manner. I thought at the time that I must be dreaming when I saw them, for, though the moonlight was behind them, they threw no shadow on the floor. They came close to me and looked at me for some time and then whispered together. Two were dark, and had high aquiline noses, like the Count's, and great dark, piercing eyes, that seemed to be almost red when contrasted with the pale yellow moon. The other was fair, as fair as can be, with great, wavy masses of golden hair and eyes like pale sapphires. I seemed somehow to know her face, and to know it in connection with some dreamy fear, but I could not recollect at the moment how or where. All three had brilliant white teeth, that shone like pearls against the ruby of their voluptuous lips. There was something about them that made me uneasy, some longing and at the same time some deadly fear. I felt in my heart a wicked, burning desire that they would kiss me with those red lips. It is not good to note this down, lest some day it should meet Mina's eyes and cause her pain; but it is the truth. They whispered together, and then they all three laughed—such a silvery, musical laugh, but as hard as though the sound never could have come through the softness of human lips. It was like the intolerable, tingling sweetness of water-glasses when played on by a cunning hand. The fair girl shook her head coquettishly, and the other two urged her on. One said:—

'Go on! You are first, and we shall follow; yours is the right to begin.' The other added:—

'He is young and strong; there are kisses for us all.' I lay quiet, looking out under my eyelashes in an agony of delightful anticipation. The fair girl advanced and bent over me till I could feel the movement of her breath upon me. Sweet it was in one sense, honey-sweet, and sent the same tingling through the nerves as her voice, but with a bitter underlying the sweet, a bitter offensiveness, as one smells in blood.

I was afraid to raise my eyelids, but looked out and saw perfectly under the lashes. The fair girl went on her knees and bent over me, fairly gloating. There was a deliberate voluptuousness which was both thrilling and repulsive, and as she arched her neck she actually licked her lips like an animal, till I could see in the moonlight the moisture shining on the scarlet lips and on the red tongue as it lapped the white sharp teeth. Lower and lower went her head as the lips went below the range of my mouth and chin and seemed about to fasten on my throat. Then she paused, and I could hear the churning sound of her tongue as it licked her teeth and lips, and could feel the hot breath on my neck. Then the skin of my throat began to tingle as one's flesh does when the hand that is to tickle it approaches nearer—nearer. I could feel the soft, shivering touch of the lips on the supersensitive skin of my throat, and the hard dents of two sharp teeth, just touching and pausing there. I closed my eyes in a languorous ecstasy and waited—waited with beating heart.

But at that instant another sensation swept though me as quick as lightning. I was conscious of the presence of the Count, and of his being as if lapped in a storm of fury. As my eyes opened involuntarily I saw his strong hand grasp the slender neck of the fair woman and with giant's power draw it back, the blue eyes transformed with fury, the white teeth champing with rage, and the fair cheeks blazing red with passion. But the Count! Never did I imagine such wrath and fury, even in the demons of the pit. His eyes were positively blazing. The red light in them was lurid, as if the flames of hell-fire blazed behind them. His face was deathly pale, and the lines of it were hard like drawn wires; the thick eyebrows that met over the nose now seemed like a heaving bar of white-hot metal. With a fierce sweep of his arm, he hurled the woman from him, and then motioned to the others, as though he were beating them back; it was the same imperious gesture that I had seen used to the wolves. In a voice which, though low and almost a whisper, seemed to cut through the air and then ring round the room, he exclaimed:—

'How dare you touch him, any of you? How dare you cast eyes on him when I had forbidden it? Back, I tell you all! This man belongs to me! Beware how you meddle with him, or you'll have to deal with me.' The fair girl, with a laugh of ribald coquetry, turned to answer him:—

'You yourself never loved; you never love!' On this the other women joined, and such a mirthless, hard, soulless laughter rang through the room that it almost made me faint to hear; it seemed like the pleasure of fiends. Then the Count turned, after looking at my face attentively, and said in a soft whisper:—

'Yes, I too can love; you yourselves can tell it from the past. Is it not so? Well, now I promise you that when I am done with him, you shall kiss him at your will. Now go! go! I must awaken him, for there is work to be done.'

'Are we to have nothing to-night?' said one of them, with a low laugh, as she pointed to the bag which he had thrown upon the floor, and which moved as though there were some living thing within it. For answer he nodded his head. One of the women jumped forward and opened it. If my ears did not deceive me there was a gasp and a low wail, as of a half-smothered child. The women closed round, whilst I was aghast with honor; but as I looked they disappeared, and with them the dreadful bag. There was no door near them, and they could not have passed me without my noticing. They simply seemed to fade into the rays of the moonlight and pass out through the window, for I could see outside the dim, shadowy forms for a moment before they entirely faded away.

Then the horror overcame me, and I sank down unconscious.

Memorandum by Abraham Van Helsing

5 November, morning.—Let me be accurate in everything, for though you and I have seen some strange things together, you may at the first think that I, Van Helsing, am mad—that the many horrors and the so long strain on nerves has at the last turn my brain.

All yesterday we travel, ever getting closer to the mountains, and moving into a more and more wild and desert land. There are great, frowning precipices and much falling water, and Nature seemed to have held sometime her carnival. Madam Mina still sleep and sleep; and though I did have hunger and appeased it, I could not waken her—even for food. I began to fear that the fatal spell of the place was upon her, tainted as she is with that Vampire baptism. 'Well,' said I to myself, 'if it be that she sleep all the day, it shall also be that I do not sleep at night.' As we travel on the rough road, for a road of an ancient and imperfect kind there was, I held down my head and slept. Again I waked with a sense of guilt and of time passed, and found Madam Mina still sleeping, and the sun low down. But all was indeed changed; the frowning mountains seemed further away, and we were near the top of a steep-rising hill, on summit of which was such a castle **as** Jonathan tell of in his diary. At once I exulted and feared; for now, for good or ill, the end was near. I woke Madam Mina, and again tried to hypnotise her; but alas! unavailing till too late. Then, ere the great dark came upon us—for even after down-sun the heavens reflected the gone sun on the snow, and all was for a time in a great twilight—I took out the horses and fed them in what shelter I could. Then I make a fire; and near it I make Madam Mina, now wake and more charming than ever, sit comfortable amid her rugs. I got ready food; but she would not eat, simply saying that she had not hunger. I did not press her, knowing her unavailingness. But I myself eat, for I must needs now be strong for all. Then, with the fear on me of what might be, I drew a ring, so big for her comfort, round where Madam Mina sat; and over the ring I passed some of the Wafer, and I broke it fine so that all was well guarded. She sat still all the time—so still as one dead; and she grew whiter and ever whiter till the snow was not more pale; and no word she said. But when I drew near, she clung to me, and I could know that the poor soul shook her from head to feet with a tremor that was pain to feel. I said to her presently, when she had grown more quiet:—

'Will you not come over to the fire?' for I wished to make a test of what she could. She rose obedient, but when she have made a step she stopped, and stood as one stricken.

'Why not go on?' I asked. She shook her head, and, coming back, sat down in her place. Then, looking at me with open eyes, as of one waked from sleep, she said simply:—

'I cannot!' and remained silent. I rejoiced, for I knew that what she could not, none of those that we dreaded could. Though there might be danger to her body, yet her soul was safe!

Presently the horses began to scream, and tore at their tethers till I came to them and quieted them. When they did feel my hands on them, they whinnied low as in joy, and licked at my hands and were quiet for a time. Many times through the night did I come to them, till it arrive to the cold hour when all nature is at lowest; and every time my coming was with quiet of them. In the cold hour the fire began to die, and I was about stepping forth to replenish it, for now the snow came in flying sweeps and with it a chill mist. Even in the dark there was a light of some kind, as there ever is over snow; and it seemed as though the snow-flurries and the wreaths of mist took shape as of women with trailing garments. All was in dead, grim silence, only that the horses whinnied and cowered, as if in terror of the worst. I began to fear—horrible fears; but then came to me the sense of safety in that ring wherein I stood. I began, too, to think that my imaginings were of the night, and the gloom, and the unrest that I have gone through, and all the terrible anxiety. It was as though my memories of all Jonathan's horrid experience were befooling me; for the snowflakes and the mist began to wheel and circle round, till I could get as though a shadowy glimpse of those women that would have kissed him. And then the horses cowered lower and lower, and moaned in terror as men do in pain. Even the madness of fright was not to them, so that they could break away. I feared for my dear Madam Mina when these weird figures drew near and circled round. I looked at her, but she sat calm, and smiled at me; when I would have stepped to the fire to replenish it, she caught me and held me back, and whispered, like a voice that one hears in a dream, so low it was:—

'No! no! Do not go without. Here you are safe!' I turned to her, and looking in her eyes, said:—

'But you? It is for you that I fear!' whereat she laughed—a laugh low and unreal, and said:—

'Fear for *me*! Why fear for me? None safer in all the world from them than I am,' and as I wondered at the meaning of her words, a puff of wind made the flame leap up, and I see the red scar on her forehead. Then, alas! I knew. Did I not, I would soon have learned, for the wheeling figures of mist and snow came closer, but keeping ever without the Holy circle. Then they began to materialise, till—if God have not take away my reason, for I saw it through my eyes— there were before me in actual flesh the same three women that Jonathan saw in the room, when they would have kissed his throat. I knew the swaying round forms, the bright hard eyes, the white teeth, the ruddy colour, the voluptuous lips. They smiled ever at poor dear Madam Mina; and as their laugh came through the silence of the night, they twined their arms and pointed to her, and said in those so sweet tingling tones that Jonathan said were of the intolerable sweetness of the water-glasses:—

'Come, sister. Come to us. Come! Come!' In fear I turned to my poor Madam Mina, and my heart with gladness leapt like flame; for oh! the terror in her sweet eyes, the repulsion, the horror, told a story to my heart that was all of hope. God be thanked she was not, yet, of them. I seized some of the firewood which was by me, and holding out some of the Wafer, advanced on them towards the fire. They drew back before me, and laughed their low horrid laugh. I fed the fire, and feared them not; for I knew that we were safe within our protections. They could not approach me, whilst so armed, nor Madam Mina whilst she remained within the ring, which she could not leave no more than they could enter. The horses had ceased to moan, and lay still on the ground; the snow fell on them softly, and they grew whiter. I knew that there was for the poor beasts no more of terror.

And so we remained till the red of the dawn began to fall through the snow-gloom. I was desolate and afraid, and full of woe and terror; but when that beautiful sun began to climb the horizon life was to me again. At the first coming of the dawn the horrid figures melted in the whirling mist and snow; the wreaths of transparent gloom moved away towards the castle, and were lost.

Instinctively, with the dawn coming, I turned to Madam Mina, intending to hypnotise her; but she lay in a deep and sudden sleep, from which I could not wake her. I tried to hypnotise through her sleep, but she made no response, none at all; and the day broke. I fear yet to stir. I have made my fire and have seen the horses; they are all dead. To-day I have much to do here, and I keep waiting till the sun is up high; for there may be places where I must go, where that sunlight, though snow and mist obscure it, will be to me a safety.

I will strengthen me with breakfast, and then I will to my terrible work. Madam Mina still sleeps; and, God be thanked! she is calm in her sleep. ...

FRANCES ISABEL (FANNY) PARNELL (1848–82)

Born at Avondale, Co. Wicklow, she was the eighth of eleven children of John Henry Parnell and Delia Tudor, daughter of Commodore Charles Stewart of the US navy. She was educated by governesses. She was Charles Stewart Parnell's* favourite sister. Her earliest poems were published under the signature 'Aleria' in *The Irish People* in 1864 and 1865. After spending time in Paris, where she cared for wounded soldiers in the Prussian siege, she travelled to America with her mother, settling in 1869 at the Stewart estate in Bordenstown, New Jersey. She took up the cause of the Land League, publishing, in 1880, *The Hovels of Ireland*, a pamphlet attacking landlordism, founding the American branch of the Ladies Land League in 1881, touring America and Canada to raise money for the league, and writing Land League verse for *The Nation* and *The Irishman*. She died from a mysterious illness on 20 July 1882. *Land League Songs* was published in America shortly after her death.

From *Land League Songs*

(1882)

Michael Davitt

Out from the grip of the slayer,
    Out from the jaws of hate,
Out from the den of bloodhounds,
    Out from Gehenna's gate;[1]
Out from the felon's bondage,
    Out from the dungeon keep,
Out from the valley of shadows,
    Out from the starless deep,
Out from the purging tortures,
    Out from the sorrow and stress,
Out from the roaring furnace,
    Out from the trodden press,—

---

1 *Gehenna's gate*: the gate of hell (cf. Matthew 5:22).

He has come for a savior of men,
   He has come on a mission of glory,
He has come to tell us again
   The olden evangelist's story!
Now blessed the poor upon earth,
   Now blessed the hungry and weeping,
For they shall have plenty for dearth,
   With joy returning and reaping;
Now blessed the outcast and slave,
   Now blessed the scorned and the hated,
The knights of the Gibbet and Grave,
   The mourners in ashes prostrated;
For they shall arise from the dust,
   Though scattered and buried for æons;
They shall know that Jehovah is just,—
   From Golgotha coming with paeans.

   Back to the grip of the slayer,
      Back to the jaws of hate,
   Back to the den of bloodhounds,
      Back to Gehenna's gate;
   Back to the dungeon's threshold–
      Now may Christ the brave soul keep!—
   Back to the valley of shadows,
      Back to the starless deep,
   Back to the doom of martyrs,
      Back to the sorrow and stress,
   Back to the fiery furnace,
      Back to the bloody press,—
He has gone for a leader of men,
   He has gone on a kingly mission,
With the prophet's fate-driven tongue and pen,
   Heralding all our hopes' fruition.
Thrice blessed the looser of chains!
   Thrice blessed the friend of the friendless!
The High-Priest whom Heaven ordains
   To sacrifice bitter and endless.
Thrice blessed the loved of the vile,
   The mean and the abject and lowly!
On him shall the Highest One smile,
   The earth that he treads shall be holy;

Thrice blessed the consecrate hands
    That beckon to Liberty's portal
The poor and despised of the lands,
    'Mid raptures and splendors immortal!

    Out of the slime and the squalor,
        Out of the slough of despond,
    Out of the yoke of Egypt,
        Out of the gyve and bond;
    Out of the Stygian darkness,
        Out of the place of tombs,
    Out of the pitiful blindness,
        Out of the gulfs and glooms,
    Up to the heights of freedom,
        Up to the hills of light,
    Up to the holy places,
        Where the dim eyes see aright,—
Up to the glory man hides from man,
    Up to the banned and shrouded altar,
Rending the veil and breaking the ban,
    With the hands that shall never falter,
Up to the truth in its inmost shrine,
    Leading the serfs that crouch and grovel.
Turning the troubled waters to wine,
    Building a fane in every hovel;
Ever and ever facing the day,
    Up and on to the radiance o'er him.
He has gone to tread the martyr's way.
    With the martyr's cross before him:
But the great white Star of Freedom's birth,
    Shall arise for the darkest nation,
And the bound, the blind, the maimed of earth,
    From his ashes shall draw salvation.

After Death

(1882)[1]

Shall mine eyes behold thy glory, O, my country!—
    Shall mine eyes behold thy glory?

---

1 This poem appeared in *The Nation*, 12 Aug. 1882, as an addendum to the recollections of Fannie Parnell by J.M., published on 29 July.

Or shall the darkness close around them ere the sun-blaze
    Break at last upon thy story?

When the nations ope for thee their queenly circle,
    As a sweet, new sister hail thee,
Shall these lips be sealed in callous death and silence,
    That have known but to bewail thee?

Shall the ear be deaf that only loved thy praises,
    When all men their tribute bring thee?
Shall the mouth be clay that sang thee in thy squalor,
    When all poets' mouths shall sing thee?

Ah! the harpings and the salvos and the shoutings
    Of thy exiled sons returning
I should hear, tho' dead and mouldered; and the grave-damps
    Should not chill my bosom's burning.

Ah! the tramp of feet victorious, I should hear them
    'Mid the shamrocks and the mosses,
And my heart should toss within the shroud, and quiver,
    As a captive dreamer tosses.

I should turn and rend the cere-cloths round me,
    Giant sinews I should borrow,
Crying, 'O my brothers! I have also loved her
    In her lowliness and sorrow.

'Let me join with you the jubilant procession,
    Let me chant with you her story;
Then contented I shall go back to the shamrocks,
    Now mine eyes have seen her glory!'

MAY LAFFAN (c. 1849-1916)

Born in Blackrock, Co. Dublin, the daughter of a mixed marriage, she was raised a Catholic, and married the Protestant Walter Hartley, a chemist, who was knighted in 1911. Her first novel, *Hogan M.P.* (3 vols, 1876) describes the shenanigans of a nationalist demagogue; she suffered a nervous breakdown due to its unfavourable reception. *Flitters, Tatters, and the Counsellor: three Waifs from the*

Dublin Streets (1879) was the most successful of her five novels, earning her the admiration of John Ruskin. She was admitted to the Bloomfield asylum in 1910, where she died, three years after her husband, and a year after her son was killed at Gallipoli.

From *Flitters, Tatters, and The Counsellor*

(1879)

Ladies first. Flitters, aged eleven, sucking the tail of a red herring, as a member of the weaker and gentler sex first demands our attention. She is older and doubly stronger than either Tatters or the Counsellor, who are seated beside her on the wall of the river, sharing with her the occupation of watching the operations of a mud-barge at work some dozen yards out in the water. Of the genus street arab Flitters is a fair type. Barefooted, of course, though, were it not for the pink lining that shows now and again between her toes one might doubt that fact—bareheaded, too, with a tangled, tufted, matted shock of hair that has never known other comb save that ten-toothed one provided by Nature, and which indeed, Flitters uses with a frequency of terrible suggestiveness.

The face consists mainly of eyes and mouth; this last-named feature is enormously wide, so wide that there seemed some foundation for a remark of the Counsellor's made in the days of their early acquaintance, before time and friendship had softened down to his unaccustomed eyes the asperities of Flitters' appearance, and which remark was to the effect that only for her ears her mouth would have gone round her head. The Counsellor was not so named without cause, for his tongue stopped at nothing. This mouth was furnished with a set of white, even teeth, which glistened when Flitters vouchsafed a smile, and gleamed like tusks when she was enraged, which she was often, for Flitters had a short temper and a very independent disposition. The eyes, close set, under overhanging, thick brows, were of a dark brown, with a lurid light in their depths. She was tall for her age, lank of limb, and active as a cat: with her tawny skin and dark eyes one might have taken her for a foreigner, were it not for the intense nationalism of the short nose and retreating chin and the mellifluousness of the Townsend Street brogue that issued from between the white teeth.

For attire she had a *princesse robe*, a cast-off perhaps of some dweller in the fashionable squares. This garment was very short in front, and disproportionately long behind, and had a bagginess as to waist and chest that suggested an arbitrary curtailment of the skirt. Viewed from a distance it seemed to have a great many pocket-holes, but on closer inspection these resolved themselves into holes without the pockets; underneath this was another old dress, much more ancient and ragged. However, as it was summer weather, Flitters felt no inconvenience from the airiness of her attire. Indeed, to look at her now with her back against a crate of cabbages which was waiting its turn to take its place on board the Glasgow steamer, one would think she had not a care in the world. She was sitting upon one foot, the other was extended over the quay wall, and the sun shone full in her eyes, and gilded the blond curls of Tatters, who, half lying, half sitting close beside her, was musingly listening to the conversation of the Counsellor. Tatters was about six years old, small and infantine of look, but with a world of guile in his far-apart blue eyes. He could smoke and chew, drink and steal, and was altogether a finished young reprobate. He wore a funny, old jerry hat, without any brim, and with the crown pinched out, doubtless with a view to its harmonizing with the rest of his attire, the most prominent portion of which was undoubtedly the shirt. The front part of this seemed not to reach much below his breast-bone; but whether to make amends for this shortcoming, or to cover deficiencies in the corduroy trousers, the hinder part hung down mid-thighs at the back. One leg of the corduroys was completely split up, and flapped loosely in front, like a lug sail in a calm. His jacket, which was a marvel of raggedness, was buttoned up tight; and seated, hugging both his knees with his hands, he looked a wonderfully small piece of goods. He had an interesting, sweet, little face; his little black nose was prettily formed; a red cherry of a mouth showed in the surrounding dirt, and gave vent to the oaths and curses of which his speech was mainly composed, in an agreeable little treble pipe.

The Counsellor, or Hoppy, for he had two names, the second derived from a personal deformity which affected his gait, was nine years old, but might have been ninety, for the *Weltkunst* his wrinkled, pock-marked countenance portrayed. He had small, bright, black eyes, and a sharp, inquisitive nose. A keen, ready intelligence seemed to exude from every feature. He was the ruling spirit of the trio. Tatters' manner to him was undisguisedly deferential, and Flitters only maintained her individuality at the expense of a bullying ostentation of superior age and strength. They were all three orphans. Flitters' father had run off to America a year before;—her mother was dead. Tatters was a foundling, whose nurse had turned him loose on the streets when she found no more money forthcoming for his maintenance, and the Counsellor's antecedents were wrapped in complete obscurity. He sometimes alluded mistily to a grandmother living in Bull Lane;[1] but he was one of those people who seem all-sufficient in themselves, and for whom one feels instinctively, and at the first glance, that no one could or ought to be responsible. He had on a man's coat, one tail of which had been removed—by force, plainly, for a good piece of the back had gone with it, giving him an odd look of a sparrow which a cat has clawed a pawful of feathers out of. He had on a great felt hat, of the kind known as billycock, which overshadowed well his small, knowing face. He wore shoes of very doubtful fit or comfort, but still shoes, and thus distinguishing him from his companions, who, to borrow a phrase from their own picturesque dialect, were both 'on the road.'

It may be asked whence they received their names. Hoppy knew of none but his nickname; his grandmother's name was Cassidy, which he did not scruple to appropriate if occasion required it. Flitters remembered to have been called Eliza once, and her father's name was Byrne; but nicknames in the arab class are more common than names, which indeed are practically useful only to people who have a fixed habitation—a luxury these creatures know nothing of. ...

Flitters could not read. The Counsellor possessed all the education as well as most of the brains of the party. Nevertheless Flitters was its chief support. She sang in the streets. The Counsellor played the Jew's harp or castanets, and sometimes sang duets with her, while Tatters stood by, looking hungry and watching for halfpence. They had other resources as well: coal-stealing along the wharfs, or sometimes sifting cinders on the waste grounds about the outskirts of the city, to sell afterwards; messages to run for workmen—a very uncertain and precarious resource, as no one ever employed them twice. Altogether, their lives were at least replete with that element so much coveted by people whose every want and comfort is supplied—to wit, excitement.

A keen observer might have remarked beneath the apparent nonchalance and lassitude of the group a certain patient pre-occupation, at once watchful and passive. They were, in fact, waiting the arrival of the passengers of an afternoon Scotch boat, in order to pick up stray coppers from such of them as might be disposed to remunerate

---

1 *Bull Lane*: near Church Street (Dublin City) and the Liffey (the neighbouring street is Cow Lane).

their musical performances. Times had been dull lately, and, with the exception of Flitters' herring-tail, which had fallen from the dinner-bundle of a dock-labourer, none of the party had dined.

The Counsellor was watching the tide as it rose nearer and nearer to the line where green slime and mud ended and dry granite began on the quay wall opposite. The boat was to leave at high tide, or thereabouts, and the greasy black ripples were rising fast with a dull, lapping sound on the stones. It was an August afternoon, and a grey, warm haze hung over the river where it widened, far below, at the Pigeon-house wall;[1] and the Custom House, with its granite pillars and goddesses, glistened and sparkled in the sun. Three gold streams seemed to gush from the arches of Carlisle Bridge; and St. Patrick's cone-like steeple and the dome of the Four Courts, far above, seemed to dance in the waving, shimmering air.

The river craft went to and fro heedlessly, tug boats gasping and quivering. A trim-looking pilot yacht, with her insignia in big black letters on the mainsail, skifted sidelong by. After it came a long-bodied, sharp-nosed, broad-beamed boat, so loaded with barrels that it was almost flush with the greasy water that swirled in great lazy curls in its wake, and puffing a thick black smoke from a tiny funnel in the stern.

The Counsellor started forward with a look of interest in his keen eyes.

'There's wan ov Guinness's barges. Look! every barrel on her's worth six shillin', widout de porther at all.'

'Ye lie!'

This courteous comment came from Flitters, and in no way conveyed any doubt as to the veracity of the statement. It was the customary expression of astonishment or negation in the gutter-language, and in this case meant the former purely, for the Counsellor was an authority on most points of general information.

'Don't I know a man found one floatin' off of the North Wall, below Martin's, and took it up to James's Street and got it!'

The six eyes followed with a longing, envious look after the piled-up treasures, each streaked with vivid red, and branded new from the famous brewery, the barge, as it swung by, keeping in the sinuous track left by the pilot.

Tatters was hungry, and his face looked pale beneath the coating of dirt.

---

1 Named after John Pidgeon, an eighteenth-century official who oversaw the construction of the South Wall, which was the main embarkation point for passengers to and from England.

'I wish 'twas five,' he said plaintively, addressing Flitters. 'I don't see wan come yet.'

But at that moment they saw a cab just in sight over the swing-bridge of the docks, loaded with trunks and parcels, and full of people. The trio waited lazily until the vehicle had drawn up at the shed below, where a herd of cows had arrived some time before, and were in process of being shipped; then all three bounced up and set out in pursuit.

They took up their post on the quay wall, opposite the saloon deck of the steamer, and waited cheerfully until the passengers should have disposed their effects below, and come up to enjoy the fresh air on the deck.

More people arrived. It was the season when Dublin empties itself periodically, and before long Flitters was singing *à-tue-tête*,[1] 'The Dark Girl Dressed in Blue.' The Counsellor played a castanet obbligato, and Tatters, leaning against the shed-wall, assumed his customary *air de circonstance*—this time without the slightest affectation.

Flitters' voice made up in volume what it lacked in *timbre*. Singing in the open air is destructive to that laryngeal membrane on which, high authorities tell us, the delicacy of modulation depends. The sea and night air, to both of which it had been recklessly exposed, are particularly harmful. However, Flitters had an ear and some turn for mimicry. She had not visited, without profit, the music-halls of the Irish metropolis and the theatres where London Boucicault companies import new varieties of Irish brogue, and she gave out the patter with surprising voice and distinctness. She soon had a crowd assembled at the bulwark, and grinned and rolled her eyes at them while she knocked off her *répertoire*—to such good purpose that before very long the pennies began flying very thickly. Then the Counsellor pocketed his castanets, and, standing at the extreme edge of the quay, made deft catches at the coins, like a practised wicket-keeper at high balls, while Tatters 'fielded' in the background. For a good hour Flitters sang and grimaced, till it seemed as if the copper harvest was all gathered. She paused, panting, at last, the perspiration rolling down her sunburnt cheeks, and, singling out with her eye a benevolent countenance among those gathered watching her, she advanced, holding out the short foreskirt of the *princesses robe*, and made a comical bob to the whole gallery.

'Wan copper for the hounour and glory of God, Miss, jewel.'

---

1 *à-tue-tête*: 'at the top of her voice'.

'You have enough,' replied some one who knew her, who had probably amused himself counting the gains.

'Me mother is lyin' sick, and me father's in hospital this two months wid a broken leg an' arm, an' she has nothin' but what me an' me little brothers takes her,' Flitters went on rapidly, without a pause even for breath.

'Who ever saw such teeth and eyes! It's a gipsy, surely,' muttered a newly-arrived tourist. Then, aloud, 'Sing another song for me, my girl.'

Flitters flashed a delighted grin back to him. She recognized his English accent, good always in the ears of her kind for double pay, and very appropriately struck up 'Come back to Erin, mavourneen,' for the bell had rung now, and they were fast clearing the ship of visitors. The Counsellor clattered the bones, and Tatters stood by with a smile of pleased expectancy on his smirched cherub countenance, while Flitters bawled out every word as clear as print, showing her thirty-two teeth like diamonds in the sun.

The first throb of the paddles made itself felt and heard as she finished with a ringing screech Killarney's 'delight.' The passenger held some money in one hand, vainly fumbling with the other among a lot of half-crowns for something smaller. He could not find any lesser coin, and, deeming these too much, was about to return them to his pocket, when he caught sight of Tatters' plaintive little figure, the shirt-tail drooping, and his head set wistfully to one side, watching him. He tossed the half-crown with such excellent aim that it went straight into one of Flitters' frock pocket-holes, whence she extricated it unceremoniously, and, waving him her thanks, set off like the wind, lest some one who had seen their luck should follow and take it from them. The Counsellor, holding on his large hat with one hand, limped after as quickly as he could; and Tatters, almost crying with impatience and hunger, trotted midway between him and Flitters ...

MARGARET BREW (?1850–?)

Little is known of Margaret Brew other than that she was born in Co. Clare, and may have been the daughter of a landowner. She contributed poems and stories to *The Irish Monthly*, and wrote two novels, *The Burtons of Dunroe* (3 vols, 1880), set in Co. Limerick in the early nineteenth century, and *The Chronicles of Castle*

Cloyne. Pictures of the Munster People (3 vols, 1885), which details the plights of an old Catholic landowning family and their tenants, the MacDermotts, during the Famine. The novel is full of descriptions of Irish peasant customs and excursions into Irish history.

From *The Chronicles of Castle Cloyne*

(1885)

The Dumb Cake

With hearts that tremble between hopes and fears,
We seek to pierce the gloom of future years,
And, with irreverent, and daring hand,
Uplift the veil that shrouds th' unseen land.

Making, baking, and eating the 'dumb cake' is a form of spell known only in Ireland, by which those who practised it sought to obtain some glimpses of the destiny that awaited them in after-life. The spell should only be wrought on All-Hallow Eve, as being the night of all the year when the 'good people' had most influence on the fate of human beings, and by three women, who should all be unmarried, and on whose maiden fame no evil shadow had ever rested. Neither a wife, nor a widow, could take any part in the mysterious rites, for their lot was fixed, their fortunes had been told long before, and they had nothing more to learn by diving into the future but what they were already well aware of, namely, that they were mortal, and must one day die.

When all in the house but themselves were asleep, the three girls proceeded to make the dumb cake. The ingredients of this magic cake consisted of an egg, which should be the first laid by a chicken, the shell of this full of flour, and another egg-shell full of salt. Those three were to be mixed by the three girls, baked by the three, and eaten by the three, in the most perfect silence. From the moment when the three put each a hand to work the cake until they awoke next morning, they were bound to observe the most rigid silence; for the utterance of even one word would have the effect of breaking the spell, and rendering its power null and void.

It was this strict and necessary silence which gave it the name of 'dumb cake.' So while the three girls were making, baking, and eating it, taking great care that not even a crumb was left behind, they never spoke a word, and in the same silence they retired to rest. It was also *de rigueur* that the three girls should sleep under the same roof, so that they should see the book of the future unfolded within reach of each other.

Early next morning the people at the farm were all astir. The farmer and his man Paddy went off to early mass; for the Feast of All Saints is a strict holy-day in the Catholic Church. Molly and the three girls were to go to a late mass; but in the meantime they were by no means idle, for the cows had to be milked, the dairy to be attended to, and the pigs and poultry fed. They were so busy that they had no time to think of their dreams of the previous night, or tell each other of the great and wonderful revelations that had been given to them while they abode in the solemn, and mysterious land of sleep.

When the morning's work was done and breakfast despatched, the farmer and his man went off to a distant part of the land to look after a sick cow, and only the women remained in the house.

Though old Molly had left her girlhood far behind her, she had her full share of the faith in the spell of the dumb cake, and a good deal of womanly sympathy with those who, by virtue of their youth and maidenhood, were privileged to perform it. She was curious, too, to know what each and all had to tell her of the working of the charm, which no doubt she had herself often tried in the long-past days of her youth.

''Tis too soon to go to mass yet,' she said to them; 'moreover, we have the place all to oursels; so sit down, girls, by the fire, and let us hear what luck the dumb cake brought to ye. 'Tis something good, or I'm greatly disappointed; for ye all desarve good luck, and ye'll get it too, never fear. Come, Oonagh *machree*,[1] let you begin, as you're the eldher; though, for that matther, there's no great differ betune any ov ye.'

'Oh, let Judy begin first, as she's the stranger. Sure, 'tis only manners to let her tell her story first.'

Judy began clearing her throat, and looked as bashful as possible, while all the others began to laugh.

'Come now, Judy, make a clane breast of it,' said Molly, entering with good-natured interest into the spirit of the fun, 'an' tell us what sort ov a boy it was that you dhramed ov last night.'

'Oh, wisha, I might as well tell it at wanst, for ye never could guess it if ye wor to be guessin' for a week,' with a burst of loud laughter, and a saucy toss of her head. 'The boy that came to me was a boy that

---

1 *machree*: 'my heart' (term of endearment).

I never would marry, if he had the estate of Castle Cloyne at his back. It was that mad Dick Considine that came to me in my dhrames; no less, if ye plase!'

'Dick Considine isn't mad at all, whatever people may say,' said Oonagh; 'though I own he's a little quare in himself at times. He's a dacent, honest boy, that minds his bisness; an', signs on, he has bisness to do when other men are wid their hands in their pockets. Sorra bit ov madness is in the same boy, but what's in the looks av him; and, sure, looks don't signify a thrawneen.[1] I heard my father say that Dick has a nice spot ov ground up in the mountains, an' that he has it well for the value too. So you needn't turn up your nose at him, Judy.'

'Well, as ye think so much ov him, you're welcome to my share ov him. I'll never marry a madman, for maybe 'tis to kill me he would.'

'But, Judy, it wasn't to me he came last night, but to yourself.'

'Well, then, he made a great mistake intirely in comin' to me; I wouldn't marry that cracked fellow—no, not if he was the Queen's eldest son. I tell ye all that, now, an' ye can remimber my words.'

There was another burst of mocking laughter from the other two girls, at which Judy's bright colour became still more bright, and her black eyes flashed indignantly.

'Who did you dhrame ov, Shusy?' said Molly, trying to pour oil on the troubled waters by changing the subject.

'Oh, then, botheration to it for a story!' replied Susie, with a pretty pout. 'I had no better luck than Judy, for if she dhramed ov a madman, I dhramed ov a fool—the biggest fool in the whole counthry.'

'An' who was he, *eroo*? Was it Mike *na Lhibe*,[2] for he's the biggest fool in the counthry?'

'It wasn't Mike *na Lhibe*.'

'An' who was it, then?'

'It was Shawn Sugagh!'[3]

'An' do you call him a fool, Shusy? He's the very handsomest boy in the three baronies, let alone the pleasantest; an' 'tis because he is so pleasant and good-humoured, that the name of 'Shawn Sugagh' was put on him. Hould your whisht, little girl, an' let no one see that you're so foolish. John Molloy is husband good enough for the first lady in the land.'

'Then the first lady in the land may have the *omadhawn*,[1] for all I

---

1 *a thrawneen*: a straw.
2 *na Lhibe*: 'the sluggard'
3 *Sugagh*: 'the merry'.

care,' said pretty Susie. 'It never'll be said ov me, that wid my eyes open I went to marry the likes ov him.'

'What is there so foolish about him?' asked Oonagh.

'Well, Oonagh, one would think, to hear you ask that question, that you hadn't an eye in your head. Why, he's full of consate an' impudence up to his very chin. Only look at the swagger ov him, and listen to his tall English, all the same as if he was an estated gentleman, an' the aiqual ov Masther Hy'cinth Dillon, ov Castle Cloyne, an' instid ov that he hasn't a majesty to bless himself wid, either goold, silver, or brass, but as his hard-workin' brother will give it to him. The poor ape thinks that all the girls are dyin' about him, an' all the time they're only makin' game ov him.'

'You're as hard to be pleased as Judy, every bit,' said the old woman, 'but 'tis no use for either ov ye to be grumblin'. What's allotted can't be blotted. Them two boys is marked out for the pair ov ye, an' mark my words, if it was in twenty years to come ye'll be married to them, an' to no one else. So ye may as well make the best of it, an' be satisfied wid what's ordained for ye. If ye're so hard to be pleased, 'tis the crooked stick ye might get instid of a husband. Did ye ever hear tell the story of the crooked stick?'

'Och! don't be botherin' about it. I'm rale sorry I had any hand in that dumb cake at all; it's nothing at all but an ould *pisherogue*.'[2]

At this sally they all laughed again.

'I'll tell you this day that you'll marry John Molloy the fool, the same day that I marry mad Dick Considine,' cries the incorrigible Judy, hardly able to speak for laughter.

'Folly on, childher, folly on; sure ye'll never be younger, or heartier, than what ye are to-day, an' the world is all on before ye,' said Molly. 'It's time enough for ye to be sorrowful when the sorra comes in the dure to ye. Now, Oonagh *Anien dheelish*,[3] 'tis your turn. Tell us who was the bachelor that came to you last night. I hope you won't be as hard to be pleased as these foolish girls here.'

'No bachelor came to me,' replied Oonagh quietly.

'Eyeh! No bachelor came to you after putting a hand in the dumb cake?'

'Sorro wan at all.'

'Well, what did you dhrame ov thin? Something sthrong, I'll go bail, you're so long in tellin' us.'

---

1 *omadhawn*: 'fool'.
2 *Pisherogue*—Superstition. [*Brew's note.*]
3 *Anien dheelish*—Dearest daughter. [*Brew's note.*]

'It was worse than sthrong, Molly, it was frightful—part ov it, I mane. I dhreamt that I was in chapel hearing mass, an' though the chapel was full ov people I didn't mind any wan there but the priest that was on the altar. He was a handsome young man, wid fair hair an' blue eyes, an' I thought I heard some one near me say that he was the new coajuther an' that that was his first mass in the parish.'

'Sure that was no bachelor at all,' cried laughing Judy, 'no wan could marry a priest.'

'Well, sure she couldn't be married without a priest, could she?' said the old woman. 'Go on, and tell us about the husband, *a rágal!*[1] You dhreamt ov something else, surely?'

'I did,' replied the girl with an expression of much gravity in her soft gray eyes. 'I thought that I was in bed, not here at home but in a strange place I never was in before, an' as I was lyin' there awake I thought two men carryin' a coffin betune 'em came in, an' laid the coffin down by the side ov my bed an' thin went away. When they were gone I ris up on my elbow, an' looked on the plate that was on the cover, an' there was 'Oonagh MacDermott,' my own name, on it! When I saw that, I was so frightened that I awoke, an' my hand to you I had no more sleep after that.'

'The Lord save us! That was a frightful dhrame to have,' cried the timid Susie with a shudder.

'Eyeh, that I mightn't die in sin, if I believe in dhrames at all!' exclaimed the good-natured Molly trying to cheer them after having heard such a weird revelation.

'They're only ould talk, an' the dumb cake is only fit for makin' fun ov it. Many a time I done it when I was a colleen oge,[2] full ov fun an' divarshun, an' the man I took wid in the ind wasn't any ov them I dhramed ov at all, though he was a good husband to me while the Lord left us together. Och! sure if I thought things would turn out so conthrary intirely, I'd set my face against the whole box and dice from the bignin.'

'Well, there's no help for spilled milk but to call the cat,' observed Oonagh philosophically. 'We may as well not be botherin' ourselves about charms and thricks on All-Hallow Eve, for they're nothing but a pack ov lies. The clergy is complately agin the like, an' as we wint agin the clergy, we couldn't expect to have better luck. For my own part, I'll larn a lesson by it, an' that's never to make or meddle wid *pisherogues* agin durin' duration.'

---

1 *a rágal*: 'my bright love' (Irish *a ghrá geal*).
2 *colleen oge*: young girl.

'Wan would think Oonagh has made up her mind to be an old maid,' said Judy, 'but don't ye mind that at all. That's an intention she won't keep when the right boy comes to the fore,' and the joyous-hearted girl sang the chorus of an old song,

'Ballinnamona oro !
The snug little wedding for me.'

'Here are my father an' Paddy comin' across the stile,' said Oonagh, starting up from her seat, 'an' tis time for us to be on the road, barrin' we want to be late for mass.'

'Oonagh is in a hurry to see if the priest that says last mass is like the priest that was in her dhrame,' said Susie.

'Faith, thin, I'm not so. I know well 'tis ould Father Rafferty that will be on the altar, an' won't he make a fine complaint ov me to Miss Grace, if I'm late for mass.'

When they were at dinner in the afternoon the farmer made several sly allusions to the spells usually done by young people on All-Hallow Eve, and ended by asking the blushing girls what bachelors did they dream of. There was a good deal of fencing on the part of the trio, and at last they boldly denied having done any charms, or dreamed of any one, or any thing in particular. At this, Martin laughed long and loud, and continued bantering and teasing them, until at last Molly came to the rescue, by asking what an old man like him knew of such things.

'Now, Molly, you may as well let the cat out ov the bag. Sure I know well that my back wasn't well turned this mornin', when you heard it all from 'em.'

'Well, an' if I did itself, you may as well take it aisy, honest man, for I don't mane to make you as wise as myself. Erra! what can an ould man like you know what young girls do be thinking ov? You know tales is'n't to be told out of school.'

'Well, girls, ye have no call to be so shamefaced about it,' said the kind old man. ''Tis only what ye're mothers an' grandmothers done before ye wor born, and what ye'r own girls will be doin' in their turn. The day will come when ye won't think ov the like at all, so while ever ye'r young, and hearty, have the bit ov divarshun, an' give no thanks to any wan o' count ov it'

When dinner was over the two visitors prepared to go away. Judy went first, having the fear of her cross stepmother before her eyes, but Susie stayed longer, waiting for her brother who was to come for her. With the shades of evening he came on horseback, with a pillion behind him for Susie. He was a good-looking young man, with a frank honest expression of countenance, that also seemed very shrewd and sensible. He was very much attached to Susie, who fully returned his affection, and thought how very happy she would be if she could succeed in 'making a match' between this dear brother and her cousin Oonagh. Her efforts in this direction, however, had up to this not been been attended with any success. Oonagh was, as Susie expressed it, 'hard to plase,' or in other words she did not see Tom Burke's perfections in the same rose-coloured light that his sister saw them, and gave a deaf ear to all the hints that Susie was constantly throwing out on the subject.

Tom Burke was obliged to dismount, for the hospitable farmer would not consent to his riding off until he had taken some refreshment, and his horse had got a feed of oats. While Tom was eating, Martin kept the two girls in an agony of bashfulness and terror, by threatening to tell him who they had dreamed of on the preceding night—an idle threat on his part, considering that he did not know it himself, though he teased them by pretending that Molly had told him privately. At last Tom, remembering that he had fifteen miles to ride before they could reach home, hurried Susie out of the house, and in a few moments the clatter of his horse's hoofs died away in the distance.

LAFCADIO HEARN (1850–1904)

He was born on Leucadio (Lefkas), one of the Ionian islands, to an Irish navy surgeon and a Greek mother. In his childhood the family moved to Dublin. The parents separated, and Lafcadio was sent to Jesuit schools in France and England. He emigrated to the United States in 1869, and published a series of unusual sketches, called 'Fantastics', in a New Orleans paper. He translated Gautier in *One of Cleopatra's Nights* (1882). In 1890 he went to Japan to write a series of travel articles. He settled there, teaching at the Imperial University. He married, and took the name Yakumo Koizumi. His view of Japanese society and culture, pervaded by the customs and beliefs of the common people, whose spiritualism had not been eroded by learning, may have influenced such modernists as Ezra Pound. Among the twelve books he wrote about Japan are *Glimpses of Unfamiliar Japan* (1894), *Kokoro* (1896), *Japanese Fairy Tales* (1902), and *Japan: An Attempt at Interpretation* (1904).

From *Glimpses of Unfamiliar Japan*
(1894)

My First Day in the Orient

II.

An ideograph does not make upon the Japanese brain any impression similar to that created in the Occidental brain by a letter or combination of letters,—dull, inanimate symbols of vocal sounds. To the Japanese brain an ideograph is a vivid picture: it lives; it speaks; it gesticulates. And the whole space of a Japanese street is full of such living characters,—figures that cry out to the eyes, words that smile or grimace like faces.

What such lettering is, compared with our own lifeless types, can be understood only by those who have lived in the farther East. For even the printed characters of Japanese or Chinese imported texts give no suggestion of the possible beauty of the same characters as modified for decorative inscriptions, for sculptural use, or for the commonest advertising purposes. No rigid convention fetters the fancy of the calligrapher or designer: each strives to make his characters more beautiful than any others; and generations upon generations of artists have been toiling from time immemorial with like emulation, so that through centuries and centuries of tireless effort and study, the primitive hieroglyph or ideograph has been evolved into a thing of beauty indescribable. It consists only of a certain number of brush-strokes; but in each stroke there is an undiscoverable secret art of grace, proportion, imperceptible curve, which actually makes it seem alive, and bears witness that even during the lightning-moment of its creation the artist felt with his brush for the ideal shape of the stroke *equally along its entire length*, from head to tail. But the art of the strokes is not all; the art of their combination is that which produces the enchantment, often so as to astonish the Japanese themselves. It is not surprising, indeed, considering the strangely personal, animate, esoteric aspect of Japanese lettering, that there should be wonderful legends of calligraphy, relating how words written by holy experts became incarnate, and descended from their tablets to hold converse with mankind.

III.

My kurumaya[1] calls himself 'Cha.' He has a white hat which looks like the top of an enormous mushroom; a short blue wide-sleeved jacket; blue drawers, close-fitting as 'tights,' and reaching to his ankles; and light straw sandals bound upon his bare feet with cords of palmetto-fibre. Doubtless he typifies all the patience, endurance, and insidious coaxing powers of his class. He has already manifested his power to make me give him more than the law allows; and I have been warned against him in vain. For the first sensation of having a human being for a horse, trotting between shafts, unwearyingly bobbing up and down before you for hours, is alone enough to evoke a feeling of compassion. And when this human being, thus trotting between shafts, with all his hopes, memories, sentiments, and comprehensions, happens to have the gentlest smile, and the power to return the least favor by an apparent display of infinite gratitude, this compassion becomes sympathy, and provokes unreasoning impulses to self-sacrifice. I think the sight of the profuse perspiration has also something to do with the feeling, for it makes one think of the cost of heart-beats and muscle-contractions, likewise of chills, congestions, and pleurisy. Cha's clothing is drenched; and he mops his face with a small sky-blue towel, with figures of bamboo-sprays and sparrows in white upon it, which towel he carries wrapped about his wrist as he runs.

That, however, which attracts me in Cha—Cha considered not as a motive power at all, but as a personality—I am rapidly learning to discern in the multitudes of faces turned toward us as we roll through these miniature streets. And perhaps the supremely pleasurable impression of this morning is that produced by the singular gentleness of popular scrutiny. Everybody looks at you curiously; but there is never anything disagreeable, much less hostile in the gaze: most commonly it is accompanied by a smile or half smile. And the ultimate consequence of all these kindly curious looks and smiles is that the stranger finds himself thinking of fairy-land. Hackneyed to the degree of provocation this statement no doubt is: everybody describing the sensations of his first Japanese day talks of the land as fairy-land, and of its people as fairy-folk. Yet there is a natural reason for this unanimity in choice of terms to describe what is almost impossible to describe more accurately at the first essay. To find one's self suddenly in a world where everything is upon a smaller and daintier scale than

---

1 *kurumaya*: 'rickshaw man' (*kuruma* is 'car').

with us,—a world of lesser and seemingly kindlier beings, all smiling at you as if to wish you well,—a world where all movement is slow and soft, and voices are hushed,—a world where land, life, and sky are unlike all that one has known elsewhere,—this is surely the realization, for imaginations nourished with English folklore, of the old dream of a World of Elves.

IV.

The traveler who enters suddenly into a period of social change—especially change from a feudal past to a democratic present—is likely to regret the decay of things beautiful and the ugliness of things new. What of both I may yet discover in Japan I know not; but to-day, in these exotic streets, the old and the new mingle so well that one seems to set off the other. The line of tiny white telegraph poles carrying the world's news to papers printed in a mixture of Chinese and Japanese characters; an electric bell in some tea-house with an Oriental riddle of text pasted beside the ivory button, a shop of American sewing-machines next to the shop of a maker of Buddhist images; the establishment of a photographer beside the establishment of a manufacturer of straw sandals: all these present no striking incongruities, for each sample of Occidental innovation is set into an Oriental frame that seems adaptable to any picture. But on the first day, at least, the Old alone is new for the stranger, and suffices to absorb his attention. It then appears to him that everything Japanese is delicate, exquisite, admirable,—even a pair of common wooden chopsticks in a paper bag with a little drawing upon it; even a package of toothpicks of cherry-wood, bound with a paper wrapper wonderfully lettered in three different colors; even the little sky-blue towel, with designs of flying sparrows upon it, which the jinrikisha[1] man uses to wipe his face. The bank bills, the commonest copper coins, are things of beauty. Even the piece of plaited colored string used by the shopkeeper in tying up your last purchase is a pretty curiosity. Curiosities and dainty objects bewilder you by their very multitude: on either side of you, wherever you turn your eyes, are countless wonderful things as yet incomprehensible.

But it is perilous to look at them. Every time you dare to look, something obliges you to buy it,—unless, as may often happen, the smiling vender invites your inspection of so many varieties of one article, each specially and all unspeakably desirable, that you flee away

1 *jinrikisha*: 'rickshaw'.

out of mere terror at your own impulses. The shopkeeper never asks you to buy; but his wares are enchanted, and if you once begin buying you are lost. Cheapness means only a temptation to commit bankruptcy; for the resources of irresistible artistic cheapness are inexhaustible. The largest steamer that crosses the Pacific could not contain what you wish to purchase. For, although you may not, perhaps, confess the fact to yourself, what you really want to buy is not the contents of a shop; you want the shop and the shopkeeper, and streets of shops with their draperies and their habitants, the whole city and the bay and the mountains begirdling it, and Fujiyama's white witchery overhanging it in the speckless sky, all Japan, in very truth, with its magical trees and luminous atmosphere, with all its cities and towns and temples, and forty millions of the most lovable people in the universe.

Now there comes to my mind something I once heard said by a practical American on hearing of a great fire in Japan: 'Oh! those people can afford fires; their houses are so cheaply built.' It is true that the frail wooden houses of the common people can be cheaply and quickly replaced; but that which was within them to make them beautiful cannot,—and every fire is an art tragedy. For this is the land of infinite hand-made variety; machinery has not yet been able to introduce sameness and utilitarian ugliness in cheap production (except in response to foreign demand for bad taste to suit vulgar markets), and each object made by the artist or artisan differs still from all others, even of his own making. And each time something beautiful perishes by fire, it is a something representing an individual idea.

Happily the art impulse itself, in this country of conflagrations, has a vitality which survives each generation of artists, and defies the flame that changes their labor to ashes or melts it to shapelessness. The idea whose symbol has perished will reappear again in other creations,—perhaps after the passing of a century,—modified, indeed, yet recognisably of kin to the thought of the past. And every artist is a ghostly worker. Not by years of groping and sacrifice does he find his highest expression; the sacrificial past is within him; his art is an inheritance; his fingers are guided by the dead in the delineation of a flying bird, of the vapors of mountains, of the colors of the morning and the evening, of the shape of branches and the spring burst of flowers: generations of skilled workmen have given him their cunning, and revive in the wonder of his drawing. What was conscious effort in the beginning became unconscious in later centuries,—

becomes almost automatic in the living man,—becomes the art instinctive. Wherefore, one colored print by a Hokusai or Hiroshige,[1] originally sold for less than a cent, may have more real art in it than many a Western painting valued at more than the worth of a whole Japanese street.

V.

Here are Hokusai's own figures walking about in straw rain-coats, and immense mushroom-shaped hats of straw, and straw sandals,— bare-limbed peasants, deeply tanned by wind and sun; and patient-faced mothers with smiling bald babies on their backs, toddling by upon their geta (high, noisy, wooden clogs), and robed merchants squatting and smoking their little brass pipes among the countless riddles of their shops.

Then I notice how small and shapely the feet of the people are,— whether bare brown feet of peasants, or beautiful feet of children wearing tiny, tiny geta, or feet of young girls in snowy tabi. The tabi, the white digitated stocking, gives to a small light foot a mythological aspect,—the white cleft grace of the foot of a fauness. Clad or bare, the Japanese foot has the antique symmetry: it has not yet been distorted by the infamous foot-gear which has deformed the feet of Occidentals.

...Of every pair of Japanese wooden clogs, one makes in walking a slightly different sound from the other, as *kring* to *krang*; so that the echo of the walker's steps has an alternate rhythm of tones. On a pavement, such as that of a railway station, the sound obtains immense sonority; and a crowd will sometimes intentionally fall into step, with the drollest conceivable result of drawling wooden noise.

XI.

'*Amma-kamishimo-go-hyakmon!*'[2]

A woman's voice ringing through the night, chanting in a tone of singular sweetness words of which each syllable comes through my open window like a wavelet of flute-sound. My Japanese servant, who speaks a little English, has told me what they mean, those words:—

---

1 *Hokusai or Hiroshige*: Hokusai Katsushika (1760–1849), famous printmaker, whose landscapes were influenced by the engravings brought into Japan by Dutch Jesuits. His most well-known work was the series of woodblock prints known as *The Thirty-six Views of Mount Fuji*. Ando Hiroshige (1797–1858), printmaker, was the most famous of the Ukiyo-E artists.

2 *Amma-kamishimo-go-hyakmon!*: 'amma-kamishimo-gohyaku-mon'—'Amma will give you a massage for 500 mon!' (Prof. Masaru Sekine notes that this is a satirical comment about the most formal of samurai garments being sold at the same price as a massage).

'*Amma-kamishimo-go-hyakmon!*'

And always between these long, sweet calls I hear a plaintive whistle, one long note first, then two short ones in another key. It is the whistle of the amma, the poor blind woman who earns her living by shampooing the sick or the weary, and whose whistle warns pedestrians and drivers of vehicles to take heed for her sake, as she cannot see. And she sings also that the weary and the sick may call her in.

'*Amma-kamishimo-go-hyakmon!*'

The saddest melody, but the sweetest voice. Her cry signifies that for the sum of 'five hundred mon' she will come and rub your weary body 'above and below,' and make the weariness or the pain go away. Five hundred mon are the equivalent of five sen (Japanese cents); there are ten rin to a sen, and ten mon to one rin. The strange sweetness of the voice is haunting,—makes me even wish to have some pains, that I might pay five hundred mon to have them driven away.

I lie down to sleep, and I dream. I see Chinese texts—multitudinous, weird, mysterious—fleeing by me, all in one direction; ideographs white and dark, upon sign-boards, upon paper screens, upon backs of sandalled men. They seem to live, these ideographs, with conscious life; they are moving their parts, moving with a movement as of insects, monstrously, like *phasmidæ*.[1] I am rolling always through low, narrow, luminous streets in a phantom jinrikisha, whose wheels make no sound. And always, always, I see the huge white mushroom-shaped hat of Cha dancing up and down before me as he runs.

At Hinomisaki

KITZUKI, August 10, 1891

My Japanese friends urge me to visit Hinomisaki, where no European has ever been, and where there is a far-famed double temple dedicated to Amaterasu-oho-mi-Kami, the Lady of Light, and to her divine brother Take-haya-susa-no-wo-no-mikoto. Hinomisaki is a little village on the Izumo coast about five miles from Kitzuki. It may be reached by a mountain path, but the way is extremely steep, rough, and fatiguing. By boat, when the weather is fair, the trip is very agreeable. So, with a friend, I start for Hinomisaki in a very cozy ryōsen,[2] skilfully sculled by two young fishermen.

---

1 *phasmidæ*: walking-stick insect.
2 *ryōsen*: 'fishing boat'.

Leaving the pretty bay of Inasa, we follow the coast to the right,—a very lofty and grim coast without a beach. Below us the clear water gradually darkens to inky blackness, as the depth increases; but at intervals pale jagged rocks rise up from this nether darkness to catch the light fifty feet under the surface. We keep tolerably close to the cliffs, which vary in height from three hundred to six hundred feet,—their bases rising from the water all dull iron-gray, their sides and summits green with young pines and dark grasses that toughen in sea-wind. All the coast is abrupt, ravined, irregular,—curiously breached and fissured. Vast masses of it have toppled into the sea; and the black ruins project from the deep in a hundred shapes of menace. Sometimes our boat glides between a double line of these, or takes a zigzag course through labyrinths of reef-channels. So swiftly and deftly is the little craft impelled to right and left, that one could almost believe it sees its own way and moves by its own intelligence. And again we pass by extraordinary islets of prismatic rock whose sides, just below the water-line, are heavily mossed with seaweed. The polygonal masses composing these shapes are called by the fishermen 'tortoise-shell stones.' There is a legend that once Oho-kuni-nushi-no-Kami, to try his strength, came here, and, lifting up one of these masses of basalt, flung it across the sea to the mountain of Sanbeyama. At the foot of Sanbe the mighty rock thus thrown by the Great Deity of Kitzuki may still be seen, it is alleged, even unto this day.

More and more bare and rugged and ghastly the coast becomes as we journey on, and the sunken ledges more numerous, and the protruding rocks more dangerous, splinters of strata piercing the sea-surface from a depth of thirty fathoms. Then suddenly our boat makes a dash for the black cliff, and shoots into a tremendous cleft of it,—an earthquake fissure with sides lofty and perpendicular as the walls of a cañon—and lo! there is daylight ahead. This is a miniature strait, a short cut to the bay. We glide through it in ten minutes, reach open water again, and Hinomisaki is before us,—a semicircle of houses clustering about a bay curve, with an opening in their centre, prefaced by a torii.[1]

Of all bays I have ever seen, this is the most extraordinary. Imagine an enormous sea-cliff torn out and broken down level with the sea, so as to leave a great scoop-shaped hollow in the land, with one original fragment of the ancient cliff still standing in the middle of the gap,—a monstrous square tower of rock, bearing trees upon its summit. And a thousand yards out from the shore rises another colossal rock, fully one hundred feet high. This is known by the name of Fumishima or

---

1 *torii*: a gate to a Shinto shrine, traditionally made of three pieces.

Okyōgashima; and the temple of the Sun-goddess, which we are now about to see, formerly stood upon that islet. The same appalling forces which formed the bay of Hinomisaki doubtless also detached the gigantic mass of Fumishima from this iron coast.

We land at the right end of the bay. Here also there is no beach; the water is black-deep close to the shore, which slopes up rapidly. As we mount the slope, an extraordinary spectacle is before us. Upon thousands and thousands of bamboo frames—shaped somewhat like our clothes-horses—are dangling countless pale yellowish things, the nature of which I cannot discern at first glance. But a closer inspection reveals the mystery. Millions of cuttlefish drying in the sun! I could never have believed that so many cuttlefish existed in these waters. And there is scarcely any variation in the dimensions of them: out of ten thousand there is not the difference of half an inch in length.

II.

The great torii which forms the sea-gate of Hinomisaki is of white granite, and severely beautiful. Through it we pass up the main street of the village,—surprisingly wide for about a thousand yards, after which it narrows into a common highway which slopes up a wooded hill and disappears under the shadow of trees. On the right, as you enter the street, is a long vision of grey wooden houses with awnings and balconies,—little shops, little two-story dwellings of fishermen,—and ranging away in front of these other hosts of bamboo frames from which other millions of freshly caught cuttlefish are hanging. On the other side of the street rises a cyclopean retaining wall, massive as the wall of a daimyō's castle, and topped by a lofty wooden parapet pierced with gates; and above it tower the roofs of majestic buildings, whose architecture strongly resembles that of the structures of Kitzuki; and behind all appears a beautiful green background of hills. This is the Hinomisaki-jinja. But one must walk some considerable distance up the road to reach the main entrance of the court, which is at the farther end of the inclosure, and is approached by an imposing broad flight of granite steps.

The great court is a surprise. It is almost as deep as the outer court of the Kitzuki-no-oho-yashiro, though not nearly so wide; and a paved cloister forms two sides of it. From the court gate a broad paved walk leads to the haiden and shamusho[1] at the opposite end of

1 *haiden and shamusho*: the hall of worship and the shrine offices.

the court—spacious and dignified structures above whose roofs appears the quaint and massive gable of the main temple, with its fantastic cross-beams. This temple, standing with its back to the sea, is the shrine of the Goddess of the Sun. On the right side of the main court, as you enter, another broad flight of steps leads up to a loftier court, where another fine group of Shintō buildings stands—a haiden and a miya;[1] but these are much smaller, like miniatures of those below. Their woodwork also appears to be quite new. The upper miya is the shrine of the god Susano-ō,[2]—brother of Amaterasu-oho-mi-Kami.

III.

To me the great marvel of the Hinomisaki-jinja is that structures so vast, and so costly to maintain, can exist in a mere fishing hamlet, in an obscure nook of the most desolate coast of Japan. Assuredly the contributions of peasant pilgrims alone could not suffice to pay the salary of a single kannushi;[3] for Hinomisaki, unlike Kitzuki, is not a place possible to visit in all weathers. My friend confirms me in this opinion; but I learn from him that the temples have three large sources of revenue. They are partly supported by the Government; they receive yearly large gifts of money from pious merchants; and the revenues from lands attached to them also represent a considerable sum. Certainly a great amount of money must have been very recently expended here; for the smaller of the two miya seems to have just been wholly rebuilt; the beautiful joinery is all white with freshness, and even the carpenters' odorous chips have not yet been all removed.

At the shamusho we make the acquaintance of the Guji of Hinomisaki, a noble-looking man in the prime of life, with one of those fine aquiline faces rarely to be met with except among the high aristocracy of Japan. He wears a heavy black moustache, which gives him, in spite of his priestly robes, the look of a retired army officer. We are kindly permitted by him to visit the sacred shrines; and a kannushi is detailed to conduct us through the buildings.

Something resembling the severe simplicity of the Kitzuki-no-oho-yashiro was what I expected to see. But this shrine of the Goddess of

---

1 *a haiden and a miya*: the hall of worship in front of a miya.
2 *Susano-ō:* This deity is seldom called by his full name, which has been shortened by common usage from Susano-ō-no-mikoto. [*Hearn's note.*]
3 *kannushi*: Shinto priest.

the Sun is a spectacle of such splendor that for the first moment I almost doubt whether I am really in a Shintō temple. In very truth there is nothing of pure Shintō here. These shrines belong to the famous period of Ryobu-Shintō, when the ancient faith, interpenetrated and allied with Buddhism, adopted the ceremonial magnificence and the marvelous decorative art of the alien creed. Since visiting the great Buddhist shrines of the capital, I have seen no temple interior to be compared with this. Daintily beautiful as a casket is the chamber of the shrine. All its elaborated woodwork is lacquered in scarlet and gold; the altar-piece is a delight of carving and color; the ceiling swarms with dreams of clouds and dragons. And yet the exquisite taste of the decorators—buried, doubtless, five hundred years ago—has so justly proportioned the decoration to the needs of surface, so admirably blended the colors, that there is no gaudiness, no glare, only an opulent repose.

This shrine is surrounded by a light outer gallery which is not visible from the lower court; and from this gallery one can study some remarkable friezes occupying the spaces above the doorways and below the eaves,—friezes surrounding the walls of the miya. These, although exposed for many centuries to the terrific weather of the western coast, still remain masterpieces of quaint carving. There are apes and hares peeping through wonderfully chiseled leaves, and doves and demons, and dragons writhing in storms. And while looking up at these, my eye is attracted by a peculiar velvety appearance of the woodwork forming the immense projecting eaves of the roof. Under the tiling it is more than a foot thick. By standing on tiptoe I can touch it; and I discover that it is even more velvety to the touch than to the sight. Further examination reveals the fact that this colossal roofing is not solid timber, only the beams are solid. The enormous pieces they support are formed of countless broad slices thin as the thinnest shingles, superimposed and cemented together into one solid-seeming mass. I am told that this composite woodwork is more enduring than any hewn timber could be. The edges, where exposed to wind and sun, feel to the touch just like the edges of the leaves of some huge thumb-worn volume; and their stained velvety yellowish aspect so perfectly mocks the appearance of a book, that while trying to separate them a little with my fingers, I find myself involuntarily peering for a running-title and the number of a folio!

We then visit the smaller temple. The interior of the sacred chamber is equally rich in lacquered decoration and gilding; and below the miya itself there are strange paintings of weird foxes,—foxes wandering in the foreground of a mountain landscape. But here the colors have been damaged somewhat by time; the paintings have a faded look. Without the shrine are other wonderful carvings, doubtless executed by the same chisel which created the friezes of the larger temple.

I learn that only the shrine-chambers of both temples are very old; all the rest has been more than once rebuilt. The entire structure of the smaller temple and its haiden, with the exception of the shrine-room, has just been rebuilt—in fact, the work is not yet quite done,—so that the emblem of the deity is not at present in the sanctuary. The shrines proper are never repaired, but simply reinclosed in the new buildings when reconstruction becomes a necessity. To repair them or restore them to-day would be impossible: the art that created them is dead. But so excellent their material and its lacquer envelope that they have suffered little in the lapse of many centuries from the attacks of time.

One more surprise awaits me,—the homestead of the high pontiff, who most kindly invites us to dine with him; which hospitality is all the more acceptable from the fact that there is no hotel in Hinomisaki, but only a kichinyado[1] for pilgrims. The ancestral residence of the high pontiffs of Hinomisaki occupies, with the beautiful gardens about it, a space fully equal to that of the great temple courts themselves. Like most of the old-fashioned homes of the nobility and of the samurai, it is but one story high,—an immense elevated cottage, one might call it. But the apartments are lofty, spacious, and very handsome—and there is a room of one hundred mats.[2] A very nice little repast, with abundance of good wine, is served up to us—and I shall always remember one curious dish, which I at first mistake for spinach. It is seaweed, deliciously prepared,—not the common edible seaweed, but a rare sort, fine like moss.

After bidding farewell to our generous host, we take an uphill stroll to the farther end of the village. We leave the cuttlefish behind; but before us the greater part of the road is covered with matting, upon which indigo is drying in the sun. The village terminates abruptly at the top of the hill, where there is another grand granite torii,—a structure so ponderous that it is almost as difficult to imag-

---

1 A *kichinyado* is an inn at which the traveler is charged only the price of the wood used for fuel in cooking his rice. [*Hearn's note.*]

2 The thick fine straw mats, fitted upon the floor of every Japanese room, are always six feet long by three feet broad. The largest room in the ordinary middle-class house is a room of eight mats. A room of one hundred mats is something worth seeing. [*Hearn's note.*]

ine how it was ever brought up the hill as to understand the methods of the builders of Stonehenge. From this torii the road descends to the pretty little seaport of U-Ryō, on the other side of the cape; for Hinomisaki is situated on one side of a great promontory, as its name implies,—a mountain-range projecting into the Japanese Sea.

IV.

The family of the Guji of Hinomisaki is one of the oldest of the Kwazoku or noble families of Izumo; and the daughters are still addressed by the antique title of Princess—O-Hime-San. The ancient official designation of the pontiff himself was Kengyō, as that of the Kitzuki pontiff was Kokuzō; and the families of the Hinomisaki and of the Kitzuki Guji are closely related.

There is one touching and terrible tradition in the long history of the Kengyōs of Hinomisaki, which throws a strange light upon the social condition of this province in feudal days.

Seven generations ago, a Matsudaira, Daimyō of Izumo, made with great pomp his first official visit to the temples of Hinomisaki, and was nobly entertained by the Kengyō,—doubtless in the same chamber of a hundred mats which we to-day were privileged to see. According to custom, the young wife of the host waited upon the regal visitor, and served him with dainties and with wine. She was singularly beautiful; and her beauty, unfortunately, bewitched the Daimyō. With kingly insolence he demanded that she should leave her husband and become his concubine. Although astounded and terrified, she answered bravely, like the true daughter of a samurai, that she was a loving wife and mother, and that, sooner than desert her husband and her child, she would put an end to her life with her own hand. The great Lord of Izumo sullenly departed without further speech, leaving the little household plunged in uttermost grief and anxiety; for it was too well known that the prince would suffer no obstacle to remain in the way of his lust or his hate.

The anxiety, indeed, proved to be well founded. Scarcely had the Daimyō returned to his domains when he began to devise means for the ruin of the Kengyō. Soon afterward, the latter was suddenly and forcibly separated from his family, hastily tried for some imaginary offense, and banished to the islands of Oki. Some say the ship on which he sailed went down at sea with all on board. Others say that he was conveyed to Oki, but only to die there of misery and cold. At all events, the old Izumo records state that, in the year corresponding to 1661 A.D., 'the Kengyō Takatoshi died in the land of Oki.'

On receiving news of the Kengyō's death, Matsudaira scarcely concealed his exultation. The object of his passion was the daughter of his own Karō, or minister, one of the noblest samurai of Matsue, by name Kamiya. Kamiya was at once summoned before the Daimyō, who said to him: 'Thy daughter's husband being dead, there exists no longer any reason that she should not enter into my household. Do thou bring her hither.' The Karō touched the floor with his forehead, and departed on his errand.

Upon the following day he reëntered the prince's apartment, and, performing the customary prostration, announced that his lord's commands had been obeyed—that the victim had arrived.

Smiling for pleasure, the Matsudaira ordered that she should be brought at once into his presence. The Karō prostrated himself, retired and presently returning, placed before his master a kubi-oke[1] upon which lay the freshly-severed head of a beautiful woman—the head of the young wife of the dead Kengyō,—with the simple utterance:

'*This is my daughter.*'

Dead by her own brave will,—but never dishonored.

Seven generations have been buried since the Matsudaira strove to appease his remorse by the building of temples and the erection of monuments to the memory of his victim. His own race died with him: those who now bear the illustrious name of that long line of daimyōs are not of the same blood; and the grim ruin of his castle, devoured by vegetation, is tenanted only by lizards and bats. But the Kamiya family endures; no longer wealthy, as in feudal times, but still highly honored in their native city. And each high pontiff of Hinomisaki chooses always his bride from among the daughters of that valiant race.

NOTE.—The Kengyo of the above tradition was enshrined by Matsudaira in the temple of Shiyekei-jinja, at Ōyama, near Matsue. This miya was built for an atonement; and the people still pray to the spirit of the Kengyō. Near this temple formerly stood a very popular theatre, also erected by the Daimyō in his earnest desire to appease the soul of his victim; for he had heard that the Kengyō was very fond of theatrical performances. The temple is still in excellent preservation; but the theatre has long since disappeared; and its site is occupied by a farmer's vegetable garden.

---

1 The *kubi-oke* was a lacquered tray with a high rim and a high cover. The name signifies 'head-box.' It was the ancient custom to place the head of a decapitated person upon a kubi-oke before conveying the ghastly trophy into the palace of the prince desirous of seeing it. [*Hearn's note.*]

WILLIAM O'BRIEN (1852–1928)

B orn in Mallow, Co. Cork, the second son of a solicitor's clerk, he was educated at Cloyne Diocesan College, and at Queen's College, Cork. He worked as a journalist for the Cork *Daily Herald* and subsequently for the *Freeman's Journal*. In 1881 Parnell appointed him editor of *United Ireland*, the weekly journal of the Land League, which O'Brien called 'an insurrection in print'. It was suppressed in October, and O'Brien was imprisoned without trial in Kilmainham, with Parnell, where he wrote the No Rent Manifesto. After his release in 1882 he acted as secretary to the National League, and was returned for Mallow the following year. With Tim Harrington, Tim Healy and John Dillon, he organized the Plan of Campaign to control rents. In the 1880s he served various prison sentences for land agitation. In 1890 he skipped bail and was raising funds in America when the revelations of Parnell's affair with Katherine O'Shea led to the split in the Irish party, O'Brien joining the anti-Parnellites. He founded the United Irish League in 1898, which advocated 'The Land for the People', and through the Land Act of 1903 led to the abolition of landlordism. Its success contributed to the reunification of the Irish Party. In 1910 he founded the All-for-Ireland League, which had as its motto 'Conference, Conciliation, Consent.' He did not contest the 1918 election in which the Parliamentary Party was annihilated by Sinn Féin, and declined a nomination to the Senate on the foundation of the Free State. *When We Were Boys* (1890), a story of the Fenian movement, was written in prison. Ken Rohan, its Catholic protagonist, asserts that 'our conquerors have managed to make us a little bit ashamed of our fathers. They did the Irish a worse injury than stealing their lands and their lives— they wrote lampoons on their tombstones.' In this novel O'Brien describes St Colman's College, which was attended by his brother, and by James Joyce's father; he gives a perceptive portrait of the President of the college, Dr Croke, later Archbishop of Cashel, who was a friend of O'Brien, and who officiated at his wedding in London on 11 June 1890. The novel proved a great success. It was followed by *A Queen of Men* (1898), which narrates the sixteenth-century exploits of the legendary pirate Grace O'Malley. He wrote several books about the era in Irish history in which he was personally involved, including *Recollections* (1908) and *The Irish Revolution* (1923). His other books include *Edmund Burke as an Irishman* (1924) and *The Parnell of Real Life* (1926).

The No Rent Manifesto

(1881)

TO THE IRISH PEOPLE,

Fellow Countrymen,

The hour has come to test whether the great organisation built up during years of patient labour and sacrifice, and consecrated by the allegiance of the whole Irish race the world over, is to disappear at the summons of a brutal tyranny.

The crisis with which we are face to face is not of our making. It has been deliberately forced upon the country, while the Land Act is as yet untested, in order to strike down the only power which might have exorted any solid benefits for the tenant-farmers of Ireland from the Act, and so leave them once more helplessly at the mercy of a law, invented to save landlordism, and administered by landlord minions. The Executive of the Irish National Land League, acting in the spirit of the resolutions of the National Convention—the most freely-elected representative body ever assembled in Ireland—was advancing steadily in the work of testing how far the administration of the Land Act might be trusted to eradicate from the rents of the Irish tenant-farmers the entire value of their own improvements, and to reduce these rents to such a figure as should for ever place our country beyond the peril of periodical famine. At the same time they took measures to secure, in the event of the Land Act proving a mere paltry mitigation of the horrors of landlordism, in order to fasten it the more securely upon the necks of the people, that the tenant-farmers should not be delivered blind-folded into the hands of hostile law courts, but should be able to fall back upon the magnificent organisation which was crushing landlordism out of existence, when Mr. Gladstone stepped to its rescue.

In either event the Irish tenant-farmers would have been in a position to exact the uttermost farthing of their just demands. It was this attitude of perfect self-command, impregnable while there remained a shadow of respect for law, and supported with unparalleled enthusiasm by the whole Irish race, that moved the rage of the disappointed English minister, upon the monstous pretext that the National Land League was forcing upon the Irish tenant-farmers an organisation which made them all-powerful, and was keeping them by intimidation from embracing an Act which offered them nothing except helplessness and uncertainty. The English Government has cast to the winds every shred of law and justice, and has plunged into an open reign of terror, in order to destroy by the foulest means an organisation which was confessedly too strong for it within the limits of its own English Constitution. Blow after blow has been struck at the Land League, in the mere wantonness of brute force.

In the face of provocation which turned men's blood to flame, the Executive of the Land League adhered calmly and steadily to the course traced out for them by the National Convention. Test cases of a varied and searching character were, with great labour, put in train for adjudication in the Land Courts. Even the arrest of our president, Mr. Charles Stewart Parnell,[1] and the excited state of popular feeling which it evoked, did not induce the Executive to swerve in the slightest from that course, for Mr. Parnell's arrest might have been accounted for by motives of personal malice, and his removal did not altogether derange the machinery for the preparation of the test cases, which he had been at much pains to perfect. But the events which have since occurred—the seizure or attempted seizure, of almost all the members of the Executive, and of the chief officials of the League, upon wild and preposterous pretences, and the violent suppression of free speech, put it beyond any possibility of doubt that the English Government, unable to declare the Land League an illegal association, defeated in the attempt to break its unity, and afraid to abide the results of test cases, watched over by a powerful popular organisation, has deliberately resolved to destroy the whole machinery of the Central League with a view to rendering an experimental trial of the Act impossible, and forcing it upon the Irish tenant-farmers, on the Government's own terms.

The brutal and arbitrary dispersion of the Central Executive has so far succeeded, that we are obliged to announce to our countrymen, that we no longer possess the machinery for adequately presenting the test cases in court, according to the policy prescribed by the National Convention.

Mr. Gladstone has, by a series of furious and wanton acts of despotism, driven the Irish tenant-farmers to choose between their own organisation and the mercy of his lawyers—between the power which

---

1 *the arrest of ... Parnell*: on 13 October 1881 Parnell was arrested at Morrison's Hotel in Dublin. They 'clapped the pride of Erin's isle into cold Kilmainham jail'. Arrests of the other prominent figures in the Land League soon followed. After this manifesto, the Government suppressed the League, on 20 October.

has reduced landlordism to almost its last gasp, and the power which strives with all the ferocity of despotism to restore the detestable ascendancy from which the Land League has delivered the Irish people. One constitutional weapon alone now remains in the hands of the Irish National Land League; it is the strongest, the swiftest, the most irresistible of all. We hesitated to advise our fellow-countrymen to employ it until the savage lawlessness of the English Government provoked a crisis, in which we must either consent to see the Irish tenant-farmers disarmed of their organisation and laid once more prostrate at the feet of the landlords, and every murmer [*sic*] of Irish public opinion suppressed with an armed hand, or appeal to our countrymen to at once resort to the only means now left in their hands of bringing this false and brutal government to its senses.

Fellow-countrymen! the hour to try your souls and to redeem your pledge has arrived. The Executive of the National Land League, forced to abandon the policy of testing the Land Act, feels bound to advise the tenant-farmers of Ireland from this forth to pay NO RENTS under any circumstances to their Landlords until the Government relinquishes the existing system of terrorism, and restores the constitutional rights of the people. Do not be daunted by the removal of your leaders. Your fathers abolished tithes by the same method without any leaders at all, and with scarcely a shadow of the magnificent organisation that covers every portion of Ireland to-day. Do not suffer yourselves to be intimidated by threats of military violence. It is as lawful to refuse to pay rents as it is to receive them. Against the passive resistance of an entire population, military power has no weapons. Do not be wheedled into compromise of any sort by the dread of eviction. If you only act together in the spirit to which, within the last two years, you have countless times solemnly pledged your vows, they can no more evict a whole nation than they can imprison them. The funds of the National Land League will be poured out unstintedly for the support of all who may endure eviction in the course of the struggle.

Our exiled brothers in America may be relied upon to contribute if necessary, as many millions of money as they have contributed thousands to starve out landlordism and bring English tyranny to its knees. You have only to show that you are not unworthy of their boundless sacrifices in your cause. No power on earth, except faint-heartedness on your part can defeat you, landlordism is already staggering under the blows which you have dealt it amidst the applause of the world. One more crowning struggle for your land, your

homes, your lives—a struggle in which you have all the memories of your race, all the hopes of your children, all the sacrifices of your imprisoned brothers, all your cravings for rent-enfranchised land, for happy homes and national freedom to inspire you;—one more heroic effort to destroy landlordism at the very source and fount of its existence and the system which was and is the curse of your race and of your existence will have disappeared for ever. The world is watching to see whether all your splendid hopes and noble courage will crumble away at the first threat of a cowardly tyranny. You have to choose between throwing yourselves upon the mercy of England, and taking your stand by the organisation which has once before proved too strong for English despotism; you have to choose between all-powerful unity, and impotent disorganisation; between the land for the landlords, and the land for the people. We cannot doubt your choice. Every tenant-farmer of Ireland is to-day the standard-bearer of the flag unfurled at Irishtown, and can bear it to a glorious victory. Stand together in the face of the brutal and cowardly enemies of your race. Pay no rents under any pretext. Stand passively, firmly, fearlessly by while the armies of England may be engaged in their hopeless struggle against a spirit, which their weapons cannot touch. Act for yourselves if you are deprived of the counsels of those who have shown you how to act. No power of legalised violence can extort one penny from your purses against your will. If you are evicted you shall not suffer, the landlord who evicts will be a ruined pauper, and the Government which supports him with its bayonets, will learn in a single winter how powerless is armed force against the will of a united, determined and self-reliant nation.
Signed,
CHARLES S. PARNELL, President, Kilmainham Gaol.
A.J. KETTLE, Hon. Sec., Kilmainham Gaol.
MICHAEL DAVITT, Hon. Sec., Portland Prison.
THOMAS BRENNAN, Hon. Sec., Kilmainham Gaol.
JOHN DILLON, Head Organiser, Kilmainham Gaol.
THOMAS SEXTON, Head Organiser, Kilmainham Gaol.
PATRICK EGAN, Treasurer, Paris.

18 October, 1881.

From *When We Were Boys*

(1890)

St. Fergal's

Ken Ronan found Mick Boohig a scarcely less amazing aerial traveler than the roc. He felt so elated with the speed, and the novelty, and the crash, that he thought he would never tire of a railway journey if Boohig were to bear them away and away through this land of enchantment until their hair should grow white. Their arrival at Clonard (in whose diocesan Seminary he was about to be installed as a pupil) was a heavy blow, until Clonard in its turn blossomed into Wonderland around him, and he found himself plucking his father's sleeve hither and thither with a rapturous: 'Just look at this!' and an: 'Oh, I say!' without the slightest regard for the dignity of his first silk hat and eclesiastically-cut garments.

Clonard was a Bishop's See. Its line of prelates extended back to the times of St. Patrick. Most of their lordships had to make shift with a mountain cave for a palace, and some with a gallows for a pulpit. Even still the older portion of the town had a curious dead-and-gone sort of air. Half-way up the main street, in the midst of a tangled graveyard, the battered ruin of a Fransiscan Abbey lay breathing out its everlasting *memento mori* through its shattered grey traceries, like an old monk on a contented death-bed, mumbling gentle words of warning to the living. The principal portion of the population seemed to reside in the surrounding graves; and the adjoining cabins, though they still breathed the turf-smoke of the living, wore a certain moribund aspect of resignation as though preparing for a general death-bed under the patronage of the reverend Franciscan ruins. There was a delightfully drowsy Spanish luxury about the whole thatched-cloister-life of the place. To think that a monthly pig fair desecrated the Main Street jarred upon one's sensibilities, like a French chorus breaking in upon a Gregorian chant. If Town Commissioners there must be at all in such a place, there was a certain æsthetic comfort in learning that they reaped a yearly crop of hay off a considerable slice of the great, empty market-place. The people ceased their chat in the street, and pulled off their hats when the Angelus bell sounded; and it seemed as if the Angelus bell never did quite finish sounding, unless when a Vesper bell was beginning, or the modest hour-bell from the Calvary Convent tinkling, or the Cathedral thundering out its chimes in full-dress majesty,

like a whole sonorous Œcumenical Council. Clonard's simple life from
dawn to dark was set to ecclesiastical music, even to the gay cherub
choirs of children playing about the gravestones, and the deep monk-
ish caw of the sober old rooks up in their ivied cloisters. The very town
band was organised under the invocation of St. Fergal, and played religious and patriotic hymns with equal spirit.

But on the breast of the hill overtopping this dozy, crumbling,
thatched, and ragged Clonard of the Penal Days there had arisen a
shiny new town of virgin limestone, all of a piece, all of a cluster, as
if it had been let down from heaven in a single night fresh from the
brain of some not-too-inventive angelic architect—the new
Cathedral, the new College, the new Convent, the new Orphanage,
the new Presbytery, glittering in naked whiteness all of a row; and
around these there had gathered the usual booths that drive a not
ungodly trade on the Way of Heaven—a wine-merchant with a spe-
ciality for Spanish altar-wines; a tailor with clerical fashion-plates; a
fancy warehouse garnished with articles of devotion 'imported direct
from Paris;' and a pastry-cook whose function in life it was to supply the funeral baked-meats for a Month's Mind at the Cathedral, or
the wedding-cake for the profession of a nun at the Convent, or the
apple-pies and waiters for a particularly large dinner-party at his
lordship's, the Bishop's. This resurrection of a faith that seemed to
have been trampled into the dust ages ago as utterly as the
Franciscans' kitchen-fire, was a source of incredible pride to a generation whose grandfathers took to the hills for worship as for an
insurrection, and whose great-grandfathers deserved to be hanged
for the capital offence of going to school. 'Like the fabled bird of the
Orient,' Mr. Mat Murrin, of the *Banner*, used to write, on speech-
day at St. Fergal's, where he annually beamed on the proceedings in
a cloudy eye-glass that required perpetual furbishing, and a silk hat
that seemed to have spent a long life in endeavouring to get properly polished, and where Mrs. Murrin's vigorous performances during
the *déjeuner*, and Mat's flowery toast of 'The President' after it, were
amongst the most valued traditions of the place—'like the fabled bird
of the Orient, temple and cloister and educational establishment
have sprung, godlike, and, so to say, full-fledged, from the ashes of
our fathers' shrines, radiant with the immortal juvenility of our faith
and race, crowning the historic hill of Clonard as with a dazzling
limestone tiara, and reflecting the utmost credit upon our enterprising townsmen, Messrs. Houlihan and Daggs, the contractors, to
whose courteous and hospitable foreman, Mr. Macdarmody, our rep-

resentative takes this opportunity of expressing his indebtedness for much interesting information and some slight, though graceful, hospitalities.' Indeed, to look up at those astonishing masses of shapely masonry, and then down over the poor little out-at-elbows town out of whose loins they had all arisen, the most whirling young Zeitgeister who decrees that the commission of Christianity was exhausted centuries ago in building churches for the Encyclopédists and Mental Physiologists to tumble down, might well bow his head as reverently as Mat Murrin before an authentic miracle of living faith. One peculiarity of all this headlong rush into stone-and-mortar was that nothing was quite finished. The Cathedral wanted a spire, and was waiting complacently until the next generation should build it, like a clergyman out under a shower of rain without his hat; there was room for another wing to the College in the architect's designs; old Mother Rosalie, of the Calvary Convent, objected totally to die until her old eyes should see an altar and reredos of Sicilian marble gleaming in the Convent Chapel; the priests' house was only roofed in for the winter until funds should come in to floor and plaster the top story; but on the Work went all the same, with funds or without them. Your Irish banker never refuses to honour *post-obit* drafts[1] upon the piety of posterity, and your Irish church-builder never fears to draw them.

'And why should they?' observed Myles Rohan, singing the praises of the various gems in the limestone tiara as he and his son rattled up to the College gate on a jaunting-car. 'If they passed a resolution to rebuild Solomon's Temple in this famished country, cedar, gold, and all, they'd manage to get the roof on by hook or crook, my hand to you, and start a Bazaar to defray the price of the precious stones.'

At St. Fergal's they were ushered into a bare, shiny, beeswaxed little reception-parlour, furnished as ascetically as a cell in the Thebaid;[2] a rough table, with a jug of cold water—it looked like ice-water—on the same; an expanse of uncarpeted floor suggestive of rigid Lenten regulations; whitewashed walls staring you out of countenance with their chastity; and a morsel of fire in the grate barely sufficient to act as a satiric sting of the flesh to anybody who should apply for comfort for unmortified appetites in that quarter. Another new pupil and his parents were seated in awful silence there before them. It was a tall shambling youth of rude country strength, writhing in his first suit of black broadcloth under the double disadvantage of having all the

---

1 *post-obit drafts*: drafts that take effect after someone's death.
2 *The Thebaid*: area of Thebes, famous for its ascetic monks.

blood in his body jostling in his cheeks, and his arms and legs glued irrevocably in the uncomfortable postures into which modesty had first contorted them. His father was one of those 'strong farmers' who emerged from the Great Famine fat with the spoils of their weaker brethren, who had departed without securing as much as a coffin in that ennobling scramble for the survival of the fittest. He was a man with quantities of straggling bright yellow hair breaking out in all directions around a very florid, very freckled face; and a pair of exuberant scarlet hands seemed to be engaged in the opposite operation of bulging out through a pair of brilliant yellow gloves, and indulging in all sorts of manifestations not provided for by the glove-maker. His partner was a comely matron, with the cheeks of a thriving milkmaid, and a 'real sealskin' jacket (which Myles enviously estimated would purchase out Mrs. Rohan's entire wardrobe), and accessories of the highest fashion to match:—to wit, a chinchilla muff through which hands and gloves of pink and green peeped in and out, a gown of sky-blue glossy silk, and a coquettish little hat of the fashionable shade of yellow, set somewhat precariously upon a lofty chignon amidst clusters of red roses and glass cherries. They sat demurely together, as though the jug of ice-water was slowly freezing them, or the stern beeswaxed floor gradually awing them into a mood to sink on their bare knees and confess their sins. They were much impressed by Myles Rohan's temerity, when they observed him stride across the room, and with a few vigorous pokes set the sickly spot of fire ablazing—he was one of those men who never poke a fire without warming the heart in it.

'I hope they don't expect people to fast from red turf of a morning like this?' he remarked. 'Wouldn't you come to the fire, ma'am, and warm your toes?'

The proposition was not in itself a startling one; but the lady in some alarm drew in one honestly proportioned foot which had strayed outside the fortifications of the sky-blue silk, as if not quite certain that that was not the topic alluded to. She blushed and smiled, and looked at her husband.

'Thank ye. It makes no odds. We're only waiting for a word with the Docthor,' said he of the scarlets-and-yellows, half apologetically and half stiffly.

As he spoke a side door opened with a whiff of warm air, laden with vague, generous suggestions, and in glided the Doctor, like the embodied spirit of those cheerier regions inside—'The Doctor' was the half-awesome, half-caressing Irish title of the Very Reverend

Marcus O'Harte, D.D., the President of St. Fergal's—a strong-built, massive-headed, precipitous-looking figure, with masses of storm-cloudy wrinkles piled over his eyebrows in the region to which phys-iognomists assign quickness of perception and swiftness of action; an upper-forehead, where the ramparts of the reflective powers were rounded off; as in all fine Celtic heads, into an imaginative arch; a square mouth, which would be a cruel mouth but for a twitch of drollery that now and again trembled at its corners; and a wonderful grey eye, which always seemed to pierce you through and through, whether with a sun-ray or a dart of lightning. With a quiet, well-bred shake-hands to the address of Myles Rohan and his son, the Doctor passed as softly as a great cat across the room, with a smile and an open hand towards the strong-farmer group.

'Ah! Mrs. Deloohery, so happy! Mr. D., you must have had a smart spin across the Bog this morning. And this is our young friend—Patsy, I believe?'

'Augustine, Docthor, Augustine,' suggested Mr. D., one of whose peculiarities was that, when he required to blush—all the natural reds being exhausted in his normal complexion—he adopted the plan of turning blue over the red, with distressingly apoplectic-looking results.

'Augustine, oh!—the English Augustine,[1] I presume? How fortu-nate! Would you believe it, Mrs. Deloohery?—he arrives just within the octave of his patron saint. A most interesting coincidence—isn't it?' The Doctor chucked Augustine under the chin, just as that mod-est youth had succeeded in completely ruffling the fur of his silk hat in a desperate endeavour to unruffle it. 'We'll make a man of him, Mrs. Deloohery, never fear,' he added, pleasantly.

From this point the conversation grew confidential, Mr. D. assum-ing an obstinate and incredulous attitude, while the lady conducted the *pourparlers* with excellent ability, albeit in unambitious English. The Doctor's face hardened into polite but icy firmness as, with his fingers playing with the tassel of his biretta, and his eyes engaged in dreamy admiration of the scenery out of windows, Ken overheard his bland, 'In advance, my dear Mrs. Deloohery—invariably in advance!' Then one of the yellow kids disappeared in a breeches pocket, and the Doctor plunged into affectionate researches as to the numbers, ages, measles, and personal adventures of the house of Deloohery, while unhappy Mr. D. who was accustomed to handle his money without kid gloves, conducted the operation of capturing the necessary number of

---

1 *the English Augustine*: Augustine, or Austin, of Canterbury (d. c.605), venerated as the evan-
gelizer of England. His feast day is 26 May.

guineas so clumsily that a gold piece tumbled through the gloves to the beeswaxed floor with a flop, and with painful deliberation rolled across to Ken Rohan's feet; whereupon there was a moment of terrific suspense, and that young gentleman presented the coin with his best bow to the afflicted owner, and the afflicted owner looked as if he did not know whether to box Ken's ears for the courtesy, and the Doctor developed a more devouring interest than ever in young Master Aloysius Deloohery's course of treatment for the rickets.

The yellow kids and their sky-blue spouse were at last satisfactorily ushered to the door, and Augustine led away in the custody of a young ecclesiastic. Doctor O'Harte, wearing an austere smile, held the door open for the departing silks and sealskins. Then he closed it briskly, and turning back into the parlour with both his hands extended, suddenly broke forth:—

'Myles, my old friend, how is every inch of you?' The earlier years of the Doctor's ministry had been spent as curate in Drumshaughlin, and a genial curate was never long in finding out that the chimney-corner at the Mill was the sunniest spot in the parish. 'And this is little Ken that used to serve my Mass and steal my pippins! Why, the young rascal is grown a man on our hands!' He twirled the stripling round in his strong grasp, like a drill-sergeant, noting with a critic's appreciation that, for all his childishness in the world's ways, and all the clumsiness of his black garments, it was a lithe, broad-shouldered, bright-complexioned lad, among whose fearless brown curls he let his broad hand rest for a moment with a rough, mastiff-like kindness— 'Come along out of those arctic regions.'

'Not to tell you a lie, Doctor, your face has a pleasanter look than your fire this morning,' said the miller, with a glance towards the dismal little grate.

There was a roguish twinkle in the Doctor's eye. 'We have to do a good deal of freezing with both of them hereabouts, I can tell you. What are you to do with people like our good friends in the rainbow liveries that were here just now? Excellent Christians, and invaluable to their parish priest, but they think their boy ought to be made a priest cheaper than their three-year-olds could be fattened for the Shrove Fair. That woman fought tooth and nail against making the piano an extra—the piano, mind you, nothing less!'

'The piano! Blood alive!—I ask your reverence's pardon,' said the miller, rubbing his hands. 'You ought to teach the young man how to dress dolls, or maybe a stitch in embroidery.'

'They *would* be serviceable accomplishments—over in Schkooil

Bog. Come, thou irreverent man, I've got the reputation of a rogue—it's my whole stock-in-trade in this wicked world—you'll spoil my character if you get me blurting out candid opinions of the faithful. Come along. Fact is, you broke in on my breakfast, and the only revenge I can have is to make you swallow a share of it cold.'

He led the way to the President's own snuggery, which, after the penitential room outside, glowed like a sunbright Easter Sunday morning after a lean Lenten season. A jovial fire of oak logs and cubes of black peat was leaping and sparkling on the hearth, and upon a table close to the warmth lay the materials of a half-finished breakfast.

'My regimen, like my ague, is chiefly derived from the Campagna,' said the Doctor, as he pressed Myles Rohan into his own easy chair and tossed aside his biretta. 'A dish of stirabout, soused in fresh milk, to begin with; then a bird, or some snack of that kind, with a glass of white wine; and a bunch of grapes or a chunk of melon to wind up with'—gently drawing the cork of his demi-bouteille of Château Yquem étampé, like a violinist drawing his bow across a delicate instrument.

'Well, sir, it may be an old-fashioned prejudice,' said the miller, 'but I like the look of a teapot on a breakfast-table, and I don't greatly fancy fruit, unless of a Snap-apple Night[1] or so, for the sake of old times.'

'As you will.' The Doctor turned to a dumb-waiter glittering with a neat little silver tea-service, whose urn was steaming merrily over a diminutive spirit-stove. It was a parting 'Testimonial' from the parishioners of Drumshaughlin. 'You ought to be able to recognise it, Myles—at least, I know it's you're responsible for most of the silver. The blackguards say I contributed the complimentary inscription myself.'

'Upon my conscience, Doctor, I never take more than one breakfast, and that's down hours ago; but, if something it must be—'

'I know—the best white wine ever grown—'

'Thank you, Doctor—a glass of grog.' There was a smack and a robust dignity about Myles Rohan's way of pronouncing 'a glass of grog'—an air of art in his apportionment of the water to a shade, and his tender poising of the tumblerful of honest gold liquor between himself and the light—a sturdy virtue and deep content in his way of settling himself out to take in the full aroma—which made the President's costly Château Yquem seem the syrup of babes and sucklings in comparison.

---

1 *Snap-apple Night*: Halloween. Snap-apple is a sport in which you try to catch in your mouth an apple which is twirling on a stick with a candle at the other end.

Ken had no invincible objection to 'more than one breakfast,' and was soon helping the Doctor through his game-pie with a heartiness for which, after disposing of a fat grouse and a huge segment of crust, he meanly sought to compound by blushing guiltily when he caught his father's eye fixed, half-comically, half-reproachfully on his performance. The truth is, our faithless young Sindbad was beginning to find the Doctor, with his hearty grips and his plump bird on the point of his fork, an even more wonderful being than Boohig.

'Don't be in dread we'll pamper him much with game-pie, Myles. Father Mulpetre has a theory that neck of mutton and vegetable soup make the best brain food going. 'Twould astonish you what medical authority he can cite for it—I am deeply impressed with his erudition myself when it comes to totting up the butcher's bill at the end of the session. Well, but now, my young friend, enough of gossip and game-pie; let's hear what better you can do than demolish pie-crust.'

The miller listened with earnest edification while the President, stern as a Grand Inquisitor, subjected his new pupil to the torture with defective Greek aorists,[1] and absurd distinctions between Pythrambic and Asclepiadean metres,[2] and details touching one Aristomenes[3] who, he rather thought, was a Messenian hero, and yet, on second thoughts, reminded him of that leather-lunged Athenian cobbler:[4]—in all of which ordeal Master Ken, whose sympathies went with the strong-winged bird rather than with the exact sciences of the ant-hill, figured less heroically than in the historical romance which his sister Katie so often constructed for him of winter evenings at the Mill. He saw the President's face darkening. Now that he looked at it more closely, it was a face that could be harsh and pitiless.

'Hark you, sir,' he said, his eye lightening from under the louring brow with a flash that made Ken Rohan, who was not a sheepish boy, drop his own eyelashes and hang down his head. 'You have breakfasted with your father's friend, not with the President of St. Fergal's. I warn you that your father's friend has no place in the business of this College, and from the President you'll get simple justice, raw and

---

1 *Greek aorists*: combinations of tense and aspect in Greek, which roughly correspond to the simple past tense in English.

2 *Pythrambic and Asclepiadean metre*: 'Pythrambic' is a compound of Pythiambic and Dythrambic (the former is indeed a metre, the latter is a processional song which lay at the foundation of Greek drama); 'Asclepiadean metre', named after the poet Asclepiades of Samos (c. 290 BC), is common in Horace's verse.

3 *Aristomenes*: hero of an aborted rising by the Messenians against the Spartans, who had enslaved them (685 BC)

4 *Athenian cobbler*: at the shop of Simon the philosophical cobbler Socratic dialogue is said to have originated (Socrates being a frequent visior).

unboiled, just as you earn it—no less, and not a grain more. Come out now and know your schoolfellows. Let me offer you two last words of advice,' he added, in a softer tone, 'for Myles Rohan's son: Never lie, and avoid Jack Harold. Come along.'

Ken's schoolfellows turned out to be better than a hundred callow country lads, who, at the President's entry into the study-hall, formed a dumb and frightened little mob around the rostrum of a peevish-looking young ecclesiastic, with beady yellow eyes and a majestic soutane.

'Hallo, a culprit!' said the President, before whom the boys shrinkingly gave way. 'What's wrong, Father Mulpetre?'

Father Mulpetre lugged forward a diminutive urchin, in still more diminutive jacket and trousers, whose little body was quivering with suppressed terror, and his little fists dug into the sockets of his streaming eyes.

'It's Master Mulloy, sir, who's been detected reading "Robinson Crusoe" during Mass, instead of his prayer-book; and'—he added in a lower tone, meant to be caught by the President alone—'it cannot be the first time, for I never could understand what made him so attentive at his prayers.'

'Who saw him do this?' demanded the President, sternly.

Father Mulpetre whispered significantly, 'It would be highly undesirable to make my informant known.' The yellowish gleams under the overhanging eyebrows were like stealthy skirmishers from the sharply-graved, perpendicular furrows which ran into a knot between the eyes, and which appeared to be the citadel of Father Mulpetre's character.

'Who saw him do this?' repeated the President, without moving a muscle.

There was a breathless little pause.

'Master Dargan, like a good boy, thought it his duty to mention to me that he watched him reading about the man Friday during the entire Mass,' said Father Mulpetre.

'Come to the front, Master Dargan.'

'Good gracious, father, it is Lionel—what a sneak!' whispered Ken, as a smartly dressed youth swaggered forward with a jaunty and offended air.

The President's face grew harsher. 'Master Mulloy, since you love "Robinson Crusoe" so much better than your prayers, you will please retire to the punishment-room, and on your bended knees recite "Robinson Crusoe" aloud from this until play-hour is over. You will probably have got enough of the author by that time. You did well, Master Dargan, if you saw your comrade do wrong, to have him corrected'—the youngster readjusted his smart necktie with complacency—'but as you could not have detected him reading his prayers out of "Robinson Crusoe" if you had been attending to your own, I must ask you to bear Master Mulloy company in the punishment-room during play-hour and read aloud "The Meditations of St. Alphonsus Liguori," which you will, no doubt, prefer to works of profane literature. Father Mulpetre will be good enough to see personally that these exercises are performed to the letter.'

'Hourra!' shouted a rebellious voice, somewhere in the thick of the crowd.

'Who spoke?' demanded the President, in a voice of thunder. The rising titter was instantly frozen up, and several boys who didn't do it blushed crimson under the Doctor's remorseless eye. 'He's a coward,whoever he is, and if I had caught him he should kneel down and beg Father Mulpetre's pardon every day before meals for a week.'

'Thank you, Doctor; I am proud to leave my boy with you,' fervently murmured Myles Rohan, squeezing the President's hand, when they were out again in the corridor. He was delighted with the Doctor's code of summary jurisdiction; delighted with the trim, snow-white dormitories fed with the free air of the hills; delighted with the elaborate heating apparatus—the Doctor's favourite *calorifère*[1]—which would do almost anything except work; delighted with the mystic little chapel, steeped in the dim religious light of pink and blue panes of glass; delighted and overawed, beyond all, by the Library which, though the shelves were of painted deal and its contents chiefly elementary schoolbooks and moral fiction, oppressed the miller only less than a church with the shadows of unknown powers. There were two topics on which Myles Rohan, the most stubborn of men, had the simple, unquestioning reverence of a child—religion and learning. Start him upon these and his indomitable spirit might be bridled and driven with a silken thread.

Dr. O'Harte perceived the direction of his thoughts. 'What humbugs we schoolmen are, to be sure,' he said, with his boisterous laugh. 'Here you are, thinking you are surrounded by ghostly regiments of Greek and Latin Fathers, and imagining— don't tell me!—that midnight finds us with wasted cheek and hollow eye poring over the secrets of their dread folios. My dear Myles, the only books I've studied these years

---

1 *calorifère*: a stove.

back are the College pass-books—these and my Breviary, and not too much of that same.'

For all that the honest miller breathed more freely when they emerged from the oppressive fumes of all this learning into the play-fields, where he amused a party of young racket-players by proposing to 'take a hand' against any champion of their naming, and covered them with confusion by beating their champion all to love.

'Hallo, the honour of St. Fergal's is at stake!' cried the President, who, on the playground, had relaxed once more into the chum and big brother of his boys. 'Just hold my soutane, O'Hara, will you?— *pro aris et focis*[1]—I'll try a bout with him myself.'

And whether it was that Myles Rohan's respect for the clergy pursued him even into the racket-court, or that he had met his match in the muscular President, certain it is that the reputation of St. Fergal's was abundantly retrieved, and the miller managed to become more popular vanquished than victorious, and was being escorted to his car in a sort of triumphal procession, when a peremptory tantarara from the Prefect's trumpet announced that play-hour and 'The Meditations of St. Liguori' were over and recalled the mutinous young enthusiasts to their allegiance.

'Come, boy, your duty now is to obey Father Mulpetre's trumpet,' said Myles Rohan. 'Be off, and—there now, God bless you!'

If Ken scorned to display a tear before the weaker sex at home, he had no scruple—nor, indeed, choice—about bursting into tears now, when he felt his father's brave hand enfolding his own for the last time; and as Myles Rohan himself strode sturdily away, I think any jury of his countrymen must have found that a certain globule trembling on the brink of his eyelid was as true and overt as ever was wrung from an honest heart, although he would have pleaded guilty to a larceny of spoons rather than to so lackadaisical a show of sentiment. His was a sort of tenderness which is never savage until it is found out.

---

1 *pro aris et focis*: correctly *pro aris atque focis*—'for altars and hearths' (Sallust, *Bellum Catilinae* 59. 5).

CANON SHEEHAN (1852–1913)

Patrick Augustine Sheehan was born in Mallow, Co. Cork, one of six children of a local shopkeeper. He was educated in the Long Room National School in Mallow, where he was a classmate of William O'Brien*, who would later describe him as 'one of the truest men of genius who have illustrated the Irish name'. After his parents' untimely death Patrick was entrusted to the guardianship of John McCarthy, the parish priest, later Bishop of Cloyne. He was sent to St. Colman's College, where he developed his love of the classics and of mathematics. He was a distinguished student in Maynooth but suffered a nervous breakdown. He was ordained in 1875, joined Bishop Vaughan's Cathedral staff in Plymouth, returned to Mallow in 1877 and became a curate in Queenstown (Cobh) in 1881. Encouraged by Father Matthew Russell, editor of *The Irish Monthly*, he wrote articles on religious instruction and Christian art, and stories for children. After a bout of ill health he returned as senior curate to Mallow; he was appointed parish priest of Doneraile in 1894 and canon of Cloyne in 1895. That year saw the anonymous publication of his first novel, *Geoffrey Austin: Student*, an exposition of defects in Irish education. It, and its sequel, *The Triumph of a Failure* (1899) were 'sermons in print'. Sheehan was to rehearse their main theme, a distrust of modern materialism, in all his fiction. He gained popular success with his picture of Father ('Daddy') Dann, the humane, conservative parish priest of Kilronan, and his impetuous curate, Father Letheby, in *My New Curate* (1900). Father Letheby's attempts to effect changes in the parish are thwarted by the ignorant greed of local girls and by modern outside forces, epitomized in the French steamer which sinks the newly-built fishing boat, *The Star of the Sea*. The eponymous hero of *Luke Delmege* (1901) is a curate, newly returned from mission work in England, whose zeal for reform brings harm to a rural Irish parish before Luke renounces his modern intellectualism. *Glenanaar* (1905) is based on the 1829 Doneraile conspiracy trials in which Daniel O'Connell defended peasants accused of agrarian crimes; it depicts the destructive greed for land. *The Blindness of Dr Gray* (1909) exposes the land grabbing after the land war of the 1880s. Sheehan's last novel, *The Graves of Kilmorna* (1915), set in 1867, is a pessimistic portrait of the futility of patriotic self-sacrifice in the face of commercial immorality. Myles Cogan, the Fenian, who was incarcerated for his part in the 1867 rising, returns to support an enthusiastic young Home Rule candidate; he is jeered by the crowd which he confronts saying 'I doubt if Ireland ever ranked lower in the sty of materialism than in the present age', and is killed by a stone thrown by a drunkard. Sheehan supported his friend William O'Brien's All-for-Ireland League. A friend of Lord Castletown of Doneraile Court, he was instrumental in affecting land transfers in Doneraile and in bringing improvements to the town.

From *My New Curate*

(1900)

Beside the Singing River

Father Letheby was coming home a few nights ago, a little after twelve o'clock, from a hurried sick-call, and he came down by the cliffs; for, as he said, he likes to see the waters when the Almighty flings his net over their depths, and then every sea-hillock is a star, and there is a moon in every hollow of the waves. As he skirted along the cliff that frowns down into the valleys of the sea on the one hand, and the valleys of the firs and poplars on the other, he thought he heard some voices deep down in the shadows, and he listened. Very soon the harsh rasp of a command came to his ears, and he heard: *"Shun! 'verse arms,'* etc. He listened very attentively, and the tramp of armed men echoed down the darkness; and he thought he saw the glint of steel here and there where the moonbeams struck the trees.

'It was a horrible revelation,' he said, 'that here in this quiet place we were nursing revolution, and had some secret society in full swing amongst us. But then, as the little bit of history brought up the past, I felt the tide of feeling sweeping through me, and all the dread enthusiasm of the race woke within me:—

> There beside the singing river
>   That dark mass of men are seen,
> Far above their shining weapons
>   Hung their own immortal green![1]

But this is a bad business, sir, for soul and body. What's to be done?'

'A bad business, indeed,' I echoed. 'But worse for soul than body. These poor fellows will amuse themselves playing at soldiers, and probably catching pneumonia; and there 'twill end. You didn't see any policemen about?'

'No. They could be hiding unknown to me.'

'Depend upon it, they were interested spectators of the midnight evolutions. I know there are some fellows in the village in receipt of secret service money, and all these poor boys' names are in the Castle archives. But what is worse, this means anti-clericalism, and consequently abstention from Sacraments, and a long train of evils besides. It must be handled gently.'

---

1 *There beside the singing river...*: from John Keegan Casey's ballad, 'The Rising of the Moon'.

'You don't mean to say, sir,' he replied, 'that that Continental poison has eaten its way in Ireland?'

'Not to a large extent; but it is there. There is no use in burying our heads in the sands and pretending not to see. But we must act judiciously. A good surgeon never acts hastily—never hurries over an operation. *Lente—lente*.'[1]

I saw a smile faintly rippling around the corners of his mouth. But I was afraid he might rush matters here, and it would be dangerous. But where's the use? He understood but one way of acting—to grapple with an abuse and strangle it. 'You drop stones,' he used to say, 'and they turn up armed men.'

How he learned their place of meeting I don't know. But Sunday afternoon was a favourite time for the rebels; and the coursing match on the black hills and the rabbit hunt in the plantations were only preliminaries to more important and secret work. Whether by accident or design, Father Letheby stumbled on such a meeting about four o'clock one Sunday afternoon. A high ditch and a strong palisade of fir trees hid him from sight, and he was able to hear a good deal, and had no scruple in playing the listener. This is what he heard. The village tailor, lame in one leg, and familiarly known as 'Hop-and-go-one,' was the orator:—

'Fellow countrymen, de time for action has come. From ind to ind of the land, the down-trodden serfs of Ireland are rising in their millions. Too long have dey been juped by false pretences; too long have the hirelings of England chated and decaved them. We know now what a shimmera,[2] what a fraud, was Home Rule. Our counthry has been dragged at the tail of English parties, who were purshuing their own interests. But 'tis all past. No more constitutional agitation, no more paceful struggle. Lead will do what fine speeches didn't. And if the black militia, wid dere ordhers from Rome, attimpt this time to interfere, we know what answer to give dem. De West's awake, and 'tisn't priests will set us to sleep agin—'

At this juncture the orator was caught by the nape of the neck, and lifted bodily off the turf ditch, which was his forum. When he looked around, and saw who was his captor, he shrieked for mercy; and Father Letheby, dropping him, as one would drop a rat, he scurried off as fast as his lame leg would permit, whilst the priest, turning round to the stupefied boys, warned them of their folly and madness:—

---

1 *lente-lente*: 'slowly, slowly' is Father Dan's motto and the advice he constantly gives to his impulsive curate.

2 *shimmera*: Chimera [*Sheehan's note.*]

'God knows, boys,' he said, 'I pity you. You are bent on a desperate and foolish course, the end of which no man can foresee. I know it is useless to reason with you on the score of danger; but I warn you that you are violating the laws of God and the Church, and that no blessing comes from such action. And yet,' he continued, placing his hand in the breast-pocket of his coat, and drawing out a blue official paper, 'this may convince you of your folly; at least, it may convince you of the fact that there is a traitor and informer in your midst. Who he is I leave yourselves to conjecture!'

He read out slowly the name of every young man that had been sworn in that secret society in the parish. The young men listened sullenly, and swore angrily between their teeth. But they could not deny their betrayal. They were vexed, humbled, disgraced; but they had to make some defence.

'The priests are always agin the people,' said one keen-looking fellow, who had been abroad.

'That's an utter falsehood,' said Father Letheby, 'and you know it. You know that priests and people for seven hundred years have fought side by side the battle of Ireland's freedom from civil and religious disabilities. I heard your own father say how well he remembered the time when the friar stole into the farmyard at night, disguised as a pedlar, and he showed me the cavern down there by the sea-shore where Mass was said, and the fishermen heard it, as they pretended to haul in their nets.'

'Thrue enough for you, your reverence,' said a few others; ''tis what our fathers, and our fathers' fathers, have told us.'

'And now,' continued Father Letheby, 'look at the consequences of your present folly. Possible imprisonment in the dungeons of Portland and Dartmoor; exile to America, enforced by the threats of prosecution; and the sense of hostility to the Church, for you know you are breaking the laws. You dare not go to confession, for you cannot receive absolution; you are a constant terror to your mothers and sisters—and all at the dictation of a few scoundrels, who are receiving secret service money from the government, and a few newspapers that are run by Freemasons and Jews.'

'Ah, now, your reverence,' said one of the boys, a littérateur, 'you are drawing the long bow. How could Irish newspapers be run by Freemasons and Jews?'

'Would you be surprised to hear,' said Father Letheby, 'that all the great Continental papers are the property of Freemasons and Jews; that all the rancour and bitterness stirred up against the Church for the past fifty years has been their work; that the anti-clerical feeling in Germany and in France has been carefully originated and fostered by them; that hatred of the Holy See is their motto; and that they have got into Ireland. You can see the cloven foot in the virulent anti-religious and anti-clerical articles that you read by the light of the fire at the forge; and yet, the very prayer-books you used at Mass to-day, and the beads that rolled through your mothers' fingers, have been manufactured by them. But the Irish are always fools—never more so than now.'

It was a magnificent leap of imagination on Father Letheby's part—that which attributed to Jews and Freemasons the manufacture of beads and prayer-books on the one hand, and anti-clericalism on the other. Yet there was truth in what he had said. Indeed, there were many indications, as I could point out to him to his surprise, which proved that the anti-Catholic agencies here in Ireland were pursuing exactly the same tactics which had led to the extinguishing of the faith in parts of France and Italy—namely, the dissemination of porno-graphic literature. They know well that there is but one thing that can destroy Irish faith, and that is the dissemination of ideas subversive of Catholic morality. Break down the earthworks that guard the purity of the nation, and the citadel of faith is taken. He was very silent all that evening, as I notice all Irish priests grow grave when this awful fact, which is under their very eyes, is made plain to them. It is so easy to look at things without seeing them. Then, as the full revelation of this new *diablerie* dawned upon him, he grew very angry. I think this is the most charming thing about my curate, that he is a thorough hater of everything cunning and concealed, and breaks out into noble philippics against whatever is foul and vicious. But I know he will be now on the alert; and God help any unfortunate that dares to peddle unwholesome wares under the necklaces and matches of his basket!

The tailor came duly to report Father Letheby for the drastic treat-ment he had received. He was rather too emphatic in demanding his immediate removal, and hinting at suspension. In lieu of that satisfac-tion, he would immediately institute proceedings in the Court of Queen's Bench for assault and battery, and place the damages at sev-eral thousand pounds. I listened to him patiently, then hinted that an illiterate fellow like him should not be making treasonable speeches. He bridled up at the word 'illiterate,' and repudiated the vile insinu-ation. He could read and write as well as any priest in Connaught.

'But you cannot read your own writing?' I said, tentatively.

'Couldn't he? Try him!'

I thrust under his eyes his last letter to the sub-inspector of the district. I thought he would get a fit of apoplexy.

'Now, you scoundrel,' I said, folding the letter and placing it beyond reach, 'I forgive you all your deception and treason. What Father Letheby has got in store for you I cannot say. But I'll never forgive you, you most unscientific and unmathematical artist, for having given me so many shocking misfits lately, until I have looked like a scarecrow in a cornfield; even now you are smelling like a distillery. And tell me, you ruffian, what right had you to say at Mrs. Haley's public house that I was 'thauto—thauto—gogical' in my preaching? If I, with all the privileges of senility, chose to repeat myself, to drive the truths of Christianity into the numskulls of this pre-Adamite village, what is that to you—you ninth part of a man? Was it not the immortal Homer that declared that every tailor— '

'For God's sake, spare me, your reverence, and I'll never do it again.'

'Do you promise to cut my garments mathematically in the future?'

'I do, your reverence.' He spoke as emphatically as if he were renewing his baptismal vows at a great mission.

'Do you promise to speak respectfully of me and my sermons for the future?'

'I do, your reverence.'

'Now, go. *Exi, erumpe, evade*, or I'll turn you into a *Sartor Resartus*.[1] I hand you over now, as the judge hands the culprit, to Father Letheby. Don't be too much surprised at eventualities. Do you know, did you ever hear, what the women of Marblehead did to a certain Floyd Ireson?[2] Well, go ask Father Letheby. He'll tell you. And I shall be much surprised if the women of Kilronan are much behind their sisters of Marblehead in dealing with such a scoundrel as you.'

I proposed this conundrum to Father Letheby that same evening: 'Why is it considered a greater crime to denounce and correct an evil than to commit it?' He looked at me as if he doubted my sanity. I put it in a more euphemistic form: 'Why is success always the test of merit? To come down from the abstract to the concrete, Why is a gigantic swindler a great financier, and a poor fellow that steals a loaf of bread a felon and a thief? Why is a colossal liar a great diplomatist, and a petty prevaricator a base and ignoble fraud? Why is Napoleon

---

1 *Sartor Resartus*: 'the tailor re-patched'—after Thomas Carlyle's *Sartor Resartus: The Life and Opinions of Herr Teufelsdröckh* (1833–34).
2 *what the women of Marblehead did to a certain Floyd Ireson*: John Greenleaf Whittier's poem, 'Skipper Ireson's Ride' recounts the plight of 'Old Floyd Ireson, for his hard heart, / Tarred and feathered and carried in a cart, / By the women of Marblehead.' (ll. 9–11).

a hero, and that wretched tramp an ever to be dreaded murderer? Why is Bismarck called great, though he crushed the French into a compost of blood and rags, ground them by taxation into paupers, jested at dying children, and lied most foully, and his minor imitators are dubbed criminals and thieves? Look here, now, young man! If you, by a quiet, firm, indomitable determination succeed in crushing out and stamping out for ever this secret society here, it will redound to your infinite credit in all men's eyes. But mark, if with all your energy and zeal you fail, or if you pass into a leaderette in some Freemason journal, and your zeal is held up as fanaticism and your energy as imprudence, the whole world will regard you as a hot-head-ed young fool, and will ask with rage and white lips, What is the Bishop doing in allowing these young men to take the reins into their own hands and drive the chariot of the sun? It is as great a crime to be a young man to-day as it was in the days of Pitt.[1] Nothing can redeem the stigma and the shame but success. Of course, all this sounds very pagan, and I am not identifying myself with it. I believe with that dear barefooted philosopher, St. Francis, who is to me more than fifty Aristotles, as à Kempis[2] is more than fifty Platos, that a man is just what he is in the eyes of God, and no more. But I am only sub-mitting to you this speculative difficulty to keep your mind from growing fallow these winter evenings. And don't be in a hurry to answer it. I'll give you six months; and then you'll say, like the inter-locutor in a Christy Minstrel entertainment:[3] 'I give it up.'

GEORGE MOORE (1852–1933)

Born at Moore Hall, Co. Mayo, he was the eldest son of George Henry Moore, a landlord, Nationalist MP and racehorse owner. After a spell at Oscott College near Birmingham, he moved to London in 1869 with the family. Intended for the army, he transferred himself to Paris on his father's death in 1873, now the owner of over 12,000 acres. Wanting to become a painter, he attended the École des Beaux Arts and the Académie Julian, but soon realised he lacked talent and decided to become a writer instead. He met many of the Impressionists in Paris, but went back to England in 1879, when returns from the estate declined.

---

1 *Pitt*: William Pitt, 1st Earl of Chatham (1708–78), was dismissed from the army for the covert satire in his maiden speech in the House of Commons, congratulating the king on the mar-riage of the Prince of Wales. Robert Walpole, the Prime Minister, is reported to have said, 'We must muzzle this terrible young cornet of horse'.

2 *à Kempis*: Thomas à Kempis (1380–1471), German Augustinian monk; author of *De Imitatione Christi*.

3 *Christy Minstrel entertainment*: a popular white blackfaced minstrel group, named after their founder Edward P. Christy (1815–62).

His verse was not successful; his first novels were *A Modern Lover* (1883) (banned by Mudie's circulating library), *A Mummer's Wife* (1885), and *A Drama in Muslin* (1886). The latter examined Irish ascendancy life critically to the disapproval of many of his fellow landlords. He followed it with *Parnell and His Island* (1887), essays that outraged nationalists. Next, he shocked bourgeois opinion with *Confessions of a Young Man* (1888), an account of his Bohemian life in Paris.

Moore wrote some lesser novels, and a good book on the Impressionists, *Modern Painting* (1893), before *Esther Waters* (1894) established his reputation; a Balzacian story of the endurance and heroism of a kitchen maid (written in reaction to Thomas Hardy's *Tess of the d'Urbervilles*), it shows how an obsession with racehorses can ruin servants as well as masters. There followed some experimental short fiction which included *Celibates* (1895), portraying the American novelist and heiress Pearl Craigie; she appears elsewhere in his writing. Impressed by Wagner, he wrote two 'musical novels', *Evelyn Innes* (1898) and *Sister Teresa* (1901), the former about illicit love, the latter about a nun who loses her faith in the sacraments. His lasting friendship with Maud Burke, later Lady Cunard, began about then. In 1900 he left England for Ireland, to join in the efforts to create an Irish literary theatre; he rewrote his cousin Edward Martyn's* play, *The Tale of a Town*, which became *The Bending of the Bough*, staged in Dublin in 1900. He collaborated the next year with Yeats* in writing *Diarmuid and Grania*. They soon quarrelled.

Moore then wrote the stories of *The Untilled Field* (1903), which had initially been serialised in Irish translation; these often bleak yet tolerantly kind stories were modelled on Turgenev. In 1905 came *The Lake*, a novel in which Moore developed what he called the melodic line which, apparently simple in its flowing ease, builds up a picture of his main character, a priest who becomes morally critical of himself and leaves his parish, swimming across the lake to find a new life.

Then Moore achieved his masterpiece in the three volumes of *Hail and Farewell*. Here he captured the atmosphere of Dublin during the literary revival, providing candid pictures of Yeats, George Russell* and Martyn—among others. This is a ruthless, forthright, very amusing book; it is controversial too, when, for instance, he attacks Irish Catholicism as being opposed to art, and regards the Gaelic movement as linked to Catholic nationalism. He left Dublin and the literary revival behind, moving to Ebury Street in London, after the first volume, *Ave*, appeared in 1911.

There he wrote *The Brook Kerith* (1916), a convincing and compelling prose piece in which he retells the New Testament with Jesus not dying on the cross (through the intervention of Joseph of Arimathea) but living among the Essenes as a shepherd, where Paul finds him. Next, Moore wrote a moving account of ill-fated love in *Héloïse and Abelard* (1921), an atmospheric and complex blend of intellectualism and human resolution set against the rich background of eleventh-century life.

Form and style continued to occupy him as he wrote further memoirs in *Avowals* (1919) and *Conversations in Ebury Street* (1924). A constant reviser of his work, he had a considerable effect on English prose, his own style deeply influenced by his knowledge of art and music, by his desire to pass on his sense of visual and aural delight to his readers.

Childhood Letters

[*Written from Oscott College to his father*]

Jan. 25, 1866.

My dear Papa, I did not wilfully disobey your commands about writing you three pages of note paper. I could not do it it was quite impossible for me to do it every day if you will only try it for a week or two you will find it more difficult than you expect just you write me three pages every day and you will soon get puzzled about [what] you would say to fill up the three pages. Keep my pocket money if you will but dont keep me here during the vac I am sure that if I could only see you half an hour that I could convince you that I could not writ that letter of three pages besides my writing is much smaller than yours and I write much closer together than yours this letter would fill up twice as much space if I write wide apart. I have made a great deel of improvement in spelling since midsummer do not be cross with me any more I will soon know how to spill perfectly the wood cocks must have been plentiful for you to shoot so many I am sure you will change your mind and take me home next summer just you try and write a letter every day and you wont find it so easy

I remain yours
George Moore.

Jan. 28th, 1866.

My dear Papa It appears to me that you think that I do not care two pins if I spell cat dog and dog cat but really the case is not so. I have made considerable progress both in spelling and writing since midsummer. It is of no good being cross with me any more if you will only correct the mistakes I make and send them to me I am sure that we by acting in concert will do a good deal more good than by scolding me and as for three pages a day it is not so easy as you might at first suppose if it was to different people it would not be so hard. I got a letter from my Aunt Browne who was kind enough to send me a post office order for a pound it was the hardest task I ever had to

read her letter I will send you her letter by post I wrote to her the day following that I got her letter. Now my dear Papa we will be friends and you will not be cross with me any more. I am sure that we will do much good if you will only follow the advice of this letter. I hope that you are all well at home I suppose that the drawing room is finished by this time You must not expect a letter of three pages every day but I will write when I can If I could get a book of those everyday letters I could write one out every day and send it to you punish me if you like but dont be cross with me any more I have got such scolding letters from you lately that it has made me very sad but I dont like to be getting sentimental I am not generally so
do not be too fast when you read this letter and send me another scolding one give my love to all at home

I remain yours affectionately

George A. Moore

Please send me a translation of my aunt's letter I could only make out a little of it.

From Flowers of Passion

(1878)

A Sapphic Dream

I love the luminous poison of the moon,
The silence of the illimitable seas,
Vast night, and all her myriad mysteries,
Perfumes that make the burdened senses swoon
And weaken will, large snakes who oscillate
Like lovely girls, immense exotic flowers,
And cats who purr through silk-enfestooned bowers
Where white-limbed women sleep in sumptuous state.

My soul e'er dreams, in such a dream as this is,
Visions of perfume, moonlight and the blisses
Of sexless love, and strange unreachéd kisses.

George Moore

From *Pagan Poems*

(1881)

Chez Moi

My white Angora cats are lying fast
Asleep, close curled together, and my snake,
My many-coloured Python, is awake,
Crawling about after a two-months' fast.

The parrot screams from time to time my last
Love's name; the atmosphere doth softly ache
With burning perfume, lazily I rake
And sift the smouldering embers of the past.

The women I have loved arise, and pass
Before me like the sun rays in a glass,—
Alice and Lizzy, Iza and Juliette;
And some are blushing, some are pale as stone:
Heigho! The world spins in a circle yet ...
My life has been a very pleasant one.

Sonnet

Idly she yawned, and threw her heavy hair
Across her flesh-filled shoulders, called the maid,
And slipped her sweet blond body out of bed,
Searching her slippers in the wintry air.

The fire shed over all a sullen glare,—
Then in her bath she sponged from foot to head,
Her body, arms, breasts, thighs, and things unsaid,
Powdered and dried herself with delicate care.

Then Zoë entered with the *Figaro*,
The chocolate, the letters, and the cat,
And drew the blinds to show the falling snow.

Upon the sofa still her mistress sat
Drawing along her legs, as white as milk,
Her long stockings of finely-knitted silk.

153

Une Fantaisie Parisienne

You whispered quickly, and your words were warm
With dreams, and down the glistening marble flight
Of steps you passed me saying, 'Come to-night,
The music told me of a tempting charm.'

I saw you turn, I saw your gorgeous arm
Amid the silk and lace; the electric light
Shed over all a mystical delight,
And vision filled my soul with sweet alarm,

Now wondering what your fancy might invent,
I pass a thickly carpeted saloon
To youward guided by the certain scent;

Lifting a curtain suddenly,—what meets
My gaze?—you, glittering like a precious stone
Amid the splendours of black satin sheets.

From A Drama in Muslin
(1886)[1]

[*Set in the turbulence of land agitation,* A Drama in Muslin *describes the transition into maturity of five girls from a convent school. The two central characters are the daughters of the upwardly mobile Mrs Barton, who has transformed her Galway farm building into a Big House, and flirts with the neighbouring Lord Dungory. She tries to marry her daughters off to ascendancy partners. Olive, pretty but shallow, abandons her earnest local suitor to become the belle of the season; despite the best efforts and financial promises of her mother, she is jilted by the impoverished Marquis of Kilcarney, who marries a less attractive and penniless girl. Alice, intelligent and plain, longs for a calling, writes articles on the Land Question, and escapes to England, where she nurses her sister, and ends up married to Dr. Reed—pat in middle-class Ealing.*]

...The principle on which the ball had been arranged was this: the forty-five spinsters who had agreed to bear the expense, which it was guaranteed would not exceed £3 10s. apiece, were supplied each with

---

1 *A Drama in Muslin* first appeared in the *Court and Society Review*, Jan. 1886. It was prefaced by an advertisement (written by Moore) praising its verisimilitude 'painted by an Irishman'. This excerpt is from the first edition published by Vizetelly & Co, London, in that year

five tickets to be distributed among their friends. To save money, the supper had been provided by the Goulds and Manlys, and day after day the rich smells of roast-beef and the salt vapours of boiling hams trailed along the passages, and ascended through the bannisters of the staircases in Beech Grove and Manly Park. Fifty chickens had been killed; presents of woodcock and snipe were received from all sides; salmon had arrived from Galway; cases of champagne from Dublin. As a wit said, 'Circe has prepared a banquet and is calling us in.'[1]

After much hesitation, a grammar-school, built by an enterprising landlord for an inappreciative population that had declined to support it, was selected as the most suitable location for the festivities. It lay about a mile from the town, and this was in itself an advantage. To the decoration of the rooms May and Fred diligently applied themselves. Off they went every morning, the carriage filled with yards of red cloth, branches of evergreen, oak and holly, flags and Chinese lanterns. You see them: Fred mounted on a high ladder, May and the maid striving to hand him a long garland which is to be hung between the windows. You see them leaning over the counter of a hardware-shop, explaining how oblong and semicircular pieces of tin are to be provided with places for candles (the illumination of the room had remained an unsolved problem until ingenious Fred had hit upon this plan); you see them running up the narrow staircases, losing themselves in the twisty passages, calling for the housekeeper; you see them trying to decide which is the gentlemen's cloakroom, which the ladies', and wondering if they will be able to hire enough furniture in the town to arrange a sitting-room for the chaperons.

As May said, 'We shall have them hanging about our heels the whole evening if we don't try to make them comfortable.'

At last the evening of the ball arrived, and, as the clocks were striking eight, dressed and ready to start, Alice knocked at May's door.

'What! dressed already?' said May, as she leaned towards the glass, illuminated on either side with wax-candles, and looked into the whiteness of her bosom. She wore a costume of Prussian-blue velvet and silk; the bodice (entirely of velvet) was pointed back and front, and a berthe of moresque lace softened the contrast between it and the cream tints of the skin. These and the flame-coloured hair were the spirits of the shadowy bedchamber; whereas Alice, in her white corded-silk, her clear candid eyes, was the truer Madonna whose ancient and inferior prototype stood on her bracket in a forgotten corner.

---

1 *Circe has prepared a banquet* ...: Circe, a goddess, is the bewitching queen of Aeaea, who in *The Odyssey* invites Ulysses' sailors into a banquet and turns them to swine.

'Oh! how nice you look!' exclaimed May; 'I don't think I ever saw anyone look so pure.'

Alice smiled; and, interpreting the smile, May said:

'I am afraid you don't think so much of me.'

'I am sure, May, you look very nice indeed, and just as you would like to look.'

To May's excitable mind it was not difficult to suggest a new train of thought, and she immediately proceeded to explain why she had chosen her present dress.

'I knew that you, and Olive, and Violet, and Lord knows how many others would be in white, and, as we shall all have to wear white at the drawing-room, I thought I would appear in this. But isn't the whole thing delightful? I am engaged already for several dances, and I have been practising the step all day with Fred.' Then, singing to herself, she waltzed in front of the glass at the immediate risk of falling into the bath.

> 'Five-and-forty spinsters baked in a pie!
> When the pie was opened the maids began to sing,
> Wasn't that a dainty dish to set before the King?'[1]

'Oh! dear, there's my garter coming down!' and, dropping on to the sofa, the girl hitched up the treacherous article of dress. 'And tell me what you think of my legs,' she said, advancing a pair of stately calves. 'Violet says they are too large.'

'They seem to me to be all right; but, May dear, you haven't got a petticoat on.'

'You can't wear petticoats with these tight dresses; one can't move one's legs as it is.'

'But don't you think you'll feel cold—catch cold?'

'Not a bit of it; no danger of cold when you have shammy-leather drawers.'

Then, overcome by her exuberant feelings, May began to sing: 'Five-and-forty spinsters baked in a pie,' etc. 'Five-and-forty,' she said, breaking off, 'have subscribed. I wonder how many will be married by this time next year. You know, I shouldn't care to be married all at once; I'd want to see the world a bit first. Even if I liked a man, I shouldn't care to marry him now; time enough in about three years' time, when one is beginning to get tired of flirtations and parties. I have often wondered what it must be like. Just fancy waking up and seeing a man's face on the pillow, or for—'

---

1 *Five-and-forty spinsters*: a variation on the refrain of the children's song, 'Sing a song of six-pence' ('Four-and-twenty blackbirds / baked in a pie ...').

'No, no, May; I will not; you must not, I will not listen to these improper conversations!'

'Now, don't get angry, there's a dear, nice girl; you are worse than Violet, 'pon my word you are; but we must be off. It is a good half-hour's drive, and we shall want to be there before nine. The people will begin to come in about that time.'

Mrs. Gould was asleep in the drawing-room, and, as they awoke her, the sound of wheels was heard on the gravel outside. The three women followed each other into the carriage. Blotted out in a far corner, Mrs. Gould thought vaguely of asking May not to dance more than three times with Fred Scully, and May chattered to Alice or looked impatiently through the misted windows for the familiar signs; the shadow of a tree on the sky, or the obscure outline of a farm-building that would tell how near they were to their destination. Suddenly the carriage turned to the right, and entered a sort of crescent. There were hedges on both sides, through which vague forms were seen scrambling, but May humorously explained that as no very unpopular landlord was going to be present, it was not thought that an attempt would be made to blow up the building: and, conscious of the beautiful night which hung like a blue mysterious flower above them, they passed through a narrow doorway draped with red-striped canvas. May called upon her mother to admire the decorations and approve of the different arrangements.

The school-hall and refectory had been transformed into ball and supper rooms, and the narrow passages intervening were hung with red cloth and green garlands of oak and holly. On crossing threads Chinese lanterns were wafted luminously.

'What taste Fred has!' said May, pointing to the huge arrangement that covered the end wall. 'And haven't my tin candelabra turned out a success? There will be no grease, and the room couldn't be better lighted.'

'But look!' said Alice, 'look at all those poor people staring in at the window. Isn't it dreadful that they, in the dark and cold, should be watching us dancing in our beautiful dresses, and in our warm bright room?'

'You don't want to ask them in, do you?'

'Of course not, but it seems very sinister; does it not seem so to you?'

'I don't know what you mean by its being sinister; but sinister or not sinister, it couldn't be helped; for if we had nailed up every window we should have simply died of heat.'

'I hope you won't think of opening the windows too soon,' said Mrs. Gould. 'You must think of us poor chaperons, who will be sitting still all night.'

Then, in the gaping silence, the three ladies listened to the melancholy harper, and the lachrymose fiddlers who, on the *estrade* in the far corner, sat tuning their instruments. At last the people began to come in. The first were a few stray black-coats, then feminine voices were heard in the passages, and necks and arms, green toilettes and white satin shoes, were seen passing and taking seats. Two Miss Duffys, the fattest of the four, were with their famous sister Bertha. Bertha was rarely seen in Galway; she lived with an aunt in Dublin, where her terrible tongue was dreaded by the *débutantes* at the Castle. Now, in a yellow dress as loud and as hard as her voice, she stood explaining that she had come down expressly for the ball. Opposite, the Honourable Miss Gores made a group of five; and a few men who preferred consideration to amusement made their way towards them. The Brennans—Gladys and Zoe—as soon as they saw Alice, asked after Lord Dungory; and all the girls were anxious to see Violet.

Hers was the charm of an infinite fragility. The bosom, whose curves were so faint that they were epicene, was set in a bodice of white *broché*, joining a skirt of white satin, with an overskirt of tulle, and the only touch of colour was a bunch of pink and white azaleas worn on the left-shoulder. And how irresistibly suggestive of an Indian carved ivory were the wee foot, the thin arm, the slender cheek!

'How sweet you look, Violet,' said Alice, with frank admiration in her eyes.

'Thanks for saying so; 'tisn't often we girls pay each other compliments; but you, you do look ever so nice in that white silk. It becomes you perfectly.'

In a few moments they were talking of the nuns they had so lately quitted. Violet had spoken also of the little play, 'King Cophetua,'[1] and of her desire to act in theatricals; but she could not keep her attention fixed, and she said abruptly:

'Do you see Mr. Burke over there? If his brother died he would be a marquis. Do you know him?'

'Yes, I met him at dinner at Dungory Castle.'

'Well, introduce him to me if you get a chance.'

---

1 *King Cophetua*: a legendary king of Africa who did not care for women until he fell in love with a beggar maid 'all in gray', and married her. They lived happily ever after.

'I am afraid you will find him stupid.'

'Oh! that doesn't matter; 'tis good form to be seen dancing with an Honourable. Do you know many men in the room?'

Alice admitted she knew no one, and, lapsing into silence, the girls scanned the ranks for possible partners. Poor Sir Richard, already very drunk, his necktie twisted under his right-ear, was vainly attempting to say something to those whom he knew, or fancied he knew. Sir Charles, forgetful of the family at home, was flirting with a young girl whose mother was probably formulating the details of a new emigration scheme. Dirty Mr. Ryan, his hands thrust deep into the pockets of his baggy trousers, whispered words of counsel to Mr. Lynch: a rumour had gone abroad that Captain Hibbert was going to hunt that season in Galway, and would want a couple of horses. Mr. Adair was making grotesque attempts to talk to a lady of dancing. On every side voices were heard speaking of the distances they had achieved: some had driven twenty, some thirty miles.

Already the first notes of the waltz had been shrieked out by the fiddle, and Mr. Fred Scully, with May's red tresses on his shoulder, was about to start, when Mrs. Barton and Olive entered. She was in white silk, so tightly drawn back that every line of her supple thighs, and every plumpness of the superb haunches was seen; and the double garland of geraniums that encircled the tulle veiling seemed like flowers of blood scattered on virgin snow. Her beauty imposed admiration; and, murmuring assent, the dancers involuntarily drew into lines, and this pale uncoloured loveliness, her high nose seen, and her silly laugh heard, by the side of her sharp brown-eyed mother, passed down the room. Lord Dungory and Lord Rosshil advanced to meet them; a moment after Captain Hibbert and Mr. Burke came up to ask for dances; a waltz was accorded to each. The triumph was complete. Such was the picture that a circling crowd of black-coats instantly absorbed; the violinist scraped, and the harper twanged intermittently; a band of foxhunters arrived; girls had been chosen, and in the small space of floor that remained the white skirts and red tail coats passed and repassed, borne along by the indomitable rhythm of Strauss.

An hour passed: perspiration had begun to loosen the work of the curling-tongs; dust had thickened the voices, but the joy of exercise was in every head and limb. A couple would rush off for a cup of tea, or an ice, and then, pale and breathless, return to the fray. Mrs. Manly was the gayest. Pushing her children out of her skirts, she called upon May:

'Now then, May, have you got a partner? We are going to have a real romp—we are going to have Kitchen Lancers. I'll undertake to see everybody through them.'

A select few, by signs, winks, and natural instinct, were drawn towards this convivial circle; but, notwithstanding all her efforts to make herself understood, Mrs. Manly was sadly hampered by the presence of a tub-like old lady who, with a small boy, was seeking a *vis-à-vis*.

'My dear May, we can't have her here, we are going to romp, anyone can see that. Tell her we are going to dance Kitchen Lancers.'

But the old lady could not be made to understand, and it was with difficulty that she was disentangled from the sixteen. At that moment the appearance of a waiter with a telegram caused the dancers to pause. Mr. Burke's name was whispered in front of the messenger; but he who, until that evening, had been Mr. Burke, was now the Marquis of Kilcarney. The smiling mouth drooped to an expression of fear as he tore open the envelope. One glance was enough; he looked about the room like one dazed; then, as his eyes fell upon the vague faces seen looking through the wet November pane, he muttered. 'Oh! you brutes! you brutes! so you have shot my brother!'

Unchecked, the harper twanged and the fiddler scraped out the tune of their lancers. Few really knew what had happened, and the newly-made marquis had to fight his way through women who, in skin-tight dresses, danced with wantoning movements of the hips, and threw themselves into the arms of men to be, in true kitchen-fashion, whirled round and round with prodigious violence.

Nevertheless, Lord Dungory and Lord Rosshill could not conceal their annoyance; both felt keenly that they had compromised themselves by remaining in the room after the news of so dreadful a catastrophe. But, as Mrs. Barton was anxious that her daughter's success should not be interfered with, nothing could be done but to express sympathy in appropriate words. Nobody, Lord Dungory declared, could regret the dastardly outrage that had been committed more than he. He had known Lord Kilcarney many years, and he had always found him a man whom no one could fail to esteem. The earldom was one of the oldest in Ireland, but the marquisate did not go back further than the last few years. Beaconsfield[1] had given him a step in the peerage; no one knew why. Most curious man—most retiring—hated society. Then Lord Rosshill related an anecdote concerning an enormous water-jump that he and Lord Kilcarney had taken together; and he

---

1 *Beaconsfield*: Benjamin Disraeli, 1st Earl of Beaconsfield (1804–81), Conservative British Prime Minister in 1868 and 1874–80.

also spoke of the late Marquis's aversion to matrimony, and hinted that he had once refused a match which would have relieved the estates of all debt. But he could not be persuaded; indeed, he had never been known to pay any woman the slightest attention.

'It is to be hoped the present Marquis won't prove so difficult to please,' said Mrs. Gould. The remark was an unfortunate one, and the chaperons present resented this violation of their secret thoughts. Mrs. Barton and Mrs. Scully suddenly withdrew their eyes, which till then had been gently following their daughters through the figures of the dance, and, forgetting what they foresaw would be the cause of future enmity, united in condemning Mrs. Gould. Obeying a glance of the Lady Hamilton eyes, Lord Dungory said:

'*On cherche amour dans les boudoirs, non pas dans les cimetières, madame.*'[1] Then he added (but this time only for the private ear of Mrs. Barton): '*La mer ne rend pas ses morts, mais la tombe nous donne souvent les écussons.*'[2]

'Ha! ha! ha!' laughed Mrs. Barton, '*ce Milord, il trouve l'esprit partout*;'[3] and her light coaxing laugh dissipated this moment of ballroom gloom.

And Alice? Although conscious of her deficiency in the *trois temps*, determined not to give in without an effort, she had allowed May to introduce her to a couple of officers; but to execute the step she knew theoretically, or to talk to her partner when he had dragged her, breathless, out of the bumping dances, she found to be equally impossible. Too clearly did she see that he thought her a plain girl, too keenly did she feel that, knowing nothing of hunting or of London theatres, and having read only one book of Ouida's,[4] it would be vain for her to hope to interest him. An impassable gulf yawned between his ideas and hers. Yet everyone else seemed happy as building birds. Behind screens, under staircases, at the end of dark passages, there were cooing couples. Girls she had known at St. Leonards as incapable of learning, or even understanding the simplest lessons, seemed suddenly to have grown bright, clever, agreeable—capable, in a word, of fulfilling that only duty which falls to the lot of women: of amusing men. But she could not do this, and must, therefore, resign herself to an aimless life of idleness, and be content in a few years to take a place amid the Miss Brennans, the Ladies Cullen, the Miss Duffys, the Honourable Miss

---

1 *On cherche amour...*: 'Love is sought in the boudoirs, not in the cemeteries, madam.'
2 *La mer ne rend pas ses morts...*: 'The sea does not give back its dead, but the tomb often gives us badges.'
3 *ce Milord...* : 'that lord finds wit everywhere'.
4 *Ouida*: Marie Louise de la Ramée (1839–1908), popular Victorian novelist.

Gores, whom she saw sitting round the walls 'waiting to be asked,' as did the women in the old Babylonian Temple.[1]

Such was the attitude of Alice's mind as she sat wearily answering Mrs. Gould's tiresome questions, not daring to approach her mother, who was laughing with Olive, Captain Hibbert, and Lord Dungory. Waltz after waltz had been played, and her ears reeked with their crying strain. One or two men had asked her 'if they might have the pleasure;' but she was determined to try dancing no more, and had refused them. At last, at the earnest request of Mrs. Gould, she had allowed Dr. Reed to take her in to supper. He was an earnest-eyed, stout, commonplace man, and looked some years over thirty. Alice, however, found she could get on with him better than with her other partners, and when they left the clattering supper-room, where plates were being broken and champagne being drunk by the gallon, sitting on the stairs, he talked to her till voices were heard calling for his services. A dancer had been thrown and had broken his leg. Alice saw something carried towards her, and, rushing towards May, whom she saw in the doorway, she asked for an explanation.

'Oh, nothing, nothing! he slipped down—has broken or sprained his ankle—that's all. Why aren't you dancing? Greatest fun in the world—just beginning to get noisy—and we are going it. Come on, Fred; come on!'

To the rowdy tune of the Posthorn polka the different couples were dashing to and fro—all a little drunk with emotion and champagne. As if fascinated, the eye followed the shoulders of a tall, florid-faced man. Doing the *deux temps*, in two or three prodigious jumps he traversed the room. His partner a tiny creature, looked a crushed bird within the circle of his terrible arm. Like a collier labouring in a heavy sea, a county doctor lurched from side to side, overpowered by the fattest of the Miss Duffys. A thin, trim youth, with bright eyes glancing hither and thither, executed a complex step, and glided with surprising dexterity in and out, and through this rushing mad mass of light toilettes and flying coat-tails. Marks, too, of conflict were visible. Mr Ryan had lost some portion of his garment in an obscure misunderstanding in the supper-room. All Mr. Lynch's studs had gone, and his shirt was in a precarious state; drunken Sir Richard had not

---

1 *the women in the old Babylonian Temple*: Herodutus, *The History of the Persian Wars* I. 199: 'The Babylonians have one most shameful custom. Every women born in the country must once in her life go and sit down in the precinct of Venus [Ishtar], and there consort with a stranger.... and here there is always a great crowd, sone coming and others going.... A woman who has once taken her seat is not allowed to return home till one of the strangers throws a silver coin into her lap, and takes her with him beyond the holy ground.'

been carried out of the room before strewing the floor with his neck-tie and fragments of his gloves. But, in the intense excitement, these details were forgotten. The harper twanged still more violently at his strings, the fiddler rasped out the agonising tune more screechingly than ever; and as the delirium of the dance fevered this horde of well-bred people the desire to exercise their animal force grew irresistible, and they charged, intent on each other's overthrow. In the onset, the vast shoulders and the *deux temps* were especially successful. One couple had gone down splendidly before him, another had fallen over the prostrate ones; and in a moment, in positions more or less recumbent, eight people were on the floor. Fears were expressed for the tight dresses, and Violet had shown more of her thin ankles than was desirable; but the climax was not reached until a young man, whose unsteady legs forbade him this part of the fun, established himself in a safe corner, and commenced to push the people over as they passed him. This was the signal for the flight of the chaperons.

'Now come along, Miss Barton,' cried Mrs. Barton, catching sight of Alice; 'and will you, Lord Dungory, look after Olive?' Lord Rosshill collected the five Honourable Miss Gores, the Miss Brennans drew around Mrs. Scully, who, without taking the least notice of them, steered her way.

And so ended, at least so far as they were concerned, the ball given by the spinsters of the county of Galway. But the real end? On this subject much curiosity was evinced.

The secret was kept for a time, but eventually they learned that, overcome by the recollections of still pleasanter evenings spent under the hospitable roof of the Mayo bachelor, Mr. Ryan, Mr. Lynch and Sir Charles had brought in the maid-servants, and that, with jigs for waltzes, and whiskey for champagne, the gaiety had not been allowed to die until the day was well begun. Bit by bit and fragment by fragment the story was pieced together, and, in the secrecy of their bedrooms, with little smothered fits of laughter, the young ladies told each other how Sir Charles had danced with the big housemaid, how every time he did the cross over he had slapped her on the stomach; and then, with more laughter they related how she had said: 'Now don't, Sir Charles, I forbid you to take such liberties.' And it also became part of the story that, when they were tired of even such pleasures as these, the gentlemen had gone upstairs to where the poor man with the broken leg was lying, and had, with whiskey and song, relieved his sufferings until the Galway train rolled into Ballinasloe.

From *Parnell and his Island*

(1887)

… The character of Dublin is the absence of any characteristic touch. Dublin is neither ugly, nor pretty, nor modern, nor ancient, but all these qualifications might be applied to it as to an 'old-clo' shop.' Yes, Dublin reminds me of an old-clothes shop where ball-dresses, dress coats, morning trowsers, riding habits, wellington boots, lace shawls are to be let or sold. Nothing seems really to belong to anyone. Everybody might have owned everything—language, dress, and manners—at one time or another. The streets are built of pale brown bricks, a pale poor brown—poor but honest. Nor are they built at hazard, improvised like London streets, but set out artificially in squares and monotonous lines, like a town that a tired child might have improvised out of a box of bricks. Here you find no architectural surprises, like in other towns; no alleys or curious courts filled with life—strange, picturesque, and enigmatic; none of those singular byways with reft of sky in the brick entanglement, sometimes bulging out into courts; where shops of fried fish, coal shops, shops of old iron and old paper, lean one against the other in giddy confusion; sometimes slipping into passages narrow and twisted, where bands of little children dance joyously to the sound of a friendly organ.

'We are poor but honest,' the houses cry aloud, and in their faded elegance they bend and bow like ladies who have seen better times. Others who would give themselves fashionable airs trail their finery like a middle-aged coquette in a provincial town. The flower-boxes rot in the windows, the rose-coloured window-blinds are torn, the railings rot with rust, the areas exhale the fœtid odours of unemptied dust-bins; add to this the noise of a hundred pianos; imagine a society of ill-bred young girls, making love to a few briefless barristers, their clerks, the employés in the breweries; beat this all up to waltz music from four o'clock in the afternoon till four in the morning, with an interval of three hours or so for dinner, and you will have realised the exterior aspect of Dublin society.

*   *   *

The great argument against the doctrine of eternal punishment is that human nature habituates itself to all things; ample proof of this has been given of late years in the West of Ireland. You would not think it an easy matter to enjoy a shooting party with a policeman walking behind you to prevent a Land Leaguer shooting you while you shot the pheasant! You would not think it an easy matter to enjoy a flirtation, with a policeman watching to see that your kissing was not interrupted by a Land Leaguer sticking a knife into you from behind—you who spend pleasant lives in the Row, think that it would be impossible to enjoy love or sport under such circumstances, but you are wrong! Notwithstanding the precautions absolutely indispensable if you would preserve a whole skin, the gentry in Mayo enjoy themselves very well indeed. And now I hear nothing talked of but a picnic—an afternoon dance which the people I am staying with are getting up. It is, I hear, to be given at a house on Lough Carra—'a house with a splendid floor for dancing,' cries one of the girls. 'And to whom does this house belong?' I ask. 'Oh! to a fellow who lives in Paris—he never comes here. Pa is his agent, and we can do what we like with his house.'

As we drove to the picnic we caught glimpses of the lake, the grey light of the beautiful mere-like lake flashing between the broken lines of rocky coast and the sloping ridges of the moorland; and then there are the blue waving lines of the Clare Mountains drawn in a circle about this landscape, this barren landscape, so suggestive of savage life and rough and barbarous minds. For in Ireland you think of border forays, wild chieftains, and tribes dressed in skins. The graft of civilisation the Anglo-Saxon has for seven hundred years striven to bind upon the island has never caught, but whether the Celt will be able to civilise himself when he gets Home Rule I do not pretend to say. At present he is a savage, eminently fitted for cattle-lifting, but ill-suited to ply the industry of farming which the law forces as the alternative of starvation upon him. Down in the wet below the edge of that bog lies the village. The cabins are built out of rough stones without mortar. Each is divided into two, rarely into three, compartments; and the windows are not so large as those of a railway carriage. And in these dens a whole family, a family consisting of husband and wife, grandfather and grandmother, and from eight to ten children herd together as best they can. The cabins are thatched or are roofed with green sods cut from the nearest field. About each doorway there is a dung-heap in which a pig wallows in the wettest and the children play on the driest part. The interior of these cabins can be imagined: a dark place from which exudes a stink; a stink which the inmates describe as a warm smell! Around the walls are vague shapes—what, you cannot quite see; like high boxes pushed out of sight are the beds. The floor is broken in places and the rain collects in the hollows, and has to be swept out every morning. A large pig, covered with lice, feeds out of a trough placed in the middle of the floor, and the beast from time to time approaches and sniffs at the child sleeping in a cot by the fireside. The old grandmother waves her palsied hands and the beast retires to his trough. As we have seen the pig, let us see the family at dinner. Of cookery, they have no idea whatever; there is not a single plate or kitchen utensil of any kind in the hovel except the black iron pot that hangs over the fire. The father and mother enter, followed by the brood. The mother, a great strong creature fit for work in the fields, dressed in a red petticoat which scarcely falls below her knees—you see the thick shapeless red legs—lifts the black pot off the fire and carries it to the threshold, one of the children holds a sieve and the water is strained off. Then the pig is hunted under one of the beds, and the family eat their dinner out of the sieve. Cold water from the well washes down this repast; sometimes well-to-do families keep a cow and there is a little butter-milk. These people are called small farmers; they possess from three to ten acres of land, for which they pay from twenty to five-and-twenty shillings an acre. In their tiny fields, not divided by luxuriant hedges like the English fields, but by miserable stone walls which give an unspeakable bleakness to the country, they cultivate oats and potatoes. With the former crop and the pig they pay the landlord, with the latter they live. As Balzac says, 'Les beaux sentiments fleurissent dans l'âme quand la fortune commence de dorer les meubles;'[1] and never have I observed in these people the slightest æsthetic intention—never was a pot of flowers seen in the cottage window of an Irish Celt.

From Confessions of a Young Man

(1888)

[*What Walter Pater called Moore's originality and delightful criticisms, his 'Aristophanic joy, or at least enjoyment in life', emerged in the memories of his 'cafe education' in Paris when he got to know Manet and Degas and their friends—Yeats described him as sitting 'among art students, young writers about to become famous, in some café; a man carved out of a turnip, looking out of astonished eyes'. In these Confessions Moore calls himself Edwin Dayne.*]

---

1 *Les beaux sentiments*…: 'Fine feelings blossom in the soul when wealth begins to gild the furniture'.

CHAPTER I.

... I was eleven years old when I first heard and obeyed this cry, or, shall I say, echo-augury?

Scene: a great family coach, drawn by two powerful country horses, lumbers along a narrow Irish road. The ever recurrent signs—long ranges of blue mountains, the streak of bog, the rotting cabin, the flock of plover rising from the desolate water. Inside the coach there are two children. They are smart, with new jackets and neckties; their faces are pale with sleep, and the rolling of the coach makes them feel a little sick. It is seven o' clock in the morning. Opposite the children are their parents, and they are talking of a novel the world is reading.[1] Did Lady Audley murder her husband? Lady Audley! What a beautiful name; and she, who is a slender, pale, fairy-like woman, killed her husband. Such thoughts flash though the boy's mind; his imagination is stirred and quickened, and he begs for an explanation. The coach lumbers along, it arrives at its destination, and Lady Audley is forgotten in the delight of tearing down fruit trees and killing a cat.

But when we returned home I took the first opportunity of stealing the novel in question. I read it eagerly, passionately, vehemently. I read its successor and its successor. I read until I came to a book called 'The Doctor's Wife'[2]—a lady who loved Shelley and Byron. There was magic, there was revelation in the name, and Shelley became my soul's divinity.

CHAPTER II.

... One day I raised my eyes, and saw there was a new-comer in the studio; and, to my surprise, for he was fashionably dressed, and my experience had not led me to believe in the marriage of genius and well-cut cloth, he was painting very well indeed. His shoulders were beautiful and broad; a long neck, a tiny head, a narrow, thin face, and large eyes, full of intelligence and fascination. And although he could not have been working more than an hour, he had already sketched in his figure, and with all the surroundings—screens, lamps, stoves, etc. I was deeply interested. I asked the young lady next me if she knew who he was. She could give me no information. But at four o'clock there was a general exodus from the studio, and we adjourned to a neigh-

---

1 *a novel the world is reading*: *Lady Audley's Secret* by Mary Elizabeth Braddon was serialized in the *Robin Goodfellow* in July 1861 and, after the magazine's discontinuance, in *The Sixpenny Magazine* from February 1862 to January 1863. The novel was immensely popular, eight, expensive, editions appearing before it had been fully published serially.

2 *The Doctor's Wife*: Mary E. Braddon's novel about an anglified Madame Bovary, transported to the little town of Graybridge-on-the-Wayverne, and married to a well-intentioned parish doctor.

bouring *café* to drink beer. The way led through a narrow passage, and as we stooped under an archway, the young man (Marshall was his name[1]) spoke to me in English. Yes, we had met before; we had exchanged a few words in So-and-So's studio—the great blonde man, whose Doré-like improvisations had awakened aspiration in me.

The usual reflections on the chances of life were of course made, and then followed the inevitable 'Will you dine with me to-night?' Marshall thought the following day would suit him better, but I was very pressing. He offered to meet me at my hotel; or would I come with him to his rooms, and he would show me some pictures—some trifles he had brought up from the country? Nothing would please me better. We got into a cab. Then every moment revealed new qualities, new superiorities, in my new-found friend. Not only was he tall, strong, handsome, and beautifully dressed, infinitely better dressed than I, but he could talk French like a native. It was only natural that he should, for he was born and had lived in Brussels all his life, but the accident of birth rather stimulated than calmed my erubescent admiration. He spoke of, and he was clearly on familiar terms with, the fashionable restaurants and actresses; he stopped at a hairdresser's to have his hair curled. All this was very exciting, and a little bewildering. I was on the tiptoe of expectation to see his apartments; and, not to be utterly outdone, I alluded to my valet.

His apartments were not so grand as I expected; but when he explained that he had just spent ten thousand pounds in two years, and was now living on six or seven hundred francs a month, which his mother would allow him until he had painted and had sold a certain series of pictures, which he contemplated beginning at once, my admiration increased to wonder, and I examined with awe the great fireplace which had been constructed at his orders, and admired the iron pot which hung by a chain above an artificial bivouac fire. This detail will suggest the rest of the studio—the Turkey carpet, the brass harem lamps, the Japanese screen, the pieces of drapery, the oak chairs covered with red Utrecht velvet, the oak wardrobe that had been picked up somewhere,—a ridiculous bargain, and the inevitable bed with spiral columns. There were vases filled with foreign grasses, and palms stood in the corners of the rooms. Marshall pulled out a few pictures; but he paid very little heed to my compliments; and, sitting down at the piano, with a great deal of splashing and dashing about the keys, he rattled off a waltz.

---

1 *Marshall was his name*: Henry Marshall is based on the painter Lewis Welldon Hawkins.

'What waltz is that?' I asked.

'Oh, nothing; something I composed the other evening. I had a fit of the blues, and didn't go out. What do you think of it?'

'I think it is beautiful; did you really compose that the other evening?'

At this moment a knock was heard at the door, and a beautiful English girl entered. Marshall introduced me. With looks that see nothing, and words that mean nothing, an amorous woman receives the man she finds with her sweetheart. But it subsequently transpired that Alice had an appointment, that she was dining out. She would, however, call in the morning, and give him a sitting for the portrait he was painting of her.

I had hitherto worked very regularly and attentively at the studio, but now Marshall's society was an attraction I could not resist. ...

*   *   *

As I picked up books, so I picked up my friends. I read friends and books with the same passion, with the same avidity; and as I discarded my books when I had assimilated as much of them as my system required, so I discarded my friends when they ceased to be of use to me. I use the word 'use' in its fullest, not in its limited and twenty-shilling sense. This reduction of the intellect to the blind unconsciousness of the lower organs will strike some as a violation of man's best beliefs, and as saying very little for the particular intellect that can be so reduced. But I am not sure these people are right. I am inclined to think that as you ascend the scale of thought to the great minds, these unaccountable impulses, mysterious resolutions, sudden, but certain knowings, falling whence, or how it is impossible to say, but falling somehow into the brain, instead of growing rarer, become more and more frequent; indeed, I think that if the really great man were to confess to the working of his mind, we should see him constantly besieged by inspiration ... inspirations? Ah! how human thought only turns in a circle, and how, when we think we are on the verge of a new thought, we slip into the enunciation of some time-worn truth. But I say again, let general principles be waived; it will suffice for the interest of these pages if it be understood that brain instincts have always been, and still are, the initial and the determining powers of my being.

CHAPTER III.

... Art was not for us then as it is now—a mere emotion, right or wrong only in proportion to its intensity; we believed then in the grammar of art, perspective, anatomy, and *la jambe qui porte*;[1] and we found all this in Julien's studio.

A year passed; a year of art and dissipation—one part art, two parts dissipation. We mounted and descended at pleasure the rounds of society's ladder. One evening we would spend at Constant's Rue de la Gaieté, in the company of thieves and housebreakers; on the following evening we were dining with a duchess or princess in the Champs Elysées. And we prided ourselves vastly on our versatility in using with equal facility the language of the 'fence's' parlour, and that of the literary salon; on being able to appear as much at home in one as in the other. Delighted at our prowess, we often whispered, 'The princess, I swear, would not believe her eyes if she saw us now;' and then in terrible slang we shouted a benediction on some 'crib' that was going to be broken into that evening. And we thought there was something very thrilling in leaving the Rue de la Gaieté, returning home to dress, and presenting our spotless selves to the *elite*. And we succeeded very well, as indeed all young men do who waltz perfectly and avoid making love to the wrong woman.

But the excitement of climbing up and down the social ladder did not stave off our craving for art; and there came about this time a very decisive event in our lives. Marshall's last and really *grande passion* had come to a violent termination, and monetary difficulties forced him to turn his thoughts to painting as a means of livelihood. This decided me. I asked him to come and live with me, and to be as near our studio as possible, I took an *appartement* in the Passage des Panoramas. It was not pleasant that your window should not open, not to the sky, but to an unclean prospect of glass roofing; nor was it agreeable to get up at seven in the morning; and ten hours of work daily are trying to the resolution even of the best intentioned. But we had sworn to forego all pleasures for the sake of art—table d'hôtes in the Rue Maubeuge, French and foreign duchesses in the Champs Elysées, thieves in the Rue de la Gaieté.

I was entering therefore on a duel with Marshall for supremacy in an art for which, as has already been said, I possessed no qualifications. It will readily be understood how a mind like mine, so keenly alive to all impulses, and so unsupported by any moral convictions,

---

1 *la jambe qui porte*: 'the supporting leg' (i.e. the leg that bears the weight).

would suffer in so keen a contest waged under such unequal and cruel conditions. It was in truth a year of great passion and great despair. Defeat is bitter when it comes swiftly and conclusively, but when defeat falls by inches like the fatal pendulum in the pit, the agony is a little out of reach of words to define. I remember the first day of my martyrdom. The clocks were striking eight; we chose our places, got into position. After the first hour, I compared my drawing with Marshall's. He had, it is true, caught the movement of the figure better than I, but the character and the quality of his work was miserable. That of mine was not. I have said I possessed no artistic facility, but I did not say faculty; my drawing was never common; it was individual in feeling, it was refined. I possessed all the rarer qualities, but not that primary power without which all is valueless;—I mean the talent of the boy who can knock off a clever caricature of his schoolmaster or make a *lifelike* sketch of his favourite horse on the barn door with a piece of chalk.

The following week Marshall made a great deal of progress; I thought the model did not suit me, and hoped for better luck next time. That time never came, and at the end of the first month I was left toiling hopelessly in the distance. Marshall's mind, though shallow, was bright, and he understood with strange ease all that was told him, and was able to put into immediate practice the methods of work inculcated by the professors. In fact, he showed himself singularly capable of education; little could be drawn out, but a great deal could be put in (using the word in its modern, not in its original sense). He showed himself anxious to learn and to accept all that was said: the ideas and feelings of others ran into him like water into a bottle whose neck is suddenly stooped below the surface of the stream. He was an ideal pupil. It was Marshall here, it was Marshall there, and soon the studio was little but an agitation in praise of him and his work, and anxious speculation arose as to the medals he would obtain. I continued the struggle for nine months. I was in the studio at eight in the morning, I measured my drawing, I plumbed it throughout, I sketched in, having regard to *la jambe qui porte*; I modelled *par les masses*.[1] During breakfast I considered how I should work during the afternoon, at night I lay awake thinking of what I might do to obtain a better result. But my efforts availed me nothing; it was like one who, falling, stretches his arms for help and grasps the yielding air. How terrible are the languors and yearnings of impotence! how wearing!

---

1 *par les masses*: 'with an eye to the mass effect'.

what an aching void they leave in the heart! And all this I suffered until the burden of unachieved desire grew intolerable.

I laid down my charcoal and said, 'I will never draw or paint again.' That vow I have kept.

Surrender brought relief, but my life seemed at an end. I looked upon a blank space of years desolate as a grey and sailless sea. 'What shall I do?' I asked myself, and my heart was weary and hopeless. Literature? my heart did not answer the question at once. I was too broken and overcome by the shock of failure; failure precise and stern, admitting of no equivocation. I strove to read: but it was impossible to sit at home almost within earshot of the studio, and with all the memories of defeat still ringing their knells in my heart. Marshall's success clamoured loudly from without; every day, almost every hour of the day, I heard of the medals which he would carry off, of what Lefevre thought of his drawing this week, of Boulanger's opinion of his talent.[1] I do not wish to excuse my conduct, but I cannot help saying that Marshall showed me neither consideration nor pity; he did not even seem to understand that I was suffering, that my nerves had been terribly shaken, and he flaunted his superiority relentlessly in my face—his good looks, his talents, his popularity. I did not know then how little these studio successes really meant.

Vanity? no, it was not his vanity that maddened me; to me vanity is rarely displeasing, sometimes it is singularly attractive; but by a certain insistence and aggressiveness in the details of life he allowed me to feel that I was only a means for the moment, a serviceable thing enough, but one that would be very soon discarded and passed over. This was intolerable. I packed up my establishment. By so doing I involved my friend in grave and cruel difficulties; by this action I imperilled his future prospects. It was a dastardly action, but his presence had grown unbearable; yes, unbearable in the fullest acceptation of the word, and in ridding myself of him I felt as if a world of misery were being lifted from me.

CHAPTER IV

After three months spent in a sweet seaside resort, where unoccupied men and ladies whose husbands are abroad happily congregate, I returned to Paris refreshed.

Marshall and I were no longer on speaking terms, but I saw him daily, in a new overcoat, of a cut admirably adapted to his figure,

---

1 *Boulanger's opinion...*: Gustave Boulanger (1824–88), French Academic painter.

sweeping past the fans and the jet ornaments of the Passage des Panoramas. The coat interested me, and I remembered that if I had not broken with him I should have been able to ask him some essential questions concerning it. Of such trifles as this the sincerest friendships are made; he was as necessary to me as I to him, and after some demur on his part a reconciliation was effected.

Then I took an *appartement* in one of the old houses in Rue de la Tour des Dames, for the windows there overlooked a bit of tangled garden with a few dilapidated statues. It was Marshall of course who undertook the task of furnishing, and he lavished on the rooms the fancies of an imagination that suggested the collaboration of a courtesan of high degree and a fifth-rate artist. Nevertheless, our salon was a pretty resort—English cretonne of a very happy design—vine leaves, dark green and golden, broken up by many fluttering jays. The walls were stretched with this colourful cloth, and the arm-chairs and the couches were to match. The drawing-room was in cardinal red, hung from the middle of the ceiling and looped up to give the appearance of a tent; a faun, in terra-cotta, laughed in the red gloom, and there were Turkish couches and lamps. In another room you faced an altar, a Buddhist temple, a statue of the Apollo, and a bust of Shelley. The bedrooms were made unconventual with cushioned seats and rich canopies; and in picturesque corners there were censers, great church candlesticks, and palms; then think of the smell of burning incense and wax and you will have imagined the sentiment of our apartment in the Rue de la Tour des Dames. I bought a Persian cat, and a python that made a monthly meal off guinea pigs; Marshall, who did not care for pets, filled his room with flowers—he used to sleep beneath a tree of gardenias in full bloom. We were so, Henry Marshall and Edwin Dayne, when we went to live in 76, Rue de la Tour des Dames, we hoped for the rest of our lives. He was to paint, I was to write.

Before leaving for the seaside I had bought some volumes of Hugo[1] and De Musset;[2] but in pleasant, sunny Boulogne poetry went flat, and it was not until I got into my new rooms that I began to read seriously. Books are like individuals; you know at once if they are going to create a sense within the sense, to fever, to madden you in blood and brain, or if they will merely leave you indifferent, or irritable, having unpleasantly disturbed sweet intimate musings as might a draught from an open window. Many are the reasons for love, but I

---

1 *Hugo*: Victor Hugo (1802–85), French Romantic poet, novelist and dramatist.
2 *De Musset*: Alfred de Musset (1810–57), French poet, playwright and novelist.

confess I only love woman or book, when it is as a voice of conscience, never heard before, heard suddenly, a voice I am at once
endearingly intimate with. This announces feminine depravities in my
affections. I am feminine, morbid, perverse. But above all perverse;
almost everything perverse interests, fascinates me. Wordsworth is the
only simple-minded man I ever loved, if that great austere mind, chill
even as the Cumberland year, can be called simple. But Hugo is not
perverse, nor even personal. Reading him was like being in church
with a strident-voiced preacher shouting from out of a terribly
sonorous pulpit, 'Les Orientales ...'[1] An East of painted card-board,
tin daggers, and a military band playing the Turkish patrol in the
Palais Royal.... The verse is grand, noble, tremendous; I liked it, I
admired it, but it did not—I repeat the phrase—awake a voice of conscience within me; and even the structure of the verse was too much
in the style of public buildings to please me....

CHAPTER VII.

The Synthesis Of The Nouvelle Athènes

Two dominant notes in my character—an original hatred of my native
country, and a brutal loathing of the religion I was brought up in. All
the aspects of my native country are violently disagreeable to me, and
I cannot think of the place I was born in without a sensation akin to
nausea. These feelings are inherent and inveterate in me. I am instinctively averse to my own countrymen; they are at once remote and
repulsive; but with Frenchmen I am conscious of a sense of nearness;
I am one with them in their ideas and aspirations, and when I am with
them, I am alive with a keen and penetrating sense of intimacy. Shall I
explain this by atavism? Was there a French man or woman in my family some half dozen generations ago? I have not inquired. The English
I love, and with a love that is foolish—mad, limitless; I love them better than the French, but I am not so near to them. Dear, sweet
Protestant England, the red tiles of the farmhouse, the elms, the great
hedgerows, and all the rich fields adorned with spreading trees, and
the weald and the wold, the very words are passionately beautiful ...
southern England, not the north—there is something Celtic in the
north,—southern England, with its quiet, steadfast faces;—a smock
frock is to me one of the most delightful things in the world; it is so
absolutely English. The villages clustered round the greens, the spires
of the churches pointing between the elm trees.... This is congenial to

1 *Les Orientales*: title of Hugo's 1829 volume of poetry.

me; and this is Protestantism. England is Protestantism, Protestantism is England. Protestantism is strong, clean, and westernly, Catholicism is eunuch-like, dirty, and Oriental.... Yes, Oriental; there is something even Chinese about it. What made England great was Protestantism, and when she ceases to be Protestant she will fall.... Look at the nations that have clung to Catholicism, starving moonlighters and starving brigands. The Protestant flag floats on every ocean breeze, the Catholic banner hangs limp in the incense silence of the Vatican. Let us be Protestant, and revere Cromwell.

* * *

Marriage—what an abomination! Love—yes, but not marriage. Love cannot exist in marriage, because love is an ideal; that is to say, something not quite understood—transparencies, colour, light, a sense of the unreal. But a wife—you know all about her—who her father was, who her mother was, what she thinks of you and her opinion of the neighbours over the way. Where, then, is the dream, the *au delà*?[1] There is none. I say in marriage an *au delà* is impossible.... the endless duet of the marble and the water, the enervation of burning odours, the baptismal whiteness of women, light, ideal tissues, eyes strangely dark with kohl, names that evoke palm trees and ruins, Spanish moonlight or maybe Persepolis. The monosyllable which epitomises the ennui and the prose of our lives is heard not, thought not there—only the nightingale-harmony of an eternal yes. Freedom limitless; the Mahometan stands on the verge of the abyss, and the spaces of perfume and colour extend and invite him with the whisper of a sweet unending yes. The unknown, the unreal.... Thus love is possible, there is a delusion, an *au delà*.

From *Esther Waters*

(1894)

[*Esther Waters is a Balzacian novel which tells how an obsession with race-horses ruins servants as well as masters. It centres upon the lasting heroism and endurance of a kitchen maid and shows Moore's concern for the position of women in society. He knew his subject well, for his father had twice owned a racing-stable and won large sums of money on the turf.*]

1 *au-delà*: 'the beyond'.

CHAPTER XXXII

It had been arranged that William should don his betting toggery at the 'Spread Eagle Inn.' It stood at the cross roads, only a little way from the station—a square house with a pillared porch. Even at this early hour the London pilgrimage was filing by. Horses were drinking in the trough, their drivers in the bar; girls in light dresses shared glasses of beer with young men. But the greater number of vehicles passed without stopping, anxious to get on the course. They went round the turn in long procession; a policeman on a strong horse occupying the middle of the road. The waggonettes and coaches had red-coated guards, and the air was rent with the tooting of the long brass horns. Every kind of dingy trap went by, sometimes drawn by two, sometimes by only one horse—shays half a century old jingled along; there were even donkey-carts. Esther and Sarah were astonished at the number of costers, but old John told them that that was nothing to what it was fifty years ago. The year that Andover won,[1] the block began seven or eight miles from Epsom. They were often half an hour without moving. Such chaffing and laughing, the coster cracked his joke with the duke, but all that was done away with now.

'Gracious!' said Esther, when William appeared in his betting toggery. 'I shouldn't have known you.'

He did seem very wonderful in his checks, green necktie, yellow flowers, and white hat with its gold inscription, 'Mr. William Latch, London.'

'It's all right,' he said; 'you never saw me before in these togs—fine, ain't they? But we're very late. Mr. North has offered to run me up to the course, but he's only two places. Teddy and me must be getting along—but you needn't hurry. The races won't begin for hours yet. It's only about a mile—a nice walk. These gentlemen will look after you. You know where to find me,' he said, turning to John and Walter. 'You'll look after my wife and Miss Tucker, won't you?' and forthwith he and Teddy jumped forthright into a waggonette and drove away.

'Well, that's what I calls cheek,' said Sarah. 'Going off by himself in a waggonette and leaving us to foot it.'

'He must look after his place on the 'ill or else he'll do no betting,' said Journeyman. 'We've plenty of time; racing don't begin till after one.'

Recollections of what the road had once been had loosened John's tongue, and he continued his reminiscences of the great days when Sir Thomas Hayward had laid fifteen thousand to ten thousand three times

---

1 *The year that Andover won*: Andover won the Epsom Derby Stakes in 1854.

over against the favourite. The third bet had been laid at this very spot, but the Duke would not accept the third bet, saying that the horse was then being backed on the course at evens. So Sir Thomas had only lost £30,000 on the race. Journeyman was deeply interested in the anecdote; but Sarah looked at the old man with a look that said, 'Well, if I'm to pass the day with you two I never want to go to the Derby again.... Come on in front,' she whispered to Esther, 'and let them talk about their racing by themselves.' The way led through a field ablaze with buttercups; it passed by a fish-pond into which three drunkards were gazing. 'Do you hear what they're saying about the fish?' said Sarah.

'Don't pay no attention to them,' said Esther. 'If you knew as much about drunkards as I do, you'd want no telling to give them a wide berth.... Isn't the country lovely? Isn't the air soft and warm?'

'Oh, I don't want no more country. I'm glad to get back to town. I wouldn't take another situation out of London if I was offered twenty a year.'

'But look,' said Esther, 'at the trees. I've hardly been in the country since I left Woodview, unless you call Dulwich the country—that's where Jackie was at nurse.'

The Cockney pilgrimage passed into a pleasant lane overhung with chestnut and laburnum trees. The spring had been late, and the white blossoms stood up like candles—the yellow dropped like tassels, and the streaming sunlight filled the leaves with tints of pale gold, and their light shadows patterned the red earth of the pathway. But very soon this pleasant pathway debouched on a thirsting roadway where tired horses harnessed to heavy vehicles toiled up a long hill leading to the downs. The trees intercepted the view, and the blown dust whitened the foliage and the wayside grass now in possession of hawker and vagrant. The crowd made way for the traps; and the young men in blue and grey trousers, and their girls in white dresses, turned and watched the four horses bringing along the tall drag crowned with London fashion. There the unwieldy omnibus and the brake filled with fat girls in pink dresses and yellow hats, and there the spring cart drawn up under a hedge. The cottage gates were crowded with folk come to see London going to the Derby. Outhouses had been converted into refreshment bars, and from these came a smell of beer and oranges; farther on there was a lamentable harmonium—a blind man singing hymns to its accompaniment, and a one-legged man holding his hat for alms; and not far away there stood an earnest-eyed woman offering tracts, warning folk of their danger, beseeching them to retrace their steps.

At last the trees ceased and they found themselves on the hill-top in a glare of sunlight, on a space of worn ground where donkeys were tethered.

'Is this the Derby?' said Sarah.

'I hope you're not disappointed?'

'No, dear; but where's all the people—the drags, the carriages?'

'We'll see them presently,' said old John, and he volunteered some explanations. The white building was the Grand Stand. The winning-post was a little further this way.

'Where do they start?' said Sarah.

'Over yonder, where you see that clump. They run through the furze right up to Tattenham Corner.'

A vast crowd swarmed over the opposite hill, and beyond the crowd the women saw a piece of open downland dotted with bushes, and rising in gentle incline to a belt of trees which closed the horizon. 'Where them trees are, that's *Tattenham Corner*.' The words seemed to fill old John with enthusiasm, and he described how the horses came round this side of the trees. 'They comes right down that 'ere 'ill—there's the dip—and they finishes opposite to where we is standing. Yonder, by Barnard's Ring.'

'What, all among the people?' said Sarah.

'The police will get the people right back up the hill.'

'That's where we shall find William,' said Esther.

'I'm getting a bit peckish; ain't you, dear? He's got the luncheon-basket … but, lor', what a lot of people! Look at that.'

What had attracted Sarah's attention was a boy walking through the crowd on a pair of stilts fully eight feet high. He uttered short warning cries from time to time, held out his wide trousers and caught pennies in his conical cap. Drags and carriages continued to arrive. The sweating horses were unyoked and grooms and helpers rolled the vehicles into position along the rails. Lackeys drew forth cases of wine and provisions, and the flutter of table-cloths had begun to attract vagrants, itinerant musicians, fortune-tellers, begging children. All these plied their trades round the fashion of grey frock-coats and silk sunshades. All along the rails rough fellows lay asleep; the place looked like a vast dormitory; they lay with their pot-hats over their faces, clay pipes sticking from under the brims, their brown red hands upon the grey grass.

Suddenly old John pleaded an appointment; he was to meet a friend who would give him the very latest news respecting a certain horse; and Esther, Sarah, and Journeyman wandered along the course in search of William. Along the rails strangely-dressed men stood on stools, satchels and race-glasses slung over their shoulders, great bouquets in their button-holes. Each stood between two poles on which was stretched a piece of white-coloured linen, on which was inscribed their name in large gold letters. Sarah read some of these names out: 'Jack Hooper, Marylebone. All bets paid.' 'Tom Wood's famous boxing-rooms, Epsom.' 'James Webster, Commission Agent, London.' And these betting men bawled the prices from the top of their high stools and shook their satchels, which were filled with money, to attract custom. 'What can I do for you to-day, sir?' they shouted when they caught the eye of any respectably dressed man. 'On the Der-by, on the Der-by, I'll bet the Der-by.... To win or a place, to win or a place, to win or a place—seven to one bar two or three, seven to one bar two or three ... the old firm, the old firm,'—like so many challenging cocks, each trying to outshrill the other.

Under the hillside in a quiet hollow had been pitched a large and commodious tent. Journeyman mentioned that it was the West London Gospel-tent. He thought the parson would have it pretty well all to himself, and they stopped before a van filled with barrels of Watford ales. A barrel had been taken from the van and placed on a small table; glasses of beer were being served to a thirsty crowd. All around were little canvas shelters, whence men shouted, ''Commodation, 'commodation.'

The sun had risen high, and what clouds remained floated away like filaments of white cotton. The Grand Stand, dotted like a ceiling with flies, stood out distinct and harsh upon a burning plain of blue. The light beat fiercely upon the booths, the carriages, the vehicles, the 'rings,' the various stands. The country around was lost in the haze and dazzle of the sunlight; but a square mile of downland fluttered with flags and canvas, and the great mob swelled, and smoked, and drank, shied sticks at Aunt Sally, and rode wooden horses. And through this crush of perspiring, shrieking humanity Journeyman, Esther, and Sarah sought vainly for William. The form of the ground was lost in the multitude, and they could only tell by the strain in their limbs whether they were walking up or down hill. Sarah declared herself to be done up, and it was with difficulty that she was persuaded to persevere a little longer. At last Journeyman caught sight of the bookmaker's square shoulders.

'Well, so here you are. What can I do for you, ladies—ten to one bar three or four. Will that suit you?'

'The luncheon-basket will suit us a deal better,' said Sarah.

At that moment a chap came up jingling two half-crowns in his hand. 'What price the favourite?' 'Two to one,' cried William. The two half-crowns were dropped into the satchel, and thus encouraged, William called out louder than ever, 'The old firm, the old firm, don't forget the old firm.' There was a smile on his lips while he halloaed, a cheery, good-natured smile, which made him popular and brought him many a customer. 'On the Der-by, on the Der-by, on the Der-by!' All kinds and conditions of men came to make bets with him; custom was brisk; he could not join the women, who were busy with the lunch-basket, but he and Teddy would be thankful for the biggest drink they could get them. 'Ginger beer with a drop of whisky in it, that's about it, Teddy?'

'Yes, guv'nor, that'll do for me.... We're getting pretty full on Dewberry; might come down a point I think.'

'All right, Teddy.... And if you'd cut us a couple each of strong sandwiches,—you can manage a couple, Teddy?'

'I think I can, guv'nor.'

There was a nice piece of beef in the basket, and Esther cut several large sandwiches, buttering the bread thickly and adding plenty of mustard. When she brought them over William bent down and whispered—

'My own duck of a wife, there's no one like her.'

Esther blushed and laughed with pleasure, and every trace of the resentment for the suffering he had occasioned her dropped out of her heart. For the first time he was really her husband; for the first time she felt that sense of unity in life which is marriage, and knew henceforth he was the one thing that she had to live for.

After luncheon Journeyman, who was making no way with Sarah, took his leave, pleading that he had some friends to meet in Barnard Ring. They were glad to be rid of him. Sarah had many a tale to tell; and, while listening to the matrimonial engagements that had been broken off, Esther shifted her parasol from time to time to watch her tall gaunt husband. He shouted the odds, willing to bet against every horse, distributed tickets to the various folk that crowded round him, each with his preference, his prejudice, his belief in omens, in tips, or in the talent and luck of a favourite jockey. Sarah continued her cursive chatter regarding the places she had served in. She felt inclined for a snooze, but was afraid it would not look well. While hesitating she ceased speaking, and both women fell asleep under the shade of their parasols. It was the shallow, glassy sleep of the open air, through which they divined easily the great blur that was the race-course.

They could hear William's voice, and they heard a bell ring and shouts of 'Here they come!' Then a lull came, and their perceptions grew a little denser, and when they awoke the sky was the same burning blue, and the multitude moved to and fro like puppets.

Sarah was in no better temper after than before her sleep. 'It's all very well for you,' she said. 'You have your husband to look after....

I'll never come to the Derby again without a young man. ... I'm tired of sitting here, the grass is roasting. Come for a walk.'...

ISABELLA AUGUSTA, LADY GREGORY (1852–1932)

Born [Isabella] Augusta Persse in Roxborough, Co. Galway, and educated private-ly, she married, in 1880, the 63-year old Sir William Gregory of the neighbour-ing Coole Park, a former MP, and Governor of Ceylon. They had one child, Robert, an artist. He was shot down over Italy when serving with the RFC in 1918, an inci-dent which was the subject of several of W.B. Yeats's elegies. In the winter of 1881, when the Gregorys were in Egypt, they supported the nationalist Arabi Bey, Lady Gregory writing *Arabi and his Household* (1882). Wilfrid Scawen Blunt, the poet, Sussex landowner and breeder of Arab horses, campaigned with her to prevent Arabi's execution. They had a passionate love affair, conducted in complete secrecy; this gave rise to her sonnets, which he published anonymously in 1892.

In 1894, two years after Sir William's death, she edited his *Autobiography*; that year she met Yeats* for the first time in London; he stayed briefly at Coole in 1896, then began the first of his twenty long summers there in 1897. Their lifelong friend-ship was based upon her desire to share in the work of the literary revival, for which her knowledge of Irish and the interest she had in common with him in Irish legends and folklore eminently suited her.

With Yeats and a neighbouring landlord, Edward Martyn*, who was interested in Ibsen and Palestrina, she planned an Irish national theatre; they founded the Irish Literary Theatre in 1899, and in 1904 the patent for the Abbey Theatre was granted in her name. Her capacity to write peasant dialogue (evinced in Yeats's *Cathleen Ni Houlihan* and *The Pot of Broth*) supplied the Abbey Theatre with many excellent comedies. Her work for the theatre was unceasing; its organization depended large-ly upon her pertinacious sense of purpose and organizing ability. She made several effective translations of Molière. Her folk history plays—notably *Kincora* (1905) and *Dervorgilla* (1907)—focussed upon crises in Irish history.

She made Coole a centre where many Irish writers came to stay. She developed her own style, known as Kiltartanese, basing it upon the English used by local Galway peo-ple and upon her own knowledge of Gaelic forms. In *Cuchulain of Muirthemne* (1902) and *Gods and Fighting Men* (1904) her achievement is impressive, for she gave life to the mythology of the Red Branch and Fenian legends, drawing upon many sources and imposing order upon their material to create masterpieces of narrative art.

The sheer volume of her work is striking. Her *Visions and Beliefs in the West of Ireland* (2 vols., 1920) resulted from work shared with Yeats; they collected materi-al for this book for over twenty years. She had an intense desire to revive Ireland's cultural heritage; her political stance shifted from the Unionism of her upbringing to a nationalist viewpoint, well exhibited in *The Rising of the Moon* (1907), in which she collaborated with Douglas Hyde*. She could argue a case forcefully, as in her attempts to get her nephew Hugh Lane's collection of Impressionist paintings returned from London to Dublin (where an unwitnessed codicil of his will had intended to place them)—something eventually achieved by a compromise solution in 1957 which shared the paintings in rotation. Her desire was to blend the best of two civilizations, two literary traditions: the Anglo-Irish and the Gaelic.

Sometimes unreasonably regarded as a frumpish, prudish Victorian, she was in fact lively, energetic, unselfish, both realistic and, in her private life, romantic and passionate. She was a woman who matched vision with unstinting service to Ireland.

From *A Woman's Sonnets*[1]

(1892)

Wild Words I Write

Wild words I write, wild words of love and pain
To lay within thy hand before we part,
For now that we may never meet again
I would make bare to thee my inmost heart.
For when I speak you answer with a jest
Or laugh and break the sentence with a kiss
And so my love is never half confessed
Nor have I told thee what has been my bliss.
And when the darkness and the clouds prevail
And I begin to know what I have lost
I would not vex thee with so sad a tale
Or tell how all too dear my love has cost.
      But now the time has come when I must go
      The tumults and the joy I fain would show.

What Have I Gained?

What have I gained? A little charity?
I never more may dare to fling a stone
Or say of any weakness I may see
That I more strength and wisdom would have shown—
And I have learned in love lore to be wise:
And knowledge of the evil and the good

---

1 *A Woman's Sonnets*: published anonymously in Wilfrid Scawen Blunt's *Love Lyrics and Songs of Proteus with the Love Sonnets of Proteus* (1892).

Have had one moment's glimpse of Paradise
And know the flavour of forbidden food.
But this, if it be gold has much alloy,
And I would gladly all the past undo
Were it not for the thought that brings me joy
That I once made some happiness for you—
That sometimes in a dark and troubled hour
I had, like Jesse's son,[1] a soothing power.

The Day Draws Near

I think the day draws near when I could stay
Within thy presence with no thought of ill—
And having put all earthliness away
Could listen to thy accents and be still,
And feel no sudden throbbing of the heart
No foolish rising of unbidden tears
Seeing thee come and go—and meet or part
Without this waste of gladness and of fears.
Only have patience for a little space.
I am not yet so wise to see unmoved
Another woman put into my place
Or loved as I was for a moment loved
Be not so cruel as to let me see
The love-light in thine eyes if not for me!

From *Lady Gregory's Diaries. 1892–1902*

1897

At the end of July, a week before the holidays, Mr. Yeats came to stay
with me, bringing his friend George Russell 'AE'—He had told me he
had described him in 'Rosa Alchemica'—& when one Monday morning I had a sudden intimation that they would be with me by lunch
time, I looked over the passage & found 'with his wild red hair, fierce
eyes & sensitive lips & rough clothes, Michael Robartes looked something between a peasant, a saint & a debauchee'[2]—so I was rather
apprehensive—& went down to meet them feeling quite shy—but to

---

1 *Jesse's son*: David, the youngest son of Jesse the Bethlehemite, would soothe King Saul's
  depression by playing the harp. David's Psalms express the passion of the human condition.
2 *with his wild red hair...*: Lady Gregory misquotes from memory a description of Michael
  Robartes, Yeats's 'fictional' character, in 'Rosa Alchemica', (*The Savoy*, April 1896), a story
  included in *The Secret Rose* (April 1897).

my relief found a gentle quiet man—apparently 'more in dread of me than I of him' as Mrs Quirk said of the leprechaun[1]—but really perfectly simple, composed—& self-restrained—8 years ago he was the most promising student in the Dublin Art schools but one day he came & said, as well as I understand, that the will is the only thing given us in this life as absolutely our own, and that we should allow no weakening of it—& that art which he cared for so much would he believed weaken his will—And so he went into Pim's shop as cashier, & had been there ever since, & Pim says he is the best cashier he has ever had—He works till 6 in the evening, has £60 a year, out of which he not only supports himself but helps others poorer than himself—edits the 'Theosophist' writing it in great part—has formed a little band of mystics believing, I think, in universal brotherhood & reincarnation—He said one evening 'this life bores me—I am waiting for a higher one'—His 'Homeward Songs by the Way' have gone into a second edition here, & have a great sale in America—On Saturday afternoon, & Sunday, his only holidays, he goes to the Wicklow hills & wanders there, sometimes lying down & seeing visions of the old Celtic Gods—of these he has done some beautiful pastel drawings— The first afternoon I took the two poets across the lake to the cromlech & there they sat until they saw a purple clad Druid appear— Next day we went to the Burren hills, to Corcomroe—a grey day— but it pleased them, & we heard fairy lore from a young man there, the [*illeg.*] on the Macnamara estate— I wish I could put down the brilliant conversation of the evenings—G. R. very quiet, but the other most brilliant —pouring out his ideas in rapid succession—hair splitting—fanciful—full of wit & poetry, deep & subtle thought—His stories of his London friends wd make us laugh till we cried—Poor Lionel Johnson[2] getting very drunk & then beginning to uphold the infallibility of the Holy Catholic church—begging him & some other not to leave him, & then, fearing they would be too much elated saying 'After all you are nothing but two fellows drinking with me'— Whibley at a literary dinner, getting into a squabble with Heinemann & saying 'All you are fit for is to put your name on the outside of

---

1 *Mrs. Quirk...*: she provided the description of the leprechaun for Lady Gregory's *Visions and Beliefs in the West of Ireland*.

2 *Lionel Johnson* (1867–1902), a close friend of Yeats in London in the 1890s. He was a cousin of Mrs Shakespear (1863–1938) with whom Yeats had an affair in 1896 and who was until her death one of his closest friends. Johnson, a fellow-member of the Rhymers' Club, impressed Yeats by his criticism and apparent learning; he introduced him to aestheticism and to the ideas of Walter Pater. Described in Yeats's *Autobiographies* as one of 'the tragic generation', he died young as a result of alcoholism.

books'[1]—Mrs. Emery[2] whose husband used to drink, & to steal half crowns from the pockets of her visitors' great coats in the hall—& who says 'I must be cynical to escape the discredit of my virtues'— ~~Bullen~~[3] the publisher who arrives at his rooms so drunk as to make a scandal in the neighbourhood—John Lane the publisher,[4] who likes to imagine he is anything else & says 'I am engaged to be married to a young lady in America & she said "I should like you to be Mr. Yeats's publisher"', & so on—

Mr. Russell left in a few days having to go back to his cash office—but Mr. Yeats stayed for two months—a most brilliant charming & lovable companion—never out of humour, simple, gentle—interested in all that went on—liking to do his work in the library in the midst of the coming & going, then if I was typing in the drawing room suddenly bursting in with some great new idea—& when it was expounded laughing & saying 'I treat you, as my father says, as an anvil, to beat out my ideas on'—Poor boy he has had a hard struggle—For some time, when he was working at his 'Usheen' & at the Blake book he had hardly enough to eat, & not enough for decent boots or clothes—& he says the bitter feeling of degredation haunted him for a long time—He got a job copying at the Bodleian once [in 1888], spent a week there, got £5—& he lived on currant buns all the time—& made himself ill thereby—Then he worked at the British Museum—& used to go gladly to an acquaintance (Countess de Bremot?[5]) near, for a cup of coffee, his ~~chief~~ only afternoon meal—until one day she proposed for him! one of her arguments being T.P. O'Connor married a woman of no character—& see what a help she has been politically to him!—So he made his escape &

---

1 *Whibley ... Heinemann ...*: Charles Whibley (1859–1930), scholar, critic and journalist, author of *A Book of Scoundrels* (1897). He had met W.B. Yeats through W.E. Henley. William Heinemann (1863–1920) founded the publishing house which bears his own surname.

2 *Mrs. Emery*: Florence Farr (1860–1917), an actress who acted in plays by Todhunter, Shaw* and Yeats. She married an actor, Edward Emery, in 1884; they divorced in 1894. A 'new woman', she had many lovers. A member of the Order of the Golden Dawn from 1890, she left it for the Theosophical Society in 1902. Ten years later she became Principal of a girls' school in Ceylon, where she died of cancer. She had been a close friend of Yeats in England.

3 *Bullen*: Arthur Henry Bullen (1857–1920) founded the publishing firm of Lawrence and Bullen, which published several of Yeats's books, including *The Celtic Twilight* (1893) and *The Secret Rose* (1897). Bullen, himself a good scholar, set up the Shakespeare Head Press, which published Yeats's *Collected Works in Verse and Prose* in eight volumes in 1908.

4 *John Lane* (1854–1925) founded the publishing firm the Bodley Head with Elkin Mathews in 1887. Mathews left the firm in 1894, and Lane published Yeats's *The Wind Among the Reeds* (1899), having also published AE's *The Earth Breath* two years earlier.

5 *Countess de Bremot*: Anna Elizabeth, née Dunphie, Countess de Brémont (1849–1922), a singer, journalist and novelist; she lived at 11 Cavendish Mansions, Portland Place. She was a friend of Lady Wilde and joined the Order of the Golden Dawn (on the same day as Oscar Wilde's wife Constance, 13 November 1888). She was expelled from the Order later).

had no more coffee—Now he has turned the corner & his name is up—
but he works very slowly—& I think starves himself—He says not—He
makes his own fire in the morning & cooks eggs & bacon—& he has a
chop for dinner—but luxury is far from him—And then there is his love
for Miss Gonne[1] preying on him—He fell in love with her ten years ago,
& for 2 or 3 years it 'broke up his life'—he did nothing but write to her
& see her & think of her—Then he grew stronger—& tho' still ideal-
ising her he did not feel it in the same way—But lately, at the Jubilee
riots it all came back to him—& he suffers tortures of hope & fear—
But I am bound to say that his healthiness of mind & body increased
while at Coole—so that he wrote afterwards 'my days at Coole passed
like a dream, a dream of peace.'

We searched for folk lore—I gave him over all I had collected, & took
him about looking for more—And whoever came to the door, fish-
woman or beggar or farmer, I would get on the subject, & if I found
the stories worth having wd call him down that he might have them
first hand—We found startling beliefs & came to the conclusion that
Ireland is Pagan, not Xtian—But this will appear in the articles he is
bringing out[2]—Then when we came in I wd write them out, & then
type them, very good training if I ever want to be private secretary!
Robert[3] & Geraldine [Beauchamp] & Henry[4] shot & bicycled & boat-
ed & cricketed & the summer flew quickly by—Robert very well &
strong—rather idle—but very keen about cricket & shooting—We
beat Gort—& then we were beaten by them—

Standish O'Grady* came to stay with us—but during dinner the first
ev[ening] he had a telegram calling him away as Revising Barrister to
Belfast—he had mistaken the time by a month! He is a fine writer—
but he has not had the recognition he deserves—If he were a Scotch
writer writing of old Scotch history his books wd be in every house—
He is now a little over excited on the Financial movement.

---

1 *Miss Gonne*: Maud Gonne (1865–1953), daughter of a British colonel, became an Irish revolutionary. She fell in love with Lucien Millevoye, a French politician and journalist, by whom
she had two children. Yeats, who fell in love with her at their first meeting in 1889, was
obsessed by her thereafter. He did not know of her relationship with Millevoye until 1898.
He wrote her many poems; she would not marry him but asked for his friendship. In 1903
she married John MacBride but sued for divorce in 1905.

2 *the articles he is bringing out*: Yeats's first article, 'The Tribes of Danu' appeared in *The New
Review*, November 1897.

3 *Robert*: Lady Gregory's only child (1881–1918), an artist who as a Major in the RFC won an
MC and the *Légion d'honneur*; he was shot down (in error) on the Italian front.

4 *Henry*: Persse (1885–1918), one of Lady Gregory's nephews, who was killed in action in the
First World War.

Next day, after his early start, another of my best countrymen arrived, Horace Plunkett[1]—He is working himself to death in his Agricultural Organization movement—but he is doing a great work in Ireland, teaching the farmers to get over their suspicions of each other, & to manage their own affairs—Even if the immediate movement should fail, this will tell in the future—We had asked the farmers to meet him, but it was a fine day after long rain, & very few came—but he came & talked to them outside the hall door, explaining the methods—with so much courtesy & earnestness that he won their hearts—His quiet manner, with so much enthusiasm underneath, strikes one very much—E. Martyn* came & stayed for his visit—I saw Mr. Plunkett off in the morning & took him to the Convent, & he gave a loom to the workroom—

The result of this little national literary stir was that Robert, near the end of the holidays said 'he would give anything to learn Irish'—We tried in vain for a teacher—all speak but none know the grammar—so we began with a primer & mastered the first exercises, taking them out to Mike to get the pronunciation right—But the partridge shooting interfered at the end, R.'s first chance, which he owed to the Jubilee extra week—He was pretty successful, getting a good many birds at Coole—& making biggest bag at Tillyra[2]—The Birch boys came for the last 10 days, very glad to find themselves back again—Then the holidays came to an end, & I was left alone—

Celtic Theatre—Edward Martyn having written a new play 'Maeve' with Celtic motive, lent it to de Basterot[3]—& I read it while with him & admired it very much—E. Martyn & Yeats drove to Duras one drenching day, & when we had had general conversation for a long time I divided the party by taking Yeats into 'Mr. Quin's office'—& there we had tea & talked, & the idea came to us that if 'Maeve' could be acted in Dublin, instead of London as E. M. thought of—& with Yeats['s] 'Countess Kathleen' it would be a development of the literary movement, & help to restore dignity to Ireland, so long vulgarised on the stage as well as in romance—& we talked until we saw Dublin as the Mecca of the Celt—This was the beginning of our movement—A day or two after Yeats came to see me at Coole—& it began to take practical shape—guarantors were thought desirable—& I

---

1 *Horace Plunkett* (1854–1932), founded the Irish Cooperative Movement in 1889.
2 *Tillyra*: Edward Martyn's castle and estate in Co. Galway.
3 *de Basterot*: Alfred Jacques Florimond, Comte de Basterot (1835–1904) had a summer house at Duras, Co. Clare.

gave the first guarantee—Then he wrote a programme, approved by E. Martyn—& then I wrote to Aubrey de Vere,[1] who sent a charming answer, with his blessing—This I added to the programme, & sent it to a few others—amongst them Lecky[2] asking him to give £1 guarantee— He was the first to respond, most warmly, promising £5—With his name, I wrote to Lord Dufferin, & he also responded amiably–& after that, except for the actual labour of typing programmes & writing letters, all went smoothly, people of all parties responded, & we had soon a splendid list of guarantors, & nearly all the money (£300) required—

Then E. M. & Yeats went to Dublin to work—found much encouragement & enthusiasm—but the way was blocked by the practical difficulty of getting a theatre—The two existing ones were engaged for the time wanted (besides demanding absurd prices) & then they thought of a hall or concert room—But there is an old act, passed just before the Union, inflicting a fine of £300 on anyone who gives a performance for gain in an unlicensed building—And a claim for a special license has to be argued before the Privy Council, & costs at least £80 in fees—I am all for having the Act repealed or a bill brought in empowering the municipality to license halls when desirable—but the matter rests so at present—[3]

I spent a few days at Tillyra to meet a 'Celtic' party—William Sharp,[4] an absurd object, in velvet coat, curled hair, wonderful ties—a good natured creature—a sort of professional patron of poets—but making himself ridiculous by stories to the men of his love affairs & entanglements, & seeing visions (instigated by Yeats)—one apparition clasped him to an elm tree from which he had to be released—Martin Morris is also there, & Dr. Moritz Bonn,[5] an odious little German, sent to me by Horace Plunkett, studying political economy & not seeing 'what relation the Celtic movement had to it'—And Dr. Douglas Hyde* came—full of enthusiasm & Irish—I took him & Sharp to the cromlech & to Kilmacduagh—& he began talking Irish to Fahy, near Cranagh— who to my pride came out with legends of Finn & Ussian galore—I was able to help Dr. Hyde to get some MS from 'one Connor', who had left

---

1 Aubrey Thomas De Vere (1814–1902), Irish poet and landlord. See Vol.2.
2 William Edward Hartpole Lecky (1838–1903), Irish historian. See Vol. 2.
3 *the Act repealed...*: the law was changed by the insertion of a clause in the 1898 Local Government Bill.
4 *William Sharp* (1855–1905) wrote various biographies and volumes of poems; in 1893 he wrote as 'Fiona Macleod'. His identity with his pseudonym remained unknown until his death.
5 *Dr Moritz Bonn*: Moritz Julius Bonn (1873–1965), a friend of Sir Horace Plunkett, the dedicatee of his *Die englische Kolonisation in Irland*.

there for Galway a year ago, & who I finally traced to a butcher's shop at Clare[n]bridge—but whether they are worth anything I know not—

Afterwards I spent 10 days at Spiddal very pleasantly, for fine weather had come at last, a sort of Indian summer, & the Atlantic was beautiful—Lord M.,[1] very cross, very violent against literature & writers, thinking Martin is going that way—I ran down to the school & had an Irish lesson when I could—& picked up some folk stories—At the end Lord M. left & E. Martyn & Yeats came—I had arranged an interview with a witch doctor for the latter of which he will doubtless give an account[2]—I tried to stir up the masters at the school to collect stories—& finally offered a prize for stories written down by the children either in English or Irish—They have since sent me eleven, not much new in them—

Then back to Coole, for some hard work alone—I had sent 'Mr. Gregory's Letter Box' re-arranged to Murray[3] at the beginning of the summer—but he was still not satisfied—I had obeyed his direction to group the letters—but he now found there were too many groups—& a harking back on dates, & that it wd not pay its way—Then I sent it to Longmans who said shortly 'It would not be a good commercial speculation.'—I showed it to de Basterot, & much like Murray, he wrote delighted with my own first chapters, but stuck when he got into the letters—Then I laid it by for the holidays, at the end trying to do a little to it, but without much time or heart—After Spiddal I set really to work, re-arranged, cut, wrote in, shed a good many letters—did my best with it—just as I was coming over sent it to Smith & Elder[4]—& they like my own part very much, but don't think much of the material—doubt its paying its way—won't publish at their own risk, but will 'put it in a special light' if I will publish on commission—

I went and consulted Murray & then Smith, Q.C.[5]—Both say it will be a literary success, & is extremely well done—at least all of my own that is in—but Irish history is at a discount— However I have decided to risk it, as I think it will be for Robert's advantage to publish—Already, Smith told me he had never heard of Mr. Gregory, & cd not

---

1 *Lord M.*: Sir Michael, Lord Morris and Killanin (1826-1901), Lord Chief Justice of Ireland. The Morris estate was in Spiddal, Co. Galway.
2 *he will doubtless give an account*: this appeared in the *Fortnightly Review*, September 1900.
3 *Murray*: John Murray (1808–1892), publisher; grandson of the founder of the famous publishing house John Murray (1745–93), whose son John (1778–1843) had succeeded him.
4 *Smith & Elder* published it in 1898.
5 *Smith, Q.C.*: Reginald John Smith Q.C., editor of the *Cornhill Magazine* and a partner in Smith and Elder.

find him in the Dict. Nat. Biography, but since he has read the MS he has directed the editor to put him in[1]—And then I wrote to Lord Peel to ask if I might use Sir R. Peel's letter to Mr. Gregory, giving his reasons for his change of front on Cat. Emancipation, & he has given it—(it had been given to Parker for his long delayed vol.) & that will be a help—& Smith is now more hopeful, & doubts that I will lose money after all—I am anxious about it, having no money to throw away, but I think I am doing right—So now the proofs have begun coming in—(I didn't lose—it paid its way).

I came over to London early in November—sorry to leave the Indian summer days & the long starlight walks with the dogs, & the beauty of the leaves—but the evenings were long & it was time to move—So I came, & was sorry—dank weather, & I was tired & depressed—& didn't know who was here & thought no one wanted me & wondered why I had come—But some cordial greetings soon changed the face of things—

I lunched with the Knowles[2] one Sunday, & Knowles asked me to write a folk lore article for the 19th Century—rather awkward as I didn't like to say I had given all my material to Yeats—so I put it off as well as I could—but Knowles followed me out saying 'I'll give you no peace or ease till you write it'—A few days afterwards I heard from Yeats that his second article had been returned by Henley,[3] who had promised to take the whole series for the New Review—as the New Review is disappearing, turning into a 3d weekly paper—& he himself retiring—A gr. blow, as it would have been so easy to write the series straight off, & wd have brought in a nice sum every month—So I asked leave to send the article to Knowles—& ask[ed] him to take it instead of one from me—& after a week he wrote having only just read it—accepting—& asking for another to follow it—So all was for the best for he will very likely take the series[4]—& this will introduce

---

1 *put him in*: the entry, written by Cæsar Litton Falkiner, appeared in Volume 22 of the *Dictionary of National Biography*, in 1901.

2 *the Knowles*: James Knowles (1831–1908) and his second wife Isabel née Hewlett. Knowles edited *The Contemporary Review* (1870–77) and founded *The Nineteenth Century* in 1877; he edited it up to his death.

3 *Henley*: William Ernest Henley (1849–1903), a good friend of Yeats in his early London days, edited (1889–94) *The Scots Observer*, which became *The National Observer* in 1892. He also edited *The New Review* (1895–97).

4 *take the series*: Only 'The Prisoners of the Gods', the second article by Yeats and Lady Gregory, appeared in *The Nineteenth Century*; 'The Broken Gates of Death', 'Irish Witch Doctors' and 'Away' were published in the *Fortnightly Review*, while 'Ireland Bewitched' appeared in the *Contemporary Review*.

W. B. Y. to another circle—He is pleased—& has been told that there is no use in approaching XIXth Century unless you have a title yourself or are introduced by someone with a title—

He has given a lecture on The Celtic Movement at the Irish Literary Society—There was some bother over it—for Graves* without consulting him asked Sharp to be chairman—W. B. Y. was furious at this—& declared it wd bring ridicule on the whole movement—so asked E. Martyn to take the chair, & on his assent wrote to tell Sharp that he had already invited him & wd not like to disappoint him—

E. Martyn told me this—& I am afraid I was not very polite for I said '*you* chairman' in an incredulous tone—but it was really too absurd— He grew uncomfortable then & said he wished to get out of it—if anything else cd. be managed—

Meanwhile Yeats had seen Sharp who refused to withdraw! so Yeats determined to change the subject of the lecture & read his folk lore article instead—& was very unhappy over it all—So one morning I telegraphed to him for Sharp's address—then to Sharp himself—& when he came I told him that Yeats's friends were of opinion the Celtic movement wd be injured by them merging into one camp—that they shd rather be allies like the Unionists & Tories—that he had determined to change the subject & read the folk lore article—that this wd probably prevent Knowles from accepting it—& this wd be a great loss 'for what is the boy to live on'—Sharp was very stiff at first—had been asked—& pressed—& had offered to resign, Graves had written back that his honour was pledged—At last, getting no 'forrarder' I thought perhaps if I pressed it wd make him turn against Yeats—so I said 'Will you come & dine on Sunday to meet Yeats & the Leckys'—'Might Mrs. Sharp come too?' said he—& of course then I knew the battle was over—& only discussed details—So Alfred Nutt[1] was put in the chair, & all went well—the lecture charming, & his delivery so good & voice, & all so natural—When it was over I had a little 'festa' in its honour at the Metropole—the Sharps—& W.'s father & sisters[2] & Miss Borthwick[3]—& Symons & Mrs. Emery—it went off very pleasantly—old Mr. Yeats charming—so all ended well.

1 *Alfred Nutt*: Alfred Trübner Nutt (1856–1910), publisher, folklorist and Celtic scholar, founded the Irish Text Society in 1898.
2 *W.'s father & sisters*: John Butler Yeats (see vol. 2), Susan Mary (Lily) and Elizabeth Corbet (Lollie).
3 *Miss Borthwick*: Mariella Norma Borthwick (1862–1934), active member of the Southwark Irish Literary Society, and of the Gaelic League.

Horace Plunkett is quite with the Celtic movement—asked E. M[artyn], & Yeats to the Ag. Organization dinner & made Yeats speak— a charming little speech 'like a rose leaf falling among a lot of agricultural implements'—And he has been very kind about the Theatre—& rushed to see the Attorney Genl. & to see me on his one day over here— And he has taken George Russell out of Pim's & made him an organiser of rural banks—I hope this may turn out well—Mr. Russell writes me a very cheery letter & sends me a portrait he has done of W. B. Y.—

I had a bad moment when I first came over....

Lecky, very encouraging about the 'Letter Box'—says he knows nothing of that period—that all is known up to the Union & after the famine, but that is a blank—Dined also with the Frederic Harrisons— & twice with the Lyalls—& with Raffy—where I was much disgusted with the greediness of W. S. Lilly,[1] calling for more food, calling for champagne out of his turn, eating like a wild beast—M. Morris says he is the same everywhere—& Henry James says having met him once at dinner he refused to meet him again—Dined also Mrs. Kay—sat between 2 pleasant adventurers—Sir Leopold McClintock[2] & Sir Alan Johnson[3]—I had some nice little dinners here too—Yeats always— partly for his sake & partly for my own, to make all go off well, for he is always brilliant & charming. ...

[December] 14—Irish lesson & proofs—Afternoon to 18 Woburn Buildings to measure W. B. Y.'s window for a curtain—Found his father there sketching him, & not very successfully—probably knows his face too well—He has been at him for 3 days—W. writes that 'it was very difficult to make him begin & now it is still more difficult to make him leave off'—The sitting room is very nice—large & low—looking on a raised flagged pavement where no traffic can come—& the bedroom, very small & draughty looks out on St. Pancras church with its caryatides & trees—But I wish poor W. cd be a little better waited on—his room had not yet been done up—& remains of breakfast (cooked by himself) still there—He received me with the announcement he had 'lost his coals'—& the fire was going out—& finally, when his father left a buck-

---

1 *W. S. Lilly*: William Samuel Lilly (1840–1919), barrister, and Secretary of the Catholic Union of Great Britain from 1875.
2 *Sir Leopold McClintock*: Francis Leopold McClintock (1819–1907), admiral and explorer. In 1859 he published *The Voyage of the Fox in the Arctic Seas: a Narrative of the Fate of Sir John Franklin and his companions*.
3 *Sir Alan Johnson*: Allen Bayard Johnson (1829–1907), general; he was the uncle of Lionel Johnson and Olivia Shakespear.

et of coal was sent in & stowed away—One cold night that he dined with me I asked him if he wd find his fire in when he went back & he said, no, he had carefully raked it out, so that the landlady when she came might make it up for lighting next morning, & otherwise he wd have to make it up himself, & the mornings are so cold for that—His father was to set out for Dublin in the evening, to paint Standish O'Grady's portrait—but I heard next day he had with W. started for the station, then found he had left his sketchbook & went back for that—& just as he had taken his ticket at Euston, the train steamed off—So then he decided to go by the next train & left his things at the cloak room & went back to Woburn Buildings—Then they set out the second time—& again he had left his sketch book—the other one, & had to return—but still they were in pretty good time at Euston, & they changed the ticket—but when he went to the cloak room, he had lost his luggage ticket & had to make a declaration—& while it was being made, the train went off & then he was ashamed to go back to his family—& so he went to the hotel for the night, & has been no more heard of....

W. B. Y. came to dine with me on the way to his '98 committee[1]—he talked much of Miss Gonne—all the old story—poor boy, it interferes sadly with his work—as he says, his reveries go to her & not to it—I advised him not to press her while she is so taken up with '98—He agrees but says 'When one is a writer one gets into the belief that a phrase will do everything'—

[December] 15—Irish lesson, the last—have got on pretty well, through the first book.... H. Lane to lunch with some pictures—I bought a nice picture by [Bristmore] of terriers & a weasel for Robert—£2.10/-& an entombing for the nuns' bazaar & a portrait of Buffon[2] for Frank—I wrote by Hugh's wish to Horsely—but have had an unsatisfactory answer—he has heard things of him since he left (probably his boasting that he made the gallery) & can't take him back 'with any self respect'—Dinner at home, Flora Shaw[3] (to interest her in the Celtic movement) Yeats—Willy Peel[4]—Sir Alan Johnson (uncle to Lionel)—young Comyn Carr[5] who has just left Oxford & is

---

1 *his '98 committee*: Yeats was elected chairman of the '98 Celebration Committee in 1897.
2 *Buffon*: George, Compte de Buffon (1707–88), French philosopher and naturalist.
3 *Flora Shaw* (1852–1929), journalist; she was Colonial Editor for the *Times*, and a friend of Cecil Rhodes.
4 *Willy Peel*: William Robert Wellesley, 1st Earl and 2nd Viscount Peel (1867–1937), statesman; grandson of Sir Robert Peel. In 1897 he was special correspondent of the *Daily Telegraph* in the Greco-Turkish war.
5 *Philip Comyn Carr* (1874–1957), drama critic and producer; he founded the Mermaid Repertory Theatre.

going in for literature—very amusing—for W. B. Y. was excited by Miss Shaw's dogmatic commonplace ultra English mind—& let off fireworks all the evening—declaiming against men of science—they are poor & paltry on every other subject, they are but a [*illeg.*] in their own discoveries—A man of letters like Goethe, of all embracing wisdom so different—Yes Parnell was a representative Irishman he lived for an idea—Englishmen will only live for an institution—Sir Frederic Leighton[1] ought to have been King of England, & the Queen President of the Royal Academy—'Oh' says Miss Shaw seriously—'but do you not confess she is an excellent constitutional monarch?' Sir A. Johnson rather amusing, meant to crush him about Mme. Blavatsky[2] who he had some stories about—& said 'Do you confess Mme. Blavatsky was an imposter?' 'Well, as to her being an imposter—it is like Newman[3] being asked if he believed that the sun really stood still in the valley of Ajalon'—& he said 'There are so many ways of interpreting the words "stood still"—that it must remain an uncertain question'—

Miss Shaw when leaving said pityingly 'He's very young'—I asked Sir A. Johnson if his nephew Lionel talked like that & he says, not to me, but I daresay he does when they're together—which amuses W. B. Y. very much—Lionel being the most gloomy, serious & discreet of men—save & except when he is drunk—Then he draws on imaginary reminiscences—including a conversation of an hour with Gladstone[4] at Oxford—which he never varies—his family who are Tory disapprove of, but are at the same time proud of this interview—

[December] 17—To see Sir F. Burton[5]—He is amused at hearing Ingram's song[6] is made so much of for the '98 centenary—as he says he never was a young Irelander or sympathized with the movement but that one evening he was roused by O'Connell in a speech throwing some disparagement on '98—& he went home & wrote the verses—

1 *Sir Frederic Leighton* (1830–96), the painter and President of the Royal Academy from 1878 to his death.
2 *Mme. Blavatsky*: Helena Petrovna Blavatsky (1831–91), Russian spiritualist; co-founded the Theosophical Society in 1875. She was declared a fraud by the London Society for Psychical Research in 1885.
3 *Newman*: John Henry Newman (1801–90), Roman Catholic theologian; author of *Apologia pro vita sua* (1864); he became a cardinal in 1879.
4 *Gladstone*: William Ewart Gladstone (1809–98), British Liberal Prime Minister (1868–74; 1880–85; 1892–94).
5 *Sir F. Burton*: Frederic William Burton (1816–1900), watercolourist and director of the National Gallery, London.
6 *Ingram's song*: 'The Memory of the Dead' [*q.v.*], a ballad beginning 'Who fears to speak of Ninety Eight,' written in 1843 by John Kells Ingram, a student at Trinity College, Dublin. His authorship was not acknowledged until 1900.

[December] 18—Stores & letters—& called on Mrs. Kay & had Hugh Lane to tea—& W. B. Y. & Mrs. Emery to dinner—

from The Felons of Our Land[1]

(1900)

... Felony is given in Johnson's dictionary as 'a crime denounced capital *by the law*,' and this is how it, or perhaps I should use the word coined for Ireland, 'treason-felony,' is defined in Ireland also—a crime in the eyes of the law, not in the eyes of the people. A thief is shunned, a murder prompted by brutality or personal malice is vehemently denounced, a sheepstealer's crime is visited on the third and fourth generations; but a 'felon' has come to mean one who has gone to death or to prison for the sake of a principle or a cause. In consequence, the prison rather lends a halo than leaves a taint. In a country that is not a reading country, 'Speeches from the Dock,'[2] the last public words of political prisoners, is in its forty-eighth edition. The chief ornament of many a cottage is the warrant for the arrest of a son of the house framed and hung up as a sort of diploma of honour. I remember an election to a dispensary district before which one candidate sent round certificates of his medical skill, the other merely a statement that several members of his family had been prosecuted by the Government. And it was the latter who won the appointment. I have known the hillsides blaze with bonfires when prisoners were released, not because they were believed to be innocent, but because they were believed to be guilty. It has been so all through the century. I find among Under-Secretary Gregory's[3] papers a letter written by Colonel Barry from Limerick in 1816 in connection with some executions that were taking place at that disturbed time. 'The Sheriff has requested that I would remark to you the propriety of appealing to Government to forbid the Bodies of all such people, or indeed any part of their clothing, being given up to their familys, who consider that these people have died as Martyrs in the cause of their country, and instead of holding them out as examples to avoid, cry them up as characters to be imitated. The

---

1 *The Felons of Our Land*: Cornhill Magazine, 3 series, 8 (Jan.–June 1900).
2 'Speeches from the Dock': *Speeches from the Dock: or, protests of Irish patriotism* had an astonishing print-run. It was initially issued, edited by A. M. Sullivan (see Vol. 2), in weekly numbers in 1867. Its 48th edition, expanded and edited by A. M., T. D. and D. B Sullivan, was published in Dublin by M. H. Gill & Son.
3 *Under-Secretary Gregory*: William Gregory (1766–1840), Co. Galway landowner, was Irish Under-secretary from 1812 to 1830. His grandson, Sir William Henry (1817–92) was born at the Under-secretary's lodge in Phoenix Park; he married Isabella Augusta in 1880.

anxiety to get the corps of the execution is very curious, it is carried to such length by the different Branches of the family as to cause very great Battles, indeed the last execution that took place here there was very nearly being a Battle, and there were as I understand upwards of a thousand people clearing for action when the Mayor threatened to turn out the main guard if they did not disperse.... Not even a shoe should be given to the family, for all the cloths the deceased had on are considered as relicks.' Then, as in later years, the act of government executioner seems often to have been a swift act of canonisation.

* * *

IV.

To the spiritual mind the spiritual truth underlying each development of Christianity is always manifest. But there is a significant contrast in the outward form in which religion appears to the peasant of England and the peasant of Ireland. In England (I quote again from the *Jail Journal*) 'is there not our venerable Church, our beautiful liturgy? There is a *department* for all that, with the excellent Archbishop of Canterbury at the head of it.'[1] To the English peasant the well-furnished village church, the pulpit cushion, the gilt-edged Bible, the cosy rectory, represent respectability, comfort, peace, a settled life. In Ireland the peasant has always before his eyes, on his own cottage walls or in his white-washed chapel, the cross, the spear, the crown of thorns, that tell of what once seemed earthly failure, that tell that He to whom he kneels was led to a felon's death.

In England the poet of to-day must, if he will gain a hearing, write of the visible and material things that appeal to a people who have made 'The Roast Beef of Old England' a fetish and whose characteristic song is:

> We don't want to fight, but by Jingo if we do,
> We've got the ships, we've got the men, *we've got the money too.*[2]

---

1 *the Jail Journal* ...: commenting on Thomas Babington Macaulay, in chapter II of his *Jail Journal* (1854), John Mitchel writes: 'Ah! but the enlightened Briton would say, "Now you talk of religion; that is our strong point in this admirable age and country. Is not there our venerable Church?—our beautiful liturgy? There is a *department* for all that, with the excellent Archbishop of Canterbury at the head of it. If information is wanted about the other world, or salvation, or anything in that line, you can apply at the head-office, or some of the subordinate stations."'

2 *We don't want to fight* ...: the chorus of a popular music hall song by George William Hunt (1829–1904); the expression 'by jingo' became the Tyrtæan ode of the (Beaconsfield) party eager to fight Russia in 1878.

In Ireland he is in touch with a people whose thoughts have long been dwelling on an idea; whose heroes have been the failures, the men 'who went out to battle and who always fell,'[1] who went out to a battle that was already lost—men who, whatever may have been their mistakes or faults, had an aim quite apart from personal greed or gain.

Some of us are inclined to reproach our younger poets with a departure from the old tradition because they no longer write patriotic and memorial ballads. But in singing of 'the dim wisdoms old and deep that God gives unto man in sleep,'[2] they have not departed from it, they have only travelled a little further on the road that leads from things seen to things unseen. And a poet is not to be shaped and trained like a yew tree and set in a hedgerow, to guard even the most hallowed ashes. He must be left to his own growth, like the tree that clings to its own hillside, that sends down its roots to find hidden waters, that sends out it branches to the winds and to the stars.

OSCAR FINGAL O'FLAHERTIE WILLS WILDE (1854–1900)

He was born in Dublin, the younger son of William Wilde and Jane Francesca Elgee. His mother contributed spirited nationalist verse to *The Nation* over the signature 'Speranza', and held a literary salon in Merrion Square; his father was a famous opthalmologist, an excellent antiquarian scholar, and a notorious womaniser. Oscar was educated at Portora Royal School, Enniskillen, at Trinity College, Dublin, where he won the Berkeley Gold Medal for Greek, and was befriended by the classical scholar and wit John Pentland Mahaffy, with whom he travelled to Ravenna and Greece in 1877, and at Magdalen College, Oxford, where he won the Newdigate Prize for poetry, and graduated BA in 1878. At Magdalen, he came under the spell of the 'Victorian prophets', Pater and Ruskin, and developed his 'Art for Art's sake' aesthetics. A master of paradox, he expressed the aspiration to live up to his blue china. His first poetry appeared in various journals, including the *Catholic Mirror*, *The Irish Monthly*, *Kottabos*, and *Time*. On leaving Oxford, Wilde was already a favourite subject for caricature in *Punch*, for his super-sensitive and ultra-refined aesthetic cult (which had an anarchic bearing on life); he was the model for Bunthorne, the 'melancholy, literary man,' in Gilbert and Sullivan's opera *Patience*. In 1882 he made a successful tour of the United States, telling the customs officers that he had nothing to declare but his genius, and concluding that

---

1 *'who went out to battle …'*: first line of a poem by the Irish-American belle-lettrist Shaemas O Sheel.
2 *'the dim wisdoms old and deep …'*: W.B. Yeats, 'Apologia addressed to Ireland in the coming days', 21–22. As Yeats himself did in this poem, Lady Gregory is defending him against the criticism that unlike Davis and Mangan he is not contributing poetically to the nationalist cause.

the English and the Americans have 'really everything in common ... except, of course, language.' *Vera, or the Nihilists*, a play with a wink at Kropotkin, the anarchist (whom he called, in admiration, 'The White Prince') was produced in New York, and flopped.

He married Constance Lloyd in 1884. The couple had two sons. Wilde wrote stories and articles for the *Pall Mall Gazette, The Dramatic Review* and the *Court and Society Review*. He edited *Woman's World* (1887–89). In 1888 he published *The Happy Prince and Other Tales*, a collection of charming, and sometimes moving, fairy tales, with distinctive Wildean idiosyncrasies. *The Picture of Dorian Gray*, his only novel, appeared in *Lippincott's Magazine* in 1890. Dorian's portrait grows older, showing the vices of its model, who retains his youth and beauty until he dies when he stabs the picture. The novel is reminiscent in its decadence of Huysmans' *À Rebours*. It was followed by the publication of his collected essays, including 'The Decay of Lying' and 'The Critic as Artist', which bear out his view that life imitates art, and that the ethics of art are a-moral. His first light comedy, *Lady Windermere's Fan* (1892), produced at St. James's Theatre, was a success, with its epigrammatic wit and paradoxical mores, as was *A Woman of no Importance*, produced at Haymarket Theatre in 1893, with Herbert Beerbohm Tree as the Wildean dandy, Lord Illingworth. *Salomé*, the one-act embodiment of *Symbolisme*, was refused a license in 1893, and was first produced in Paris in 1896. Written in French, it was translated in 1894 by Lord Alfred Douglas, who was Wilde's lover. It would serve as the libretto of Richard Strauss' haunting opera, and inform several of Yeats's plays for dancers. Wilde continued his popular success in 1895 at the Haymarket with *An Ideal Husband*, and at St. James's Theatre with *The Importance of being Earnest: a trivial comedy for serious people*, a play about the importance of names, in which it is discovered that the protagonist was replaced in his youth by a three-penny novel. That year he unsuccessfully sued the Marquis of Queensberry for libel after the Marquis, Lord Alfred Douglas's father, had left a card in the Albemarle Club which read, 'To Oscar Wilde, posing as a somdomite' [sic]. Wilde in turn was charged with gross indecency and sentenced to two years' hard labour. In Reading Gaol he wrote an apologia to, and about Lord Alfred Douglas, published by his loyal friend Robert Ross in 1905. After his release in 1897, Wilde, bankrupt, went to live in France, off a small annuity provided by his friends. He adopted the name 'Sebastian Melmoth', after Maturin's eponymous wanderer. At Berneval he wrote the *Ballad of Reading Gaol* (1898), with its haunting line, 'But each man kills the thing he loves'. He died at the Hôtel d'Alsace.

From *Poems*

(1881)

Requiescat[1]

Tread lightly, she is near
 Under the snow,
Speak gently, she can hear
 The daisies grow.
All her bright golden hair
 Tarnished with rust,
She that was young and fair
 Fallen to dust.

Lily-like, white as snow,
 She hardly knew
She was a woman, so
 Sweetly she grew.

Coffin-board, heavy stone,
 Lie on her breast,
I vex my heart alone,
 She is at rest.

Peace, peace, she cannot hear
 Lyre or sonnet,
All my life's buried here,
 Heap earth upon it.

Avignon

The Harlot's House

(1885)[2]

We caught the tread of dancing feet,
We loitered down the moonlit street,
And stopped beneath the harlot's house.

---

1 The poem was written in 1875, in memory of Wilde's younger sister Isola who died on 23 February 1867, at the age of 8. Wilde regularly visited her grave.
2 Published in the *Dramatic Review*, 11 April 1885.

Inside, above the din and fray,
We heard the loud musicians play
The 'Treues Liebes Herz' of Strauss.[1]

Like strange mechanical grotesques,
Making fantastic arabesques,
The shadows raced across the blind.

We watched the ghostly dancers spin
To sound of horn and violin,
Like black leaves wheeling in the wind.

Like wire-pulled automatons,
Slim silhouetted skeletons
Went sidling through the slow quadrille.

They took each other by the hand,
And danced a stately saraband;
Their laughter echoed thin and shrill.

Sometimes a clockwork puppet pressed
A phantom lover to her breast,
Sometimes they seemed to try to sing.

Sometimes a horrible marionette
Came out, and smoked its cigarette
Upon the steps like a live thing.

Then, turning to my love, I said,
'The dead are dancing with the dead,
The dust is whirling with the dust.'

But she—she heard the violin,
And left my side, and entered in:
Love passed into the house of lust.

Then suddenly the tune went false,
The dancers wearied of the waltz,
The shadows ceased to wheel and whirl.

---

1 *The 'Treues Liebes Herz' of Strauss*: 'The True Loving Heart', supposedly a waltz by
Johann Strauss.

And down the long and silent street,
The dawn, with silver-sandalled feet,
Crept like a frightened girl.

From *Intentions*

(1891)

from The Decay of Lying

CYRIL: ... I should like to ask you a question. What do you mean by saying that life, 'poor, probable, uninteresting human life,' will try to reproduce the marvels of art? I can quite understand your objection to art being treated as a mirror. You think it would reduce genius to the position of a cracked looking-glass. But you don't mean to say that you seriously believe that Life imitates Art, that Life in fact is the mirror, and Art the reality?

VIVIAN: Certainly I do. Paradox though it may seem—and paradoxes are always dangerous things—it is none the less true that Life imitates art far more than Art imitates life. We have all seen in our own day in England how a certain curious and fascinating type of beauty, invented and emphasised by two imaginative painters,[1] has so influenced Life that whenever one goes to a private view or to an artistic salon one sees, here the mystic eyes of Rossetti's dream, the long ivory throat, the strange square-cut jaw, the loosened shadowy hair that he so ardently loved, there the sweet maidenhood of 'The Golden Stair,' the blossom-like mouth and weary loveliness of the 'Laus Amoris,' the passion-pale face of Andromeda, the thin hands and lithe beauty of the Vivien in 'Merlin's Dream.' And it has always been so. A great artist invents a type, and Life tries to copy it, to reproduce it in a popular form, like an enterprising publisher. Neither Holbein nor Vandyck[2] found in England what they have given us. They brought their types with them, and Life with her keen imitative faculty set herself to supply the master with models. The Greeks, with their quick artistic instinct, understood this, and set in the bride's chamber the statue of

1 *Two imaginative painters*: the Pre-Raphaelite painters, Dante Gabriel Rossetti (1828–82) and Edward Burne-Jones (1833–98); Vivian refers to the latter's *The Golden Stairs* (1872–80), *Laus Veneris* (1870–75) and *The Beguiling of Merlin* (1870–74).
2 *Neither Holbein nor Vandyck*: the German Hans Holbein, the Younger (1497–1543) and the Flemish artist, Anthony van Dyck (1599–1641); both painted in England.

Hermes or of Apollo, that she might bear children as lovely as the works of art that she looked at in her rapture or her pain. They knew that Life gains from Art not merely spirituality, depth of thought and feeling, soul-turmoil or soul-peace, but that she can form herself on the very lines and colours of Art, and can reproduce the dignity of Pheidias as well as the grace of Praxiteles.[1] Hence came their objection to realism. They disliked it on purely social grounds. They felt that it inevitably makes people ugly, and they were perfectly right. We try to improve the conditions of the race by means of good air, free sunlight, wholesome water, and hideous bare buildings for the better housing of the lower orders. But these things merely produce health, they do not produce beauty. For this, Art is required, and the true disciples of the great artist are not his studio-imitators, but those who become like his works of art, be they plastic as in the Greek days, or pictorial as in modern times: in a word. Life is Art's best, Art's only pupil.

As it is with the visible arts, so it is with literature. The most obvious and the vulgarest form in which this is shown is in the case of the silly boys who, after reading the adventures of Jack Sheppard or Dick Turpin,[2] pillage the stalls of unfortunate applewomen, break into sweet-shops at night, and alarm old gentlemen who are returning home from the city by leaping out on them in suburban lanes, with black masks and unloaded revolvers. This interesting phenomenon, which always occurs after the appearance of a new edition of either of the books I have alluded to, is usually attributed to the influence of literature on the imagination. But this is a mistake. The imagination is essentially creative and always seeks for a new form. The boy-burglar is simply the inevitable result of life's imitative instinct. He is Fact, occupied as Fact usually is, with trying to reproduce Fiction, and what we see in him is repeated on an extended scale throughout the whole of life. Schopenhauer[3] has analysed the pessimism that char-

---

1 *Pheidias ... Praxiteles*: famous Athenian sculptors of the fifth and mid-fourth century BC.

2 *Jack Sheppard or Dick Turpin*: Jack Sheppard (1702–24) and Dick Turpin (1706–39), a popular criminal and a highwayman. Jack Sheppard was the model for MacHeath in John Gay's *The Beggar's Opera* (1728); he formed the subject of a melodrama, *Jack Sheppard the House-Breaker* (1825), and is the eponymous hero of a novel by William Harrison Ainsworth (1839). Dick Turpin, the hero of Henry Downes Miles' popular novel (1840), formed the subject of various novels and plays.

3 *Schopenhauer*: Arthur Schopenhauer (1788–1860), German philosopher, who presents an atheistic and pessimistic world view in *The World as Will and Idea* (1818).

acterises modern thought, but Hamlet invented it. The world has become sad because a puppet was once melancholy. The Nihilist, that strange martyr who has no faith, who goes to the stake without enthusiasm, and dies for what he does not believe in, is a purely literary product. He was invented by Tourgénieff, and completed by Dostoieffski.[1] Robespierre came out of the pages of Rousseau as surely as the People's Palace rose out of the *débris* of a novel.[2] Literature always anticipates life. It does not copy it, but moulds it to its purpose. The nineteenth century, as we know it, is largely an invention of Balzac. Our Luciens de Rubempré, our Rastignacs, and De Marsays made their first appearance on the stage of the *Comédie Humaine*.[3] We are merely carrying out, with footnotes and unnecessary additions, the whim or fancy or creative vision of a great novelist. I once asked a lady, who knew Thackeray intimately, whether he had had any model for Becky Sharp.[4] She told me that Becky was an invention, but that the idea of the character had been partly suggested by a governess who lived in the neighbourhood of Kensington Square, and was the companion of a very selfish and rich old woman. I inquired what became of the governess, and she replied that, oddly enough, some years after the appearance of *Vanity Fair*, she ran away with the nephew of the lady with whom she was living, and for a short time made a great splash in society, quite in Mrs. Rawdon Crawley's style, and entirely by Mrs. Rawdon Crawley's methods. Ultimately she came to grief, disappeared to the Continent, and used to be occasionally seen at Monte Carlo and other gambling places. The noble gentleman from whom

---

1 *Invented by Tourgénieff ... Dostoieffski*: Russian author Ivan Turgenev (1818–83) invented the word *nihilist* to describe the central character Evgenii Bazarov in his novel *Fathers and Sons* (1862); in his novels, Fyodor Dostoevsky (1821–81) gives a comprehensive picture of nihilists and nihilism.

2 *Robespierre ... Rousseau ... débris of a novel*: Robespierre (1758–94), French revolutionary politician; Jean-Jacques Rousseau (1712–78), French social philosopher. *The People's Palace for East London* (1887) was a museum open to the general public, based on a scheme of Barber Beaumont's Philosophical Institute, and promoted in Sir Walter Besant's novel, *All Sorts and Conditions of Men* (1882).

3 Honoré de Balzac (1799–1850) wrote the ninety-one novels and stories of *La Comédie Humaine* between 1827 and 1847. Lucien de Rubempré is the unhappy hero of *Les illusions perdues* (1843) and *Splendeurs et misères des courtisanes* (1847); Eugène de Rastignac, a type of the ambitious young man, appears in twenty-six novels or stories, and Henri de Marsay, a type of the dandy, in twenty-eight.

4 *Thackeray ... Becky Sharp*: Becky Sharp, the heroine of William Makepeace Thackeray's novel *Vanity Fair* (1847–48), secretly marries Rawdon Crawley, against the wishes of her family.

the same great sentimentalist drew Colonel Newcome died, a few months after *The Newcomes* had reached a fourth edition, with the word 'Adsum' on his lips.[1] Shortly after Mr. Stevenson published his curious psychological story of transformation,[2] a friend of mine, called Mr. Hyde, was in the north of London, and being anxious to get to a railway station, took what he thought would be a short cut, lost his way, and found himself in a network of mean, evil-looking streets. Feeling rather nervous he began to walk extremely fast, when suddenly out of an archway ran a child right between his legs. It fell on the pavement, he tripped over it, and trampled upon it. Being of course very much frightened and a little hurt, it began to scream, and in a few seconds the whole street was full of rough people who came pouring out of the houses like ants. They surrounded him, and asked him his name. He was just about to give it when he suddenly remembered the opening incident in Mr. Stevenson's story. He was so filled with horror at having realised in his own person that terrible and well written scene, and at having done accidently, though in fact, what the Mr. Hyde of fiction had done with deliberate intent, that he ran away as hard as he could go. He was, however, very closely followed, and finally he took refuge in a surgery, the door of which happened to be open, where he explained to a young assistant, who happened to be there, exactly what had occurred. The humanitarian crowd were induced to go away on his giving them a small sum of money, and as soon as the coast was clear he left. As he passed out, the name on the brass door-plate of the surgery caught his eye. It was 'Jekyll'. At least it should have been.

Here the imitation, as far as it went, was of course accidental. In the following case the imitation was self-conscious. In the year 1879, just after I had left Oxford, I met at a reception at the house of one of the Foreign Ministers a woman of very curious exotic beauty. We became great friends, and were constantly together. And yet what interested most in her

---

1 *Adsum' on his lips*: the famous last word of Colonel Newcome in *The Newcomes* (1853–55): 'As the last bell struck, a peculiar sweet smile shone over his face, and he lifted up his head a little, and quickly said, "Adsum!" and fell back. It was the word we used at school, when names were called; and lo, he, whose heart was as that of a little child, had answered to his name, and stood in the presence of The Master.'

2 *Mr. Stevenson ... story of transformation*: In Chapter One of Robert Louis Stevenson's *The Strange Case of Dr Jekyll and Mr Hyde* (1886), Mr Enfield describes how at three in the morning Mr Hyde tramples a child in a London slum.

was not her beauty, but her character, her entire vagueness of character. She seemed to have no personality at all, but simply the possibility of many types. Sometimes she would give herself up entirely to Art, turn her drawing-room into a studio, and spend two or three days a week at picture-galleries or museums. Then she would take to attending race-meetings, wear the most horsey clothes, and talk about nothing but betting. She abandoned religion for mesmerism, mesmerism for politics, and politics for the melodramatic excitements of philanthropy. In fact, she was a kind of Proteus, and as much a failure in all her transformations as was that wondrous sea-god when Odysseus laid hold of him. One day a serial began in one of the French magazines. At that time I used to read serial stories, and I well remember the shock of surprise I felt when I came to the description of the heroine. She was so like my friend that I brought her the magazine, and she recognised herself in it immediately, and seemed fascinated by the resemblance. I should tell you, by the way, that the story was translated from some dead Russian writer, so that the author had not taken his type from my friend. Well, to put the matter briefly, some months afterwards I was in Venice, and finding the magazine in the reading-room of the hotel, I took it up casually to see what had become of the heroine. It was a most piteous tale, as the girl had ended by running away with a man absolutely inferior to her, not merely in social station, but in character and intellect also. I wrote to my friend that evening about my views on John Bellini,[1] and the admirable ices at Florio's, and the artistic value of gondolas, but added a postscript to the effect that her double in the story had behaved in a very silly manner. I don't know why I added that, but I remember I had a sort of dread over me that she might do the same thing. Before my letter had reached her, she had run away with a man who deserted her in six months. I saw her in 1884 in Paris, where she was living with her mother, and I asked her whether the story had had anything to do with her action. She told me that she had felt an absolutely irresistible impulse to follow the heroine step by step in her strange and fatal progress, and that it was with a feeling of real terror that she had looked

---

1 *John Bellini*: Giovanni Bellini (1431?–1516), Venetian painter; Ruskin refers to him as 'John Bellini'.

forward to the last few chapters of the story. When they appeared, it seemed to her that she was compelled to reproduce them in life, and she did so. It was a most clear example of this imitative instinct of which I was speaking, and an extremely tragic one.

However, I do not wish to dwell any further upon individual instances. Personal experience is a most vicious and limited circle. All that I desire to point out is the general principle that Life imitates Art far more than Art imitates Life, and I feel sure that if you think seriously about it you will find that it is true. Life holds the mirror up to Art, and either reproduces some strange type imagined by painter or sculptor, or realises in fact what has been dreamed in fiction. Scientifically speaking, the basis of life—the energy of life, as Aristotle would call it—is simply the desire for expression, and Art is always presenting various forms through which this expression can be attained. Life seizes on them and uses them, even if they be to her own hurt. Young men have committed suicide because Rolla did so, have died by their own hand because by his own hand Werther died.[1] Think of what we owe to the imitation of Christ, of what we owe to the imitation of Cæsar.

CYRIL: The theory is certainly a very curious one, but to make it complete you must show that Nature, no less than Life, is an imitation of Art. Are you prepared to prove that?

VIVIAN: My dear fellow, I am prepared to prove anything.

CYRIL: Nature follows the landscape painter then, and takes her effects from him?

VIVIAN: Certainly. Where, if not from the Impressionists, do we get those wonderful brown fogs that come creeping down our streets, blurring the gas-lamps and changing the houses into monstrous shadows? To whom, if not to them and their master, do we owe the lovely silver mists that brood over our river, and turn to faint forms of fading grace curved bridge and swaying barge? The extraordinary change that has taken place in the climate of London during the last ten years is entirely due to this particular school of Art. You smile. Consider the matter from a scientific or a metaphysical point

---

1 *Rolla ... Werther died*: the eponymous heroes of Goethe's tragic romance *Die Leiden des jungen Werthers* (1774) and of Alfred de Musset's long poem *Rolla* (1833) committed suicide; their example was indeed followed by young men in real life.

of view, and you will find that I am right. For what is Nature? Nature is no great mother who has borne us. She is our creation. It is in our brain that she quickens to life. Things are because we see them, and what we see, and how we see it, depends on the Arts that have influenced us. To look at a thing is very different from seeing a thing. One does not see anything until one sees its beauty. Then, and then only, does it come into existence. At present, people see fogs, not because there are fogs, but because poets and painters have taught them the mysterious loveliness of such effects. There may have been fogs for centuries in London. I dare say there were. But no one saw them, and so we do not know anything about them. They did not exist till Art had invented them. Now, it must be admitted, fogs are carried to excess. They have become the mere mannerism of a clique, and the exaggerated realism of their method gives dull people bronchitis. Where the cultured catch an effect, the uncultured catch cold. And so, let us be humane, and invite Art to turn her wonderful eyes elsewhere. She has done so already, indeed. That white quivering sunlight that one sees now in France, with its strange blotches of mauve, and its restless violet shadows, is her latest fancy, and, on the whole, Nature produces it quite admirably. Where she used to give us Corots and Daubignys, she gives us now exquisite Monets and entrancing Pisaros.[1] Indeed there are moments, rare, it is true, but still to be observed from time to time, when Nature becomes absolutely modern. Of course she is not always to be relied upon. The fact is that she is in this unfortunate position. Art creates an incomparable and unique effect, and, having done so, passes on to other things. Nature, upon the other hand, forgetting that imitation can be made the sincerest form of insult, keeps on repeating this effect until we all become absolutely wearied of it. Nobody of any real culture, for instance, ever talks now-a-days about the beauty of the sunset. Sunsets are quite old-fashioned. They belong to the time when Turner[2] was the last note in Art. To admire them is a distinct sign of provincialism of temperament. Upon the

1 *Corots ... Pisaros*: Jean Baptiste Corot (1796–1875) and Charles François Daubigny (1817–78) were *plein air* painters who influenced the Impressionists, Claude Monet (1840–1926) and Camille Pisarro (1831–1903).
2 *Turner*: Joseph Turner (1775–1851), English landscape painter whose later works anticipated Impressionism.

207

other hand they go on. Yesterday evening Mrs Arundel insisted on my going to the window, and looking at the glorious
sky, as she called it. Of course I had to look at it. She is one
of those absurdly pretty Philistines, to whom one can deny
nothing. And what was it? It was simply a very second-rate
Turner, a Turner of a bad period, with all the painter's worst
faults exaggerated and over-emphasized. Of course, I am
quite ready to admit that Life very often commits the same
error. She produces her false Renés and her sham Vautrins,
just as Nature gives us, on one day a doubtful Cuyp, and on
another a more than questionable Rousseau.[1] Still, Nature
irritates one more when she does things of that kind. It seems
so stupid, so obvious, so unnecessary. A false Vautrin might
be delightful. A doubtful Cuyp is unbearable. However, I
don't want to be too hard on Nature. I wish the Channel,
especially at Hastings, did not look quite so often like a
Henry Moore, grey pearl with yellow lights,[2] but then, when
Art is more varied, Nature will, no doubt, be more varied
also. That she imitates Art, I don't think even her worst
enemy would deny now. It is the one thing that keeps her in
touch with civilized man. But have I proved my theory to
your satisfaction.

CYRIL: You have proved it to my dissatisfaction, which is better. But
even admitting this strange imitative instinct in Life and Nature,
surely you would acknowledge that Art expresses the temper of
its age, the spirit of its time, the moral and social conditions that
surround it, and under whose influence it is produced.

VIVIAN: Certainly not! Art never expresses anything but itself. This is
the principle of my new æsthetics; and it is this, more than
that vital connection between form and substance, on which
Mr. Pater dwells, that makes music the type of all the arts.[3]
Of course, nations and individuals, with that healthy natural

---

1 *False Renés ... questionable Rousseau*: René is the eponymous hero of an autobiographically
tinted novel by François-René de Chateaubriand (1768–1848), which has traces of Goethe's
Werther. Vautrin is the formidable criminal character who appears in three of Balzac's novels
(*Le Père Goriot*, *Les illusions perdues*, and *Splendeurs et misères des courtisanes*). He is also
the main character in Balzac's play *Vautrin* (1840), the original performance of which was
delayed because the eponymous villain bore an uncanny resemblance to King Louis Philippe.
Albert Cuyp (1620–91) was a Dutch painter of land- and seascapes to whom many paintings
seem spuriously attributed. Théodore Rousseau (1812–67) was one of the Barbizon School of
landscape painters.
2 *Grey pearl with yellow lights*: skit on the titles of the seascapes by Henry Moore (1831–95).
3 *Mr. Pater ... the arts*: Walter Pater (1839–94) postulated his famous dictum, '*All art constantly aspires towards the condition of music*', in 'The School of Giorgione' (*Studies in the
Renaissance*—1873).

vanity which is the secret of existence, are always under the impression that it is of them that the Muses are talking, always trying to find in the calm dignity of imaginative art some mirror of their own turbid passions, always forgetting that the singer of life is not Apollo, but Marsyas.[1] Remote from reality, and with her eyes turned away from the shadows of the cave.[2] Art reveals her own perfection, and the wondering crowd that watches the opening of the marvellous, many-petalled rose fancies that it is its own history that is being told to it, its own spirit that is finding expression in a new form. But it is not so. The highest art rejects the burden of the human spirit, and gains more from a new medium or a fresh material than she does from any enthusiasm for art, or from any lofty passion, or from any great awakening of the human consciousness. She develops purely on her own lines. She is not symbolic of any age. It is the ages that are her symbols.

Even those who hold that Art is representative of time and place and people, cannot help admitting that the more imitative an art is, the less it represents to us the spirit of its age. The evil faces of the Roman emperors look out at us from the foul porphyry and spotted jasper in which the realistic artists of the day delighted to work, and we fancy that in those cruel lips and heavy sensual jaws we can find the secret of the ruin of the Empire. But it was not so. The vices of Tiberius could not destroy that supreme civilization, any more than the virtues of the Antonines could save it. It fell for other, for less interesting reasons. The sibyls and prophets of the Sistine may indeed serve to interpret for some that new birth of the emancipated spirit that we call the Renaissance; but what do the drunken boors and brawling peasants of Dutch art tell us about the great soul of Holland? The more abstract, the more ideal an art is, the more it reveals to us the temper of its age. If we wish to understand a nation by means of its art, let us look at its architecture or its music.

* * *

---

1 *The singer of life is not Apollo but Marsyas*: Phoebus Apollo, the Olympian god of light, was challenged by the Phrygian flute-player Marsyas to a contest judged by the Muses. Apollo won, and Marsyas was flayed alive, whereupon according to Ovid all the woodland gods and animals wept for him. The contest became symbolical for the struggle between divine harmony and earthly passions.
2 *Remote from reality ... the cave*: a reference to Plato's *Republic*.

The Ballad of Reading Gaol

(1898)[1]

In Memoriam

C. T. W.

Sometime Trooper Of The Royal Horse Guards
Obiit H. M. Prison, Reading, Bershire
July 7, 1896[2]

I

He did not wear his scarlet coat,[3]
  For blood and wine are red,
And blood and wine were on his hands
  When they found him with the dead,
The poor dead woman whom he loved,
  And murdered in her bed.

He walked amongst the Trial Men
  In a suit of shabby grey;
A cricket cap was on his head,
  And his step seemed light and gay;
But I never saw a man who looked
  So wistfully at the day.

I never saw a man who looked
  With such a wistful eye
Upon that little tent of blue
  Which prisoners call the sky,
And at every drifting cloud that went
  With sails of silver by.

I walked, with other souls in pain,
  Within another ring,
And was wondering if the man had done
  A great or little thing,
When a voice behind me whispered low,
  'That fellow's got to swing.'

---

1 In the first six printings, by Leonard Smithers in 1898 (5,800 copies), Wilde used his cell-number, C.3.3, as *his nom de plume.*

2 C. T. W.: Charles Thomas Wooldridge, a fellow prisoner, who had been a trooper in the Royal Horse Guards, was hanged for cutting the throat of his wife.

3 *He did not wear his scarlet coat*: the Royal Horse Guards wore a dark blue uniform; when Wilde was alerted to this he is said to have replied, 'I could hardly have written "He did not wear his azure coat, for blood and wine are blue"'.

Dear Christ! the very prison walls
   Suddenly seemed to reel,
And the sky above my head became
   Like a casque of scorching steel;
And, though I was a soul in pain,
   My pain I could not feel.

I only knew what hunted thought
   Quickened his step, and why
He looked upon the garish day
   With such a wistful eye;
The man had killed the thing he loved,
   And so he had to die.

ᔟ

Yet each man kills the thing he loves,
   By each let this be heard,
Some do it with a bitter look,
   Some with a flattering word.
The coward does it with a kiss,
   The brave man with a sword!

Some kill their love when they are young,
   And some when they are old;
Some strangle with the hands of Lust,
   Some with the hands of Gold:
The kindest use a knife, because
   The dead so soon grow cold.

Some love too little, some too long,
   Some sell, and others buy;
Some do the deed with many tears,
   And some without a sigh:
For each man kills the thing he loves,
   Yet each man does not die.

He does not die a death of shame
   On a day of dark disgrace,
Nor have a noose about his neck,
   Nor a cloth upon his face,

Nor drop feet foremost through the floor
    Into an empty space.

He does not sit with silent men
    Who watch him night and day;
Who watch him when he tries to weep,
    And when he tries to pray;
Who watch him lest himself should rob
    The prison of its prey.

He does not wake at dawn to see
    Dread figures throng his room,
The shivering Chaplain robed in white,
    The Sheriff stern with gloom,
And the Governor all in shiny black,
    With the yellow face of Doom.

He does not rise in piteous haste
    To put on convict-clothes,
While some coarse-mouthed Doctor gloats, and notes
    Each new and nerve-twitched pose,
Fingering a watch whose little ticks
    Are like horrible hammer-blows.

He does not know that sickening thirst
    That sands one's throat, before
The hangman with his gardener's gloves
    Slips through the padded door,
And binds one with three leathern thongs,
    That the throat may thirst no more.

He does not bend his head to hear
    The Burial Office read,
Nor, while the terror of his soul
    Tells him he is not dead,
Cross his own coffin, as he moves
    Into the hideous shed.[1]

He does not stare upon the air
    Through a little roof of glass:

---

1 *into the hideous shed*: 'it is a wooden oblong narrow shed with a glass roof' (Wilde to Robert Ross).

He does not pray with lips of clay
    For his agony to pass;
Nor feel upon his shuddering cheek
    The kiss of Caiaphas.[1]

II

Six weeks our guardsman walked the yard,
    In the suit of shabby grey:
His cricket cap was on his head,
    And his step seemed light and gay,
But I never saw a man who looked
    So wistfully at the day.

I never saw a man who looked
    With such a wistful eye
Upon that little tent of blue
    Which prisoners call the sky,
And at every wandering cloud that trailed
    Its ravelled fleeces by.

He did not wring his hands, as do
    Those witless men who dare
To try to rear the changeling Hope
    In the cave of black Despair:
He only looked upon the sun,
    And drank the morning air.

He did not wring his hands nor weep,
    Nor did he peek or pine,
But he drank the air as though it held
    Some healthful anodyne;
With open mouth he drank the sun
    As though it had been wine!

And I and all the souls in pain,
    Who tramped the other ring,
Forgot if we ourselves had done

---

1 *the kiss of Caiaphas*: Joseph Caiaphas, in the New Testament, was the high priest to whom
Jesus was taken after his arrest in the garden of Gethsemane, where Judas had betrayed Jesus
with a kiss. Wilde explained to Leonard Smithers, the publisher: 'By "Caiaphas" I do not
mean the present Chaplain of Reading ... I mean any priest of God who assists at the cruel
and unjust punishment of man'.

A great or little thing,
And watched with gaze of dull amaze
The man who had to swing.

And strange it was to see him pass
With a step so light and gay,
And strange it was to see him look
So wistfully at the day,
And strange it was to think that he
Had such a debt to pay.

ಜ

For oak and elm have pleasant leaves
That in the spring-time shoot:
But grim to see is the gallows-tree,
With its adder-bitten root,
And, green or dry, a man must die
Before it bears its fruit!

The loftiest place is that seat of grace
For which all worldlings try:
But who would stand in hempen band
Upon a scaffold high,
And through a murderer's collar take
His last look at the sky?

It is sweet to dance to violins
When Love and Life are fair:
To dance to flutes, to dance to lutes
Is delicate and rare:
But it is not sweet with nimble feet
To dance upon the air!

So with curious eyes and sick surmise
We watched him day by day,
And wondered if each one of us
Would end the self-same way,
For none can tell to what red Hell
His sightless soul may stray.

&

At last the dead man walked no more
   Amongst the Trial Men,
And I knew that he was standing up
   In the black dock's dreadful pen,
And that never would I see his face
   In God's sweet world again.

Like two doomed ships that pass in storm
   We had crossed each other's way:
But we made no sign, we said no word,
   We had no word to say;
For we did not meet in the holy night,
   But in the shameful day.

A prison wall was round us both,
   Two outcast men we were:
The world had thrust us from its heart,
   And God from out His care:
And the iron gin[1] that waits for Sin
   Had caught us in its snare.

III

In Debtors' Yard the stones are hard,
   And the dripping wall is high,
So it was there he took the air
   Beneath the leaden sky,
And by each side a Warder walked,
   For fear the man might die.

Or else he sat with those who watched
   His anguish night and day;
Who watched him when he rose to weep,
   And when he crouched to pray;
Who watched him lest himself should rob
   Their scaffold of its prey.

The Governor was strong upon
   The Regulations Act:

---

1 *iron gin*: metal trap.

The Doctor said that Death was but
  A scientific fact:

And twice a day the Chaplain called,
  And left a little tract.
And twice a day he smoked his pipe,
  And drank his quart of beer:
His soul was resolute, and held
  No hiding-place for fear;
He often said that he was glad
  The hangman's hands were near.

But why he said so strange a thing
  No Warder dared to ask:
For he to whom a watcher's doom
  Is given as his task,
Must set a lock upon his lips,
  And make his face a mask.

Or else he might be moved, and try
  To comfort or console:
And what should Human Pity do
  Pent up in Murderer's Hole?
What word of grace in such a place
  Could help a brother's soul?

છ

With slouch and swing around the ring
  We trod the Fools' Parade!
We did not care: we knew we were
  The Devil's Own Brigade:
And shaven head and feet of lead
  Make a merry masquerade.

We tore the tarry rope to shreds
  With blunt and bleeding nails;[1]
We rubbed the doors, and scrubbed the floors,
  And cleaned the shining rails:

---

1 *We tore the tarry rope ... nails*: In Pentonville Prison, Oscar Wilde had to pick the 'tarry rope' (old rope, known as 'oakum').

And, rank by rank, we soaped the plank,
　　And clattered with the pails.

We sewed the sacks,[1] we broke the stones,
　　We turned the dusty drill:[1]
We banged the tins, and bawled the hymns,
　　And sweated on the mill:[1]
But in the heart of every man
　　Terror was lying still.

So still it lay that every day
　　Crawled like a weed-clogged wave:
And we forgot the bitter lot
　　That waits for fool and knave,
Till once, as we tramped in from work,
　　We passed an open grave.

With yawning mouth the yellow hole
　　Gaped for a living thing;
The very mud cried out for blood
　　To the thirsty asphalte ring:
And we knew that ere one dawn grew fair
　　Some prisoner had to swing.

Right in we went, with soul intent
　　On Death and Dread and Doom:
The hangman, with his little bag,
　　Went shuffling through the gloom:
And I trembled as I groped my way
　　Into my numbered tomb.

❧

That night the empty corridors
　　Were full of forms of Fear,
And up and down the iron town
　　Stole feet we could not hear,
And through the bars that hide the stars
　　White faces seemed to peer.

---

1 *We sewed the sacks*: mail bags.
2 *the dusty drill*: a narrow iron drum which, when turned, scooped up, and emptied, sand.
3 *sweated on the mill*: a treadmill which revolved as the prisoners stepped on it.

217

He lay as one who lies and dreams
    In a pleasant meadow-land,
The watchers watched him as he slept,
    And could not understand
How one could sleep so sweet a sleep
    With a hangman close at hand.

But there is no sleep when men must weep
    Who never yet have wept:
So we— the fool, the fraud, the knave—
    That endless vigil kept,
And through each brain on hands of pain
    Another's terror crept.

ᘓ

Alas! it is a fearful thing
    To feel another's guilt!
For, right, within, the sword of Sin
    Pierced to its poisoned hilt,
And as molten lead were the tears we shed
    For the blood we had not spilt.

The Warders with their shoes of felt
    Crept by each padlocked door,
And peeped and saw, with eyes of awe,
    Grey figures on the floor,
And wondered why men knelt to pray
    Who never prayed before.

All through the night we knelt and prayed,
    Mad mourners of a corse!
The troubled plumes of midnight were
    The plumes upon a hearse:
And bitter wine upon a sponge
    Was the savour of Remorse.[1]

ᘓ

---

1 *bitter wine upon a sponge*…: John 19:29: 'Now there was set a vessel full of vinegar: and they filled a spunge with vinegar, and put it upon hyssop, and put it to his mouth.'

Oscar Fingal O'Flahertie Wills Wilde

The gray cock crew, the red cock crew,
　But never came the day:
And crooked shapes of Terror crouched,
　In the corners where we lay:
And each evil sprite that walks by night
　Before us seemed to play.

They glided past, they glided fast,
　Like travellers through a mist:
They mocked the moon in a rigadoon[1]
　Of delicate turn and twist,
And with formal pace and loathsome grace
　The phantoms kept their tryst.

With mop and mow, we saw them go,
　Slim shadows hand in hand:
About, about, in ghostly rout
　They trod a saraband:
And the damned grotesques made arabesques,
　Like the wind upon the sand!

With the pirouettes of marionettes,
　They tripped on pointed tread:
But with flutes of Fear they filled the ear,
　As their grisly masque they led,
And loud they sang, and long they sang,
　For they sang to wake the dead.

'Oho!' they cried, 'The world is wide,
　But fettered limbs go lame!
And once, or twice, to throw the dice
　Is a gentlemanly game,
But he does not win who plays with Sin
　In the secret House of Shame.'

❧

No things of air these antics were,
　That frolicked with such glee:
To men whose lives were held in gyves,

---
1 *rigadoon*: a lively dance, supposedly invented by a Frenchman called Rigaud.

And whose feet might not go free,
Ah! wounds of Christ! they were living things,
   Most terrible to see.

Around, around, they waltzed and wound;
   Some wheeled in smirking pairs;
With the mincing step of a demirep[1]
   Some sidled up the stairs:
And with subtle sneer, and fawning leer,
   Each helped us at our prayers.

❧

The morning wind began to moan,
   But still the night went on:
Through its giant loom the web of gloom
   Crept till each thread was spun:
And, as we prayed, we grew afraid
   Of the Justice of the Sun.

The moaning wind went wandering round
   The weeping prison-wall:
Till like a wheel of turning steel
   We felt the minutes crawl:
O moaning wind! what had we done
   To have such a seneschal?[2]

At last I saw the shadowed bars,
   Like a lattice wrought in lead,
Move right across the whitewashed wall
   That faced my three-plank bed,
And I knew that somewhere in the world
   God's dreadful dawn was red.

❧

At six o'clock we cleaned our cells,
   At seven all was still,
But the sough and swing of a mighty wing

---

1 *demirep*: woman of doubtful reputation.
2 *seneschal*: official entrusted with the administration of justice.

Oscar Fingal O'Flahertie Wills Wilde

The prison seemed to fill,
For the Lord of Death with icy breath
  Had entered in to kill.

He did not pass in purple pomp,
  Nor ride a moon-white steed.
Three yards of cord and a sliding board
  Are all the gallows' need:
So with rope of shame the Herald came
  To do the secret deed.

ಬ

We were as men who through a fen
  Of filthy darkness grope:
We did not dare to breathe a prayer,
  Or to give our anguish scope:
Something was dead in each of us,
  And what was dead was Hope.

For Man's grim Justice goes its way,
  And will not swerve aside:
It slays the weak, it slays the strong,
  It has a deadly stride:
With iron heel it slays the strong,
  The monstrous parricide!

ಬ

We waited for the stroke of eight:
  Each tongue was thick with thirst:
For the stroke of eight is the stroke of Fate
  That makes a man accursed,
And Fate will use a running noose[1]
  For the best man and the worst.

We had no other thing to do,
  Save to wait for the sign to come:
So, like things of stone in a valley lone,
  Quiet we sat and dumb:

---

1 *running noose*: a loop formed with a running knot, which tightens as the rope is pulled.

But each man's heart beat thick and quick,
  Like a madman on a drum!

⁖

With sudden shock the prison-clock
  Smote on the shivering air,
And from all the gaol rose up a wail
  Of impotent despair,
Like the sound that frightened marches hear
  From some leper in his lair.

And as one sees most fearful things
  In the crystal of a dream,
We saw the greasy hempen rope
  Hooked to the blackened beam,
And heard the prayer the hangman's snare
  Strangled into a scream.

And all the woe that moved him so
  That he gave that bitter cry,
And the wild regrets, and the bloody sweats,
  None knew so well as I:
For he who lives more lives than one
  More deaths than one must die.

IV

There is no chapel on the day
  On which they hang a man:
The Chaplain's heart is far too sick,
  Or his face is far too wan,
Or there is that written in his eyes
  Which none should look upon.

So they kept us close till nigh on noon,
  And then they rang the bell,
And the Warders with their jingling keys
  Opened each listening cell,
And down the iron stair we tramped,
  Each from his separate Hell.

Out into God's sweet air we went
  But not in wonted way,
For this man's face was white with fear,
  And that man's face was gray,
And I never saw sad men who looked
  So wistfully at the day.

I never saw sad men who looked
  With such a wistful eye
Upon that little tent of blue
  We prisoners called the sky,
And at every careless cloud that passed
  In happy freedom by.

But there were those amongst us all
  Who walked with downcast head,
And knew that, had each got his due,
  They should have died instead:
He had but killed a thing that lived,
  Whilst they had killed the dead.

For he who sins a second time
  Wakes a dead soul to pain,
And draws it from its spotted shroud,
  And makes it bleed again,
And makes it bleed great gouts of blood,
  And makes it bleed in vain!

❦

Like ape or clown, in monstrous garb
  With crooked arrows starred,
Silently we went round and round,
  The slippery asphalte yard;
Silently we went round and round,
  And no man spoke a word.

Silently we went round and round,
  And through each hollow mind
The Memory of dreadful things
  Rushed like a dreadful wind,

And Horror stalked before each man,
  And Terror crept behind.

⚘

The Warders strutted up and down,
  And kept their herd of brutes,
Their uniforms were spick and span,
  And they wore their Sunday suits,
But we knew the work they had been at,
  By the quicklime on their boots.[1]

For where a grave had opened wide,
  There was no grave at all:
Only a stretch of mud and sand
  By the hideous prison-wall,
And a little heap of burning lime,
  That the man should have his pall.

For he has a pall, this wretched man,
  Such as few men can claim:
Deep down below a prison-yard,
  Naked for greater shame,
He lies, with fetters on each foot,
  Wrapt in a sheet of flame!

And all the while the burning lime
  Eats flesh and bone away,
It eats the brittle bone by night,
  And the soft flesh by day,
It eats the flesh and bone by turns,
  But it eats the heart alway.

⚘

For three long years they will not sow
  Or root or seedling there:
For three long years the unblessed spot
  Will sterile be and bare,
And look upon the wondering sky
  With unreproachful stare.

---

1 *the quicklime on their boots*: quicklime was scattered over a corpse to accelerate decomposition.

They think a murderer's heart would taint
　　Each simple seed they sow.
It is not true! God's kindly earth
　　Is kindlier than men know,
And the red rose would but blow more red,
　　The white rose whiter blow.

Out of his mouth a red, red rose!
　　Out of his heart a white!
For who can say by what strange way,
　　Christ brings His will to light,
Since the barren staff the pilgrim bore
　　Bloomed in the great Pope's sight?[1]

❧

But neither milk-white rose nor red
　　May bloom in prison air;
The shard, the pebble, and the flint,
　　Are what they give us there:
For flowers have been known to heal
　　A common man's despair.

So never will wine-red rose or white,
　　Petal by petal, fall
On that stretch of mud and sand that lies
　　By the hideous prison-wall,
To tell the men who tramp the yard
　　That God's Son died for all.

❧

Yet though the hideous prison-wall
　　Still hems him round and round,
And a spirit may not walk by night
　　That is with fetters bound,
And a spirit may but weep that lies
　　In such unholy ground,

---

1 *the barren staff ... bloomed in the great Pope's sight*: In Wagner's opera *Tannhaüser* the Pope
tells Tannhaüser that he can expect no more forgiveness than his staff can blossom. In the last
act a band of pilgrims carry the papal staff, which has put forth leaves.

He is at peace—this wretched man—
  At peace, or will be soon:
There is no thing to make him mad,
  Nor does Terror walk at noon,
For the lampless Earth in which he lies
  Has neither Sun nor Moon.

            ઠ

They hanged him as a beast is hanged:
  They did not even toll
A requiem that might have brought
  Rest to his startled soul,
But hurriedly they took him out,
  And hid him in a hole.

They stripped him of his canvas clothes,
  And gave him to the flies:
They mocked the swollen purple throat,
  And the stark and staring eyes:
And with laughter loud they heaped the shroud
  In which their convict lies.

The Chaplain would not kneel to pray
  By his dishonoured grave:
Nor mark it with that blessed Cross
  That Christ for sinners gave,
Because the man was one of those
  Whom Christ came down to save.

Yet all is well; he has but passed
  To Life's appointed bourne:
And alien tears will fill for him
  Pity's long-broken urn,
For his mourners will be outcast men,
  And outcasts always mourn.

           V
I know not whether Laws be right,
  Or whether Laws be wrong;
All that we know who lie in gaol

Is that the wall is strong;
And that each day is like a year,
 A year whose days are long.

But this I know, that every Law
 That men have made for Man,
Since first Man took his brother's life,
 And the sad world began,
But straws the wheat and saves the chaff
 With a most evil fan.

This too I know—and wise it were
 If each could know the same—
That every prison that men build
 Is built with bricks of shame,
And bound with bars lest Christ should see
 How men their brothers maim.

With bars they blur the gracious moon,
 And blind the goodly sun:
And they do well to hide their Hell,
 For in it things are done
That Son of God nor son of Man
 Ever should look upon!

℘

The vilest deeds like poison weeds,
 Bloom well in prison-air;
It is only what is good in Man
 That wastes and withers there:
Pale Anguish keeps the heavy gate,
 And the Warder is Despair.

For they starve the little frightened child
 Till it weeps both night and day:
And they scourge the weak, and flog the fool,
 And gibe the old and grey,
And some grow mad, and all grow bad,
 And none a word may say.

Each narrow cell in which we dwell
   Is a foul and dark latrine,
And the fetid breath of living Death
   Chokes up each grated screen,
And all, but Lust, is turned to dust
   In Humanity's machine.

The brackish water that we drink
   Creeps with a loathsome slime,
And the bitter bread they weigh in scales
   Is full of chalk and lime,
And Sleep will not lie down, but walks
   Wild-eyed, and cries to Time.

ꙮ

But though lean Hunger and green Thirst
   Like asp with adder fight,
We have little care of prison fare,
   For what chills and kills outright
Is that every stone one lifts by day
   Becomes one's heart by night.

With midnight always in one's heart,
   And twilight in one's cell,
We turn the crank, or tear the rope,
   Each in his separate Hell,
And the silence is more awful far
   Than the sound of a brazen bell.

And never a human voice comes near
   To speak a gentle word:
And the eye that watches through the door
   Is pitiless and hard:
And by all forgot, we rot and rot,
   With soul and body marred.

And thus we rust Life's iron chain
   Degraded and alone:
And some men curse, and some men weep,
   And some men make no moan:

But God's eternal Laws are kind
    And break the heart of stone.

ᛯ

And every human heart that breaks,
    In prison-cell or yard,
Is as that broken box that gave
    Its treasure to the Lord,[1]
And filled the unclean leper's house
    With the scent of costliest nard.

Ah! happy they whose hearts can break
    And peace of pardon win!
How else may man make straight his plan
    And cleanse his soul from Sin?
How else but through a broken heart
    May Lord Christ enter in?

ᛯ

And he of the swollen purple throat,
    And the stark and staring eyes,
Waits for the holy hands that took
    The Thief to Paradise;[2]
And a broken and a contrite heart
    The Lord will not despise.[3]

The man in red who reads the Law[4]
    Gave him three weeks of life,
Three little weeks in which to heal
    His soul of his soul's strife,
And cleanse from every blot of blood
    The hand that held the knife.

---

1 ... *that broken box*...: Mark 14:3: 'And being in Bethany in the house of Simon the leper, as he sat at meat, there came a woman having an alabaster box of ointment of spikenard very precious; and she brake the box, and poured it on his head'.

2 *that took / the Thief to Paradise*: one of the thieves crucified beside Jesus cursed him; the other asked him for forgiveness, and was shriven—Luke 23:42–3: 'And he said unto Jesus, Lord, remember me when thou comest into thy kingdom. And Jesus said unto him, Verily I say unto thee, To day shalt thou be with me in paradise'.

3 *a broken and a contrite heart*...: Psalm 51:17: 'The sacrifices of God are a broken spirit: a broken and a contrite heart, O God, thou wilt not despise'.

4 *The man in red who reads the Law*: the judge who sentenced Woolridge.

And with tears of blood he cleansed the hand,
  The hand that held the steel:
For only blood can wipe out blood,
  And only tears can heal:
And the crimson stain that was of Cain
  Became Christ's snow-white seal.

VI

In Reading gaol by Reading town
  There is a pit of shame,
And in it lies a wretched man
  Eaten by teeth of flame,
In a burning winding-sheet he lies,
  And his grave has got no name.

And there, till Christ call forth the dead,
  In silence let him lie:
No need to waste the foolish tear,
  Or heave the windy sigh:
The man had killed the thing he loved,
  And so he had to die.

And all men kill the thing they love,
  By all let this be heard,
Some do it with a bitter look,
  Some with a flattering word,
The coward does it with a kiss,
  The brave man with a sword!

C.3.3

Oscar Fingal O'Flahertie Wills Wilde

From *De Profundis*

[Letter to Lord Alfred Douglas, January–March 1897[1]]

H. M. Prison
Reading

Dear Bosie,

... Suffering is one long moment. We cannot divide it by seasons. We can only record its moods, and chronicle their return. With us time itself does not progress. It revolves. It seems to circle round one centre of pain. The paralysing immobility of a life, every circumstance of which is regulated after an unchangeable pattern, so that we eat and drink and walk and lie down and pray, or kneel at least for prayer, according to the inflexible laws of an iron formula; this immobile quality, that makes each dreadful day in the very minutest detail like its brother, seems to communicate itself to those external forces the very essence of whose existence is ceaseless change. Of seed-time or harvest, of the reapers bending over the corn, or the grape-gatherers threading through the vines, of the grass in the orchard made white with broken blossoms or strewn with fallen fruit, we know nothing, and can know nothing. For us there is only one season, the season of Sorrow. The very sun and moon seem taken from us. Outside, the day may be blue and gold, but the light that creeps down through the thickly-muffled glass of the small iron-barred window beneath which one sits is grey and niggard. It is always twilight in one's cell, as it is always midnight in one's heart. And in the sphere of thought, no less than in the sphere of time, motion is no more. The thing that you personally have long ago forgotten, or can easily forget, is happening to me now, and will happen to me again to-morrow. Remember this, and you will be able to understand a little of why I am writing, and in this manner writing.

A week later, I am transferred here.[1] Three more months go over and my mother dies. You knew, none better, how deeply I loved and

---

1 Excerpts of this letter were first published in 1905 by Robert Ross. That Douglas was the addressee was first revealed when he brought an action to the High Court for libel against Arthur Ransome, who, in *Oscar Wilde: A Critical Study* (1912), had identified him implicitly as the 'man to whom Wilde felt that he owed some, at least, of the circumstances of his public disgrace'. In 1908 Ross published an enlarged edition of *De Profundis*; in 1909 he deposited the full letter in the British Museum, to be kept under seal for fifty years. Vyvyan Holland, Oscar Wilde's younger son, published a version in 1949 from a typescript which had been bequeathed to him by Ross. The whole letter was first published in Rupert Hart-Davis's *The Letters of Oscar Wilde* (1962).

2 *A week later, I am transferred here*: Wilde originally wrote 'On the 13th of November'. After Wilde had been sentenced on 15 May 1895, he was taken to Pentonville, London; on 4 July he was transferred to Wandsworth. A week after his bankruptcy proceedings, on 20 November 1895, he was transferred again for health reasons to Reading.

honoured her. Her death was so terrible to me that I, once a lord of language, have no words in which to express my anguish and my shame. Never, even in the most perfect of days of my development as an artist, could I have had words fit to bear so august a burden, or to move with sufficient stateliness of music through the purple pageant of my incommunicable woe. She and my father had bequeathed me a name they had made noble and honoured not merely in Literature, Art, Archæology and Science, but in the public history of my own country in its evolution as a nation. I had disgraced that name eternally. I had made it a low byword among low people. I had dragged it through the very mire. I had given it to brutes that they might make it brutal, and to fools that they might turn it into a synonym for folly. What I suffered then, and still suffer, is not for pen to write or paper to record. My wife, at that time kind and gentle to me, rather than that I should hear the news from indifferent or alien lips, travelled, ill as she was, all the way from Genoa to England to break to me herself the tidings of so irreparable, so irredeemable, a loss. Messages of sympathy reached me from all who had still affection for me. Even people who had not known me personally, hearing what a new sorrow had come into my broken life, wrote to ask that some expression of their condolence should be conveyed to me. You alone stood aloof, sent me no message, and wrote me no letter. Of such actions, it is best to say what Virgil says to Dante of those whose lives have been barren in noble impulse and shallow of intention: 'Non ragioniam di lor, ma guarda, e passa.'[2]

Three months go over. The calendar of my daily conduct and labour that hangs on the outside of my cell-door, with my name and sentence written upon it, tells me that it is Maytime. My friends come to see me again. I enquire, as I always do, after you. I am told that you are in your villa at Naples, and are bringing out a volume of poems. At the close of the interview it is mentioned casually that you are dedicating them to me. The tidings seemed to give me a sort of nausea of life. I said nothing, but silently went back to my cell with contempt and scorn in my heart. How could you dream of dedicating a volume of poems to me without first asking my permission? Dream, do I say? How could you dare to do such a thing? Will you give as your answer that in the days of my greatness and fame I had consented to receive the dedication of your early work? Certainly, I did so; just as I would have accepted the homage of any other young man beginning the difficult and beautiful art of literature. All homage is delightful to an artist, and doubly sweet

---

1 *Non ragioniam di lor, ma guarda, e passa*: 'Let us not talk of them, but look thou, and pass by' (*Inferno*, iii, 51).

when youth brings it. Laurel and bay leaf wither when aged hands pluck them. Only youth has a right to crown an artist. That is the real privilege of being young, if youth only knew it. But the days of abasement and infamy are different from those of greatness and of fame. You have yet to learn that Prosperity, Pleasure and Success may be rough of grain and common in fibre, but Sorrow is the most sensitive of all created things. There is nothing that stirs in the whole world of thought to which Sorrow does not vibrate in terrible if exquisite pulsation. The thin beaten-out leaf of tremulous gold that chronicles the direction of forces that the eye cannot see is in comparison coarse. It is a wound that bleeds when any hand but that of Love touches it and even then must bleed again, though not for pain....

Where there is Sorrow there is holy ground. Some day you will realise what that means. They will know nothing of life till you do. Robbie[1] and natures like his can realise it. When I was brought down from my prison to the Court of Bankruptcy, between two policemen, Robbie waited in the long dreary corridor, that before the whole crowd, whom an action so sweet and simple hushed into silence, he might gravely raise his hat to me, as handcuffed and with bowed head, I passed him by. Men have gone to heaven for smaller things than that. It was in this spirit, and with this mode of love that the saints knelt down to wash the feet of the poor, or stooped to kiss the leper on the cheek. I have never said one single word to him about what he did. I do not know to the present moment whether he is aware that I was even conscious of his action. It is not a thing for which one can render formal thanks in formal words. I store it in the treasury-house of my heart. I keep it there as a secret debt that I am glad to think I can never possibly repay. It is embalmed and kept sweet by the myrrh and cassia of many tears. When Wisdom has been profitless to me, and Philosophy barren, and the proverbs and phrases of those who have sought to give me consolation as dust and ashes in my mouth, the memory of that little lowly silent act of Love has unsealed for me all the wells of pity, made the desert blossom like a rose, and brought me out of the bitterness of lonely exile into harmony with the wounded, broken, and great heart of the world. When people are able to understand, not merely how beautiful Robbie's action was, but why it meant so much to me, and always will mean so much, then, perhaps, you will realise how and in what spirit you should have approached me for permission to dedicate to me your verses.[2]

*   *   *

---

1 *Robbie*: Robert Ross, Wilde's faithful friend, who would become his literary executor.

2 *permission to dedicate to me your verses*: Lord Alfred Douglas' *Poems* appeared in 1896, without dedication.

Other miserable men, when they are thrown into prison, if they are robbed of the beauty of the world, are at least safe, in some measure, from the world's most deadly slings, most awful arrows. They can hide in the darkness of their cells, and of their very disgrace make a mode of sanctuary. The world, having had its will, goes its way, and they are left to suffer undisturbed. With me it has been different. Sorrow after sorrow has come beating at the prison door in search of me. They have opened the gates wide and let them in. Hardly, if at all, have my friends been suffered to see me. But my enemies have had full access to me always. Twice in my public appearances at the Bankruptcy Court, twice again in my transferences from one prison to another, have I been shown under conditions of unspeakable humiliation to the gaze and mockery of men. The messenger of Death has brought me tidings and gone his way, and in entire solitude, and isolated from all that could give me comfort, or suggest relief, I have had to bear the intolerable burden of misery and remorse that the memory of my mother placed upon me, and places on me still. Hardly has that wound been dulled, not healed, by time, when violent and bitter and harsh letters come to me from my wife through her solicitor. I am, at once, taunted and threatened with poverty. That I can bear. I can school myself to worse than that. But my two children are taken from me by legal procedure.[1] That is and always will remain to me a source of infinite distress, of infinite pain, of grief without end or limit. That the law should decide, and take upon itself to decide, that I am one unfit to be with my own children is something quite horrible to me. The disgrace of prison is as nothing compared to it. I envy the other men who tread the yard along with me. I am sure that their children wait for them, look for their coming, will be sweet to them.

The poor are wiser, more charitable, more kind, more sensitive than we are. In their eyes prison is a tragedy in a man's life, a misfortune, a casualty, something that calls for sympathy in others. They speak of one who is in prison as of one who is '*in trouble*' simply. It is the phrase they always use, and the expression has the perfect wisdom of Love in it. With people of our own rank it is different. With us prison makes a man a pariah. I, and such as I am, have hardly any right to air and sun. Our presence taints the pleasures of others. We

---

1 *my two children are taken from me by legal procedure*: Constance Wilde applied for custody and guardianship of their two children, Vyvyan (aged 10) and Cyril (aged 12), on 12 February 1897; the judge made her and her cousin by marriage, Adrian Hope, joint guardians. Wilde was not allowed to communicate with them without the guardians' permission.

are unwelcome when we reappear. To revisit the glimpses of the moon[1] is not for us. Our very children are taken away. Those lovely links with humanity are broken. We are doomed to be solitary, while our sons still live. We are denied the one thing that might heal us and help us, that might bring balm to the bruised heart, and peace to the soul in pain. ...

I must say to myself that neither you nor your father, multiplied a thousand times over, could possibly have ruined a man like me: that I ruined myself: and that nobody, great or small, can be ruined except by his own hand. I am quite ready to do so. I am trying to do so, though you may not think it at the present moment. If I have brought this pitiless indictment against you, think what an indictment I bring without pity against myself. Terrible as what you did to me was, what I did to myself was far more terrible still.

I was a man who stood in symbolic relations to the art and culture of my age. I had realised this for myself at the very dawn of my manhood, and had forced my age to realise it afterwards. Few men hold such a position in their own lifetime and have it so acknowledged. It is usually discerned, if discerned at all, by the historian, or the critic, long after both the man and his age have passed away. With me it was different. I felt it myself, and made others feel it. Byron[2] was a symbolic figure, but his relations were to the passion of his age and its weariness of passion. Mine were to something more noble, more permanent, of more vital issue, of larger scope.

The gods had given me almost everything. I had genius, a distinguished name, high social position, brilliancy, intellectual daring: I made art a philosophy, and philosophy an art: I altered the minds of men and the colours of things: there was nothing I said or did that did not make people wonder: I took the drama, the most objective form known to art, and made it as personal a mode of expression as the lyric or the sonnet, at the same time that I widened its range and enriched its characterisation: drama, novel, poem in rhyme, poem in prose, subtle or fantastic dialogue, whatever I touched, I made beautiful in a new mode of beauty: to truth itself I gave what is false no

---

1 *revisit the glimpses of the moon*: Hamlet I. iv. 51–6:
        ...What may this mean
    That thou, dead corse, again in complete steel
    Revisits thus the glimpses of the moon,
    Making night hideous; and we fools of nature
    So horridly to shake our disposition
    With thoughts beyond the reaches of our souls?
2 *Byron*: George Gordon, 6th Baron Byron (1788–1824), English poet; the symbol of Romanticism, the adjective 'Byronic' was first released in 1823.

less than what is true as its rightful province, and showed that the false and the true are merely forms of intellectual existence. I treated Art as the supreme reality, and life as a mere mode of fiction: I awoke the imagination of my century so that it created myth and legend around me: I summed up all systems in a phrase, and all existence in an epigram.

Along with these things, I had things that were different. I let myself be lured into long spells of senseless and sensual ease. I amused myself with being a *flâneur*, a dandy, a man of fashion. I surrounded myself with the smaller natures and the meaner minds. I became the spendthrift of my own genius, and to waste an eternal youth gave me a curious joy. Tired of being on the heights I deliberately went to the depths in the search for new sensations. What the paradox was to me in the sphere of thought, perversity became to me in the sphere of passion. Desire, at the end, was a malady, or a madness, or both. I grew careless of the lives of others. I took pleasure where it pleased me and passed on. I forgot that every little action of the common day makes or unmakes character, and that therefore what one has done in the secret chamber one has some day to cry aloud on the housetops. I ceased to be Lord over myself. I was no longer the Captain of my Soul, and did not know it. I allowed you to dominate me, and your father to frighten me. I ended in horrible disgrace. There is only one thing for me now, absolute Humility: just as there is only one thing for you, absolute Humility also. You had better come down into the dust and learn it beside me.

I have lain in prison for nearly two years. Out of my nature has come wild despair; an abandonment to grief that was piteous even to look at: terrible and impotent rage: bitterness and scorn: anguish that wept aloud: misery that could find no voice: sorrow that was dumb. I have passed through every possible mood of suffering. Better than Wordsworth himself I know what Wordsworth meant when he said—

> 'Suffering is permanent, obscure, and dark
> And has the nature of infinity.'[1]

But while there were times when I rejoiced in the idea that my sufferings were to be endless, I could not bear them to be without meaning. Now I find hidden away in my nature something that tells me that nothing in the whole world is meaningless, and suffering least of

---

1 The lines are spoken by Oswald in Wordsworth's play *The Borderers*, III.v.90–91, but Wilde quotes them as they appear in Wordsworth's 'The White Doe of Rylstone, or the Fate of the Nortons'.

all. That something hidden away in my nature, like a treasure in a field, is Humility.

It is the last thing left in me, and the best: the ultimate discovery at which I have arrived: the starting-point for a fresh development. It has come to me right out of myself, so I know that it has come at the proper time. It could not have come before, nor later. Had any one told me of it, I would have rejected it. Had it been brought to me, I would have refused it. As I found it, I want to keep it. I must do so. It is the one thing that has in it the elements of life, of a new life, a *Vita Nuova*[1] for me. Of all things it is the strangest. One cannot give it away, and another may not give it to one. One cannot acquire it, except by surrendering everything that one has. It is only when one has lost all things, that one knows that one possesses it.

Now that I realise that it is in me, I see quite clearly what I have got to do, what, in fact, I must do. And when I use such a phrase as that, I need not tell you that I am not alluding to any external sanction or command. I admit none. I am far more of an individualist than I ever was. Nothing seems to me of the smallest value except what one gets out of oneself. My nature is seeking a fresh mode of self-realisation. That is all I am concerned with. And the first thing that I have got to do is to free myself from any possible bitterness of feeling against you.

I am completely penniless, and absolutely homeless. Yet there are worse things in the world than that. I am quite candid when I tell you that rather than go out from this prison with bitterness in my heart against you or against the world I would gladly and readily beg my bread from door to door. If I got nothing from the house of the rich, I would get something at the house of the poor. Those who have much are often greedy. Those who have little always share. I would not a bit mind sleeping in the cool grass in summer, and when winter came on sheltering myself by the warm close-thatched rick, or under the penthouse of a great barn, provided I had love in my heart. The external things of life seem to me now of no importance at all. You can see to what intensity of individualism I have arrived, or am arriving rather, for the journey is long, and 'where I walk there are thorns.'[2]

Of course I know that to ask for alms on the highway is not to be my lot, and that if ever I lie in the cool grass at night-time it will be

---

1 Dante's collection of love poems to Beatrice, *La Vita Nuova* (1283–93).

2 *where I walk there are thorns*: 'For me the world is shrivelled to a palm's breath, and where I walk there are thorns' (Mrs Arbuthnot in *A Woman of No Importance*, Act IV).

to write sonnets to the Moon. When I go out of prison, Robbie will be waiting for me on the other side of the big iron-studded gate, and he is the symbol not merely of his own affection, but of the affection of many others besides. I believe I am to have enough to live on for about eighteen months at any rate, so that, if I may not write beautiful books, I may at least read beautiful books; and what joy can be greater? After that, I hope to be able to recreate my creative faculty. But were things different: had I not a friend left in the world: were there not a single house open to me in pity: had I to accept the wallet and ragged cloak of sheer penury: still as long as I remained free from all resentment, hardness, and scorn, I would be able to face life with much more calm and confidence than I would were my body in purple and fine linen, and the soul within it sick with hate. And I shall really have no difficulty in forgiving you. But to make it a pleasure for me you must feel that you want it. When you really want it you will find it waiting for you.

I need not say that my task does not end there. It would be comparatively easy if it did. There is much more before me. I have hills far steeper to climb, valleys much darker to pass through. And I have to get it all out of myself. Neither Religion, Morality, nor Reason can help me at all.

Morality does not help me. I am a born antinomian. I am one of those who are made for exceptions, not for laws. But while I see that there is nothing wrong in what one does, I see that there is something wrong in what one becomes. It is well to have learned that.

Religion does not help me. The faith that others give to what is unseen, I give to what one can touch, and look at. My Gods dwell in temples made with hands, and within the circle of actual experience is my creed made perfect and complete: too complete it may be, for like many or all of those who have placed their Heaven in this earth, I have found in it not merely the beauty of Heaven, but the horror of Hell also. When I think about Religion at all, I feel as if I would like to found an order for those who cannot believe: the Confraternity of the Fatherless one might call it, where on an altar, on which no taper burned, a priest, in whose heart peace had no dwelling, might celebrate with unblessed bread and a chalice empty of wine. Every thing to be true must become a religion. And agnosticism should have its ritual no less than faith. It has sown its martyrs, it should reap its saints, and praise God daily for having hidden Himself from man. But whether it be faith or agnosticism, it must be nothing external to me. Its symbols must be of my own creating.

Only that is spiritual which makes its own form. If I may not find its secret within myself, I shall never find it. If I have not got it already, it will never come to me.

Reason does not help me. It tells me that the laws under which I am convicted are wrong and unjust laws, and the system under which I have suffered a wrong and unjust system. But, somehow, I have got to make both of these things just and right to me. And exactly as in Art one is only concerned with what a particular thing is at a particular moment to oneself, so it is also in the ethical evolution of one's character. I have got to make everything that has happened to me good for me. The plank-bed, the loathsome food, the hard ropes shredded into oakum till one's finger-tips grow dull with pain,[1] the menial offices with which each day begins and finishes, the harsh orders that routine seems to necessitate, the dreadful dress that makes sorrow grotesque to look at, the silence, the solitude, the shame— each and all of these things I have to transform into a spiritual experience. There is not a single degradation of the body which I must not try and make into a spiritualising of the soul.

I want to get to the point when I shall be able to say, quite simply and without affectation, that the two great turning-points in my life were when my father sent me to Oxford, and when society sent me to prison. I will not say that prison is the best thing that could have happened to me, for that phrase would savour of too great bitterness towards myself. I would sooner say, or hear it said of me, that I was so typical a child of my age, that in my perversity, and for that perversity's sake, I turned the good things of my life to evil, and the evil things of my life to good. What is said, however, by myself or by others matters little. The important thing, the thing that lies before me, the thing that I have to do, or be, for the brief remainder of my days are maimed, marred, and incomplete, is to absorb into my nature all that has been done to me, to make it part of me, to accept it without complaint, fear, or reluctance. The supreme vice is shallowness. Whatever is realised is right. . . .

---

1 *the hard ropes shredded into oakum*...: At Pentonville Prison, Wilde had to pick oakum.

PERCY FRENCH (1854–1920)

Born in Cloonyquin, Co. Roscommon, the second son of Christopher French, L.D., J.P., he was educated at Kirk Langley (Derbyshire), Windermere College, Foyle College, and Trinity College, Dublin, where he took a BA in 1876 and a BE in 1880. While a student he wrote 'Abdallah Bulbul Ameer', selling the rights for £5; it became a music-hall hit. In 1883 he joined the Board of Works as a surveyor in Cavan, and styled himself an 'Inspector of Drains'; in the meantime he painted watercolours and wrote songs. He was made redundant in 1887, and became editor of the comic weekly journal *The Jarvey*. It folded within two years, and French wrote the librettos for two comic operas, the music being provided by W. Houston Collinson. In 1891 his wife Ettie died in childbirth, their baby daughter dying a few days later. Three years later he married Helen Sheldon; they had three daughters. They moved to London in 1900. French produced a popular revue show called 'Dublin Up to Date'. With Collinson he toured North America and the West Indies to great acclaim, and he continued to tour Ireland every year. During the First World War he gave charity performances in England and on the Continent. Many of his songs, such as 'Are Ye Right There, Michael', 'The Mountains of Mourne' and 'Come Back, Paddy Reilly', have retained their popularity.

Abdallah Bulbul Ameer

(1877)[1]

I.

Oh, the sons of the Prophet are hardy and grim,
    And quite unaccustom'd to fear;
But none were so reckless of life or of limb
    As Abdallah Bulbul Ameer.[2]
When they wanted a man to encourage the van,

---

1 Percy French wrote about the publication of this lyric: 'My only contribution to contemporary literature during my college career was a ballad called *Abdallah Bulbul Ameer*. It described a duel between a Turk and a Russian during the Russo-Turkish War, and became so popular at college smokers that I determined to publish it. To borrow a fiver from Archie West, the only man of means in my class, was the work of a moment, and when Messrs Cramer and Co. handed me 200 copies to be disposed of at 1s. 6d. a copy, Eldorado seemed round the corner. But alas! We had forgotten to take out the copyright, and a London firm, finding out our mistake, brought out a pirated edition without even my name on the cover! As they had taken care to copyright *their* version, I was tricked out of all rights to my song, though words and music were both mine.'
    The poem refers light-heartedly to the Russo-Turkish War (1877–78). Following the unrest in the Turkish dominions in the Balkan, the cruel repression of two Bulgarian risings, and the Ottoman victory in the Turco-Serbian war, Russia declared war on Turkey on 24 April, avowedly to come to the aid of Christians in Turkey.

2 *Abdallah Bulbul Ameer*: Sultan Abd-Ul-Hamir II (1842–1918) succeeded to the Ottoman throne on 31 August 1876. French calls him 'Bulbul' (nightingale of the East) because the sultan was a translator and composer of opera.

Or to harass the foe in the rear,
    Or to take a redoubt, they would always send out
For Abdallah Bulbul Ameer.

II.

There are heroes in plenty and well known to fame
    In the army that's led by the Czar
But none were so brave as a man by the name
    Of Ivan Potschjinski Skidar.
He could imitate Toole,[1] play euchre[2] and pool
    And perform on the Spanish guitar.
In fact quite the cream of the Muscovite team
    Was Ivan Potschjinksi Skidar.

III.

One morning the Russian had shouldered his gun
    And assumed his most truculent sneer,
And was walking down town when he happened to run
    Into Abdallah Bulbul Ameer.
'Young man,' says Bulbul, 'Can your life be so dull
    That you're anxious to end your career?
For, infidel, know you have trod on the toe
    Of Abdallah Bulbul Ameer.'

IV.

'Take your ultimate look upon sunshine and brook
    Make your latest remarks on the war;
Which I mean to imply that you're going to die
    Mr. Count Caskowhisky Cigar.'
Said the Russian, 'My friend your remarks in the end
    Would only be wasted I fear,
For you'll never survive to repeat them alive
    Mr. Abdallah Bulbul Ameer.'

V.

Then the bold Mameluke drew his trusty chibouque,[3]
    And shouted 'Il Allah Ackbar'
And being intent upon slaughter he went

---

1 *Toole*: John Lawrence Toole (1832–1906), popular English comic actor.
2 *euchre*: a nineteenth-century American card game.
3 *chibouque*: long Turkish tobacco-pipe.

For Ivan Potschjinki Skidar.
But just as his knife had abstracted his life,
    In fact he was shouting 'Huzza',
When he found he was struck by that subtle Calmuck
    Young Ivan Potschjinksi Skidar.

VI.

The Consul drove up in red crescent fly
    To give the survivor a cheer,
He arrived just in time to exchange a goodbye
    With Abdallah Bulbul Ameer.
And Skobeleff, Gourko and Gortschakoff too[1]
    Drove up in the Emperor's car
But all they could do was cry 'Och-whilliloo'
    For Ivan Potschjinksi Skidar.

VII.

There's a grave where the waves of the blue Danube roll,[2]
    And on it in characters clear
Is 'Stranger, remember to pray for the soul
    Of Abdallah Bulbul Ameer.'
And a Muscovite maiden her vigil doth keep
    By the light of the true lover's star
And the name that she murmurs so oft in her sleep
    Is Ivan Potschjinksi Skidar.

Phil the Fluther's Ball

(1889)

Have you heard of Phil the Fluther, of the town of Ballymuck?
The times were going hard with him, in fact the man was bruk,
So he just sent out a notice to his neighbours, one and all,
As how he'd like their company that ev'nin' at a ball.
And when writin' out, he was careful to suggest to them,
That if they found a hat of his convaniant to the dure,
The more they put in, whenever he requested them,
'The better would the music be for battherin' the flure.'

---

1 *Skobeleleff, Gourko and Gortschakoff too*: Mikael Skobelev (1841–82) and Count Joseph Vladimirovich Gourko (1828–1901) were, respectively, a prominent Russian general and a Field Marshal in the Russo-Turkish War; Prince Aleksandr Mikhailovich Gorchakov (1798–1883), Russian statesman, was chancellor of the Russian empire (1863–82).
2 *blue Danube roll*: the Danube formed the Turkish frontier.

CHORUS.

With the foot of the flute,
And the twiddle of the fiddle, O
Hoppin' in the middle, like a herrin' on a griddle O—
Up, down, hand a-rown'
Crossin' to the wall
Oh—hadn't we the gaiety at Phil the Fluther's Ball!

There was Mishter Denis Dogherty, who kep' 'The Runnin' Dog';
There was little crooked Paddy, from the Tiraloughett bog;
There were boys from every Barony, and girls from ev'ry 'art,'
And the beautiful Miss Bradys, in a private ass an' cart,
And along with them came bouncin' Mrs Cafferty,
Little Micky Mulligan was also to the fore,
Rose, Suzanne, and Margaret O'Rafferty,
The flower of Ardragullian, and the pride of Pethravore.

CHORUS.

First, litte Micky Mulligan get up to show them how,
And then the Widda' Cafferty steps out and makes her bow.
'I could dance you off your feet,' sez she, 'as sure as you are born,
If ye'll only make the piper play "the hare was in the corn".'
So Phil plays up to the best of his ability,
The lady and the gentleman begin to do their share;
'Faith then, Mick, it's you that has agility!'
'Begorra! Mrs Cafferty, yer leppin' like a hare!'

CHORUS.

Then Phil the Fluther tipped a wink to little crooked Pat,
'I think it's nearly time,' sez he, 'for passin' round the hat.'
So Paddy passed the caubeen round, and looking mighty cute
Sez, 'Ye've got to pay the piper when he toothers on the flute.'
Then all joined in wid the greatest joviality,
Coverin' the buckle, and the shuffle, and the cut;
Jigs were danced, of the very finest quality,
But the Widda' bet the company at 'handeling the fut'.

CHORUS.

Shlathery's Mounted Fut

(1889)

You've heard o' Julius Cæsar, an' the great Napoleon, too,
An' how the Cork Militia beat the Turks at Waterloo;
But there's a page of glory that, as yet, remains uncut,
An' that's the Martial story o' the Shlathery's Mounted Fut.
This gallant corps was organized by Shlathery's eldest son.
A noble-minded poacher, wid a double-breasted gun;
An' many a head was broken, aye, an' many an eye was shut,
When practisin' manœuvres in the Shlathery's Mounted Fut.

CHORUS.

An' down the mountains came the squadrons an' platoons,
Four-an'-twinty fightin' min, an' a couple o' sthout gossoons,
An' whin we marched behind the dhrum to patriotic tunes,
We felt that fame would gild the name o' Shlathery's Light Dragoons.

Well, first we reconnoithered round o' O'Sullivan's Shebeen—
It used to be 'The Shop House,' but we call it, 'The Canteen;'
But there we saw a notice which the bravest heart unnerved—
'All liquor must be settled for before the dhrink is served.'
So on we marched, but soon again each warrior's heart grew pale,
For risin' high in front o' us we saw the County Jail;
An' whin the army faced about, 'twas just in time to find
A couple o' policemin had surrounded us behind.

CHORUS.

Still from the mountains came the squadrons an' platoons,
Four-an'-twinty fightin' min, an' a couple o' sthout gossoons,
Says Shlathery, 'We must circumvent these bludgeonin' bosthoons,
Or else it sames they'll take the names o' Shlathery's Light Dragoons.

'We'll cross the ditch,' our leader cried, 'an' take the foe in flank,'
But yells of consthernation here arose from every rank,
For posted high upon a tree we very plainly saw,
'Threspassers prosecuted, in accordance wid' the law.'
'We're foiled!' exclaimed bowld Shlathery, 'here ends our grand campaign,
'Tis merely throwin' life away to face that mearin' dhrain,
I'm not as bold as lions, but I'm braver nor a hin,
An' he that fights and runs away wil live to fight agin.'

CHORUS.
An' back to the mountains came the squadrons an' platoons,
Four-an'-twinty fightin' men, an' a couple o' sthout gossoons,
The band was playing cautiously their patriotic tunes,
To sing the fame, if rather lame, o' Shlathery's Light Dragoons.

From *The First Lord Liftinant and Other Tales*

(1890)

The First Lord Liftinant
AN HISTORICAL SKETCH
As Related by Andrew Geraghty (Philomath.)

'Essex,'[1] said Queen Elizabeth, as the two of them sat at breakwhist in the back parlour of Buckingham Palace, 'Essex, me haro, I've got a job that I think would suit you. Do you know where Ireland is?'

'I'm no great fist at jografy,' says his Lordship, 'but I know the place you mane. Population, three million; exports, emigrants.'

'Well,' says the Queen, 'I've been reading the Dublin *Evening Mail* and the *Telegraft* for some time back, and sorra one o' me can get at the trooth o' how things is goin', for the leadin' articles is as contradictory as if they wor husband and wife.'

'That's the way wid papers all the world over,' says Essex. 'Columbus told me it was the same in Amirikay when he was there, abusin' and contradictin' each other at every turn—it's the way they make their livin'. Thrubble you for an egg spoon.'

'It's addled they have me betune them,' says the Queen. 'Not a know I know what's goin' on. So now what I want you to do is to run over to Ireland, like a good fella, and bring me word how matters stand.'

'Is it me?' says Essex, leppin' up off his chair. 'It's not in airnest ye are, ould lady. Sure it's the hoight of the London season. Every one's

---

1 *Essex*: Robert Devereux, 2nd Earl of Essex (1567–1601), the hot-headed favourite of Queen Elizabeth. After Hugh O'Neill's victory at the Yellow Ford, Essex was appointed lord lieutenant and governor-general of Ireland, heading a force of sixteen thousand foot and thirteen hundred horse. He arrived in Dublin on 15 April, after a rough passage. Essex made incursions into Munster, contrary to the official plan of campaign, and was ordered to oppose O'Neill in the north. He met O'Neill secretly at the ford of Bellaclinthe, and arranged a ceasefire, which Elizabeth dismissed as 'full of scandal to our realm and future peril to the state'. Abandoning his command, he threw himself, mud-bespattered, at the Queen's feet at Nonsuch, but was placed under house arrest. Among the charges levelled at him by the Council, next day, were his disobedience in deserting his post, his writing presumptuous letters to the Queen, and his intrusion into her bedchamber. Following his half-hearted attempt at a rising he was executed on 25 February 1601. He was indeed renowned for his dalliances.

in town, and Shake's new fairy piece, 'The Midsummer's Night Mare' billed for next week.'

'You'll go when yer told,' says the Queen, fixin' him with her eye. 'If you know which side yer bread's buttered on. See here, now,' says she, seein' him chokin' wid vexation and a slice of corned beef, 'you ought to be as pleased as Punch about it, for you'll be at the top of the walk over there as vice-regent representin' me.'

'I ought to have a title or two,' says Essex, pluckin' up a bit. 'His Gloriosity the Great Panjandhrum, or the like o' that.'

'How would "His Excellency the Lord Liftinant of Ireland" strike you?' says Elizabeth.

'First class,' cries Essex. 'Couldn't be betther; it doesn't mean much, but it's allitherative, and will look well below the number on me hall door.'

Well, boys, it didn't take him long to pack his clothes and start away for the Island o' Saints. It took him a good while to get there, though, through not knowing the road; but by means of a pocket compass and a tip to the steward, he was landed at last contagious to Dalkey Island.

Going up to an ould man who was sitting on a rock he took off his hat, and says he:

'That's great weather we're havin'?'

'Good enough for the times that's in it,' says the ould man, cockin' one eye at him.

'Any divarshan goin' on?' says Essex.

'You're a stranger in these part, I'm thinking,' says the ould man, 'or you'd know this was a "band night" in Dalkey.'

'I wasn't aware of it,' says Essex. 'The fact is,' says he, 'I only landed from England just this minute.'

'Aye,' says the ould man bitterly,' it's little they know about us over there. I'll howld you,' says he with a slight thrimble in his voice, 'that the Queen herself doesn't know there is to be fireworks in the Sorrento Gardins[1] this night.'

Well, when Essex heard that, he disremembered entirely he was sent over to Ireland to put down rows and ructions, and haway wid him to see the fun and flirt with all the pretty girls he could find.

And he found plenty of them—thick as bees they were, and each one as beautiful as the day and the morra.

---

1 *Sorrento Gardins*: fashionable area in Dalkey.

He wrote two letters home next day—one to Queen Elizabeth and the other to Lord Montaigle,[1] a play-boy like himself.

I'll read you the one to the Queen first:—

Dame Sthreet,
April 16, 1599.

FAIR ENCHANTRESS,—

I wish I was back in London, baskin' in your sweet smiles and listenin' to your melodious voice once more. I got the consignment of men and the post-office order all right. I was out all the mornin' looking for the inimy, but sor a taste of Hugh O'Neil or his men can I find.[2] A policeman at the corner of Nassau Street told me they were hiding in Wicklow. So I am making up a party to explore the Dargle[3] on Easter Monda'. The girls here are as ugly as sin, and every minute of the day I do be wishing it was your good-lookin' self I was gazin' at instead of these ignorant scare-crows.

Hoppin' soon to be back in ould England, I remain, your lovin' subjec',

ESSEX.

P.S.—I hear Hugh O'Neil was seen on the top of the Donnybrook tram yesterday mornin'. If I have any luck the head'll be off him before you get this.

E.

The other letter read this way—

DEAR MONTY.—This is a great place all out. Come over here if you want fun. Divil such play-boys ever I seen, and the girls—oh, don't be talkin'—'pon me secret honour you'll see more loveliness at a tay and supper ball in Ra'mines than there is in the whole of England. Tell Ned Spencer[4] to send me a love-song to sing to a young girl who

---

1 *Lord Montaigle*: William Parker, 14th Baron Monteagle (1575–1622) joined the Earl of Essex in Ireland in 1599, where he was knighted the following year. He took part in Essex's failed rebellion, was imprisoned in the Tower, and released on paying a substantial fine.

2 *Hugh O'Neil or his men…*: Hugh O'Neill (c. 1550–1616), 2nd Earl of Tyrone, rose against the English Government in 1594. His victory over the English at the battle of the Yellow Ford in August 1598 urged Elizabeth to crush the rebellion. He was defeated at the battle of Kinsale in 1601, and surrendered at Mellifont in 1603, gaining a pardon and retaining control of his title, six days after Elizabeth had died. O'Neill fled to the Continent in 1607, and received asylum in Rome, where he died. The 'Flight of the Earls' marked the end of the old order.

3 The River Dargle rises in the Wicklow mountains, and flows east for twelve miles to enter the Irish Sea at Bray.

4 *Ned Spencer*: Edmund Spenser (?1552–99), English poet, who accompanied Lord Grey, Viceroy of Ireland, to Dublin. He stayed on in Ireland, where he wrote *The Fairy Queene* (1590–96).

seems taken with my appearance. Her name's Mary, and she lives in Dunlary, so he oughtent to find it hard.

I hear Hugh O'Neil's a terror, and hits a powerful welt, especially when you're not lookin'. If he tries any of his games on wid me, I'll give him in charge. No brawling for yours truly,

ESSEX.

Well, me bould Essex stopped for odds of six months, in Dublin, purtendin' to be very busy subjugatin' the country, but all the time only losin' his time and money without doin' a hand's turn, and doin' his best to avoid a ruction with 'Fighting Hugh.'

If a messenger came in to tell him that O'Neill was campin' out on the North Bull, Essex would up stick and away for Sandycove, where, after draggin' the forty-foot hole,[1] he'd write off to Elizabeth, sayin' that 'owing to their suparior knowledge of the country, the dastard foe had once more eluded him.'

The Queen got mighty tired of these letters, especially as they always ended with a request to send stamps by return, and told Essex to finish up his business, and not be makin' a fool of himself.

'Oh, that's the talk, is it', says Essex. 'Very well, me ould sauce-box' (that was the name he had for her ever since she gev him the clip on the ear for turnin' his back on her).[2] 'Very well, me ould sauce-box,' says he, 'I'll write off to O'Neil this very minit, and tell him to send in his lowest terms for peace at ruling prices.' Well, the treaty was a bit of a one-sided one.

The terms proposed were:—

1. Hugh O'Neil to be King of Great Britain.
2. Lord Essex to return to London and remain there as Viceroy of England.
3. The O'Neil family to be supported by Government, with free passes to all theatres and places of entertainment.
4. The London markets to buy only from Irish dealers.
5. All taxes to be sent in stamped envelope, directed to H. O'Neil, and marked 'private.'

Cheques crossed and made payable to H. O'Neil. Terms cash.

---

1 *the forty-foot hole*: Named after the 40th Regiment of Foot, which was stationed in a tower above it, the Forty Foot in Sandycove was a men-only swimming hole, where nude bathing was the rule. The Martello Tower and the bathing place are the scene of the Telemachus episode of Joyce's *Ulysses*.

2 *she gev him the clip on the ear*...: in a dispute in July 1598 over the appointment of a lord deputy for Ireland, Essex turned his back on the queen. Elizabeth struck him a blow on the ear and told him to go and be hanged. Neither side ever fully forgot the quarrel.

Well, if Essex had had the sinse to read through this treaty, he'd have seen it was of too graspin' a nature to pass with any sort of a respectable sovereign, but he was that mad he just stuck the document in the pocket of his pot-metal overcoat, and haway wid him hot foot for England.

'Is the Queen within?' says he to the butler, when he opened the door of the Palace.

He's clothes was that dirty and disorthered wid travellin' all night, and his boots that muddy, that the butler was for not littin' him in at the first go off, so says he very grand:

'Her Meejisty is abow stairs and can't be seen till she'd had her brekwish,'

'Tell her the Lord Liftinant of Oirland desires an enterview,' says Essex.

'Oh, beg parden, me lord,' says the butler, steppin' to one side. 'I didn't know 'twas yourself was in it; come inside, sir; the Queen's in the dhrawin' room.'

Well, Essex leps up the stairs and into the dhrawin' room wid him, muddy boots and all; but not a sight of Elizabeth was to be seen.

'Where's your Missus?' says he to one of the maids of honour that was dustin' the chimbley piece.

'She's not out of her bed yet,' says the maid with a toss of her head; 'but if you write your message on the slate beyant, I'll see'—but before she had finished, Essex was up the second flight and knockin' at the Queen's bed-room door.

'Is that the hot wather?' says the Queen.

'No; it's me—Essex. Can you see me?'

'Faith I can't,' says the Queen. 'Howld on till I draw the bed curtains. Come in now,' says she, 'and say your say, for I can't have you stoppin' long—you young Lutharian.'[1]

'Bedad, yer Majesty,' says Essex, droppin' on his knees before her (the delutherer he was) 'small blame to me if I am a Lutharian, for you have a face on you that would charum a bird off a bush.'

'Hold your tongue, you young reprobate,' says the Queen, blushing up to her curl papers wid delight, 'and tell me what improvements you med in Ireland.'

'Faith, I taught manners to O'Neil,' cries Essex.

'He had a bad masther, then,' says Elizabeth, looking at his dirty boots; 'couldn't you wipe yer feet before ye desthroyed me carpets, young man?'

'Oh, now,' says Essex, 'is is wastin' me time shufflin' about on a

1 *young Lutharian*: after 'gay Lothario'—a libertine or rake.

mat you'd have me, when I might be gazin' on the loveliest faymale the world ever saw.'

'Well,' says the Queen, 'I'll forgive you this time as you've been so long away, but remimber in future that Kidderminster isn't oilcolth. Tell me,' says she, 'is Westland Row Station finished yet?'[1]

'There's a side wall or two wanted yet, I believe,' says Essex.

'What about the Loop Line?' says she.

'Oh, they're gettin' on with that,' says he, 'only some people think the girders is a disfigurement to the city.'

'Is there any talk about that esplanade from Sandycove to Dunlary?'[2]

'There's talk about it, but that's all,' says Essex, ''twould be an odious fine improvement to house property, and I hope they'll see to it soon.'

'Sorra much you seem to have done, beyant spending me men and me money. Let's have a look at that threaty I see stickin' out of your pocket.'

Well, when the Queen read the terms of Hugh O'Neil, she just gave him one look, and jumping from off the bed, put her head out of the window, and called out to the policeman on duty—'Is the Head below?'

'I'll tell him you want him, ma'am,' says the policeman.

'Do,' says the Queen.

'Hello,' says she, as a slip of paper dropped out of the dispatches.' What's this? "Lines to Mary?" Ho! ho! me gay fella, that's what you've been up to, is it?'

> Mrs. Brady's
> A widow lady,
> And she has a charming daughter I adore;
> I went to court her
> Across the water,
> And her mother keeps a little candy store.
> She's such a darlin',
> She's like a starlin,'
> And in love with her I'm getting more and more.
> Her name is Mary,
> She's from Dunlary;
> And her mother keeps a little candy store.

---

1 *Is Westland Row...*: Westland Row Station was linked with Connolly Station in 1891.
2 *that esplanade...*:the esplanade was first proposed in 1863, but it was not built until 1922.

'That settles it,' says the Queen. 'It's the gaoler you'll serenade next.'

When Essex heard that, he trhimbled so much that the button of his cuirass shook off and rowled under the dressin' table.

'Arrest that man!' says the Queen, when the Head-Constable came to the door. 'Arrest that thrater,' says she, 'and never let me set eyes on him again.'

And indeed she never did, for soon after that he met with his death from the skelp of an axe he got when he was standin' on Tower Hill.

SARAH GRAND (1854–1943)

Frances Elizabeth Clarke was born at Donaghadee, Co. Down, of English parents. After her father's death, in 1861, the family moved to Yorkshire. She was educated at home and was sent to a boarding school at 14. At 16 she married David MacFall, an army surgeon, who was twenty-three years her senior. It was not a happy marriage; after the financial success of her first novel, *Ideala: A Study from Life* (1888), she went to live in London, leaving her husband and their son, and becoming an influential 'New Woman' writer. She was active in the Women's Writers' Suffrage League, the Women's Suffrage Society and the National Council of Women. She moved to Bath in 1920, and became the city's mayoress for six years. *Ideala*, narrated by a male friend of the eponymous heroine, challenges the goals of women in Victorian society. It was the first of a controversial trilogy which exposed the oppression of women in male-dominated Victorian society. *The Heavenly Twins* (1893) presents an intricate web of tales dealing with the difficulties of self-development for women in a society where female education is grossly inadequate, and where marital abuse is rife. It contrasts the opportunities for Theodore (Diavolo) with the want of them for his twin sister Angelica, and it presents the plight of Evadne, self-educated by necessity, who is deluded into marrying Major Colquohon, a syphilitic brute ('a very fine, manly fellow', according to her father). *The Beth Book: A Study in the Life of a Woman of Genius* (1897), the third in the trilogy, is largely autobiographical. The heroine emerges from a Victorian upbringing in a violent Ulster household, and from an unhappy marriage to a domineering doctor, with a resolution not to serve—she finds a room in which to write 'for women, not for men'. Among her later novels, *Adnam's Orchard* (1912) and *Winged Victory* (1916) deal with the problems of land reform.

From *The Heavenly Twins*

(1893)

BOOK I

Childhoods and Girlhoods

On the third day after Evadne's wedding, in the afternoon, Mrs. Orton Beg was sitting alone in her long, low drawing room by the window which looked out into the high-walled garden. She had found it difficult to occupy herself with books and work that day. Her sprained ankle had been troublesome during the night, and she had risen late, and when her maid had helped her to dress, and she had limped downstairs on her crutches, and settled herself in her long chair, she found herself disinclined for any further exertion, and just sat, reclining upon pale pink satin cushions, her slender hands folded upon her lap, her large, dark luminous eyes and delicate, refined features all set in a wistful sadness.

There was a singular likeness between herself and Evadne in some things, a vague, haunting family likeness which continually obtruded itself but could not be defined. It had been more distinct when Evadne was a child, and would doubtless have grown greater had she lived with her aunt, but the very different mental attitude which she gradually acquired had melted the resemblance, as it were, so that at nineteen, although her slender figure, and air, and carriage continually recalled Mrs. Orton Beg, who was then in her thirty-fifth year, the expression of her face was so different that they were really less alike than they had been when Evadne was four years younger. Evadne's disposition, it must be remembered, was essentially swift to act. She would, as a human being, have her periods of strong feeling, but that was merely a physical condition in no way affecting her character; and the only healthy minded happy state for her was the one in which thought instantly translated itself into action.

With Mrs. Orton Beg it was different. Her spiritual nature predominated, her habits of mind were dreamy. She lived for the life to come entirely, and held herself in constant communion with another world. She felt it near her, she said. She believed that its inhabitants visit the earth, and take cognizance of all we do and suffer; and she cherished the certainty of one day assuming a wondrous form, and entering upon a new life, as vivid and varied and as real as this, but far more perfect. Her friends were chiefly of her own way of thinking; but her faith was so profound, and the charm of her conversation so entrancing, that the hardest headed materialists were apt to feel strange delicious thrills in her presence, forebodings of possibilities beyond the test of reason and knowledge; and they would return time after time to dispute her conclusions and argue themselves out of the impression she had produced, but only to relapse into their former state of blissful sensation so soon as they once more found themselves within range of her influence. Opinions are germs in the moral atmosphere which fasten themselves upon us if we are predisposed to entertain them; but some states of feeling are a perfume which every sentient being must perceive with emotions that vary from extreme repugnance to positive pleasure through diverse intermediate strata of lively interest or mere passive perception; and the feeling which emanated from Mrs. Orton Beg is one that is especially contagious. For, in the first place, the beauty of goodness appeals pleasurably to the most depraved; to be elevated above themselves for a moment is a rare delight to them; and, in the second, there is a deeply implanted leaning in the heart of man toward the something beyond everything, the impalpable, impossible, imperceptible, which he cannot know and will not credit, but is nevertheless compelled to feel in some of his moods, or in certain presences, and having once felt, finds himself fascinated by it, and so returns to the subject for the sake of the sensation. In that long, low drawing room of Mrs. Orton Beg's, with the window at either end, in view of the gray old cathedral towering above the gnarled elms of the Lower Close, itself the scene of every form of human endeavour, every expression of human passion, in surroundings so heavy with memories of the past, and listening to the quiet tone of conviction in which Mrs. Orton Beg spoke, with the double charm of extreme polish and simplicity combined—in that same room even the worldliest had found themselves rise into the ecstasy of the higher life, spiritually freed for the moment, and with the desire to go forth and do great deeds of love.

Mrs. Orton Beg had sat idle an hour looking out of the window, her mind in the mood for music, but bare of thought.

A gale was blowing without. The old elms in the Close were tossing their stiff, bare arms about, the ground was strewed with branches and leaves from the limes, and a watery wintry sun made the misery of the muddy ground apparent, and accentuated the blight of the flowers and torn untidiness of the creepers, and all the items which make autumn gardens so desolate. The equinoctial gales had set in early that year. They began on Evadne's wedding day with a fearful storm which raged all over the country, and burst with especial violence upon Morningquest, and the wind continued high, and showed no sign of abating. It was depressing weather, and Mrs. Orton Beg sighed more than once unconsciously.

* * *

When her friends had gone that day Mrs. Orton Beg sat long in the gathering dusk, watching the newly lighted fire burn up, and thinking. She was thinking of Evadne chiefly, wondering why she had had no news of her, why her sister Elizabeth did not write, and tell her all about the wedding; and she was just on the verge of anxiety—in that state when various possibilities of trouble that might have occurred to account for delays begin to present themselves to the mind, when all at once, without hearing anything, she became conscious of a presence near her, and looking up she was startled to see Evadne herself.

'My dear child!' she gasped, 'what has happened? Why are you here?'

'Nothing has happened, auntie; don't be alarmed,' Evadne answered. 'I am here because I have been a fool.'

She spoke quietly but with concentrated bitterness, then sat down and began to take off her gloves with that exaggerated show of composure which is a sign in some people of suppressed emotion.

Her face was pale, but her eyes were bright, and the pupils were dilated.

'I have come to claim your hospitality, auntie,' she pursued, 'to ask you for shelter from the world for a few days, *because* I have been a fool. May I stay?'

'Surely, dear child,' Mrs. Orton Beg replied, and then she waited, mastering the nervous tremor into which the shock of Evadne's sudden appearance had thrown her with admirable self-control. And here again the family likeness between aunt and niece was curiously apparent. Both masked their agitation because both by temperament were shy, and ashamed to show strong feeling.

Evadne looked into the fire for a little, trying to collect herself. 'I knew what was right,' she began at last in a low voice, 'I knew we should take nothing for granted, we should never be content merely to feel and suppose and hope for the best in matters about which we should know exactly. And yet I took no trouble to ascertain. I fell in love, and liked the sensation, and gave myself up to it unreservedly. Certainly, I was a fool—there is no other word for it.'

'But are you married, Evadne?' Mrs. Orton Beg asked in a voice rendered unnatural by the rapid beating of her heart.

'Let me tell you, auntie, all about it,' Evadne answered hoarsely. She drew her chair a little closer to the fire, and spread her hands out to the blaze. There was no other light in the room by this time. The wind without howled dismally still, but at intervals, as if with an effort. During one of its noisiest bursts the cathedral clock began to strike, and hushed it, as it were, suddenly. It seemed to be listening, to be waiting, and Evadne waited and listened too, raising her head....

When the last reverberation of the last note had melted out of hearing, Evadne sighed; then she straightened herself, as if collecting her energy, and began to speak.

'Yes, I am married,' she said, 'but when I went to change my dress after the ceremony I found this letter. It was intended, you see, to reach me some days before it did, but unfortunately it was addressed to Fraylingay, and time was lost in forwarding it.' She handed it to her aunt, who raised her eyebrows when she saw the writing, as if she recognized it, hastily drew the letter from its envelope, and held it so that the blaze fell upon it while she read. Evadne knelt on the hearthrug, and stirred the fire, making it burn up brightly.

Mrs. Orton Beg returned the letter to the envelope when she had read it. 'What did you do?' she said.

'I read it before I went downstairs, and at first I could not think what to do, so we drove off together, but on the way to the station it suddenly flashed upon me that the proper thing to do would be to go at once and hear all that there was to tell, and fortunately Major Colquhoun gave me an opportunity of getting away without any dispute. He went to see about something, leaving me in the carriage, and I just got out, walked round the station, took a hansom, and drove off to the General Post Office to telegraph to my people.'

'But why didn't you go home?'

'For several reasons,' Evadne answered, 'the best being that I never thought of going home. I wanted to be alone and think. I fancied that at home they either could not or would not tell me anything of Major Colquhoun's past life, and I was determined to know the truth exactly. And I can't tell you how many sayings of my father's recurred to me all at once with a new significance, and made me fear that there was some difference between his point of view and mine on the subject of a suitable husband. He told me himself that Major Colquhoun had been quite frank about his past career, and then, when I came to think, it appeared to me clearly that it was the frankness which had satisfied my father; the career itself was nothing. You heard how pleased they were about my engagement?'

'Yes,' Mrs. Orton Beg answered slowly, 'and I confess I was a little surprised when I heard from your mother that your *fiancé* had been "wild" in his youth, for I remembered some remarks you made last year about the kind of man you would object to marry, and it seemed to me from the description that Major Colquhoun was very much that kind of man.'

'Then why didn't you warn me?' Evadne exclaimed.

'I don't know whether I quite thought it was a subject for warning,' Mrs. Orton Beg answered, 'and at any rate, girls *do* talk in that way sometimes, not really meaning it. I thought it was mere *youngness* on our part, and theory; and I don't know now whether I quite approve of your having been told—of this new departure,' she added, indicating the letter.

'*I* do,' said Evadne decidedly. 'I would stop the imposition, approved of custom, connived at by parents, made possible by the state of ignorance in which we are carefully kept—the imposition upon a girl's innocence and inexperience of a disreputable man for a husband.'

Mrs. Orton Beg was startled by this bold assertion, which was so unprecedented in her experience that for a moment she could not utter a word; and when she did speak she avoided a direct reply, because she thought any discussion on the subject of marriage, except from the sentimental point of view, was indelicate.

'But tell me your position exactly,' she begged—'what you did next: why you are here!'

'I went by the night mail North,' Evadne answered, 'and saw them. They were very kind. They told me everything. I can't repeat the details; they disgust me.'

'No, pray don't!' Mrs. Orton Beg exclaimed hastily. She had no mind for anything unsavoury.

'They had been abroad, you know,' Evadne pursued; 'Otherwise I should have heard from them as soon as the engagement was announced. They hoped to be in time, however. They had no idea the marriage would take place so soon.'

Mrs. Orton Beg reflected for a little, and then she asked in evident trepidation, for she had more than a suspicion of what the reply would be: 'And what are you going to do?'

'Decline to live with him,' Evadne answered.

This was what Mrs. Orton Beg had begun to suspect, but there is often an element of surprise in the confirmation of our shrewdest suspicions, and now she sat upright, leant forward, and looked at her niece aghast. '*What*?' she demanded.

'I shall decline to live with him,' Evadne repeated with emphasis.

Mrs. Orton Beg slowly resumed her reclining position, acting as one does who has heard the worst, and realizes that there is nothing to be done but to recover from the shock.

'I thought you loved him,' she ventured, after a prolonged pause.

'Yes, so did I,' Evadne answered, frowning—'but I was mistaken. It was a mere affair of the senses, to be put off by the first circumstance calculated to cause a revulsion of feeling by lowering him in my estimation—a thing so slight that, after reading the letter, as we drove to the station—even so soon! I could see him as he is. I noticed at once—but it was for the first time—I noticed that, although his face is handsome, the expression of it is not noble at all.' She shuddered as at the sight of something repulsive. 'You see,' she explained, 'my taste is cultivated to so fine an extent, I require something extremely well-flavoured for the dish which is to be the *pièce de resistance* of my life-feast. My appetite is delicate, it requires to be tempted, and a husband of that kind, a moral leper'—she broke off with a gesture, spreading her hands, palms outward, as if she would fain put some horrid idea far from her. 'Besides, marrying a man like that, allowing him an assured position in society, is countenancing vice, and'—she glanced round apprehensively, then added in a fearful whisper—'*helping to spread it.*'

Mrs. Orton Beg knew in her head that reason and right were on Evadne's side, but she felt in her heart the full force of the custom and prejudice that would be against her, and shrank appalled by the thought of what the cruel struggle to come must be if Evadne persisted in her determination. In view of this, she sat up in her chair once more energetically, prepared to do her best to dissuade her; but then again she relapsed, giving in to a doubt of her own capacity to advise in such an emergency, accompanied by a sudden and involuntary feeling of respect for Evadne's principles, however peculiar and unprecedented they might be, and for the strength of character which had enabled her so far to act upon them. 'You must obey your own conscience, Evadne,' was what she found herself saying at last. 'I will help you to do that. I would rather not influence you. You may be right. I cannot be sure—and yet—I don't agree with you. For I know if I could have my husband back with me, I would welcome him, even if he were—a leper.' Evadne compressed her lips in steady disapproval. 'I should think only of his future. I should forgive the past.'

'That is the mistake you good women all make,' said Evadne. 'You set a detestably bad example. So long as women like you will forgive anything, men will do anything. You have it in your power to set up a high standard of excellence for men to reach in order to have the privilege of associating with you. There is this quality in men, that they will have the best of everything; and if the best wives are only to be obtained by being worthy of them, they will strive to become so. As it is, however, why should they? Instead of punishing them for their depravity, you encourage them in it by overlooking it; and besides,' she added, 'you must know that there is no past in the matter of vice. The consequences become hereditary, and continue from generation to generation.'

Again Mrs. Orton Beg felt herself checked.

'Where did you hear all this, Evadne!' she asked,

'I never heard it. I read—and I thought,' she answered. 'But I am only now beginning to understand,' she added. 'I suppose moral axioms are always the outcome of pained reflection. Knowledge cries to us in vain as a rule before experience has taken the sharp edge off our egotism—by experience, I mean the addition of some personal feeling to our knowledge.'

'I don't understand you in the least, Evadne,' Mrs. Orton Beg replied.

'Your husband was a good man,' Evadne answered indirectly. 'You have never thought about what a woman ought to do who has married a bad one—in an emergency like mine, that is. You think I should act as women have been always advised to act in such cases, that I should sacrifice myself to save that one man's soul. I take a different view of it. I see that the world is not a bit the better for centuries of self-sacrifice on the woman's part and therefore I think it is time we tried a more effectual plan. And I propose now to sacrifice the man instead of the woman.'

Mrs. Orton Beg was silent.

'Have you nothing to say to me, auntie?' Evadne asked at last, caressingly.

'I do not like to hear you talk so, Evadne. Every word you say seems to banish something—something from this room—something from my life to which I cling. I think it is my faith in love—and loving. You may be right, but yet—the consequences! the struggle, if we must resist! It is best to submit. It is better not to know.'

'It is easier to submit—yes; it is disagreeable to know,' Evadne translated.

There was another pause, then Mrs. Orton Beg broke out: 'Don't make me think about it. Surely I have suffered enough? Disagreeable to know! It is torture. If I ever let myself dwell on the horrible depravity that goes on unchecked, the depravity which you say we women license by ignoring it when we should face and unmask it, I should go out of my mind. I do know—we all know; how can we live and not know? But we don't think about it—we can't—we daren't. See! I try always to keep my own mind in one attitude, to keep it filled for ever with holy and beautiful thoughts. When I am alone, I listen for the chime, and when I have repeated it to myself slowly—

He, watching over Israel, slumbers not nor sleeps—[1]

my heart swells. I leave all that is inexplicable to Him, and thank him for the love and the hope with which he feeds my heart and keeps it from hardening. I thank him too,' she went on hoarsely, 'for the terrible moments when I feel my loss afresh, those early morning moments, when the bright sunshine and the beauty of all things only make my own barren life look all the more bare in its loneliness; when my soul struggles to free itself from the shackles of the flesh that it may spread its wings to meet that other soul which made earth heaven for me here, and will, I know, make all eternity ecstatic as a dream for me hereafter. It is good to suffer, yes; but surely I suffer enough? My husband—if I cry to him, he will not hear me; if I go down on my knees beside his grave, and dig my arms in deep, deep, I shall not reach him. I cannot raise him up again to caress him, or move the cruel weight of earth from off his breast. The voice that was always kind will gladden me no more; the arms that were so willing to protect—the world—just think how big it is! and if I traverse it every yard, I shall not find him. He is not anywhere in all this huge expanse. Ah, God! the agony of yearning, the ache, the ache; why must I live?'

'Auntie!' Evadne cried. 'I am selfish.' She knelt down beside her and held her hand. 'I have made you think of your own irreparable loss, compared with which I know my trouble is so small. Forgive me.'

Mrs. Orton Beg put her arms round the girl's neck and kissed her: 'Forgive *me*' she said. 'I am so weak, Evadne, and you—ah! you are strong.'

(GEORGE) BERNARD SHAW (1856–1950)

Born at 3 Upper Synge Street, Dublin, one of three children, and the only son, of an alcoholic insolvent grain merchant, and the stoic Lucinda Elizabeth (Bessie) Gurly, a gifted musician, he was educated by his uncle, Rev. William Carroll, rector of St Bride's, at the Wesley Connexional, the Central Model Boys' School and the Dublin English Scientific and Commercial Day School—all of which he hated. His parents' marriage was unconventional; when Shaw suspected he was an illegitimate child he shed his first name

---

1 *He, watching over Israel, slumbers not nor sleeps*: from the chorus of Felix Mendelsohn Bartholdy's *Elijah*. It is repeated in its musical score as a leitmotiv throughout book I.

George. From 1866 to 1873, when his parents' marriage broke up, the Shaws lived with the conductor George (Vandeleur) Lee at his house in Hatch Street and his summer cottage on Dalkey Hill. Shaw was found employment in 1871 in a land agency, first as office boy, then as cashier. His mother followed Lee to London, Shaw and his father moving to 61 Harcourt Street in 1873. Shaw then went to London, and tried to build up a career as a novelist, publishing four books in serial form, including *Cashel Byron's Profession* (1882–83), about a prize-fighter (Shaw entered the English Amateur Boxing Association Championship as middleweight), and *The Unsocial Socialist* (1884), which led to his acquaintance with William Morris. These books received no critical acclaim, and Shaw 'set to work to find out what the world was really like'. He educated himself at the British Museum, and, in 1884, joined the recently established Fabian Society. He collaborated with William Archer on *Widowers' Houses*, promoting Ibsenism. He fashioned an alter ego in the art and music critic 'G.B.S.', writing for *The World* (1886–89), and as 'Corno di Bassetto' for the *Star* (1888–90) and *The World* (1890–95). He wrote *The Quintessence of Ibsenism* (1891), and a treatise on *Der Ring des Nibelungen*, entitled *The Perfect Wagnerite* (1898).

Widower' Houses, with his lover Florence Farr as Blanche, began his dramatic career; it was produced at the recently founded Independent Theatre in December 1892, and got an unfavourable reception from the critics. The first of his *Plays Unpleasant*, it exposed the cynical heartlessness beneath the civilized veneer of bourgeois society; and it was the first of many plays in which Shaw aired his mistrust of idealism. *Plays Pleasant* formed a counterbalance; the first, *Arms and the Man* (1894), was staged with W.B. Yeats's* *The Land of Heart's Desire* (after the joint production Yeats had a nightmare vision of Shaw as a laughing sewing machine). Shaw became drama critic for the *Saturday Review* (1895–98). *The Man of Destiny* (1897) dealt with Napoleon and the 'one universal passion: fear', while in *Three Plays for Puritans* (1901) he attacked, in *The Devil's Discipline*, the 'idolatry of sensuousness', and, in *Caesar and Cleopatra*, portrayed Julius Caesar as a 'psychological woman-tamer'. *Man and Superman* (1903) is 'Shavian' in its insistence on creative evolution. *John Bull's Other Island* (1904) is Shaw's paradoxical comedy (1904) of idealized and pragmatic—inside and outside—views of Ireland; it was the first of a series of his play, including *Major Barbara* (1905), and *The Doctor's Dilemma* (1906), which were successfully produced at the Court Theatre. *The Shewing-Up of Blanco Posnet* (1909), banned in England, was staged in Dublin, and reviewed by James Joyce. Henry Higgins in *Pygmalion* (1912) is loosely modelled on the phonetician Daniel Jones (Shaw advocated spelling reform); a blending of Pygmalion and Faust, the play remains the most successful of his comedies; a film version appeared in 1939.

No stranger to controversy, Shaw caused outrage with such essays as *Common Sense About the War* (14 Nov. 1914). He also protested against the execution of the leaders of the Easter Rising, and his letter 'Shall Roger Casement Hang?' was rejected by *The Times*. *Heartbreak House*, which ends with a bombing raid, was written during the War;

it was first produced in 1921. The two 'demon daughters' of its Lear-like male lead, Captain Shotover, were based on Erica Cotterill and Mrs Patrick Campbell, with whom he had affairs. Joan of Arc in *Saint Joan* (1921) embodies the hope of Humanity (the 'entirely mystic force of evolution') which is crushed by the reactionary Inquisition. The play was a great success on both sides of the Atlantic. His later plays are experimental and abstract. He was impressed by Russia, which he visited the year he published *The Intelligent Women's Guide to Socialism and Capitalism*. In 1925 he received the Nobel Prize for Literature.

Two Letters to Ellen Terry[1]

24 June 1892
29 Fitzroy Square, W.

Dear Miss Terry—I went to the Lyric Club today, and listened to your young Italian friend. The only thing I can do is to give you my exact opinion, which you can take for what it is worth, and communicate to her or not, as you may think best. In every respect except the purely musical one, you will understand the position better than I do myself. To begin with, you know that you do not hold your present position because you possess this, that, and the other personal attraction, but because you have made yourself one of the six best actresses in the fourteen thousand millions of people (I think that is the figure) in the world. And you therefore know that nothing short of being one of the six best singers in the world would enable your novice to get praised as you get praised. At the concert, for instance, although I was morbidly alive to every weakness in Lewis's poem,[2] guessing all the bads and sads beforehand, and being tickled beyond measure by the line beginning 'My language &c.,' yet you brought tears to my eyes, not, you will understand, by the imaginary sorrows of the lunatic (sorrow does not make me cry, even when it is real) but by doing the thing beautifully. My whole claim to be a critic of art is that I can be touched in that way. Now your friend did not touch me in the least. I liked her at once: she is very amiable, very clever, and very good-looking. But— and now the murder is coming out—she is not interesting as an artist.

1 *Ellen Alice Terry* (1847–1928) was a leading English actress. She had made her debut in 1856 at the Princess Theatre. She became the leading Shakespeare actress from 1874, striking up a partnership with Henry Irving at the Lyceum Theatre, where she first appeared as Ophelia in 1878. At the time of these letters she had not yet met Shaw. She had asked Shaw, as music critic of the *Saturday Review*, for his opinion of the prospects of a young composer-singer friend. He went to the afternoon concert in the Lyric Club where she recited and her friend sang. The latter subsequently became a teacher.
2 *Lewis's poem*: 'The Captive' by Monk Lewis.

She sang the bolero from The Sicilian Vespers[1] prettily and fluently, just as she would, I dare say, repeat one of Ophelia's speeches if you taught it to her. What is more, she sang it intelligently. You know, however, that this is not enough. The quality of execution that makes apparently trivial passages interesting, the intense grip of one's work that rouses all the attention of an audience: these she has not got to anything like a sufficient degree to make a career for her; and what is more, she will never acquire them in drawing-rooms or in the Lyric Club. What she does is not convincing to me: it is only a development of that facility in music which clever children acquire when they are brought up in a musical atmosphere. You must know how children who grow up amid theatrical surroundings catch up a certain familiarity with stage ways which inexperienced people easily mistake for genuine artistic talent. Bedford Park[2] is full of such imps, who will nevertheless be hopelessly beaten in the long run by comparatively unpromising competitors. Now singing is to your signorina partly what acting is to the imps: more a picked-up habit than an art. She has got to turn the habit into an art—to put purpose into it—to make it the means of realizing herself, concentrating herself, throwing herself completely and exhaustively into action—I cannot express it; but you will perhaps recognize what I mean. I therefore think she ought to work on the stage if she can obtain an opening. All her drawing-room beauty and charm will vanish at once behind the footlights; and she will have to remake herself, build herself up from the foundation, instead of taking herself down from a peg as she was hung up by Nature, and wearing herself at the Lyric Club before audiences more or less packed. She has a certain resemblance to Trebelli[3] both in facial expression and musical style; and she might, if she worked hard enough, succeed her as Cherubino, Zerlina,[4] &c. Her voice is all stifled by singing into carpets and curtains: it wants large spaces to develop in; and what is true of her voice is true also of herself. She will never be a dazzling vocal executant any more than Trebelli was: her success, if it is to come at all, will be in sympathetic, intelligent dramatic singing. The most unpromising thing about her is her grace in her present uncultivated state. When Nature intends anyone to be a highly cultivated artist, she generally forces them on by condemning them to fiendishness or loutishness until they fulfil her intention.

---

1 *The Sicilian Vespers: I Vespri Siciliani* by Giuseppe Verdi. The 'Bolero' ('*Mercè, dilette amiche*') is a coloratura of thanks in ¾ time sung by Duchess Elena in Act Five.
2 *Bedford Park*: artists' quarters in London. John Butler Yeats lived there.
3 Trebelli: Zélia Trebelli (Gloria Caroline Gillebert or Le Bert) (1834–92), French mezzo-soprano. She was the first to sing Carmen at the Metropolitan Opera, in 1884.
4 *Cherubino, Zerlina*: characters in Mozart's operas *Le nozze di Figaro* and *Don Giovanni*.

However, there must be exceptions to this, except perhaps as to the fiendishness.

I really must not make this letter any longer: you must be out of patience already. My verdict briefly is that as a drawingroom singer the signorina is no better than many others; and I would not walk a hundred yards to hear her sing again. But if she takes good care of herself and her voice, ten years work on the stage may make something of her. There is a certain humanity about her, to the development of which I should be sorry to prophesy any limit. At the same time, if she prefers to take things easy, and sing and compose in her present fashion, she may, with her social talent, get on very peacefully and comfortably, which you will perhaps tell her is better than being a great artist. If you do, you will be guilty of a most awful falsehood; but you must settle that with your own conscience.

My chief concern about this letter is the likelihood of its putting you to the trouble of acknowledging it. If writing is a trouble to you (my own correspondence drives me stark mad) pray do not mind me, or at least do not go beyond saying 'Thank you for nothing' on a postcard.— Yours very truly,

G. Bernard Shaw

6 April 1896
Stocks Cottage, Aldbury, Tring

There is a song of Schubert's in which the gentleman (who is, I think, Scott's Imprisoned Huntsman translated and retranslated and translated back again from English to German) wants 'to sun himself in Ellen's eyes.'[1] That is what I am going to do for a while this evening in my Easter cottage. The weather has frowned; but Fortune has smiled. Ten splendid things have happened: to wit, 1, a letter from Ellen Terry; 2, a cheque for my Chicago royalties, swollen by the dollars of the thousands of people who were turned away from the doors where Ellen was acting and had to go to Arms and the Man *faute de mieux*; 3, a letter from Ellen Terry; 4, the rolling away of the clouds from the difficult second act of my new play,[2] leaving the view clear and triumphant right on to the curtain; 5, a letter from Ellen Terry;

---

1 *a song of Schubert's*: 'Malcolm Graeme's song—Lay of the Imprisoned Huntsman' ('Lied des gefangenen Jägers') (D843): 'No more at dawning morn I rise, / And sun myself in Ellen's eyes (ll. 17–18).

2 *my new play*: You Never Can Tell, a comedy of manners (1897) with echoes of Wilde's *The Importance of Being Earnest*.

6, a beautiful sunset ride over the hills and far away, thinking of Ellen Terry; 7, a letter from Ellen Terry; 8, a letter from Ellen Terry; 9, a letter from Ellen Terry; 10, a letter from Ellen Ellen Ellen Ellen Ellen Ellen Ellen Ellen Ellen Eleanor Ellenest Terry.

Who has told you that Mrs Pat is to have my Strange Lady?[1] He lies in his throat whoever he is. And yet I suspect Henry Irving1[2]—oh, I suspect him. Why, you ask, should everybody think everybody else corruptible? Because everybody *is* corruptible: is not that simple?[3] He would buy me in the market like a rabbit, wrap me up in brown paper and put me by on his shelf if I offered myself for sale—and how else does a critic offer himself except by writing his little play, or his adaptation or what not? And it would be such a sly way to send it through you. Oh, twenty thousand million devils!—But 'it *is* not so, and it *was* not so, and indeed God forbid that it should be so.'[4] You see the devil can quote Shakespear for his own purpose. If he wants to do the play the least bit in the world, why, I know his value, and will reserve it for him though the next best man covered his offer ten times. But if not, do not let the rabbit be bought and wrapped up. He will not produce it for your sake: no man ever does anything for a woman's sake: from our birth to our death we are women's babies, always wanting something from them, never giving them anything except something to keep *for us*. After all, why should he be fond of people? People are always talking of love and affection and the like—just as they talk of religion—as if they were the commonest things in the world; but the Frenchman was nearer the truth when he said that a great passion is as rare as a man of genius. Has he ever loved you for the millionth fraction of a moment? if so, for that be all his sins forgiven unto him. I do not know whether women ever love. I rather doubt it: they pity a man, *mother* him, delight in making him love them; but I always suspect that their tenderness is deepened by their remorse for being unable to love him. Man's one gift is that at his best he *can* love—not constantly, nor faithfully, nor often, nor for long,—but for a moment—a few minutes perhaps out of years. It is because I have had a glimpse or two that I am such a hopelessly impious person; for when

---

1 *my Strange Lady*: the 'Strange Lady' in *The Man of Destiny* had Ellen's appearance—'tall and extraordinarily graceful, with a delicately intelligent, apprehensive, questioning face: perception in the brow, sensitiveness in the nostrils, character in the chin: all keen, refined and original....'
2 *Sir Henry Irving* (1838–1905), legendary actor and manager of the Lyceum. Shaw objected to his influence over the London theatre; the two men wrangled over the production of *The Man of Destiny* at the Lyceum.
3 *everybody* is *corruptible*: Shaw had written in the *Saturday Review*, 'I am to all intents and purposes incorruptible'.
4 *it* is *not so* ...: *Much Ado About Nothing*, I. i. 200–01.

God offers me heaven as the reward of piety, I simply reply. 'I know. I've been there. You can do nothing further for me, thank you.'

You boast that you are a fool (it is at bottom, oh, such a tremendous boast: do you know that in Wagner's last drama, Parsifal, the redeemer is 'der reine Thor,' 'the pure fool?') but you have the wisdom of the heart, which makes it possible to say deep things to you. You say I'd be sick of you in a week; but this is another boast: it implies that you could entertain me for a whole week. Good heavens! with what? With art? with politics? with philosophy? or with any other department of culture? I've written more about them all (for my living) than you ever thought about them. On that plane I would exhaust you before you began, and could bore you dead with my own views in two hours. But one does not get tired of adoring the Virgin Mother. Bless me! you will say, the man is a Roman Catholic. Not at all: the man is the author of Candida; and Candida, between you and me, is the Virgin Mother and nobody else.[1] And my present difficulty is that I want to reincarnate her—to write another Candida play *for* YOU. Only, it wont come. Candida came easily enough; but after her came that atrocious Man of Destiny, a mere stage brutality, and my present play brings life and art together and strikes showers of sparks from them as if they were a knife and a grindstone. Heaven knows how many plays I shall have to write before I earn one that belongs of divine right to you. Some day, when you have two hours to spare, you must let me read Candida to you. You will find me a disagreeably cruel-looking middle-aged Irishman with a red beard; but that cannot be helped. By the way, you once spoke to me, although, as you were evidently woolgathering at the time, you wont remember the circumstance. It was at one of the performances at the new opera house which is now the Palace Music Hall. You were in the stalls; so was I; and it happened that we were almost the last persons to leave and were kept standing together for a moment waiting for the doorway into the corridor to clear. I was highly conscious of your illustrious presence and identity, but of course took care not to appear conscious. You seemed very much in earnest and even affected about something; and my theory is that you were in imagination impersonating some unfortunate young village girl of lowly station—Hetty in Adam Bede perhaps[2]—and that you suddenly took it into your head

1 *Candida*: in the Preface to *Plays Pleasant* (1898), Shaw decribed *Candida* (1895) as a socialist-religious play. A variation on Ibsen's *A Doll's House*, it was initially subtitled 'A Mystery'. The play was written for the voluptuous Janet Achurch.
2 *Hetty in Adam Bede*: Hetty Sorrel in George Eliot's *Adam Bede* (1859) is distracted by the idle attentions of Captain Arthur Donnithorne; she is imprisoned for murdering her own child. Adam Bede retains his loyalty to her.

that I was the squire, or perhaps the parson. At all events you most unexpectedly raised your eyes to mine for a moment and said, with the deepest respect, 'Good evening, sir.' I nearly sat down on the floor in confusion; but by good luck I managed not to wake you out of your dream. What I did was to instinctively fall into your drama (whatever it was) by saying 'Good evening' so exactly in the manner of the squire acknowledging a salutation from the gamekeeper's daughter (a most respectable, promising, well conducted young woman) that you passed unsuspectingly on up the avenue, with the squirrels and rabbits scampering away as you approached; and I watched you until you turned into the path leading to the dairy and vanished. I suppose you dont happen to remember, in the course of your transmigrations, meeting a squire or a parson with a red beard and a nasty expression about the corners of his mouth? But I must not ask you questions, as you have written me enough to live on until you come back; and your precious forces must not be wasted in writing letters to me. I wish this ink—a penny a bottle at the village shop—were blacker and my writing bolder. If you have a magnifying glass, it will all come out beautifully legible....

G. B. S.

From *Widowers' Houses*[1]

(1892)

[*Act One is set in Germany, where 24-year-old Dr Harry Trench and his middle-aged companion William de Burgh Cokane make the acquaintance of Sartorius, a moneyed man, and his good-looking and strong-minded daughter Blanche. Trench proposes, and is given permission to marry Blanche if his family (and particularly his aunt, Lady Roxdale) give their written consent to the marriage.*]

---

1 The title alludes to the second Book of Esdras 16 (a disputed book in the King James version): 'O my people, hear my word: make you ready to thy battle, and in those evils be even as pilgrims upon the earth. He that selleth, let him be as he that fleeth away: and he that buyeth, as one that will lose: He that occupieth merchandise, as he that hath no profit by it: and he that buildeth, as he that shall not dwell therein: He that soweth, as if he should not reap: so also he that planteth the vineyard, as he that shall not gather the grapes: They that marry, as they that shall get no children; and they that marry not, as the widowers. And therefore they that labour labour in vain: For strangers shall reap their fruits, and spoil their goods, overthrow their houses, and take their children captives, for in captivity and famine shall they get children.' (2 Esdras 16:40–6).

Act II

In the library of a handsomely appointed villa at Surbiton on a sunny forenoon in September. Sartorius is busy at a writing table littered with business letters. The fireplace, decorated for summer, is close behind him: the window is in the opposite wall. Between the table and the window Blanche, in her prettiest frock, sits reading The Queen. The door is in the middle. All the walls are lined with shelves of smartly tooled books, fitting into their places like bricks.

SARTORIUS. Blanche.

BLANCHE. Yes, papa.

SARTORIUS. I have some news here.

BLANCHE. What is it?

SARTORIUS. I mean news for you—from Trench.

BLANCHE *[with affected indifference]* Indeed?

SARTORIUS. 'Indeed?'! is that all you have to say to me? Oh very well.
He resumes his work. Silence.

BLANCHE. What do his people say, papa?

SARTORIUS. His people? I dont know. *[Still busy]*
Another pause.

BLANCHE. What does he say?

SARTORIUS. He! He says nothing. *[He folds a letter leisurely, and looks at the envelope]*. He prefers to communicate the result of his—where did I put?—oh, here. Yes: he prefers to communicate the result in person.

BLANCHE *[springing up]* Oh, papa! When is he coming?

SARTORIUS. If he walks from the station, he may arrive in the course of the next half-hour. If he drives, he may be here any moment.

BLANCHE *[making hastily for the door]* Oh!

SARTORIUS. Blanche.

BLANCHE. Yes, papa.

SARTORIUS. You will of course not meet him until he has spoken to me.

BLANCHE *[hypocritically]* Of course not, papa. I shouldn't have thought of such a thing.

SARTORIUS. That is all. *[She is going, when he puts out his hand, and says with fatherly emotion]* My dear child. *[She responds by going over to kiss him. A tap at the door]*. Come in.
Lickcheese enters, carrying a black handbag. He is a shabby, needy man, with dirty face and linen, scrubby beard

and whiskers, going bald. A nervous, wiry, pertinacious human terrier, judged by his mouth and eyes, but miserably apprehensive and servile before Sartorius. He bids Blanche 'Good morning, miss'; and she passes out with a slight and contemptuous recognition of him.

LICKCHEESE. Good morning, sir.

SARTORIUS [*harsh and peremptory*] Good morning.

LICKCHEESE [*taking a little sack of money from his bag*] Not much this morning, sir. I have just had the honor of making Dr Trench's acquaintance, sir.

SARTORIUS [*looking up from his writing, displeased*] Indeed?

LICKCHEESE. Yes, sir. Dr Trench asked his way of me, and was kind enough to drive me from the station.

SARTORIUS. Where is he, then?

LICKCHEESE. I left him in the hall, with his friend, sir. I should think he is speaking to Miss Sartorius.

SARTORIUS. Hm! What do you mean by his friend?

LICKCHEESE. There is a Mr Cokane with him, sir.

SARTORIUS. I see you have been talking to him, eh?

LICKCHEESE. As we drove along: yes, sir.

SARTORIUS [*sharply*] Why did you not come by the nine o'clock train?

LICKCHEESE. I thought—

SARTORIUS. It cannot be helped now; so never mind what you thought. But do not put off my business again to the last moment. Has there been any further trouble about the St Giles property?

LICKCHEESE. The Sanitary Inspector has been complaining again about No. 13 Robbins's Row. He says he'll bring it before the vestry.

SARTORIUS. Did you tell him that I am on the vestry?

LICKCHEESE. Yes, sir.

SARTORIUS. What did he say to that?

LICKCHEESE. Said he supposed so, or you wouldnt dare to break the law so scand'lous. I only tell you what he said.

SARTORIUS. Hm! Do you know his name?

LICKCHEESE. Yes, sir. Speakman.

SARTORIUS. Write it down in the diary for the day of the next meeting of the Health Committee. I will teach Mr Speakman his duty to members of the vestry.

LICKCHEESE [*doubtfully*] The vestry cant hurt him, sir. He's under the Local Government Board.

SARTORIUS. I did not ask you that. Let me see the books. [*Lickcheese produces the rent book, and hands it to Sartorius; then makes the desired entry in the diary on the table, watching Sartorius with misgiving as the rent book is examined. Sartorius rises, frowning*]. One pound four for repairs to number thirteen! What does this mean?

LICKCHEESE. Well, sir, it was the staircase on the third floor. It was downright dangerous: there werent but three whole steps in it, and no handrail. I thought it best to have a few boards put in.

SARTORIUS. Boards! Firewood, sir, firewood! They will burn every stick of it. You have spent twenty-four shillings of my money on firewood for them.

LICKCHEESE. There ought to be stone stairs, sir: it would be a saving in the long run. The clergyman says—

SARTORIUS. What! Who says?

LICKCHEESE. The clergyman, sir, only the clergyman. Not that I make much account of him; but if you knew how he has worried me over that staircase—

SARTORIUS. I am an Englishman; and I will suffer no priest to interfere in my business. [*He turns suddenly on Lickcheese*]. Now look here, Mr Lickcheese! This is the third time this year that you have brought me a bill of over a pound for repairs. I have warned you repeatedly against dealing with these tenement houses as if they were mansions in a West-End square. I have had occasion to warn you too against discussing my affairs with strangers. You have chosen to disregard my wishes. You are discharged.

LICKCHEESE [*dismayed*] Oh, sir, dont say that.

SARTORIUS [*fiercely*] You are discharged.

LICKCHEESE. Well, Mr Sartorius, it is hard, so it is. No man alive could have screwed more out of them poor destitute devils for you than I have, or spent less in doing it. I have dirtied my hands at it until theyre not fit for clean work hardly; and now you turn me—

SARTORIUS [*interrupting him menacingly*] What do you mean by dirtying your hands? If I find that you have stepped an inch outside the letter of the law, Mr Lickcheese, I will prosecute you myself. The way to keep your hands clean is to gain the confidence of your employers. You will do well to bear that in mind in your next situation.

THE PARLORMAID [*opening the door*] Mr Trench and Mr Cokane.

> *Cokane and Trench come in: Trench festively dressed and in buoyant spirits: Cokane highly self-satisfied.*

SARTORIUS. How do you do, Dr Trench? Good morning, Mr Cokane. I am pleased to see you here. Mr Lickcheese: you will place your accounts and money on the table: I will examine them and settle with you presently.

Lickcheese retires to the table, and begins to arrange his accounts, greatly depressed. The parlormaid withdraws.

TRENCH [*glancing at Lickcheese*] I hope we're not in the way.

SARTORIUS. By no means. Sit down, pray. I fear you have been kept waiting.

TRENCH [*taking Blanche's chair*] Not at all. Weve only just come in. [*He takes out a packet of letters, and begins untying them*].

COKANE [*going to a chair nearer the window, but stopping to look admiringly round before sitting down*] You must be happy here with all these books, Mr Sartorius. A literary atmosphere.

SARTORIUS [*resuming his seat*] I have not looked into them. They are pleasant for Blanche occasionally when she wishes to read. I chose the house because it is on gravel. The death-rate is very low.

TRENCH [*triumphantly*] I have any amount of letters for you. All my people are delighted that I am going to settle. Aunt Maria wants Blanche to be married from her house. [*He hands Sartorius a letter*].

SARTORIUS. Aunt Maria?

COKANE. Lady Roxdale, my dear sir: he means Lady Roxdale. Do express yourself with a little more tact, my dear fellow.

TRENCH. Lady Roxdale, of course. Uncle Harry—

COKANE. Sir Harry Trench. His godfather, my dear sir, his godfather.

TRENCH. Just so. The pleasantest fellow for his age you ever met. He offers us his house at St Andrews for a couple of months, if we care to pass our honeymoon there. [*He hands Sartorius another letter*]. It's the sort of house nobody can live in, you know; but it's a nice thing for him to offer. Dont you think so?

SARTORIUS [*dissembling a thrill at the titles*] No doubt. These seem very gratifying, Dr Trench.

TRENCH. Yes, arnt they? Aunt Maria has really behaved like a brick.

	If you read the postscript youll see she spotted Cokane's hand in my letter. [*Chuckling*] He wrote it for me.
SARTORIUS	[*glancing at Cokane*] Indeed! Mr Cokane evidently did it with great tact.
COKANE	[*returning the glance*] Dont mention it.
TRENCH	[*gleefully*] Well, what do you say now, Mr Sartorius? May we regard the matter as settled at last?
SARTORIUS.	Quite settled. [*He rises and offers his hand. Trench, glowing with gratitude, rises and shakes it vehemently, unable to find words for his feelings*].
COKANE	[*coming between them*]. Allow me to congratulate you both. [*He shakes hands with the two at the same time.*]
SARTORIUS.	And now, gentlemen, I have a word to say to my daughter. Dr Trench: you will not, I hope, grudge me the pleasure of breaking this news to her: I have had to disappoint her more than once since I last saw you. Will you excuse me for ten minutes?
COKANE	[*in a flush of friendly protest*] My dear sir: can you ask?
TRENCH.	Certainly.
SARTORIUS.	Thank you. [*He goes out*].
TRENCH	[*chuckling again*] He wont have any news to break, poor old boy: she's seen all the letters already.
COKANE.	I must say your behavior has been far from straightforward. Harry. You have been carrying on a clandestine correspondence.
LICKCHEESE	[*stealthily*] Gentlemen—
TRENCH } COKANE	[*turning: they had forgotten his presence*] Hallo!
LICKCHEESE	[*coming between them very humbly, but in mortal anxiety and haste*] Look here, gentlemen. [*To Trench*] You, sir, I address myself to more particlar. Will you say a word in my favor to the guvnor? He's just given me the sack; and I have four children looking to me for their bread. A word from you, sir, on this happy day, might get him to take me on again.
TRENCH	[*embarrassed*] Well, you see, Mr Lickcheese, I dont see how I can interfere. I'm very sorry, of course.
COKANE	Certainly you cannot interfere. It would be in the most execrable taste.
LICKCHEESE.	Oh, gentlemen, youre young; and you dont know what loss of employment means to the like of me. What harm

271

would it do you to help a poor man? Just listen to the circumstances, sir. I only—

TRENCH [*moved, but snatching at an excuse for taking a high tone in avoiding the unpleasantness of helping him*] No: I had rather not. Excuse my saying plainly that I think Mr Sartorius is not a man to act hastily or harshly. I have always found him very fair and generous; and I believe he is a better judge of the circumstances than I am.

COKANE [*inquisitive*] I think you ought to hear the circumstances, Harry. It can do no harm. Hear the circumstances by all means.

LICKCHEESE. Never mind, sir: it aint any use. When I hear that man called generous and fair!—well, never mind.

TRENCH [*severely*] If you wish me to do anything for you, Mr Lickcheese, let me tell you that you are not going the right way about it in speaking ill of Mr Sartorius.

LICKCHEESE. Have I said one word against him, sir? I leave it to your friend: have I said a word?

COKANE. True: true. Quite true. Harry: be just.

LICKCHEESE. Mark my words, gentlemen: he'll find what a man he's lost the very first week's rents the new man'll bring him. Youll find the difference yourself, Dr Trench, if you or your children come into the property. Ive took money there when no other collector alive would have wrung it out. And this is the thanks I get for it! Why, see here, gentlemen! Look at that bag of money on the table. Hardly a penny of that but there was a hungry child crying for the bread it would have bought. But I got it for him—screwed and worried and bullied it out of them. I—look here, gentlemen: I'm pretty seasoned to the work; but theres money there that I couldnt have taken if it hadnt been for the thought of my own children depending on me for giving him satisfaction. And because I charged him four-and-twenty shillin to mend a staircase that three women have been hurt on, and that would have got him prosecuted for manslaughter if it had been let go much longer, he gives me the sack. Wouldnt listen to a word, though I would have offered to make up the money out of my own pocket: aye, and am willing to do it still if you will only put in a word for me.

TRENCH [*aghast*] You took money that ought to have fed starving children! Serve you right! If I had been the father of one of those children, I'd have given you something worse than the sack. I wouldnt say a word to save your soul, if you have such a thing. Mr Sartorius was quite right.

LICKCHEESE [*staring at him, surprised into contemptuous amusement in the midst of his anxiety*] Just listen to this! Well, you are an innocent young gentleman. Do you suppose he sacked me because I was too hard? Not a bit on it; it was because I wasnt hard enough. I never heard him say he was satisfied yet: no, nor he wouldnt, not if I skinned em alive. I dont say he's the worst landlord in London: he couldnt be worse than some; but he's no better than the worst I ever had to do with. And, though I say it, I'm better than the best collector he ever done business with. Ive screwed more and spent less on his properties than anyone would believe, that knows what such properties are. I know my merits, Dr Trench, and will speak for myself if no one else will.

COKANE. What description of properties? Houses?

LICKCHEESE. Tenement houses, let from week to week by the room or half room: aye, or quarter room. It pays when you know how to work it, sir. Nothing like it. It's been calculated on the cubic foot of space, sir, that you can get higher rents letting by the room than you can for a mansion in Park Lane.

TRENCH. I hope Mr Sartorius hasnt much of that sort of property, however it may pay.

LICKCHEESE. He has nothing else, sir; and he shews his sense in it, too. Every few hundred pounds he could scrape together he bought old houses with: houses that you wouldnt hardly look at without holding your nose. He has em in St Giles's: he has em in Marylebone: he has em in Bethnal Green. Just look how he lives himself, and youll see the good of it to him. He likes a low deathrate and a gravel soil for himself, he does. You come down with me to Robbins's Row; and I'll shew you a soil and a deathrate, I will! And, mind you, it's me that makes it pay him so well. Catch him going down to collect his own rents! Not likely!

TRENCH. Do you mean to say that all his property—all his means— come from this sort of thing?

LICKCHEESE. Every penny of it, sir.

Trench, overwhelmed, has to sit down.

COKANE   [*looking compassionately at him*] Ah, my dear fellow, the love of money is the root of all evil.

LICKCHEESE. Yes, sir; and we'd all like to have the tree growing in our garden.

COKANE   [*revolted*] Mr Lickcheese: I did not address myself to you. I do not wish to be severe with you; but there is something peculiarly repugnant to my feelings in the calling of a rent collector.

LICKCHEESE. It's no worse than many another. I have my children looking to me.

COKANE.   True: I admit it. So has our friend Sartorius. His affection for his daughter is a redeeming point—a redeeming point, certainly.

LICKCHEESE. She's a lucky daughter, sir. Many another daughter has been turned out upon the streets to gratify his affection for her. Thats what business is, sir, you see. Come, sir: I think your friend will say a word for me now he knows I'm not in fault.

TRENCH   [*rising angrily*] I will not. It's a damnable business from beginning to end; and you deserve no better luck for helping in it. I've seen it all among the out-patients at the hospital; and it used to make my blood boil to think that such things couldnt be prevented.

LICKCHEESE   [*his suppressed spleen breaking out*] Oh indeed, sir. But I suppose youll take your share when you marry Miss Blanche, all the same. [*Furiously*] Which of us is the worse, I should like to know? me that wrings the money out to keep a home over my children, or you that spend it and try to shove the blame on to me?

COKANE.   A most improper observation to address to a gentleman, Mr Lickcheese! A most revolutionary sentiment!

LICKCHEESE. Perhaps so. But then Robbins's Row aint a school for manners. You collect a week or two there—youre welcome to my place if I cant keep it for myself—and youll hear a little plain speaking, you will.

COKANE   [*with dignity*] Do you know to whom you are speaking, my good man ?

LICKCHEESE   [*recklessly*] I know well enough who I'm speaking to. What do I care for you, or a thousand such? I'm poor: thats enough to make a rascal of me. No consideration for me! nothing to be got by saying a word for me! [*Suddenly cringing to Trench*] Just a word, sir. It would cost you nothing. [*Sartorius appears at the door, unobserved*] Have some feeling for the poor.

TRENCH.   I'm afraid you have shewn very little, by your own confession.

LICKCHEESE [*breaking out again*] More than your precious father-in-law, anyhow. I—[*Sartorius's voice, striking in with deadly coldness, paralyzes him*].

SARTORIUS.   You will come here tomorrow not later than ten, Mr Lickcheese, to conclude our business. I shall trouble you no further today. [*Lickcheese, cowed, goes out amid dead silence. Sartorius continues, after an awkward pause*] He is one of my agents, or rather was; for I have unfortunately had to dismiss him for repeatedly disregarding my instructions. [*Trench says nothing. Sartorius throws off his embarrassment, and assumes a jocose, rallying air, unbecoming to him under any circumstances, and just now almost unbearably jarring*]. Blanche will be down presently, Harry [*Trench recoils*]—I suppose I must call you Harry now. What do you say to a stroll through the garden, Mr Cokane? We are celebrated here for our flowers.

COKANE.   Charmed, my dear sir, charmed. Life here is an idyll—a perfect idyll. We were just dwelling on it.

SARTORIUS [*slyly*] Harry can follow with Blanche. She will be down directly.

TRENCH   [*hastily*] No. I cant face her just now.

SARTORIUS [*rallying him*] Indeed! Ha, ha!

The laugh, the first they have heard from him, sets Trench's teeth on edge. Cokane is taken aback, but instantly recovers himself.

COKANE.   Ha! ha! ha! Ho! ho!

TRENCH.   But you dont understand.

SARTORIUS.   Oh, I think we do, I think we do. Eh, Mr Cokane? Ha! ha!

COKANE.   I should think we do. Ha! ha! ha!

They go out together, laughing at him. He collapses into a chair shuddering in every nerve. Blanche appears at the door. Her face lights up when she sees that he is alone. She trips noiselessly to the back of his chair and clasps her hands over his eyes. With a convulsive start and exclamation he springs up and breaks away from her.

BLANCHE   [*astonished*] Harry!

TRENCH	[*with distracted politeness*] I beg your pardon. I was thinking—wont you sit down?
BLANCHE	[*looking suspiciously at him*] Is anything the matter? [*She sits down slowly near the writing table. He takes Cokane's chair*].
TRENCH.	No. Oh no.
BLANCHE.	Papa has not been disagreeable, I hope.
TRENCH	No: I have hardly spoken to him since I was with you. [*He rises; takes up his chair; and plants it beside hers. This pleases her better. She looks at him with her most winning smile. A sort of sob breaks from him; and he catches her hands and kisses them passionately. Then, looking into her eyes with intense earnestness, he says*] Blanche: are you fond of money?
BLANCHE	[*gaily*] Very. Are you going to give me any?
TRENCH	[*wincing*] Dont make a joke of it: I'm serious. Do you know that we shall be very poor?
BLANCHE.	Is that what made you look as if you had neuralgia?
TRENCH	[*pleadingly*] My dear: it's no laughing matter. Do you know that I have a bare seven hundred a year to live on?
BLANCHE.	How dreadful!
TRENCH.	Blanche: it's very serious indeed: I assure you it is.
BLANCHE.	It would keep me rather short in my housekeeping, dearest boy, if I had nothing of my own. But papa has promised me that I shall be richer than ever when we are married.
TRENCH.	We must do the best we can with seven hundred. I think we ought to be self-supporting.
BLANCHE.	Thats just what I mean to be. Harry. If I were to eat up half your seven hundred, I should be making you twice as poor; but I'm going to make you twice as rich instead. [*He shakes his head*]. Has papa made any difficulty?
TRENCH	[*rising with a sigh and taking his chair back to its former place*] No. None at all. [*He sits down dejectedly. When Blanche speaks again her face and voice betray the beginning of a struggle with her temper*].
BLANCHE.	Harry: are you too proud to take money from my father?
TRENCH.	Yes, Blanche: I am too proud.
BLANCHE	[*after a pause*] That is not nice to me. Harry.
TRENCH.	You must bear with me, Blanche. I—I cant explain. After all, it's very natural.

BLANCHE. Has it occurred to you that I may be proud too?

TRENCH. Oh, thats nonsense. No one will accuse you of marrying for money.

BLANCHE. No one would think the worse of me if I did, or of you either. [*She rises and begins to walk restlessly about*]. We really cannot live on seven hundred a year, Harry; and I dont think it quite fair of you to ask me merely because you are afraid of people talking.

TRENCH. It's not that alone, Blanche.

BLANCHE. What else is it, then?

TRENCH. Nothing. I—

BLANCHE [*getting behind him, and speaking with forced playfulness as she bends over him, her hands on his shoulders*] Of course it's nothing. Now dont be absurd, Harry: be good; and listen to me: I know how to settle it. You are too proud to owe anything to me; and I am too proud to owe anything to you. You have seven hundred a year. Well, I will take just seven hundred a year from papa at first; and then we shall be quits. Now, now. Harry, you know youve not a word to say against that.

TRENCH. It's impossible.

BLANCHE. Impossible!

TRENCH. Yes, impossible. I have resolved not to take any money from your father.

BLANCHE. But he'll give the money to me, not to you.

TRENCH. It's the same thing. [*With an effort to be sentimental*] I love you too well to see any distinction. [*He puts up his hand halfheartedly: she takes it over his shoulder with equal indecision. They are both trying hard to conciliate one another*].

BLANCHE. Thats a very nice way of putting it. Harry; but I'm sure theres something I ought to know. Has papa been disagreeable?

TRENCH. No: he has been very kind—to me, at least. It's not that. It's nothing you can guess, Blanche. It would only pain you—perhaps offend you. I dont mean, of course, that we shall live always on seven hundred a year. I intend to go at my profession in earnest, and work my fingers to the bone.

BLANCHE [*playing with his fingers, still over his shoulder*] But I shouldnt like you with your fingers worked to the bone,

Harry. I must be told what the matter is. [*He takes his hand quickly away: she flushes angrily; and her voice is no longer even an imitation of the voice of a lady as she exclaims*] I hate secrets; and I dont like to be treated as if I were a child.

TRENCH [*annoyed by her tone*] Theres nothing to tell. I dont choose to trespass on your father's generosity: thats all.

BLANCHE. You had no objection half an hour ago, when you met me in the hall, and shewed me all the letters. Your family doesnt object. Do you object?

TRENCH [*earnestly*] I do not indeed. It's only a question of money.

BLANCHE [*imploringly, the voice softening and refining for the last time*] Harry: theres no use in our fencing in this way. Papa will never consent to my being absolutely dependent on you; and I dont like the idea of it myself. If you even mention such a thing to him you will break off the match: you will indeed.

TRENCH [*obstinately*] I cant help that.

BLANCHE [*white with rage*] You cant help—! Oh, I'm beginning to understand. I will save you the trouble. You can tell papa that *I* have broken off the match; and then there will be no further difficulty.

TRENCH [*taken aback*] What do you mean, Blanche? Are you offended?

BLANCHE. Offended! How dare you ask me?

TRENCH. Dare!

BLANCHE. How much more manly it would have been to confess that you were trifling with me that time on the Rhine! Why did you come here today? Why did you write to your people?

TRENCH. Well, Blanche, if you are going to lose your temper—

BLANCHE. Thats no answer. You depended on your family to get you out of your engagement; and they did not object: they were only too glad to be rid of you. You were not mean enough to stay away, and not manly enough to tell the truth. You thought you could provoke me to break the engagement: thats so like a man—to try to put the woman in the wrong. Well, you have your way: I release you. I wish youd opened my eyes by downright brutality; by striking me; by anything rather than shuffling as you have done.

TRENCH [*hotly*] Shuffling! If I'd thought you capable of turning on me like this, I'd never have spoken to you. Ive a good mind never to speak to you again.

BLANCHE. You shall not—not ever. I will take care of that [*going to the door*].

TRENCH [*alarmed*] What are you going to do?

BLANCHE. To get your letters: your false letters, and your presents: your hateful presents, to return them to you. I'm very glad it's all broken off; and if—[*as she puts her hand to the door it is opened from without by Sartorius, who enters and shuts it behind him*].

SARTORIUS [*interrupting her severely*] Hush, pray, Blanche: you are forgetting yourself: you can be heard all over the house. What is the matter?

BLANCHE [*too angry to care whether she is overheard or not*] You had better ask him. He has some excuse about money.

SARTORIUS. Excuse! Excuse for what?

BLANCHE. For throwing me over.

TRENCH [*vehemently*] I declare I never—

BLANCHE [*interrupting him still more vehemently*] You did. You did. You are doing nothing else—

TRENCH. ⎫ [*together: each trying to* ⎧ I am doing nothing
BLANCHE.⎭ *shout down the other*] ⎩ What else is it but

⎧ of the sort. You know very well what you are saying
⎩ throwing me over? But I dont care for you. I hate you.

⎰ is disgracefully untrue. It's a damned lie. I wont stand—
⎱ I always hated you. Beastly—dirty—vile—

SARTORIUS [*in desperation at the noise*] Silence! [*Still more formidably*] Silence!! [*They obey. He proceeds firmly*] Blanche: you must control your temper: I will not have these repeated scenes within hearing of the servants. Dr Trench will answer for himself to me. You had better leave us. [*He opens the door, and calls*] Mr Cokane: will you kindly join us here?

COKANE [*in the conservatory*] Coming, my dear sir, coming. [*He appears at the door*].

BLANCHE. I'm sure I have no wish to stay. I hope I shall find you alone when I come back. [*An inarticulate exclamation bursts from Trench. She goes out, passing Cokane resentfully. He looks after her in surprise; then looks questioningly at the two men. Sartorius shuts the door with an*

279

angry stroke, and turns to Trench].

SARTORIUS [*aggressively*] Sir—

TRENCH [*interrupting him more aggressively*] Well, sir?

COKANE [*getting between them*] Gently, dear boy, gently. Suavity, Harry, suavity.

SARTORIUS [*mastering himself*] If you have anything to say to me, Dr Trench, I will listen to you patiently. You will then allow me to say what I have to say on my part.

TRENCH [*ashamed*] I beg your pardon. Of course, yes. Fire away.

SARTORIUS. May I take it that you have refused to fulfil your engagement with my daughter?

TRENCH. Certainly not: your daughter has refused to fulfil her engagement with me. But the match is broken off, if thats what you mean.

SARTORIUS. Dr Trench: I will be plain with you. I know that Blanche has a quick temper. It is part of her strong character and her physical courage, which is greater than that of most men, I can assure you. You must be prepared for that. If this quarrel is only Blanche's temper, you may take my word for it that it will be over before tomorrow. But I understood from what she said just now that you have made some difficulty on the score of money.

TRENCH [*with renewed excitement*] It was Miss Sartorius who made the difficulty. I shouldnt have minded that so much, if it hadnt been for the things she said. She shewed that she doesnt care that [*snapping his fingers*] for me.

COKANE [*soothingly*] Dear boy—

TRENCH. Hold your tongue. Billy: it's enough to make a man wish he'd never seen a woman. Look here, Mr Sartorius: I put the matter to her as delicately and considerately as possible, never mentioning a word of my reasons, but just asking her to be content to live on my own little income; and yet she turned on me as if I'd behaved like a savage.

SARTORIUS. Live on your income! Impossible: my daughter is accustomed to a proper establishment. Did I not expressly undertake to provide for that? Did she not tell you I promised her to do so?

TRENCH. Yes, I know all about that, Mr Sartorius; and I'm greatly obliged to you; but I'd rather not take anything from you except Blanche herself.

SARTORIUS. And why did you not say so before?

TRENCH.   No matter why. Let us drop the subject.

SARTORIUS.   No matter! But it does matter, sir. I insist on an answer. Why did you not say so before?

TRENCH.   I didnt know before.

SARTORIUS   [*provoked*] Then you ought to have known your own mind on a point of such vital importance.

TRENCH   [*much injured*] I ought to have known! Cokane: is this reasonable? [*Cokane's features are contorted by an air of judicial consideration; but he says nothing; and Trench again addresses Sartorius, this time with a marked diminution of respect*]. How the deuce could I have known? You didnt tell me.

SARTORIUS.   You are trifling with me, sir. You said that you did not know your own mind before.

TRENCH.   I said nothing of the sort. I say that I did not know where your money came from before.

SARTORIUS.   That is not true, sir. I—

COKANE.   Gently, my dear sir. Gently, Harry, dear boy. Suaviter in modo: fort—[1]

TRENCH.   Let him begin, then. What does he mean by attacking me in this fashion?

SARTORIUS.   Mr Cokane: you will bear me out. I was explicit on the point. I said I was a self-made man; and I am not ashamed of it.

TRENCH.   You are nothing of the sort. I found out this morning from your man—Lickcheese, or whatever his confounded name is—that your fortune has been made out of a parcel of unfortunate creatures that have hardly enough to keep body and soul together—made by screwing, and bullying, and threatening, and all sorts of pettifogging tyranny.

SARTORIUS   [*outraged*] Sir! [*They confront one another threateningly*].

COKANE   [*softly*] Rent must be paid, dear boy. It is inevitable, Harry, inevitable. [*Trench turns away petulantly. Sartorius looks after him reflectively for a moment; then resumes his former deliberate and dignified manner, and addresses Trench with studied consideration, but with a perceptible condescension to his youth and folly*].

SARTORIUS.   I am afraid, Dr Trench, that you are a very young hand at business; and I am sorry I forgot that for a moment or so. May I ask you to suspend your judgment until we have

---

1 *Suaviter in modo, fortiter in re*: 'Gentle in manner, resolute [in execution]'.

had a little quiet discussion of this sentimental notion of yours? if you will excuse me for calling it so. [*He takes a chair, and motions Trench to another on his right*].

COKANE. Very nicely put, my dear sir. Come, Harry: sit down and listen; and consider the matter calmly and judicially. Dont be headstrong.

TRENCH. I have no objection to sit down and listen; but I dont see how that can make black white; and I am tired of being turned on as if I were in the wrong. [*He sits down*].

Cokane sits at Trench's elbow, on his right. They compose themselves for a conference.

SARTORIUS. I assume, to begin with, Dr Trench, that you are not a Socialist, or anything of that sort.

TRENCH. Certainly not. I'm a Conservative. At least, if I ever took the trouble to vote, I should vote for the Conservative and against the other fellow.

COKANE. True blue. Harry, true blue!

SARTORIUS. I am glad to find that so far we are in perfect sympathy. I am, of course, a Conservative. Not a narrow or preju-diced one, I hope, not at all opposed to true progress. Still, a sound Conservative. As to Lickcheese, I need say no more about him than that I have dismissed him from my service this morning for a breach of trust; and you will hardly accept his testimony as friendly or disinterested. As to my business, it is simply to provide homes suited to the small means of very poor people, who require roofs to shelter them just like other people. Do you suppose I can keep up those roofs for nothing?

TRENCH. Yes: thats all very fine; but the point is, what sort of homes do you give them for their money? People must live somewhere, or else go to jail. Advantage is taken of that to make them pay for houses that are not fit for dogs. Why dont you build proper dwellings, and give fair value for the money you take?

SARTORIUS [*pitying his innocence*] My young friend: these poor peo-ple do not know how to live in proper dwellings: they would wreck them in a week. You doubt me: try it for yourself. You are welcome to replace all the missing ban-isters, handrails, cistern lids and dusthole tops at your own expense; and you will find them missing again in less than three days: burnt, sir, every stick of them. I do not blame the poor creatures: they need fires, and often have no other way of getting them. But I really cannot spend pound after pound in repairs for them to pull down, when I can barely get them to pay me four and sixpence a week for a room, which is the recognized fair London rent. No, gentlemen: when people are very poor, you cannot help them, no matter how much you may sympathize with them. It does them more harm than good in the long run. I prefer to save my money in order to provide additional houses for the homeless, and to lay by a little for Blanche. [*He looks at them. They are silent: Trench unconvinced, but talked down; Cokane humanely perplexed. Sartorius bends his brows; comes forward in his chair as if gathering himself for a spring; and addresses himself, with impressive significance, to Trench*]. And now, Dr Trench, may I ask what your income is derived from?

TRENCH [*defiantly*] From interest: not from houses. My hands are clean as far as that goes. Interest on a mortgage.

SARTORIUS [*forcibly*] Yes: a mortgage on my property. When I, to use your own words, screw, and bully, and drive these people to pay what they have freely undertaken to pay me, I cannot touch one penny of the money they give me until I have first paid you your seven hundred a year out of it. What Lickcheese did for me, I do for you. He and I are alike intermediaries: you are the principal. It is because of the risks I run through the poverty of my tenants that you exact interest from me at the monstrous and exorbitant rate of seven per cent, forcing me to exact the uttermost farthing in my turn from the tenants. And yet, Dr Trench, you, who have never done a hand's turn of work in connection with the place, you have not hesitated to speak contemptuously of me because I have applied my industry and forethought to the management of our property, and am maintaining it by the same honorable means.

COKANE [*greatly relieved*] Admirable, my dear sir, excellent! I felt instinctively that Trench was talking unpractical nonsense. Let us drop the subject, my dear boy: you only make an ass of yourself when you meddle in business matters. I told you it was inevitable.

TRENCH [*dazed*] Do you mean to say that I am just as bad as you are?

COKANE. Shame, Harry, shame! Grossly bad taste! Be a gentleman. Apologize.

SARTORIUS. Allow me, Mr Cokane. [*To Trench*] If, when you say you are just as bad as I am, you mean that you are just as powerless to alter the state of society, then you are unfortunately quite right.

Trench does not at once reply. He stares at Sartorius, and then hangs his head and gazes stupidly at the floor, morally beggared, with his clasped knuckles between his knees, a living picture of disillusion. Cokane comes sympathetically to him and puts an encouraging hand on his shoulder.

COKANE [*gently*] Come, Harry, come! Pull yourself together. You owe a word to Mr Sartorius.

TRENCH [*still stupefied, slowly unlaces his fingers; puts his hands on his knees, and lifts himself upright; pulls his waistcoat straight with a tug; and tries to take his disenchantment philosophically as he says, turning to Sartorius*] Well, people who live in glass houses have no right to throw stones. But, on my honor, I never knew that my house was a glass one until you pointed it out. I beg your pardon. [*He offers his hand*].

SARTORIUS. Say no more. Harry: your feelings do you credit: I assure you I feel exactly as you do, myself. Every man who has a heart must wish that a better state of things was practicable. But unhappily it is not.

TRENCH [*a little consoled*] I suppose not.

COKANE. Not a doubt of it, my dear sir: not a doubt of it. The increase of the population is at the bottom of it all.

SARTORIUS [*to Trench*] I trust I have convinced you that you need no more object to Blanche sharing my fortune than I need object to her sharing yours.

TRENCH [*with dull wistfulness*] It seems so. We're all in the same swim, it appears. I hope youll excuse my making such a fuss.

SARTORIUS. Not another word. In fact, I thank you for refraining from explaining the nature of your scruples to Blanche: I admire that in you. Harry. Perhaps it will be as well to leave her in ignorance.

TRENCH [*anxiously*] But I must explain now. You saw how angry she was.

SARTORIUS. You had better leave that to me. [*He looks at his watch,*

and rings the bell]. Lunch is nearly due: while you are getting ready for it I can see Blanche; and I hope the result
will be quite satisfactory to us all. [*The parlormaid
answers the bell: he addresses her with his habitual
peremptoriness*]. Tell Miss Blanche I want her.

THE PARLORMAID [*her face falling expressively*] Yes, sir. [*She turns reluctantly to go*].

SARTORIUS [*on second thoughts*] Stop. [*She stops*]. My love to Miss
Blanche; and I am alone here and would like to see her
for a moment if she is not busy.

THE PARLORMAID [*relieved*] Yes sir. [*She goes out*].

SARTORIUS. I will shew you your room, Harry. I hope you will soon
be perfectly at home in it. You also, Mr Cokane, must
learn your way about here. Let us go before Blanche
comes. [*He leads the way to the door*].

COKANE [*cheerily, following him*] Our little discussion has given
me quite an appetite.

TRENCH [*moodily*] It's taken mine away.

*The two friends go out, Sartorius holding the door for them. He is fol-
lowing when the parlormaid reappears. She is a snivelling sympathetic
creature, and is on the verge of tears.*

SARTORIUS. Well: is Miss Blanche coming?

THE PARLORMAID. Yes, sir. I think so, sir.

SARTORIUS. Wait here until she comes; and tell her that I will be back
in a moment. I have to shew Dr Trench his room.

THE PARLORMAID. Yes, sir. [*She comes into the room. A sound between
a sob and a sniff escapes her*].

Sartorius looks suspiciously at her. He half closes the door.

SARTORIUS. [*lowering his voice*] Whats the matter with you?

THE PARLORMAID [*whimpering*] Nothing, sir.

SARTORIUS [*at the same pitch, more menacingly*] Take care how you
behave yourself when there are visitors present. Do you
hear.

THE PARLORMAID. Yes, sir. [*Sartorius goes out*].

SARTORIUS [*outside*] Excuse me: I had a word to say to the servant.

Trench is heard replying 'Not at all,' *and Cokane* 'Dont mention it, my
dear sir.'

*Their voices pass out of hearing. The parlormaid sniffs; dries her
eyes; and takes some brown paper and a ball of string from a cupboard
under the bookcase. She puts them on the table, and wrestles with
another sob. Blanche comes in, with a jewel box in her hands. Her*

expression is that of a strong and determined woman in an intense passion. The maid looks at her with abject wounded affection and bodily terror.

BLANCHE   [*looking round*] Wheres my father?

THE PARLORMAID [*tremulously propitiatory*] He left word he'd be back directly, miss. I'm sure he wont be long. Heres the paper and string all ready, miss. [*She spreads the paper on the table*]. Can I do the parcel for you, miss?

BLANCHE.   No. Mind your own business. [*She empties the box on the sheet of brown paper. It contains a packet of letters and some jewellery. She plucks a ring from her finger and throws it down on the heap so angrily that it rolls away and falls on the carpet. The maid submissively picks it up and puts it on the table, again sniffing and drying her eyes*]. What are you crying for?

THE PARLORMAID [*plaintively*] You speak so brutal to me, Miss Blanche; and I do love you so. I'm sure no one else would stay and put up with what I have to put up with.

BLANCHE.   Then go. I dont want you. Do you hear? Go.

THE PARLORMAID [*piteously, falling on her knees*] Oh no, Miss Blanche. Dont send me away from you: dont—

BLANCHE   [*with fierce disgust*] Agh! I hate the sight of you. [*The maid, wounded to the heart, cries bitterly*]. Hold your tongue. Are those two gentlemen gone?

THE PARLORMAID [*weeping*] Oh, how could you say such a thing to me. Miss Blanche: me that—

BLANCHE   [*seizing her by the hair and throat*] Stop that noise, I tell you, unless you want me to kill you.

THE PARLORMAID [*protesting and imploring, but in a carefully subdued voice*] Let me go. Miss Blanche: you know youll be sorry: you always are. Remember how dreadfully my head was cut last time.

BLANCHE   [*raging*] Answer me, will you. Have they gone?

THE PARLORMAID. Lickcheese has gone, looking dreadf—[*she breaks off with a stifled cry as Blanche's fingers tighten furiously on her*].

BLANCHE.   Did I ask you about Lickcheese? You beast: you know who I mean: you're doing it on purpose.

THE PARLORMAID [*in a gasp*] Theyre staying to lunch.

BLANCHE   [*looking intently into her face*] He?

THE PARLORMAID [*whispering with a sympathetic nod*] Yes, miss.

[*Blanche lets her drop, and stands forlorn, with despair in her face. The parlormaid, recognizing the passing of the crisis of passion, and fearing no further violence, sits discomfitedly on her heels, and tries to arrange her hair and cap, whimpering a little with exhaustion and soreness*]. Now youve set my hands all trembling; and I shall jingle the things on the tray at lunch so that everybody will notice me. It's too bad of you, Miss Bl—[*Sartorius coughs outside*].

BLANCHE   [*quickly*] Sh! Get up. [*The parlormaid hastily rises, and goes out as demurely as she can. Sartorius glances sternly at her and comes to Blanche*].

SARTORIUS   [*mournfully*] My dear: can you not make a little better fight with your temper?

BLANCHE   [*panting with the subsidence of her fit*] No I cant. I wont. I do my best. Nobody who really cares for me gives me up because of my temper. I never shew my temper to any of the servants but that girl; and she is the only one that will stay with us.

SARTORIUS.   But, my dear, remember that we have to meet our visitors at luncheon presently. I have run down before them to say that I have arranged that little difficulty with Trench. It was only a piece of mischief made by Lickcheese. Trench is a young fool; but it is all right now.

BLANCHE.   I dont want to marry a fool.

SARTORIUS.   Then you will have to take a husband over thirty, Blanche. You must not expect too much, my child. You will be richer than your husband, and, I think, cleverer too. I am better pleased that it should be so.

BLANCHE   [*seizing his arm*] Papa.

SARTORIUS.   Yes, my dear.

BLANCHE.   May I do as I like about this marriage; or must I do as you like?

SARTORIUS   [*uneasily*] Blanche—

BLANCHE.   No, papa: you must answer me.

SARTORIUS   [*abandoning his self-control, and giving way recklessly to his affection for her*] You shall do as you like now and always, my beloved child. I only wish to do as my own darling pleases.

BLANCHE.   Then I will not marry him. He has played fast and loose with me. He thinks us beneath him: he is ashamed of us:

he dared to object to being benefited by you—as if it were not natural for him to owe you everything; and yet the money tempted him after all. [*She throws her arms hysterically about his neck*] Papa: I dont want to marry: I only want to stay with you and be happy as we have always been. I hate the thought of being married: I dont care for him: I dont want to leave you. [*Trench and Cokane come in; but she can hear nothing but her own voice and does not notice them*]. Only send him away: promise me that you will send him away and keep me here with you as we have always—[*seeing Trench*] Oh! [*She hides her face on her father's breast*].

TRENCH   [*nervously*] I hope we are not intruding.

SARTORIUS   [*formidably*] Dr Trench: my daughter has changed her mind.

TRENCH   [*disconcerted*] Am I to understand—

COKANE   [*striking in in his most vinegary manner*] I think, Harry, under the circumstances, we have no alternative but to seek luncheon elsewhere.

TRENCH.   But, Mr Sartorius, have you explained?

SARTORIUS   [*straight in Trench's face*] I have explained, sir. Good morning. [*Trench, outraged, advances a step. Blanche sinks away from her father into a chair. Sartorius stands his ground rigidly*].

TRENCH   [*turning away indignantly*] Come on, Cokane.

COKANE.   Certainly, Harry, certainly. [*Trench goes out, very angry. The parlormaid, with a tray jingling in her hands, passes outside*]. You have disappointed me, sir, very acutely. Good morning. [*He follows Trench*].

Act III

The drawing room in Sartorius's house in Bedford Square, London. Winter evening: fire burning, curtains drawn, and lamps lighted. Sartorius and Blanche are sitting glumly near the fire. The parlormaid, who has just brought in coffee, is placing it on a small table between them. There is a large table in the middle of the room. Looking from it towards the two windows, the pianoforte, a grand, is on the right, with a photographic portrait of Blanche on a miniature easel on a sort of bedspread which covers the top, shewing that the instrument is seldom, if ever, opened. There are two doors: one on the left, further for-

ward than the fireplace, leading to the study; the other by the corner nearest the right hand window, leading to the lobby. Blanche has her workbasket at hand, and is knitting. Sartorius, closer to the fire, has a newspaper. The parlormaid goes out.

SARTORIUS. Blanche, my love.

BLANCHE. Yes.

SARTORIUS. I had a long talk to the doctor today about our going abroad.

BLANCHE [*impatiently*] I am quite well; and I will not go abroad. I loathe the very thought of the Continent. Why will you bother me so about my health?

SARTORIUS. It was not about your health, Blanche, but about my own.

BLANCHE [*rising*] Yours! [*She goes anxiously to him*]. Oh, papa, theres nothing the matter with you, I hope?

SARTORIUS. There will be: there must be, Blanche, long before you begin to consider yourself an old woman.

BLANCHE. But theres nothing the matter now?

SARTORIUS. Well, my dear, the doctor says I need change, travel, excitement—

BLANCHE. Excitement! You need excitement! [*She laughs joyously, and sits down on the rug at his feet*]. How is it, papa, that you, who are so clever with everybody else, are not a bit clever with me? Do you think I cant see through your little plan to take me abroad? Since I will not be the invalid and allow you to be the nurse, you are to be the invalid and I am to be the nurse.

SARTORIUS. Well, Blanche, if you will have it that you are well and have nothing preying on your spirits, I must insist on being ill and have something preying on mine. And indeed, my girl, there is no use in our going on as we have for the last four months. You have not been happy; and I have been very far from comfortable. [*Blanche's face clouds: she turns away from him, and sits dumb and brooding. He waits in vain for some reply; then adds in a lower tone*] Need you be so inflexible, Blanche?

BLANCHE. I thought you admired inflexibility: you have always prided yourself on it.

SARTORIUS. Nonsense, my dear, nonsense! I have had to give in often enough. And I could shew you plenty of soft fellows who have done as well as I, and enjoyed themselves more, perhaps. If it is only for the sake of inflexibility that you are standing out—

BLANCHE.   I am not standing out. I dont know what you mean. [*She tries to rise and go away*].

SARTORIUS   [*catching her arm and arresting her on her knees*] Come, my child! you must not trifle with me as if I were a stranger. You are fretting because—

BLANCHE   [*violently twisting herself free and speaking as she rises*] If you say it, papa, I will kill myself. It is not true. If he were here on his knees tonight, I would walk out of the house sooner than endure it. [*She goes out excitedly*].

Sartorius, greatly troubled, turns again to the fire with a heavy sigh.

SARTORIUS   [*gazing gloomily into the glow*] Now if I fight it out with her, no more comfort for months! I might as well live with my clerk or my servant. And if I give in now, I shall have to give in always. Well! I cant help it. I have stuck to having my own way all my life; but there must be an end to that drudgery some day. She is young: let her have her turn at it.

The parlormaid comes in, evidently excited.

THE PARLORMAID. Please, sir, Mr Lickcheese wants to see you very particlar. On important business. Your business, he told me to say.

SARTORIUS. Mr Lickcheese! Do you mean Lickcheese who used to come here on my business?

THE PARLORMAID. Yes, sir. But indeed, sir, youd scarcely know him.

SARTORIUS   [*frowning*] Hm! Starving, I suppose. Come to beg?

THE PARLORMAID. [*intensely repudiating the idea*] O-o-o-o-h NO, sir. Quite the gentleman, sir! Sealskin overcoat, sir! Come in a hansom, all shaved and clean! I'm sure he's come into a fortune, sir.

SARTORIUS. Hm! Shew him up.

Lickcheese, who has been waiting at the door, instantly comes in. The change in his appearance is dazzling. He is in evening dress, with an overcoat lined throughout with furs presenting all the hues of the tiger. His shirt is fastened at the breast with a single diamond stud. His silk hat is of the glossiest black; a handsome gold watch-chain hangs like a garland on his filled-out waistcoat; he has shaved his whiskers and grown a moustache, the ends of which are waxed and pointed. As Sartorius stares speechless at him, he stands, smiling, to be admired, intensely enjoying the effect he is producing. The parlormaid, hardly less pleased with her own share in this coup-de-théâtre, goes out beam-

ing, full of the news for the kitchen. Lickcheese clinches the situation by a triumphant nod at Sartorius.

SARTORIUS [*bracing himself: hostile*] Well?

LICKCHEESE. Quite well, Sartorius, thankee.

SARTORIUS. I was not asking after your health, sir, as you know, I think, as well as I do. What is your business?

LICKCHEESE. Business that I can take elsewhere if I meet with less civility than I please to put up with, Sartorius. You and me is man and man now. It was money that used to be my master, and not you: dont think it. Now that I'm independent in respect of money—

SARTORIUS [*crossing determinedly to the door, and holding it open*] You can take your independence out of my house, then. I wont have it here.

LICKCHEESE [*indulgently*] Come, Sartorius: dont be stiff-necked. I come here as a friend to put money in your pocket. No use your lettin on to me that youre above money. Eh?

SARTORIUS [*hesitates, and at last shuts the door saying guardedly*] How much money?

LICKCHEESE [*victorious, going to Blanche's chair and taking off his overcoat*] Ah! there you speak like yourself, Sartorius. Now suppose you ask me to sit down and make myself comfortable.

SARTORIUS [*coming from the door*] I have a mind to put you downstairs by the back of your neck, you infernal blackguard.

LICKCHEESE [*not a bit ruffled, hangs his overcoat on the back of Blanche's chair, pulling a cigar case out of one of the pockets as he does so*] You and me is too much of a pair for me to take anything you say in bad part, Sartorius. Ave a cigar?

SARTORIUS. No smoking here: this is my daughter's room. However, sit down, sit down. [*They sit*].

LICKCHEESE. I' bin gittin on a little since I saw you last.

SARTORIUS. So I see.

LICKCHEESE. I owe it partly to you, you know. Does that surprise you?

SARTORIUS. It doesnt concern me.

LICKCHEESE. So you think, Sartorius; because it never did concern you how *I* got on, so long as I got you on by bringin in the rents. But I picked up something for myself down at Robbins's Row.

SARTORIUS. I always thought so. Have you come to make restitution?

LICKCHEESE. You wouldnt take it if I offered it to you, Sartorius. It wasnt money: it was knowledge: knowledge of the great public question of the Ousing of the Working Classes. You know theres a Royal Commission on it, dont you?

SARTORIUS. Oh, I see. Youve been giving evidence.

LICKCHEESE. Giving evidence! Not me. What good would that do me? Only my expenses; and that not on the professional scale, neither. No: I gev no evidence. But I'll tell you what I did. I kep it back, jast to oblige one or two people whose feelins would 'a bin urt by seeing their names in a bluebook as keepin a fever den. Their Agent got so friendly with me over it that he put his name on a bill of mine to the tune of—well, no matter: it gev me a start; and a start was all I ever wanted to get on my feet. Ive got a copy of the first report of the Commission in the pocket of my overcoat. [*He rises and gets at his overcoat, from a pocket of which he takes a bluebook*]. I turned down the page to shew you: I thought youd like to see it. [*He doubles the book back at the place indicated, and hands it to Sartorius*].

SARTORIUS. So blackmail is the game, eh? [*He puts the book on the table without looking at it, and strikes it emphatically with his fist*]. I don't care that for my name being in blue-books. My friends don't read them; and I'm neither a Cabinet Minister nor a candidate for Parliament. Theres nothing to be got out of me on that lay.

LICKCHEESE [*shocked*] Blackmail! Oh, Mr Sartorius, do you think I would let out a word about your premises? Round on an old pal! no: that aint Lickcheese's way. Besides, they know all about you already. Them stairs that you and me quarrelled about, they was a whole arternoon examinin the clergyman that made such a fuss—you remember?— about the women that was urt on it. He made the worst he could of it, in an ungentlemanly, unchristian spirit. I wouldnt have that clergyman's disposition for worlds. Oh no: thats not what was in my thoughts.

SARTORIUS. Come, come, man! what was in your thoughts? Out with it.

LICKCHEESE [*with provoking deliberation, smiling and looking myste-riously at him*] You aint spent a few hundreds in repairs since we parted, ave you? [*Sartorius, losing patience, makes a threatening movement*]. Now dont fly out at me. I know a landlord that owned as beastly a slum as you

292

could find in London, down there by the Tower. By my advice that man put half the houses into first-class repair, and let the other half to a new Company: the North Thames Iced Mutton Depot Company, of which I hold a few shares: promoter's shares. And what was the end of it, do you think?

SARTORIUS. Smash, I suppose.

LICKCHEESE. Smash! not a bit of it. Compensation, Mr Sartorius, compensation. Do you understand that?

SARTORIUS. Compensation for what?

LICKCHEESE. Why, the land was wanted for an extension of the Mint; and the Company had to be bought out, and the buildings compensated for. Somebody has to know these things beforehand, you know, no matter how dark theyre kept.

SARTORIUS [*interested, but cautious*] Well?

LICKCHEESE. Is that all you have to say to me, Mr Sartorius? Well! as if I was next door's dog! Suppose I'd got wind of a new street that would knock down Robbins's Row and turn Burke's Walk into a frontage worth thirty pound a foot! would you say no more to me than [*mimicking*] 'Well'? [*Sartorius hesitates, looking at him in great doubt. Lickcheese rises and exhibits himself*]. Come! look at my get-up, Mr Sartorius. Look at this watch-chain! Look at the corporation Ive got on me! Do you think all that came from keeping my mouth shut? No: it came from keeping ears and eyes open.

Blanche comes in, followed by the parlormaid, who has a silver tray on which she collects the coffee cups. Sartorius, impatient at the interruption, rises and motions Lickcheese to the door of the study.

SARTORIUS. Sh! We must talk this over in the study. There is a good fire there; and you can smoke. Blanche: an old friend of ours.

LICKCHEESE. And a kind one to me. I hope I see you well, Miss Blanche.

BLANCHE. Why, it's Mr Lickcheese! I hardly knew you.

LICKCHEESE. I find you a little changed yourself, miss.

BLANCHE [*hastily*] Oh, I am the same as ever. How are Mrs Lickcheese and the chil—

SARTORIUS. [*impatiently*] We have business to transact, Blanche. You can talk to Mr Lickcheese afterwards. Come on.

Sartorius and Lickcheese go into the study. Blanche, surprised at her father's abruptness, looks after them for a moment. Then, seeing Lickcheese's overcoat on her chair, she takes it up, amused and looks at the fur.

THE PARLORMAID. Oh, we are fine, aint we. Miss Blanche? I think Mr Lickcheese must have come into a legacy. [*Confidentially*] I wonder what he can want with the master, Miss Blanche! He brought him this big book. [*She shews the bluebook to Blanche*].

BLANCHE [*her curiosity roused*] Let me see. [*She takes the book and looks at it*]. Theres something about papa in it. [*She sits down and begins to read*].

THE PARLORMAID [*folding the tea-table and putting it out of the way*] He looks ever s'much younger, Miss Blanche, dont he? I couldnt help laughing when I saw him with his whiskers shaved off: it do look so silly when youre not accustomed to it. [*No answer from Blanche*]. You havnt finished your coffee, miss: I suppose I may take it away? [*No answer*]. Oh, you are interested in Mr Lickcheese's book, miss.

Blanche springs up. The parlormaid looks at her face, and instantly hurries out of the room on tiptoe with her tray.

BLANCHE. So that was why he would not touch the money. [*She tries to tear the book across. Finding this impossible she throws it violently into the fireplace. It falls into the fender*]. Oh, if only a girl could have no father, no family, just as I have no mother! Clergyman! beast! 'The worst slum landlord in London.' 'Slum landlord.' Oh! [*She covers her face with her hands, and sinks shuddering into the chair on which the overcoat lies. The study door opens*].

LICKCHEESE [*in the study*] You just wait five minutes: I'll fetch him. [*Blanche snatches a piece of work from her basket, and sits erect and quiet, stitching at it. Lickcheese comes back, speaking to Sartorius, who follows him*]. He lodges round the corner in Gower Street; and my private ansom's at the door. By your leave, Miss Blanche [*pulling gently at his overcoat*].

BLANCHE [*rising*] I beg your pardon. I hope I havnt crushed it.

LICKCHEESE [*gallantly, as he gets into the coat*] Youre welcome to crush it again now, Miss Blanche. Dont say good evenin to me, miss: I'm comin back presently: me and a friend or two. Ta ta, Sartorius: I shant be long. [*He goes out*].

Sartorius looks about for the bluebook.

BLANCHE. I thought we were done with Lickcheese.

SARTORIUS. Not quite yet, I think. He left a book here for me to look over: a large book in a blue paper cover. Has the girl put it away? [*He sees it in the fender; looks at Blanche; and adds*] Have you seen it?

BLANCHE. No. Yes. [*Angrily*] No: I have not seen it. What have I to do with it?

Sartorius picks the book up and dusts it; then sits down quietly to read. After a glance up and down the columns, he nods assentingly, as if he found there exactly what he expected.

SARTORIUS. It's a curious thing, Blanche, that the Parliamentary gentlemen who write such books as these should be so ignorant of practical business. One would suppose, to read this, that we are the most grasping, grinding heartless pair in the world, you and I.

BLANCHE. Is it not true? About the state of the houses, I mean?

SARTORIUS [*calmly*] Oh, quite true.

BLANCHE. Then it is not our fault?

SARTORIUS. My dear: if we made the houses any better, the rents would have to be raised so much that the poor people would be unable to pay, and would be thrown homeless on the streets.

BLANCHE. Well, turn them out and get in a respectable class of people. Why should we have the disgrace of harboring such wretches?

SARTORIUS [*opening his eyes*] That sounds a little hard on them, doesnt it, my child?

BLANCHE. Oh, I hate the poor. At least, I hate those dirty, drunken, disreputable people who live like pigs. If they must be provided for, let other people look after them. How can you expect any one to think well of us when such things are written about us in that infamous book?

SARTORIUS [*coldly and a little wistfully*] I see I have made a real lady of you, Blanche.

BLANCHE [*defiantly*] Well? Are you sorry for that?

SARTORIUS. No, my dear: of course not. But do you know, Blanche, that my mother was a very poor woman, and that her poverty was not her fault?

BLANCHE. I suppose not; but the people we want to mix with now dont know that. And it was not my fault; so I dont see why *I* should be made to suffer for it.

SARTORIUS [*enraged*] Who makes you suffer for it, miss? What would

295

you be now but for what your grandmother did for me when she stood at her wash-tub for thirteen hours a day and thought herself rich when she made fifteen shillings a week?

BLANCHE   [*angrily*] I suppose I should have been down on her level instead of being raised above it, as I am now. Would you like us to go and live in that place in the book for the sake of grandmamma? I hate the idea of such things. I dont want to know about them. I love you because you brought me up to something better. [*Half aside, as she turns away from him*] I should hate you if you had not.

SARTORIUS   [*giving in*] Well, my child, I suppose it is natural for you to feel that way, after your bringing up. It is the ladylike view of the matter. So dont let us quarrel, my girl. You shall not be made to suffer any more. I have made up my mind to improve the property, and get in quite a new class of tenants. There! does that satisfy you? I am only waiting for the consent of the ground landlord, Lady Roxdale.

BLANCHE.   Lady Roxdale!

SARTORIUS.   Yes. But I shall expect the mortgagee to take his share of the risk.

BLANCHE.   The mortgagee! Do you mean—[*She cannot finish the sentence: Sartorius does it for her*].

SARTORIUS.   Harry Trench. Yes. And remember, Blanche: if he consents to join me in the scheme, I shall have to be friends with him.

BLANCHE.   And to ask him to the house?

SARTORIUS.   Only on business. You need not meet him unless you like.

BLANCHE   [*overwhelmed*] When is he coming?

SARTORIUS.   There is no time to be lost. Lickcheese has gone to ask him to come round.

BLANCHE   [*in dismay*] Then he will be here in a few minutes! What shall I do?

SARTORIUS.   I advise you to receive him as if nothing had happened, and then go out and leave us to our business. You are not afraid to meet him?

BLANCHE.   Afraid! No: most certainly not. But—

LICKCHEESE'S VOICE [*without*] Straight in front of you, doctor. You never bin here before; but I know the house better than my own.

BLANCHE.   Here they are. Dont say I'm here, papa. [*She rushes away into the study].*

Lickcheese comes in with Trench and Cokane. Both are in evening dress. Cokane shakes hands effusively with Sartorius. Trench who is coarsened and sullen, and has evidently not been making the best of his disappointment, bows shortly and resentfully. Lickcheese covers the general embarrassment by talking cheerfully until they are all seated round the large table: Trench nearest the fireplace; Cokane nearest the piano; and the other two between them, with Lickcheese next Cokane].

LICKCHEESE. Here we are, all friends round St Paul's. You remember Mr Cokane? he does a little business for me now as a friend, and gives me a help with my correspondence: sekketerry we call it. Ive no litery style, and thats the truth; so Mr Cokane kindly puts it into my letters and draft prospectuses and advertisements and the like. Dont you, Cokane? Of course you do: why shouldnt you? He's been helping me to pursuade his old friend, Dr Trench, about the matter we were speaking of.

COKANE   [*austerely*] No, Mr Lickcheese, not trying to persuade him. No: this is a matter of principle with me. I say it is your duty, Henry—your duty—to put those abominable buildings into proper and habitable repair. As a man of science you owe it to the community to perfect the sanitary arrangements. In questions of duty there is no room for persuasion, even from the oldest friend.

SARTORIUS   [*to Trench*] I certainly feel, as Mr Cokane puts it, that it is our duty: one which I have perhaps too long neglected out of regard for the poorest class of tenants.

LICKCHEESE. Not a doubt of it, gents: a dooty. I can be as sharp as any man when it's a question of business; but dooty's another pair o' shoes.

TRENCH.   Well, I dont see that it's any more my duty now than it was four months ago. I look at it simply as a question of so much money.

COKANE.   Shame, Harry, shame! Shame!

TRENCH.   Oh, shut up, you fool. [*Cokane springs up*].

LICKCHEESE   [*catching his coat and holding him*] Steady! steady! Mr Sekketerry. Dr Trench is only joking.

COKANE.   I insist on the withdrawal of that expression. I have been called a fool.

TRENCH   [*morosely*] So you are a fool.

COKANE.   Then you are a damned fool. Now, sir!

TRENCH.   All right. Now weve settled that. [*Cokane, with a snort, sits down*]. What I mean is this. Dont lets have any nonsense about this job. As I understand it, Robbins's Row is to be pulled down to make way for the new street into the Strand; and the straight tip now is to go for compensation.

LICKCHEESE [*chuckling*] That'so, Dr Trench. Thats it.

TRENCH   [*continuing*] Well, it appears that the dirtier a place is the more rent you get; and the decenter it is, the more compensation you get. So we're to give up dirt and go in for decency.

SARTORIUS. I should not put it exactly in that way; but—

COKANE.   Quite right, Mr Sartorius, quite right. The case could not have been stated in worse taste or with less tact.

LICKCHEESE. Sh-sh-sh-sh!

SARTORIUS. I do not quite go with you there, Mr Cokane. Dr Trench puts the case frankly as a man of business. I take the wider view of a public man. We live in a progressive age; and humanitarian ideas are advancing and must be taken into account. But my practical conclusion is the same as his. I should hardly feel justified in making a large claim for compensation under existing circumstances.

LICKCHEESE. Of course not; and you wouldnt get it if you did. You see, it's like this, Dr Trench. Theres no doubt that the Vestries has legal powers to play old Harry with slum properties, and spoil the houseknacking game if they please. That didnt matter in the good old times, because the Vestries used to be us ourselves. Nobody ever knew a word about the election; and we used to get ten of us into a room and elect one another, and do what we liked. Well, that cock wont fight any longer; and, to put it short, the game is up for men in the position of you and Mr Sartorius. My advice to you is, take the present chance of getting out of it. Spend a little money on the block at the Cribbs Market end: enough to make it look like a model dwelling, you know; and let the other block to me on fair terms for a depot of the North Thames Iced Mutton Company. Theyll be knocked down inside of two years to make room for the new north and south main thoroughfare; and youll be compensated to the tune of double the present valuation, with the cost of the improvements thrown in. Leave things as they are; and you stand a good chance of being fined, or condemned, or pulled down before long. Now's your time.

COKANE. Hear, hear! Hear, hear! Hear, hear! Admirably put from the business point of view! I recognize the uselessness of putting the moral point of view to you, Trench; but even you must feel the cogency of Mr Lickcheese's business statement.

TRENCH. But why cant you act without me? What have I got to do with it? I'm only a mortgagee.

SARTORIUS. There is a certain risk in this compensation investment, Dr Trench. The County Council may alter the line of the new street. If that happens, the money spent in improving the houses will be thrown away: simply thrown away. Worse than thrown away, in fact; for the new buildings may stand unlet or half let for years. But you will expect your seven per cent as usual.

TRENCH. A man must live.

COKANE. Je n'en vois pas la nécessité.[1]

TRENCH. Shut up. Billy; or else speak some language you understand. No, Mr Sartorius: I should be very glad to stand in with you if I could afford it; but I cant; so you may leave me out of it.

LICKCHEESE. Well, all I can say is that youre a very foolish young man.

COKANE. What did I tell you, Harry?

TRENCH. I dont see that it's any business of yours, Mr Lickcheese.

LICKCHEESE. It's a free country: every man has a right to his opinion.

COKANE. Hear, hear!

LICKCHEESE. Come! wheres your feelins for them poor people, Dr Trench? Remember how it went to your heart when I first told you about them. What! are you going to turn hard?

TRENCH. No: it wont do: you cant get over me that way. You proved to me before that there was no use in being sentimental over that slum shop of ours; and it's no good your turning round on the philanthropic tack now that you want me to put my capital into your speculation. I've had my lesson; and I'm going to stick to my present income. It's little enough for me as it is.

SARTORIUS. It really matters nothing to me, Dr Trench, how you decide. I can easily raise the money elsewhere and pay you off. Then since you are resolved to run no risks, you can invest your ten thousand pounds in Consols and get two hundred

---

1 *Je n'en vois pas la nécessité*: 'I don't see the need'.

and fifty pounds a year for it instead of seven hundred.
*Trench, completely outwitted, stares at them in consternation. Cokane
breaks the silence.*

COKANE. This is what comes of being avaricious, Harry. Two thirds
of your income gone at one blow. And I must say it serves
you right.

TRENCH. Thats all very fine; but I dont understand it. If you can do
this to me, why didnt you do it long ago?

SARTORIUS. Because, as I should probably have had to borrow at the
same rate, I should have saved nothing; whereas you
would have lost over four hundred a year: a very serious
matter for you. I had no desire to be unfriendly; and even
now I should be glad to let the mortgage stand, were it
not that the circumstances mentioned by Mr Lickcheese
force my hand. Besides, Dr Trench, I hoped for some time
that our interests might be joined by closer ties than those
of friendship.

LICKCHEESE [*jumping up, relieved*] There! Now the murder's out.
Excuse me, Dr Trench. Ex - cuse me, Mr Sartorius: excuse
my freedom. Why not Dr Trench marry Miss Blanche,
and settle the whole affair that way?

Sensation. Lickcheese sits down triumphant.

COKANE. You forget, Mr Lickcheese, that the young lady, whose
taste has to be considered, decisively objected to him.

TRENCH. Oh! Perhaps you think she was struck with you.

COKANE. I do not say so, Trench. No man of any delicacy would
suggest such a thing. You have an untutored mind,
Trench, an untutored mind.

TRENCH. Well, Cokane: Ive told you my opinion of you already.

COKANE [*rising wildly*] And I have told you my opinion of you. I
will repeat it if you wish. I am ready to repeat it.

LICKCHEESE. Come, Mr Sekketerry: you and me, as married men, is out
of the unt as far as young ladies is concerned. I know Miss
Blanche: she has her father's eye for business. Explain this
job to her; and she'll make it up with Dr Trench. Why not
have a bit of romance in business when it costs nothing?
We all have our feelins: we aint mere calculatin machines.

SARTORIUS [*revolted*] Do you think, Lickcheese, that my daughter is
to be made part of a money bargain between you and
these gentlemen?

LICKCHEESE. Oh come, Sartorius! dont talk as if you was the only

| | father in the world. I have a daughter too; and my feelins in that matter is just as fine as yours. I propose nothing but what is for Miss Blanche's advantage and Dr Trench's. |

COKANE. Lickcheese expresses himself roughly, Mr Sartorius; but his is a sterling nature; and what he says is to the point. If Miss Sartorius can really bring herself to care for Harry, I am far from desiring to stand in the way of such an arrangement.

TRENCH. Why, what have you got to do with it?

LICKCHEESE. Easy, Dr Trench, easy. We want your opinion. Are you still on for marrying Miss Blanche if she's agreeable?

TRENCH [*shortly*] I dont know that I am. [*Sartorius rises indignantly*].

LICKCHEESE. Easy one moment, Mr Sartorius. [*To Trench*] Come now, Dr Trench! you say you don't know that you are. But do you know that you aint? thats what we want to know.

TRENCH [*sulkily*] I wont have the relations between Miss Sartorius and myself made part of a bargain. [*He rises to leave the table*].

LICKCHEESE [*rising*] Thats enough: a gentleman could say no less. [*Insinuatingly*] Now, would you mind me and Cokane and the guvnor steppin into the study to arrange about the lease to the North Thames Iced Mutton Company?

TRENCH. Oh, *I* dont mind. I'm going home. Theres nothing more to say.

LICKCHEESE. No: dont go. Only just a minute: me and Cokane will be back in no time to see you home. Youll wait for us, wont you?

TRENCH. Oh well, if you wish, yes.

LICKCHEESE [*cheerily*] Didnt I know you would!

SARTORIUS [*at the study door, to Cokane*] After you, sir.

Cokane bows formally and goes into the study.

LICKCHEESE [*at the door, aside to Sartorius*] You never ad such a managin man as me, Sartorius. [*He goes into the study chuckling, followed by Sartorius*].

Trench, left alone, looks round carefully and listens a moment. Then he goes on tiptoe to the piano and leans upon it with folded arms, gazing at Blanche's portrait. Blanche herself appears presently at the study door. When she sees how he is occupied, she closes it softly and steals over to him, watching him intently. He rises from his leaning attitude, and takes the portrait from the easel, and is about to kiss it when, tak-

ing a second look round to reassure himself that nobody is watching him, he finds Blanche close upon him. He drops the portrait, and stares at her without the least presence of mind.

BLANCHE   [*shrewishly*] Well? So you have come back here. You have had the meanness to come into this house again. [*He flushes and retreats a step. She follows him up remorselessly*]. What a poor spirited creature you must be! Why dont you go? [*Red and wincing, he starts huffily to get his hat from the table; but when he turns to the door with it she deliberately stands in his way; so that he has to stop*]. I dont want you to stay. [*For a moment they stand face to face, quite close to one another, she provocative, taunting, half defying, half inviting him to advance, in a flush of undisguised animal excitement. It suddenly flashes on him that all this ferocity is erotic: that she is making love to him. His eye lights up: a cunning expression comes into the corners of his mouth: with a heavy assumption of indifference he walks straight back to his chair, and plants himself in it with his arms folded. She comes down the room after him*]. But I forgot: you have found that there is some money to be made here. Lickcheese told you. You, who were so disinterested, so independent, that you could not accept anything from my father! [*At the end of every sentence she waits to see what execution she has done*]. I suppose you will try to persuade me that you have come down here on a great philanthropic enterprise—to befriend the poor by having those houses rebuilt, eh? [*Trench maintains his attitude and makes no sign*]. Yes: when my father makes you do it. And when Lickcheese has discovered some way of making it profitable. Oh, I know papa; and I know you. And for the sake of that, you come back here—into the house where you were refused—ordered out. [*Trench's face darkens: her eyes gleam as she sees it*]. Aha! you remember that. You know it's true: you cant deny it. [*She sits down, and softens her tone a little as she affects to pity him*]. Well, let me tell you that you cut a poor figure, a very, very poor figure, Harry. [*At the word Harry he relaxes the fold of his arms; and a faint grin of anticipated victory appears on his face*]. And you, too, a gentleman! so highly connected! with such distinguished relations! so particular as to where your money comes from! I wonder at you. I really wonder at you. I should have thought that if your fine family gave you nothing else, it might at least have given you some sense of personal dignity. Perhaps you think you look dignified at present: eh? [*No reply*]. Well, I can assure you that you dont: you look most ridiculous—as foolish as a man could look—you don't know what to say; and you don't know what to do. But after all, I really dont see what any one could say in defence of such conduct. [*He looks straight in front of him, and purses up his lips as if whistling. This annoys her; and she becomes affectedly polite*]. I am afraid I am in your way, Dr Trench. [*She rises*]. I shall not intrude on you any longer. You seem so perfectly at home that I need make no apology for leaving you to yourself. [*She makes a feint of going to the door; but he does not budge; and she returns and comes behind his chair*]. Harry. [*He does not turn. She comes a step nearer*]. Harry: I want you to answer me a question. [*Earnestly, stooping over him*] Look me in the face. [*No reply*]. Do you hear? [*Seizing his cheeks and twisting his head round*] Look—me—in—the—face. [*He shuts his eyes tight and grins. She suddenly kneels down beside him with her breast against his shoulder*]. Harry: what were you doing with my photograph just now, when you thought you were alone? [*He opens his eyes: they are full of delight. She flings her arms around him, and crushes him in an ecstatic embrace as she adds, with furious tenderness*] How dare you touch anything belonging to me?

The study door opens and voices are heard.

TRENCH.   I hear some one coming.

She regains her chair with a bound, and pushes it back as far as possible. Cokane, Lickcheese, and Sartorius come from the study. Sartorius and Lickcheese come to Trench. Cokane crosses to Blanche in his most killing manner.

COKANE.   How do you do. Miss Sartorius? Nice weather for the return of l'enfant prodigue, eh?

BLANCHE.   Capital, Mr Cokane. So glad to see you. [*She gives him her hand, which he kisses with gallantry*].

LICKCHEESE [*on Trench's left, in a low voice*] Any noos for us, Dr Trench?

TRENCH   [*to Sartorius, on his right*] I'll stand in, compensation or no compensation. [*He shakes Sartorius's hand*].

The parlormaid has just appeared at the door.

THE PARLORMAID. Supper is ready, miss.

COKANE.   Allow me.

Exeunt omnes: Blanche on Cokane's arm; Lickcheese jocosely taking Sartorius on one arm, and Trench on the other.

From *The Perfect Wagnerite*

(1898)

from Siegfried as Protestant

The philosophically fertile element in the original project of Siegfried's Death[1] was the conception of Siegfried himself as a type of the healthy man raised to perfect confidence in his own impulses by an intense and joyous vitality which is above fear, sickliness of conscience, malice, and the makeshifts and moral crutches of law and order which accompany them. Such a character appears extraordinarily fascinating and exhilarating to our guilty and conscience-ridden generations, however little they may understand him. The world has always delighted in the man who is delivered from conscience. From Punch and Don Juan down to Robert Macaire,[2] Jeremy Diddler[3] and the pantomime clown, he has always drawn large audiences; but hitherto he has been decorously given to the devil at the end. Indeed eternal punishment is sometimes deemed too high a compliment to his nature. When the late Lord Lytton, in his Strange Story,[4] introduced a character personifying the joyousness of intense vitality, he felt bound to deny him the immortal soul which was at that time conceded even to the humblest characters in fiction, and to accept mischievousness, cruelty, and utter incapacity for sympathy as the inevitable consequence of his magnificent bodily and mental health.

In short, though men felt all the charm of abounding life and abandonment to its impulses, they dared not, in their deep self-mistrust, conceive it otherwise than as a force making for evil—one which must lead to universal ruin unless checked and literally mortified by self-renunciation in obedience to superhuman guidance, or at least to some

---

1 *Siegfried's death*: Siegfried, the hero of Wagner's *Der Ring des Nibelungen*, is killed by Hagen as he regains his memory and recalls his love for Brünnhilde, whom he has rescued from the magic fire to which her father Wotan, chief of the gods, had consigned her.

2 *Robert Macaire*: a clever rogue, depicted in a series of lithographs by Honoré Daumier. He was a minor character in the melodrama *L'Auberge des Adrets* (1823), written by Benjamin Antier, Saint-Amand and Paulyanthe; the actor Frederic Lemaitre transformed him into the dubious hero of social satire in his play *Robert Macaire, ce cynique scapin de crime* (1834).

3 *Jeremy Diddler*: a cunning trickster in James Kenney's farce, *Raising the Wind* (1803).

4 *his Strange Story*:Margrave, in Edward Bulwer Lytton, *A Strange Story* (1861) is a malevolent character who wants to live forever.

reasoned system of morals. When it became apparent to the cleverest of them that no such superhuman guidance existed, and that their secularist systems had all the fictitiousness of 'revelation' without its poetry, there was no escaping the conclusion that all the good that man had done must be put down to his arbitrary will as well as all the evil he had done; and it was also obvious that if progress were a reality, his beneficent impulses must be gaining on his destructive ones. It was under the influence of these ideas that we began to hear about the joy of life where we had formerly heard about the grace of God or the Age of Reason, and that the boldest spirits began to raise the question whether churches and laws and the like were not doing a great deal more harm than good by their action in limiting the freedom of the human will. Four hundred years ago, when belief in God and in revelation was general throughout Europe, a similar wave of thought led the strongest-hearted peoples to affirm that every man's private judgment was a more trustworthy interpreter of God and revelation than the Church. This was called Protestantism; and though the Protestants were not strong enough for their creed, and soon set up a Church of their own, yet the movement, on the whole, has justified the direction it took. Nowadays the supernatural element in Protestantism has perished; and if every man's private judgment is still to be justified as the most trustworthy interpreter of the will of Humanity (which is not a more extreme proposition than the old one about the will of God) Protestantism must take a fresh step in advance, and become Anarchism. Which it has accordingly done, Anarchism being one of the notable new creeds of the eighteenth and nineteenth centuries.

The weak place which experience finds out in the Anarchist theory is its reliance on the progress already achieved by 'Man.' There is no such thing as Man in the world: what we have to deal with is a multitude of men, some of them great rascals, some of them great statesmen, others both, with a vast majority capable of managing their personal affairs, but not of comprehending social organization, or grappling with the problems created by their association in enormous numbers. If 'Man' means this majority, then 'Man' has made no progress: he has, on the contrary, resisted it. He will not even pay the cost of existing institutions: the requisite money has to be filched from him by 'indirect taxation.' Such people, like Wagner's giants, must be governed by laws; and their assent to such government must be secured by deliberately filling them with prejudices and practising on their imaginations by pageantry and artificial eminences and dignities. The government is of course established by the few who are capable of government, though, its mechanism once complete, it may be, and generally is, carried on unintelligently by people who are incapable of it, the capable people repairing it from time to time when it gets too far behind the continuous advance or decay of civilization. All these capable people are thus in the position of Wotan, forced to maintain as sacred, and themselves submit to, laws which they privately know to be obsolescent makeshifts, and to affect the deepest veneration for creeds and ideals which they ridicule among themselves with cynical scepticism. No individual Siegfried can rescue them from this bondage and hypocrisy; in fact, the individual Siegfried has come often enough, only to find himself confronted with the alternative of governing those who are not Siegfrieds or risking destruction at their hands. And this dilemma will persist until Wotan's inspiration comes to our governors, and they see that their business is not the devising of laws and institutions to prop up the weaknesses of mobs and secure the survival of the unfittest, but the breeding of men whose wills and intelligences may be depended on to produce spontaneously the social well-being our clumsy laws now aim at and miss. The majority of men at present in Europe have no business to be alive; and no serious progress will be made until we address ourselves earnestly and scientifically to the task of producing trustworthy human material for society. In short, it is necessary to breed a race of men in whom the life-giving impulses predominate, before the New Protestantism becomes politically practicable.[1]

The most inevitable dramatic conception, then, of the nineteenth century is that of a perfectly naïve hero upsetting religion, law and order in all directions, and establishing in their place the unfettered action of Humanity doing exactly what it likes, and producing order instead of confusion thereby because it likes to do what is necessary for the good of the race. This conception, already incipient in Adam Smith's Wealth of Nations,[2] was certain at last to reach some great artist, and be embodied by him in a masterpiece. It was also certain that if that master happened to be a German, he should take delight in describing his hero as the Freewiller of Necessity, thereby beyond measure exasperating Englishmen with a congenital incapacity for metaphysics.

JANE BARLOW (1857–1917)

1 The necessity for breeding the governing class from a selected stock has always been recognized by Aristocrats, however erroneous their methods of selection. We have changed our system from Aristocracy to Democracy without considering that we were at the same time changing, as regards our governing class, from Selection to Promiscuity. Those who have taken a practical part in modern politics best know how farcical the result is. [*Shaw's note.*]
2 *Adam Smith's Wealth of Nations*: in *The Wealth of Nations* (1776), Adam Smith propounded the doctrine that society is the sum of its members, each motivated by a self-interest which helps to benefit society at large.

Jane Barlow

Born in Clontarf, Co. Dublin, the daughter of Rev. James Barlow, later vice-provost of Trinity College, Dublin, she spent most of her life in a thatched cottage in Raheny, Dublin. *Bog-land Studies* (1892), her first poetry collection, is wholly written in the Hiberno English spoken in the west of Ireland. Her best-known works, *Irish Idylls* (1892) and *Strangers at Lisconnel* (1895), are sketches set in the Connemara village of Lisconnel which stands 'in the common light of day ... with no fantastic myths to embellish or disprove it'. They were followed by *Maureen's Fairing and Other Stories* (1895), *Mrs. Martin's Company and Other Stories* (1896), and *A Creel of Irish Stories* (1897), and various other collections, which were popular in Britain and America, but were largely ignored in Ireland. Her novel *Kerrigan's Quality* (1894) presents the ordeals of the Famine through the eyes of a returning emigrant.

From *Bog-land Studies*

(1894)

Past Praying For: Or, The Souper's Widow[1]

'Horribili super aspectu mortalibus instans.'[2]

(A.D. 184–)

I.

Sure he'd never ha' done it, not he, if I'd on'y but held o' me tongue;
Och, the fool that I was, the black fool—for the same I'd deserve to be hung;
But, bedad thin, the tongue o' ye's harder than aught in the world else to hould,
An' that mornin' we all was disthracted an' perished wid hunger an' could.

II.

It was right in the worst o' the famine, the first years the praties wint black—
Tho' ye're scarce of an age, Sisther Frances, to remember o' things so far back;
But in coorse ye've heard tell o' thim times, whin the people was dyin' be the score,
Ay, be hundrids an' thousinds, the like was ne'er seen in the counthry before.
An' what else should the crathurs ha' done, wid the food o' thim rotted to dirt?
Och, to see thim—ye'd meet ne'er a man but his face was as white as his shirt.
And ourselves had been starved all the winther, the childher, an' Micky, an' me,

---

1 *Souper* is a term applied to the few Irish Catholic peasants who, during famine years, professed Protestantism in order to obtain the relief, often intrusted for distribution to the clergy of the then Established Church, who occasionally made a grant conditional upon attendance at their services, etc., though as a rule acting impartially and humanely. [*Barlow's note.*]
2 Titus Lucretius Carus, from *De rerum natura*—'Its horrible face glowering over mankind born to die'.

307

An' poor Micky's ould mother, till, comin' on spring, not a chance could we see;
For there wasn't a house far or near where they'd give ye the black o' your eye,
And our Praste he was down wid the fever, an' clane ruinated forby.

III.

So it's rale delighted we were on that evenin' Pat Murphy brought word
How the people o' Lunnon had sint some relief to our townland he heard;
Relief—that was oatmale, an' loaves, an' a grand sup o' broth in a bowl,
An' to git it ye'd stip down to Parson, who'd tuk to disthribit the whole.
So full early we started next day, sin' the road's a long sthretch to his place,
An' we hadn't a scrap in the house but a crust for the childher. And in case
We got out the big bag for the male, Mick an' I, while the rest, lookin' on,
Did be wishin' we'd bring it back full, an' a-wondhrin' how long we'd be gone.
Sure, the laste o' thim all, little Larry, that scarce was a size to run sthraight,
Tuk a notion to come wid us too, whin he heard 'twas for somethin' to ait.
I remember the look of it yit, skytin' afther us the lenth o' the lane.
Thin I mind, comin' into the town, meetin' cart-loads and cart-loads o' grain,
That Lord Athmore was sindin' in sthrings to be shipped off from Westport by say;
An' the people stood watchin' thim pass like as if 'twas a corpse on its way.
An' sez Mick, whin we met thim: 'Look, Norah,' sez he, 'that's not aisy to stand:
It's the lives of our childher th' ould naygur's a-cartin' off out o' the land.'
An' sez I, just to pacify Mick: 'Thin good luck to the folks as ha' sint
What 'ill keep o' the sowls in their bodies; if we can but do that I'm contint.'

IV.

But, och, Sisther darlin', at Parson's we got sorra a bit afther all;
Not a taste in the world save the smell o' the soup that was sthrong in the hall.
For whin Parson come out from his breakfast, he said the relief that he'd got
Was for thim who wint reg'lar to church—where he'd ne'er seen a wan of our lot;
An' he'd liefer throw bread to the dogs than to childher o' papists, whose thricks
Were no better than haythins' brought up to be worshippin' ould bits o' sticks.
Howsome'er, if we'd give him our word we'd attind the next Sunday, why thin
He'd considher. But who could ha' promised the like? Such a shame and a sin:
Turn a souper in sight o' thim all, an' throop off to the place where they curse
The ould Pope, an' the Virgin, an' jeer at the Mass—why, what haythin'd do worse?
Yet that hape o' big loaves. Sisther Frances, thim folk's in a manner to blame
Who know whin ye're starvin' an' tempt ye. So we wint back the way that we came.
But, ochone, it seemed double the lenth, an' it's never a word Micky said,
An' the ould empty bag on me arm was that light it felt heavy as lead;
An' the childher, that ran out to meet us as far as the top o' the hill,

Whin they found we'd brought nothin' at all—I could cry now to think o' thim still.

V.

An' twyst afther that Mick wint down there to thry if a bit could be had,
But onless that we promised to turn, not a scrapeen we'd git good or bad.
Och, the long hungry days. So wan mornin' we'd ate all the breakfast o'er night,
And I hoped we'd be late wakin' up, but it seemed cruel soon gittin' light.
An' the March win' was ice, an' the sun on'y shinin' to show it its road,
An' the fire was gone out on us black, an' no turf till wan thramped for a load.
Thin the childher, an' Mick's mother herself, were that starvin', the crathurs, an' could,
That they all fell to keenin' together most woeful, the young an' the ould;
Until Mick, that was lyin' in bed for the hunger, an' half the week long
Had scarce tasted a bit, he laned up on his elbow to ax what was wrong.
An' sez I—God forgive me, 'twas just the first thing that come into me head—
'Sure it's cryin' they are, man,' sez I, 'for the want of a mouthful o' bread,
And it's dyin' they may be next thing, for what help I can see. Och, it's quare,
But if Parson had knowed how we're kilt, an' ye'd on'y ha' spoken him fair,
He'd allow us a thrifle at laste.' An' sez he: 'Woman, whisht! what's the use?
I might spake him as fair as ye plase, or might give him the heighth of abuse,
All as wan, he's that bitther agin us. But throth will I stand it no more;
I'll turn souper this day for the male.' And he ups wid himself off the floor;
For 'twas Sunday that mornin', worse luck: 'It's a sin, sure,' sez he, 'I know well,
'Siver, sooner than watch thim disthroyed, I'd say prayers to the Divil in Hell,'
Sez he, goodness forgive him—but, mind you, meself's every ha'porth as bad,
For thin, watchin' him off down the lane, I dunno was I sorry or glad.

VI.

And he wint, sure enough, to the church. Widdy Mahon she tould me next day
How she'd gone there herself for the victuals, an' met wid him comin' away;
And how afther the service they stepped up to Parson's to thry what they'd git,
An' they got a half loaf, an' the full o' the male-bag; an' never a bit
Would he touch, but made off wid him sthraight, tho' she said he seemed hard-set to crawl—
Och, ye see 'twas for us that he turned, for himself he'd ne'er do it at all.
An' it's wishful he was to slip home in a hurry, poor lad, wid his pack,
An' to bring us the best that he had. But och, Sisther, he never got back.

VII.

For the boys comin' up from the Mass down at Moyna, a while later on,
Found him dhropped of a hape be the path past Kilogue wid the life of him gone;
An' th' ould male-bag gripped close in his hand, that he thought to ha' carried us home.

309

Och, I mind it, the place where he lay, 'tis the lonesomest road ye can roam,
Wid the bog black an' dhreary around ye, an' sorra a wall or a hedge,
Sthretchin' out till the hill-top lifts up like a fear-ful great face o'er the edge;
An' the breadths o' the big empty sky, wid no end, look as far as ye will,
Seem just dhrawin' an' dhrainin' your life out, if weak-like ye're feelin' an' ill;
An' it's that way poor Mick was. Och, Sisther, there's scarcely a day's gone by
In the years ever since, but I'm thinkin' how desolit he happint to die,
And I dhrame it o' nights—be himself, starin' lonesome an' lost 'nathe thim skies,
Wid the could creepin' into his heart, an' the cloud comin' over his eyes,
An' that sin on his sowl—would ye say there's a chance for him? Look, now, at me,
Wid a bed to die aisy on here in the House, betther off, sure, than he,
An' me fau't just as bad. Cock me up! to lie here where I've help widin call,
An' poor Mick out o' rache on the road—where's the manin' or sinse in't at all?

VIII.

Ay, in troth, 'twas no thing to go do; ay, a scandal it was and a sin;
But mayhap they'd scarce judge him so hard if they knew all the sthraits we were in.
There's the Mother o' Mercy, sez I to meself, sure, it's childher she's had—
May they ne'er want the bite or the sup, if she'll spake a good word for me lad.
Och, me head's gittin' doitered an' quare, or I'd know they've tuk off out o' this,
And is settled in glory above, where there's nought can befall them amiss.
But suppose she remembers her time down below, if she even lived where
The ould blight never come on their praties an' dhruv the whole land to despair,
Yet I'm thinkin' there's always been plenty o' throuble about on this earth,
An' for sure 'twill ha' happint her whiles to ha' never a sod on the hearth,
Or a scrap for the pot, an' the childher around her all famished an' white,
An' they cryin', an' she nothin' to give them, save bid them to whisht an' be quite.

IX.

But, indeed, for that matther, the Lord, who'd enough to contind wid those times,
Might ha' some sort o' notion himself how the poor people's tempted to crimes,
Whin they're watchin' their own folk a-starvin', an' no help for it, strive as they may.
For himself set a dale by his mother, accordin' as I've heard say,
An' remembered her last thing of all in the thick of his throuble, an' thought
To make sure she'd ha' some wan to care her an' heed that she wanted for nought,
An' be keepin' the roof o'er her head while she lived, all the same as her son—
But, ye see, he'd a frind he could trust to, an' Micky, the crathur, had none.
An' that same would be vexin' his heart while he lay dyin' there on the road;
For the sorra a sowl would be left in the world to purtect us, he knowed;
An' I mind when the fever he had, an' was wandh'rin' a bit in his head,
He kep' ravin' continyal as how 'twas desthroyed we'd be wanst he was dead.

An' poor Mick was that kind in his heart, he'd be put past his patience outright
Whin th' ould mother an' childher was frettin' wid hunger from mornin' till night;
An' it's that was the raison he done it—nought else. So, belike, if above
They'd considher the hardships he met, till it's desprit, bedad, he was dhruv,
An' no hope o' relief for the crathurs at home, mind you, barrin' he wint
An' let on a bit now an' agin—they'd believe 'twas no harm that he mint;
An' that wan sin he done, an' he starvin', they'd maybe forgive an' forget—
Och, Sisther Frances, me honey, would ye say there's a chance for him yet?

From *Strangers at Lisconnel*

(1896)

Jerry Dunne's Basket

So it is worth while to tell the reason why people at Lisconnel some-times respond with irony to a question: 'What have I got? Sure, all that Jerry Dunne had in his basket.' The saying is of respectable antiquity, for it originated while Bessy Joyce, who died a year or so back, at 'a great ould age entirely,' was still but a slip of a girl. In those days her mother used often to say regretfully that she didn't know when she was well off, like Rody O'Rourke's pigs, quoting a proverb of obscurer ante-cendents. When she did so she was generally thinking of the fine little farm in the county Clare, which they had not long since exchanged for the poor tiny holding away in the heart of the black bog; and of how, among the green fields, and thriving beasts, and other good things of Clonmena, she had allowed her content to be marred by such a detail as her Bessy's refusal to favour the suit of Jerry Dunne.

Mrs. Joyce eagerly desired a brilliant alliance for Bessy, who was rather an important daughter, being the only grown-up girl, and a very pretty one, among a troop of younger brethren; so it seemed contrary enough that she wouldn't look the same side of the road as young Jerry, who was farming prosperously on his own account, and whose family were old friends and neighbours, and real respectable people, including a first cousin nothing less than a parish priest. Yet Bessy ran away and hid her-self in as ingeniously unlikely places as a strayed calf whenever she heard of his approach, and if brought by chance into his society became most discouragingly deaf and dumb.

It is true that at the time I speak of Bessy's prospects fully entitled her to as opulent a match, and no one apparently foresaw how speedi-ly they would be overcast by her father's improvidence. But Andy Joyce had an ill-advised predilection for seeing things what he called 'dacint and proper' about him, and it led him into several imprudent acts. For instance, he built some highly superior sheds in the bawn, to the bettering, no doubt, of his cattle's condition, but very little to his own purpose, which he would indeed have served more advantageously by spending the money they cost him at Moriarty's shebeen. Nor was he left without due warning of the consequences likely to result from such courses. The abrupt raising of his rent by fifty per cent, was a broad hint which most men would have taken; and it did keep Andy quiet, ruefully, for a season or two. Then, however, having again saved up a trifle, he could not resist the temptation to drain the swampy corner of the farthest river-field, which was as kind a bit of land as you could wish, only for the water lying on it, and in which he afterwards raised himself a remarkably fine crop of white oats. The sight of them 'done his heart good,' he said, exultantly, nothing recking that it was the last touch of farmer's pride he would ever feel. Yet on the next quarter-day the Joyces received notice to quit, and their landlord determined to keep the vacated holding in his own hands; those new sheds were just the thing for his young stock. Andy, in fact, had done his best to improve himself off the face of the earth, and he should therefore have been thankful to retain a foothold, even in a loose-jointed, rush-roofed cabin away at stony Lisconnel. Whether thankful or no, there, at any rate, he presently found himself established with all his family, and the meagre remnant of his hastily sold-off gear, and the black doors of the 'house'[1] seeming to loom ahead whenever he looked into the murky future.

The first weeks and months of their new adversity passed slowly and heavily for the transplanted household, more especially for Andy and his wife, who had outgrown a love of paddling in bogholes, and had acquired a habit of wondering 'what at all 'ud become of the childer, the crathurs.' One shrill-blasted March morning Andy trudged off to the fair down below at Duffclane—not that he had any business to transact there, unless we reckon as such a desire to gain a respite from regretful boredom. He but partially succeeded in doing this, and returned at dusk so fagged and dispirited that he had not energy to relate his scraps of news until he was half through his plate of stirabout. Then he observed: 'I seen a couple of boys from home in it.'

'Whethen now, to think of that,' said Mrs. Joyce with mournful interest, 'which of them was it?'

---

1 *the 'house'*: the workhouse.

'The one of them was Terence Kilfoyle,' said Andy.

Mrs. Joyce's interest flagged, for young Kilfoyle was merely a good-looking lad with the name of being rather wild. 'Ah sure *he* might as well be in one place as another,' she said indifferently. 'Bessy, honey, as you're done, just throw the scraps to the white hin where she's sittin'.'

'He sez he's thinkin' to settle hereabouts,' said Andy. 'I tould him he'd a right to go thry his fortin' somewhere outlandish, but he didn't seem to fancy the idee, and small blame to him. A man's bound to get his heart broke one way or the other anywheres, as far as I can see. I met Jerry Dunne too.'

'Och and did you indeed?' said Mrs. Joyce, kindling into eagerness again.

Jerry had been absent from Clonmena at the time of their flitting, and they had heard nothing of him since; but she still cherished a flicker of hope in his connection, which the tidings of his appearance in the neighbourhood fanned and fed.

'And he's quit out of it himself,' Andy continued, 'for the ould uncle of his he's been stoppin' wid this while back at Duffclane's after dyin' and lavin' him a fine farm and a hantle of money, and I dunno what all besides. So it's there he's goin' to live, and he's gave up the ould place at Clonmena, as well he may, and no loss to him on it, for he sez himself he niver spent a pinny over it beyont what he'd be druv to, if he wanted to get e'er a crop out of it at all, and keep things together in any fashion: he wasn't such a fool.' Andy hesitated, as if on the brink of a painful theme, and resumed with an effort: 'He's bought Magpie and the two two-year-olds off of Peter Martin. Chape enough he got them, too, though he had to give ten shillin's a head more for them than Martin ped me.'

'Mavrone, but some people have the luck,' said Mrs. Joyce.

'And Jerry bid me tell you,' said Andy, the memory of his lost cattle still saddening his tone, 'that he might be steppin' up here to see you tomorra or next day.'

At this Mrs. Joyce's face suddenly brightened, as if she had been summoned to share Jerry Dunne's good luck. She felt almost as if that had actually happened. For his visit could surely signify nothing else than that he meant to continue his suit; and under the circumstances, Bessy's misliking was a piece of folly not to be taken into account. Besides that, the girl, she thought, looked quite heartened up by the news. So she replied to her husband: ''Deed then, he'll be very welcome,' and the sparkle was in her eyes all the rest of the evening.

On the morrow, which was a bright morning with a far-off pale blue sky, Mrs. Joyce hurried over her readying-up, that she might be prepared for her possible visitor. She put on her best clothes, and as her wardrobe had not yet fallen to a level with her fortune, she was able to array herself in a strong steel-grey mohair gown, a black silk apron with three rows of velvet ribbon on it besides the binding, a fine small woollen shawl of very brilliant scarlet and black plaid, with a pinkish cornelian brooch to pin it at the throat, all surmounted by a snowy high-caul cap, in those days not yet out of date at Lisconnel, where fashions lag somewhat. She noticed, well-pleased, Bessy's willingness to fall in with the suggestion that she should re-arrange her hair and change her gown after the morning's work was done; and the inference drawn grew stronger, when, for the first time since their troubles, the girl began to sing 'Moll Dhuv in Glanna'[1] while she coiled up her long tresses.

All that forenoon Mrs. Joyce had happy dreams about the mending of the family fortunes, which would be effected by Bessy's marriage with Jerry Dunne. When her neighbour, Mrs Ryan looked in, she could not forebear mentioning the expected call, and was further elated because Mrs. Ryan at once remarked: 'Sure, 'twill be Bessy he's after,' though she herself of course, disclaimed the idea, saying: 'Och musha,[2] ma'am, not at all.' The Ryans were tenants who had also been put out of Clonmena, and they occupied a cabin adjoining the Joyces', these two dwellings, backed by the slopes of the Knockawn, forming the nucleus of Lisconnel.

About noon, Paddy, the eldest boy, approached at a hand gallop, bestriding a donkey which belonged to the gang of men who were still working on the unfinished road. As soon as the beast reached the open-work stone wall of the potato-field it resolutely scraped its rider off, a thing it had been vainly wishing to do all along the fenceless track. Paddy, however, alighted unconcerned among the clattering stones, and ran on with his tidings. These were to the effect that he was 'after seein' Jerry Dunne shankin' up from Duffclane ways, a goodish bit below the indin' of the road, and he wid a great big basket carryin', fit to hould a young turf-stack.'

The intelligence created an agreeable excitement, which was undoubtedly heightened by the fact of the basket. 'Very belike,' said Mrs. Ryan, 'he's bringin' somethin' to you, or it might be Bessy.' And while Mrs. Joyce rejoined deprecatingly: 'Ah sure, woman alive, what would the poor lad be troublin' himself to bring us all this way?' she was really answering her own question with a dozen flattering con-

---

1 *'Moll Dhuv in Glanna'*: 'The Dark Maiden of the Valley', a slow air.
2 *musha*: Hiberno-English for 'indeed', 'well'.

jectures. The basket must certainly contain *something*, and there were so few by any means probable things that would not at this pinch have come acceptably to the Joyces' household, where the heavy pitaty sack grew light with such alarming rapidity, and the little hoard of corn dwindled, and the childer's appetites seemed to wax larger day by day. She had not quite made up her mind, when Jerry arrived, whether she would wish for a bit of bacon—poor Andy missed an odd taste of it so bad—or for another couple of hens, which would be uncommonly useful now that her own few had all left laying.

Mrs. Ryan having discreetly withdrawn, Mrs. Joyce stood alone in her dark doorway to receive her guest, and, through all her flutter of hope, she felt a bitter twinge of housewifely chagrin at being discovered in such miserable quarters. The black earth flooring at her threshold gritted hatefully under her feet, and the gusts whistling through the many chinks of her rough walls seemed to skirl derisively. She was nevertheless resolved to put the best possible face upon the situation.

'Well, Mrs Joyce, ma'am. and how's yourself this long while?' said Jerry Dunne, coming up. 'Bedad I'm glad to see you so finely, and it's an iligant place you've got up here.'

'Ah, it's not too bad whatever,' said Mrs. Joyce, 'on'y 'twas a great upset on us turnin' out of the ould house at home. Himself had a right to ha' left things the way he found them, and then it mightn't iver ha' happened him. But sure, poor man, he niver thought he'd be ruinatin' us wid his conthrivances. It's God's will. Be steppin' inside to the fire, Jerry lad; there's a thin feel yet in the win'.'

Jerry, stepping inside, deposited his basket, which did not appear to be very heavy, rather disregardfully by him on the floor. Mrs. Joyce would not allow herself to glance in its direction. It struck her that the young man seemed awkward and flustered, and she considered this a favourable symptom.

'And what way's Mr. Joyce?' said Jerry. 'He was lookin' grand whin I seen him yesterday.'

''Deed, he gits his health middlin' well enough, glory be to goodness,' she said; 'sometimes he'll be frettin' a bit, thinkin' of diffrent things, and when I tell him he'd better lave botherin' his head wid them, he sez he might as aisy bid a blast of win' to not be blowin' through a houle. Och, Andy's a quare man. He's out and about now somewheres on the farm.'

Mrs. Joyce put a spaciousness into her tone wholly disproportionate to their screed of tussocks and boulders; and then paused, hoping that the next inquiry might relate to Bessy.

But what young Jerry said was. 'You've got a great run, anyway, for the fowls.'

The irrelevance of the remark disappointed Mrs. Joyce, and she replied a little tartly: 'A great run you may call it, for begorrah our hearts is broke huntin' after the crathurs, and they strayin' off wid themselves over the width of the bog there, till you've as much chance of catchin' them as the sparks flyin' up the chimney.'

'That's unhandy, now,' said Jerry. He sat for some moments reflectively ruffling up his flaxen hair with both hands, and then he said. 'Have you the big white hin yit that you got from me a while ago?'

'We have so bedad,' said Mrs. Joyce, not loth to enlarge upon this subject. 'Sure we made a shift to bring a few of the best chickens we had along wid us, and sorry we'd ha' been to lose her, and she a won'erful layer, and after you a-givin' her to us in a prisint that way.'

'There was some talk that time,' said Jerry, 'about me and Bessy.'

'Ay, true for you, there was,' said Mrs. Joyce, in eager assent, 'plinty of talk.' She would have added more, but he was evidently in a hurry to speak again.

'Well, there's none now.' he said. 'Things is diff'rent altogether. If I'd ha' known, I'd ha' kep'the hin. The fact of the matter is I'm about gettin' married to Sally Coghlan, that's me poor uncle's wife's niece. He's after leavin' her what he had saved up. She's a fine figure of a girl as iver you saw, and as good as gould, and the bit of lan' and the bit of money had a right to go the one way. So I was thinkin', Mrs. Joyce, I might as well be takin' home the ould hin wid me—things bein' diff'rent now, and no talk of Bessy. Sally has a great wish for a white hin, and we've ne'er a one of that sort at our place. I've brought a wad of hay in the basket meself, for 'fraid yous might be short of it up here.' Jerry gave a kick to the basket, which betrayed the flimsy nature of its contents by rolling over with a wobble on its side.

At this critical moment Mrs. Joyce's pride rallied loyally to the rescue of her dignity and self-respect, proving as effectual as the ice-film which keeps the bleakest pool unruffled by the wildest storm wind. With the knell of all her hope clanging harshly in her ears, she smiled serenely, and said gaily: 'Ay, bedad, himself was tellin' us somethin' about it last night. Sure, I'm rael glad to hear tell of your good luck, and I wish you joy of it. And will you be gettin' married agin Shrovetide? Och, that's grand. But the white hin now—the on'y thing is the crathur's been sittin' on a clutch of eggs since Monday week. So what are we to do at all?'

'There's hapes of room for the whole of them in the basket, for that matter,' Jerry suggested promptly.

'Ah, sure, it's distroyed they'd be, jogglin' along, and the crathur herself 'ud go distracted entirely; sorra a bit of good you'd get of her. But look here, Mr. Dunne, I've got another out there as like her as if the both of them had come out of the one egg, and you could be takin' that instid. It's a lucky thing I didn't set her to sit the way I was intendin'; on'y I niver could get a clutch gathered for her, be raison of the lads aitin' up the eggs on me. Sure, I can't keep them from the little bosthoons when they are hungry.'

"Twould be all the same thing to me, in coorse, supposin' she was equally so good,' Jerry admitted with caution.

'Ivery feather she is,' said Mrs. Joyce. 'I seen her runnin' about there just this minute; you can be lookin' at her yourself.'

She went towards the door as she spoke, and was somewhat taken aback to perceive her husband leaning against the wall close outside. How much of the discussion he might have heard, she could not tell. The white hen also appeared within easy reach, daintily resplendent under the sunshine on a back-ground of black turf. And Mrs. Ryan, standing darkly framed in her doorway, was very certain to be an interested observer of events. For a moment Mrs. Joyce's uppermost anxiety was to avoid any betrayal of discomfiture, and she according-ly said in a loud and cheerful tone:

'Och, and are you there, Andy? Jerry Dunne's wishful for the loan of a clockin' hin, so I'm about catchin' him the young white one to take home wid him.'

But, to her intense disgust, Jerry, who had followed her with his basket, said remonstrantly: 'Whethen now, Mrs. Joyce, the way I understand the matter there's no talk in it of borryin' at all. I'm on'y takin' her back instid of the ould one, and I question would any rea-sonable body stand me out I don't own her be rights. It's an unjust thing to be spakin' of loans.'

Mrs. Joyce was so dumfoundered by this rebuff that she could only hide her confusion by displaying an exaggerated activity in the cap-ture of the hen.

Her husband, however, said blandly, 'Och, don't make yourself onaisy, man. Loan or no loan, you needn't be under any apperhinsion we'll be comin' after her wid a basket. Divil a much. Stir yourself, Kitty, and be clappin' her in under the lid. He's in a hurry to get home to his sweetheart wid the iligant prisint he's after pickin' up for her. Ay, that's right, woman alive; give a tie to the bit of string, and then there's nothin' to be delayin' him.'

After this everybody said good-bye with much politeness and affability, though withal a certain air of despatch, as if they were conscious of handling rather perishable goods. And when Jerry was beyond earshot, Andy, looking after him, remarked, 'I niver liked a bone in that fellow's skin. Himself and his ould basket. The lads 'ill be prisintly comin' in to their dinners.'

'D'you know where Bessy is?' said Mrs. Joyce, her heart sinking still lower at the thought of the disappointment, which she had presumably been helping to prepare for her daughter.

'When I seen her a while back, she was out there wid the childer, discoorsin' to Terence Kilfoyle,' Andy said contentedly.

'Musha, good gracious, Terence Kilfoyle, and what's *he* come after?' she said in a bitter tone.

'He stepped up wid a couple of pounds of fresh butter and a dozen of eggs. He said he minded Bessy havin' a fancy for duck-eggs, and he thought we mightn't happen to have e'er a one up here. She seemed as pleased as anythin'. But if you ax *me*, Kitty,' he said, with a twinkle, 'I've a notion he's come after somethin' more than our ould hin.'

'He's a great young rogue,' said Mrs. Joyce. Yet there was an accent of relief in her voice, and on her face a reflection of her husband's smile.

And Jerry Dunne's basket still occupies its niche in the stores of our proverbial philosophy.

EDITH ŒNONE SOMERVILLE (1858–1949) AND MARTIN ROSS (VIOLET MARTIN) (1861–1915)

Somerville and Ross formed the most famous partnership in Irish literature. Somerville was born on Corfu, the eldest child of an army officer, grew up at the family home Drishane, West Carbery, Co. Cork, and was educated at Alexandra College, Dublin. She studied art in London, Düsseldorf and Paris. In 1886 she met her cousin Violet Martin (they were both granddaughters of Charles Kendal Bushe), with whom she formed the partnership of Somerville and Ross. Violet Martin was born in Ross House, Oughterard, Co. Galway, and educated in Alexandra College, Dublin. On the death of her father, a bankrupt, the family home was closed, and Martin moved to Dublin with her mother. They returned to Ross House in 1888, as tenants of part of the mansion.

Together, Somerville and Martin produced the playful unpublished 'Budh Dictionary', a lexicon of odd family words and phrases. Their first published joint venture was *An Irish Cousin* (1889), which had been planned as a Gothic horror novel, and appeared under the names 'Giles Herring' and 'Martin Ross' (Somerville taking another name because her mother was shocked that her daughter was a writer). It was followed by a series of Big House novels, of which *The Real Charlotte* is the masterpiece, and by the comic 'Irish R.M.' stories—greatly enhanced by Violet Martin's absolute memory for dialect. The latter proved so popular that they hardly had time to write serious fiction. They also wrote short stories and accounts of their travels, such as *Through Connemara in a Governess Cart* (1892) and *Beggars on Horseback* (1895). After a horse-riding accident in 1898 Martin Ross was in constant pain; she died from a brain tumour in 1915, but Somerville maintained contact with her spiritually, and kept publishing under their joint names, the most impressive novel being *The Big House at Inver* (1925), which records the rise and fall of the Prenderville family, and was based on her memories of Tyrone House, Co. Galway.

From *The Real Charlotte*

(1894)

[*The action in* The Real Charlotte *is dominated by two women: the pretty, unassuming, light-hearted Francie; and her guardian, the complex, heavy-set Charlotte, whose heart breaks over her unrequited love for Roddy Lambert, the widowed land agent, who is in love with Francie. Katharine Tynan* described the novel as 'written in acid'.*]

CHAPTER 34.

...'Leave me alone! What is it to you who I marry?' [Francie] cried; passionately; 'I'll marry who I like, and no thanks to you!'

'Oh, indeed,' said Charlotte, breathing hard and loud between the words; 'it's nothing to me, I suppose, that I've kept the roof over your head and put the bit into your mouth, while ye're carrying on with every man that ye can get to look at ye!'

'I'm not asking you to keep me,' said Francie, starting up in her turn and standing in the window facing her cousin; 'I'm able to keep myself, and to wait as long as I choose till I get married; *I'm* not afraid of being an old maid!'

They glared at each other, the fire of anger smiting on both their faces, lighting Francie's cheek with a malign brilliance, and burning in ugly purple-red on Charlotte's leathery skin. The girl's aggressive beauty was to Charlotte a keener taunt than the rudimentary insult of her words; it brought with it a swarm of thoughts that buzzed and stung in her soul like poisonous flies.

'And might one be permitted to ask how long you're going to wait?' she said, with quivering lips drawn back; 'will six months be enough for you, or do you consider the orthodox widower's year too long to wait? I daresay you'll have found out what spending there is

319

in twenty-five pounds before that, and ye'll go whimpering to Roddy Lambert, and asking him to make ye Number Two, and to pay your debts and patch up your character!'

'Roddy Lambert!' cried Francie, bursting out into shrill unpleasant laughter; 'I think I'll try and do better than that, thank ye, though you're so kind in making him a present to me!' Then, firing a random shot, 'I'll not deprive you of him, Charlotte; you may keep him all to yourself!'

It is quite within the bounds of possibility that Charlotte might at this juncture have struck Francie, and thereby have put herself for ever into a false position, but her guardian angel, in the shape of Susan, the grey tomcat, intervened. He had jumped in at the window during the discussion, and having rubbed himself unnoticed against Charlotte's legs with stiff, twitching tail, and cold eyes fixed on her face, he, at this critical instant, sprang upwards at her, and clawed on to the bosom of her dress, hanging there in expectation of the hand that should help him to the accustomed perch on his mistress's shoulder. The blow that was so near being Francie's descended upon the cat's broad confident face and hurled him to the ground. He bolted out of the window again, and when he was safely on the gravel walk, turned and looked back with an expression of human anger and astonishment.

When Charlotte spoke her voice was caught away from her as Christopher Dysart's had been the day before. All the passions have but one instrument to play on when they wish to make themselves heard, and it will yield but a broken sound when it is too hardly pressed.

'Dare to open your mouth to me again, and I'll throw you out of the window after the cat!' was what she said in that choking whisper. 'Ye can go out of this house tomorrow and see which of your lovers will keep ye the longest, and by the time that they're tired of ye, maybe ye'll regret that your impudence got ye turned out of a respectable house!' She turned at the last word, and, like a madman who is just sane enough to fear his own madness, flung out of the room without another glance at her cousin.

Susan sat on the gravel path, and in the intervals of licking his paws in every crevice and cranny, surveyed his mistress's guest with a stony watchfulness as she leaned her head against the window sash and shook in a paroxysm of sobs.

CHAPTER 39.

It was a cold east-windy morning near the middle of March, when the roads were white and dusty, and the clouds were grey, and Miss Mullen, seated in her new dining room at Gurthnamuckla, was finishing her Saturday balancing of accounts. Now that she had become a landed proprietor, the process was more complicated than it used to be. A dairy, pigs, and poultry cannot be managed and made to pay without thought and trouble, and, as Charlotte had every intention of making Gurthnamuckla pay, she spared neither time nor account books, and was beginning to be well satisfied with the result. She had laid out a good deal of money on the house and farm, but she was going to get a good return for it, or know the reason why; and as no tub of skim milk was given to the pigs, or barrow of turnips to the cows, without her knowledge, the chances of success seemed on her side.

She had just entered, on the page headed Receipts, the sale of two pigs at the fair, and surveyed the growing amount in its neat figures with complacency; then, laying down her pen, she went to the window, and directed a sharp eye at the two men who were spreading gravel on the reclaimed avenue, and straightening the edges of the grass.

"Pon my word, it's beginning to look like a gentleman's avenue,' she said to herself, eyeing approvingly the arch of the elm tree branches, and the clumps of yellow daffodils, the only spots of light in the colourless landscape, while the cawing of the building rooks had a pleasant manorial sound in her ears. A young horse came galloping across the lawn, with floating mane and tail, and an intention to jump the new wooden railings that only failed him at the last moment, and resulted in two soapy slides in the grass, that Charlotte viewed from her window with wonderful equanimity. 'I'll give Roddy a fine blowing up when he comes over,' she thought, as she watched the colt cutting capers among the daffodils; 'I'll ask him if he'd like me to have his four precious colts in to tea. He's as bad about them as I am about the cats!' Miss Mullen's expression denoted that the reproof would not be of the character to which Louisa was accustomed, and Mrs Bruff, who had followed her mistress into the window, sprang on a chair, and, arching her back, leaned against the well-known black alpaca apron with a feeling that the occasion was exceptionally propitious. The movements of Charlotte's character, for it cannot be said to possess the power of development, were akin to those of some amphibious thing, whose strong, darting course under the water is only marked by a bubble or two, and it required almost an animal instinct to note them. Every bubble betrayed the creature below, as well as the limitations of its power of hiding itself, but people never thought of looking out for these indications in Charlotte, or even suspected that she had anything to conceal. There was an almost blatant simplicity about her, a humorous rough and readiness which, joined with her literary culture, proved business capacity, and dreaded temper, seemed to leave no room for any further aspect, least of all of a romantic kind.

Having opened the window for a minute to scream abusive directions to the men who were spreading gravel, she went back to the table, and, gathering her account books together, she locked them up in her davenport. The room that, in Julia Duffy's time, had been devoted to the storage of potatoes, was now beginning life again, dressed in the faded attire of the Tally Ho dining room. Charlotte's books lined one of its newly-papered walls; the foxhunting prints that dated from old Mr Butler's reign at Tally Ho hung above the chimney-piece, and the maroon rep curtains were those at which Francie had stared during her last and most terrific encounter with their owner. The air of occupation was completed by a basket on the rug in front of the fire with four squeaking kittens in it, and by the Bible and the grey manual of devotion out of which Charlotte read daily prayers to Louisa the orphan and the cats. It was an ugly room, and nothing could ever make it anything else, but with the aid of the brass-mounted grate, a few bits of Mrs Mullen's silver on the sideboard, and the deep-set windows, it had an air of respectability and even dignity that appealed very strongly to Charlotte. She enjoyed every detail of her new possessions, and, unlike Norry and the cats, felt no regret for the urban charms and old associations of Tally Ho. Indeed, since her aunt's death, she had never liked Tally Ho. There was a strain of superstition in her that, like her love of land, showed how strongly the blood of the Irish peasant ran in her veins; since she had turned Francie out of the house she had not liked to think of the empty room facing her own, in which Mrs Mullen's feeble voice had laid upon her the charge that she had not kept; her dealings with table-turning and spirit-writing had expanded for her the boundaries of the possible, and made her the more accessible to terror of the supernatural. Here, at Gurthnamuckla, there was nothing to harbour these suggestions; no brooding evergreens rustling outside her bedroom window, no rooms alive with the little incidents of a past life, no doors whose opening and shutting were like familiar voices reminding her of the footsteps that they had once heralded. This new house was peopled only by the pleasant phantoms of a future that she had fashioned for herself out of the slightest and vulgarest materials, and her wakeful nights were spent in schemings in which the romantic and the practical were logically blended. ...

*   *   *

... Charlotte unlocked the bag and drew forth its contents. There were three letters for her, and she laid one of them aside at once while she read the other two. One was from a resident in Ferry Lane, an epistle that began startlingly, 'Honored Madman,' and slanted over two sides of the notepaper in lamentable entreaties for a reduction of the rent and a little more time to pay it in. The other was an invitation from Mrs Corkran to meet a missionary, and tossing both down with an equal contempt, she addressed herself to the remaining one. She was in the act of opening it when she caught sight of the printed name of a hotel upon its flap, and she suddenly became motionless, her eyes staring at the name, and her face slowly reddening all over.

'Bray!' she said between her teeth, 'what takes him to Bray, when he told me to write to him to the Shelbourne?'[1]

She opened the letter, a long and very neatly written one, so neat, in fact, as to give to a person who knew Mr Lambert's handwriting in all its phases the idea of very unusual care and a rough copy.

'My dear Charlotte,' it began, 'I know you will be surprised at the news I have to tell you in this letter, and so will many others; indeed I am almost surprised at it myself.' Charlotte's left hand groped backwards till it caught the back of a chair and held on to it, but her eyes still flew along the lines. 'You are my oldest and best friend, and so you are the first I would like to tell about it, and I would value your good wishes far beyond any others that might be offered to me, especially as I hope you will soon be my relation as well as my friend. I am engaged to Francie Fitzpatrick, and we are to be married as soon as possible.'

The reader sat heavily down upon the chair behind her, her colour fading from red to a dirty yellow as she read on. 'I am aware that many will say that I am not showing proper respect towards poor dear Lucy in doing this, but you, or any one that knew her well, will support me in saying that I never was wanting in that to her when she was alive, and that she would be the last to wish I should live a lonely and miserable life now that she is gone. It is a great pleasure to me to think that she always had such a liking for Francie, for her own sake as well as because she was your cousin. It was my intention to have put off the marriage for a year, but I heard a couple of days ago

---

1 'Bray! ...: Bray is a seaside resort south of Dublin; the Shelbourne Hotel is on Stephen's Green in the heart of Dublin.

from Robert Fitzpatrick that the investment that Francie's little fortune had been put into was in a very shaky state, and that there is no present chance of dividends from it. He offered to let her live with them as usual, but they have not enough to support themselves. Francie was half starved there, and it is no place for her to be, and so we have arranged to be married very quietly down here at Bray, on the twentieth—just a week from today. I will take her to London, or perhaps a little further for a week or so, and about the first or second week in April I hope to be back in Rosemount. I know, my dear Charlotte, my dear old friend, that this must appear a sudden and hasty step, but I have considered it well and thoroughly. I know too that when Francie left your house there was some trifling little quarrel between you, but I trust you will forget all about that, and that you will be the first to welcome her when she returns to her new home. She begs me to say that she is sorry for anything she said to annoy you, and would write to you if she thought you would like to hear from her. I hope you will be as good a friend to her as you have always been to me, and will be ready to help and advise her in her new position. I would be greatly obliged to you if you would let the Lismoyle people know of my marriage, and of the reasons that I have told you for hurrying it on this way; you know yourself how glad they always are to get hold of the wrong end of a story. I am going to write to Lady Dysart myself. Now, my dear Charlotte, I must close this letter. The above will be my address for a week, and I will be very anxious to hear from you. With much love from Francie and myself, I remain your attached friend,

'RODERICK LAMBERT.'

A human soul, when it has broken away from its diviner part and is left to the anarchy of the lower passions, is a poor and humiliating spectacle, and it is unfortunate that in its animal want of self-control it is seldom without a ludicrous aspect. The weak side of Charlotte's nature was her ready abandonment of herself to fury that was, as often as not, wholly incompatible with its cause, and now that she had been dealt the hardest blow that life could give her, there were a few minutes in which rage, and hatred, and thwarted passion took her in their fierce hands, and made her for the time a wild beast. When she came to herself she was standing by the chimney-piece, panting and trembling; the letter lay in pieces on the rug, torn by her teeth, and stamped here and there with the semicircle of her heel; a chair was lying on its side on the floor, and Mrs Bruff was crouching aghast under the sideboard, looking out at her mistress with terrified inquiry.

Charlotte raised her hand and drew it across her mouth with the unsteadiness of a person in physical pain, then, grasping the edge of the chimney-piece, she laid her forehead upon it and drew a few long shuddering breaths. It is probable that if anyone had then come into the room, the human presence, with its mysterious electric quality, would have drawn the storm outwards in a burst of hysterics; but solitude seems to be a non-conductor, and a parched sob, that was strangled in its birth by an imprecation, was the only sound that escaped from her. As she lifted her head again her eyes met those of a large cabinet photograph of Lambert that stared brilliantly at her with the handsome fatuity conferred by an over-touched negative. It was a recent one, taken during one of those visits to Dublin whose object had been always so plausibly explained to her, and as she looked at it, the biting thought of how she had been hoodwinked and fooled, by a man to whom she had all her life laid down the law, drove her half mad again. She plucked it out of its frame with her strong fingers, and thrust it hard down into the smouldering fire.

'If it was hell I'd do the same for you!' she said, with a moan like some furious feline creature, as she watched the picture writhe in the heat, 'and for her too!' She took up the poker, and with it drove and battered the photograph into the heart of the fire, and then, flinging down the poker with a crash that made Louisa jump as she crossed the hall, she sat down at the dinner table and made her first effort at self-control.

'His old friend!' she said, gasping and choking over the words; 'the cur, the double-dyed cur! Lying and cringing to me, and borrowing my money, and—and—' even to herself she could not now admit that he had gulled her into believing that he would eventually marry her—'and sneaking after her behind my back all the time! And now he sends me her love—her love! Oh, my God Almighty—' she tried to laugh, but instead of laughter came tears as she saw herself helpless, and broken, and aimless for the rest of her life—'I won't break down—I won't break down—'she said, grinding her teeth together with the effort to repress her sobs. She staggered blindly to the sideboard, and, unlocking it, took out a bottle of brandy. She put the bottle to her mouth and took a long gulp from it, while the tears ran down her face.

CHAPTER 41.

The morning after Lambert received the telegram announcing Sir Benjamin's death, he dispatched one to Miss Charlotte Mullen at Gurthnamuckla, in which he asked her to notify his immediate return to his household at Rosemount. He had always been in the habit of relying on her help in small as well as great occasions, and now that he had had that unexpectedly civil letter from her, he had turned to her at once without giving the matter much consideration. It was never safe to trust to a servant's interpretation of the cramped language of a telegram, and moreover, in his self-sufficient belief in his own knowledge of women, he thought that it would flatter her and keep her in good humour if he asked her to give directions to his household. He would have been less confident of his own sagacity had he seen the set of Miss Mullen's jaw as she read the message, and heard the laugh which she permitted to herself as soon as Louisa had left the room.

'It's a pity he didn't hire me to be his major-domo as well as his steward and stud groom!' she said to herself, 'and his financier into the bargain! I declare I don't know what he'd do without me!'

The higher and more subtle side of Miss Mullen's nature had exacted of the quivering savage that had been awakened by Lambert's second marriage that the answer to his letter should be of a conventional and non-committing kind; and so, when her brain was still on fire with hatred and invective, her facile pen glided pleasantly over the paper in stale felicitations and stereotyped badinage. It is hard to ask pity for Charlotte, whose many evil qualities have without pity been set down, but the seal of ignoble tragedy had been set on her life; she had not asked for love, but it had come to her, twisted to burlesque by the malign hand of fate. There is pathos as well as humiliation in the thought that such a thing as a soul can be stunted by the trivialities of personal appearance, and it is a fact not beyond the reach of sympathy that each time Charlotte stood before her glass her ugliness spoke to her of failure, and goaded her to revenge.

It was a wet morning, but at half-past eleven o'clock the black horse was put into the phaeton, and Miss Mullen, attired in a shabby mackintosh, set out on her mission to Rosemount. A cold north wind drove the rain in her face as she flogged the old horse along through the shelterless desolation of rock and scrub, and in spite of her mackintosh she felt wet and chilled by the time she reached Rosemount yard. She went into the kitchen by the back door, and delivered her message to Eliza Hackett, whom she found sitting in elegant leisure, retrimming a bonnet that had belonged to the late Mrs Lambert.

'And is it the day after tomorrow. Miss, please?' demanded Eliza Hackett with cold resignation.

'It is, me poor woman, it is,' replied Charlotte, in the tone of facetious intimacy that she reserved for other people's servants. 'You'll have to stir your stumps to get the house ready for them.'

'The house is cleaned down and ready for them as soon as they like to walk into it,' replied Eliza Hackett with dignity, 'and if the new lady faults the drawing-room chimbley for not being swep, the master will know it's not me that's to blame for it, but the sweep that's gone dhrilling with the Mileetia.'

'Oh, she's not the one to find fault with a man for being a soldier any more than yourself, Eliza!' said Charlotte, who had pulled off her wet gloves and was warming her hands. 'Ugh! How cold it is! Is there any place upstairs where I could sit while you were drying my things for me?'

The thought had occurred to her that it would not be uninteresting to look round the house, and as it transpired that fires were burning in the dining room and in Mr Lambert's study she left her wet cloak and hat in the kitchen and ascended to the upper regions. She glanced into the drawing room as she passed its open door, and saw the blue rep chairs ranged in a solemn circle, gazing with all their button eyes at a three-legged table in the centre of the room; the blinds were drawn down, and the piano was covered with a sheet; it was altogether as inexpressive of everything, except bad taste, as was possible. Charlotte passed on to the dining room and stationed herself in front of an indifferent fire there, standing with her back to the chimney-piece and her eyes roving about in search of entertainment. Nothing was changed, except that the poor turkey-hen's medicine bottles and pill boxes no longer lurked behind the chimney-piece ornaments; the bare dinner table suggested only how soon Francie would be seated at its head, and Charlotte presently prowled on to Mr Lambert's study at the end of the passage, to look for a better fire, and a room less barren of incident.

The study grate did not fail of its reputation of being the best in the house, and Mr Lambert's chair stood by the hearthrug in wide-armed invitation to the visitor. Charlotte sat down in it and slowly warmed one foot after the other, while the pain rose hot and unconquerable in her heart. The whole room was so gallingly familiar, so inseparably connected with the time when she had still a future, vague and improbable as it was, and could live in sufficient content on its slight sustenance. Another future had now to be constructed, she had already traced out some lines of it, and in the perfecting of these she would henceforward find the cure for what she was now suffering. She roused herself, and glancing towards the table saw that on it lay a heap of unopened newspapers and letters; she got up with alacrity and addressed herself to the congenial task of examining each letter in succession.

'H'm! They're of a very bilious complexion,' she said to herself. 'There's one from Langford,' turning it over and looking at the name on the back. 'I wonder if he's ordering a Victoria[1] for her ladyship? I wouldn't put it past him. Perhaps he'd like me to tell her whose money it was paid Langford's bill last year!'

She fingered the letter longingly, then, taking a hairpin from the heavy coils of her hair, she inserted it under the flap of the envelope. Under her skilful manipulation it opened easily, and without tearing, and she took out its contents. They consisted of a short but severe letter from the head of the firm, asking for 'a speedy settlement of this account, now so long overdue,' and of the account in question. It was a bill of formidable amount, from which Charlotte soon gathered the fact that twenty pounds only of the money she had lent Lambert last May had found its way into the pockets of the coachbuilder. She replaced the bill and letter in the envelope, and, after a minute of consideration, took up for the second time two large and heavy letters that she had thrown aside when first looking through the heap. They had the stamp of the Lismoyle bank upon them, and obviously contained bank books. Charlotte saw at a glance that the hairpin would be of no avail with these envelopes, and after another pause for deliberation she replaced all the letters in their original position, and went down the passage to the top of the kitchen stairs.

'Eliza,' she called out, 'have ye a kettle boiling down there? Ah, that's right—' as Eliza answered in the affirmative. 'I never knew a well kept kitchen yet without boiling water in it! I'm chilled to me bones, Eliza,' she continued. 'I wonder could you put your hand on a drop of spirits anywhere, and I'd ask ye for a drop of hot grog to keep the life in me, and'—as Eliza started with hospitable speed in search of the materials,—'let me mix it meself, like a good woman; I know very well I'd be in the lock-up before night if I drank what *you'd* brew for me!'

Retiring on this jest, Miss Mullen returned to the study, and was sitting over the fire with a newspaper when the refreshment she had asked for was brought in.

'I cut ye a sandwich to eat with it. Miss,' said Eliza Hackett, on whom Charlotte's generosity in the matter of Mrs Lambert's clothing had not been thrown away; 'I know meself that as much as the smell o' sperrits would curdle under me nose, takin' them on an empty stomach. Though, indeed, if ye walked Lismoyle's ye'd get no better

---

1 *a Victoria*: an elegant carriage, popular among wealthy families.

brandy than what's in that little bottle. 'Tis out o'the poor mistress's medicine chest I got it. Well, well, she's where she won't want brandy now!'

Eliza withdrew with a well-ordered sigh, that, as Charlotte knew, was expressive of future as well as past regret, and Mr Lambert's 'oldest friend' was left in sole possession of his study. She first proceeded to mix herself a tumbler of brandy and water, and then she lifted the lid of the brass punch kettle, and taking one of the envelopes that contained the bank books, she held it in the steam till the gum of the flap melted. The book in it was Lambert's private banking account, and Charlotte studied it for some time with greedy interest, comparing the amounts of the drafts and cash payments with the dates against each. Then she opened the other envelope, keeping a newspaper ready at hand to throw over the books in case of interruption, and found, as she had anticipated, that it was the bank book of the Dysart estate. After this she settled down to hard work for half an hour, comparing one book with another, making lists of figures, sipping her brandy and water meanwhile, and munching Eliza Hackett's sandwiches. Having learned what she could of the bank books, she fastened them up in their envelopes, and, again having recourse to the kettle that was simmering on the hob, she made, with slow, unslaked avidity, an examination of some of the other letters on the table. When everything was tidy again she leaned back in the chair, and remained in deep meditation over her paper of figures, until the dining-room clock sent a muffled reminder through the wall that it was two o'clock....

CHAPTER 51.

The floor of the potato loft at Gurthnamuckla had for a long time needed repairs, a circumstance not in itself distressing to Miss Mullen, who held that effort after mere theoretical symmetry was unjustifiable waste of time in either housekeeping or farming. On this first of June, however, an intimation from Norry that 'there's ne'er a pratie ye have that isn't ate with the rats,' given with the thinly-veiled triumph of servants in such announcements, caused a truculent visit of inspection to the potato loft; and in her first spare moment of the afternoon Miss Mullen set forth with her tool basket, and some boards from a packing case, to make good the breaches with her own hands. Doing it herself saved the necessity of taking the men from their work, and moreover ensured its being properly done.

So she thought, as, having climbed the ladder that led from the cowhouse to the loft, she put her tools on the floor and surveyed with a workman's eye the job she had set herself. The loft was hot and air-less, redolent of the cowhouse below, as well as of the clayey musti-ness of the potatoes that were sprouting in the dirt on the floor, and even sending pallid, worm-like roots down into space through the cracks in the boards. Miss Mullen propped the window shutter open with the largest potato, and, pinning up her skirt, fell to work.

She had been hammering and sawing for a quarter of an hour when she heard the clatter of a horse's hoofs on the cobblestones of the yard, and, getting up from her knees, advanced to the window with caution and looked out. It was Mr Lambert, in the act of pulling up his awk-ward young horse, and she stood looking down at him in silence while he dismounted, with a remarkable expression on her face, one in which some acute mental process was mixed with the half-unconscious and yet all-observant recognition of an intensely familiar object.

'Hullo, Roddy!' she called out at last, 'is that you? What brings you over so early?'

Mr Lambert started with more violence than the occasion seemed to demand.

'Hullo!' he replied, in a voice not like his own, 'is that where you are?'

'Yes, and it's where I'm going to stay. This is the kind of fancy work I'm at,' brandishing her saw; 'so if you want to talk to me you must come up here.'

'All right,' said Lambert, gloomily, 'I'll come up as soon as I put the colt in the stable.'

It is a fact so improbable as to be worth noting, that before Lambert found his way up the ladder, Miss Mullen had unpinned her skirt and fastened up the end of a plait that had escaped from the mas-sive coils at the back of her head.

'Well, and where's the woman that owns you?' she asked, begin-ning to work again, while her visitor stood in obvious discomfort, with his head touching the rafters, and the light from the low window striking sharply up against his red and heavy eyes.

'At home,' he replied, almost vacantly. 'I'd have been here half an hour ago or more,' he went on after a moment or two, 'but the colt cast a shoe, and I had to go on to the forge beyond the cross to get it put on.'

Charlotte, with a flat pencil in her mouth, grunted responsively, while she measured off a piece of board, and, holding it with her knee on the body of a legless wheelbarrow, began to saw it across. Lambert looked on, provoked and disconcerted by this engrossing industry.

With his brimming sense of collapse and crisis, he felt that even this temporary delay of sympathy was an unkindness.

'That colt must be sold this week, so I couldn't afford to knock his hoof to bits on the hard road.' His manner was so portentous that Charlotte looked up again, and permitted herself to remark on what had been apparent to her the moment she saw him.

'Why, what's the matter with you, Roddy? Now I come to see you, you look as if you'd been at your own funeral.'

'I wish to God I had! It would be the best thing could happen to me.'

He found pleasure in saying something to startle her, and in seeing that her face became a shade hotter than the stifling air and the stooping over her work had made it.

'What makes you talk like that?' she said, a little strangely, as it seemed to him.

He thought she was moved, and he immediately felt his position to be more pathetic than he had believed. It would be much easier to explain the matter to Charlotte than to Francie, he felt at once; Charlotte understood business matters, a formula which conveyed to his mind much comfortable flexibility in money affairs.

'Charlotte,' he said, looking down at her with eyes that self-pity and shaken self-control were moistening again, 'I'm in most terrible trouble. Will you help me?'

'Wait till I hear what it is and I'll tell you that,' replied Charlotte, with the same peculiar, flushed look on her face, and suggestion in her voice of strong and latent feeling. He could not tell how it was, but he felt as if she knew what he was going to say.

'I'm four hundred pounds in debt to the estate, and Dysart has found out,' he said, lowering his voice as if afraid that the spiders and wood lice might repeat his secret.

'Four hundred,' thought Charlotte; 'that's more than I reckoned;' but she said aloud, 'My God! Roddy, how did that happen?'

'I declare to you I don't know how it happened. One thing and another came against me, and I had to borrow this money, and before I could pay it he found out.'

Lambert was a pitiable figure as he made his confession, his head, his shoulders, and even his moustache drooping limply, and his hands nervously twisting his ash plant.

'That's a bad business,' said Charlotte reflectively, and was silent for a moment, while Lambert realized the satisfaction of dealing with an intelligence that could take in such a situation instantaneously, without alarm or even surprise.

'Is he going to give you the sack?' she asked.

'I don't know yet. He didn't say anything definite.'

Lambert found the question hard to bear, but he endured it for the sake of the chance it gave him to lead up to the main point of the interview. 'If I could have that four hundred placed to his credit before I see him next, I believe there'd be an end of it. Not that I'd stay with him,' he went on, trying to bluster, 'or with any man that treated me this kind of way, going behind my back to look at the accounts.'

'Is that the way he found you out?' asked Charlotte, taking up the lid of the packing case and twisting a nail out of it with a hammer, 'He must be smarter than you took him for.'

'Someone must have put him up to it,' said Lambert, 'someone who'd got at the books. It beats me to make it out. But what's the good of thinking of that? The thing that's setting me mad is to know how to pay him.' He waited to see if Charlotte would speak, but she was occupied in straightening the nail against the wall with her hammer, and he went on with a dry throat, 'I'm going to sell all my horses. Charlotte, and I daresay I can raise some money on the furniture; but it's no easy job to raise money in such a hurry as this, and if I'm to be saved from being disgraced, I ought to have it at once to stop his mouth. I believe if I could pay him at once he wouldn't have spunk enough to go any further with the thing.' He waited again, but the friend of his youth continued silent. 'Charlotte, no man ever had a better friend, through thick and thin, than I've had in you. There's no other person living that I'd put myself under an obligation to but yourself. Charlotte, for the sake of all that's ever been between us, would you lend me the money?'

Her face was hidden from him as she knelt, and he stooped and placed a clinging, affectionate hand upon her shoulder. Miss Mullen got up sharply, and Lambert's hand fell.

'All that's ever been between us is certainly a very weighty argument, Roddy,' she said with a smile that deepened the ugly lines about her mouth, and gave Lambert a chilly qualm. 'There's a matter of three hundred pounds between us, if that's what you mean.'

'I know, Charlotte,' he said hastily. 'No one remembers that better than I do. But this is a different kind of thing altogether. I'd give you a bill of sale on everything at Rosemount—and there are the horses out here too. Of course, I suppose I might be able to raise the money at the bank or somewhere, but it's a very different thing to deal with a friend, and a friend who can hold her tongue too. You never failed me yet, Charlotte, old girl, and I don't believe you'll do it now!'

His handsome, dark eyes were bent upon her face with all the pathos he was master of, and he was glad to feel tears rising in them.

'Well, I'm afraid that's just what I'll have to do,' she said, flinging away the nail that she had tried to straighten, and fumbling in her pocket for another; 'I may be able to hold my tongue, but I don't hold with throwing good money after bad.'

Lambert stood quite still, staring at her, trying to believe that this was the Charlotte who had trembled when he kissed her, whose love for him had made her his useful and faithful thrall.

'Do you mean to say that you'll see me ruined and disgraced sooner than put out your hand to help me?' he said passionately.

'I thought you said you could get the money somewhere else,' she replied, with undisturbed coolness, 'and you might know that coming to me for money is like going to the goat's house for wool. I've got nothing more to lend, and no one ought to know that better than yourself!'

Charlotte was standing, yellow-faced and insolent, opposite to Lambert, with her hands in the pockets of her apron; in every way a contrast to him, with his flushed forehead and suffused eyes. The dull, white light that struck up into the roof from the whitewashed kitchen wall showed Lambert the furrowed paths of implacability in his adversary's face as plainly as it showed her his defeat and desperation.

'*You've* got no more money to lend, d'ye say!' he repeated, with a laugh that showed he had courage enough left to lose his temper; 'I suppose you've got all the money you got eighteen months ago from the old lady lent out? 'Pon my word, considering you got Francie's share of it for yourself, I think it would have been civiller to have given her husband the first refusal of a loan! I daresay I'd have given you as good interest as your friends in Ferry Lane!'

Charlotte's eyes suddenly lost their exaggerated indifference.

'And if she ever had the smallest claim to what ye call a share!' she vociferated, 'haven't you had it twenty times over? Was there ever a time that ye came cringing and crawling to me for money that I refused it to ye? And how do you thank me? By embezzling the money I paid for the land, and then coming to try and get it out of me over again, because Sir Christopher Dysart is taught sense to look into his own affairs, and see how his agent is cheating him!'

Some quality of triumph in her tone, some light of previous knowledge in her eye, struck Lambert.

'Was it you told him?' he said hoarsely, 'was it you spoke to Dysart ?'

Every now and then in the conduct of her affairs Miss Mullen permitted the gratification of her temper to take the place of the slower pleasure of secrecy.

'Yes, I told him,' she answered, without hesitation.

'You went to Dysart, and set him on to ruin me!' said Lambert, in a voice that had nearly as much horror as rage in it.

'And may I ask you what you've ever done for me,' she said, gripping her hammer with a strong, trembling hand, 'that I was to keep your tricks from being found out for you? What reason was there in God's earth that I wasn't to do my plain duty by those that are older friends than you?'

'What reason!' Lambert almost choked from the intolerable audacity and heartlessness of the question. 'Are you in your right mind to ask me that? You, that's been like a—a near relation to me all these years, or pretending to be! There was a time you wouldn't have done this to me, you know it damned well, and so do I. You were glad enough to do anything for me then, so long as I'd be as much as civil to you, and now, I suppose, this is your dirty devilish spite, because you were cut out by someone else!'

She did not flinch as the words went through and through her.

'Take care of yourself!' she said, grinning at him, 'perhaps you're not the one to talk about being cut out! Oh, I don't think ye need look as if ye didn't understand me. At all events, all ye have to do is to go home and ask your servants—or, for the matter of that, anyone in the streets of Lismoyle—who it is that's cut ye out, and made ye the laughing stock of the country!'

She put her hands on the dusty beam beside her, giddy with her gratified impulse, as she saw him take the blow and wither under it.

She scarcely heard at first the strange and sudden sound of commotion that had sprung up like a wind in the house opposite. The windows were all open, and through them came the sound of banging doors and running footsteps, and then Norry's voice screaming something as she rushed from room to room. She was in the kitchen now, and the words came gasping and sobbing through the open door.

'Where's Miss Charlotte? Where is she? O God! O God! Where is she? Miss Francie's killed, her neck's broke below on the road! O God of Heaven, help us!'

Neither Charlotte nor Lambert heard clearly what she said, but the shapeless terror of calamity came about them like a vapour and blanched the hatred in their faces. In a moment they were together at the window, and at the same instant Norry burst out into the yard, with outflung arms and grey hair streaming. As she saw Lambert, her strength seemed to go from her. She staggered back, and, catching at the door for support, turned from him and hid her face in her cloak.

From *Some Experiences of an Irish R.M.*

(1899)

Great-Uncle McCarthy

A resident Magistracy in Ireland is not an easy thing to come by nowadays; neither is it a very attractive job; yet on the evening when I first propounded the idea to the young lady who had recently consented to become Mrs. Sinclair Yeates, it seemed glittering with possibilities. There was, on that occasion, a sunset, and a string band playing 'The Gondoliers',[1] and there was also an ingenuous belief in the omnipotence of a godfather of Philippa's—(Philippa was the young lady) who had once been a member of the Government.

I was then climbing the steep ascent of the Captains towards my Majority. I have no fault to find with Philippa's godfather; he did all and more than even Philippa had expected; nevertheless, I had attained to the dignity of mud major, and had spent a good deal on postage stamps, and on railway fares to interview people of influence, before I found myself in the hotel at Skebawn, opening long envelopes addressed to 'Major Yeates, R.M.'[2]

My most immediate concern, as anyone who has spent nine weeks at Mrs. Raverty's hotel will readily believe, was to leave it at the earliest opportunity; but in those nine weeks I had learned, amongst other painful things, a little, a very little, of the methods of the artisan in the west of Ireland. Finding a house had been easy enough. I had had my choice of several, each with some hundreds of acres of shooting, thoroughly poached, and a considerable portion of the roof intact. I had selected one; the one that had the largest extent of roof in proportion to the shooting, and had been assured by my landlord that in a fortnight or so it would be fit for occupation.

'There's a few little odd things to be done,' he said easily; 'a lick of paint here and there, and a slap of plaster——'

I am short-sighted; I am also of Irish extraction; both facts that make for toleration—but even I thought he was understating the case. So did the contractor.

---

1 'The Gondoliers': a comic operetta by Gilbert and Sullivan (1889) about two gondoliers running a kingdom in a spirit of 'republican quality'.

2 R.M.: Resident Magistrate. The RMs were in charge of the petty sessions and coordinated the police in the district to which they were appointed; they reported directly to the Chief Secretary. Many resident magistrates were, or had been, military officers. Their appointment was sometimes a reward for services rendered.

At the end of three weeks the latter reported progress, which mainly consisted of the facts that the plumber had accused the carpenter of stealing sixteen feet of his inch-pipe to run a bell wire through, and that the carpenter had replied that he wished the devil might run the plumber through a wran's quill. The plumber having reflected upon the carpenter's parentage, the work of renovation had merged in battle, and at the next Petty Sessions I was reluctantly compelled to allot to each combatant seven days, without the option of a fine.

These and kindred difficulties extended in an unbroken chain through the summer months, until a certain wet and windy day in October, when, with my baggage, I drove over to establish myself at Shreelane. It was a tall, ugly house of three stories high, its walls faced with weather-beaten slates, its windows staring, narrow, and vacant. Round the house ran an area, in which grew some laurustinus and holly bushes among ash heaps, and nettles, and broken bottles. I stood on the steps, waiting for the door to be opened, while the rain sluiced upon me from a broken eaveshoot that had, amongst many other things, escaped the notice of my landlord. I thought of Philippa, and of her plan, broached in today's letter, of having the hall done up as a sitting-room.

The door opened, and revealed the hall. It struck me that I had perhaps overestimated its possibilities. Among them I had certainly not included a flagged floor, sweating with damp, and a reek of cabbage from the adjacent kitchen stairs. A large elderly woman, with a red face, and a cap worn helmet-wise on her forehead, swept me a magnificent curtsy as I crossed the threshold.

'Your honour's welcome——' she began, and then every door in the house slammed in obedience to the gust that drove through it. With something that sounded like 'Mend ye for a back door!' Mrs. Cadogan abandoned her opening speech and made for the kitchen stairs. (Improbable as it may appear, my housekeeper was called Cadogan, a name made locally possible by being pronounced Caydogawn.)

Only those who have been through a similar experience can know what manner of afternoon I spent. I am a martyr to colds in the head, and I felt one coming on. I made a laager in front of the dining-room fire, with a tattered leather screen and the dinner table, and gradually, with cigarettes and strong tea, baffled the smell of must and cats, and fervently trusted that the rain might avert a threatened visit from my landlord. I was then but superficially acquainted with Mr. Florence McCarthy Knox and his habits.

At about 4.30, when the room had warmed up, and my cold was yielding to treatment, Mrs. Cadogan entered and informed me that 'Mr. Flurry' was in the yard, and would be thankful if I'd go out to him, for he couldn't come in. Many are the privileges of the female sex; had I been a woman I should unhesitatingly have said that I had a cold in my head.

My landlord was there on horseback, and with him there was a man standing at the head of a stout grey animal. I recognized with despair that I was about to be compelled to buy a horse.

'Good afternoon. Major,' said Mr. Knox in his slow, sing-song brogue; 'it's rather soon to be paying you a visit, but I thought you might be in a hurry to see the horse I was telling you of.'

I could have laughed. As if I were ever in a hurry to see a horse! I thanked him, and suggested that it was rather wet for horse-dealing.

'Oh, it's nothing when you're used to it.' replied Mr. Knox. His gloveless hands were red and wet, the rain ran down his nose, and his covert coat was soaked to a sodden brown. I thought that I did not want to become used to it. My relations with horses have been of a purely military character. I have endured the Sandhurst riding-school, I have galloped for an impetuous general, I have been steward at regimental races, but none of these feats has altered my opinion that the horse, as a means of locomotion, is obsolete. Nevertheless, the man who accepts a resident magistracy in the south-west of Ireland voluntarily retires into the prehistoric age; to institute a stable became inevitable.

'You ought to throw a leg over him,' said Mr. Knox, 'and you're welcome to take him over a fence or two if you like. He's a nice flippant jumper.'

Even to my unexacting eye the grey horse did not seem to promise flippancy, nor did I at all desire to find that quality in him. I explained that I wanted something to drive, and not to ride.

'Well, that's a fine raking horse in harness,' said Mr. Knox, looking at me with his serious grey eyes, 'and you'd drive him with a sop of hay in his mouth. Bring him up here, Michael.'

Michael abandoned his efforts to kick the grey horse's forelegs into becoming position, and led him up to me.

I regarded him from under my umbrella with a quite unreasonable disfavour. He had the dreadful beauty of a horse in a toy-shop, as chubby, as wooden, and as conscientiously dappled, but it was unreasonable to urge this as an objection, and I was incapable of finding any more technical drawbacks. Yielding to circumstance, I 'threw my leg' over the brute, and after pacing gravely round the quadrangle that formed the yard, and jolting to my entrance gate and back, I decided that as he had neither fallen down nor kicked me off, it was worth paying twenty-five pounds for him, if only to get in out of the rain.

Mr. Knox accompanied me into the house and had a drink. He was a fair, spare young man, who looked like a stableboy among gentlemen, and a gentleman among stableboys. He belonged to a clan that cropped up in every grade of society in the county, from Sir Valentine Knox of Castle Knox down to the auctioneer Knox, who bore the attractive title of Larry the Liar. So far as I could judge, Florence McCarthy of that ilk occupied a shifting position about midway in the tribe. I had met him at dinner at Sir Valentine's, I had heard of him at an illicit auction, held by Larry the Liar, of brandy stolen from a wreck. They were 'Black Protestants', all of them, in virtue of their descent from a godly soldier of Cromwell, and all were prepared at any moment of the day or night to sell a horse.

'You'll be apt to find this place a bit lonesome after the hotel,' remarked Mr. Flurry, sympathetically, as he placed his foot in its steaming boot on the hob, 'but it's a fine sound house anyway, and lots of rooms in it, though indeed, to tell you the truth, I never was through the whole of them since the time my great-uncle, Denis McCarthy, died here. The dear knows I had enough of it that time.' He paused, and lit a cigarette—one of my best, and quite thrown away upon him. 'Those top floors, now,' he resumed, 'I wouldn't make too free with them. There's some of them would jump under you like a spring bed. Many's the night I was in and out of those attics, following my poor uncle when he had a bad turn on him—the horrors, y'know—there were nights he never stopped walking through the house. Good Lord! will I ever forget the morning he said he saw the devil coming up the avenue! "Look at the two horns on him", says he, and he out with his gun and shot him, and, begad, it was his own donkey!'

Mr. Knox gave a couple of short laughs. He seldom laughed, having in unusual perfection the gravity of manners that is bred by horse-dealing, probably from the habitual repression of all emotion save disparagement.

The autumn evening, grey with rain, was darkening in the tall windows, and the wind was beginning to make bullying rushes among the shrubs in the area; a shower of soot rattled down the chimney and fell on the hearth-rug.

'More rain coming,' said Mr. Knox, rising composedly; 'you'll have to put a goose down these chimneys some day soon, it's the only way in the world to clean them. Well, I'm for the road. You'll come out on the grey next week, I hope; the hounds'll be meeting here. Give a roar at him coming in at his jumps.' He threw his cigarette into the fire and extended a hand to me. 'Good-bye, Major, you'll see plenty of me and my hounds before you're done. There's a power of foxes in the plantations here.'

This was scarcely reassuring for a man who hoped to shoot wood-cock, and I hinted as much.

'Oh, is it the cock?' said Mr. Flurry; 'b'leeve me, there never was a woodcock yet that minded hounds, now, no more than they'd mind rabbits! The best shoots ever I had here, the hounds were in it the day before.'

When Mr. Knox had gone, I began to picture myself going across country roaring, like a man on a fire-engine, while Philippa put the goose down the chimney; but when I sat down to write to her I did not feel equal to being humorous about it. I dilated ponderously on my cold, my hard work, and my loneliness, and eventually went to bed at ten o'clock full of cold shivers and hot whisky-and-water.

After a couple of hours of feverish dozing, I began to understand what had driven Great-Uncle McCarthy to perambulate the house by night. Mrs. Cadogan had assured me that the Pope of Rome hadn't a better bed undher him than myself; wasn't I down on the new flog mattherass the old masther bought in Father Scanlan's auction? By the smell I recognized that 'flog' meant flock, otherwise I should have said my couch was stuffed with old boots. I have seldom spent a more wretched night. The rain drummed with soft fingers on my window panes; the house was full of noises. I seemed to see Great-Uncle McCarthy ranging the passages with Flurry at his heels; several times I thought I heard him. Whisperings seemed borne on the wind through my keyhole, boards creaked in the room overhead, and once I could have sworn that a hand passed, groping, over the panels of my door. I am, I may admit, a believer in ghosts; I even take in a paper that deals with their culture, but I cannot pretend that on that night I looked for-ward to a manifestation of Great-Uncle McCarthy with any enthusiasm.

The morning broke stormily, and I woke to find Mrs. Cadogan's understudy, a grimy nephew of about eighteen, standing by my bed-side, with a black bottle in his hand.

'There's no bath in the house, sir,' was his reply to my command; 'but me a'nt said, would you like a taggeen?'

This alternative proved to be a glass of raw whisky. I declined it.

I look back to that first week of housekeeping at Shreelane as to a comedy excessively badly staged, and striped with lurid melodrama. Towards its close I was positively home-sick for Mrs. Raverty's, and I had not a single clean pair of boots. I am not one of those who hold the convention that in Ireland the rain never ceases, day or night, but I must say that my first November at Shreelane was composed of weather of which my friend Flurry Knox remarked that you wouldn't meet a Christian out of doors, unless it was a snipe or a dispensary doctor. To this lamentable category might be added a resident magistrate. Daily, shrouded in mackintosh, I set forth for the Petty Sessions Courts of my wide district; daily, in the inevitable atmosphere of wet frieze and perjury, I listened to indictments of old women who plucked geese alive, of publicans whose hospitality to their friends broke forth uncontrollably on Sunday afternoons, of 'parties' who, in the language of the police sergeant, were subtly defined as 'not to say dhrunk, but in good fighting thrim'.

I got used to it all in time—I suppose one can get used to anything—I even became callous to the surprises of Mrs. Cadogan's cooking. As the weather hardened and the woodcock came in, and one by one I discovered and nailed up the rat holes, I began to find life endurable, and even to feel some remote sensation of home-coming when the grey horse turned in at the gate of Shreelane.

The one feature of my establishment to which I could not become inured was the pervading subpresence of some thing or things which, for my own convenience, I summarized as Great-Uncle McCarthy. There were nights on which I was certain that I heard the inebriate shuffle of his foot overhead, the touch of his fumbling hand against the walls. There were dark times before the dawn when sounds went to and fro, the moving of weights, the creaking of doors, a far-away rapping in which was a workmanlike suggestion of the undertaker, a rumble of wheels on the avenue. Once I was impelled to the perhaps imprudent measure of cross-examining Mrs. Cadogan. Mrs. Cadogan, taking the preliminary precaution of crossing herself, asked me fatefully what day of the week it was.

'Friday!' she repeated after me. 'Friday! The Lord save us! 'Twas a Friday the old masther was buried!'

At this point a saucepan opportunely boiled over, and Mrs. Cadogan fled with it to the scullery, and was seen no more.

In the process of time I brought Great-Uncle McCarthy down to a fine point. On Friday nights he made coffins and drove hearses; during the rest of the week he rarely did more than patter and shuffle in the attics over my head.

One night, about the middle of December, I awoke, suddenly aware that some noise had fallen like a heavy stone into my dreams. As I felt for the matches it came again, the long, grudging groan and the uncompromising bang of the cross door at the head of the kitchen stairs. I told myself that it was a draught that had done it, but it was a perfectly still night. Even as I listened, a sound of wheels on the avenue shook the stillness. The thing was getting past a joke. In a few minutes I was stealthily groping my way down my own staircase, with a box of matches in my hand, enforced by scientific curiosity but none the less armed with a stick. I stood in the dark at the top of the back stairs and listened; the snores of Mrs. Cadogan and her nephew Peter rose tranquilly from their respective lairs. I descended to the kitchen and lit a candle; there was nothing unusual there, except a great portion of the Cadogan wearing apparel, which was arranged at the fire, and was being serenaded by two crickets. Whatever had opened the door, my household was blameless.

The kitchen was not attractive, yet I felt indisposed to leave it. None the less, it appeared to be my duty to inspect the yard. I put the candle on the table and went forth out into the outer darkness. Not a sound was to be heard. The night was very cold, and so dark that I could scarcely distinguish the roofs of the stables against the sky; the house loomed tall and oppressive above me; I was conscious of how lonely it stood in the dumb and barren country. Spirits were certainly futile creatures, childish in their manifestations, stupidly content with the old machinery of raps and rumbles. I thought how fine a scene might be played on a stage like this; if I were a ghost, how bluely I would glimmer at the windows, how whimperingly chatter in the wind. Something whirled out of the darkness above me, and fell with a flop on the ground, just at my feet. I jumped backwards, in point of fact I made for the kitchen door, and, with my hand on the latch, stood still and waited. Nothing further happened; the thing that lay there did not stir. I struck a match. The moment of tension turned to pathos as the light flickered on nothing more fateful than a dead crow.

Dead it certainly was. I could have told that without looking at it; but why should it, at some considerable period after its death, fall from the clouds at my feet? But did it fall from the clouds? I struck another match and stared up at the impenetrable face of the house. There was no hint of solution in the dark windows, but I determined to go up and search the rooms that gave upon the yard.

How cold it was! I can feel now the frozen musty air of those attics, with their rat-eaten floors and wallpapers furred with damp. I went softly from one to another, feeling like a burglar in my own house, and found nothing in elucidation of the mystery. The windows were hermetically shut, and sealed with cobwebs. There was no furniture, except in the end room, where a wardrobe without doors stood in a corner, empty save for the solemn presence of a monstrous tall hat. I went back to bed, cursing those powers of darkness that had got me out of it, and heard no more.

My landlord had not failed of his promise to visit my coverts with his hounds; in fact, he fulfilled it rather more conscientiously than seemed to me quite wholesome for the cock-shooting. I maintained a silence which I felt to be magnanimous on the part of a man who cared nothing for hunting and a great deal for shooting, and wished the hounds more success in the slaughter of my foxes than seemed to be granted to them. I met them all, one red frosty evening, as I drove down the long hill to my demesne gates. Flurry at their head, in his shabby pink coat and dingy breeches, the hounds trailing dejectedly behind him and his half-dozen companions.

'What luck?' I called out, drawing rein as I met them.

'None,' said Mr. Flurry briefly. He did not stop, neither did he remove his pipe from the down-twisted corner of his mouth; his eye at me was cold and sour. The other members of the hunt passed me with equal hauteur; I thought they took their ill luck very badly.

On foot, among the last of the straggling hounds, cracking a carman's whip, and swearing comprehensively at them all, slouched my friend Slipper. Our friendship had begun in Court, the relative positions of the dock and the judgement-seat forming no obstacle to its progress, and had been cemented during several days' tramping after snipe. He was, as usual, a little drunk, and he hailed me as though I were a ship.

'Ahoy, Major Yeates!' he shouted, bringing himself up with a lurch against my cart; 'it's hunting you should be, in place of sending poor divils to gaol!'

'But I hear you had no hunting,' I said.

'Ye heard that, did ye?' Slipper rolled upon me an eye like that of a profligate pug. 'Well, begor, ye heard no more than the thruth.'

'But where are all the foxes?' said I.

'Begor, I don't know no more than your honour. And Shreelane— that there used to be as many foxes in it as there's crosses in a yard of check! Well, well, I'll say nothin' for it, only that it's quare! Here,

Vaynus! Naygress!' Slipper uttered a yell, hoarse with whisky, in adjuration of two elderly ladies of the pack who had profited by our conversation to stray away into an adjacent cottage. 'Well, good-night, Major. Mr. Flurry's as cross as briars, and he'll have me ate!'

He set off at a surprisingly steady run, cracking his whip, and whooping like a madman. I hope that when I also am fifty I shall be able to run like Slipper.

That frosty evening was followed by three others like unto it, and a flight of woodcock came in. I calculated that I could do with five guns, and I dispatched invitations to shoot and dine on the following day to four of the local sportsmen, among whom was, of course, my landlord. I remember that in my letter to the latter I expressed a facetious hope that my bag of cock would be more successful than his of foxes had been.

The answers to my invitations were not what I expected. All, without so much as a conventional regret, declined my invitation; Mr. Knox added that he hoped the bag of cock would be to my liking, and that I need not be 'affraid' that the hounds would trouble my coverts any more. Here was war! I gazed in stupefaction at the crooked scrawl in which my landlord had declared it. It was wholly and entirely inexplicable, and instead of going to sleep comfortably over the fire and my newspaper as a gentleman should, I spent the evening in irritated ponderings over this bewildering and exasperating change of front on the part of my friendly squireens.

My shoot the next day was scarcely a success. I shot the woods in company with my gamekeeper, Tim Connor, a gentleman whose duties mainly consisted in limiting the poaching privileges to his personal friends, and whatever my offence might have been, Mr. Knox could have wished me no bitterer punishment than hearing the unavailing shouts of 'Mark cock!' and seeing my birds winging their way from the coverts, far out of shot. Tim Connor and I got ten couple between us; it might have been thirty if my neighbours had not boycotted me, for what I could only suppose was the slackness of their hounds.

I was dog-tired that night, having walked enough for three men, and I slept the deep, insatiable sleep that I had earned. It was somewhere about 3 a.m. that I was gradually awakened by a continuous knocking, interspersed with muffled calls. Great-Uncle McCarthy had never before given tongue, and I freed one ear from blankets to listen. Then I remembered that Peter had told me the sweep had promised to arrive that morning, and to arrive early. Blind with sleep and fury I went to the passage window, and thence desired the sweep to go to the devil. It availed me little. For the remainder of the night I could hear him pacing round the house, trying the windows, banging at the doors, and calling upon Peter Cadogan as the priests of Baal called upon their god. At six o'clock I had fallen into a troubled doze, when Mrs. Cadogan knocked at my door and imparted the information that the sweep had arrived. My answer need not be recorded, but in spite of it the door opened, and my housekeeper, in a weird *déshabille*, effectively lighted by the orange beams of her candle, entered my room.

'God forgive me, I never seen one I'd hate as much as that sweep!' she began; 'he's these three hours—arrah, what three hours!—no, but all night, raising tally-wack and tandem round the house to get at the chimbleys.'

'Well, for Heaven's sake let him get at the chimneys and let me go to sleep,' I answered, goaded to desperation, 'and you may tell him from me that if I hear his voice again I'll shoot him!'

Mrs. Cadogan silently left my bedside, and as she closed the door she said to herself, 'The Lord save us!'

Subsequent events may be briefly summarized. At seven-thirty I was awakened anew by a thunderous sound in the chimney, and a brick crashed into the fireplace, followed at a short interval by two dead jackdaws and their nests. At eight, I was informed by Peter that there was no hot water, and that he wished the divil would roast the same sweep. At nine-thirty, when I came down to breakfast, there was no fire anywhere, and my coffee, made in the coach-house, tasted of soot. I put on an overcoat and opened my letters. About fourth or fifth in the uninteresting heap came one in an egregiously disguised hand.

'Sir,' it began, 'this is to inform you your unsportsmanlike conduct has been discovered. You have been suspected this good while of shooting the Shreelane foxes, it is known now that you do worse. Parties have seen your gamekeeper going regular to meet the Saturday early train at Salters Hill Station, with your grey horse under a cart, and your labels on the boxes, and we know as well *as your agent in Cork* what it is you have in those boxes. Be warned in time.—Your Wellwisher.'

I read this through twice before its drift became apparent, and I realized that I was accused of improving my shooting and my finances by the simple expedient of selling my foxes. That is to say, I was in a worse position than if I'd stolen a horse, or murdered Mrs. Cadogan, or got drunk three times a week in Skebawn.

For a few moments I fell into wild laughter, and then, aware that

344

it was rather a bad business to let a lie of this kind get a start, I sat down to demolish the preposterous charge in a letter to Flurry Knox. Somehow, as I selected my sentences, it was borne in upon me that, if the letter spoke the truth, circumstantial evidence was rather against me. Mere lofty repudiation would be unavailing, and by my infernal facetiousness about the woodcock had effectively filled in the case against myself. At all events, the first thing to do was to establish a basis and have it out with Tim Connor. I rang the bell.

'Peter, is Tim Connor about the place?'

'He is not, sir. I heard him say he was going west the hill to mend the bounds fence.' Peter's face was covered with soot, his eyes were red, and he coughed ostentatiously. 'The sweep's after breaking one of his brushes within in yer bedroom chimney, sir,' he went on, with all the satisfaction of his class in announcing domestic calamity; 'he's above on the roof now, and he'd be thankful to you to go up to him.'

I followed him upstairs in that state of simmering patience that any employer of Irish labour must know and sympathize with. I climbed the rickety ladder and squeezed through the dirty trapdoor involved in the ascent to the roof, and was confronted by the hideous face of the sweep, black against the frosty blue sky. He had encamped with all his paraphernalia on the flat top of the roof, and was good enough to rise and put his pipe in his pocket on my arrival.

'Good morning. Major. That's a grand view you have up here,' said the sweep. He was evidently far too well bred to talk shop. 'I travelled every roof in this country and there isn't one where you'd get as handsome a prospect!'

Theoretically he was right, but I had not come up to the roof to discuss scenery, and demanded brutally why he had sent for me. The explanation involved a recital of the special genius required to sweep the Shreelane chimneys; of the fact that the sweep had in infancy been sent up and down every one of them by Great-Uncle McCarthy; of the three ass-loads of soot that by his peculiar skill he had this morning taken from the kitchen chimney; of its present purity, the draught being such that it would 'dhraw up a young cat with it'. Finally—realizing that I could endure no more—he explained that my bedroom chimney had got what he called 'a wynd' in it, and he proposed to climb down a little way in the stack to try 'would he get to come at the brush'. The sweep was very small, the chimney very large. I stipulated that he should have a rope round his waist, and despite the illegality, I let him go. He went down like a monkey, digging his toes and fingers into the niches made for the purpose in the old chimney; Peter held the rope. I lit a cigarette and waited.

Certainly the view from the roof was worth coming up to look at. It was rough, heathery country on one side, with a string of little blue lakes running like a turquoise necklet round the base of a firry hill, and patches of pale green pasture were set amidst the rocks and heather. A silvery flash behind the undulations of the hills told where the Atlantic lay in immense plains of sunlight. I turned to survey with an owner's eye my own grey woods and straggling plantations of larch, and espied a man coming out of the western wood. He had something on his back, and he was walking very fast; a rabbit poacher no doubt. As he passed out of sight into the back avenue he was beginning to run. At the same instant I saw on the hill beyond my western boundaries half a dozen horsemen scrambling by zigzag ways down towards the wood. There was one red coat among them; it came first at the gap in the fence that Tim Connor had gone out to mend, and with the others was lost to sight in the covert, from which, in another instant, came clearly through the frosty air a shout of 'Gone to ground!' Tremendous horn blowings followed, then, all in the same moment, I saw the hounds break in full cry from the wood, and come stringing over the grass and up the back avenue towards the yard gate. Were they running a fresh fox into the stables?

I do not profess to be a hunting-man, but I am an Irishman, and so, it is perhaps superfluous to state, is Peter. We forgot the sweep as if he had never existed, and precipitated ourselves down the ladder, down the stairs, and out into the yard. One side of the yard is formed by the coach-house and a long stable, with a range of lofts above them, planned on the heroic scale in such matters that obtained in Ireland formerly. These join the house at the corner by the back door. A long flight of stone steps leads to the lofts, and up these, as Peter and I emerged from the back door, the hounds were struggling helter-skelter. Almost simultaneously there was a confused clatter of hoofs in the back avenue, and Flurry Knox came stooping at a gallop under the archway followed by three or four other riders. They flung themselves from their horses and made for the steps of the loft; more hounds pressed, yelling, on their heels, the din was indescribable, and justified Mrs. Cadogan's subsequent remark that 'when she heard the noise she thought 'twas the end of the world and the divil collecting his own!'

I jostled in the wake of the party, and found myself in the loft, wading in hay, and nearly deafened by the clamour that was bandied about the high roof and walls. At the farther end of the loft the hounds were raging in the hay, encouraged thereto by the whoops and screeches of Flurry and his friends. High up in the gable of the loft, where it joined the main wall of the house, there was a small door, and I noted with a transient surprise that there was a long ladder leading up to it. Even as it caught my eye a hound fought his way out of a drift of hay and began to jump at the ladder, throwing his tongue vociferously, and even clambered up a few rungs in his excitement.

'There's the way he's gone!' roared Flurry, striving through hounds and hay towards the ladder. Trumpeter has him! What's up there, back of the door, Major? I don't remember it at all.'

My crimes had evidently been forgotten in the supremacy of the moment. While I was futilely asserting that had the fox gone up the ladder he could not possibly have opened the door and shut it after him, even if the door led anywhere which, to the best of my belief, it did not, the door in question opened, and to my amazement the sweep appeared at it. He gesticulated violently, and over the tumult was heard to asseverate that there was nothing above there, only a way into the flue, and anyone would be destroyed with the soot——

'Ah, go to blazes with your soot!' interrupted Flurry, already halfway up the ladder.

I followed him, the other men pressing up behind me. That Trumpeter had made no mistake was instantly brought home to our noses by the reek of fox that met us at the door. Instead of a chimney, we found ourselves in a dilapidated bedroom, full of people. Tim Connor was there, the sweep was there, and a squalid elderly man and woman on whom I had never set eyes before. There was a large open fireplace, black with the soot the sweep had brought down with him, and on the table stood a bottle of my own special Scotch whisky. In one corner of the room was a pile of broken packing-cases, and beside these on the floor lay a bag in which something kicked.

Flurry, looking more uncomfortable and nonplussed than I could have believed possible, listened in silence to the ceaseless harangue of the elderly woman. The hounds were yelling like lost spirits in the loft below, but her voice pierced the uproar like a bagpipe. It was an unspeakable vulgar voice, yet it was not the voice of a countrywoman, and there were frowsy remnants of respectability about her general aspect.

'And is it you. Flurry Knox, that's calling me a disgrace! Disgrace, indeed, am I? Me that was your poor mother's own uncle's daughter and as good a McCarthy as ever stood in Shreelane!'

What followed I could not comprehend, owing to the fact that the sweep kept up a perpetual undercurrent of explanation to me as to how he had got down the wrong chimney. I noticed that his breath stank of whisky—Scotch, not the native variety.

Never, as long as Flurry Knox lives to blow a horn, will he hear the last of the day that he ran his mother's first cousin to ground in the attic. Never, while Mrs. Cadogan can hold a basting spoon, will she cease to recount how, on the same occasion, she plucked and roasted ten couple of woodcock in one torrid hour to provide luncheon for the hunt. In the glory of this achievement her confederacy with the stowaways in the attic is wholly slurred over, in much the same manner as the startling outburst of summons for trespass, brought by Tim Connor during the remainder of the shooting season, obscured the unfortunate episode of the bagged fox. It was, of course, zeal for my shooting that induced him to assist Mr. Knox's disreputable relations in the deportation of my foxes; and I have allowed it to remain at that.

In fact, the only things not allowed to remain were Mr. and Mrs. McCarthy Gannon. They, as my landlord informed me, in the midst of vast apologies, had been permitted to squat at Shreelane until my tenancy began, and having then ostentatiously and abusively left the house, they had, with the connivance of the Cadogans, secretly returned to roost in the corner attic, to sell foxes under the ægis of my name, and to make inroads on my belongings. They retained connection with the outer world by means of the ladder and the loft, and with the house in general, and my whisky in particular, by a door into the other attics—a door concealed by the wardrobe in which reposed Great-Uncle McCarthy's tall hat.

It is with the greatest regret that I relinquish the prospect of writing a monograph on Great-Uncle McCarthy for a Spiritualistic Journal, but with the departure of his relations he ceased to manifest himself and neither the nailing up of packing-cases, nor the rumble of the cart that took them to the station, disturbed my sleep for the future.

I understand that the task of clearing out the McCarthy Gannons' effects was of a nature that necessitated two glasses of whisky per man; and if the remnants of rabbit and jackdaw disinterred in the process were anything like the crow that was thrown out of the window at my feet, I do not grudge the restorative.

As Mrs. Cadogan remarked to the sweep, 'A Turk couldn't stand it.'

ROSE KAVANAGH (1859–91)

Born in Killadroy, Co. Tyrone, and educated at Loreto Convent, Omagh, she died of consumption on a visit to her mother at Knockmany, February 26, 1891. Like Yeats* and AE*, she went to the Metropolitan School of Art, Dublin. She tended Charles Kickham, who called her 'Rose of Knockmany', in his final illness. She shared his patriotism, and wrote for *The Shamrock*, under the pseudonym 'Ruby'. She contributed a children's section to *The Irish Fireside* and *The Weekly Freeman* under the name 'Uncle Remus'. She became one of Father Matthew Russell's protégées—he wrote an appreciative foreword to *Rose Kavanagh and Her Verses* (1909). She was an active member of the Pan-Celtic society. Yeats called her poetry 'meditative and sympathetic, rather than stirring and energetic', adding that it was 'easy to be unjust to such poetry, but very hard to write it'.

Knockmany

(1884)[1]

Knockmany, my darling, I see you again,
    As the sunrise has made you a king;
And your proud face looks tenderly down on the plain
    Where my young larks are learning to sing.

At your feet lies our vale, but sure that's no disgrace;
    If your arms had their will, they would cover
Every inch of the ground, from Dunroe to Millrace,
    With the sweet, silent care of a lover.

To that green heart of yours have I stolen my way,
    With my first joy and pain and misgiving.
Dear mountain! old friend, ah! I would that to-day
    You could thus share the life I am living!

For one draught of your breath would flow into my heart,
    Like the rain to the thirsty green corn;
And I know 'neath your smile all my cares would depart,
    As the night shadows flee from the morn.

---

1 Published in *The Irish Monthly* Vol. VIII (1884), p. 315.

EDWARD MARTYN (1859–1923)

Born in Tulira, Co. Galway, the last in the line of a wealthy Catholic family exempt-ed from the Penal Laws by an Act of Queen Anne, he was educated in Beaumont and Oxford, and returned to his ancestral home. He encouraged his cousin George Moore* to return to Ireland. With his neighbour Lady Gregory* and W.B. Yeats* he co-founded the Irish Literary Theatre in 1899, to which he contributed *The Heather Field* (1899) and *Maeve: A Psychological Drama* (1900). He acted as the theatre's chief guarantor, and wrote a plea for a national theatre in *Samhain* in 1901, but, disliking peasant drama and Yeats's symbolist theatre, he resolved to finance none but his own plays. These plays show an indebtedness to Ibsen's theatre of ideas, and contain as standard fare a conflict between idealistic men and uncompromising women. In 1906, with George Russell* and others, he co-founded the break-away Theatre of Ireland, and in 1914, with Joseph Mary Plunkett and Thomas MacDonagh, the Irish Theatre, producing continental drama in translation and modern Irish plays without 'peasant quality', some in Irish.

He endowed the Pro-Cathedral Palestrina choir (which counted among its members John McCormack, whose musical training he had sponsored), and supported church architecture reform and ecclesiastical art. He supported the protest against the visit of Edward VII in 1903, and served as the first president of Sinn Féin (1904–08). Black-balled in the Kildare Street Club in 1906, he took a successful court action against its protestant members. He ridiculed West-Britons in *The Place-Hunters* (1902) and *The Tale of a Town* (1905). *The Dream Physician* (1914) and *Romulus and Remus* (1916) lampoon personalities of the Literary Renaissance (Yeats the poseur, Moore the egotist). In *Regina Eyre* (1919), an unpublished play, he reverses the genders of the characters in *Hamlet* and transports the scene from Elsinore to Kerry.

From *The Heather Field*

(1899)[1]

CHARACTERS

BARRY USSHER, *a landowner, student, philosopher, etc.*
LORD SHRULE, *a neighbouring landowner*
LADY SHRULE (LILIAN), *his wife*
CARDEN TYRRELL
MRS. GRACE TYRRELL (*born* DESMOND), *his wife*
KIT, *their son, nine years old*
MILES TYRRELL, *scholar of Trinity College, Dublin, and brother of Carden*
DOCTOR DOWLING, ⎱ *physicians*
DOCTOR ROCHE, ⎰

1 Premièred at the Antient Concert Rooms, Dublin, 9 May 1899.

The action takes place about the year 1890, in CARDEN TYRRELL'S *house on the West coast of Ireland.*

from ACT I

SCENE:—CARDEN TYRRELL'S *library. On the right a door leads to the dining-room and rest of house. On the left is a large empty fire-place. At back through open glass folding-doors a small garden is visible, below which the Atlantic Ocean, flanked by a mountain at left, stretches out to the horizon. Between fire-place and folding-doors stands a writing-table with chairs on either side. At the opposite part of the room near folding-doors is a large sofa. Books in shelves line all walls. In front at the right is another table covered with papers, magazines, &c., which are likewise thrown negligently over other chairs in the room. It is a bright afternoon in the Autumn.*

MILES TYRRELL, *a young light-haired man of about nineteen, dressed in a blue serge suit, is seated at the writing-table in deep study with several books around him. After a pause he looks up wearily, then again bends over his books.*

> BARRY USSHER, *a lean man of about two and thirty, of medium height, with dark hair, a short pointed beard, and dressed in a riding-costume of sombre grey, enters from garden at back.*

MILES: (*Starting*) Ah, Barry.

USSHER: (*Throwing his hat and hunting-whip on the sofa*) Hallo, Miles, good morning. I see you are determined to win that gold-medal at Trinity—and become one day Lord Chancellor of Ireland, too, I'll be bound.

MILES: (*With a faint smile*) Lord Chancellor, indeed! I shall be lucky if I can pass my examination and then find just so many briefs as will afford me a living.

USSHER: Why are you so despondent? You have ability.

MILES: Perhaps—if there was an opportunity for displaying it. Oh, this is no place to work.

USSHER: I know what you mean. But why not study in your room upstairs?

MILES: I might do that. Still, it is not so much the interruptions. It is the knowledge of what goes on, perpetually.

USSHER: Are things as bad as ever?

MILES: Yes—my brother and his wife cannot agree.

USSHER: How sad it is.

MILES: Oh, if only I had a quiet house to study in like yours. You live there like a sage absorbed in your books and ideas.

USSHER: I fear I also find difficulties in cultivating the tastes that are congenial to me.

MILES: Why?

USSHER: You see. Miles, an unfortunate landowner must devote all his attention to keeping a little of his belongings together in these bad times.

MILES: As if you were affected by bad times—you, with that fine place here joining us, and with your unencumbered estate, and no one depending upon you. You're a lucky fellow. No wonder the luck of Barry Ussher is a byword with the country people.

USSHER: They know nothing about it.

MILES: Well, in any case you seem able to live as you please. You have always means to travel, and never want for anything.

USSHER: So that is your idea of luck, Miles?

MILES: Well, somewhat, I fancy. Isn't it yours?

USSHER: I don't think these things make much difference either way.

MILES: Oh, come, Barry, you can't expect me to believe that.

USSHER: Yes, I mean that what we have on one side is taken away from the other; so the world's lots are more fairly divided than you imagine. Our natures remain much the same at their root. There is always the original pain.

MILES: I suppose you cynical philosophers must invent some grievance from lack of real troubles.

USSHER: No, Miles.

MILES: Well, if you only knew how my brother envies your good fortune.

USSHER: There are others Carden Tyrrell might envy, but he need not envy me. By the way, where is he?

MILES: He is out—I suppose in the heather field.

USSHER: Oh—(*After a short pause*) He has finished all his work there, hasn't he?

MILES: Yes, the young grass is coming up beautifully now. Do you want to see him at once? I can send for him. In any case he is sure to be back soon.

USSHER: That will do. I am in no great hurry.

MILES: You have some business with him?

USSHER: Well, yes. It is about this very subject of land reclamation. I hear he is about to raise another large loan from Government, in order to extend these operations of his.

MILES: Really?

USSHER: So they told me yesterday in Dublin at the Board of Works.

MILES: When Grace hears this, there will be more troubles and disputes.

USSHER: Most likely. What a pity your sister-in-law defeats all her objects by her manner towards Carden.

MILES: Oh indeed, she is very impatient with him. Yet she is good enough in her way too.

USSHER: Precisely; and would probably have made an excellent wife for almost any other man; but for your brother—well, it might have been better if he had never thought of marriage at all.

MILES: What? Surely he might have found some one to suit him. Why should you say such a thing?

USSHER: (*with a frightened look*). Why?

MILES: Yes, Barry. But what is the matter with you?

USSHER: (*quickly recovering himself*). Oh, nothing. Miles, nothing. I merely meant to say that it would be very difficult for anyone to suit Carden. He is a person so much of himself, you know.

MILES: Ah, it is certainly a great misfortune he ever met Grace. And this estrangement is so extraordinary for he once used to be so fond of her.

USSHER: Yes, they generally begin that way. I remember just before he became engaged he told me that he thought till then he should never marry, but that at last he had found real happiness. They all say that, you know.

MILES: You may very well philosophise over what is past, Barry. But why did you not then try to dissuade him?

USSHER: Of course I tried to dissuade him then. I did my best.

MILES: Oh, you did, did you?

USSHER: Yes, of course. I warned him against the danger of marrying a girl with whom he was only acquainted so short a time. I entreated him to wait a while at all events, as he was then only twenty-one and she something younger. But all to no purpose. Ah, if he had waited, he could not have failed to discover that she was only marrying him for his means and position, and that she did not in the least care for him. Besides I was certain from the first that he had no real affection or respect for her.

MILES: Indeed? What made you so certain of that, Barry?

USSHER: Well, you see. Carden and I had been intimate so long. We had been brought up together in fact, so that I fancy I understood him better than anyone. The sudden overturning of all his ideas at that time seemed to me strange and unnatural. He was like one bewitched. A man's whole nature somehow does not change in a moment. You were too young. Miles, to know him in those days; but he was so ideal, so imaginative, as engaging as some beautiful child who saw nothing real in the world outside his own fairy dreams.

MILES: *(with a baffled look)*. I have memories of those days!

USSHER: They are vivid with me. Oh, he always did *so* fascinate and interest me. What poetry he put into those days of my youth—the days that are dead. *(Pause)* Then to see him suddenly changed, grown even prosy under the power of her influence, it made it impossible for me to consider this attachment of his genuine or likely to endure. And has not the result proved that I was right?

MILES: I fear I must admit, Barry, that you were, alas, a reliable prophet.

USSHER: Oh, I foresaw all. I knew this change could not last. The old, wild nature had to break out again when the novelty was over. It was a misfortune since he was married, but it was inevitable. There are some dispositions too eerie, too ethereal, too untamable for good, steady, domestic cultivation, and if so domesticated they avenge themselves in after time. Ah, foolishly his wife and her friends thought they were going to change Carden to their model of a young man, but the latent, untamable nature was not to be subdued. Its first sign of revolt against suppression was when he began this vast work in the heather field.

MILES: *(with a puzzled look)*. Barry, I—I do not understand.

USSHER: Miles, you must admit it was rather an extravagant work. He has sunk a fortune of borrowed capital in the reclamation of that mountain. Look at all the men he employed to root up rocks, and the steam ploughs, too, that have been working during these last years.

MILES: But surely he will obtain a large rent for the rich grass he has made to grow there. That ought to more than compensate for his outlay.

USSHER: Meanwhile interest is accruing. The grass has not grown sufficiently for letting as yet. Then payment of rent cannot

follow till long after, always supposing that it ever produces much rent.

MILES: (*surprised*). Why do you say that? Is not the land good now.

USSHER: Ah, Miles, do you not know that the soil in such places is
very wild and untamable? If heather lands are brought into
cultivation for domestic use, they must be watched, they
must have generous and loving treatment, else their old
wild nature may avenge itself.

                              [*He averts his look.*

MILES: (*with mingled wonder and uneasiness*). Avenge itself? How,
Barry?

USSHER: Why, the wild heather may break out upon them soon
again.

MILES: Oh—(*Then eagerly*) But don't you think Carden has given
the best of treatment to the heather field?

USSHER: (*slowly and gently*). I do not know whether his treatment
was sufficiently kind, as farmers say here in West Ireland.
Somehow he seemed too impatient for the change. He was
hardly considerate enough, perhaps, in the accomplishment of his will.

MILES: (*with dejection*). You evidently think there is something
unsatisfactory in the business.

USSHER: Let us hope for the best, Miles. In any case we ought to try
and prevent him from embarking on further schemes.

MILES: Do, Barry. If there is one person in the world he will listen to,
it is you. Besides you will remove a fresh cause of quarrels
with Grace: and who knows but you may be able to do more
afterwards. Stop—I see him coming now through the garden.

       CARDEN TYRRELL, *a rather powerfully built man of one and
thirty, with light hair, spare growth of beard, unsteady eyes,
very large forehead, and lower part of face small, dressed
negligently in a dark suit, enters from the back.*

TYRRELL: (*smiling*). Oh, how goes it with you, Barry? You have not
favoured us with visits much of late. What have you been
doing?

USSHER: Well, I have been in Dublin for one thing.

TYRRELL: So I heard. But is it true you are reducing all your rents?

USSHER: Yes, I *have* been reducing them somewhat.

TYRRELL: My goodness. I suppose you will end by making the tenants a present of your property. You call me a dreamer, but
it seems that I am the practical man.

USSHER: (*laughing*). Oh, that does not follow at all. I consider it wiser to give a little in time, than later on to have perhaps more wrung from me by the Land Commission.[1]

TYRRELL: But one should never depreciate the value of one's property. I am afraid, Barry, you are mismanaging your affairs. Have you begun yet to reclaim that bog outside your demesne, as I advised?

USSHER: No, Carden.

TYRRELL: There, you see. Well, a fortune is to be made by such work. You would be much better employed at it than at reducing your rents. But, my dear old Barry, there is no use in arguing with you, when you are once set upon a thing. I suppose it is because you knew I would not approve of what you are doing that you have not been to see me for so long.

USSHER: Always suspicious, Carden. But, may I ask why you never come to see me?

TYRRELL: You forget all I have undertaken—all my responsibilities. I have little time.

USSHER: And one would think my time was of no value. Perhaps, Carden, the real reason is that I might possibly not appreciate some of your undertakings and responsibilities.

TYRRELL: (*with a swift shy glance*). Why should you think so?

USSHER: (*smiling*). Oh, I don't know. I was only wondering.

TYRRELL: But why should that prevent me from going to you?

USSHER: Precisely, why indeed? I should never have thought of it, if you had not first suggested the thought.

TYRRELL: Well, you have no reason to think anything of the kind. Just as if I could be occupied in the way you imagine.

USSHER: It seems odd that you should. Carden.

TYRRELL: Yet you have an idea all the same, that I could.

USSHER: Well, to tell you the truth, I heard yesterday that you were contemplating what seems to me certainly most rash.

TYRRELL: Oh, you did, did you? Let us hear what seems to you most rash.

USSHER: It is true, is it not, that you are about to borrow another large sum of money for new land improvements?

TYRRELL: (*somewhat confused*). Yes, it is true—well?

USSHER: Well—don't you think you had better not?

TYRRELL: Why not?

---

1 *the Land Commission*: Established under the 1881 Land Act, it regulated fair rents and oversaw land purchase by tenants.

USSHER: Don't you think you have done enough work—for the present, at all events? Would it not be better to rest for a time and be sure whether what you have already accomplished is going to be successful?

MILES: Yes, Carden, don't you think you ought to wait for a while longer?

TYRRELL: Wait? Why wait, when I know the work must be successful—nay, is already successful?

USSHER: You can scarcely be sure of that yet, Carden.

TYRRELL: Why not?

USSHER: (*rather confused*). Oh, the nature—

[*He hesitates.*

MILES: You can scarcely yet be sure of what the land is capable, you know.

TYRRELL: Can I not see what grass it has produced?

USSHER: Yes, but will that continue?

TYRRELL: (*scornfully*). Will that continue? Who ever heard so absurd a question. As well ask will the air continue to bear up the birds? Will its myriad life continue to pant underneath the sea? Come—my old friend, my brother, I will not have you talk in this discouraging way and make such insinuations, as if you were indeed nothing more than mere country neighbours, who cannot understand my ideas. No, you must believe in me, and inspire me with heart.

MILES: We do believe in you. Carden—but——

USSHER: We only suggest prudence.

MILES: Be prudent. Carden.

TYRRELL: Oh, but when you understand the matter, you will see how prudent I have been. For it was absolutely necessary to obtain this further loan unless the value of the previous one was to be destroyed.

USSHER: I do not follow you. Will you explain?

TYRRELL: Well, you see, the drainage of the heather field has practically swamped the lands below it; so I now must necessarily drain the water off from them right down to the sea. When I have finished all that grand ramification of drains, I shall have created a whole vast tract of fertile pasture which will double the value of my property. What do you think of that? Why, I believe all you people imagine that I am working in the dark, that I do not know what I am about. But I tell you I have excellent reasons for everything I undertake.

USSHER: Yes, Carden, of course—but you have borrowed a vast sum of money. Take care that the interest you will have to pay the Board of Works does not exceed your income.

TYRRELL: There is no danger, Barry. Have I not told you that my income must be greatly increased?

USSHER: You have indeed. I can only hope most sincerely that it will be so.

TYRRELL: But you still seem to doubt it all the same. (USSHER *is silent*). Oh, come, Barry, this is unfriendly of you. Barry, you are a prophet of evil. Heaven grant that your doubts may be vain, else—Oh, I should be the most miserable of men. But they are vain—they are, they are—even despite your other memorable prophecy that, alas, has come too true. Ah, do you remember your warning to me ten years ago?

USSHER: You mean just before your marriage? Yes.

TYRRELL: (*gloomily*). I wonder had that anything to do with its unhappiness. I wonder if these doubts now will bring misfortune on my present undertakings.

USSHER: (*in a frightened voice*). Carden, for pity's sake stop. Don't speak like that. Forget any doubts I may have now expressed. Forget them—forget them. I was wrong ever to have interfered with my advice. Never will I do so again. No—I have not the right. See, Carden, for all I know you may succeed now. I heartily hope you will. You are determined to, and discouragement might only cause you to fail. No, you must not have a second misfortune to cast at me. Good-bye.   [*He prepares to go*].

MILES: Oh, Barry, do not leave us in this way. Think—

TYRRELL: Oh, I am sorry you should take anything I said in that light. I did not mean, Barry, really, to——

USSHER: No, Carden, forgive me, but I was for the moment unnerved by the thought that you should attribute to me any of your ill-luck. No—I hope you will always find me a help to you instead, whenever you may require me.

TYRRELL: Ah, now you are like yourself again—the Barry of other days. I knew you would understand me when I explained everything to you.

USSHER: I hope, Carden, at least I may never be to you the cause of ill-luck.

[*Exit at back.*

*　*　*

from ACT III

SCENE:—*The same as last.... A fire of fresh ashwood in the large fire-place burns cheerfully, while sunlight streams in through the window-doors at back. A sheet of the ordnance map lies on writing table at left. Several months have passed; and it is now Spring.*

[*Kit Tyrrell has gone to the heather field on the pony which Ussher has just brought him, to pluck wild flowers for his father. Ussher tries to convince Tyrrell to settle his affairs—at least with his tenants—but Tyrrell is intransigent. Grace Tyrrell takes up Lord and Lady Shrule's invitation to stay with them and leave her husband, who, financially ruined, is being watched by the police.*]

TYRRELL:	(*starting*). Well, what is the matter?
GRACE:	(*holding out a paper*). A dreadful-looking man has just handed me this.
TYRRELL:	Let me see. (*takes paper*). Ah——
GRACE:	I have so often asked you for money to pay this person.
TYRRELL:	I am very sorry. I had nothing to give you.
GRACE:	Alas, you always had plenty to squander on that mountain.
TYRRELL:	That was Government money, and it could not honestly be expended except on the object for which it was advanced.
GRACE:	I am afraid I must have some of it now. I cannot be left in this condition.
TYRRELL:	Indeed you shall not have one penny of it.
GRACE:	What—you mean to leave me under the stigma of such an insult?
TYRRELL:	(*impatiently*). There is no particular urgency. I will see if I can possibly meet this writ by some money of my own. (*With a painfully distracted look*) Oh, this worry—this worry.

[Exit by door at right.

GRACE:	Well, Mr. Ussher, I hope you are satisfied now. We are ruined; and my husband is becoming stranger in his behaviour every day. But for you, he might have been cured by this, and the estate in a very different condition.
USSHER:	I have nothing, Mrs. Tyrrell, to reproach myself with. I did all for the best.
GRACE:	Yes, of course. That is the only satisfaction one ever receives for injuries done through gratuitous interference.

USSHER: Nothing has since happened to convict me of having acted wrongly. I have done you no injury.

GRACE: No injury? Well!

USSHER: You cannot lay to my account this quarrel with the tenants which is the cause of your present difficulties. Goodness knows I have done my best to mend it.

GRACE: (*impatiently*). Oh, that is only a temporary difficulty. But the estate will be ruined for ever by the great debt from which we should have saved it, if you had not interfered. (*Pause*) Yes—I see how it all will be. The child and I will be driven out, ruined, to battle with the world.

USSHER: Oh, don't think of such a thing, Mrs. Tyrrell. It can never come to that.

GRACE: (*sadly*). Ah, yes, you destroyed my last chance of saving our home. I might have kept it lovingly for Kit until he grew to be a man; but now I see it must go from us. I shall have to bid everything farewell—the familiar rooms—the garden where I found an occupation for my life—even those common useless things about the house I have been accustomed to look at for years. Oh, you don't know what it is—this parting from those everyday things of one's life.

USSHER: Yes, yes—indeed I do—and from my heart I feel for you.

GRACE: And yet you could have acted as you have.

USSHER: I acted only in good faith. Heaven knows that is the truth.

GRACE: The injury remains still the same.

USSHER: (*with strong emotions*). If it is I who have injured you, Mrs. Tyrrell, you must allow me to make amends.

GRACE: Alas, what amends are possible?

USSHER: Who can tell? I promise you, at least, you shall never, *never* bid farewell to your home.

GRACE: (*in a trembling voice*). If only what you say might come true.

LADY SHRULE, LORD SHRULE, *and* CARDEN TYRRELL *enter by door at right.*

LORD SHRULE: Carden, I believe the butler was actually going to say 'not at home' to us, if I had not caught sight of you in the hall. Ha, ha.

360

LADY SHRULE: What a shame, Mr. Tyrrell, to try and prevent me from seeing Grace. How do you do, Grace dear? (*Giving her hand apathetically to* USSHER). How do you do?

LORD SHRULE: (*shakes hands with* GRACE *and* USSHER). We should have been so disappointed.

TYRRELL: I assure you. Lord Shrule, my attempt to escape is purely an imagination on your part.

LORD SHRULE: Oh, you sly fellow, you think I do not know. You are just like your father when people used to call—although he would never run away from me, I can tell you.

TYRRELL: No more did I. I was only surprised to see you; that was all. When I heard the bell I thought it was Miles come from Dublin. I am anxiously expecting him now at any moment.

LORD SHRULE: Ah, it will be a pleasure to see Miles again. We have all heard of his University triumphs. How proud your poor father would have been.

TYRRELL: Yes, and how delighted to share his satisfaction with you.

LORD SHRULE: Poor Marmaduke—we were such friends. At our very last interview he asked me to keep you and your brother always in mind after he was gone. So I have always felt somewhat like a father towards you both, you know, and with a father's privilege occasionally have given advice.

GRACE: Yes, Lord Shrule, and how I wish your good advice occasionally had been followed.

LORD SHRULE: Ah, we cannot help that, Mrs. Tyrrell. Nothing will ever teach the young save bitter experience.

GRACE: I am sure there has been enough bitter experience; but it seems to have taught nothing at all.

LORD SHRULE: Well, well, I hope it won't be so. Eh, Carden?

TYRRELL: I do not see how my experience can teach me to act differently from my present way of acting. (*Aside to* USSHER) Miles ought to have arrived by this. Oh, I am nearly dead with anxiety to know the news he will bring.

USSHER: (*aside to* TYRRELL). I hope there will be good news.

LORD SHRULE: Never mind, Mrs. Tyrrell. Carden will come by degrees to see his mistakes.

GRACE: I fear we are now in so bad a way that it does not much matter whether he sees them or not.

LADY SHRULE: No—really, Grace, you do not say so?

GRACE: Oh, Lilian, we are ruined.

LORD SHRULE: Come, come, I am sure it cannot be as bad as that.

TYRRELL: Goodness me, of course, Lord Shrule. On the contrary, in the near future we shall make a fortune.

GRACE: I say we are ruined, utterly, irretrievably.

TYRRELL: No—no——

USSHER: What noise is that? (*Listens, then opens doors at right.*) Why, Miles has arrived.

TYRRELL: Miles—oh!

USSHER: There, Carden, for goodness sake be calm.
Enter MILES TYRRELL *by door at right.*

MILES: Carden. (*he grasps his brother by the hand, then greets all the rest.*)

TYRRELL: What news. Miles? Will he wait?

MILES: (*turning away dejectedly*). I did my best, Carden. There is no hope, I fear.

GRACE: No hope? What is this new misfortune? Who won't wait?

MILES: The chief mortgagee.

GRACE: Is he going to foreclose?

MILES: He says so.

LORD SHRULE: Ha—this is a most serious matter.

TYRRELL: But Miles, didn't you explain to him all about the heather field?

MILES: Yes.

TYRRELL: Didn't you assure him that it would soon bring in what would more than pay his interest?

MILES: Indeed I did. Carden.

TYRRELL: Well?

MILES: Well, that only seemed to make him impatient with me. But I used every argument I could think of, and pleaded with him for nearly an hour in his office, until at last he had to get rid of me almost brutally.

TYRRELL: (*with a look of humiliation and despair*). Oh, ruin! ruin!

USSHER: No, no. Carden—it is not yet that. We must see how we can help you through this difficulty.

TYRRELL: (*quietly*). With all your goodwill, Barry, what can you do now?

USSHER: Who knows? Just keep quiet, and do not distress yourself. Leave it all to me.

TYRRELL: (*almost staggering*). Yes—such a severe blow—this. It has quite upset me. I am sure you will all excuse me. You, Barry, will see what you can do, won't you? Yes— (*He goes to door at right.*)

USSHER: Yes, Carden, I hope all will come well.

LORD SHRULE: How much of the property does this mortgage cover?

GRACE: Oh, pretty nearly all, I should think.

TYRRELL: (*suddenly turning*) All, do you say? No—not all. This vulture cannot touch the heather field! My hope—it is my only hope now, and it will save me in the end. Ha, ha! these wise ones! They did not think the barren mountain of those days worth naming in their deed. But now that mountain is a great green field worth more than all they can seize (*with a strange intensity*) and it is mine—all mine!

[*Exits by door at right.*

LORD SHRULE: (*throwing up his hands*). Oh dear, oh dear, what infatuation!

GRACE: Yes, indeed, it has caused us all to be cast adrift in the world. Oh, what is to become of me—what is to become of me? (*She sobs in her handkerchief.*)

LADY SHRULE: Grace, you must not lose heart.

GRACE: Ah, the final misfortune has come.

LADY SHRULE: We shall try and help you, dear—there.

USSHER: Yes, we must lose no time now to see what can be done for Carden.

LADY SHRULE: You should indeed bestir yourself, Mr Ussher, and save him; for we have you to thank that he was left in a position to ruin himself.

USSHER: And have not you too, Lady Shrule, to thank yourself for the same thing?

LADY SHRULE: I? How so, pray?

USSHER: Why did you and Lord Shrule disappear so suddenly on that day the doctors were here? Your advocacy would doubtless have made them heedless of my objections—

LADY SHRULE: Ha—why indeed? You know, Shrule, I wanted you to——

LORD SHRULE: Well, well, I could not bear to act in such a way to the son of my old friend. But I suppose in my weakness I did wrong.

USSHER: No, Lord Shrule, you did right. You never could be suspected by anyone of doing otherwise.

LORD SHRULE: I hope not, Ussher! Still, I am inclined to think it might have been wiser then to have taken some definite step.

LADY SHRULE: I should think so. Just see what has happened since.

GRACE: Nothing less than the ruin of a helpless woman and her child.

LADY SHRULE: You have, indeed, incurred a nice responsibility, Mr. Ussher.

GRACE: (*to* USSHER). What—what right had you to do my child and me this wrong?

USSHER: I only prevented what I thought a grievous wrong from being done to my friend.

GRACE: It was no wrong—it was for his good—for all our good. In your heart you must know I was right.

USSHER: I have often said, Mrs. Tyrrell, I know nothing of the sort.

LADY SHRULE: Still, you must admit that his actions since more than justify Mrs. Tyrrell in the course she adopted.

LORD SHRULE: Alas, I fear that is the case.

USSHER: I admit he is very wilful and extravagant, but no more. I cannot discover any mental infirmity. His mind has a perfect grasp of ideas.

GRACE: Don't talk of ideas. I have heard enough about them since I was married to give me a horror of them for the rest of my life.

LADY SHRULE: They have certainly caused the wreck of this household.

LORD SHRULE: Oh, I hope not. We must not be too pessimistic.—Who can tell?—Perhaps the heather field may turn out a success after all!

GRACE: (*with contempt*). The heather field.

LORD SHRULE: If it were to, there can be no doubt but that all would be saved. I wonder how it is going on. Have you been there lately, Mrs. Tyrrell?

GRACE: Of course not. Lord Shrule. The very thought of the place fills me with despair.

MILES: That is a pity, Grace—a great pity, when so much depends upon the success of the heather field.

GRACE: No good can ever come of that abominable work.

MILES: You must not speak such words; no luck can come from such words.

GRACE: I cannot help it.

MILES: Oh, I know you have much to endure, but I cannot remain here and listen to such denunciation of what

	my brother holds nearest to his heart.
GRACE:	I have only said the truth.
MILES:	You cannot be certain of this truth. It is not right to speak such words.

[*Exit by door at right.*

LADY SHRULE:	My poor Grace.
GRACE:	Oh, Lilian.
LADY SHRULE:	These troubles are driving you to distraction. You had better leave this place for a while. Will you not come and stay with us?
LORD SHRULE:	Oh, yes, won't you stay with us, Mrs Tyrrell? You might be saved much annoyance and worry.
GRACE:	You are both so kind—I should like to for a little while, certainly. This house has become unbearable of late with debts and difficulties on every side.
LADY SHRULE:	Oh dear, how terrible. You had better leave at once, Grace. Perhaps you might have some of your things seized. Anyhow, bring with you those that you most value. We will take care of them.
GRACE:	Thanks, Lilian.
LORD SHRULE:	Well then, that is agreed, Mrs Tyrrell. I am so glad we may be of use to you.
LADY SHRULE:	We shall expect you this evening, dear.
GRACE:	Yes, I shall get ready at once.
LADY SHRULE:	And it is time for us to return home. Good-bye, Mr Ussher.
USSHER:	Good-bye, Lady Shrule.
LORD SHRULE:	Good-bye.

[*Exeunt* LADY SHRULE, GRACE TYRRELL *and* LORD SHRULE
by door at right.

USSHER:	(*gloomily*). Heaven help her—help them all. What is to be done? Stay—I might go security, I would do anything to help them. But would it really be of use? Other difficulties must follow these, so that my whole fortune would not suffice. I will think the matter over.—I wonder how the heather field is going on. No one seems to have been there lately.

KIT TYRRELL, *carrying a small white bundle, enters
through door at back.*

KIT:	(*placing the bundle on sofa*). Barry, the pony is splendid. I had such galloping over the heather field.

USSHER:	Well, did you bring back any flowers?
KIT:	They have not yet come out. All I could find there were these little buds in my handkerchief. (*Unties the bundle*) Look.
USSHER:	(*with a start*). What—buds of heather? Has your father seen these, Kit?
KIT:	Yes, I told him I found them growing all over the heather field.
USSHER:	You did, boy—and what did he say?
KIT:	Nothing for a while. But he looked—he looked—well, I have never seen him look like that before.
USSHER:	Ha—and then—?
KIT:	Oh, then he seemed to forget all about it. He became so kind, and oh, Barry, what do you think, he called me, his 'little brother Miles.' So I am really his brother, he says, after all—
	MILES TYRRELL, *in haste and violent trepidation, enters through door at back.*
MILES:	Barry, for pity's sake. (*Sees* KIT *and suddenly checks himself, then brings* USSHER *over to fireplace*). Barry, something dreadful has come over Carden. He does not know me.
USSHER:	(*in a trembling voice, as he gazes fixedly before him*). The vengeance of the heather field.

*   *   *

KATHARINE TYNAN (1859–1931)

She was born in South Richmond Street, Dublin, the fifth of twelve children of Andrew Cullen Tynan, a dairy-farmer. Andrew became a successful cattle farmer, supplying the British army, and in 1868 the family moved to Whitehall in Clondalkin (the house had belonged to John Philpott Curran, the patriot lawyer). At the age of five, Katharine was sent to a 'young ladies' school'. At seven she developed ulcers on her eyes, which left her purblind. In 1871 she went to the boarding school of the Dominican Siena Convent in Drogheda, leaving in 1874 because her father wanted her company.

Her father was an enthusiastic and generous supporter of Parnell*; Katharine became the books editor of the Parnellite *Irish Daily Independent*, and joined the Ladies Land League. Her first poem, 'A Dream' appeared in 1878. It was soon followed by a host of publications, as her lists of poetic acquaintances grew to include Christina Rossetti, Alice and Wilfrid Meynell, Francis Thompson, and Lionel Johnson.

After the publication of *Louise de la Vallière and Other Poems* (1885), her father set up a literary salon for her, which was frequented by many Irish writers—including AE* (who remained a life-long friend) and W.B. Yeats*).

In 1893 she married Henry Albert Hinkson, a handsome barrister who wrote an important book on copyright law, and had literary ambitions. They moved to Ealing, where she wrote her best poetry: *Cuckoo Songs* (1894), *A Lover's Breast-Knot* (1896), *The Wind in the Trees* (1898), *Innocencies* (1905); *Irish Poems* (1908), with its simple, loving celebration of nature, remains her finest book. The couple had three children. Hinkson did not find steady employment, and Tynan had to boil the pot, writing a staggering number of novels, poetry collections, collections of stories, memoirs, biographies, *in memoria*, anthologies, etc., while contributing regularly to popular newspapers and magazines.

The couple returned to Ireland in 1911, settling in Killiney, Co. Dublin, before Tynan persuaded Lord Aberdeen, the Lord-Lieutenant, to confer the Resident Magistracy of Mayo on her husband. She had a remarkable gift for solace; her early poem 'Sheep and Lambs', put to music by Sir Hugh Roberton, became a very popular hymn. With her War poetry, she offered succour to a large number of bereaved. After her husband's death in 1919, she led a nomadic existence, travelling through Germany and France with her daughter Pamela (herself a successful novelist under the pseudonym 'Peter Deane'), before settling in a flat in Wimbledon, where she died.

Letter to Rev. Matthew Russell[1]

446 Camden Road, London N.
April 22nd. 1884.

... I have come to describe you to people in a sort of stock phrase; I laugh now when I catch myself using it. I always say 'my dear Father Russell; the most unweariedly kind friend a young writer ever had.'... I enjoyed my visit [at Lady Wilde's] very much. She is a very imposing woman (Mr Sexton to whom I described her said my description made her more imposing than fascinating, but I hope you won't think so, because she is very nice, very tall, and with iron grey hair falling a little at the back, and with a very strongly marked face; a noble looking old woman I thought her. She was very kind to me but she overawed me a little; I sent her my 'Joan of Arc'[2] afterwards and she wrote

---

1 *Revd Matthew Russell* (1834–1912), founder and editor of *The Irish Monthly*. He was the brother of Lord Russell of Killowen, the first Catholic Lord Chief Justice of England since the Reformation. This letter is part of Matthew Russell's correspondence in the Irish Jesuit Archive.

2 'Joan of Arc': a poetic monologue, which appeared in *Louise de la Vallière*. It was first published in *Hibernia* Vol. II (1883).

me such a nice letter. She says it is as perfect as anything William Morris[1] has written and a great deal more and signs herself, 'my friend in love and sympathy.'... Oscar[2] honoured me with not a little notice; he talked to me for about 20 minutes of poets and poetry in a very amusing way rather as if he were lecturing.... He spoke of *The Irish Monthly*; said it was a charming little magazine. I said astutely that the best Irish writers had worked for it, and concluded with 'and I think you graduated on it Mr Wilde.' He laughed at my transparent flattery, and said he was afraid he had written for some of the Oxford Magazines earlier. I said 'Oh! Mr Wilde, we always claim you for the Irish Monthly', and he replied that he was very glad indeed to be so claimed. What do you think of me now? Miss C. Lloyd to whom he is to be married next month was there also; she is a very nice graceful girl. Philip Burke Marston,[3] the blind poet was there also, and I had a little talk with him, but it is very sad the way he stares at you with his sightless eyes. I am going there again next Saturday. I met an old clergyman at Lady Wilde's a Mr. Ponsonby Lyons[4] who is very kind to me. He is editing the Ancient manuscripts in the British Museum and he made me take a ticket for the fine reading room there. I go whenever I have an off day, and he has introduced me to a good many literary people, among others to Mr. Furnivall[5] the founder and secretary of the Browning Society. He was delighted with my 'Joan' of which I gave a copy to Mr Lyons who showed it to him, and he asked me to write a paper on Browning for the Society. I am going to their meeting tomorrow night when Mr Cotter Morison[6] will read a paper on 'Caliban on Setebos' and Mr Russell Lowell[7] will take the chair. I was introduced to a great many other people, some frightfully learned men who knew Coptic and Sanscrit better than English.

---

1 *William Morris* (1834–96), English poet, designer and socialist.

2 *Oscar*: Oscar Wilde* published seven poems, mostly religious, in the *Irish Monthly* between 1876 and 1878.

3 *Philip Burke Marston*: Philip Bourke Marston (1850–87) partially lost sight at the age of three, due to the administration of belladonna; he went blind later in life.

4 *Ponsonby Lyons*: Ponsonby Annesley Lyons, scholar, translated Ernest Nys' *The Papacy Considered in relation to International Law* (1879), co-authored *Cartularium Monasterii de Rameseia* (with William Henry Hart, 1884) and published *Two 'Compoti' of the Lancashire and Cheshire Manors of Henry de Lacy* (1884); he also wrote an article on the origins and history of the *Encyclopaedia Britannica*.

5 *Mr Furnivall*: Frederick James Furnivall (1825–1910), scholar and critic.

6 *Mr Cotter Morison*: John Cotter Morison (d.1888), author of *The Service of Man*, described by *The Athenaeum* as 'the most powerful attack on Christianity that has been produced in England during this generation'.

7 *Mr Russell Lowell*: James Russell Lowell (1819–91), American author and diplomat.

Do you know anything about a man named Fitzgerald Molloy,[1] a novelist. He has written several books. I found him rather nice. I almost forgot to tell you of a girl I met there a Miss Nellie Hellis,[2] who writes children's stories, and who had an adoration almost like mine for my beautiful Rosa.[3] She had some correspondence with her at one time, and when she found out I knew her she carried me off to tea, and I had to describe her minutely. She is so anxious to see her. How is she? she wrote to me after I came here; will you tell her that I asked you for her. I am going back to Great Cressingham[4] for a week or ten days. They have the bad taste to be very fond of me and I love Mr Fagan very much, and I like all the others greatly also. When are you going to print Mary's poem?[5] I fear she begins to think you will not print it. Will you write to her about it, and about the corrections you want her to make. Her address at present is St Elmo, Christ Church Rd, Bournemouth, but she will be going home soon. Please write to her. I had such a kind letter from Mrs Meynell lately. I think they would have been very kind to me, if things had been more fortuitous but Mr Meynell has been sick ever since I have been here and she is very delicate. She said she hoped I would stay till late in May when she expected to be strong again, and she and Mr Meynell would like to have me to dine with them, with Mr. Charlie Fagan, Mr Fagan's poet son who is a great friend of mine and who is one of the new contributors to *Merry England*. I don't know that I shall be here, but it is so kind of them, and I believe it is almost unprecedented to be asked to dine in Meynells'[6]—they are such hard-working people. I am going next Wednesday to a dinner party in Mrs Rae's she is 'Melusine''s sister.[7]

---

1 *Fitzgerald Molloy*: Joseph Fitzgerald Molloy (1858–1909), Irish writer, friend of Mr and Mrs S.C. Hall, and private secretary to Sir Charles Gavan Duffy.
2 *Nellie Hellis* wrote children's books for the Religious Tract Society and the Christian Knowledge Society.
3 *Rosa*: Rosa Mulholland* (Lady Gilbert) (1841–1921), the writer, was the sister-in-law of Father Matthew Russell.
4 *Great Cressingham*: the rectory of the Revd Henry Stuart Fagan (1827–90), an ardent supporter of Irish Home Rule. His son, the poet Charles Gregory Fagan (1860–85), an Oxford graduate and aesthete poet, went to India to teach, and died there from typhoid.
5 Mary Fagan, Charles' sister.
6 Meynells': The poet and essayist Alice Meynell (1847–1922) and her husband Wilfrid (1852–1948), editor of *Merry England*, became Katharine Tynan's closest friends.
7 *Mrs Rae....*: 'Mrs [Katharine] Rae was a grand-daughter of John Foster, the last Speaker of the Irish House of Commons, and she and her sister, Miss Skeffington Thompson, were ardent Irish patriots. At that time they were watching over and tending a little Society at Southwark which had begun to teach the London Irish children Irish history, Irish poems, Irish songs and dances— the seed of the Irish Literary Society, and of a bigger growth, the Gaelic League' (*Twenty-Five Years: Reminiscences* [London: Smith, Elder & Co, 1913], p.123). 'Melusine' was the pseudonym of Emily Skeffington Thompson, author of *Moy O'Brien. A Tale of Irish Life* and *The Irish Birthday Book: Selections from the speeches and writings of Irish men and women, both Catholic and Protestant* (1884).

Will you please send a copy of April 'Monthly' to Mr Fagan at Gt Cressingham. He has not seen my 'Eastertide'. If you have the *Merry England* with Mrs Meynell's article on 'Poetesses' please send it to me,

your attached child
Katie Tynan

Not Lovers Then

(c. 1887)[1]

Not lovers then but friends
Until our world's glimpse ends
   Dear, take my hand on this;
Since you have willed it so
   I am content you know
   Let's part without a kiss.

For love is full of smart
To wound and break a heart
   The heart it sets to beat
Ever so; your words are wise
Look once into my eyes
   Was not the old way sweet?

Let the old love lie there
With hidden face and hair.
   While you and I forget
So dead and piteous
He will not trouble us
   Making our eyes wet.

From *Ballads and Lyrics*

(1891)

Sheep and Lambs

All in the April evening,
   April airs were abroad,

---

1 Holograph poem in exercise book of Katharine Tynan (in possession of editor).

The sheep with their little lambs
  Passed me by on the road.

The sheep with their little lambs
  Passed me by on the road;
All in the April evening
  I thought on the Lamb of God.

The lambs were weary, and crying
  With a weak, human cry.
I thought on the Lamb of God
  Going meekly to die.

Up in the blue, blue mountains
  Dewy pastures are sweet
Rest for the little bodies,
  Rest for the little feet

But for the Lamb of God,
  Up on the hill-top green,
Only a Cross of shame
  Two stark crosses between.

All in the April evening,
  April airs were abroad,
I saw the sheep with their lambs,
  And thought on the Lamb of God.

Only in August

Only in August I have not seen you.
    August comes with his wheat and poppies;
    Ruddy sunlight in corn and coppice:
Only in August I have not seen you.

Autumn beckons far-off like a greeting.
    I and Autumn have secrets of you,
    All the Winter was long to love you;
Wintry winds have a song of meeting.

Dear is Summer, but Spring is dearer.

In the Spring there was heavenly weather;
Love and sunshine and you together.
Dear is Summer, but Spring is dearer.

June is fled with her rose and pansies.
More is gone than a drift of roses,
More than the may that the May uncloses,
More than April—with songs and dances.

Only in August I have not seen you.
Every month hath its share of graces,
Flowers, and song, and beloved faces.
Only in August I have not seen you.

From *The Wind in the Trees*

(1897)

Lambs

He sleeps as a lamb sleeps,
Beside his mother.
Somewhere in yon blue deeps
His tender brother
Sleeps like a lamb and leaps.

He feeds as a lamb might,
Beside his mother.
Somewhere in fields of light
A lamb, his brother,
Feeds, and is clothed in white.

William Butler Yeats

(1893)[1]

When Mr. W. B. Yeats is in London he lives at his father's residence, 3, Blenheim Road, Bedford Park. Most people know that pleasant Queen Anne village, which would be altogether delightful if it had a surrounding meadow and boscage instead of brickfields, alternated by

---

1 *The Sketch*, 29 November 1893.

raw sections of new villa residences. Fortunately, London does not long content the finer part of the young poet, though when he is in London he is a gadabout, to be seen at all the literary gatherings. He says in one of his most exquisite poems, 'The Lake Isle of Inisfree'—

> I will arise and go now, for always, night and day,
>   I hear lake-water lapping with low sounds on the shore;
> While I stand in the roadway, or on the pavements grey,
>   I hear it in the deep heart's core.

His 'Inisfree' is Sligo, in Connaught, to which belong his mother's people, a race of shippers and sailors. But even Dublin, where a stir of literary movements rises about his presence, has many an Inisfree within walking distance—deep glens in the dove-grey hills; lonely country lanes sunk between high hedges, with marshy ditches, full of yellow iris and purple foxglove; cliffs above the sea, where there are only the gulls for companionship. To have been a citizen of Dublin makes one disbelieve in English country or seaside, nearer than Wales or Cornwall—which, if one thinks of it, are scarce English at all.

Mr. Yeats's study is at the back of the quaint and charming house, in which, outside the poet's den, order reigns. It opens on a little balcony, twined about and overhung with the Virginia creeper. When he is in London he has generally a few plants there, of which he is inordinately jealous. Indeed, one of the few occasions on which I have seen his placid temper roused was when some teasing person pretended to annex the faint blossoms he had coaxed into existence.

In the study confusion reigns paramount. The fireplace, which makes a slanting projection, is littered with papers. The mantelpiece is buried in layers of them. Books are everywhere—on shelves, chairs, table, and mantelpiece. When the poet wishes to invite your attention to any particular book or paper, he sweeps the dusky hair with his hand from his beautiful forehead—a gesture telling of effort and endeavour. On the ceiling he has painted a map of Sligo, with a ship at each corner. How he achieved the painting—unless he lay slung on his back on a plank—I can't imagine, and I omitted to ask him. The books cover a large range, but are mainly either poetry or books on occult subjects, for, as Mr. Yeats's readers well know, he loves magic and mystery. Of books, papers, letters, and proof-sheets there is such a confusion that one wonders how he can disentangle anything.

Prominent in the disorder is a book bound like a mediæval missal in cherry-coloured brocade and tarnished gold.

'What may that fine thing be?' I ask.

He answers with a slight blush, 'That is my MS. Book. A friend brought me the cover from Paris, and I had the book made to fit it.'

I inspect the book. It is such thick paper as one finds in *editions de luxe*, and, one imagines, must be rather uncomfortable to write upon.

The fine book is a part of the literary dandyism which rather distinguishes Mr. Yeats. In the old Dublin days he was as untidy as a genius newly come from the backwoods. He was an art student then, and generally bore the stains of the studio. I have observed him with sympathy devote patient hour after hour to scrubbing at a paint stain with what he took to be turpentine, but which was really linseed oil. He used to affect scarlet ties, which lit up his olive face. They were tied most carelessly. Ordinary young men who had been at school with him, and resented his being a genius, used to say that the carelessness was the result of long effort; but one never believed them. Now he wears the regulation London costume, plus a soft hat, and his ties are dark silk, knotted in a soft bow. He is extremely handsome in his strange way; he is very tall and very slender; so dark, that he was once taken for a Hindu by a Hindu; a long, delicate, oval face, beautiful brows, and large, melancholy, velvety brown eyes that see visions.

He reads to me one of the poems from the fine book, a fantastic thing which, he says, he actually dreamt. He has a beautiful voice, full of rich cadences. Some people enjoy his queer chanting of poetry. For me, I do not; the method distracts my attention from the poetry.

'Tell me what you are doing,' I say, with the imperativeness of a very old friend.

'I have two books coming out with Lawrence and Bullen,' he answers; 'one is a volume of Irish sketches, the source of many of which you will recognise. It is to be called "Celtic Twilight." I believe I have some of the proofs'—and searching his many pockets he produces a sheaf of proofs. The form looks very pretty; it is a long, slender page, very old-fashioned. I turn the sheets over. The sketches are mostly portraits, with variations. Yes, I recognise them, nearly all: 'The Visionary,' 'The Coward,' 'The Farmer,' they are all portraits, beautifully rendered.[1]

'And the other book?' I ask.

'The other is to be called 'The Secret Rose,' and is to be a collection of weird stories of the Middle Ages in Ireland; some of them have appeared in the *National Observer*. Also,' he adds, 'I am in treaty about a new volume of poems.'

---

1 'A Knight of the Sheep', in *The Celtic Twilight* (1893) was based on Katharine Tynan's father.

'Tell me,' I say, 'about your early poems. What did you write first?'

'The first attempt at serious poetry I made,' he says 'was when I was about seventeen, and much under the influence of Shelley. It was a dramatic poem, about a magician who set up his throne in Central Asia, and who expressed himself with Queen Mab-like heterodoxy. It was written in rivalry with G——,'[1] mentioning a schoolfellow of his I knew; 'I forget what he wrote.'

'And your second?' I ask.

'The second was 'Time and the Witch Vivien,' which you will remember in "The Wanderings of Ossian."'

I do remember that exquisite fragment, and on expressing my surprise that it should be such young work he assures me that he never re-touched it.

'And your first reading?' I ask. 'What interested you most as a boy?'

'Scott first,' he answers, 'and then Macaulay.' So he had had the common school-boy idols, albeit he was so uncommon.

'I am going back to Dublin this week,' he volunteers, 'and intend to stay there. I want my work to be as Irish as possible, and I find that here my impressions get blunted.'

It is good for his work that he is to be away from London and the literary coteries. Ireland is the country of faiths; not alone the supreme faith, which is religion, but the faiths in ghosts and fairies, in old customs, in the Motherland and her future, in lost causes, in heroes who were always defeated and slain. In London these things have little but a remote and literary interest. But no dry-rot of disbelief or cynicism is likely to affect 'Willie Yeats,' as his friends call him, so long as he has with him his father's sweetening and saving influence. The father is instinct with poetry and idealism, a man of beautiful and lovable character. Father and son have always been dear friends. I have many memories of them in the father's studio in Dublin, where I sat week after week for a portrait, and never grumbled at the prolonged sittings, because the talk was so delightful, and the atmosphere so full of sweetness and sunny temper. There used to be a picture of Willie in his boyhood on an easel over against me as I sat. The dusky face had carnations in the cheeks which now are pale olive. If it was at all representative of him, he must have been a beautiful boy, full of rich Eastern colour. I did not meet him till a year or two later, when he had assumed the man's colourless cheeks, with the silky, dark, very youthful beard he then wore.

---

1 Frederick Gregg, a friend at the High School, Dublin; Yeats and he had written (or attempted) a verse play together.

GEORGE EGERTON (MARY CHAVELITA BRIGHT, NÉE DUNNE) (1859–1945)

Born in Melbourne, Australia, the daughter of an Irish officer, she was educated in Chile, Ireland and Germany. She trained as a nurse before moving to Norway, in 1887 with Henry Higginson, who was a friend of her father's—and a drunken bigamist. Here she met Knut Hamsun, the novelist, and fell under the spell of Ibsen's cult of the New Woman. Higginson died in 1889; 'Chav' returned to London, cut her losses, and married Clairmonte Egerton, a Canadian, who left for America not long after the birth of their son. She became the mistress of John Lane of the *Yellow Book*, who published her (as would Grant Richards). In all she wrote four collections of stories under the name of George Egerton, of which *Keynotes* (1893) established her reputation as a shockingly frank writer, for whom marriage was 'legal prostitution'. It was followed by *Discords* (1894), *Symphonies* (1897), and *Fantasias* (1898). Her novels include the semi-autobiographical *The Wheel of God* (1898) and *Rosa Amorosa: The Love-Letters of a Woman* (1901). She also wrote four plays, and several biographies. She married the literary agent and drama critic, Reginald Golding Bright, and herself became agent for such writers as Bernard Shaw* and Somerset Maugham.

From *Keynotes*

(1893)

An Empty Frame

It was a simple pretty little frame, such as you may buy at any sale cheaply; its ribbed wood, aspinalled white, with an inner frame of pale blue plush; its one noticeable feature, that it was empty. And yet it stood on the middle of the bedroom mantel-board.

It was not a luxurious room, none of the furniture matched, it was a typical boarding-house bedroom.

Any one preserving the child habit of endowing inanimate objects with human attributes might fancy that the flickering flames of the fire took a pleasure in bringing into relief the bright bits in its dinginess. For they played over the silver-backed brushes, and the cut-glass perfume-bottles on the dressing-table; flicked the bright beads on the toes of coquettish small shoes and the steel clasps of a travelling bag in the corner; imparting a casual air of comfort, such as the touch of certain dainty women lends to a common room.

A woman enters, a woman wondrously soft and swift in all her movements. She seems to reach a place without your seeing how, no motion of elbow or knee betrays her. Her fingers glide swiftly down the buttons of her gown; in a second she has freed herself from its ensheathing, garment after garment falls from her until she stands almost free. She gets into night-dress and loose woollen dressing-gown, and slips her naked feet into fur-lined slippers with a movement that is somehow the expression of an intense nervous relief from a thrall. Everything she does is done so swiftly that you see the result rather than the working out of each action.

She sinks into a chair before the fire, and, clasping her hands behind her head, peers into the glowing embers. The firelight, lower than her face, touches it cruelly; picks out and accentuates as remorselessly as a rival woman the autographs past emotions have traced on its surface; deepens the hollows of her delicate thoughtful temples and the double furrow between her clever irregular eyebrows. Her face is more characteristic than beautiful. Nine men would pass it, the tenth sell his immortal soul for it. The chin is strong, the curve of jaw determined; there is a little full place under the chin's sharp point. The eyes tell you little; they are keen and inquiring, and probe others' thoughts rather than reveal their own. The whole face is one of peculiar strength and self-reliance. The mouth is its contradiction—the passionate curve of the upper lip with its mobile corners, and the tender little under lip that shelters timidly beneath it, are encouraging promises against its strength.

The paleness of some strong feeling tinges her face, a slight trembling runs through her frame. Her inner soul-struggle is acting as a strong developing fluid upon a highly sensitized plate; anger, scorn, pity, contempt chase one another like shadows across her face. Her eyes rest upon the empty frame, and the plain white space becomes alive to her. Her mind's eye fills it with a picture it once held in its dainty embrace. A rare head amongst the rarest heads of men, with its crest of hair tossed back from the great brow, its proud poise and the impress of grand confident compelling genius that reveals itself one scarce knows how; with the brute possibility of an untamed, natural man lurking about the mouth and powerful throat. She feels the subduing smile of eyes that never failed to make her weak as a child under their gaze, and tame as a hungry bird. She stretches out her hands with a pitiful little movement, and then, remembering, lets them drop and locks them until the knuckles stand out whitely. She shuts her eyes, and one tear after the other starts from beneath her lids, trickles down her cheeks, and drops with a splash into her lap. She does not sob, only cries quietly, and she sees, as if she held the letter in her hand, the words that decided her fate—

'You love me; I know it, you other half of me. You want me to complete your life as I you, you good, sweet woman. You slight, weak thing, with your strong will and your grand, great heart. You witch with a soul of clean white fire. I kiss your hands (such little hands! I never saw the like), slim child-hands, with a touch as cool and as soft as a snow-flake! You dear one, come to me, I want you, now, always. Be with me, work with me, share with me, live with me, my equal as a creature; above me as my queen of women! I love you, I worship you, but you know my views. I cannot, I will not bind myself to you by any legal or religious tie. I must be free and unfettered to follow that which I believe right for me. If you come to me in all trust, I can and will give myself to you in all good faith, yours as much as you will, for ever! I will kneel to you. Why should I always desire to kneel to you? It is not that I stand in awe of you, or that I ever feel a need to kneel at all; but always to you, and to you alone. Come—I will crouch at your feet and swear myself to you,'—and she had replied 'No!' and in her loneliness of spirit married him who seemed to need her most out of those who admired her....

The door opens and he comes in. He looks inquiringly at her, touches her hair half hesitatingly, and then stands with his hands thrust in his pockets and gnaws his moustache.

'Are you angry, little woman?'

'No' (very quietly), 'why should I be?'

She closes her eyes again, and after five minutes' silence he begins to undress. He does it very slowly, watching her perplexedly. When he has finished he stands with his back to the fire, an unlovely object in sleeping suit.

'Would you like to read her letter?'

She shakes her head.

'I suppose I ought to have sent her back her letters before, you know. She hadn't heard I was married.'

'Yes,' she interjects, 'it would have been better to start with a clean bill; but why talk about it?'

He looks at her a while, then gets into bed and watches her from behind the pages of the *Field*. It seems unusually quiet. His watch, that he has left in his waistcoat pocket, thrown across the back of a chair, seems to fill the whole room with a nervous tick.

He tosses the paper on to the floor. She looks up as it falls, rises, turns off the gas-jet, sinks back into her old position, and stares into the fire. He gets up, goes over, and kneels down next her.

'I am awfully sorry you are put out, old girl. I saw you were when

I answered you like that, but I couldn't help feeling a bit cut up, you know. She wrote such an awfully nice letter, you know, wished'——

'you all sorts of happiness (with a snap) and hopes you'll meet in a better world?'

He rises to his feet and stares at her in dumb amazement. How could she know? She smiles with a touch of malicious satisfaction, as she sees the effect of her chance shot.

'It's a pity, isn't it, that you both have to wait so long?'

He imagines he sees light, and blunders ahead like an honest man.

'I wouldn't have sent those things back now if I had thought you cared. By Jove, it never entered my head that you'd be jealous!'

'Jealous? (she is on her feet like a red white flash). I, jealous of her? (each word is emphasised). I couldn't be jealous of her, *Nur die Dummen sind bescheiden!*[1] Why, the girl isn't fit to tie my shoe-strings!'

This is too much; he feels he must protest.

'You don't know her (feebly). She is an awfully nice girl!'

'Nice girl! I don't doubt it, and she will be an awfully nice woman, and under each and every circumstance of life she will behave like an awfully nice person. Jealous! Do you think I cried because I was jealous? Good God, no! I cried because I was sorry, fearfully sorry for myself. She' (with a fine thin contempt) 'would have suited you better than I. Jealous! no, only sorry. Sorry because any nice average girl of her type, who would model her frocks out of the *Lady's Pictorial*, gush over that dear Mr. Irving,[2] paint milking-stools, try poker work, or any other fashionable fad, would have done for you just as well. And I' (with a catch of voice) 'with a great man might have made a great woman—and now those who know and understand me' (bitterly) 'think of me as a great failure.'

She finishes wearily, the fire dies out of eyes and voice. She adds half aloud as if to herself:

'I don't think I quite realised this until I saw how you took that letter. I was watching your face as you read it, and the fact that you could put her on the same level, that if it had not been for a mistake, she would have suited you as well, made me realise, don't you see? that I should have done better for some one else!'

He is looking at her in utter bewilderment, and she smiles as she notes his expression; she touches his cheek gently and leans her head against his arm.

---

1 *Nur die Dummen sind bescheiden*: 'Only the dumb ones are modest'.
2 *dear Mr. Irving*: the famous actor, Sir Henry Irving (1838–1905), whose picture appeared frequently in women's magazines.

'There, it's all right, boy! Don't mind me, I have a bit of a complex nature; you couldn't understand me if you tried to; you'd better not try!'

She has slipped, whilst speaking, her warm bare foot out of her slipper, and is rubbing it gently over his chilled ones.

'You are cold, better go back to bed, I shall go too!'

She stands a moment quietly as he turns to obey, and then takes the frame, and kneeling down puts it gently into the hollowed red heart of the fire. It crackles crisply, and little tongues of flame shoot up, and she gets into bed by their light.

*   *   *

When the fire has burnt out, and he is sleeping like a child with his curly head on her breast, she falls asleep too and dreams that she is sitting on a fiery globe rolling away into space. That her head is wedged in a huge frame, the top of her head touches its top, the sides its sides, and it keeps growing larger and larger and her head with it, until she seems to be sitting inside her own head, and the inside is one vast hollow.

From *Discords*

(1894)

Virgin Soil

The bridegroom is waiting in the hall; with a trifle of impatience he is tracing the pattern of the linoleum with the point of his umbrella. He curbs it and laughs, showing his strong white teeth at a remark of his best man; then compares the time by his hunter[1] with the clock on the stairs. He is florid, bright-eyed, loose-lipped, inclined to stoutness, but kept in good condition; his hair is crisp, curly, slightly grey; his ears peculiar, pointed at their tops like a faun's. He looks very big and well-dressed, and, when he smiles, affable enough.

Upstairs a young girl, with the suns of seventeen summers on her brown head, is lying with her face hidden on her mother's shoulder; she is sobbing with great childish sobs, regardless of reddened eyes and the tears that have splashed on the silk of her grey, going-away gown.

The mother seems scarcely less disturbed than the girl. She is a

---

1 *hunter*: Hunter cased pocket watch.

fragile-looking woman with delicate fair skin, smoothly parted thin chestnut hair, dove-like eyes, and a monotonous piping voice. She is flushing painfully, making a strenuous effort to say something to the girl, something that is opposed to the whole instincts of her life.

She tries to speak, parts her lips only to close them again, and clasp her arms tighter round the girl's shoulders; at length she manages to say with trembling, uncertain pauses:

'You are married now, darling, and you must obey'—she lays a stress upon the word—'your husband in all things—there are—there are things you should know—but—marriage is a serious thing, a sacred thing'– with desperation—'you must believe that what your husband tells you is right— let him guide you—tell you—'

There is such acute distress in her usually unemotional voice that the girl looks up and scans her face—her blushing, quivering, faded face. Her eyes are startled, fawn-like eyes as her mother's, her skin too is delicately fair, but her mouth is firmer, her jaw squarer, and her piquant, irregular nose is full of character. She is slightly built, scarcely fully developed in her fresh youth.

'What is it that I do not know, mother? What is it ?'—with anxious impatience. 'There is something more—I have felt it all these last weeks in your and the others' looks—in his, in the very atmosphere— but why have you not told me before—I——' Her only answer is a gush of helpless tears from the mother, and a sharp rap at the door, and the bridegroom's voice, with an imperative note that it strikes the nervous girl is new to it, that makes her cling to her mother in a close, close embrace, drop her veil and go out to him.

She shakes hands with the best man, kisses the girl friend who has acted as bridesmaid—the wedding has been a very quiet one—and steps into the carriage. The Irish cook throws an old shoe after them from the side door, but it hits the trunk of an elder-tree, and falls back on to the path, making that worthy woman cross herself and mutter of ill-omens and bad luck to follow; for did not a magpie cross the path first thing this morning when she went to open the gate, and wasn't a red-haired woman the first creature she clapped eyes on as she looked down the road?

Half an hour later the carriage pulls up at the little station and the girl jumps out first; she is flushed, and her eyes stare helplessly as the eyes of a startled child, and she trembles with quick running shudders from head to foot. She clasps and unclasps her slender, grey-gloved hands so tightly that the stitching on the back of one bursts.

He has called to the station-master, and they go into the refreshment-room together; the latter appears at the door and, beckoning to a porter, gives him an order.

She takes a long look at the familiar little place. They have lived there three years, and yet she seems to see it now for the first time; the rain drips, drips monotonously off the zinc roof, the smell of the dust is fresh, and the white pinks in the borders are beaten into the gravel.

Then the train runs in; a first-class carriage, marked 'engaged,' is attached, and he comes for her; his hot breath smells of champagne, and it strikes her that his eyes are fearfully big and bright, and he offers her his arm with such a curious amused proprietary air that the girl shivers as she lays her hand in it.

The bell rings, the guard locks the door, the train steams out, and as it passes the signal-box, a large well-kept hand, with a signet ring on the little finger, pulls down the blind on the window of an engaged carriage.

*   *   *

Five years later, one afternoon on an autumn day, when the rain is falling like splashing tears on the rails, and the smell of the dust after rain fills the mild air with freshness, and the white chrysanthemums struggle to raise their heads from the gravel path into which the sharp shower has beaten them, the same woman, for there is no trace of girlhood in her twenty-two years, slips out of a first-class carriage; she has a dressing-bag in her hand.

She walks with her head down and a droop in her shoulders; her quickness of step is due rather to nervous haste than elasticity of frame. When she reaches the turn of the road, she pauses and looks at the little villa with the white curtains and gay tiled window-boxes. She can see the window of her old room; distinguish every shade in the changing leaves of the creeper climbing up the south wall; hear the canary's shrill note from where she stands.

Never once has she set foot in the peaceful little house with its air of genteel propriety since that eventful morning when she left it with him; she has always framed an excuse.

Now as she sees it a feeling of remorse fills her heart, and she thinks of the mother living out her quiet years, each day a replica of the one gone before, and her resolve weakens; she feels inclined to go back, but the waning sun flickers over the panes in the window of the room she occupied as a girl. She can recall how she used to run to the open window on summer mornings and lean out and draw in the dewy freshness and welcome the day, how she has stood on moonlight nights and danced with her bare white feet in the strip of moonlight, and let her fancies fly out into the silver night, a young girl's dreams of the beautiful, wonderful world that lay outside.

A hard dry sob rises in her throat at the memory of it, and the fleeting expression of softness on her face changes to a bitter disillusion.

She hurries on, with her eyes down, up the neat gravelled path, through the open door into the familiar sitting-room.

The piano is open with a hymn-book on the stand; the grate is filled with fresh green ferns, a bowl of late roses perfume the room from the centre of the table. The mother is sitting in her easy chair, her hands folded across a big white Persian cat on her lap; she is fast asleep. Some futile lace work, her thimble, and bright scissor are placed on a table near her.

Her face is placid, not a day older than that day five years ago. Her glossy hair is no greyer, her skin is clear, she smiles in her sleep. The smile rouses a sort of sudden fury in the breast of the woman standing in her dusty travelling cloak at the door, noting every detail in the room. She throws back her veil and goes over and looks at herself in the mirror over the polished chiffonnier—scans herself pitilessly. Her skin is sallow with the dull sallowness of a fair skin in ill-health, and the fringe of her brown hair is so lacking in lustre that it affords no contrast. The look of fawn-like shyness has vanished from her eyes, they burn sombrefully and resentfully in their sunken orbits, there is a dragged look about the mouth; and the keynote of her face is a cynical disillusion. She looks from herself to the reflection of the mother, and then turning sharply with a suppressed exclamation goes over, and shaking the sleeping woman not too gently, says:

'Mother, wake up, I want to speak to you!'

The mother starts with frightened eyes, stares at the other woman as if doubting the evidence of her sight, smiles, then cowed by the unresponsive look in the other face, grows grave again, sits still and stares helplessly at her, finally bursting into tears with a

'Flo, my dear, Flo, is it really you?'

The girl jerks her head impatiently and says drily:

'Yes, that is self-evident. I am going on a long journey. I have something to say to you before I start! Why on earth are you crying?'

There is a note of surprised wonder in her voice mixed with impatience.

The older woman has had time to scan her face and the dormant motherhood in her is roused by its weary anguish. She is ill, she thinks, in trouble. She rises to her feet; it is characteristic of the habits of her life, with its studied regard for the observance of small proprieties, and distrust of servants as a class, that she goes over and closes the room door carefully.

This hollow-eyed, sullen woman is so unlike the fresh girl who left her five years ago that she feels afraid. With the quiet selfishness that has characterised her life she has accepted the excuses her daughter has made to avoid coming home, as she has accepted the presents her son-in-law has sent her from time to time. She has found her a husband well-off in the world's goods, and there her responsibility ended. She approaches her hesitatingly; she feels she ought to kiss her, there is something unusual in such a meeting after so long an absence; it shocks her, it is so unlike the one she has pictured; she has often looked forward to it, often; to seeing Flo's new frocks, to hearing of her town life.

'Won't you take off your things? You will like to go to your room?'

She can hear how her own voice shakes; it is really inconsiderate of Flo to treat her in this strange way.

'We will have some tea,' she adds.

Her colour is coming and going, the lace at her wrist is fluttering. The daughter observes it with a kind of dull satisfaction, she is taking out her hat-pins carefully. She notices a portrait in a velvet case upon the mantelpiece; she walks over and looks at it intently. It is her father, the father who was killed in India in a hill skirmish when she was a little lint-locked maid barely up to his knee. She studies it with new eyes, trying to read what man he was, what soul he had, what part of him is in her, tries to find herself by reading him. Something in his face touches her, strikes some underlying chord in her, and she grinds her teeth at a thought it rouses.

'She must be ill, she must be very ill,' says the mother, watching her, 'to think I daren't offer to kiss my own child!' She checks the tears that keep welling up, feeling that they may offend this woman who is so strangely unlike the girl who left her. The latter has turned from her scrutiny of the likeness and sweeps her with a cold criticising look as she turns towards the door, saying:

'I *should* like some tea. I will go upstairs and wash off the dust'

*   *   *

Half an hour later the two women sit opposite one another in the pretty room. The younger one is leaning back in her chair watching the mother pour out the tea, following the graceful movements of the white, blue-veined hands amongst the tea things—she lets her wait on her; they have not spoken beyond a commonplace remark about the heat, the dust, the journey.

'How is Philip, is he well?' The mother ventures to ask with a feeling of trepidation, but it seems to her that she ought to ask about him.

'He is quite well, men of his type usually are; I may say he is particularly well just now, he has gone to Paris with a girl from the Alhambra!'[1]

The older woman flushes painfully, and pauses with her cup half way to her lips and lets the tea run over unheeded on to her dainty silk apron.

'You are spilling your tea,' the girl adds with malicious enjoyment.

The woman gasps: 'Flo, but Flo, my dear, it is dreadful! What would your poor father have said! *no wonder* you look ill, dear, how shocking! Shall I—ask the vicar to—to remonstrate with him?——'

'My dear mother, what an extraordinary idea! These little trips have been my one solace. I assure you, I have always hailed them as lovely oases in the desert of matrimony, resting-places on the journey. My sole regret was their infrequency. That is very good tea, I suppose it is the cream.'

The older woman puts her cup on the tray and stares at her with frightened eyes and paled cheeks.

'I am afraid I don't understand you, Florence. I am old-fashioned'—with a little air of frigid propriety—'I have always looked upon matrimony as a sacred thing. It is dreadful to hear you speak this way; you should have tried to save Philip—from—from such a shocking sin.'

The girl laughs, and the woman shivers as she hears her. She cries—

'I would never have thought it of Philip. My poor dear, I am afraid you must be very unhappy.'

'Very,' with a grim smile, 'but it is over now, I have done with it. I am not going back.'

If a bomb had exploded in the quiet, pretty room the effect could hardly have been more startling than her almost cheerful statement. A big bee buzzes in and bangs against the lace of the older woman's cap and she never heeds it, then she almost screams:

'Florence, Florence, my dear, you can't mean to desert your husband! Oh, think of the disgrace, the scandal, what people will say, the'—with an uncertain quaver—'the sin. You took a solemn vow, you know, and you are going to break it—'

'My dear mother, the ceremony had no meaning for me, I simply

---

1 *the Alhambra*: the name of several English music halls.

did not know what I was signing my name to, or what I was vowing to do. I might as well have signed my name to a document drawn up in Choctaw.[1] I have no remorse, no prick of conscience at the step I am taking; my life must be my own. They say sorrow chastens, I don't believe it; it hardens, embitters; joy is like the sun, it coaxes all that is loveliest and sweetest in human nature. No, I am not going back.'

The older woman cries, wringing her hands helplessly:

'I can't understand it. You must be very miserable to dream of taking such a serious step.'

'As I told you, I am. It is a defect of my temperament. How many women really take the man nearest to them as seriously as I did! I think few. They finesse and flatter and wheedle and coax, but truth there is none. I couldn't do that, you see, and so I went to the wall. I don't blame them; it must be so, as long as marriage is based on such unequal terms, as long as man demands from a wife as a right, what he must sue from a mistress as a favour; until marriage becomes for many women a legal prostitution, a nightly degradation, a hateful yoke under which they age, mere bearers of children conceived in a sense of duty, not love. They bear them, birth them, nurse them, and begin again without choice in the matter, growing old, unlovely, with all joy of living swallowed in a senseless burden of reckless maternity, until their love, granted they started with that, the mystery, the crowning glory of their lives, is turned into a duty they submit to with distaste instead of a favour granted to a husband who must become a new lover to obtain it.'

'But men are different, Florence; you can't refuse a husband, you might cause him to commit sin.'

'Bosh, mother, he is responsible for his own sins, we are not bound to dry-nurse his morality. Man is what we have made him, his very faults are of our making. No wife is bound to set aside the demands of her individual soul for the sake of imbecile obedience. I am going to have some more tea.'

The mother can only whimper:

'It is dreadful! I thought he made you such an excellent husband, his position too is so good, and he is so highly connected.'

'Yes, and it is as well to put the blame in the right quarter. Philip is as God made him, he is an animal with strong passions, and he avails himself of the latitude permitted him by the laws of society. Whatever of blame, whatever of sin, whatever of misery is in the whole matter

---

1 *Choctaw*: language of North American Indian tribe from Mississippi and Alabama.

rests *solely* and *entirely* with you, mother'—the woman sits bolt upright—'and with no one else—that is why I came here—to tell you that—I have promised myself over and over again that I would tell you. It is with you, and you alone the fault lies.'

There is so much of cold dislike in her voice that the other woman recoils and whimpers piteously:

'You must be ill, Florence, to say such wicked things. What have I done? I am sure I devoted myself to you from the time you were little; I refused—dabbing her eyes with her cambric handkerchief—'ever so many good offers. There was young Fortescue in the artillery, such a good-looking man, and such an elegant horseman, he was quite infatuated about me; and Jones, to be sure he was in business, but he was most attentive. Every one said I was a devoted mother; I can't think what you mean, I——'

A smile of cynical amusement checks her.

'Perhaps not. Sit down, and I'll tell you.'

She shakes off the trembling hand, for the mother has risen and is standing next to her, and pushes her into a chair, and paces up and down the room. She is painfully thin, and drags her limbs as she walks.

'I say it is your fault, because you reared me a fool, an idiot, ignorant of everything I ought to have known, everything that concerned me and the life I was bound to lead as a wife; my physical needs, my coming passion, the very meaning of my sex, my wifehood and motherhood to follow. You gave me not one weapon in my hand to defend myself against the possible attacks of man at his worst. You sent me out to fight the biggest battle of a woman's life, the one in which she ought to know every turn of the game, with a white gauze'—she laughs derisively—'of maiden purity as a shield.'

Her eyes blaze, and the woman in the chair watches her as one sees a frog watch a snake when it is put into its case.

'I was fourteen when I gave up the gooseberry-bush theory as the origin of humanity; and I cried myself ill with shame when I learnt what maternity meant, instead of waking with a sense of delicious wonder at the great mystery of it. You gave me to a man, nay more, you told me to obey him, to believe that whatever he said would be right, would be my duty; knowing that the meaning of marriage was a sealed book to me, that I had no real idea of what union with a man meant. You delivered me body and soul into his hands without preparing me in any way for the ordeal I was to go through. You sold me for a home, for clothes, for food; you played upon my ignorance,

I won't say innocence, that is different. You told me, you and your sister, and your friend the vicar's wife, that it would be an anxiety off your mind if I were comfortably settled——'

'It is wicked of you to say such dreadful things!' the mother cries, 'and besides'—with a touch of asperity—'you married him willingly, you seemed to like his attentions——'

'How like a woman! What a thorough woman you are, mother! The good old-fashioned kitten with a claw in her paw! Yes, I married him willingly; I was not eighteen, I had known no men; was pleased that you were pleased—and, as you say, I liked his attentions. He had tact enough not to frighten me, and I had not the faintest conception of what marriage with him meant. I had an idea'—with a laugh—'that the words of the minister settled the matter. Do you think that if I had realised how fearfully close the intimacy with him would have been that my whole soul would not have stood up in revolt, the whole woman in me cried out against such a degradation of myself?' Her words tremble with passion, and the woman who bore her feels as if she is being lashed by a whip. 'Would I not have shuddered at the thought of *him* in such a relationship?—and waited, waited until I found the man who would satisfy me, body and soul—to whom I would have gone without any false shame, of whom I would think with gladness as the father of a little child to come, for whom the white fire of love or passion, call it what you will, in my heart would have burned clearly and saved me from the feeling of loathing horror that has made my married life a nightmare to me—ay, made me a murderess in heart over and over again. This is not exaggeration. It has killed the sweetness in me, the pure thoughts of womanhood— has made me hate myself and *hate you*. Cry, mother, if you will; you don't know how much you have to cry for—I have cried myself barren of tears. Cry over the girl you killed'—with a gust of passion— 'why didn't you strangle me as a baby? It would have been kinder; my life has been a hell, mother—I felt it vaguely as I stood on the platform waiting, I remember the mad impulse I had to jump down under the engine as it came in, to escape from the dread that was chilling my soul. What have these years been? One long crucifixion, one long submittal to the desires of a man I bound myself to in ignorance of what it meant; every caress'—with a cry—'has only been the first note of that. Look at me'—stretching out her arms—'look at this wreck of my physical self; I wouldn't dare to show you the heart or the soul underneath. He has stood on his rights; but do you think, if I had known, that I would have given such insane obedience, from a mistaken sense of duty, as would lead to this? I have my rights too, and my duty to myself; if I had only recognised them in time.'

'Sob away, mother; I don't even feel for you—I have been burnt too badly to feel sorry for what will only be a tiny scar to you; I have all the long future to face with all the world against me. Nothing will induce me to go back. Better anything than that; food and clothes are poor equivalents for what I have had to suffer—I can get them at a cheaper rate. When he comes to look for me, give him that letter. He will tell you he has only been an uxorious husband, and that you reared me a fool. You can tell him too, if you like, that I loathe him, shiver at the touch of his lips, his breath, his hands; that my whole body revolts at his touch; that when he has turned and gone to sleep, I have watched him with such growing hatred that at times the temptation to kill him has been so strong that I have crept out of bed and walked the cold passage in my bare feet until I was too benumbed to feel anything; that I have counted the hours to his going away, and cried out with delight at the sight of the retreating carriage!'

'You are very hard, Flo; the Lord soften your heart! Perhaps'—with trepidation—'if you had had a child—'

'Of his—that indeed would have been the last straw—no, mother.'

There is such a peculiar expression of satisfaction over something—of some inner understanding, as a man has when he dwells on the successful accomplishment of a secret purpose—that the mother sobs quietly, wringing her hands.

'I did not know, Flo, I acted for the best; you are very hard on me!'

*   *   *

Later, when the bats are flitting across the moon, and the girl is asleep—she has thrown herself half-dressed on the narrow white bed of her girlhood, with her arms folded across her breast and her hands clenched—the mother steals into the room. She has been turning over the contents of an old desk; her marriage certificate, faded letters on foreign paper, and a bit of Flo's hair cut off each birthday, and a sprig of orange-blossom she wore in her hair. She looks faded and grey in the silver light, and she stands and gazes at the haggard face in its weary sleep. The placid current of her life is disturbed, her heart is roused, something of her child's soul-agony has touched the sleeping depths of her nature. She feels as if scales have dropped from her eyes, as if the instincts and conventions of her life are toppling over, as if all the needs of protesting women of whom she has read with a vague displeasure have come home to her. She covers the girl tenderly, kisses her hair, and slips a little roll of notes into the dressing-bag on the table and steals out, with the tears running down her cheeks.

When the girl looks into her room as she steals by, when the morning light is slanting in, she sees her kneeling, her head, with its straggling grey hair, bowed in tired sleep. It touches her. Life is too short, she thinks, to make any one's hours bitter; she goes down and writes a few kind words in pencil and leaves them near her hand, and goes quickly out into the road.

The morning is grey and misty, with faint yellow stains in the east, and the west wind blows with a melancholy sough in it—the first whisper of the fall, the fall that turns the world of nature into a patient suffering from phthisis[1]—delicate season of decadence, when the loveliest scenes have a note of decay in their beauty; when a poisoned arrow pierces the marrow of insect and plant, and the leaves have a hectic flush and fall, fall and shrivel and curl in the night's cool; and the chrysanthemums, the 'good-bye summers' of the Irish peasants, have a sickly tinge in their white. It affects her, and she finds herself saying: 'Wither and die, wither and die, make compost for the loves of the spring, as the old drop out and make place for the new, who forget them, to be in their turn forgotten.' She hurries on, feeling that her autumn has come to her in her spring, and a little later she stands once more on the platform where she stood in the flush of her girlhood, and takes the train in the opposite direction.

ANNA MARGARET (AMANDA) MCKITTRICK ROS
(1860–1939)

Born at Drumaness, Co. Down, the fourth child of Edward Amlane M'Kittrick, principal of Drumaness high school. She described herself as the 'high-bred daughter of distinguished effeminacy', claiming that the McKittricks were descended from King Sitric of Denmark. She was named Amanda by her mother, after the heroine of the popular novel by Regina Maria Roche, a writer of romance. Amanda was educated at home and at Marlborough Teacher's Training College, Dublin, and became a teacher at Milbrook national school, Larne. In 1887 she married Andrew Ross, the Larne stationmaster, who, Amanda boasted, 'was a fine English scholar [and] could speak Russian, French and Norwegian fluently.' He became stationmaster at Larne Harbour. Amanda claimed that she began writing *Irene Iddesleigh*, a tragic tale, at the

1 *phthisis*: tuberculosis.

age of 12; her husband paid for its printing as a wedding anniversary gift, and it was published in 1897 under her pen-name Amanda Ros (the surname of an ancient Co. Down family). The book was brought to the attention of the literary world by Barry Pain, who hailed her 'magnificent incongruities' in an engaging review in *Black and White* (February 1898) as 'The Book of the Century'. She responded by vituperating against her reviewers in her bulky second novel, *Delina Delaney* (1898). Amanda Ros appreciation societies sprang up, her 'admirers' including Herbert Henry Asquith, St John Ervine, Siegfried Sassoon, Osbert Sitwell, Mark Twain, and Aldous Huxley, who in 'Eupheus Revividus' (1923) commented on her 'magical and delicious intoxication', 'the result of the discovery of art by an unsophisticated mind'.

She was notorious for savage attacks upon lawyers and critics. The vituperation permeated the collections *Poems of Puncture* (1913) and *Fumes of Formation* (1933); the latter was 'hatched within a mind fringed with Fumes of Formation, the Ingenious Innings of Inspiration and Thorny Tincture of Thought'. Her letters—selections appeared in *Bayonets of Bastard* (1954)—were pointed and pungent ('Sir, your letter is before me, shortly it will be behind me.'). Her posthumous writings included *St Scandalbegs* (1954) as well as her last novel, *Helen Huddleston* (1969), which her biographer Jack Loudan completed. She described herself as 'the personality who has disturbed the bowels of millions'.

From *Irene Iddesleigh*

(1897)

[*The eponymous heroine, widely known as 'The Southern Beauty', is the adopted daughter of Lord and Lady Dilworth. She marries Sir John Dunfern, a dependable 48-year old bachelor, and gives birth to a son, but she feels constrained by her husband's retiring lifestyle. She discovers that she is the only child of Colonel Iddesleigh, 'who fell a victim to a gunshot wound inflicted by the hand of his wife, who had fallen into the pit of intemperance'. She runs away with her tutor, Oscar Otwell, who is driven to drink, wife-beating and suicide (in that order). In the final chapters she revisits her old homes.*]

CHAPTER EIGHTEEN

Mocking Angel! The trials of a tortured throng are naught when weighed in the balance of future anticipations. The living sometimes learn the touchy tricks of the traitor, the tardy, and the tempted; the dead have evaded the flighty earthly future, and form to swell the retinue of retired rights, the righteous school of the invisible, and the rebellious roar of raging nothing.

The night was dark and tempestuous; the hill rather inclined to be steep; the clouds were bathed in wrinkled furrows of vapoury smoke; the traffic on the quiet and lonely roads surrounding Dunfern Mansion was utterly stopped, and nature seemed a block of obstruction to the eye of the foreigner who drudged so wearily up the slope that led to the home of Mrs Durand, who had been confined to bed for the past three years, a sufferer from rheumatism.

Perceiving the faint flicker of light that occasionally flung its feeble rays against the dim fanlight of faithful Fanny's home—the aged sister of the late Tom Hepworth—the two-fold widowed wanderer, with trembling step, faltered to the door of uncertain refuge, and, tapping against it with fingers cold and stiff, on such a night of howling wind and beating rain, asked, in weakened accents, the woman who opened to her the door, 'if she could be allowed to remain for the night?'—a request that was granted through charity alone. After relieving herself of some outer garments, and partaking of the slight homely fare kindly ordered by Mrs Durand, the widow of Oscar Otwell and Sir John Dunfern warmed herself and dried her saturated clothing before going to bed. She had just arrived the day previous, and hastened to take up her abode as near her former home of exquisiteness as she could, without detection.

On extinguishing the light before retiring, and casting one glance in the direction of the little window, the innumerable recollections of the abundant past swept across the mind of the snowy-haired widow, and were further augmented by the different star-like lights which shone from the numerous windows in Dunfern Mansion, directly opposite where she lay.

A couple of days found her almost rested after such a trying night as that on which she arrived, and observing the sharpest reticence lest she might be known, she nerved herself to appear next day at Dunfern Mansion, to accomplish the last wish of her late lover and husband, for whom she ventured so much and gained so little, and particularly to try and see her son.

The morning was warm and fine; numerous birds kept chirping outside the little cottage of Mrs Durand. The widow, with swollen eyes and face of faded fear, prepared herself for the trying moment, which she was certain of achieving. Partaking of a very slight breakfast, she told Mrs Durand not to expect her for dinner.

Marching down the hill's face, she soon set foot on the main road that led directly to Dunfern Mansion. Being admitted by Nancy Bennet, a prim old dame, who had been in charge of the lodge for the last eighteen years, the forlorn widow, whose heart sank in despair as she slowly walked up the great and winding avenue she once claimed, reached the huge door through which she had been unconsciously carried by Marjory Mason a good many years ago.

Gently ringing the bell, the door was attended by a strange face. Reverently asking to have an interview with Sir John Dunfern, how the death-like glare fell over the eyes of the disappointed as the foot-man informed her of his demise! 'Madam, if you cast your eyes thence'—here the sturdy footman pointed to the family graveyard, lying quite adjacent, and in which the offcast of effrontery had often-times trodden—'you can with ease behold the rising symbol of death which the young nobleman, Sir Hugh Dunfern, has lavishly and unscrupulously erected to his fond memory.'

The crushed hopes of an interview with the man she brought with head of bowed and battered bruises, of blasted untruths and astound-ing actions, to a grave of premature solitude were further crumbled to atoms in an instant. They were driven beyond retention, never again to be fostered with feverish fancy. After the deplorable news of her rightful husband's death had been conveyed to the sly and shameless questioner, who tried hard to balance her faintish frame unobserved, she asked an interview with Sir Hugh Dunfern. This also was denied, on the ground of absence from home.

Heavily laden with the garb of disappointment did the wandering woman of wayward wrong retrace her footsteps from the door for ever, and leisurely walked down the artistic avenue of carpeted care, never more to face the furrowed frowns of friends who, in years gone by, bestowed on her the praises of poetic powers. Forgetful almost of her present movements, the dangerous signal of widowhood was seen to float along the family graveyard of the Dunferns.

Being beforehand acquaint with the numerous and costly tomb-stones erected individually, regardless of price, the wearied and sick-ly woman of former healthy tread was not long in observing the lat-est tablet, of towering height, at the north-east end of the sacred plot.

There seemed a touchy stream of gilded letters carefully cut on its marble face, and on reading them with watery eye and stooping form, was it anything remarkable that a flood of tears bathed the verdure that peeped above the soil?

The lines were these:

I

The hand of death hath once more brought
    The lifeless body here to lie,
Until aroused with angels' voice,
    Which call it forth, no more to die.

II

This man, of health and honest mind,
    Had troubles great to bear whilst here,
Which cut him off, in manhood's bloom,
    To where there's neither frown nor tear.

III

His life was lined with works of good
    For all who sought his affluent aid;
His life-long acts of charity
    Are sure to never pass unpaid.

IV

Sir John Dunfern, whose noble name
    Is heard to echo, far and wide;
In homes of honour, truth, and right,
    With which he here lies side by side.

V

The wings of love and lasting strength
    Shall flap above his hollow bed;
Angelic sounds of sweetest strain
    Have chased away all tears he shed.

VI

Then, when the glorious morn shall wake
    Each member in this dust of ours,
To give to each the sentence sure
    Of everlasting Princely Power—

VII

He shall not fail to gain a seat
    Upon the bench of gloried right,
To don the crown of golden worth
    Secured whilst braving Nature's fight.

After carefully reading these lines the figure of melting woe sat for a long time in silence until a footstep came up from behind, which alarmed her not a little. Looking up she beheld the face of a youth whose expression was very mournful, and asking after her mission, was informed she had been casting one last look on the monument of her lamented husband.

'Mighty Heavens!' exclaimed Sir Hugh Dunfern, 'are you the vagrant who ruined the very existence of him whom you now profess to have loved? You, the wretch of wicked and wilful treachery, and formerly the wife of him before whose very bones you falsely kneel! Are you the confirmed traitoress of the trust reposed in you by my late lamented, dearest, and most noble of fathers? Are you aware that the hypocrisy you manifested once has been handed down to me as an heirloom of polluted possession, and stored within this breast of mine, an indelible stain for life, or, I might say, during your known and hated existence?

'False woman! Wicked wife! Detested mother! Bereft widow!

'How darest thou set foot on the premises your chastity should have protected and secured! What wind of transparent touch must have blown its blasts of boldest bravery around your poisoned person and guided you within miles of the mansion I proudly own?

'What spirit but that of evil used its influence upon you to dare to bend your footsteps of foreign tread towards the door through which they once stole unknown? Ah, woman of sin and stray companion of tutorism, arise, I demand you, and strike across that grassy centre as quickly as you can, and never more make your hated face appear within these mighty walls. I can never own you; I can never call you mother; I cannot extend the assistance your poor, poverty-stricken attire of false don silently requests; neither can I ever meet you on this side of the grave, before which you so pityingly kneel!'

Speechless and dogged did the dishonoured mother steal for ever from the presence of her son, but not before bestowing one final look at the brightened eye and angry countenance of him who loaded on her his lordly abuse. The bowed form of former stateliness left for ever the grounds she might have owned without even daring to offer one word of repentance or explanation to her son.

Walking leisurely along the road that reached Dilworth Castle, how the trying moments told upon her who shared in pangs of insult and poverty!—how the thoughts of pleasant days piled themselves with parched power upon the hilltop of remembrance and died away in the distance! The whirling brain became more staid as she heard the approach of horses' feet, and stopping to act the part of Lot's wife, gave such a haggard stare at the driver of the vehicle as caused him to make a sudden halt. Asking her to have a seat, the weary woman gladly mounted upon its cushion with thankfulness, and alighted on reaching its journey's end, about three miles from Audley Hall. The drive was a long one, and helped to rest the tired body of temptation.

Returning thanks to the obliging driver, she marched wearily along until she reached the home of her first refuge after flight.

Perceiving the yellow shutters firmly bolted against the light admitters of Audley Hall, she feared disappointment was also waiting her. Knocking loudly twice before any attempt was made to open the door, there came at last an aged man with halting step and shaking limb.

'Is Major Iddesleigh at home?' asked the saddened widow.

'Oh, madam, he has been dead almost twelve years, and since then no one has occupied this Hall save myself, who am caretaker. The Marquis of Orland was deceived by his nephew, who sold it in an underhand manner to the major, and he resolved that never again would he allow it to be occupied since the major's death by any outsider.'

'You are rather lonely,' said the widow.

'Yes, yes,' replied he, 'but I have always been accustomed living alone, being an old bachelor, and wish to remain so. It is better to live a life of singleness than torture both body and soul by marrying a woman who doesn't love you, like the good Sir John Dunfern—a nobleman who lived only some miles from this, and who died lately broken-hearted—who became so infatuated with an upstart of unknown parentage, who lived in Dilworth Castle, with one Lord Dilworth, the previous owner, that he married her offhand, and, what was the result, my good woman?—why she eventually ran off with a poor tutor! and brought the hairs of hoary whiteness of Sir John Dunfern to the grave much sooner than in all probability they would have, had he remained like me.'

Facing fumes of insult again, thought the listener. And asking after Major Iddesleigh's will, eagerly awaited his reply.

Placing one hand upon her shoulder, and pointing with the other, 'Behold,' said he, 'yonder church? that was his last will—Iddesleigh Church. It was only when the jaws of death gaped for their prey that the major was forced to alter his will, having had it previously prepared in favour of his niece, whose whereabouts could never be traced until after his death.'

'Enough—enough, I must go,' said the painful listener, and thanking the old man for his information, which, like her son's, had screwed its bolts of deadly weight more deeply down on the lid of abstract need, turned her back on Audley Hall for ever.

CHAPTER NINETEEN

Hope sinks a world of imagination. It in almost every instance never fails to arm the opponents of justice with weapons of friendly defence, and gains their final fight with peaceful submission. Life is too often stripped of its pleasantness by the steps of false assumption, marring the true path of life-long happiness which should be pebbled with principle, piety, purity, and peace.

Next morning, after the trying adventure of the lonely outcast, was the scene of wonder at Dilworth Castle. Henry Hawkes, the head gardener under the Marquis of Orland, on approaching the little summer-house in which Irene Iddesleigh so often sat in days of youth, was horrified to find the dead body of a woman, apparently a widow, lying prostrate inside its mossy walls. 'Lord, protect me!' shouted poor Hawkes, half distractedly, and hurried to Dilworth Castle to inform the inmates of what he had just seen.

They all rushed towards the little rustic building to verify the certainty of the gardener's remarks. There she lay, cold, stiff, and lifeless as Nero, and must have been dead for hours. They advised the authorities, who were soon on the spot.

What stinging looks of shame the Marquis cast upon her corpse on being told that it was that of the once beautiful Lady Dunfern—mother of the present heir to Dunfern estate.

Lying close at hand was an old and soiled card, with the words almost beyond distinction, 'Irene Iddesleigh'. In an instant her whole history flashed before the unforgiving mind of the Marquis, and being a sharer in her devices, through his nephew Oscar Otwell, ordered her body to be conveyed to the morgue, at the same time intimating to Sir Hugh Dunfern her demise.

It transpired at the inquest, held next day, that she was admitted the previous night to the grounds of Dilworth Castle by the porter at the lodge, giving her name as 'Irene Iddesleigh'.

She must have taken refuge in the little construction planned under her personal supervision whilst inhabiting Dilworth Castle during her girlhood, and, haunted with the never-dying desire to visit once more its lovely grounds, wandered there to die of starvation.

No notice whatever was taken of her death by her son, who obeyed to the last letter his father's instructions, and carried them out with tearless pride.

The little narrow bed at the lowest corner on the west side of Seaforde graveyard was the spot chosen for her remains. Thus were laid to rest the orphan of Colonel Iddesleigh, the adopted daughter and imagined heiress of Lord and Lady Dilworth, what might have been the proud wife of Sir John Dunfern, the unlawful wife of Oscar Otwell, the suicidal outcast, and the despised and rejected mother.

She who might have swayed society's circle with the sceptre of nobleness—she who might still have shared in the greatness of her position and defied the crooked stream of poverty in which she so long sailed—had she only been, first of all, true to self, then the honourable name of Sir John Dunfern would have maintained its standard of pure and noble distinction, without being spotted here and there with heathenish remarks inflicted by a sarcastic public on the administerer of proper punishment; then the dignified knight of proud and upright ancestry would have been spared the pains of incessant insult, the mockery of equals, the haunted diseases of mental trials, the erring eye of harshness, and the throbbing twitch of constant criticism.

It was only the lapse of a few minutes after the widowed waif left Dunfern Mansion until the arrival of her son from London, who, after bidding his mother quit the grounds owned by him, blotted her name for ever from his book of memory; and being strongly prejudiced by a father of faultless bearing, resolved that the sharers of beauty, youth, and false love should never have the slightest catch on his affections.

DOUGLAS HYDE (1860–1949)

Born at Frenchpark, Co. Roscommon, the third son of a Church of Ireland rector, Hyde spent his childhood at his father's rectory in Tibohine, learning Irish from native speakers there. He was an exceptional student of languages, theology, and law at Trinity College, Dublin, graduating with a gold medal in modern literature in 1884 and taking his LLD in 1888. At college he began to publish original poetry in Irish written under the signature *An Craobhinn Aobhinn* (the delightful little branch). After a year as interim professor of modern languages in Canada, he devoted himself to preserving the Irish language and its folk literature.

Hyde became the first president of the National Literary Society in 1891, delivering his famous 'The Necessity for De-Anglicising Ireland' as his inaugural address.

In 1893 he published the *Love Songs of Connacht* (with his own verse translations), and was elected president of the Gaelic League at its first meeting. In 1897 he became assistant editor of the New Irish Library. He was the president of the Irish Text Society. Among his many publications, *A Literary History of Ireland* (1899) stands out as a comprehensive survey of Irish-language literature from the beginning to the nineteenth century. In 1905 he was appointed Professor of Modern Irish at University College Dublin. He served as Senator in the Irish Free State (1925–26), and was elected first president of Ireland (1938–45).

From *Love Songs of Connacht*
(1893)

I shall now give a piece which is to be found in every place throughout the country—the Red Man's Wife. I do not know why the people took so much pleasure in this song, unless it is the air which is on it. I do not see myself much music or poetry in the words, but this piece is so well known North and South that I cannot omit it. A friend of mine got the words which follow from an old man in the County Galway, and I got them from him. I leave out a verse or two which are not very clear.

The Red Man's Wife[1]

'Tis what they say,
    Thy little heel fits in a shoe.
'Tis what they say,
    Thy little mouth kisses well, too.
'Tis what they say,
    Thousand loves that you leave me to rue;
That the tailor went the way
    That the wife of the Red man knew.

Nine months did I spend
    In a prison penned tightly and bound;
Bolts on my smalls[2]
    And a thousand locks frowning around;

---

1 A translation of 'Bean an Fir Ruaid'. The entire text of *Love Songs of Connacht*, poems and prose commentary, is in parallel translation, with the Irish on the left, the English on the right side of the page.
2 *smalls*: There are three 'smalls,' the wrists, elbows and ankles. In Irish romantic literature we often meet with mention of men being bound 'with the binding of the three smalls.' [*Hyde's note.*]

But o'er the tide
    I would leap with the leap of a swan,
Could I once set my side
    By the bride of the Red-haired man.

I thought, O my life,
    That one house between us love would be;
And I thought I would find
    You once coaxing my child on your knee;
But now the curse of the High One,
    On him let it be,
And on all of the band of the liars
    Who put silence between you and me.

There grows a tree in the garden
    With blossoms that tremble and shake,
I lay my hands on its bark
    And I feel that my heart must break.
On one wish alone
    My soul through the long months ran,
One little kiss
    From the wife of the Red-haired man.

But the Day of Doom shall come,
    And hills and harbours be rent;
A mist shall fall on the sun
    From the dark clouds heavily sent;
The sea shall be dry,
    And earth under mourning and ban;
Then loud shall he cry
    For the wife of the Red-haired man.[1]

Here is a good song I found in my own old manuscript, one which I have never met anywhere else—

---

1 ... *For the wife of the Red-haired man*: This translation is in the curious broken metre of the original. *Literally*: They are saying it, That thou art the thin little mouth of the kisses. They are saying it, Thousand loves, that thou hast turned thy back on me, Though a man may be had. The tailor's is the wife of the red man, etc. The other verses offer no difficulty. There is no mention of a tailor in the older copy. It may have been altered to suit local circumstance. [*Hyde's note.*]

Douglas Hyde

Young Breed of the Tresses[1]

Unto God I pray
Every night and day
Not to leave me pining, but to speed me on my way;
Oh, come my love to-day
Where the ravens seek their prey,
We shall sorrow in the valley where you set my heart astray.

For gone it is and strayed,
My love is on a maid,
I think her nine times sweeter than the cuckoo in the glade,
Or, thrush, within the shade,
Or blackbird when he played
His sweetest notes to cheer us, and my soul is dismayed.

Oh, have you heard them say
How arch and bright and gay
Is my lady, how she writes with a pen in her play?
There is not, so they say,
In France or Spain to-day,
A man who would not leap to take the hand of my may.[2]

Girls I'd get, I swear,
Who silk and satins wear,
Hats both dark and glossy, and rings rich and rare;
But see, I leave them there,
Thou only art my care,
Sister of Antrim's Earldom, so fragrant and so fair.

---

1 This translation is in the metre of the original ['Brigid óg na g-ciabh']. *Literally:*—
   I put to his guardianship Upon God, and I request, Smooth for me the way and do not suffer me (to be) in pain. If thou wert to come with me under the mountains, Where the raven dwells, Making melancholy through the valleys, and with you I have lost my senses.
   I have love for a woman, And she ruined my heart. I thought her nine times sweeter than the cuckoo on the branch Or the blackbird of the yellow mouth, And the song-finch (?) at his side. She is the melodious coaxing little thrush that bitter-burned my heart, etc.
   The next verses offer no difficulty and need not be translated. 'Diol fin' in the third verse, means 'a sufficiency for any husband;' that is, one good enough to satisfy the most exacting. [*Hyde's note.*]
2 *may*: maiden (archaic).

I Shall Not Die for Thee[1]

For thee I shall not die
    Woman high of fame and name;
Foolish men thou mayest slay
    I and they are not the same.

Why should I expire
    For the fire of any eye,
Slender waist or swan-like limb,
    Is't for them that I should die?

The round breasts, the fresh skin,
    Cheeks crimson, hair so long and rich;
Indeed, indeed, I shall not die,
    Please God, not I, for any such.

The golden hair, the forehead thin,
    The chaste mien, the gracious ease,
The rounded heel, the languid tone,
    Fools alone find death from these.

Thy sharp wit, thy perfect calm,
    Thy thin palm like foam of sea;
Thy white neck, thy blue eye,
    I shall not die for thee.

Woman, graceful as the swan,
    A wise man did nurture me.
Little palm, white neck, bright eye,
    I shall not die for ye.

---

1 The translation [of 'Ní bhrág mise bás duit'] is exactly in the metre of the original, *Literally*. I shall not die for thee, O woman yonder, of body like a swan. Silly people (were they) thou hast ever slain. They and myself are not the same. Why should I go to die For the red lip, for the teeth like blossoms; The gentle figure, the breast like a swan, Is it for them I myself should die. The pointed (?) breasts, the fresh skin; The scarlet cheeks, the undulating cool; Indeed, then, I shall not die For them, may it please God. Thy narrow brows, thy tresses like gold, Thy chaste secret, thy languid voice, Thy heel round, thy calf smooth. They shall slay none but a silly person. Thy delightful mien, thy free spirit, Thy thin palm, thy side like foam. Thy blue eye, thy white throat!—I shall not die for thee. O woman of body like a swan, I was nurtured by a cunning man, O thin palm, O white bosom—I shall not die for thee. [*Hyde's note.*]

Douglas Hyde

Like a Star in the Night

(1896)[1]

Like a star in the night that guides a ship,
On rising of the wind and tide heavily,
It shows her, her way through the struggling of her waves,
And she goes straight over through the flood.

Like a light in the night on a cold scald mountain,
To the wayfarer who is ever travelling it is delightful to his eye;
It increases and it strengthens his courage and his walk;
He rises and blesses the glorious king of the elements.

My star in the night, it is you who are
My light on the cold mountain, it is you, are it, agra;[2]
Rise up, and I entreat the Virgin each day
To protect you and to guide you for ever and always.

The Necessity for De-Anglicising Ireland

(1892)[3]

When we speak of 'The Necessity for De-Anglicising the Irish Nation'
we mean it, not as a protest against imitating what is *best* in the English
people, for that would be absurd, but rather to show the folly of
neglecting what is Irish, and hastening to adopt, pell-mell, and indis-
criminately, everything that is English simply because it *is* English.

This is a question which most Irishmen will naturally look at from
a National point of view, but it is one which ought also to claim the
sympathies of every intelligent Unionist, and which, as I know, does
claim the sympathy of many.

If we take a bird's-eye view of our island to-day, and compare it
with what it used to be, we must be struck by the extraordinary fact
that the nation which was once, as every one admits, one of the most
classically learned and cultured nations in Europe, is now one of the
least so; how one of the most reading and literary peoples has become

1 From *The Shan Van Vocht*, 4 September 1896—the poem is a translation of 'Mar reult ann
san oidche a treóraigheas long'.
2 *agra*: 'my dear'.
3 An address delivered before the Irish National Literary Society, Dublin, 25 Nov. 1892.
Published in *The Revival of Irish Literature. Addresses by Sir Charles Gavan Duffy, K.C.M.G.,
Dr. George Sigerson, and Dr. Douglas Hyde* (1894).

one of the *least* studious and most *un*-literary, and how the present art products of one of the quickest, most sensitive, and most artistic races on earth are now only distinguished for their hideousness.

I shall endeavour to show that this failure of the Irish people in recent times has been largely brought about by the race diverging during this century from the right path, and ceasing to be Irish without becoming English. I shall attempt to show that with the bulk of the people this change took place quite recently, much more recently than most people imagine, and is, in fact, still going on. I should also like to call attention to the illogical position of men who drop their own language to speak English, of men who translate their euphonious Irish names into English monosyllables, of men who read English books, and know nothing about Gaelic literature, nevertheless protesting as a matter of sentiment that they hate the country which at every hand's turn they rush to imitate.

I wish to show you that in Anglicising ourselves wholesale we have thrown away with a light heart the best claim which we have upon the world's recognition of us as a separate nationality. What did Mazzini[1] say? What is Goldwin Smith[2] never tired of declaiming? What do the *Spectator* and *Saturday Review* harp on? That we ought to be content as an integral part of the United Kingdom because we have lost the notes of nationality, our language and customs.

It has always been very curious to me how Irish sentiment sticks in this half-way house—how it continues to apparently hate the English, and at the same time continues to imitate them; how it continues to clamour for recognition as a distinct nationality, and at the same time throws away with both hands what would make it so. If Irishmen only went a little farther they would become good Englishmen in sentiment also. But—illogical as it appears—there seems not the slightest sign or probability of their taking that step. It is the curious certainty that come what may Irishmen will continue to resist English rule, even though it should be for their good, which prevents many of our nation from becoming Unionists upon the spot. It is a fact, and we must face it as a fact, that although they adopt English habits and copy England in every way, the great bulk of Irishmen and Irishwomen

---

1 *Mazzini*: Giuseppe Mazzini (1805–72), Italian patriot and revolutionary, who advocated the unification of Italy. He founded the Young Italy movement, and the Young Europe Association 'of men believing in a future of liberty, equality and fraternity for all mankind'. He lived in London for a substantial part of his life, and contributed to various English journals.
2 *Goldwin Smith*: English historian and publicist (1823–1910); author of *Irish History and Irish Character* (1861). He supported Irish Disestablishment but opposed 'the dismemberment of the great Anglo-Saxon community'.

over the whole world are known to be filled with a dull, ever-abiding animosity against her, and—right or wrong—to grieve when she prospers, and joy when she is hurt. Such movements as Young Irelandism, Fenianism, Land Leagueism, and Parliamentary obstruction[1] seem always to gain their sympathy and support. It is just because there appears no earthly chance of their becoming good members of the Empire that I urge that they should not remain in the anomalous position they are in, but since they absolutely refuse to become the one thing, that they become the other; cultivate what they have rejected, and build up an Irish nation on Irish lines.

But you ask, why should we wish to make Ireland more Celtic than it is—why should we de-Anglicise it at all?

I answer because the Irish race is at present in a most anomalous position, imitating England and yet apparently hating it. How can it produce anything good in literature, art, or institutions as long as it is actuated by motives so contradictory? Besides, I believe it is our Gaelic past which, though the Irish race does not recognise it just at present, is really at the bottom of the Irish heart, and prevents us becoming citizens of the Empire, as, I think, can be easily proved.

To say that Ireland has not prospered under English rule is simply a truism; all the world admits it, England does not deny it. But the English retort is ready. You have not prospered, they say, because you would not settle down contentedly, like the Scotch, and form part of the Empire. 'Twenty years of good, resolute, grandfatherly government', said a well-known Englishman, will solve the Irish question.[2] He possibly made the period too short, but let us suppose this. Let us suppose for a moment—which is impossible—that there were to arise a series of Cromwells[3] in England for the space of one hundred years, able administrators of the Empire, careful rulers of Ireland, developing to the utmost our national resources, whilst they unremittingly stamped out every spark of national feeling, making Ireland a land of

---

1 *Young Irelandism, Fenianism, Land Leagueism, and Parliamentary obstruction*: movements and tactics intended to gain Irish independence from England. The Young Irelanders of the 1840s propagated cultural nationalism; the Fenians, founded by John O'Mahony in 1858, used physical force; the Land League, founded in 1879, led the violent struggle of tenants with lanlords, and the Irish Parliamentary party used filibustering.

2 *Twenty years ... Irish question*: in May 1886, some three months before his second office as Prime Minister, the conservative Lord Salisbury declared 'that Parliament should enable the Government of England to govern Ireland.... Apply that recipe honestly, consistently, and resolutely for 20 years, and at the end of time you will find Ireland will be fit to accept any gift in the way of local government or repeal of Coercion Laws that you may wish to give.' (Joseph Hendershot Park, *British Prime Ministers of the Nineteenth Century: Politics and Speeches* (New York University Press, 1916), p.294.)

3 *Cromwells*: Oliver Cromwell (1599–1658), Lord Protector of the Commonwealth (1653–58), detested in Ireland for his savage campaign of 1649–50.

wealth and factories, whilst they extinguished every thought and every idea that was Irish, and left us, at last, after a hundred years of good government, fat, wealthy, and populous, but with all our characteristics gone, with every external that at present differentiates us from the English lost or dropped; all our Irish names of places and people turned into English names; the Irish language completely extinct; the O's and the Macs dropped; our Irish intonation changed, as far as possible by English schoolmasters into something English; our history no longer remembered or taught; the names of our rebels and martyrs blotted out; our battlefields and traditions forgotten; the fact that we were not of Saxon origin dropped out of sight and memory, and let me now put the question—How many Irishmen are there who would purchase material prosperity at such a price? It is exactly such a question as this and the answer to it that shows the difference between the English and Irish race. Nine Englishmen out of ten would jump to make the exchange, and I as firmly believe that nine Irishmen out of ten would indignantly refuse it.

And yet this awful idea of complete Anglicisation, which I have here put before you in all its crudity is, and has been, making silent inroads upon us for nearly a century.

Its inroads have been silent, because, had the Gaelic race perceived what was being done, or had they been once warned of what was taking place in their own midst, they would, I think, never have allowed it. When the picture of complete Anglicisation is drawn for them in all its nakedness Irish sentimentality becomes suddenly a power and refuses to surrender its birthright.

What lies at the back of the sentiments of nationality with which the Irish millions seem so strongly leavened, what can prompt them to applaud such sentiments as:

> 'They say the British empire owes much to Irish hands,
> That Irish valour fixed her flag o'er many conquered lands;
> And ask if Erin takes no pride in these her gallant sons,
> Her Wolseleys and her Lawrences, her Wolfes and Wellingtons.[1]
>
> Ah! these were of the Empire—we yield them to her fame,
> And ne'er Erin's orisons are heard their alien name;
> But those for whom her heart beats high and benedictions swell,
> They died upon the scaffold and they pined within the cell.

---

1 *Her Wolseleys and Lawrences, her Wolfes and Wellingtons*: Irishmen who gained fame in the British army.

Of course it is a very composite feeling which prompts them; but I believe that what is largely behind it is the half unconscious feeling that the race which at one time held possession of more than half Europe, which established itself in Greece, and burned infant Rome, is now—almost extirpated and absorbed elsewhere— making its last stand for independence in this island of Ireland; and do what they may the race of to-day cannot wholly divest itself from the mantle of its own past. Through early Irish literature, for instance, can we best form some conception of what that race really was, which, after over-throwing and trampling on the primitive peoples of half Europe, was itself forced in turn to yield its speech, manners, and independence to the victorious eagles of Rome. We alone of the nations of Western Europe escaped the claws of those birds of prey; we alone developed ourselves naturally upon our own lines outside of and free from all Roman influence; we alone were thus able to produce an early art and literature, *our* antiquities can best throw light upon the pre-Romanised inhabitants of half Europe, and—we are our father's sons.

There is really no exaggeration in all this, although Irishmen are sometimes prone to overstating as well as to forgetting. ...

What we must endeavour to never forget is this, that the Ireland of today is the descendant of the Ireland of the seventh century, then the school of Europe and the torch of learning. It is true that Northmen made some minor settlements in it in the ninth and tenth centuries, it is true that the Normans made extensive settlements during the suc-ceeding centuries, but none of those broke the continuity of the social life of the island. Dane and Norman drawn to the kindly Irish breast issued forth in a generation or two fully Irishised, and more Hibernian than the Hibernians themselves, and even after the Cromwellian plantation the children of numbers of the English sol-diers who settled in the south and midlands, were, after forty years' residence, and after marrying Irish wives, turned into good Irishmen, and unable to speak a word of English, while several Gaelic poets of the last century have, like Father English, the most unmistakably English names. In two points only was the continuity of the Irishism of Ireland damaged. First, in the north-east of Ulster, where the Gaelic race was expelled and the land planted with aliens, whom our dear mother Erin, assimilative as she is, has hitherto found it difficult to absorb, and in the ownership of the land, eight-ninths of which belongs to people many of whom always lived, or live, abroad, and not half of whom Ireland can be said to have assimilated.

During all this time the continuation of Erin's national life centred, according to our way of looking at it, not so much in the Cromwellian or Williamite[1] landholders who sat in College Green,[2] and governed the country, as in the mass of the people whom Dean Swift[3] considered might be entirely neglected, and looked upon as hewers of wood and drawers of water; the men who, nevertheless constituted the real working population, and who were living on in the hopes of better days; the men who have since made America, and have within the last ten years proved what an important factor they may be in wrecking or building the British Empire. These are the men of whom our merchants, artisans, and farmers mostly consist, and in whose hands is today the making or marring of an Irish nation. But alas, *quantum mutates ab illo!*[4] What the battle axes of the Dane, the sword of the Norman, the wile of the saxon were unable to perform, we have accomplished ourselves. We have at last broken the continuity of Irish life, and just at the moment when the Celtic race is presumably about to largely recover possession of its own country, it finds itself deprived and stript of its Celtic characteristics, cut off from the past, yet scarcely in touch with the present. ... Just when we should be starting to build up anew the Irish race and the Gaelic nation—as within our own recollection Greece had been built up anew—we find ourselves despoiled of the bricks of nationality. The old bricks that lasted eighteen hundred years are destroyed; we must now set to, to bake new ones, if we can, on other ground and of other clay. Imagine for a moment the restoration of a German-speaking Greece.

The bulk of the Irish race really lived in the closest contact with the traditions of the past and the national life of nearly nineteen hundred years, until the beginning of this century. Not only so, but during the whole of the dark Penal times they produced amongst themselves a most vigorous literary development. Their schoolmasters and wealthy farmers, unwearied scribes, produced innumerable manuscripts in beautiful writing, each letter separated from another as in Greek, transcripts both of the ancient literature of their sires and of the more modern literature produced by themselves. Until the beginning of the present century there was no country, no barony, and, I may almost say, no townland which did not boast of an Irish poet, the

---

1 *Williamite*: Followers of William III (1650–1702), who defeated James II at the Boyne in 1690.

2 *College Green*: the Irish Parliament sat in College Green, Dublin, until the Act of Union in 1800.

3 *Dean Swift*: Jonathan Swift (1667–1745), towering literary figure in the eighteenth century (author of *Gulliver's Travels*) and Anglican Dean of St Patrick's Cathedral, Dublin.

4 *quantum mutates ab illo!*: 'How changed from that!'—Virgil, *Aeneid* 2, 274 (Aeneas's remark about his maimed brother-in-law Hector).

people's representative of those ancient bards who died out with the extirpation of the great Milesian families. The literary activity of even the eighteenth century among the Gaels was very great, not in the South alone, but also in Ulster—the number of poets it produced was something astonishing. It did not, however, produce many works in Gaelic prose, but it propagated translations of many pieces from the French, Latin, Spanish, and English. Every well-to-do farmer could read and write Irish, and many of them could understand even archaic Irish. I have myself heard persons reciting the poems of Donogha More O'Daly,[1] Abbot of Boyle, in Roscommon, who died sixty years before Chaucer was born. To this very day the people have a word for archaic Irish, which is much the same as though Chaucer's poems were handed down amongst the English peasantry, but required a special training to understand. This training, however, nearly every one of fair education during the Penal times possessed, nor did they begin to lose their Irish training and knowledge until after the establishment of Maynooth[2] and the rise of O'Connell.[3] These two events made an end of the Gaelicism of the Gaelic race, although a great number of poets and scribes existed even down to the forties and fifties of the present century, and a few may linger on yet in remote localities. But it may be said, roughly speaking, that the ancient Gaelic civilization died with O'Connell, largely, I am afraid, owing to his example and his neglect of inculcating the necessity of keeping alive racial customs, language, and traditions, in which with the one notable exception of our scholarly idealist, Smith O'Brien,[4] he has been followed until a year ago by almost every leader of the Irish race.[5]

Thomas Davis[6] and his brilliant band of Young Irelanders came just at the dividing of the line, and tried to give to Ireland a new literature in English to replace the literature which was just being discarded. It succeeded and it did not succeed. It was a most brilliant effort, but the old bark had been too recently stripped off the Irish tree, and the trunk could not take as it might have done to a fresh one. It was a new

1 *Donogha More O'Daly* (d. 1244), religious poet trained in the bardic school.
2 *the establishment of Maynooth*: St Patrick's, the catholic seminary in Kildare, was established in 1795.
3 *the rise of O'Connell*: as early as the first decade of the nineteenth century, Daniel O'Connell (1775–1847) became the most famous advocate of Catholic rights.
4 *Smith O'Brien*: William Smith O'Brien (1803–64), Irish nationalist and leader of the Young Ireland movement. He was transported to Tasmania for his leading role in the failed rising of 1848. He returned to Ireland in 1856 and contributed articles to *The Nation* condemning militantism.
5 *he has been followed until a year ago* …: an oblique reference to the death of Charles Stewart Parnell, leader of the Irish Parliamentary party.
6 *Thomas Davis*: Thomas Osborne Davis (1814–45), co-founder of *The Nation*, and architect of the Young Ireland movement.

departure, and at first produced a violent effect. Yet in the long run it failed to properly leaven our peasantry who might, perhaps, have been reached upon other lines. I say they *might* have been reached upon other lines, because it is quite certain that even well on into the beginning of this century, Irish poor scholars and schoolmasters used to gain the greatest favour and applause by reading out manuscripts in the people's houses at night, some of which manuscripts had an antiquity of a couple of hundred years or more behind them, and which, when they got illegible from age, were always recopied. The Irish peasantry at that time were all to some extent cultured men, and many of the better off ones were scholars and poets. What have we now left of all that? Scarcely a trace. Many of them read newspapers indeed, but who reads, much less recites, an epic poem, or chants an elegiac or even a hymn?

Wherever Irish throughout Ireland continued to be spoken, there the ancient MSS. continued to be read, there the epics of Cuchullain, Conor MacNessa, Déirdre, Finn, Oscar, and Ossian continued to be told, and there poetry and music held sway. Some people may think that I am exaggerating in asserting that such a state of things existed down to the present century, but it is no exaggeration. ...

So much for the greatest stroke of all in our Anglicisation, the loss of our language. I have often heard people thank God that if the English gave us nothing else they gave us at least their language. In this way they put a bold face upon the matter, and pretend that the Irish language is not worth knowing, and has no literature. But the Irish language *is* worth knowing, or why would the greatest philologists of Germany, France, and Italy be emulously studying it, and it *does* possess a literature, or why would a German savant have made the calculation that the books written in Irish between the eleventh and seventeenth centuries, and still extant, would fill a thousand octavo volumes.

I have no hesitation at all in saying that every Irish-feeling Irishman, who hates the reproach of West-Britonism, should set himself to encourage the efforts, which are being made to keep alive our once great national tongue. The losing of it is our greatest blow, and the sorest stroke that the rapid Anglicisation of Ireland has inflicted upon us. In order to de-Anglicise ourselves we must at once arrest the decay of the language. We must bring pressure upon our politicians not to snuff it out by their tacit discouragement merely because they do not happen themselves to understand it. We must arouse some spark of patriotic inspiration among the peasantry who still use the language, and put an end to the shameful state of feeling—a thousand-tongued reproach to our leaders and statesmen—which makes young men and women blush and hang their heads when overheard speaking their own language.[1] Maynooth has at last come splendidly to the front, and it is now incumbent upon every clerical student to attend lectures in the Irish language and history during the first three years of his course. But in order to keep the Irish language alive where it is still spoken—which is the utmost we can at present aspire to—nothing less than a house-to-house visitation and exhortation of the people themselves will do, something—though with a very different purpose—analogous to the procedure that James Stephens[2] adopted throughout Ireland when he found her like a corpse on the dissecting table. This and some system of giving medals or badges of honour to every family who will guarantee that they have always spoken Irish amongst themselves during the year. But, unfortunately, distracted as we are and torn by contending factions, it is impossible to find either men or money to carry out this simple remedy, although to a dispassionate foreigner—to a Zeuss, Jubainville, Zimmer, Kuno Meyer, Windisch, or Ascoli,[3] and the rest—this is of greater importance than whether Mr. Redmond or Mr. MacCarthy lead the largest wing of the Irish party for the moment,[4] or Mr. So-and-So succeed with his election petition. To a person taking a

---

1 As an instance of this, I mention the case of a young man I met on the road coming from the fair of Tuam, some ten miles away. I saluted him in Irish, and he answered me in English. 'Don't you speak Irish', said I. 'Well, I declare to God, sir', he said, 'my father and mother hasn't a word of English, but still, I don't speak Irish.' This was absolutely true for him. There are thousands upon thousands of houses all over Ireland today where the old people invariably use Irish in addressing the children, and the children as invariably answer in English, the children understanding Irish but not speaking it, the parents understanding their children's English but unable to use it themselves. In a great many cases, I should almost say most, the children are not conscious of the existence of two languages. I remember asking a gossoon a couple of miles west of Ballaghaderreen in the Co. Mayo, some questions in Irish and he answered them in English. At last I said to him, '*Nach labhrann tu Gaedheilg?*' (i.e., 'Don't you speak Irish?') and his answer was, 'And isn't it Irish I'm spaking?' 'No *a-chuisle*,' said I, 'it's not Irish you're speaking, but English.' 'Well then', said he, 'that's how I spoke it ever!' He was quite unconscious that I was addressing him in one language and he answering in another. On a different occasion I spoke Irish to a little girl in a house near Kilfree Junction, Co. Sligo, into which I went while waiting for a train. The girl answered me in Irish until her brother came in. 'Arrah now, Mary', said he, with what was intended to be a most bitter sneer; 'and isn't that a credit to you!' And poor Mary—whom I had with difficulty persuaded to begin—immediately hung her head and changed to English. This is going on from Malin Head to Galway, and from Galway to Waterford, with the exception possibly of a few spots in Donegal and Kerry, where the people are wiser and more national. [*Hyde's note.*]
2 *James Stephens* (1825–1901), aide-de-camp of William Smith O'Brien, and founder of the Fenian movement.
3 *Zeuss. ... Ascoli*: foreign Celtic scholars.
4 *whether Mr. Redmond or Mr. MacCarthy* lead...: after the fall of Parnell in 1890, the Irish Parliamentary party spilt into several factions. John Redmond (1856–1918) headed the Parnellites, with the support of his brother William (1861–1917); Justin McCarthy was the compromise leader of the anti-Parnellites.

bird's-eye view of the situation a hundred or five hundred years hence, believe me, it will also appear of greater importance than any mere temporary wrangle, but, unhappily, our countrymen cannot be brought to see this.

We can, however, insist, and we *shall* insist if Home Rule be carried, that the Irish language, which so many foreign scholars of the first calibre find so worthy of study, shall be placed on a par with—or even above—Greek, Latin, and modern languages, in all examinations held under the Irish Government. We can also insist, and we *shall* insist, that in those baronies where the children speak Irish, Irish shall be taught, and that Irish-speaking schoolmasters, petty sessions clerks, and even magistrates be appointed in Irish-speaking districts. If all this were done, it should not be very difficult, with the aid of the foremost foreign scholars, to bring about a tone of thought which would make it disgraceful for an educated Irishman—especially of the old Celtic race, MacDermotts, O'Conors, O'Sullivans, MacCarthys, O'Neills— to be ignorant of his own language—would make it at least as disgraceful as for an educated Jew to be quite ignorant of Hebrew.

[*Hyde goes on to show the Anglicisation of Ireland in its surnames and Christian names, place names, and in its games and dress.*]

I have now mentioned a few of the principal points on which it would be desirable for us to move, with a view to de-Anglicising ourselves; but perhaps the principal point of all I have taken for granted. That is the necessity for encouraging the use of Anglo-Irish literature instead of English books, especially instead of English periodicals. We must set our face sternly against penny dreadfuls, shilling shockers, and still more, the garbage of vulgar English weeklies like *Bow Bells* and the *Police Intelligence*. Every house should have a copy of Moore[1] and Davis. In a word, we must strive to cultivate everything that is most racial, most smacking of the soil, most Gaelic, most Irish, because in spite of the little admixture of Saxon blood in the northeast corner, this island *is* and will *ever* remain Celtic at the core, far more Celtic than most people imagine, because, as I have shown you, the names of our people are no criterion of their race. On racial lines, then, we shall best develop, following the bent of our own natures; and, in order to do this, we must create a strong feeling against West-Britonism, for it—if we give it the least chance, or show it the small-

---

1 *Moore*: Thomas Moore (1779–1852), poet, author of the *Irish Melodies* (1807–35) and of *Lalla Rookh* (1817).

est quarter—will overwhelm us like a flood, and we shall find ourselves toiling painfully behind the English at each step following the
same fashions, only six months behind the English ones; reading the
same books, only months behind them; taking up the same fads, after
they have become stale *there*, following *them* in our dress, literature,
music, games, and ideas, only a long time after them and a vast way
behind. We will become, what, I fear, we are largely at present, a
nation of imitators, the Japanese of Western Europe, lost to the power
of native initiative and alive only to second-hand assimilation. I do
not think I am overrating this danger. We are probably at once the
most assimilative and the most sensitive nation in Europe. A lady in
Boston said to me that the Irish immigrants had become Americanised
on the journey out before ever they landed at Castle Gardens. And
when I ventured to regret it, she said, shrewdly, 'If they did not at
once become Americanised they would not be Irish.' I knew fifteen
Irish workmen who were working in a haggard in England give up
talking Irish amongst themselves because the English farmer laughed
at them. And yet O'Connell used to call us the 'finest peasantry in
Europe.' Unfortunately, he took little care that we should remain so.
We must teach ourselves to be less sensitive, we must teach ourselves
not to be ashamed of ourselves, because the Gaelic people can never
produce its best before the world as long as it remains tied to the
apron-strings of another race and another island, waiting for *it* to
move before it will venture to take any step itself.

In conclusion, I would earnestly appeal to every one, whether
Unionist or Nationalist, who wishes to see the Irish nation produce its
best—and surely whatever our politics are we all wish that—to set his
face against this constant running to England for our books, literature, music, games, fashions, and ideas. I appeal to every one whatever his politics— for this is no political matter—to do his best to help
the Irish race to develop in future upon Irish lines, even at the risk of
encouraging national aspirations, because upon Irish lines alone can
the Irish race once more become what it was of yore—one of the most
original, artistic, literary and charming peoples of Europe.

SHAN F[ADH] BULLOCK (1865–1935)

John William Bullock was born in Crom, Co. Fermanagh, the son of a small-farmer
who became agent to the Earl of Fermanagh; he was educated in Farra School, Co.
Westmeath. He worked as a civil servant in London, where he attended King's
College. He adopted the name Shan Fadh, a character in William Carleton's *Traits*

413

and Stories* out of sympathy with the Catholic Irish community. He was awarded an MBE for his work as a secretary of the Irish Home Rule Convention. In his fiction, Bullock couples naturalism with melodrama. He wrote over a dozen novels, mostly with unattractive characters; but he also wrote poems, stories and autobiographies. His first collection, *The Awkward Squads And Other Stories* (1893), deals with tribal rivalry in the face of a changing Ireland. The title story describes the fumbled attempts of rivalling religious factions to organize themselves into militias. His first novel, *By Thrasna River; The Story of a Townland* (1895), is narrated by John Farmer, a recurrent character in Bullock's fiction, the son of the formidable 'Master', who was modelled on Bullock's father. It vividly depicts the hardship of living off the land. 'The Master' is the central figure in his autobiography *After Sixty Years* (1931). *Robert Thorne: The Story of a London Clerk* (1917) documents at first hand the drudgery of poor 'pen-drivers'. Bullock collaborated with Emily Lawless* on *The Race of Castlebar* (1913), each author writing alternate chapters. His best-known work is *Thomas Andrews, Shipbuilder* (1912), the story of the Ulsterman who built the Titanic, and was drowned when she sank.

From *The Awkward Squads*

(1893)

A State Official

Right in the heart of Cavan, sheltered on all sides by hills, and scattered aimlessly along two roads which there meet, cross, and wander on, stands the village of Raheen. In a generous moment you might say it numbered twenty houses, all thickly whitewashed, heavily thatched, and preserving a stillness that might be taken as peaceful or dull as the humour required.

Coming down the hill on which, amid its mouldering graves, stands the parish church, and over which lies the road to the railway, you see right in front, under an arch of spreading beech branches, the village shop cleverly placed on an angle made by the crossing roads; and to the left a low grey wall over which peep the white chimneys of a row of thatched cottages. These last really make the village; without them (and the shop maybe) two roads would meet at a hamlet after their wanderings across the hills.

But, besides this mere numerical and purely local importance, the cottages still preserve a certain air of distinction, first assumed when a tyrannical, to be sure, yet, on the whole, intelligent, Government decided that they should shelter a branch of the Imperial post office.

It is gone now; but some time, say ten years ago, if, one evening in June, you had leant over the low grey wall and looked down, you would have seen, across a trim, gay little garden and behind a wealth of hanging creepers, an open window framing the bent head of old Dan the cobbler and village postmaster. The *tip tap* of his hammer would have come with a soothing regularity and seemed to be the only sign of life—at that hour it would certainly be the only sound— in the place. After the dust of the road you would have found it pleasant to lean there on the cool stones, and, with that dull beating in your ears, let your eyes wander idly over the homely garden, the old brown thatch, then across the roof towards the fading green of the hills.

But presently the sound would cease; then, looking, you would have seen Dan lean forward, turn a leaf in a book that lay on the window-ledge before him, read fixedly for a moment, and, with a smile on his old face, look up at yourself. For your elbows would rest on stones that were shiny from long rubbing by the coats of gossips who had stood there, sometimes by the hour, cracking a sly joke with the garrulous old man.

Had you remained longer that evening, however, you would have seen a thin, ugly man turn down by the end of the wall, cross the garden, and, regardless of tender flowers, tramp clumsily to Dan's window.

'Hello!' said Dan, looking up and pushing his spectacles up his brow; 'that's sudden. Ah, it's you, Micky! Well, God be with ye, me son, anyway; but you're a powerful bad friend to the light.'

'Yis,' said the man, 'I suppose I am—but no matter. I want to say a word to ye.'

'Say on, me son,' said Dan, reaching to close his book, and putting down his hammer. 'As the wise man said: "There's a time for all things".'

'I want to know, Dan,' said the other, stooping and resting his hands on the window-sill, 'if you've thought better o' what ye said th' other night? Ha' ye changed yir mind?'

'Eh, avick?[1] What's that?' said Dan sharply. 'Changed me mind?— that's what I seldom do. What about?'

'Ye know.'

'I forgot then.'

'About the man that's occupyin' Widow Reilly's farm—are ye goin' to do lek another?'

---

1 *avick*: 'my son' (term of endearment).

'Ah!' said Dan, 'that's it, is it? An' why should I do like another? Eh?'

'It's no use bleatherin'!' answered the man irritably. 'Ye know what I mane—In plain words will ye quit spakin' or havin' anythin' to do wi' the man?'

'Why should I, Micky? Answer me that. Why *should* I luk your way for advice?'

'It's not me. I do as I'm bid—so must you. The man's betrayed the cause be takin' an evicted woman's farm—ye know that. So long as he's there he's a traitor to the cause, an' them that has dealin's with him are worse.'

'The *cause*!' broke in Dan with a scornful laugh. 'Ye call it a cause to leave a man without a bite to eat, or a dud to wear, or a soul to cross words with! D'ye call it a cause to let wee childer starve an' a woman to fret?'

'Ye may quit!' said the man abruptly. 'Say no more; ivery word takes ye deeper. Is that your answer?'

'Micky Flynn,' said Dan, rising and, the better to look severe, dragging his spectacles down to his nose, 'from you or any other man I take no counsel when I try to do right. Ye call it a *cause*. I say it's hellish persecution! The man has harmed no one, neither have his childer; he's only done what *you* think wrong. An' who are you, Micky Flynn, to judge another? *I* think he's done no harm, Micky; an' cause or no cause I'm goin' to think lek that.' He stooped and laid his hand on the closed book. 'Here's where I get me counsel, Micky—here I read'—he shook a warning finger at the man—' *"This above all—to thine own self be true, and it must—"*'[1]

The man turned away with a foul exclamation of disgust and spat on the flowers, walked to the gate, and there wheeled round.

'Ye may talk yir fool's clack to yirself, now,' he shouted back. 'Be God, yi'll have time enough, ye bleatherin' ould rogue!'

Dan leaned across the sill and looked at his flowers.

'Ah!' said he, 'it's well there's rain comin'; it'll help to wipe out the divil's hoof-tracks.' Then he laughed, and closing the window lit a candle and sat down on his stool.

The unsteady light fell softly on all the mad disorder of the room— the litter on the floor, the rolls of leather in the corner, the lasts on the wall hanging over pictured newspaper cuttings, the little official desk strewn with old pens, cheap stationery, dirty copies of rules and regu-

---

1 *This above all*...: Polonius' oft-quoted advice to Laertes in *Hamlet* I. iii. 78–9.

lations—fell softly on all that and on the sturdy old figure of the postmaster. He laughed softly to himself, and wagged his head gravely.

'Well, well,' said he, 'after all these years o' peace an' quiet to come to this! Spoke to lek that! What next? What's goin' to come to me? Well, well; time'll tell "*This above all*",' he muttered slowly, '"*To thine own self be true—to thine own self be true*".'

He reached for his book, and, holding the candle close to his face, began turning the leaves and reading a line here and there on a chance page.

"*My way of life is fallen into the sere, the yellow leaf*"—ah, ah!'[1]

'"*Rude am I in my speech.*"[2] Just so, just so!'

"*I am a very foolish, fond old man . . . climbing sorrow . . . serpent's tooth.*"[3] Poor old Lear, Lord help all like him!'

Presently he looked up, and, pushing back his glasses, declaimed in a measured sing-song:

'"*There's a divinity that shapes our ends, rough-hew them how we will.*"[4] That's good, that's what I wanted—that's somethin' to sleep on—that an' th' other. What's this it is? Oh, ay! "*This above all . . . There's a divinity.*"'

Repeating the phrases over and over to himself, he rose and busied himself about the room, arranging his tools, tidying his desk, looking out his work for the morrow.

"*There's a divinity*",' he kept on repeating; then suddenly stopped, and holding up a piece of wax-end: "*Shapes our ends!*"' he said with a soft chuckle. 'I wonder if it takes a divinity to shape this?'

And laughing at his little joke he bolted the door and went to bed.

The next morning, his flowers watered and wed,[5] his frugal breakfast over, and his little kitchen swept and tidied, Dan with his book open before him, and breathing the sweet morning freshness of his garden, was again at his work, hammering and sewing, reading and muttering, laughing softly betimes to himself and looking up through his spectacles at the wall. But though he looked up often no one that morning leant on the stones to exchange greetings or jokes; sometimes footsteps sounded from the road; sometimes a neighbour passed close to the wall; once or twice someone looked furtively towards the open window; but no one spoke; and for the first time

---

1 *My way of life...*: *Macbeth* V. iii. 22–3.

2 *Rude am I in my speech*: *Othello* I. iii. 80.

3 *I am a very foolish old man...*: *King Lear* IV. vii. 60; 'Down, thou climbing sorrow!': II. iv. 55; 'How sharper than a serpents tooth it is, To have a thankless child!': I. iv. 285–6.

4 *There's a divinity that shapes our ends...*: *Hamlet* V. ii. 10–11.

5 *wed*: weeded.

for many years the stool at Dan's elbow, where usually his neighbours waited for the post, was vacant.

'Eh?' he would say, looking round at the empty stool and up at the wall. 'Eh? well, well!'

Then the post came, carried by a lad who that morning seemed peculiarly gruff and silent, and Dan, for a while sinking his trade and putting on the air of importance becoming a state official, carefully sorted the letters and placed them in order on his desk.

'Now,' said he, turning to his work again, '*now* they'll come—they *must* come now; they *must*.'

Only children came that morning—children who seemed suddenly to be smitten with an unusual awkwardness and shyness, as they stopped before the window or came to the door of Dan's room and asked if there were any letters for Mammy, please.

'Come in, Mary, agra!'[1] Dan called cheerily to the first who came; 'come in, me girl, an' I'll give ye a flower.—Ye can't come?—Well, well!—Where's your Daddy the day?—Eh? Where's your tongue, Mary?'

The child suddenly raised her hand from her lips to her eyes, and began to cry.

'Oh!' she sobbed, 'please Dan, Mammy says I mustn't spake to ye.'

Dan's eyes swiftly became grave behind his spectacles.

'Ah!' he said. 'Well, well!'—then, without a word, handed the child the letter.

With the next it was the same, and the next—after that he questioned no more. And all that day he sat silent, his book for the most part neglected, and his heart heavy; not one came to his little room, not one paused to speak to him, not one looked over the wall, except towards evening, when Dan, more by habit than will, raising his eyes, saw a dark, ugly face, that scowled on him for a moment and was gone.

So three days passed; and the fourth morning saw Dan cobbler no longer, but post-master only. The last job of mending had been taken away (by a child, as usual); for the first time in his working life he had not a stitch to sew. For three days he had been left to his thoughts and his book—in that time only once had he heard a friendly voice, and that belonged to the man for whom he was suffering. His heart was heavy; his flowers had not their old sweet power over him; even Shakespeare could not wholly catch his thoughts; his eyes were grown very sorrowful, and his brow was troubled.

---

1 *agra*: 'my love'.

'Well, well!' he would say, 'well, well!—Am I asleep or awake? Is it me at all?—What have I done?—What am I to do?'

For the hundredth time he reviewed his position. He was cut off from the world—a social outlaw. He had no work, would have none. He could only get food by walking far to a town where he was not known. He had the few shillings a week that made his official salary, and a few pounds in the savings bank—could he keep life with that? He had that one friend—a dull fellow, as it happened, without a laugh in his body, whom, besides, it was dangerous just then to visit. His own thoughts, himself, bare life, his little cottage and garden—could he do with just that?

Such was his position, and such it would be for long and long—till he yielded. Was it worth while? he asked. Should he yield? He did no one any good by holding out—not one, not even that dull friend. He was pleasing himself, injuring himself. Should he yield? he asked himself that fourth morning, sitting on his stool beside his open window waiting for the children to come for the letters. Mechanically his hand reached for his book of wisdom and opened its old, tattered pages.

'"*This above all*",' he said in a little while, raising his beaming face to the wall. '"*This above all, to thine own self be true*"—an' what's th' other? "*There's a divinity that shapes our ends*."—Just so, Dan; that's your reason. By the Lord, Dan, you're a sinner at heart; only for the old book you'd be a limb of Satan!'

So he accepted his position; and for a time bore his lot cheerfully, passing the long days as best he might—working in his garden, white-washing his cottage inside and out and repairing its thatch, reading his one book by the open window; sometimes, at night, dressing in his Sunday clothes, and, with his hat jauntily cocked and a flower in his coat, whistling and singing defiantly as he slowly paraded up and down the street or past his neighbours' open doors.

For a time—say, a few weeks longer—he bore himself bravely; then, with a sudden rush, was borne in upon him a full sense of his cruel, unutterable loneliness. A living man shut in a tomb; a tongue quickly smitten dumb; a world suddenly changed from life and laugh-ter to grim, gloomy silence: as such, in such, he found himself. Could he endure that—he by nature so sociable and kindly, who, lately, had been the life of the village—its half-understood (crazy, indeed, people said) wit, sage, politician; he who had delighted in the talk and socie-ty of his neighbours as much as in his own musings? Could he endure silence, loneliness, not for a day or a week, but for long, perhaps very long? He was doing right; but that did not bring comfort enough—

indeed was but cold comfort, seeing that doing right brought only trouble. He could bear hunger, privation, neglect; but silence, loneliness, this death in life, these he could not bear. He felt he must talk or go mad. And all round him for miles and miles there was not one with whom he could chat pleasantly for an hour in the day, only an hour; not one but the dull, distant fellow for whom he was denying himself.

Yes, there was another; he, at least, would listen patiently.

So Dan took his book, and, climbing the hill behind the shop, came at last to a hovel by the wayside, where, bending over a small peat fire, he found a miserable old man, clad in rags, crippled with age, dirty beyond belief, and with only bare life lighting his eyes. Here was someone who would listen, even if he could not answer; a relic almost of life, mumbling childishly about himself and his pains, sometimes knitting his brows as his tongue fashioned an old-time phrase, or his mind was troubled with a sudden, half-realized memory.

'Ah!' he would mutter, 'it's shivery cowld the day—Tell me, did—did—was it true that they disestablished the Church, the Prodestan'?—ach, no!—ach, a bad man!'[1]

And so he muttered now and then, whilst Dan read by the hour, or stopped to expound a passage, or, coming at last to his favourite lines, made them the text of a long harangue in which his tongue freed his mind of the irritating, ugly burden gathered through those days of silence.

'Ach, a bad man!' was the response, or one equally vague. 'Ach, a bad man!'

But for all his squalor and witlessness, the old cripple was a human being who listened to Dan and did not keep his face from him; who turned his head and said 'Good morning' when Dan entered, and followed him with lifeless old eyes as he went—a human being to whom Dan could talk, and who answered as best he could.

This was very well, so far; but, returning one day from one of these morning visits; feeling, for all his recent effort, a great desire to talk (really, it may be, a craving for fellowship and sympathy), an almost irresistible impulse to shout aloud, or to go to the nearest house and there compel conversation, and wondering betimes how best he should put behind him the long remaining hours of the day; suddenly, right in view of the village, the thought came to him—Why not go and talk? Who might hinder him? People might not answer; but they could not refuse to hear.

---

1 *disestablished the Church, the Prodestan'*: 'the Prodestan' is William Ewart Gladstone (1809–98), the Prime Minister who carried through Disestablishment of the Church of Ireland in 1869.

The notion made him laugh and slap his leg as he stood pondering on the road. It would be a good way to pay back men's cruelty; it would give himself pleasure and them annoyance; perhaps—yes, perhaps!—he might be able to mingle wisdom with his talk, and so gradually bring them round to his charitable point of view.

'Yes,' he said aloud, slapping his leg once more, and beaming at the thought of the funny, clever, old codger he still was; 'yes, begob, it's a good idea—a good idea, me son! Dan, you're not done with yet! I'll try it this very night—Mebbe, mebbe—' And, turning over the maybes in his mind, he went slowly, but not sadly, home.

That evening, with his book under his arm, and a big rose in his black chapel coat, Dan went out; and, taking his stand about the crossing of the roads, before the shop and within hearing of the cottages, there, with a humorous glint in his eye which sometimes belied the seriousness of his face, read, expounded, and discoursed.

Had you been in Raheen that fine summer's evening; enjoying the rich warmth of the sunset, perhaps, as you leaned at the old spot across the wall; you must certainly have watched the scene with interest—the laughing, bare-armed women at the doors; the men lounging against the wall, wondering whether Dan were knave or fool; the children in the dusty, yellow street, clustering, open-eyed, round the old man just then raising his voice in a part serious, part humorous discourse on Truth even in politics to one's self, and the Divinity that even in politics shapes man's ends. You would have found the scene interesting; perhaps, had you known what lay behind it all, you might have found it pathetic.

Only, the villagers clearly found in it nothing but amusement and a little welcome excitement; for, a night or two after saw Dan talking to bare white walls, the doors all closed, the children's voices coming merrily over the roofs from the back. But Dan was not discomfited. He moved closer to the cottages, and raised his voice louder in a more personal and less humorous harangue—yes! waxed bold; and one night, entering a house, stood with his back to the door and spoke his soul concerning the cause and its adherents.

This, in the opinion of his neighbours, was more than amusing and not to be tolerated. He might talk nonsense outside as much as he chose; but a man's hearthstone was private, and the cause was sacred. He might be cracked—no doubt he was; but he had sense enough left to do harm and talk black heresy.

He had one more chance; and, recklessly, almost foolishly abused it. Then a party of men, with blackened faces and carrying guns, visited him as he sat in his kitchen reading by candle light. They entered silently; and, having surrounded him with a ring of threatening muzzles, one of their number, in forcible language, made clear to the trembling, haggard old man the character and blackness of his offence and the swift punishment that would follow its repetition.

Did he hear? shouted the man, and fired at the roof.

Then, silently they went out, and left the old man to stagger to bed with a pain at his heart.

The next morning another opened the postbag; and now, people say that sometimes at night, if you lean over the wall, across the rotting flower-beds you will see a laughing, muttering old man behind a closed window, hammering and reading away.

WILLIAM BUTLER YEATS (1865–1939)

The son of John Butler Yeats, born in Dublin, he was educated at the Godolphin School, Hammersmith, the High School, Dublin and the Metropolitan School of Art, Dublin. Deeply interested in Theosophy, Indian thought, Rosicrucianism, Buddhism, magic, spiritualism and astrology, he determined to give new expression to Irish legends and mythology and was a shaping force, along with George Russell (AE)*, Douglas Hyde* and Standish O'Grady* in the Irish Literary Revival. He managed to support himself on literary journalism while writing his 'Celtic Twilight' poetry; misty and melancholic, it culminated in *The Wind Among the Reeds* (1899). His obsession with Maud Gonne, whom he first met in 1889 and who refused all his proposals of marriage, runs through his poetry. He met Lady Gregory* in 1894, spent summers at her Galway house, Coole Park, and with her and Edward Martyn* created the Irish Literary Theatre, which became the Abbey Theatre in 1904, with Yeats as its manager. In his middle period, the poems were less decorative, and included complex narrative poems. Stronger, more political, often bitter in tone, it heralded the powerful mature verse of *Michael Robartes and the Dancer* (1921), with its bleak vision of 'The Second Coming'. *The Tower* (1928) and *The Winding Stair and Other Poems* (1933) contained much magnificent poetry, its rhetoric embracing love, fatherhood, civil war and the constant drama of impending destruction. He married Georgie Hyde Lees in 1917; her automatic writing led to *A Vision* (1925; 1937), which provided a sanction and scaffolding for his symbolism, enhanced by the purchase (in 1917) and restoration of a medieval tower in Co. Galway in which many of his poems are set. He became a Senator of the Irish Free State in 1922, won the Nobel Prize for Literature in 1923 and, despite frequent illnesses, continued to write with passion about love, sex, history and politics until his death.

William Butler Yeats

The Stolen Child

(1886)[1]

Where dips the rocky highland
    Of Slewth Wood in the lake,
There lies a leafy island
    Where flapping herons wake
The drowsy water rats;
There we've hid our fairy vats
Full of berries
And of reddest stolen cherries.
Come away, O human child!
To the woods and waters wild
With a fairy, hand in hand,
For the world's more full of weeping than you can understand.

Where the wave of moonlight glosses
    The dim grey sands with light,
Far off by furthest Rosses
    We foot it all the night,
Weaving olden dances,
Mingling hands and mingling glances
    Till the moon has taken flight;
To and fro we leap
    And chase the frothy bubbles
    While the world is full of troubles
And is anxious in its sleep.
Come away, O human child!
To the woods and waters wild
With a fairy, hand in hand,
For the world's more full of weeping than you can understand.

Where the wandering water gushes
    From the hills above Glen-Car,
In pools among the rushes
    That scarce could bathe a star,
We seek for slumbering trout
    And whispering in their ears

---

1 First published in *The Irish Monthly*, Dec. 1886. Cf. William Allingham's 'The Fairies', *Irish Literature: The Nineteenth Century* Vol.II.

We give them evil dreams,
  Leaning softly out
 From ferns that drop their tears
   Of dew on the young streams.
Come, O human child!
To the woods and waters wild
With a fairy, hand in hand,
For the world's more full of weeping than you can understand.

Away with us he's going,
  The solemn-eyed—
He'll hear no more the lowing
  Of the calves on the warm hill side
Or the kettle on the hob
  Sing peace into his breast,
Or see the brown mice bob
  Round and round the oatmeal chest.
For he comes, the human child,
To the woods and waters wild
With a fairy, hand in hand,
For the world's more full of weeping than he can understand.

William Butler Yeats

From *The Wanderings of Usheen*[1]
(1889)[2]

from Book I

ST. PATRICK
You who are bent, and bald, and blind,
With a heavy heart and a wandering mind,
Have known three centuries, poets sing,
Of dalliance with a demon thing.

USHEEN.[3]
Sad to remember, sick with years,
The swift innumerable spears,
The horsemen with their floating hair,
And bowls of barley, honey, and wine,
And feet of maidens dancing in tune,
And the white body that lay by mine;
But the tale, though words be lighter than air,
Must live to be old like the wandering moon.

---

1 This poem is founded upon the Middle Irish dialogues of St. Patrick and Usheen and a certain Gaelic poem of the last century. The events it describes, like the events in most of the
poems in this volume, are supposed to have taken place rather in the indefinite period, made
up of many periods, described by the folk-tales, than in any particular century; it therefore,
like the later Fenian stories themselves, mixes much that is mediaeval with other matters that
are ancient. The Gaelic poems do not make Usheen go to more than one island, but tradition
speaks of three islands. A story in the *Silva Gadelica* describes 'four paradises,' an island to
the north, an island to the west, an island to the south, and Adam's paradise in the east.
Another tradition, which puts one of the paradises under the sea, is perhaps a memory of the
fabled kingdom of the shadowy Fomoroh, whose name proves that they came from the great
waters. [*Yeats's note.*]
  Yeats's main source was Bryan O'Looney's adaptation of an eighteenth-century Gaelic
poem, *Laoi Oisin i dTir na nOg* (*The Lay of Oisin in the Land of Youth*), by Micheál Coimín.
Coimín's poem is based on the medieval Irish 'Colloquy of the Old Men', which is part of the
Ossianic Cycle. Usheen (Oisin), son of Finn (Fionn) Mac Cumhaill, was a warrior and poet
of the Fenians (Fianna). According to the Finn Cycle, he and his followers were defeated at
the Battle of Gabhra by King Carbery. After a century-long sojourn in the Land of Youth,
Usheen returns, topples from his horse, and grows old.
2 The version provided here is from *Poems* (London and Boston, 1895), which is considerably
closer to the final shape the poem took in *The Selected Poems* (1929) and *The Collected Poems*
(1950) than the first in *The Wanderings of Oisin and other Poems* (London, 1889).
3 *Usheen*: The poet of the Fenian cycle of legend, as Fergus was the poet of the Red Branch
cycle. [*Yeats's note.*]

Caolte,[1] and Conan,[2] and Finn[3] were there,
When we followed a deer with our baying hounds,
With Bran, Sgeolan, and Lomair,[4]
And passing the Firbolgs' burial mounds,[5]
Came to the cairn-heaped grassy hill
Where passionate Maive[6] is stony still;
And found on the dove-gray edge of the sea
A pearl-pale, high-born lady, who rode
On a horse with bridle of findrinny;[7]
And like a sunset were her lips,
A stormy sunset on doomed ships;
A citron colour gloomed in her hair,
But down to her feet white vesture flowed,
And with the glimmering crimson glowed
Of many a figured embroidery;
And it was bound with a pearl-pale shell
That wavered like the summer streams,
As her soft bosom rose and fell.

ST. PATRICK.

You are still wrecked among heathen dreams.

USHEEN.

'The hunting of heroes should be glad:
'Why do you wind no horn?' she said.
'And every hero droop his head?
'The hornless deer is not more sad
'That many a peaceful moment had,
'More sleek than any granary mouse,

---

1 *Caolte*: Caoilte mac Rónáin, a swift-footed giant-killer and minstrel; he was Finn's favourite warrior.
2 *Conan*: The Thersites of the Fenian cycle. [*Yeats's note.*] Conan the Bald was a comic braggart; Lady Gregory calls him Conan of the Bitter Tongue'.
3 *Finn*: chief of the Leinster Fianna; father of Usheen.
4 *Bran, Sgeolan, and Lomair*: Finn's favourite hunting dogs. They were the children of Finn's sister Uirne, who had been turned into a dog by her jilted lover; she regained her human form, but her children did not.
5 *Firbolgs…*: An early race who warred vainly upon the Fomorians, or Fomoroh, before the coming of the Tuath de Danaan. Certain Firbolg kings, killed at Southern Moytura, are supposed to be buried at Ballisodare. It is by their graves that Usheen and his companions rode. [*Yeats's note.*]
6 *Maive*: A famous queen of the Red Branch cycle. She is rumoured to be buried under the cairn on Knocknarea. Ferguson speaks of 'the shell-heaped cairn of Maive high up on haunted Knocknarea,' but inaccurately, for the cairn is of stones. [*Yeats's note.*]
7 *findrinny*: A kind of red bronze. [*Yeats's note.*]

'In his own leafy forest house
'Among the waving fields of fern.'

'O pleasant maiden,' answered Finn,
'We think on Oscar's pencilled urn,[1]
'And on the heroes lying slain,
'On Gavra's raven-covered plain;[2]
'But where are your noble kith and kin,
'And into what country do you ride?'

'I am Neave, a child of the mighty Shee,[3]
'And was born where the sun drops down in the tide,
'O worn deed-doer.'
                    'What may bring
'To this dim shore those gentle feet?
'Did your companion wander away?'

Then did you answer, pearl-pale one,
With laughter low, and tender, and sweet:
'I have not yet, war-weary king,
'Been spoken of with any man.
'For love of Usheen my feet ran
'Over the glossy sea.'

            'O, wild
'Young princess, when were you beguiled
'By this young man, Usheen my son?'

'I loved no man, though canns[4] besought,
'And many a prince of lofty name,
'Until the Danaan[5] poets came,

1 *Oscar's pencilled urn*: the urn that contained the ashes of Usheen's son Oscar had writing on it. Yeats may have taken this reference from Sir Samuel Ferguson's poem 'Aideen's Grave'.
2 *Gavra's raven-covered plain*: The great battle in which the power of the Fenians was broken. [*Yeats's note.*]
3 *Neave, a child of the mighty Shee*: Niamh Chinn Óir ('Niamh of the Golden Hair') in Micheál Coimín's text. Her name denotes brightness and beauty. The Shee (*Sidhe*), the Fairies, were the *Tuatha Dé Dannan* who fled underground after their defeat by the Milesians (see note 5 below). In this poem Niamh has a fair bit in common with Keats's 'Belle Dame Sans Merci'.
4 *Canns*: A kind of chieftain. [*Yeats's note.*] Cf. 'Khan' in J. C. Mangan's 'A Vision of Connaught in the Thirteenth Century', l.17 (Vol. II).
5 *Danaan*: Tuath De Danaan means the Race of the Gods of Dana. Dana was the mother of all the ancient gods of Ireland. They were the powers of light and life and warmth, and did battle with the Fomoroh, or powers of night and death and cold. Robbed of offerings and honour, they have gradually dwindled in the popular imagination until they have become the Faeries. [*Yeats's note.*]

'Bringing me honeyed, wandering thought
'Of noble Usheen and his fame,
'Of battles broken by his hands,
'Of stories builded by his words
'That are like coloured Asian birds
'At evening in their rainless lands.'

O Patrick, by your brazen bell,[1]
There was no limb of mine but fell
Into a desperate gulph of love!
'You only will I wed,' I cried,
'And I will make a thousand songs,
'And set your name all names above,
'And captives bound with leathern thongs
'Shall kneel and praise you, one by one,
'At evening in my western dun.'[2]

'O Usheen, mount by me and ride
'To shores by the wash of the tremulous tide,
'Where men have heaped no burial mounds,
'And the days pass by like a wayward tune,
'Where broken faith has never been known,
'And the blushes of first love never have flown;
'And there I will give you a hundred hounds,—
'No mightier creatures bay at the moon—
'And a hundred robes of murmuring silk,
'And a hundred calves and a hundred sheep
'Whose long wool whiter than sea froth flows,
'And a hundred spears and a hundred bows,
'And oil and wine and honey and milk,
'And always never-anxious sleep;
'While a hundred youths, mighty of limb,
'By knowing nor tumult nor hate nor strife,
'And a hundred maidens, merry as birds,
'Who when they dance to a fitful measure
'Have a speed like the speed of the salmon herds,
'Shall follow your horn and obey your whim,
'And you shall know the Danaan leisure:

---

1 O *Patrick, by your brazen bell*: St Patrick was supposed to have introduced these bells into Ireland.
2 *dun*: 'stronghold'.

'And Neave be with you for a wife.'

Then she sighed gently, 'It grows late,
'And many a mile is the faery state,
'Where I would be when the white moon climbs,
'The red sun falls, and the world grows dim.'

And then I mounted and she bound me
With her triumphing arms around me,
And whispering to herself enwound me;
But when the horse had felt my weight,
He shook himself, and neighed three times:
Caolte, Conan, and Finn came near,
And wept, and raised their lamenting hands,
And bid me stay, with many a tear;
But we rode out from the human lands.

In what far kingdom do you go,
Ah, Fenians, with the shield and bow?
Or are you phantoms white as snow,
Whose lips had life's most prosperous glow?
O you, with whom in sloping valleys,
Or down the dewy forest alleys,
I chased at morn the flying deer,
With whom I hurled the hurrying spear,
And heard the foemen's bucklers rattle,
And broke the heaving ranks of battle!
And Bran, Sgeolan, and Lomair,
Where are you with your long rough hair?
You go not where the red deer feeds,
Nor tear the foemen from their steeds.

ST. PATRICK.
Boast not, nor mourn with drooping head
Companions long accurst and dead.
And hounds for centuries dust and air.

USHEEN.
We galloped over the glossy sea:
I know not if days passed or hours,
For Neave sang continually

429

Danaan songs, and their dewy showers
Of pensive laughter, unhuman sound,
Lulled weariness, and softly round
My human sorrow her white arms wound.

On! on! and now a hornless deer
Passed by us, chased by a phantom hound
All pearly white, save one red ear;
And now a maiden rode like the wind
With an apple of gold in her tossing hand,
And with quenchless eyes and fluttering hair
A beautiful young man followed behind.[1]

'Were these two born in the Danaan land,
'Or have they breathed the mortal air?'

'Vex them no longer,' Neave said,
And sighing bowed her gentle head,
And sighing laid the pearly tip
Of one long finger on my lip.

But now the moon like a white rose shone
In the pale west, and the sun's rim sank,
And clouds arrayed their rank on rank
About his fading crimson ball:
The floor of Emen's hosting hall[2]
Was not more level than the sea,
As full of loving phantasy,
And with low murmurs we rode on,
Where many a trumpet-twisted shell
That in immortal silence sleeps
Dreaming of her own melting hues,
Her golds, her ambers, and her blues,
Pierced with soft light the shallowing deeps.
But now a wandering land breeze came
And a far sound of feathery quires;
It seemed to blow from the dying flame,

1 *a hornless deer...*: the mythical images in this stanza are also in Micheál Coimín's original. In a headnote to 'He mourns for the Change that has come upon him and his Beloved...' Yeats interpets them as 'images of the desire of the man, and of the desire of woman "which is for the desire of the man"' (*The Dome*, June 1897).
2 *Emen's hosting hall*: The capital of the Red Branch kings. [Yeats's note.]

They seemed to sing in the smouldering fires:
The horse towards the music raced,
Neighing along the lifeless waste;
Like sooty fingers, many a tree
Rose ever out of the warm sea;
And they were trembling ceaselessly,
As though they all were beating time,
Upon the centre of the sun,
To that low laughing woodland rhyme.
And, now our wandering hours were done,
We cantered to the shore, and knew
The reason of the trembling trees:
Round every branch the song-birds flew,
Or clung thereon like swarming bees;
While round the shore a million stood
Like drops of frozen rainbow light,
And pondered, in a soft vain mood,
Upon their shadows in the tide,
And told the purple deeps their pride,
And murmured snatches of delight;
And on the shores were many boats
With bending sterns and bending bows,
And carven figures on their prows
Of bitterns, and fish-eating stoats,[1]
And swans with their exultant throats:
And where the woods and waters meet
We tied the horse in a leafy clump,
And Neave blew three merry notes
Out of a little silver trump;
And then an answering whisper flew
Over the bare and woody land,
A whisper of impetuous feet,
And ever nearer, nearer grew;
And from the woods rushed out a band
Of men and maidens, hand in hand,
And singing, singing all together;
Their brows were white as the fragrant milk,
Their brattas[2] made out of yellow silk,
And trimmed with many a crimson feather:

---

1 *stoats*: larger weasels; the European ermines.
2 *brattas*: robes, cloaks.

And when they saw that the bratta I wore
Was dim with the mire of a mortal shore,
They fingered it and gazed on me
And laughed like murmurs of the sea;
But Neave with a swift distress
Bid them away and hold their peace;
And when they heard her voice they ran
And knelt them, every maid and man,
And kissed, as they would never cease,
Her pearl-pale hand and the hem of her dress.
She bade them bring us to the hall
Where Angus[1] dreams, from sun to sun,
A Druid dream of the end of days
When the stars are to wane and the world be done;

They lead us by long and shadowy ways
Where drops of dew in myriads fall,
And tangled creepers every hour
Blossom in some new crimson flower;
And once a sudden laughter sprang
From all their lips, and once they sang
Together, while the dark woods rang,
And made in all their distant parts,
With boom of bees in honey marts,
A rumour of delighted hearts.
And once a maiden by my side
Gave me a harp, and bid me sing,
And touch the laughing silver string;
But when I sang of human joy
A sorrow wrapped each merry face,
And, Patrick! by your beard, they wept,
Until one came, a tearful boy;
'A sadder creature never stept
'Than this strange human bard,' he cried;
And caught the silver harp away,
And, weeping over the white strings, hurled
It down in a leaf-hid, hollow place
That kept dim waters from the sky;
And each one said with a long, long sigh,

---

1 *Angus*: The god of youth, beauty, and poetry. He reigned in Tir-nan-Oge, the country of the young. [*Yeats's note.*]

'O saddest harp in all the world,
'Sleep there till the moon and the stars die!'

And now still sad we came to where
A beautiful young man dreamed within
A house of wattles, clay, and skin;
One hand upheld his beardless chin,
And one a sceptre flashing out
Wild flames of red and gold and blue,
Like to a merry wandering rout
Of dancers leaping in the air;
And men and maidens knelt them there
And showed their eyes with teardrops dim,
And with low murmurs prayed to him,
And kissed the sceptre with red lips,
And touched it with their finger-tips.

He held that flashing sceptre up.
'Joy drowns the twilight in the dew,
'And fills with stars night's purple cup,
'And wakes the sluggard seeds of corn,
'And stirs the young kid's budding horn,
'And makes the infant ferns unwrap,
'And for the peewit paints his cap,
'And rolls along the unwieldy sun,
'And makes the little planets run:
'And if joy were not on the earth,
'There were an end of change and birth,
'And earth and heaven and hell would die,
'And in some gloomy barrow lie
'Folded like a frozen fly;
'Then mock at Death and Time with glances
'And waving arms and wandering dances.

'Men's hearts of old were drops of flame
'That from the saffron morning came,
'Or drops of silver joy that fell
'Out of the moon's pale twisted shell;
'But now hearts cry that hearts are slaves,
'And toss and turn in narrow caves;
'But here there is nor law nor rule,

'Nor have hands held a weary tool;
'And here there is nor Change nor Death,
'But only kind and merry breath,
'For joy is God and God is joy.'
With one long glance on maid and boy
And the thin crescent of the moon,
He fell into a Druid swoon.

And in a wild and sudden dance
We mocked at Time and Fate and Chance,
And swept out of the wattled hall
And came to where the dewdrops fall
Among the foamdrops of the sea,
And there we hushed the revelry;
And, gathering on our brows a frown,
Bent all our swaying bodies down,
And to the waves that glimmer by
That sloping green De Danaan sod
Sang, 'God is joy and joy is God,
'And things that have grown sad are wicked,
'And things that fear the dawn of the morrow,
'Or the gray wandering osprey Sorrow.'

We danced to where in the winding thicket
The damask roses, bloom on bloom,
Like crimson meteors hang in the gloom,
And bending over them softly said,
Bending over them in the dance,
With a swift and friendly glance
From dewy eyes: 'Upon the dead
'Fall the leaves of other roses,
'On the dead, dim earth encloses:
'But never, never on our graves,
'Heaped beside the glimmering waves,
'Shall fall the leaves of damask roses.
'For neither Death nor Change comes near us,
'And all listless hours fear us,
'And we fear no dawning morrow,
'Nor the gray wandering osprey Sorrow.'

The dance wound through the windless woods—

The ever-summered solitudes—
Until the tossing arms grew still
Upon the woody central hill;
And, gathered in a panting band,
We flung on high each waving hand,
And sang unto the starry broods:
In our raised eyes there flashed a glow
Of milky brightness to and fro
As thus our song arose: 'You stars,
'Across your wandering ruby cars
'Shake the loose reins: you slaves of God,
'He rules you with an iron rod,
'He holds you with an iron bond,
'Each one woven to the other,
'Each one woven to his brother
'Like bubbles in a frozen pond;
'But we in a lonely land abide
'Unchainable as the dim tide,
'With hearts that know nor law nor rule,
'And hands that hold no wearisome tool,
'Folded in love that fears no morrow,
'Nor the gray wandering osprey Sorrow.'

O Patrick! for a hundred years
I chased upon that woody shore
The deer, the badger, and the boar.
O Patrick! for a hundred years
At evening on the glimmering sands,
Beside the piled-up hunting spears,
These now outworn and withered hands
Wrestled among the island bands.
O Patrick! for a hundred years
We went a-fishing in long boats
With bending sterns and bending bows,
And carven figures on their prows
Of bitterns and fish-eating stoats.
O Patrick! for a hundred years
The gentle Neave was my wife;
But now two things devour my life—
The things that most of all I hate—
Fasting and prayers.

*   *   *

from Book II.

. . . .
                              We sought the part
That was most distant from the door; green slime
Made the way slippery, and time on time
Showed prints of sea-born scales, while down through it
The captives' journeys to and fro were writ
Like a small river, and, where feet touched, came
A momentary gleam of phosphorus flame.
Under the deepest shadows of the hall
That maiden found a ring hung on the wall,
And in the ring a torch, and with its flare
Making a world about her in the air,
Passed under a dim doorway, out of sight,
And came again, holding a second light
Burning between her fingers, and in mine
Laid it and sighed: I held a sword whose shine
No centuries could dim: and a word ran
Thereon in Ogham[1] letters, 'Mananan':[2]
That sea-god's name, who in a deep content
Sprang dripping, and, with captive demons sent
Out of the seven-fold seas, built the dark hall
Rooted in foam and clouds, and cried to all
The mightier masters of a mightier race;
And at his cry there came no milk-pale face[3]
Under a crown of thorns and dark with blood,
But only exultant faces.

                              Neave stood
With bowed head, trembling when the white blade shone,
But she whose hours of tenderness were gone
Had neither hope nor fear. I bade them hide
Under the shadows till the tumults died
Of the loud crashing and earth shaking fight,
Lest they should look upon some dreadful sight;
And thrust the torch between the slimy flags.
A dome made out of endless carven jags,

---

1 Ogham: ancient Irish alphabet of twenty characters.
2 *'Mananan'*: Mananan, the sea-god, was a son of Lir, the infinite waters. [*Yeats's note.*] He is a shape-shifter.
3 *milk-pale face*: the face of Christ.

Where shadowy face flowed into shadowy face,
Looked down on me; and in the self-same place
I waited hour by hour, and the high dome
Windowless, pillarless, multitudinous home
Of faces, waited; and the leisured gaze
Was loaded with the memory of days
Buried and mighty: when through the great door
The dawn came in, and glimmered on the floor
With a pale light, I journeyed round the hall
And found a door deep sunken in the wall,
The least of doors; beyond on a dim plain
A little runnel made a bubbling strain,
And on the runnel's stony and bare edge
A dusky demon dry as a withered sedge
Swayed, crooning to himself an unknown tongue:
In a sad revelry he sang and swung
Bacchant and mournful, passing to and fro
His hand along the runnel's side, as though
The flowers still grew there: far on the sea's waste;
Shaking and waving, vapour vapour chased,
While high frail cloudlets, fed with a green light,
Like drifts of leaves, immovable and bright,
Hung in the passionate dawn. He slowly turned:
A demon's leisure: eyes, first white, now burned
Like wings of kingfishers; and he arose
Barking. We trampled up and down with blows
Of sword and brazen battle-axe, while day
Gave to high noon and noon to night gave way;
But when at withering of the sun he knew
The Druid sword of Mananan, he grew
To many shapes; I lunged at the smooth throat
Of a great eel; it changed, and I but smote
A fir-tree roaring in its leafless top;
I held a dripping corpse, with livid chop
And sunken shape, against my face and breast,
When I had torn it down; but when the west
Surged up in plumy fire, I lunged and drave
Through heart and spine, and cast him in the wave,
Lest Neave shudder.

Full of hope and dread
Those two came carrying wine and meat and bread,
And healed my wounds with unguents out of flowers
That feed white moths by some De Danaan shrine;
Then in that hall, lit by the dim sea shine,
We lay on skins of otters, and drank wine,
Brewed by the sea gods, from huge cups that lay
Upon the lips of sea gods in their day;
And then on heaped-up skins of otters slept.
But when the sun once more in saffron stept,
Rolling his flagrant wheel out of the deep,
We sang the loves and angers without sleep,
And all the exultant labours of the strong:

But now the lying clerics murder song
With barren words and flatteries of the weak.
In what land do the powerless turn the beak
Of ravening Sorrow, or the hand of Wrath?
For all your croziers, they have left the path
And wander in the storms and clinging snows,
Hopeless for ever: ancient Usheen knows,
For he is weak and poor and blind, and lies
On the anvil of the world.

ST. PATRICK.
Be still: the skies
Are choked with thunder, lightning, and fierce wind,
For God has heard and speaks His angry mind;
Go cast your body on the stones and pray,
For He has wrought midnight and dawn and day.

USHEEN.
Saint, do you weep? I hear amid the thunder
The Fenian horses—armour torn asunder—
Laughter and cries: the armies clash and shock—
All is done now—I see the ravens flock—
Ah, cease, you mournful, laughing Fenian horn!

We feasted for three days. On the fourth morn
I found, dropping sea foam on the wide stair,
And hung with slime, and whispering in his hair,

That demon dull and unsubduable;
And once more to a day-long battle fell,
And at the sundown threw him in the surge,
To lie until the fourth morn saw emerge
His new healed shape: and for a hundred years
So warred, so feasted, with nor dreams, nor fears,
Nor languor nor fatigue: an endless feast,
An endless war.

          The hundred years had ceased;
I stood upon the stair: the surges bore
A beech bough to me, and my heart grew sore,
Remembering how I stood by white-haired Finn
While the woodpecker made a merry din,
The hare leaped in the grass.

          Young Neave came
Holding that horse, and sadly called my name;
I mounted, and we passed over the lone
And drifting grayness, while this monotone,
Surly and distant, mixed inseparably
Into the clangour of the wind and sea.

'I hear my soul drop down into decay,
'And Mananan's dark tower, stone by stone,
'Gather sea slime and fall the seaward way,
'And the moon goad the waters night and day,
    'That all be overthrown.

'But till the moon has taken all, I wage
'War on the mightiest men under the skies,
'And they have fallen or fled, age after age:
'Light is man's love and lighter is man's rage;
    'His purpose drifts away.'

And then lost Neave murmured, 'Love, we go
'To the Island of Forgetfulness, for lo!
'The Islands of Dancing and of Victories
'Are empty of all power.'

'And which of these
'Is the Island of Content?'

'None know,' she said;
And on my bosom laid her weeping head.

The Lake Isle of Innisfree

(1890)[1]

I will arise and go now, and go to Innisfree,
And a small cabin build there, of clay and wattles made;
Nine bean rows will I have there, a hive for the honey bee,
And live alone in the bee-loud glade.

And I shall have some peace there, for peace comes dropping slow,
Dropping from the veils of the morning to where the cricket sings;
There midnight's all a-glimmer, and noon a purple glow,
And evening full of the linnets' wings.

I will arise and go now, for always night and day
I hear lake water lapping with low sounds on the shore;
While I stand on the roadway or on the pavements grey,
I hear it in the deep heart's core.

The Sorrow of Love

(1892)[2]

The quarrel of the sparrows in the eaves,
    The full round moon and the star-laden sky,
And the loud song of the ever-singing leaves
    Had hid away earth's old and weary cry.

And then you came with those red mournful lips,
    And with you came the whole of the world's tears,
And all the sorrows of her labouring ships,
    And all burden of her myriad years.

---

1 Published in *The National Observer*, 13 Dec. 1890.
2 From *The Countess Kathleen and Various Legends and Lyrics* (1892).

And now the sparrows warring in the eaves,
    The crumbling moon, the white stars in the sky,
And the loud chanting of the unquiet leaves,
    Are shaken with earth's old and weary cry.

Apologia addressed to Ireland in the coming days

(1892)[1]

Know that I would accounted be
True brother of that company
Who sang to sweeten Ireland's wrong,
Ballad and story, rann[2] and song;
Nor be I any less of them,
Because the red rose bordered hem
Of her whose history began
Before God made the angelic clan,
Trails all about the written page,
For in the world's first blossoming age
The light fall of her flying feet
Made Ireland's heart begin to beat,
And still the starry candles flare
To help her light foot here and there,
And still the thoughts of Ireland brood,
Upon her holy quietude.

Nor may I less be counted one
With Davis, Mangan, Ferguson,[3]
Because to him who ponders well
My rhymes more than their rhyming tell
Of the dim wisdoms old and deep,
That God gives unto man in sleep.
For round about my table go
The magical powers to and fro.
In flood and fire and clay and wind,
They huddle from man's pondering mind,
Yet he who treads in austere ways

---

1 From *The Countess Kathleen and Various Legends and Lyrics* (1892).
2 rann: Irish for 'verse' or 'quatrain'.
3 Davis, Mangan, Ferguson: Thomas Davis (1814–45), James Clarence Mangan (1803–49) and Samuel Ferguson (1810–86), the three major figures of the nineteenth century associated with Irish cultural nationalism (see Vol. II). Yeats had been rebuked by nationalists for being disparaging about Davis's ballad poetry.

May surely meet their ancient gaze.
Man ever journeys on with them
After the red rose bordered hem.
Ah, fairies, dancing under the moon,
A druid land, a druid tune!

While still I may I write out true
The love I lived, the dream I knew.
From our birthday until we die,
Is but the winking of an eye.
And we, our singing and our love,
The mariners of night above,
And all the wizard things that go
About my table to and fro,
Are passing on to where may be,
In truth's consuming ecstasy,
No place for love and dream at all,
For God goes by with white foot-fall.
I cast my heart into my rhymes,
That you in the dim coming times
May know how my heart went with them
After the red rose bordered hem.

The Fiddler of Dooney

(1892)[1]

When I play on my fiddle in Dooney,
Folk dance like a wave o' the sea—
My brother is priest of Kilbarnet,
My cousin of Rosnaree.

I passed my brother and cousin,
They read in a book of prayer,
I read in a book of songs
I bought at the Sligo fair.

When we come at the close of Time
To Peter sitting in state,
He will smile on the three old spirits,

---

1 First published in *The Bookman*, Dec. 1892

But call me first through the gate.

For the good are always the merry,
Save by an evil chance,
And the merry love the fiddle,
And the merry love to dance.

And the folk there when they spy me
Will all come up to me,
With, 'Here is the fiddler of Dooney,'
And dance like a wave o' the sea.

The Hosting of the Sidhe

(1893)[1]

The powerful and wealthy called the gods of ancient Ireland the Tuatha De Danaan, or the Tribes of the goddess Danu, but the poor called them, and still sometimes call them, the Sidhe, from Aes Sidhe, or Sluagh Sidhe, the people of the Faery Hills, as these words are usually explained. Sidhe is also Gaelic for wind, and certainly the Sidhe have much to do with the wind. They journey in whirling winds, the winds that were called the dance of the daughters of Herodias in the Middle Ages, Herodias doubtless taking the place of some old goddess. When the country people see the leaves whirling on the road they bless themselves, because they believe the Sidhe to be passing by....

... The great of the old times are among the Tribes of Danu, and are kings and queens among them. Caolte was a companion of Fiann; and years after his death he appeared to a king in a forest, and was a flaming man, that he might lead him in the darkness. When the king asked him who he was, he said, 'I am your candlestick.' I do not remember where I have read this story, and I have maybe, half forgotten it. Niam was a beautiful woman of the Tribes of Danu, that led Oisin to the Country of the Young, as their country is called; I have written about her in 'The Wanderings of Usheen;' and he came back, at last, to bitterness and weariness.

Knocknarea is in Sligo, and the country people say that Maeve, still a great queen of the western Sidhe, is buried in the cairn of stones upon it. I have written of Clooth-na-bare in 'The Celtic Twilight.' She 'went all over the world, seeking a lake deep enough to drown her faery life, of which she had grown weary, leaping from hill to hill, and setting up a cairn of stones wherever her feet lighted, until, at last, she found the deepest water in the world in little Lough Ia, on the top of the bird mountain, in

---

1 First published in *The National Observer*, 7 Oct. 1893. The version provided here is from *The Wind Among the Reeds* (1899).

Sligo.' I forget, now, where I heard this story, but it may have been from a priest at Collooney. Clooth-na-Bare would mean the old woman of Bare, but is evidently a corruption of Cailleac Bare, the old woman Bare, who, under the names Bare, and Berah, and Beri, and Verah, and Dera, and Dhira, appears in the legends of many places....

> The host is riding from Knocknarea
> And over the grave of Clooth-na-bare;
> Caolte tossing his burning hair
> And Niamh calling *Away, come away:*
> *Empty your heart of its mortal dream.*
> *The winds awaken, the leaves whirl round,*
> *Our cheeks are pale, our hair is unbound,*
> *Our breasts are heaving, our eyes are a-gleam,*
> *Our arms are waving, our lips are apart;*
> *And if any gaze on our rushing band,*
> *We come between him and the deed of his hand,*
> *We come between him and the hope of his heart.*
> The host is rushing 'twixt night and day,
> And where is there hope or deed as fair?
> Caolte tossing his burning hair,
> And Niamh calling *Away, come away.*

'The Valley of the Black Pig'

(1896)[1]

The Irish peasantry have for generations comforted themselves, in their misfortunes, with visions of a great battle, to be fought in a mysterious valley, called 'The Valley of the Black Pig,' and to break at last the power of their enemies. A few years ago, in the barony of Lisadell, in county Sligo, an old man would fall entranced upon the ground from time to time, and rave out a description of the battle; and I have myself heard said that the girths shall rot from the bellies of the horses, because of the few men that shall come alive out of the vallies.

> The dews drop slowly; the dreams gather; unknown spears
> Suddenly hurtle before my dream-awakened eyes;
> And then the clash of fallen horsemen, and the cries
> Of unknown perishing armies beat about my ears.
> We, who are labouring by the cromlech on the shore,
> The gray cairn on the hill, when day sinks drowned in dew,

---

1 First published in *The Savoy*, April 1896.

Being weary of the world's empires, bow down to you,
Master of the still stars, and of the flaming door.

The Song of Wandering Aengus[1]

(1897)[2]

I went out to the hazel wood,
Because a fire was in my head,
And cut and peeled a hazel wand,
And hooked a berry to a thread;
And when white moths were on the wing,
And moth-like stars were flickering out,
I dropped the berry in a stream,
And caught a little silver trout.

When I had laid it on the floor,
I went to blow the fire a-flame;
But something rustled on the floor,
And someone called me by my name:
It had become a glimmering girl
With apple-blossom in her hair
Who called me by my name and ran
And faded through the brightening air.

---

1 The Tribes of the goddess Danu can take all shapes, and those that are in the waters take often the shape of fish. A woman of Burren, in Galway, says, 'There are more of them in the sea than on the land, and they sometimes try to come over the side of the boat in the form of fishes, for they can take their choice shape.' At other times they are beautiful women; and another Galway woman says, 'Surely those things are in the sea as well as on land. My father was out fishing one night off Tyrone. And something came beside the boat that had eyes shining like candles. And then a wave came in, and a storm rose all in a minute, and whatever was in the wave, the weight of it had like to sink the boat. And then they saw that it was a woman in the sea that had the shining eyes. So my father went to the priest, and he bid him always to take a drop of holy water and a pinch of salt out in the boat with him, and nothing could harm him.'

The poem was suggested to me by a Greek folk song; but the folk belief of Greece is very like that of Ireland, and I certainly thought, when I wrote it, of Ireland, and of the spirits that are in Ireland. An old man who was cutting a quickset hedge near Gort, in Galway, said, only the other day, 'One time I was cutting timber over in Inchy, and about eight o'clock one morning, when I got there, I saw a girl picking nuts, with her hair hanging down over her shoulders; brown hair; and she had a good, clean face, and she was tall, and nothing on her head, and her dress no way gaudy, but simple. And when she felt me coming she gathered herself up, and was gone, as if the earth had swallowed her up. And I followed her, and looked for her, but I never could see her again from that day to this, never again.'

The county Galway people use the word 'clean' in its old sense of fresh and comely. [Yeats's note.]

2 First published in *The Sketch*, 4 Aug. 1897. This version is from *The Wind Among the Reeds* (1899).

Though I am old with wandering
Through hollow lands and hilly lands,
I will find out where she has gone,
And kiss her lips and take her hands;
And walk among long dappled grass,
And pluck till time and times are done,
The silver apples of the moon,
The golden apples of the sun.

To the Secret Rose

(1897)[1]

Far off, most secret, and inviolate Rose,
Enfold me in my hour of hours; where those
Who sought thee at the Holy Sepulchre,
Or in the wine-vat, dwell beyond the stir
And tumult of defeated dreams; and deep
Among pale eyelids heavy with the sleep
Men have named beauty. Your great leaves enfold
The ancient beards, the helms of ruby and gold
Of the crowned Magi; and the king whose eyes
Saw the Pierced Hands and Rood of Elder rise
In druid vapour and make the torches dim;
Till vain frenzy awoke and he died;[2] and him
Who met Fand[3] walking among flaming dew,
By a grey shore where the wind never blew,

---

1 First published in *The Savoy*, Sept. 1896. This version is the poem in *The Secret Rose* (1897).

2 *Vain frenzy ... died*: after killing his son, whom Emer in her envy sent out to fight her former lover, Cú Chullain, mad with grief, fought 'the ungovernable sea' (hence, perhaps, Hamlet's 'to take arms against a sea of troubles' in Shakespeare's most famous soliloquy [III. i. 59]).

3 *Fand*: I have imagined Cuchullain meeting Fand 'walking among flaming dew.' The story of their love is one of the most beautiful of our old tales. Two birds, bound one to another with a chain of gold, came to a lake side where Cuchullain and the host of Uladh was encamped, and sang so sweetly that all the host fell into a magical sleep. Presently they took the shape of two beautiful women, and cast a magical weakness upon Cuchullain, in which he lay for a year. At the year's end an Aengus, who was probably Aengus the master of love, one of the greatest children of the goddess Danu, came and sat upon his bedside, and sang how Fand, the wife of Mannannan, the master of the sea, and of the islands of the dead, loved him; and that if he would come into the country of the gods, where there was wine and gold and silver, Fand, and Laban her sister, would heal him of his magical weakness. Cuchullain went to the country of the gods, and, after being for a month the lover of Fand, made her a promise to meet her at a place called 'the Yew at the Strand's End,' and came back to the earth. Emer, his mortal wife, won his love again, and Mannannan came to 'the Yew at the Strand's End,' and carried Fand away. When Cuchullain saw her going, his love for her fell upon him again, and he went mad, and wandered among the mountains without food or drink, until he was at last cured by a Druid drink of forgetfulness.... [*Yeats's note in* The Wind Among the Reeds.]

And lost the world and Emir for a kiss;
And him who drove the gods out of their liss[1]
And till a hundred morns had flowered red
Feasted, and wept the barrows of his dead;
And the proud dreaming king who flung the crown
And sorrow away, and calling bard and clown
Dwelt among wine-stained wanderers in deep woods;[2]
And him who sold tillage and house and goods,[3]
And sought through lands and islands numberless years
Until he found with laughter and with tears
A woman of so shining loveliness
That men threshed corn at midnight by a tress,
A little stolen tress. I too await
The hour of thy great wind of love and hate.
When shall the stars be blown about the sky,
Like the sparks blown out of a smithy, and die?
Surely thine hour has come, thy great wind blows,
Far off, most secret, and inviolate Rose?

---

1 *him who drove the gods out of their liss*: I have founded the man 'who drove the gods out of their Liss,' or fort, upon something I have read about Caolte after the battle of Gabra, when almost all his companions were killed, driving the gods out of their Liss, either at Osraighe, now Ossory, or at Eas Ruaidh, now Asseroe, a waterfall at Ballyshannon, where Ilbreac, one of the children of the goddess Danu, had a Liss ... [*Yeats's note in* The Wind Among the Reeds.]

2 *the proud dreaming king...*: Fergus, the son of Roigh, the legendary poet of 'the quest of the bull of Cualge,' as he is in the ancient story of Deirdre, and in modern poems by Ferguson. He married Nessa.... Presently, because of his great love, he gave up his throne to Conchobar, her son by another, and lived out his days, feasting, and fighting, and hunting.... [*Yeats's note in* The Wind Among the Reeds.]

3 *him who sold tillage, and house, and goods*: ... A young man 'saw a light before him on the high road. When he came as far, there was an open box on the road, and a light coming up out of it. He took up the box. There was a lock of hair in it. Presently he had to go to become the servant of a king for his living. There were eleven boys. When they were going out into the stable at ten o'clock, each of them took a light but he. He took no candle at all with him. Each of them went into his own stable. When he went into his stable he opened the box. He left it in a hole in the wall. The light was great. It was twice as much as in the other stables.' The king hears of it, and makes him show the box. The king says, 'You must go and bring me the woman to whom the hair belongs.' In the end, the young man, and not the king, marries the woman. [*Yeats's note in* The Wind Among the Reeds.] Yeats quotes from William Larminie's *West Irish Folk Tales and Romances*.

Aedh wishes for the Cloths of Heaven[1]

(1899)[2]

Had I the heavens' embroidered cloths,
Enwrought with golden and silver light,
The blue and the dim and the dark cloths
Of night and light and the half light,
I would spread the cloths under your feet:
But I, being poor, have only my dreams;
I have spread my dreams under your feet;
Tread softly because you tread on my dreams.

The Crucifixion of the Outcast[3]

(1894)[4]

A man, with thin brown hair and a pale face, half ran, half walked,
along the road that wound from the south to the Town of the Shelly
River. Many called him Cumhal, the son of Cormac, and many called
him the Swift, Wild Horse; and he was a gleeman, and he wore a
short parti-coloured doublet, and had pointed shoes, and a bulging
wallet. Also he was of the blood of the Ernaans, and his birth-place
was the Field of Gold; but his eating and sleeping places were the four
provinces of Eri, and his abiding place was not upon the ridge of the
earth. His eyes strayed from the Abbey tower of the White Friars and
the town battlements to a row of crosses which stood out against the
sky upon a hill a little to the eastward of the town, and he clenched
his fist, and shook it at the crosses. He knew they were not empty, for
the birds were fluttering about them; and he thought how, as like as
not, just such another vagabond as himself was hanged on one of
them; and he muttered: 'If it were hanging or bow-stringing, or ston-
ing or beheading, it would be bad enough. But to have the birds peck-
ing your eyes and the wolves eating your feet! I would that the red

---

1 ... It is probable that only students of the magical tradition will understand me when I say
that ... 'Aedh,' whose name is not merely the Irish form of Hugh, but the Irish for fire, is fire
burning by itself. To put it in a different way ... Aedh is the myrrh and frankinscence that the
imagination offers continually before all that it loves. [*Yeats's note.*]
2 From *The Wind Among the Reeds* (1899).
3 *The Crucifixion of the Outcast*: This story was suggested by the opening incidents of the
eleventh century poem, *The Vision of Maconglinne*. [*Yeats's note to the 1894 version.*]
4 First published in *The National Observer*, 24 March 1894. The version provided here is from
The Secret Rose (1897).

wind of the Druids had withered in his cradle the soldier of Dathi,[3] who brought the tree of death out of barbarous lands, or that the lightning, when it smote Dathi at the foot of the mountain, had smitten him also, or that his grave had been dug by the green-haired and green-toothed merrows deep at the roots of the deep sea.'

While he spoke, he shivered from head to foot, and the sweat came out upon his face, and he knew not why, for he had looked upon many crosses. He passed over two hills and under the battlemented gate, and then round by a left-hand way to the door of the Abbey. It was studded with great nails, and when he knocked at it, he roused the lay brother who was the porter, and of him he asked a place in the guest-house. Then the lay brother took a glowing turf on a shovel, and led the way to a big and naked outhouse strewn with very dirty rushes; and lighted a rush-candle fixed between two of the stones of the wall, and set the glowing turf upon the hearth and gave him two unlighted sods and a wisp of straw, and showed him a blanket hanging from a nail, and a shelf with a loaf of bread and a jug of water, and a tub in a far corner. Then the lay brother left him and went back to his place by the door. And Cumhal the son of Cormac began to blow upon the glowing turf, that he might light the two sods and the wisp of straw; but his blowing profited him nothing, for the sods and the straw were damp. So he took off his pointed shoes, and drew the tub out of the corner with the thought of washing the dust of the highway from his feet; but the water was so dirty that he could not see the bottom. He was very hungry, for he had not eaten all that day; so he did not waste much anger upon the tub, but took up the black loaf, and bit into it, and then spat out the bite, for the bread was hard and mouldy. Still he did not give way to his wrath, for he had not drunken these many hours; having a hope of heath beer or wine at his day's end, he had left the brooks untasted, to make his supper the more delightful. Now he put the jug to his lips, but he flung it from him straightway, for the water was bitter and ill-smelling. Then he gave the jug a kick, so that it broke against the opposite wall, and he took down the blanket to wrap it about him for the night. But no sooner did he touch it than it was alive with skipping fleas. At this, beside himself with anger, he rushed to the door of the guest-house, but the lay brother, being well accustomed to such outcries, had locked it on the outside; so Cumhal emptied the tub and began to beat the door with it, till the lay brother came to the door, and asked what ailed him, and why he woke him

1 *Dathi*: fifth-century king of Connacht; he was struck by lightning after occupying the tower of Formenus, King of Thrace, who lived in the Alps as a hermit. Dathi's Bough was a sacred tree in early Ireland.

out of sleep. 'What ails me!' shouted Cumhal, 'are not the sods as wet as the sands of the Three Headlands? and are not the fleas in the blanket as many as the waves of the sea and as lively? and is not the bread as hard as the heart of a lay brother who has forgotten God? and is not the water in the jug as bitter and as ill-smelling as his soul? and is not the foot-water the colour that shall be upon him when he has been charred in the Undying Fires?' The lay brother saw that the lock was fast, and went back to his niche, for he was too sleepy to talk with comfort. And Cumhal went on beating at the door, and presently he heard the lay brother's foot once more, and cried out at him, 'O cowardly and tyrannous race of friars, persecutors of the bard and the gleeman, haters of life and joy! O race that does not draw the sword and tell the truth! O race that melts the bones of the people with cowardice and with deceit!'

'Gleeman,' said the lay brother, 'I also make rhymes; I make many while I sit in my niche by the door, and I sorrow to hear the bards railing upon the friars. Brother, I would sleep, and therefore I make known to you that it is the head of the monastery, our gracious Coarb, who orders all things concerning the lodging of travellers.'

'You may sleep,' said Cumhal, 'I will sing a bard's curse on the Coarb.' And he set the tub upside down under the window, and stood upon it, and began to sing in a very loud voice. The singing awoke the Coarb, so that he sat up in bed and blew a silver whistle until the lay brother came to him. 'I cannot get a wink of sleep with that noise,' said the Coarb. 'What is happening?'

'It is a gleeman,' said the lay brother, 'who complains of the sods, of the bread, of the water in the jug, of the foot-water, and of the blanket. And now he is singing a bard's curse upon you, O brother Coarb, and upon your father and your mother, and your grandfather and your grandmother, and upon all your relations.'

'Is he cursing in rhyme?'

'He is cursing in rhyme, and with two assonances in every line of his curse.'

The Coarb pulled his night-cap off and crumpled it in his hands, and the circular brown patch of hair in the middle of his bald head looked like an island in the midst of a pond, for in Connaught they had not yet abandoned the ancient tonsure for the style then coming into use. 'If we do not somewhat,' he said, 'he will teach his curses to the children in the street, and the girls spinning at the doors, and to the robbers on the mountain of Gulben.'

'Shall I go then,' said the other, 'and give him dry sods, a fresh loaf, clean water in a jug, clean foot-water, and a new blanket, and make him swear by the blessed St. Benignus,[1] and by the sun and moon, that no bond be lacking, not to tell his rhymes to the children in the street, and the girls spinning at the doors, and the robbers on the mountain of Gulben?'

'Neither our blessed Patron nor the sun and the moon would avail at all,' said the Coarb: 'for to-morrow or the next day the mood to curse would come upon him, or a pride in those rhymes would move him, and he would teach his lines to the children, and the girls, and the robbers. Or else he would tell another of his craft how he fared in the guest-house, and he in his turn would begin to curse, and my name would wither. For learn there is no steadfastness of purpose upon the roads, but only under roofs, and between four walls. Therefore I bid you go and awaken Brother Kevin, Brother Dove, Brother Little Wolf, Brother Bald Patrick, Brother Bald Brandon, Brother James and Brother Peter. And they shall take the man, and bind him with ropes, and dip him in the river that he may cease to sing. And in the morning, lest this but make him curse the louder, we will crucify him.'

'The crosses are all full,' said the lay brother.

'Then we must make another cross. If we do not make an end of him another will, for who can eat and sleep in peace while men like him are going about the world? Ill should we stand before blessed St. Benignus, and sour would be his face when he comes to judge us at the Last Day, were we to spare an enemy of his when we had him under our thumb! Brother, the bards and the gleemen are an evil race, ever cursing and ever stirring up the people, and immoral and immoderate in all things, and heathen in their hearts, always longing after the Son of Lir, and Angus, and Bridget, and the Dagda, and Dana the Mother, and all the false gods of the old days; always making poems in praise of those kings and queens of the demons, Finvaragh of the Hill in the Plain, and Red Aodh of the Hill of the Shee, and Cleena of the Wave, and Eiveen of the Grey Rock, and him they call Don of the Vats of the Sea; and railing against God and Christ and the blessed Saints.' While he was speaking he crossed himself, and when he had finished he drew the nightcap over his ears, to shut out the noise, and closed his eyes, and composed himself to sleep.

The lay brother found Brother Kevin, Brother Dove, Brother Little Wolf, Brother Bald Patrick, Brother Bald Brandon, Brother James and Brother Peter sitting up in bed, and he made them get up. Then they bound Cumhal, and they dragged him to the river, and they dipped him in it at the place which was afterwards called Buckley's Ford.

---

1 *St. Benignus*: martyred saint of the second century.

'Gleeman,' said the lay brother, as they led him back to the guest-house, 'why do you ever use the wit which God has given you to make blasphemous and immoral tales and verses? For such is the way of your craft. I have, indeed, many such tales and verses well nigh by rote, and so I know that I speak true! And why do you praise with rhyme those demons, Finvaragh, Red Aodh, Cleena, Eiveen and Don? I, too, am a man of great wit and learning, but I ever glorify our gracious Coarb, and Benignus our Patron, and the princes of the province. My soul is decent and orderly, but yours is like the wind among the salley gardens. I said what I could for you, being also a man of many thoughts, but who could help such a one as you?'

'My soul, friend,' answered the gleeman, 'is indeed like the wind, and it blows me to and fro, and up and down, and puts many things into my mind and out of my mind, and therefore am I called the Swift, Wild Horse.' And he spoke no more that night, for his teeth were chattering with the cold.

The Coarb and the friars came to him in the morning, and bade him get ready to be crucified, and led him out of the guest-house. And while he still stood upon the step a flock of great grass-barnacles passed high above him with clanking cries. He lifted his arms to them and said, 'O great grass-barnacles, tarry a little, and mayhap my soul will travel with you to the waste places of the shore and to the ungovernable sea!' At the gate a crowd of beggars gathered about them, being come there to beg from any traveller or pilgrim who might have spent the night in the guest-house. The Coarb and the friars led the gleeman to a place in the woods at some distance, where many straight young trees were growing, and they made him cut one down and fashion it to the right length, while the beggars stood round them in a ring, talking and gesticulating. The Coarb then bade him cut off another and shorter piece of wood, and nail it upon the first. So there was his cross for him; and they put it upon his shoulder, for his crucifixion was to be on the top of the hill where the others were. A half-mile on the way he asked them to stop and see him juggle for them: for he knew, he said, all the tricks of Angus the Subtle-Hearted. The old friars were for pressing on, but the young friars would see him: so he did many wonders for them, even to the drawing of live frogs out of his ears. But after a while they turned on him, and said his tricks were dull and a shade unholy, and set the cross on his shoulders again. Another half-mile on the way, and he asked them to stop and hear him jest for them, for he knew, he said, all the jests of Conan the Bald, upon whose back a sheep's wool grew. And the young friars, when they had heard his merry tales, again bade him take up his cross, for it ill became them to listen to such follies. Another half-mile on the way, he asked them to stop and hear him sing the story of White-Breasted Deirdre, and how she endured many sorrows, and how the sons of Usna died to serve her. And the young friars were mad to hear him, but when he had ended, they grew angry, and beat him for waking forgotten longings in their hearts. So they set the cross upon his back, and hurried him to the hill.

When he was come to the top, they took the cross from him, and began to dig a hole to stand it in, while the beggars gathered round, and talked among themselves. 'I ask a favour before I die,' says Cumhal.

'We will grant you no more delays,' says the Coarb.

'I ask no more delays, for I have drawn the sword, and told the truth, and lived my vision, and am content.'

'Would you then confess?'

'By sun and moon, not I; I ask but to be let eat the food I carry in my wallet. I carry food in my wallet whenever I go upon a journey, but I do not taste of it unless I am well-nigh starved. I have not eaten now these two days.'

'You may eat, then,' says the Coarb, and he turned to help the friars dig the hole.

The gleeman took a loaf and some strips of cold fried bacon out of his wallet and laid them upon the ground. 'I will give a tithe to the poor,' says he, and he cut a tenth part from the loaf and the bacon. 'Who among you is the poorest?' And thereupon was a great clamour, for the beggars began the history of their sorrows and their poverty, and their yellow faces swayed like the Shelly River when the floods have filled it with water from the bogs.

He listened for a little, and, says he, 'I am myself the poorest, for I have travelled the bare road, and by the glittering footsteps of the sea; and the tattered doublet of particoloured cloth upon my back and the torn pointed shoes upon my feet have ever irked me, because of the towered city full of noble raiment which was in my heart. And I have been the more alone upon the roads and by the sea, because I heard in my heart the rustling of the rose-bordered dress of her who is more subtle than Angus, the Subtle-Hearted, and more full of the beauty of laughter than Conan the Bald, and more full of the wisdom of tears than White-Breasted Deirdre, and more lovely than a bursting dawn to them that are lost in the darkness. Therefore, I award the tithe to myself; but yet, because I am done with all things, I give it unto you.'

So he flung the bread and the strips of bacon among the beggars, and they fought with many cries until the last scrap was eaten. But meanwhile the friars nailed the gleeman to his cross, and set it upright in the hole, and shovelled the earth in at the foot, and trampled it level and hard. So then they went away, but the beggars stared on, sitting round the cross. But when the sun was sinking, they also got up to go, for the air was getting chilly. And as soon as they had gone a little way, the wolves, who had been showing themselves on the edge of a neighbouring coppice, came nearer, and the birds wheeled closer and closer. 'Stay, outcasts, yet a little while,' the crucified one called in a weak voice to the beggars, 'and keep the beasts and the birds from me.' But the beggars were angry because he had called them outcasts, so they threw stones and mud at him, and went their way. Then the wolves gathered at the foot of the cross, and the birds flew lower and lower. And presently the birds lighted all at once upon his head and arms and shoulders, and began to peck at him, and the wolves began to eat his feet. 'Outcasts,' he moaned, 'have you also turned against the outcast?'

The Adoration Of The Magi

(1897)[1]

I was sitting reading late into the night a little after my last meeting with Aherne,[2] when I heard a light knocking on my front door; and found upon the doorstep three very old men with stout sticks in their hands, who said they had been told I should be up and about, and that they were to tell me important things. I brought them into my study, and when the peacock curtains had closed behind us, I set their chairs for them close to the fire, for I saw that the frost was on their great-coats of frieze and upon the long beards that flowed almost to their waists. They took off their great-coats, and leaned over the fire warming their hands, and I saw that their clothes had much of the country of our time, but a little also, as it seemed to me, of the town life of a more courtly time. When they had warmed themselves; and they warmed themselves, I thought, less because of the cold of the night than because of a pleasure in warmth for the sake of warmth; they turned towards me, so that the light of the lamp fell full upon their

1 First published together with 'The Tables of the Law' in 1897.
2 *Aherne*: Owen Aherne is, like Michael Robartes, one of Yeats's fictional alter egos.

weather-beaten faces, and told the story I am about to tell. Now one talked and now another, and they often interrupted one another, with a desire, like that of peasants, when they tell a story, to leave no detail untold. When they had finished they made me take notes of whatever conversation they had quoted, so that I might have the exact words, and got up to go, and when I asked them where they were going and what they were doing and by what names I should call them, they would tell me nothing, except that they had been commanded to travel over Ireland continually, and upon foot and at night, that they might live close to the stones and the trees and at the hours when the immortals are awake.

I have let some years go by before writing out this story, for I am always in dread of the illusions which come of that inquietude of the veil of the Temple, which M. Mallarmé considers a characteristic of our times;[1] and only write it now because I have grown to believe that there is no dangerous idea, which does not become less dangerous when written out in sincere and careful English.

The three old men were three brothers, who had lived in one of the western islands from their early manhood, and had cared all their lives for nothing except for those classical writers and old Gaelic writers who expounded an heroic and simple life; night after night in winter, Gaelic story-tellers would chant old poems to them over the poteen; and night after night in summer, when the Gaelic story-tellers were at work in the fields or away at the fishing, they would read to one another Virgil and Homer, for they would not enjoy in solitude, but as the ancients enjoyed. At last a man who told them he was Michael Robartes came to them in a fishing-boat, like St. Brandan[2] drawn by some vision and called by some voice; and told them of the coming again of the gods and the ancient things; and their hearts, which had never endured the body and pressure of our time, but only of distant times, found nothing unlikely in anything he told them, but accepted all simply and were happy. Years passed, and one day; when the oldest of the old men, who had travelled in his youth and thought sometimes of other lands, looked out on the grey waters, on which the peasants see the dim outline of the Islands of the Young, the Happy Islands where the Gaelic heroes live the lives of Homer's Phæacians; a voice

1 *veil of the Temple*: at a reading given by his friend, the Symbolist poet and critic Arthur Symons, Yeats had written down a line by the French symbolist poet Stephan Mallarmé: 'The whole age is troubled by the trembling of the veil of the Temple'. Yeats would use the phrase as the title of his 1922 autobiographical collection.
2 *St. Brandan*: St. Brendan the Navigator (c. 486–578) Irish abbot renowned for his seafaring adventures.

came out of the air over the waters and told him of the death of Michael Robartes. While they were still mourning, the next oldest of the old men fell asleep whilst he was reading out the Fifth Eclogue of Virgil, and a strange voice spoke through him, and bid them set out for Paris, where a woman lay dying, who would reveal to them the secret names of the immortals, which can be perfectly spoken only when the mind is steeped in certain colours and certain sounds and certain odours; but at whose perfect speaking the immortals cease to be cries and shadows, and walk and talk with one like men and women.

They left their island, and were at first troubled at all they saw in the world, and came to Paris, and there the youngest met a person in a dream, who told him they were to wander about at hazard until the immortals, who would guide their footsteps, had brought them to a street and a house, which the person showed him in the dream. They wandered hither and thither for many days, until one morning they wandered into some narrow and shabby streets, on the south of the Seine, where women with pale faces and untidy hair looked at them out of the windows; and just as they were about to turn back because Wisdom could not have alighted in so foolish a neighbourhood, they came to the street and the house of the dream. The oldest of the old men, who still remembered some of the modern languages he had known in his youth, went up to the door and knocked, and when he had knocked, the next oldest of the old men said it was not a good house, and could not be the house they were looking for, and urged him to ask for some one who they knew was not there and go away. The door was opened by an old over-dressed woman, who said, 'O, you are her three cousins from Ireland. She has been expecting you all day.' The old men looked at one another and followed her upstairs, passing doors from which pale and untidy women thrust out their heads, and into a room where a beautiful woman lay asleep in a bed, with another woman sitting by her.

The old woman said: 'Yes, they have come at last; now she will be able to die in peace,' and went out.

'We have been deceived by Dhouls,' said one of the old men, for the immortals would not speak through a woman like this.'

'Yes,' said another, 'we have been deceived by Dhouls, and we must go away quickly.'

'Yes,' said the third, 'we have been deceived by Dhouls, but let us kneel down for a little, for we are by the death-bed of one who was beautiful.' They knelt down, and the woman who sat by the bed and seemed overcome with fear and awe, lowered her head. They watched for a little the face upon the pillow and wondered at its look, as of unquenchable desire, and at the porcelain-like refinement of the vessel in which so malevolent a flame had burned.

Suddenly the second oldest of the old men crowed like a cock, and until the room seemed to shake with the crowing. The woman in the bed still slept on in her death-like sleep, but the woman who sat by her head crossed herself and grew pale, and the youngest of the old men cried out: 'A Dhoul has gone into him, and we must begone or it will go into us also.' Before they could rise from their knees, a resonant chanting voice came from the lips that had crowed and said: 'I am not a Dhoul, but I am Hermes the Shepherd of the Dead, and I run upon the errands of the gods, and you have heard my sign, that has been my sign from the old days. Bow down before her from whose lips the secret names of the immortals, and of the things near their hearts, are about to come that the immortals may come again into the world. Bow down, and understand that when the immortals are about to overthrow the things that are to-day and bring the things that were yesterday, they have no one to help them, but one whom the things that are to-day have cast out. Bow down and very low, for they have chosen for their priestess, this woman in whose heart all follies have gathered, and in whose body all desires have awaked; this woman who has been driven out of Time and has lain upon the bosom of Eternity. After you have bowed down the old things shall be again, and another Argo shall carry heroes over the deep, and another Achilles beleaguer another Troy.'

The voice ended with a sigh, and immediately the old man awoke out of sleep, and said: 'Has a voice spoken through me, as it did when I fell asleep over my Virgil, or have I only been asleep?'

'A voice has spoken through you,' said the oldest of the old men. 'Where has your soul been while the voice was speaking through you?'

'I do not know where my soul has been, but I dreamed I was under the roof of a manger, and I looked down and I saw an ox and an ass; and I saw a red cock perching on the hay-rack; and a woman hugging a child; and three old men, in armour studded with rubies, kneeling with their heads bowed very low in front of the woman and the child. While I was looking the cock crowed and a man with wings on his heels swept up through the air, and as he passed me, cried out: 'Foolish old men, you had once all the wisdom of the stars.' I do not understand my dream or what it would have us do, but you who have heard the voice out of the wisdom of my sleep know what we have to do.'

Then the oldest of the old men told him they were to take the parchments they had brought with them out of their pockets and to spread them on the ground. When they had spread them on the ground they took out of their pockets their pens, made of three feathers which had fallen from the wing of the old eagle, that is believed to have talked of wisdom with St. Patrick.

'He meant, I think,' said the youngest of the old men, as he put their ink-bottles by the side of the rolls of parchment, 'that when people are good the world likes them and takes possession of them, and so eternity comes through people who are not good or who have been forgotten. Perhaps Christianity was good and the world liked it, so now it is going away and the immortals are beginning to awake.'

'What you say has no wisdom,' said the oldest of the old men, 'because if there are many immortals there cannot be only one immortal.'

Then the woman in the bed sat up and looked about her with wild eyes; and the oldest of the old men said: 'Lady, we have come to write down the names of the immortals,' and at his words a look of great joy came into her face. Presently she began to speak slowly, and yet eagerly, as though she knew she had but a little while to live, and, in English, with the accent of their own country; and she told them the secret names of the immortals of many lands, and of the colours, and odours, and weapons, and instruments of music and instruments of handicraft they held dearest; but most about the immortals of Ireland and of their love for the cauldron, and the whetstone, and the sword, and the spear, and the hills of the Shee,[1] and the horns of the moon, and the Grey Wind, and the Yellow Wind, and the Black Wind, and the Red Wind. Then she tossed feebly a while and moaned, and when she spoke again it was in so faint a murmur that the woman who sat by the bed leaned down to listen, and while she was listening the spirit went out of the body.

Then the oldest of the old men said in French to the woman who was still bending over the bed: 'There must have been yet one name which she had not given us, for she murmured a name while the spirit was going out of the body,' and the woman said, 'She was merely murmuring over the name of a symbolist painter she was fond of. He used to go to something he called the Black Mass, and it was he who

---

1 *the Shee*: The powerful and wealthy called the gods of ancient Ireland the Tuatha De Danaan, or the Tribes of the goddess Danu, but the poor called them, and still sometimes call them, the Sidhe, from Aes Sidhe, or Sluagh Sidhe, the people of the Faery Hills, as these words are usually explained. Sidhe is also Gaelic for wind, and certainly the Sidhe have much to do with the wind. They journey in whirling winds, the winds that were called the dance of the daughters of Herodias in the Middle Ages. ... [*Yeat's note to* The Wind Among the Reeds.]

taught her to see visions and to hear voices. She met him for the first time a few months ago, and we have had no peace from that day because of her talk about visions and about voices. Why! It was only last night that I dreamed I saw a man with a red beard and red hair and dressed in red standing by my bedside. He held a rose in one hand and tore it in pieces with the other hand, and the petals drifted about the room, and became beautiful people who began to dance slowly. When I woke up I was all in a heat with terror.'

This is all the old man told me, and when I think of their speech and of their silence, of their coming and of their going, I am almost persuaded that had I gone out of the house, after they had gone out of it, I should have found no footsteps on the snow. They may, for all I or any man can say, have been themselves immortals: immortal demons, come to put an untrue story into my mind for some purpose I do not understand. Whatever they were, I have turned into a pathway which will lead me from them, and from the Order of the Alchemical Rose. I no longer live an elaborate and haughty life, but seek to lose myself among the prayers and the sorrows of the multitude. I pray best in poor chapels where frieze coats brush against me as I kneel, and when I pray against the demons I repeat a prayer which was made I know not how many centuries ago to help some poor Gaelic man or woman who had suffered with a suffering like mine:—

> *Seacht b-páidreacha fó seacht*
> *Chuir Muire faoi n-a Mac,*
> *Chuir Brighid faoi n-a brat,*
> *Chuir Dia faoi n-a neart,*
> *Eidir sinn 'san Sluagh. Sidhe,*
> *Eiair sinn, 'san Sluagh Gaoith.*

> [Seven Paters seven times,[1]
> Send Mary by her Son,
> Send Bridget by her mantle,
> Send God by His strength,
> Between us and the faery host,
> Between us and the demons of the air.]

---

1 *Seven Paters*: seven prayers.

The Autumn of the Flesh

(1898)[2]

Our thoughts and emotions are often but spray flung up from hidden tides that follow a moon no eye can see. I remember that when I first began to write I desired to describe outward things as vividly as possible, and took pleasure, in which there was, perhaps, a little discontent, in picturesque and declamatory books. And then, quite suddenly, I lost the desire of describing outward things, and found that I took little pleasure in a book unless it was spiritual and unemphatic. I did not then understand that the change was from beyond my own mind, but I understand now that writers are struggling all over Europe, though not often with a philosophic understanding of their struggle, against picturesque and declamatory way of writing, against that 'externality' which a time of scientific and political thought has brought into literature. This struggle has been going on for some years, but it has only just become strong enough to draw within itself the little inner world which alone seeks more than amusement in the arts. In France, where movements are more marked, because the people are pre-eminently logical, 'The Temptations of S. Anthony,' the last great dramatic invention of the old romanticism, contrasts very plainly with 'Axel,' the first great dramatic invention, of the new; and Maeterlinck has followed Count Villiers de L'Isle Adam.[1] Flaubert wrote unforgettable descriptions of grotesque, bizarre, and beautiful scenes and persons, as they show to the ear and to the eye, and crowded them with historic and ethnographical details; but Count Villiers de L'Isle Adam swept together, by what seemed a sudden energy, words, behind which glimmered a spiritual and passionate mood, as the flame glimmers behind the dusky blue and red glass in an Eastern lamp; and created persons from whom has fallen all even of personal characteristic except a thirst for that hour when all things shall pass away like a vapour, and a pride like that of the Magi following their star over many mountains; while Maeterlinck has plucked away even this thirst and this pride and set before us faint souls, naked and pathetic shadows already half vapour and sighing to one another

---

1 Part of a polemic with John Eglinton*, AE* and William Larminie, about legend as the subject matter of Irish drama, in the *Daily Express* (1898), published the following year as *Literary Ideals in Ireland*, edited by Eglinton.

2 *The Temptations of S. Anthony'... de L'Isle Adam: La tentation de Saint-Antoine* (1874) by Gustave Flaubert (1821–80); *Axel* (1890), by Philippe Auguste, comte de Villiers de l'Isle Adam (1838–89); Maurice Maeterlinck (1862–1949) met Villiers l'Isle Adam in Paris and was greatly influenced by his esotericism.

upon the border of the last abyss. There has been, as I think, a like change in French painting, for one sees everywhere, instead of the dramatic stories, and picturesque moments of an older school, frail and tremulous bodies unfitted for the labour of life, and landscape where subtle rhythms of colour and of form have overcome the clear outline of things as we see them in the labour of life.

There has been a like change in England, but it has come more gradually and is more mixed with lesser changes than in France. The poetry which found its expression in the poems of writers like Browning and of Tennyson, and even of writers, who are seldom classed with them, like Swinburne, and like Shelley in his earlier years, pushed its limits as far as possible, and tried to absorb into itself the science and politics, the philosophy and morality of its time; but a new poetry, which is always contracting its limits, has grown up under the shadow of the old. Rossetti began it, but was too much of a painter in his poetry to follow it with a perfect devotion; and it became a movement when Mr. Lang and Mr. Gosse and Mr. Dobson[1] devoted themselves to the most condensed of lyric forms, and when Mr. Bridges,[2] a more considerable poet, elaborated a rhythm too delicate for any but an almost bodiless emotion, and repeated over and over the most ancient notes of poetry, and none but these. The poets who followed have either, like Mr. Kipling,[3] turned from serious poetry altogether, and so passed out of the processional order, or speak out of some personal or spiritual passion in words and types and metaphors that draw one's imagination as far as possible from the complexities of modern life and thought. The change has been more marked in English painting, which, when intense enough to belong to the processional order, began to cast out things, as we see them in the labour of life, so much before French painting, that ideal painting is sometimes called English upon the Continent.

I see, indeed, in the arts of every country those faint lights and faint colours and faint outlines and faint energies which many call 'the decadence,' and which I, because I believe that the arts lie dreaming of things to come, prefer to call the autumn of the flesh. An Irish poet

1 *Mr. Lang and Mr. Gosse and Mr. Dobson*: Andrew Lang (1844–1912), English poet, novelist, anthropologist, Greek scholar and historian; Edmund Gosse (1849–1928), English poet and literary scholar (he summed up a lecture of Yeats's which he chaired at the Irish Literary Society in 1892, 'We did not so much haer a lecture as overhear a poet preparing a lecture'); Austin Dobson (1840–1921), English writer of popular light verse and literary historian.

2 *Mr. Bridges*: Robert Bridges (1844–1930), appointed poet laureate in 1913; gained his reputation with a series of 'Shorter Poems', published between 1873 and 1893. He was indeed a consummate metrist.

3 *Mr. Kipling*: Rudyard Kipling (1865–1936), author of popular stories and verse and winner of the Nobel Prize (1907).

whose rhythms are like the cry of a sea bird in autumn twilight has told its meaning in the line, 'The very sunlight's weary, and it's time to quit the plough.'[4] Its importance is the greater because it comes to us at the moment when we were beginning to be interested in many things which positive science, the interpreter of exterior law, has always denied: communion of mind with mind in thought and without words, foreknowledge in dreams and in visions, and the coming amongst us of the dead, and of much else. We are, it may be, at a crowning crisis of the world, at the moment when man is about to ascend, with his arms full of the wealth he has been so long gathering: the stairway he has been descending from the first days. The poets, if one may find their images in the Kalavala,[2] had not Homer's preoccupation with things, and he was not so full of their excitement as Virgil. Dante added to poetry a dialectic which, although he made it serve his laborious ecstacy, was the invention of minds trained by the labour of life, by a traffic among many things, and not a spontaneous expression of an interior life; while Shakespeare shattered the symmetry of verse and of drama that he might fill them with things and their accidental relations.

Each of these writers had come further down the stairway than those who had lived before him, but it was only with the modern poets, with Goethe and Wordsworth and Browning, that poetry gave up the right to consider all things in the world as a dictionary of types and symbols and began to call itself a critic of life and an interpreter of things as they are. Painting, music, science, politics, and even religion, because they have felt a growing belief that we know nothing but the fading and flowering of the world, have changed, too, in numberless elaborate ways. Man has wooed and won the world, and has fallen weary, and not, I think, for a time, but with a weariness that will not end until the last autumn, when the stars shall be blown away like withered leaves. He grew weary when he said—'These things that I touch and see and hear are alone real,' for he saw them without illusion at last, and found them but air and dust and moisture. And now he must be philosophical about everything, even about the arts, for he can only return the way he came and so escape from weariness, by philosophy. The arts are, I believe, about to take upon their shoulders the burdens that have lain upon the shoulders of priests, and to lead us back upon our journey by filling our thoughts with the essences of

---

1 *'Tis the twilight of the ages and it's time to quit the plough. / Oh, the very sunlight's weary ere it lightens up the dew'*: 'Carrowmore Lake' by AE (George Russell).

2 *the Kalavala*: an old Finnish epic poem which was recorded by Elias Lönnrot (1802–84) and published in 1835 and in 1849. It inspired Finnish nationalism.

things, and not with things.[1] We are about to substitute once more
the distillation of alchemy for the analysis of chemistry and for the
method of some other sciences; and certain of us are looking everywhere for the perfect alembic that no silver or golden drop may
escape. Mr. Symons has written lately on M. Mallarmé's method,
and has quoted him as saying that we should 'abolish the pretension,
æsthetically an error, despite its dominion over almost all the masterpieces, to enclose within the subtle pages other than—the horror
of the forest or the silent thunder in the leaves, not the intrinsic
dense wood of the trees,' and as desiring to substitute for 'the old
lyric afflatus or the enthusiastic personal direction of the phrase'
words 'that take light from mutual reflection, like an actual trail of
fire over precious stones,' and 'to make an entire word hitherto
unknown to the language' 'out of many vocables.'[2] Mr. Symons
understands these and other sentences to mean that poetry will
henceforth be a poetry of essences, separated one from another in little and intense poems. I think there will be much poetry of this kind,
because of an ever more arduous search for an almost disembodied
ecstacy, but I think we will not cease to write long poems, but rather
that we will write them more and more as our new belief makes the
world plastic under our hands again. I think that we will learn how
to describe at great length an old man wandering among enchanted
islands, his return home at last, his slow gathering vengeance, a flitting shape of a goddess, and a flight of arrows, and yet to make all
of these so different things 'take light by mutual reflection, like an
actual trail of fire over precious stones,' and become 'an entire
word,' the signature, or symbol of a mood of the divine imagination
as imponderable as 'the horror of the forest or the silent thunder in
the leaves.'[3]

---

1 This marks a change in Yeats's aesthetics; reviewing Katharine Tynan's *Shamrocks* in the *Irish Fireside* (12 March 1887), Yeats had echoed Goethe when he wrote 'I now write of the metaphors of things; some day I shall write of the things themselves'.
2 *Mr. Symons… vocables*: Yeats is misquoting from the essay on Mallarmé by his friend, the Symbolist poet and critic Arthur Symons (published in *The Fortnightly Review*, Nov. 1898, and in *The Symbolist Movement in Literature*—1899).
3 'take light.… the horror of the forest or the silent thunder in the leaves': Yeats once again misquotes Mallarmé through Arthur Symons.

'Dust Hath Closed Helen's Eye'[1]

(1899)[2]

I have been lately to a little group of houses, not many enough to be called a village, in the barony of Kiltartan in County Galway, whose name, Baile-laoi, is known through all the west of Ireland. There is the old square castle, Baile-laoi,[3] inhabited by a farmer and his wife, and a cottage where their daughter and their son-in-law live, and a little mill with an old miller, and old ash-trees throwing green shadows upon a little river and great stepping-stones. I went there two or three times last year to talk to the miller about Biddy Early, a wise woman that lived in Clare some years ago, and about her saying, 'There is a cure for all evil between the two mill-wheels of Baile-laoi,' and to find out from him or another whether she meant the moss between the running waters or some other herb. I have been there this summer, and I shall be there again before it is autumn, because Mary Hynes, a beautiful woman whose name is still a wonder by turf fires, died there sixty years ago; for our feet would linger where beauty has lived its life of sorrow to make us understand that it is not of the world. An old man brought me a little way from the mill and the castle, and down a long, narrow boreen that was nearly lost in brambles and sloe bushes, and he said, 'That is the little old foundation of the house, but the most of it is taken for building walls, and the goats have ate those bushes that are growing over it till they've got cranky, and they won't grow any more. They say she was the handsomest girl in Ireland, her skin was like dribbled snow'—he meant driven snow, perhaps,—'and she had blushes in her cheeks. She had five handsome brothers, but all are gone now!' I talked to him about a poem in Irish, Raftery,[4] a famous poet, made about her, and how it said, 'there is a strong cellar in Baile-laoi.' He said the strong cellar was the great hole where the river sank under ground, and he brought me to a deep pool, where an otter hurried away under a grey boulder, and told me that

---

1 *Duth Hath Closed Helen's Eye*: Thomas Nashe (1567–1601), 'In Time of Pestilence', l. 19. Thirty-eight years later, Yeats alluded to this poem in 'The Lady's Second Song' (*New Poems*, 1938) by counterpointing the sentiments of the song with a slight variation on Nashe's refrain line, '*Lord, have mercy on us!*'

2 First published in *The Dome*, Oct. 1899.

3 *the old square castle, Baile-laoi* Ballylee Castle, or Thoor Ballylee, as I have named it to escape from the too magnficient word 'castle,' is now my property, and I spend my summers or some part of them there. [*Yeats's note, added in 1924.*]

4 *Raftery*: Antoine Raiftearaí (1779–1835) was born in Killedan, near Kiltimagh, Co. Mayo. He was blinded by smallpox in childhood, and was illiterate. He features in Yeats's 'The Tower'.

many fish came up out of the dark water at early morning 'to taste the fresh water coming down from the hills.'

I first heard of the poem from an old woman who lives about two miles further up the river, and who remembers Raftery and Mary Hynes. She says, 'I never saw anybody so handsome as she was, and I never will till I die,' and that he was nearly blind, and had 'no way of living but to go round and to mark some house to go to, and then all the neighbours would gather to hear. If you treated him well he'd praise you, but if you did not, he'd fault you in Irish. He was the greatest poet in Ireland, and he'd make a song about that bush if he chanced to stand under it. There was a bush he stood under from the rain, and he made verses praising it, and then when the water came through he made verses dispraising it.' She sang the poem to a friend and to myself in Irish, and every word was audible and expressive, as the words in a song were always, as I think, before music grew too proud to be the garment of words, flowing and changing with the flowing and changing of their energies. The poem is not as natural as the best Irish poetry of the last century, for the thoughts are arranged in a too obviously traditional form, so the old poor half-blind man who made it, has to speak as if he were a rich farmer offering the best of everything to the woman he loves, but it has naïve and tender phrases. The friend that was with me has made some of the translation, but some of it has been made by the country people themselves. I think it has more of the simplicity of the Irish verses than one finds in most translations.

Going to Mass by the will of God,
The day came wet and the wind rose;
I met Mary Hynes at the cross of Kiltartan,
And I fell in love with her then and there.

I spoke to her kind and mannerly,
As by report was her own way;
And she said, 'Raftery, my mind is easy,
You may come to-day to Baile-laoi.'

When I heard her offer I did not linger,
When her talk went to my heart my heart rose.
We had only to go across the three fields,
We had daylight with us to Baile-laoi.

The table was laid with glasses and a quart measure,

She had fair hair, and she sitting beside me;
And she said, 'Drink, Raftery, and a hundred welcomes,
There is a strong cellar in Baile-laoi.'

O star of light and O sun in harvest,
O amber hair, O my share of the world,
Will you come with me upon Sunday
Till we agree together before all the people?

I would not grudge you a song every Sunday evening,
Punch on the table, or wine if you would drink it.
But, O King of Glory, dry the roads before me,
Till I find the way to Baile-laoi.

There is sweet air on the side of the hill
When you are looking down upon Baile-laoi;
When you are walking in the valley picking nuts and blackberries,
There is music of the birds in it and music of the Sidhe.

What is the worth of greatness till you have the light
Of the flower of the branch that is by your side?
There is no good to deny it or to try and hide it,
She is the sun in the heavens who wounded my heart.

There was no part of Ireland I did not travel,
From the rivers to the tops of the mountains,
To the edge of Lough Greine whose mouth is hidden,
And I saw no beauty but was behind hers.

Her hair was shining, and her brows were shining too;
Her face was like herself, her mouth pleasant and sweet.
She is the pride, and I give her the branch,
She is the shining flower of Baile-laoi.

It is Mary Hynes, this calm and easy woman,
Has beauty in her mind and in her face.
If a hundred clerks were gathered together,
They could not write down a half of her ways.

An old weaver, whose son is supposed to go away among the
Sidhe (the faeries) at night, says:—'Mary Hynes was the most beau-

tiful thing ever made. My mother used to tell me about her, for she'd be at every hurling, and wherever she was she was dressed in white. As many as eleven men asked her in marriage in one day, but she wouldn't have any of them. There was a lot of men up beyond Kilbecanty one night, sitting together, drinking, and talking of her, and one of them got up and set out to go to Baile-laoi and see her; but Cloon bog was open then, and when he came to it he fell into the water, and they found him dead there in the morning. She died of the fever that was before the famine.' Another old man says he was only a child when he saw her, but he remembered that 'the strongest man that was among us, one John Madden, got his death of the head of her, cold he got, crossing rivers in the night-time to get to Baile-laoi.' This is perhaps the man the other remembered, for tradition gives the one thing many shapes. There is an old woman who remembers her, at Derrybrien among the Echtge hills, a vast desolate place, which has changed little since the old poem said, 'the stag upon the cold summit of Echtge hears the cry of the wolves,' but still mindful of many poems and of the dignity of ancient speech. She says, 'The sun and the moon never shone on anybody so handsome, and her skin was so white that it looked blue, and she had two little blushes on her cheeks.' And an old wrinkled woman who lives close by Baile-laoi, and has told me many tales of the Sidhe, says, 'I often saw Mary Hynes, she was handsome indeed. She had two bunches of curls beside her cheeks, and they were the colour of silver. I saw Mary Molloy that was drowned in the river beyond, and Mary Guthrie that was in Ardrahan, but she took the sway of them both, a very comely creature. I was at her wake too—she had seen too much of the world. She was a kind creature. One day I was coming home through that field beyond, and I was tired, and who should come out but the *Poisin Glegeal* (the shining flower), and she gave me a glass of new milk.' This old woman meant no more than some beautiful bright colour by the colour of silver, for though I knew an old man— he is dead now—who thought she might know 'the cure for all the evils in the world,' that the Sidhe knew, she has seen too little gold to know its colour. But a man by the shore at Kinvara, who is too young to remember Mary Hynes, says, 'Everybody says there is no one at all to be seen now so handsome; it is said she had beautiful hair, the colour of gold. She was poor, but her clothes every day were the same as Sunday, she had such neatness. And if she went to any kind of a meeting, they would all be killing one another for a sight of her, and there was a great many in love with her, but she died young. It is said that no one that has a song made about them will ever live long.'

Those who are much admired are, it is held, taken by the Sidhe, who can use ungoverned feeling for their own ends, so that a father, as an old herb doctor told me once, may give his child into their hands, or a husband his wife. The admired and desired are only safe if one says 'God bless them' when one's eyes are upon them. The old woman that sang the song thinks too that Mary Hynes was 'taken,' as the phrase is, 'for they have taken many that are not handsome, and why would they not take her, and people came from all parts to look at her, and maybe there were some that did not say "God bless her."' An old man, who lives by the sea at Duras, has as little doubt that she was taken, 'for there are some living yet can remember her coming to the pattern[1] there beyond, and she was said to be the handsomest girl in Ireland.' She died young because the gods loved her, for the Sidhe are the gods, and it may be that the old saying, which we forget to understand literally, meant her manner of death in old times. These poor countrymen and countrywomen in their beliefs, and in their emotions are many years nearer to that old Greek world, that set beauty beside the fountain of things, than are our men of learning. She 'had seen too much of the world,' but these old men and women when they tell of her blame another and not her, and though they can be hard they grow gentle as the old men of Troy grew gentle when Helen passed by on the walls.

The poet who helped her to so much fame has himself a great fame throughout the west of Ireland. Some think that Raftery was half blind, and say, 'I saw Raftery, a dark man, but he had sight enough to see her,' or the like, but some think he was wholly blind, as he may have been at the end of his life. Fable makes all things perfect in their kind, and her blind people must never look on the world and the sun. I asked a man I met one day, when I was looking for a pool *na mna Sidhe* where women of faery have been seen, how Raftery could have admired Mary Hynes so much if he had been altogether blind. He said, 'I think Raftery was altogether blind, but those that are blind have a way of seeing things, and have the power to know more, and to feel more, and to do more, and to guess more than those that have their sight, and a certain wit and a certain wisdom is given to them.' Everybody indeed will tell you that he was very wise, for was he not only blind but a poet? The weaver whose words about Mary Hynes I have already given, says, 'His poetry was the gift of the Almighty, for there are three things that are the gift of the Almighty, poetry and

---

1 *the pattern*: the festival of a patron saint.

dancing and principles. That is why in the old times an ignorant man coming down from the hillside would be better behaved and have better learning than a man with education you'd meet now, for they got it from God'; and a man at Coole says, 'When he put his finger to one part of his head everything would come to him as if it was written in a book'; and an old pensioner at Kiltartan says, 'he was standing under a bush one time and he talked to it and it answered him back in Irish. Some say it was the bush that spoke, but it must have been an enchanted voice in it, and it gave him the knowledge of all the things of the world. The bush withered up afterwards, and it is to be seen on the roadside now between this and Rahasane.' There is a poem of his about a bush, which I have never seen, and it may have come out of the cauldron of fable in this shape. A friend of mine met a man once who had been with him when he died, but the people say that he died alone, and one Maurteen Gillane told Dr. Hyde[1] that all night long a light was seen streaming up to heaven from the roof of the house where he lay, and 'that was the angels who were with him'; and all night long there was a great light in the hovel, 'and that was the angels who were waking him. They gave that honour to him because he was so good a poet, and sang such religious songs.' It may be that in a few years Fable, who changes mortalities to immortalities in her cauldron, will have changed Mary Hynes and Raftery to perfect symbols of the sorrow of beauty and of the magnificence and penury of dreams.

Letter to Katharine Tynan, 17 or 24 September 1887

Rosses Point
Sligo
Saturday

My dear Miss Tynan

... 'Oisin'[2] goes a head famously the country helps one to think.

I went last Wednesday up Ben Belban to see the place where Dermot died,[3] a dark pool fabulously deep and still haunted—1732 feet above the sea line, open to all winds. Tracks of sheep and deer and smaller tracks of hares converging from all sides, made as they go to drink. All peasants at the foot of the mountain know the legend, and know that Dermot still haunts the pool, and fear it. Every hill and stream is some way or other connected with the story.

---

1 *Dr. Hyde*: Douglas Hyde* (1860–1949), Celtic scholar, first president of the Gaelic League (1893).
2 'The Wanderings of Usheen' [*q.v.*].
3 'The Pursuit of Diarmuid and Grainne' is one of the principal poems in Katharine Tynan's *Shamrocks* (1887).

... I lived some days in a haunted house a little while ago, heard nothing but strange knockings on the walls and on the glass of an old mirror. The servent one evening before I heard anything heard the stamping of heavy feet the house being empty.[1]

... Am as usual fighting that old snake—revery to get from him a few hours each day for my writing.

Your friend
W B Yeats

Letter to Katharine Tynan, 18 November 1887

Charlemont
Sligo
Friday.

My dear Miss Tynan

Oison having come to an end—nothing now remaining but the copying out, if quite convenient to you I will be with you Tuesday next by the train that reaches the Broadstone[2] at 4.15 in the afternoon—This finishing of Oison is a great releaf—never has any poem given me such a trouble—making me sleepless a good deel, it has kept me out of spirits and nervous—the thing always on my mind—these several weeks back. It seems better now than when I was working it out. I suppose my thinking so badly of it was mainly because of colds and head aches mixing themselves up with the depression that comes when one idia has been long in the mind, for now it seems one of my successes. Two days ago it seemed the worst thing I ever wrote. A long poem is like a fever—especially when I am by myself as I am down here. This to me is the lonliest place in the world. Going for a walk is a continual meeting with ghosts for Sligo for me has no flesh and blood attractions— only memories and sentimenttalities accumulated here as a child making it more dear than any other place.

I was going along the side of the river a few days ago when a man stopped me and said 'I think I should know you sir'. I found out he knew me well as a child. He asked me to go for a row with him saying 'come we will tell old yarns' and with old yarns mainly fairy yarns collected round about here I have filled two note books. You shall hear the best when we meet....

You have not told me this long while what you are writing—so

---

1 ... *a haunted house* ...: This was Elsinore Lodge, at Rosses Point in Co. Sligo, formerly owned by John Black, a smuggler. It belonged to Yeats's great-uncle William Middleton.
2 *The Broadstone*: terminus in North Dublin of the Midland Great Western Railway.

when I see you you may expect many questions on that head. I myself
have nothing to read you but Oisin, Dhoya and some few scraps, but
have much to tell of. You have many poems to read I hope.

Your friend
W B Yeats

from Letter to Katharine Tynan, ?22–28 September 1888

3 Blenheim Road
Bedford Park
Turnham Green

Dear Miss Tynan

... I enclose a couple of lyrics of my own for your opinion. One is
made out of three lines of verse I picked up in Sligo—old Irish verse.[1]

... You would have been much amused to have seen my departure
from Oxford.[2] All the while I was there one thing only troubled my
peace of mind—the politeness of the man servent. It was perpetually
'Wine sir, coffey sir, any thing sir'. At every 'sir' I said to my self 'that
means an extra shilling in his mind at least'. When I was going I did
not know what to give him, but gave him five shillings. Then suddenly
thought I had given too little. I tried a joke. My jokes had all been failures so far with him. It went explosively. And I departed sadly knowing I had given too much.

I have corrected the two first parts of Oisin. The second part is much
more coherent than I had hoped. You did not hear the second part. It is
the most inspired but the least artistic of the three. The last has most art.
Because I was in complete solitude—no one near me but old and reticent
people—when I wrote it. It was the greatest effort of all my things.
When I had finished I brought it round to read to my uncle George
Pollexfen, and could hardly read so collapsed I was. My voice quite broken. It really was a kind of a vision it beset me day and night. Not that
I ever wrote more than a few lines in a day. But those few lines took me
hours. And all the rest of the time, I walked about the roads thinking of
it. I wait impatiently the proofs of it. With the other parts I am much dis-
apointed—they seem only shadows of what I saw. But the third must
have got itself expressed—it kept me from my sleep too long. Yet the sec-

---

1 *I enclose a couple of lyrics of my own*: These were 'To an Isle in the Water' and 'Down by the
  Salley Gardens'. The latter was described by Yeats as 'an attempt to reconstruct an old song
  from three lines imperfectly remembered by an old peasant woman in the village of
  Ballysodare, Sligo, who often sings them to herself'. It was based on a Sligo ballad.

2 *my departure from Oxford*: Yeats was there copying Caxton's 1484 edition of *Aesop's Fables* for
  Joseph Jacobs, a literary journalist and friend of the Yeats family's friend Professor York Powell.

ond part is more deep and poetic. It is not inspiration that exhausts one, but art. The first parts I felt. I saw the second. Yet there too perhaps only shaddows have got them selves onto paper. And I am like the people who dream some wonderful things and get up in the middle of the night and write it, and find next day only scribling on the paper.

I have added to the book the last scene of the *Island of Statues* with a short argument to make all plain. I am sure the Island is good of its kind. I was then living a quite harmonius poetic life. Never thinking out of my depth. Always harmonius narrow, calm. Taking small interest in people but most ardently moved by the more minute kinds of natural beauty. Mosada[1] was then written and a poem called Time & Vivien[2] which you have not seen—it is second in my book. Every thing done then was quite passionless. The 'Island' was the last. Since I have left the 'Island' I have been going about on shoreless seas. Nothing anywhere has clear outline. Everywhere is cloud and foam. Oisin and the Seaker are the only ... readable result. In the second part of Oisin under disguise of symbolism I have said severel things, to which I only have the key. The romance is for my readers, they must not even know there is a symbol anywhere. They will not find out. If they did it would spoil the art. Yet the whole poem is full of symbols—if it be full of aught but clowds. The early poems I know to be quite choherent and at no time are there clouds in my details for I hate the soft modern manner. The clouds began about 4 years ago. I was finishing the Island. They came and robbed Nachina of her Shaddow as you will see, the rest is cloudless narrow and calm....[3]

Your Friend Always
W B Yeats

Letter to John O'Leary, ?25 November 1891

3 Blenheim Road
Bedford Park
Chiswick—W
Wednesday

Dear Mr O'Leary

Could you lend me £1? I will return it to you as soon as any body

---

1 *Mosada*, a poetic drama, appeared in the *Dublin University Review*, June 1886.

2 *Time & Vivien*: 'Time and the Witch Vivien', a dialogue poem, was published in *The Wanderings of Oisin and Other Poems*.

3 *They came and robbed Nachina of her Shaddow...*: At the apparently happy close of the play *The Island of Statues*, published serially April–July 1885 in the *Dublin University Review*, Naschina the heroine has defeated the Enchantress, regaining her lover Almintor but losing her humanity, her soul, when she is shadowless.

pays me anything. I am owed various amounts by various people but my only regular & certain paymaster 'the Providence Journal' has either not taken or has post poned my article sent last month. The late editor Williams[1] is now doing most of the literary work himself. Hence the rest of us are elbowed out to some extent.[2] I can't trouble the 'National Observer' until there proper pay day comes round as they rather resent one's doing so I think. They have asked me, by the by for stories like Dhoya if I can make them short enough to fit their pages.[3] I doubt if it can be done but mean to try. You need not return the copy of John Sherman which you have, as I have got a few more copies.[4] Did Ash King[5] like it? Henley[6] praises it & it seems generally to be liked. If you meet Taylor[7] ask him what he thought of it.

Blake goes on slowly[8]—A good big bundle of MSS has gone to the printer. I am bringing the MS of my new book of poems to Fisher Unwin today but do not think they will be out until next April as the man who is publishing 'the Book of the Rhymers' Club' wants to keep the copyright of the poems it contains until the end of March. Some of my best lyrics are to be in it so I must wait until April to reprint them.[9] What of The Young Ireland League? I wrote to Lavelle[10] for information & got no answer. If you meet him please stir him up. Miss Gonne will be in Dublin in 10 days or less—She returns to London from Paris in two or three days. The main reasen why I ask you for the loan of this £1 is that I do not want to be without the price of cabs Etc while she is here & I have promised to take her to one or two places. Some times post me a United Ireland as I never see an Irish paper here by any chance—

Yours Always
W B Yeats

1 *the late editor Williams*: Alfred Williams (1840–96) retired as editor of the *Providence Journal* in 1891.

2 *the rest of us are elbowed out…*: Yeats's last article for the *Providence Journal* appeared on 26 July 1891.

3 *They have asked me … for stories*: Yeats contributed several stories to the *National Observer*.

4 *John Sherman & Dhoya*, two tales, were first published in 1891, in the Pseudonym Library under the name Ganconagh.

5 *Ash King*: Richard Ashe King (1839–1932), novelist, editor of *Truth*, a London weekly, for 38 years; he was then living in Blackrock, Co. Dublin.

6 *Henley*: William Ernest Henley (1849–1903), poet, critic and editor, was a friend of R.L. Stevenson, who based Long John Silver in *Treasure Island* on him. He met Yeats in 1888, the year he fell out with Stevenson. He was editor of the *National Observer*.

7 *Taylor*: John F. Taylor (1850–1902), an Irish barrister and journalist—an eloquent orator. He was antagonistic to Yeats.

8 *Blake goes on slowly*: with Edwin Ellis (1848–1916), a friend of his father, Yeats collaborated on an edition of the works of William Blake. They started the project in 1889; the three-volume Quaritch edition appeared in 1893.

9 *The Book of the Rhymers' Club*, suggested by Yeats, was published by Elkin Mathews in February 1892.

10 Patrick Lavelle (b. 1866) was secretary of the National Club Literary Society.

Letter to George Russell (AE), 22 January 1898

18 Woburn Buildings
Euston Road.
Saturday
22 Jan.

My dear Russell: I feel certain that things will greatly improve with you in a month or so.[1] I do intreat you to give this work a fair trial. It is so unlike all you have done that it was certain to trouble you & absorb your thoughts at first. Every change of life, everything that takes one out of old habits, even a change for the better troubles one at first. But remember always that now you are face to face with Ireland, its tragedy & its poverty, & if we would express Ireland we must know her to the heart & in all her moods. You will be a far more powerful mystic & poet & teacher because of this knowledge—This change of life will test you as a man & a thinker & a will & if you can gradually build up a strong life out of it you will be a bigger soul in all things. You are face to face with the herterogenous & the test of one's harmony is ones power to absorb it & make it harmonius. Gradually these bars hotels & cottages & strange faces will become familiar, gradually you will come to see them through a mist of half humerous, half ironical, half poetical half affectionate memories & hopes. The arguments you use, & the methods you adopt, will become familiar too & then your mind will be free again. When I began speaking on politics first my mind used to be absorbed for days before & very anxious, & now I hardly think of what I am to say until I get to the meeting & when it is over it goes straight out of my mind. Do not be troubled because you cannot write. I confess I did not expect you would be able to write just at first.

Do you know I now think the 'Earth Breath' quite your best work.[2] There are great poems in it. It is an enormous advance in Art too. 'Janus' cannot help being immortal & 'dream love' is as fine in style as a Jacobean lyric & has a far finer style than many Jacobean writers ever had. I think you will yet outsing us all & sing in the ears of many generations to come. Absorb Ireland & her tragedy & you will be the poet of a people, perhaps the poet of a new inspiration.

I am deep in 'Celtic Mysticism'. The whole thing is forming in elaborate vision. Maud Gonne & myself are going for a week or two presently to some country place in Ireland to get as you do the forces

---

1 AE* had taken up a post with Sir Horace Plunket's Irish Agricultural Organization Society at Yeats's persuasion and was exhausted by his work in Mayo, as he had told Yeats in a letter to which this is a reply. He was to play a leading role in the Irish Cooperative Movement.
2 *'Earth Breath* ... best work: *The Earth Breath and Other Poems* was published in September 1897; it was AE's first distinctly Irish collection.

of gods & spirits & too get sacred earth for our invocation. Perhaps
we can arrange to go some where where you are so that we can all
work togeather. Maud Gonne has seen visions of a little temple of the
heroes which she proposes to build some where in Ireland when 98 is
over & to make the centre of our mystical & literary movement.[1]

I shall be in Ireland about the 20 or 23 of Feb & will be in Dublin
for a week or two arranging 98 work.[2] If you like I think I could
arrange, though I am not altogeather sure, to join you where ever you
are then & we would make time to work at the celtic mysticism
togeather. I feel pretty sure I could arrange this.

I have just finished my review of you for 'the Sketch'.[3]

Yr ever
W B Yeats

How much a week could I live for in the country if I stayed a couple
of weeks or so? Could I do it for 30/-? Please let me know about this
soon.

I have a lot to say about the mysticism but will write later on.

ETHNA CARBERY (ANNA MACMANUS, NÉE JOHNSON) (1866–1902)

Ethna Carbery was born Anna Johnson in Ballymena, Co. Antrim, of a Fenian family. Her father, a successful businessman, was claimed to have been a member of
the Supreme Council of the IRB. The family moved to Belfast during Anna's childhood. She spent most of her life there. She contributed nationalist poetry to *The
Nation*, *The Shamrock*, and *Young Ireland*. With Alice Milligan, she edited *The
Northern Patriot*—until her Fenian sympathies were discovered, and she was asked to
leave. In 1896 the two women founded the nationalist monthly *The Shan Van Vocht*.
In 1901 she married the writer, and former teacher, Seumas MacManus, who had been
a frequent contributor to her journal. The couple moved to Co. Donegal. Her collection *The Four Winds of Eirinn* (1902) was very popular; it includes the well-known
patriotic ballad 'Rody McCorley'. After her death, her husband collected her stories
and published them as *The Passionate Hearts* (1903) and *In the Celtic Past* (1904).

---

1 *to make the centre of our mystical & literary movement*: 'On a visit to Dr Hyde I had seen
the Castle Rock, as it was called in Lough Key.... I believed that the castle could be hired for
little money, and had long been dreaming of making it an Irish Eleusis or Samothrace.... I
meant to initiate young men and women in this worship, which would unite the radical truths
of Christianity to those of a more ancient world, and to use the Castle Rock for their occa-
sional retirement from the world.' (Yeats, *Memoirs*, 123–4).
2 *when 98 is over.... arranging 98 work*: celebrations for the centenary of the 1798 uprising;
Yeats was selected chairman of the '98 Celebration Committee' in 1897.
3 *my review of you ...*: AE's *The Earth Breath* was dedicated to Yeats; the review appeared in
The Sketch, 6 April 1898.

From *In the Celtic Past*

The Last Battle of Iliach of the Clanna Rury

(1898)[1]

Hark! The war-trumpet of Queen Maeve has sent forth its challenge from the borders of Uladh,[2] where she lies encamped with her vast army of invasion into the Northern province. She has come to reave the Brown Bull of Coolney from its pasturage and carry it—the pride of the foray—back with her to the valleys of Connacht as a rival to the famous White Bull which her husband, Ailil, numbers amongst his kingly herds. Her challenge had penetrated to the Court of the Red Branch at Emania,[3] where Conor, the King, reigned nobly and well, but alas! It found the son of Nessa and his brave warriors lying in a state of torpidity under the spells of a woman whom they had, once upon a time, wronged. Macha was her name, and sadly did the Ultonians[4] rue the day on which they condemned her to a trial of speed with the swiftest chariot of the King. Her husband's life was the price of the wife's fleet-footedness, and when the woman, having won, sank down, dying in giving birth to her twin children, before Conor, she laid a bitter curse upon him and his knights because of this evil eric they had devised for her undoing. And the curse had wrought itself out in the strange debility which had overtaken them year after year since that day at the same fateful time; so that now, when the red spectre of war came knocking upon their gates and shouting the battle-cry of Connacht in their unheeding ears, they reclined upon their skin-covered couches, half asleep, nor made a move towards the spear and shield that dangled overhead against the wall; nor did even one listless hand stretch gropingly for the short sharp sword that held its place in the leather belt above the thigh of each fallen warrior.

Evil, in truth, was the deed that had brought about this spell on the flower of the Red Branch chivalry; and evil was the curse that had led the borders of Uladh unguarded to the encroachment of a hostile clan. Only the youths who were in training in the great military school of Emania—children of those spell-bound chieftains—bright-faced lads with flowing hair and white unwounded limbs, and the

---

1 Published in *The Shan Van Vocht*, 4 July 1898, as part of a series titled *In* [or *From*] *the Celtic Past*.
2 *Uladh*: Ulster
3 *Emania*: Latinized spelling of Emain Macha, capital of Ulster, royal seat of Conchobar (Conor) mac Nessa and the warriors of the Red Branch.
4 *Ultonians*: Ulstermen (*Obs.*).

very old fighting men whose day of prowess was over long since, were left to meet the onslaught of the fierce fair Queen and her wild tribes from the Western kingdom.

Yet, of those who were untouched in Uladh by the curse of Macha but two came swiftly towards the Ford of Watching at the challenge of the Connacht marauders. One was in the flower of his youth, smooth-skinned and blue-eyed. His golden curls fell down upon his young shoulders and blew backwards on the wind with the speed of his approach. He wore a shirt and tunic of saffron colour closely fastened around his body with a strong supple belt of leather, and over this was his battle-girdle, also of hard-tanned leather, which encircled him from his hips to his arm-pits, so that neither javelins, nor sharp-pointed irons, nor spears, nor darts could pierce through it, but bounded away from it as if from a rock.

In his right hand he held a tall bronze spear, and on his left arm a great curved black-red shield with a scalloped keen-edged rim, so sharp that whenever he used it as a weapon he cut equally with it as with his spear or his sword. As he stood up straight in his chariot behind the flying horses, which guided by the unerring hand of Laegh, his charioteer, bore him like a lightening shaft towards the Ford, Queen Maeve leaning forward in her chariot-seat on the opposite brink of the river, turned her proud eyes, full of his questioning, on a tall dark youth who stood anear.

'Is it but a boy they send to stay my progress,' she exclaimed in scornful wonder. Dost thou know his name, Ferdia? Thou hadst knowledge of the Ultonian lads in thy younger days.'

'I know him, O Queen, and thou wilt find him a foeman worthy of thy steel. Setanta, the son of Sualtainn, was his name ere he was my comrade at the Military School of the Lady Scathach over the seas in Alba.[1] But afterwards, because of a wondrous feat, in which he tore the watch-dog of Culand, the Armourer of King Conor, asunder when it strove to prevent his entrance into the Smith's house in the wake of the King, he hath been called Cuchullin, that is the Hound of Culand. His strength shall yet be felt in this battle as I and others have felt it in the wrestle, and his feats of championship are many and marvellous.'

'Yet he is but a boy,' repeated the Queen softly, 'a boy, and oh! the pity that against him our javelins shall fly, and our blue sharp-pointed spears be set. Can he be won to us, O Ferdia?'

'Nay, nay, my Queen, he is pledged to Conor, who is his mother's brother; and Cuchullin was never known to forsake his friend, or break his plighted word.'

---

1 *Alba*: Scotland

While all eyes were fixed upon the young hero, the rumbling noise of another chariot, hastily driven, reached their ears across the Ford. Then a great mocking shout of laughter rose from Maeve and her attendant warriors, and in a moment it had spread throughout the army. A second champion had come to guard the borders of Uladh, and it was at his appearance their mirth had broken forth.

He drove forward to the margin of the Ford beside Cuchullin, and stayed his horses in full view of the invaders. Their laughter rang louder and longer at nearer sight of him.

Iliach, the Son of Cas, of the Clanna Rury, was his name, and in his youth he had been one of the chief fighters of that royal race. But now, alas, he had grown very old, and being exempted by age from active warfare he had settled down into ways of peace. As he sat by the fireside in his *caiséal*,[1] he fought once more, in memory, the battles of his youth and manhood. The sword that he never hoped to wield again rusted in its scabbard, his spears swung idly to and fro upon the wall, the two old steeds that had borne him into the core of conflict many a time and oft, were turned out loose for life into the green, wide-spreading meadows round his home, where the river rippled between high banks of sheltering trees, and the battle-car which had withstood the dint of many a shock in his fierce fighting days was lying, almost decaying, hard by in a corner of his bawn.

Yet, when Iliach heard of the hostile descent upon Uladh, the old war-anger wakened in his heart again, until he felt that the strength had come back to his arm and the keen, far-seeing vision to his dimmed and weary eye. He called his clansmen around him from the high hills and deep glens of that Northern tribe-land, exhorting them to follow whither he led, that the Clanna Rury might stand, as it had often stood before, for the defence of Uladh in the face of the enemy.

And while the clansmen were gathering and making ready, the old chieftain, impatient for the fray, set out alone. He had caused the venerable speckled steeds to be yoked once more to the shattered chariot, which had neither cushions nor skins to it, for in his earlier days a warrior looked upon these as luxuries unbefitting his manly hardihood. He slung over his shoulder his rough dark shield of iron with its thick rim of silver, and round his waist, by its leathern girdle, he fastened his gray-hilted heavy-striking sword to his left side. In his hand he took his shaky-headed, many-gapped spears, and because that his armament was ancient and scanty, his people filled the chari-

---

1 *caiséal*: mantle

ot around him with stones and rocks and great flags that he might, with these, defend himself to the last.

It was the sight of this shaggy, strangely-equipped champion beside the young Cuchullin that awakened the mirth of the Olne-Machta. Great, indeed, was their merriment as he waved his rusty spear threateningly across the water, and Maeve's shrill womanly laughter rang clearest of all.

'A boy and a dotard—Uladh is, in truth, well guarded.' She stood up in her seat and looked round upon her immense army which darkened the plain as far as eye could reach.

'The Bull of Coolney is mine, O Ailell,' she cried to her husband, 'won without blood or loss, only by this pleasant journey from our own territories to those of King Conor. Let us cross the Ford.'

But, straight as a young poplar, on the other side stood Cuchullin challenging her bravest to single combat, and on a level with him, Iliach raised his battle-shout of defiance.

Then the fight began, and it shall be related hereafter how the Hound of Uladh kept his guaranty while the Red Branch slept. It is with Iliach of the Clanna Rury our tale is concerned, and how he fought and died.

When the heat of the fray made men pant and strain and wrestle agonisingly in the trial of single combat with Cuchullin, Iliach held his own against the lesser champions that approached him. The strength of youth had, indeed, been renewed in him, and he fought as in the bygone days, when his name was revered throughout Uladh as that of a warrior of renown. Nay, he fought better than ever in that heroic time, for it seemed as if a magic skill pervaded his being, so quick-darting was he to avoid a blow, so strong was his body to withstand the assaults of those ferocious Connacians, and so supple was the hand that held his long shaky spear as it darted hither and thither under and above the shields of his enemies, piercing, hacking, and hewing them until the dead lay piled in heaps around. And when the spear, through excess of use, broke off in two, he mounted into his chariot again, and picking up the heavy large stones with which it was filled hurled them on the heads of Maeve's men, crushing, grinding, and bruising them until those who had fallen were covered as with a cairn.

Many wounds did he receive from lance and javelin as he stood holding the Ford of Watching with Cuchullin—many and grievious [sic] wounds, through which his life-blood swiftly flowed. And when he felt the icy hand of Death clutch at his heart-strings he groped his way, barely alive, to the spot where Doche Mac Magach, of

Connacht, stood, one who had been his brother in arms in their boyhood. Now, they were on different sides in this great encounter.

When Doche saw Iliach approach he went to meet him.

'Well hast thou fought this day, old friend,' said he. 'Yet it has been against heavy odds, and many are the gaping wounds upon thee. Wherefore dost thou seek me?'

'To beg thee for one last favour, O Doche Mac Magach,' replied Iliach, 'since my day is over and the night of Death is creeping fast in my track. I have fought my last battle, and no longer can I stand against King Conor's foes. In memory of the friendship that was between thee and me, who never lifted hands against one another until this day, I pray thee grant my request.'

'It is granted, O my friend,' said Doche.

'Then since I would not be led a prisoner to the camp of Queen Maeve, but would rather, of a surety, die upon the field, do thou strike off my head with thy sword that I may pass through the Dark Gates speedily and reach the heroes waiting beyond. And yet another favour I would ask, O Doche, that thou wilt convey my sword, now broken and edgeless, to thy friend and mine, Leury of Uladh, as a parting token of my affection.'

'I promise,' said the other, mournfully.

'Then farewell, friend of my heart. Strike swift and sure.'

He knelt on the bloody ground before Doche and bent his withered neck for the blow. Swift and sure it came, and the head of Iliach of the Clanna Rury bounded forward till it reached the feet of Cuchullin, who saw it without ceasing one moment in his terrible slaughter of his enemies.

'For thee, and for thee,' he cried loudly, 'for thee, and for thee, O brave chieftain, who had been my mainstay, I shall deal havoc on those who have slain thee.' And the clansmen of Connacht fell as grass falls beneath the scythe of the mower around him, because of his pity for the old warrior whose last battle was done.

* * *

In the Northern Glen on the sea-swept eastern coast of Uladh the Clanna Rury raised the *caoine* for their chieftain, and over his body, which had been tenderly conveyed from the Ford of Watching, they raised the monumental mound.

Ethna Carbery

From *The Four Winds of Eirinn*
(1902)

Rody M'Corley[1]
(1896)

Ho! see the fleet-foot host of men
Who speed with faces wan,
From farmstead and from fishers' cot
Upon the banks of Bann!
They come with vengeance in their eyes—
Too late! Too late are they—
For Rody M'Corley goes to die
On the bridge of Toome to-day.

Oh Ireland, Mother Ireland,
You love them still the best,
The fearless brave who fighting fall
Upon your hapless breast;
But never a one of all your dead
More bravely fell in fray,
Than he who marches to his fate
On the Bridge of Toome to-day.

Up the narrow street he stepped
Smiling and proud and young;
About the hemp-rope on his neck
The golden ringlets clung;
There's ne'er a tear in his blue, blue eyes,
Both glad and bright are they—
As Rody M'Corley goes to die
On the bridge of Toome to-day.

Ah! when he last stepped up that street,
His shining pike in hand,
Behind him marched, in grim array
An earnest stalwart band!
To Antrim town! for Antrim town!

---

1 Rody (or Roddy) M'Corley, a member of the Catholic Defenders, became a martyr of the 1798 Rebellion; he was hanged on 28 February 1800.

He led them to the fray—
And Rody M'Corley goes to die
On the bridge of Toome to-day.

The grey coat and its sash of green
Were brave and stainless then;
A banner flashed beneath the sun
Over the marching men—
The coat hath many a rent this noon
The sash is torn away,
And Rody McCorley goes to die
On the bridge of Toome to-day.

Oh! how his pike flashed to the sun!
Then found a foeman's heart!
Through furious fight, and heavy odds,
He bore a true man's part;
And many a red-coat bit the dust
Before his keen pike-play—
But Rody M'Corley goes to die
On the bridge of Toome to-day.

Because he loved the Motherland,
Because he loved the Green,
He goes to meet the martyr's fate
With proud and joyous mien,
True to the last, true to the last,
He treads the upward way—
Young Rody M'Corley goes to die
On the Bridge of Toome to-day.

GEORGE W. RUSSELL (AE) (1867–1935)

Born in Lurgan, Co. Armagh, he was the youngest son of a bookkeeper. When he was about 10 the family moved to Dublin, where he attended Rathmines School and, from the age of 15, the Metropolitan School of Art. Here he befriended W.B. Yeats*, who introduced him to Theosophy. He took evening classes in the school of the Royal Hibernian Academy, but, having joined the Inner Circle of the Theosophists, he decided against a full-time career as a painter. Like Blake, he developed eidetic vision; his *nom de plume* AE is the first sound in *Æon*, the mystic word which came to Russell at the start of his spiritual journey—inadvertently split by a printer. His mysticism, which informs such books as *The Candle of Vision* (1918), has been dubbed AEtheism.

Russell worked in the Phoenix brewery from 1884, and from 1890 as a clerk in Pim's drapery, in Dublin. Charles Weekes, the theosophist and private publisher, persuaded him to publish his *Homeward: Songs by the Way* (1894), which launched him as a leading figure in literary Dublin. It was followed by *The Earth Breath and Other Poems* (1897), *The Divine Vision and Other Poems* (1904) and various collections of mystical, visionary verse. His play *Deirdre* (1902) was double-billed with Yeats's *Cathleen ni Houlihan*. AE took delight in discovering new literary talent.

In 1897 he joined the Irish Agricultural Organization Society, becoming Horace Plunkett's right-hand man and editing its organ *The Irish Homestead* from 1906; in 1923 it merged with *The Irish Statesman*, which was edited by AE until it ceased publication in 1930. His interest in cooperative economics is attested in *Co-Operation and Nationality* (1912) and *The National Being* (1916). He attacked the employers of Dublin for the Lock-Out strike in 1913. He served on the Convention of 1917–18, trying to conciliate England. He refused, in 1922, to become a member of the Senate of the Irish Free State. Disillusioned by the new state's Jansenist mentality and deeply depressed by the death of his wife Violet, he moved to England in 1933, living first in London and then in Bournemouth, where he died in 1935.

From *The Earth Breath and Other Poems*
(1897)

The Earth Breath

From the cool and dark-lipped furrows
    breathes a dim delight
Through the woodland's purple plumage
    to the diamond night.
Aureoles of joy encircle
    every blade of grass
Where the dew-fed creatures silent
    and enraptured pass.
And the restless ploughman pauses,
    turns and, wondering,
Deep beneath his rustic habit
    finds himself a king;
For a fiery moment looking
    with the eyes of God

Over fields a slave at morning
    bowed him to the sod.
Blind and dense with revelation
    every moment flies,
And unto the mighty mother,
    gay, eternal, rise
All the hopes we hold, the gladness,
    dreams of things to be.
One of all thy generations,
    mother, hails to thee.
Hail, and hail, and hail for ever,
    though I turn again
From thy joy unto the human
    vestiture of pain.
I, thy child who went forth radiant
    in the golden prime,
Find thee still the mother-hearted
    through my night in time;
Find in thee the old enchantment
    there behind the veil
Where the gods, my brothers, linger.
    hail, forever, hail!

Janus[1]

Image of beauty, when I gaze on thee,
Trembling I waken to a mystery,
How through one door we go to life or death
By spirit kindled or the sensual breath.

Image of beauty, when my way I go;
No single joy or sorrow do I know:
Elate for freedom leaps the starry power,
The life which passes mourns its wasted hour.

And, ah, to think how thin the veil that lies
Between the pain of hell and paradise!
Where the cool grass my aching head embowers
God sings the lovely carol of the flowers.

---

1 *Janus*: Roman god who kept the gate of Heaven.

George W. Russell

The Grey Eros

(1897)[1]

We are desert leagues apart;
   Time is misty ages now
Since the warmth of heart to heart
   Chased the shadows from my brow.
Oh, I am so old, meseems
   I am next of kin to Time,
The historian of her dreams
   From the long-forgotten prime.
You have come a path of flowers.
   What a way was mine to roam!
Many a fallen empire's towers,
   Many a ruined heart my home.
No, there is no comfort, none.
   All the dewy tender breath
Idly falls when life is done
   On the starless brow of death.
Though the dream of love may tire,
   In the ages long agone
There were ruby hearts of fire—
   Ah, the daughters of the dawn!
Though I am so feeble now,
   I remember when our pride
Could not to the Mighty bow;
   We would sweep His stars aside.
Mix thy youth with thoughts like those—
   It were but to wither thee,
But to graft the youthful rose
   On the old and flowerless tree.
Age is no more near than youth
   To the sceptre and the crown.
Vain the wisdom, vain the truth;
   Do not lay thy rapture down.

---

1 Published in *The Nuts of Knowledge* (1903); it was included in a letter to W.B. Yeats, 3 April
1897.

Nationality and Cosmopolitanism in Literature

(1898)[1]

As one of those who believe that the literature of a country is for ever creating a new soul among its people, I do not like to think that literature with us must follow an inexorable law of sequence, and gain a spiritual character only after the bodily passions have grown weary and exhausted themselves. Whether the art of any of the writers of the decadence does really express spiritual things is open to doubt. The mood in which their work is conceived, a sad and distempered emotion through which no new joy quivers, seems too often to tell rather of exhausted vitality than of the ecstacy of a new life. However much, too, their art refines itself, choosing ever rarer and more exquisite forms of expression, underneath it all an intuition seems to disclose only the old wolfish lust hiding itself beneath the golden fleece of the spirit. It is not the spirit breaking through corruption, but the life of the senses longing to shine with the light which makes saintly things beautiful; and it would put on the jewelled raiment of seraphim, retaining still a heart of clay smitten through and through with the unappeasable desire of the flesh: so Rossetti's women,[2] who have around them all the circumstances of poetry and romantic beauty, seem through their sucked-in lips to express a thirst which could be allayed in no spiritual paradise. Art in the decadence in our times might be symbolized as a crimson figure undergoing a dark crucifixion; the hosts of light are overcoming it, and it is dying filled with anguish and despair at a beauty it cannot attain. All these strange emotions have a profound psychological interest. I do not think because a spiritual flaw can be urged against a certain phase of life that it should remain unexpressed. The psychic maladies which attack all races when their civilization grows old must needs be understood to be dealt with; and they cannot be understood without being revealed in literature or art. But in Ireland we are not yet sick with this sickness. As psychology it concerns only the curious. As expressing a literary ideal, I think a consideration of it was a mere side-issue in the discussion Mr. Yeats' article[3] continued. The discussion on the one side was really a plea for nationality in our literature, and on the

---

1 This essay was part of a polemic with John Eglinton*, W.B. Yeats* and William Larminie, about legend as the subject matter of Irish drama, which appeared in the *Daily Express* (1898); it was published the following year as *Literary Ideals in Ireland*, edited by Eglinton.
2 *Rossetti's women*: the women painted by the Pre-Raphaelite artist Dante Gabriel Rossetti (1828–82).
3 *Mr. Yeats' article*: 'The Autumn of the Flesh' [*q.v.*].

other a protest on behalf of individualism. It is true that nationality may express itself in many ways; it may not be at all evident in the subject matter, but may be very evident in the sentiment. But a literature loosely held together by some emotional characteristics common to the writers, however great it may be, does not fulfil the purpose of a literature or art created by a number of men who have a common aim in building up an overwhelming ideal—who create, in a sense, a soul for their country, and who have a common pride in the achievement of all. The world has not seen this since the great antique civilizations of Egypt and Greece passed away. We cannot imagine an Egyptian artist daring enough to set aside the majestic attainment of many centuries. An Egyptian boy as he grew up must have been overawed by the national tradition and have felt that it was not to be set aside; it was beyond his individual rivalry. The soul of Egypt incarnated in him, and, using its immemorial language and its mysterious lines, the efforts of the least workman who decorated a tomb seem to have been directed by the same hand that carved the Sphinx. This adherence to a traditional form is true of Greece, though to a less extent. The little Tanagra terra-cottas might have been done by Phidias,[1] and in literature Ulysses and Agamemnon were not the heroes of one epic, but appeared endlessly in epic and drama. Since the Greek civilization no European nation has had an intellectual literature which was genuinely national. In the present century, leaving aside a few things in outward circumstance, there is little to distinguish the work of the best English writers or artists from that of their Continental contemporaries. Millais, Leighton, Rossettti, Turner[2]—how different from each other, and yet they might have painted the same pictures as born Frenchmen and it would not have excited any great surprise as a marked divergence from French art. The cosmopolitan spirit, whether for good or for evil, is hastily obliterating distinctions. What is distinctly national in these countries is less valuable than the immense wealth of universal ideas; and the writers who use this wealth appeal to no narrow circle: the foremost writers, the Tolstois[3] and Ibsens,[4] are conscious of addressing a European audience.

If nationality is to justify itself in the face of all this, it must be because the country which preserves its individuality does so with the profound conviction that its peculiar ideal is nobler than that

---

1 *Phidias*: Greek sculptor of the mid-fifth century BC.

2 *Millais, Leighton, Rossettti, Turner*: English painters of the Victorian era.

3 *the Tolstois:* Leo Nikolaievisch Tolstoy (1828–1910), Russian novelist; author of *War and Peace* (1863–69) *and Anna Karenina* (1873–77).

4 *Ibsens*: Henrik Johan Ibsen (1828–1906), Norwegian playwright and poet; author of *Peer Gynt* (1867), *A Doll's House* (1879), *Ghosts* (1881) and *Hedda Gabler* (1891).

which the cosmopolitan spirit suggests—that this ideal is so precious to it that its loss would be as the loss of the soul, and that it could not be realised without an aloofness from, if not an actual indifference to, the ideals which are spreading so rapidly over Europe. Is it possible for any nationality to make such a defence of its isolation? If not, let us read Goethe,[1] Balzac,[2] Tolstoi, men so much greater than any we can show, try to absorb their universal wisdom and no longer confine ourselves to local traditions. But nationality was never so strong in Ireland as at the present time. It is beginning to be felt, less as a political movement than as a spiritual force. It seems to be gathering itself together, joining men, who were hostile before, in a new intellectual fellowship; and if all these could unite on fundamentals it would be possible in a generation to create a national ideal in Ireland, or rather to let that spirit incarnate fully which began among the ancient peoples, which has haunted the hearts and whispered a dim revelation of itself through the lips of the bards and peasant story-tellers.

Every Irishman forms some vague ideal of his country, born from his reading of history, or from contemporary politics, or from an imaginative intuition; and this Ireland in the mind it is, not the actual Ireland, which kindles his enthusiasm. For this he works and makes sacrifices; but because it has never had any philosophical definition, or a supremely beautiful statement in literature which gathered all aspirations about it, the ideal remains vague. This passionate love cannot explain itself; it cannot make another understand its devotion. To reveal Ireland in clear and beautiful light, to create the Ireland in the heart, is the province of a national literature. Other arts would add to this ideal hereafter, and social life and politics must in the end be in harmony. We are yet before our dawn, in a period comparable to Egypt before the first of her solemn temples constrained its people to an equal mystery, or to Greece before the first perfect statue had fixed an ideal of beauty which mothers dreamed of to mould their yet unborn children. We can see, however, as the ideal of Ireland grows from mind to mind it tends to assume the character of a sacred land. The Dark Rosaleen of Mangan[3] expresses an almost religious adoration, and to a later writer it seems to be nigher to the Spiritual Beauty than other lands:—

---

1 *Goethe*: Johann Wolfgang von Goethe (1749–1832), German poet, novelist, and playwright; leader of the *Sturm und Drang* movement; author of *Die Leiden des jungen Werthers* (1774) and *Faust* (1808).

2 *Balzac*: Honoré de Balzac (1799–1850), French novelist; author of *La Comédie humaine* (in eighty volumes).

3 *The Dark Rosaleen of Mangan*: 'Dark Rosaleen' by James Clarence Mangan (1803–49) is an *asiling*—a poem in which Ireland is revered as a beloved (see Vol. II).

> And still the thoughts of Ireland brood
> Upon her holy quietude.[1]

The faculty of abstracting from the land their eyes behold, another Ireland through which they wandered in dream, has always been a characteristic of the Celtic poets. This inner Ireland which the visionary eye saw, was the Tir-na-noge, the country of immortal youth, for they peopled it only with the young and beautiful. It was the Land of the Living Heart, a tender name which showed that it had become dearer than the heart of woman, and overtopped all other hopes as the last dream of the spirit, the bosom where it would rest after it had passed from the fading shelter of the world. And sure a strange and beautiful land this Ireland is, with a mystic beauty which closes the eyes of the body as in sleep, and opens the eyes of the spirit as in dreams; and never a poet has lain on our hillsides but gentle, stately figures, with hearts shining like the sun, move through his dreams, over radiant grasses, in an enchanted world of their own; and it has become alive through every haunted rath and wood and mountain and lake, so that we can hardly think of it otherwise than as the shadow of the thought of God. The last Celtic poet who has appeared shows the spiritual qualities of the first, when he writes of the grey rivers in their 'enraptured' wanderings, and when he sees in the jewelled bow which arches the heavens

> The Lord's seven spirits that shine through the rain.

This mystical view of nature, peculiar to but one English poet, Wordsworth, is a national characteristic; and much in the creation of the Ireland in the mind is already done, and only needs retelling by the new writers. More important, however, for the literature we are imagining as an offset to the cosmopolitan ideal, would be the creation of heroic figures, types, whether legendary or taken from history, and enlarged to epic proportions by our writers, who would use them in common, as Cuculain, Fionn, Ossian, and Oscar, were used by the generations of poets who have left us the bardic history of Ireland, wherein one would write of the battle fury of a hero, and another of a moment when his fire would turn to gentleness, and another of his love for some beauty of his time, and yet another tell how the rivalry of a spiritual beauty made him tire of love; and so from iteration and persistent dwelling on a few heroes their imaginative images found echoes in life, and other heroes arose continuing their tradition of chivalry.

That such types are of the highest importance and have the most

---

1 *and still ... quietude*: Yeats, 'To Ireland in the Coming Times', 15–16.

ennobling influence on a country, cannot be denied. It was this idea
led Whitman[1] to 'exploit' himself as the typical American. He felt that
what he termed a 'stock personality' was needed to elevate and har-
monise the incongruous human elements in the States. English literature has always been more sympathetic with actual beings than with
ideal types, and cannot help us much. A man who loves Dickens, for
example, may grow to have a great tolerance for the grotesque characters which are the outcome of the social order in England, but he
will not be assisted in the conception of a higher humanity; and this
is true of very many English writers who lack a fundamental philosophy, and are content to take man, as he seems to be for the moment,
rather than as the pilgrim of eternity—as one who is flesh to-day but
who may hereafter grow divine, and who may shine at last like the
stars of the morning, triumphant among the sons of God.

Mr. Standish O'Grady, in his notable epic of Cuculain, was the first
in our time to treat the Celtic traditions worthily. He has contributed
one hero who awaits equal comrades, if, indeed, the tales of the Red
Branch chivalry do not absorb the thoughts of many imaginative writers, and Cuculain remain the typical hero of the Gael, becoming to
every boy who reads the story a revelation of what his own spirit is.

I have written at some length on the two paths which lie before us,
for we have arrived at a parting of ways. One path leads, and has
already led many Irishmen, of whom Professor Dowden[2] is a type, to
obliterate all nationality from their work. The other path winds spi-
rally upwards to a mountain-top of our own, which may be in the
future the Meru to which many worshippers will turn.[3] To remain
where we are as a people, indifferent to literature, to art, to ideas,
wasting the precious gift of public spirit we possess so abundantly in
the sordid political rivalries, without practical or ideal ends, is to justify those who have chosen the other path and followed another star
than ours. I do not wish anyone to infer from this a contempt for
those who, for the last hundred years or so, have guided public opinion in Ireland. If they failed in one respect, it was out of a passionate
sympathy for wrongs of which many are memories, thanks to them.
And to them is due the creation of a force which may be turned in

---

1 *Whitman*: Walt Whitman (1819–92), American poet, author of *Leaves of Grass* (1855) and
  Specimen Days and Collect (1882), a prose work, set himself to incorporating the whole of
  modern life in poetry.
2 *Professor Dowden*: Edward Dowden (1843–1913), Professor of English at Trinity College,
  Dublin; an influential critic who wrote on Shakespeare, Shelley, Southey and French literature; a friend of W.B. Yeats's father—and the butt of his son's criticism.
3 *The Meru ... turn*: Mount Meru, the old name of a holy mountain in Tibet. It would become
  the subject of a poem by W.B. Yeats in *Parnell's Funeral and Other Poems* (1935).

other directions, not without a memory of those pale sleepers to whom we may turn in thought, placing

> 'A kiss of fire on the dim brow of failure,
> A crown upon her uncrowned head.'

Two Letters to W.B. Yeats

3 Up Ely Place
2.6.96

Dear W. B. Y—

I am not going to bother you about any derned thing this time but simply to tell you some things about the Ireland behind the veil. You remember my writing to you about the awakening of the ancient fires which I knew about. Well, it has been confirmed from other sources and we are likely to publish it. The gods have returned to Erin and have centred themselves in the sacred mountains and blow the fires through the country. They have been seen by several in vision, they will awaken the magical instinct everywhere, and the universal heart of the people will turn to the old druidic beliefs. I note through the country the increased faith in faery things. The bells are heard from the mounds and sounding in the hollows of the mountains. A purple sheen in the inner air, perceptible at times in the light of day, spreads itself over the mountains. All this I can add my own testimony to. Furthermore, we were told that though now few we would soon be many, and that a branch of the school for the revival of the ancient mysteries to teach real things would be formed here soon. Out of Ireland will arise a light to transform many ages and peoples. There is a hurrying of forces and swift things going out and I believe profoundly that a new Avatar is about to appear and in all spheres the forerunners go before him to prepare. It will be one of the kingly Avatars, who is at once ruler of men and magic sage. I had a vision of him some months ago and will know him if he appears. America is on fire with mysticism just now and the new races are breaking the mould of European thought and psychics abound. Their light reflects itself in Ireland, and the path of connection has been seen. Now I wish you could come over to this county Sligo or wherever you like and absorb this new force. To me enchantment and fairyland are real and no longer dreams....

By the way I want to spend a week or ten days in the neighbourhood of Sligo this year to hunt up some old currents. Can you tell me some moderate priced hotel to put up at. I wish you could be there. I

will start I think about the 4th or 5th of August. My holidays beginning then. Would there be any chance of your roaming about there for
a while with me and talking over magic, the Celt, and the old country amid the ancient sites of the mysteries?... May the Opal Fire Kings
have you in their keeping. Yours ever, Geo. W. Russell

5 Seapoint Terrace
3rd April 1897

Dear Willie,

I came home last night big with radiant ideas and full of wrath over
the priests. Ah wicked wizard, it will take me weeks to get together the
'Will to do' you have dissolved in dream. There I have been trying to
disentangle myself from the Enchanted World, and nerving myself for
deeds, and you send up a spray of lovely colours to draw me away again
into the byways where these shadowy beauties create only endless
desire and there is nothing for the will to do. I must forgive you for
many reasons, mainly for the stories of the Red One.[1] Many things
which I used to think were due in your work to a perverted fancy for
the grotesque I see now in another way. Your visionary faculty has an
insight more tender than the moralist knows of. Just in the same way as
O'Grady[2] always seems to detect under the rude act the spirit of defiant
and heroic manhood, so you unveil beneath excess and passion a love
for spiritual beauty expressing itself pathetically in the life of this wayward outcast. That insight is indeed an ennobling thing to impart, and
I suppose just because the highest things are the most dangerous you
will find a number of people, who have not got your mental balance,
using your visionary revelation of a hidden spirit seeking for beauty as
justification and defence of passions which have no justification,
except that they are the radiations of a spirit which can find no higher outlet. The *Rosa Alchemica* is a most wonderful piece of prose.[3]
Everything in it thought and word are so rich that they seem the gathering in the temple of the mind of thousands of pilgrim rays returning and leaving there their many experiences.

A book sustained at that level throughout would be one of the
greatest things in literature. I notice a change in your lyrics. They are

---

1 *The stories of the Red One*: Yeats's Stories of Red Hanrahan were published as part of *The Secret Rose* (1897); several stories of Hanrahan the Red had appeared in periodical publication from 1892 onwards.
2 *O'Grady*: Standish James O'Grady* (1846–1928).
3 *Rosa Alchemica...*: W.B. Yeats's *Rosa Alchemica, The Tables of the Law* and *The Adoration of the Magi* (1897) was dedicated 'to A.E.'

much simpler, more classic, and with a better feeling for the form of the idea, nothing of unnecessary beauty in them. You used to be carried away by every lovely fancy into side images which marred a little the directness and effect of the central plan. The little song in the *Rose in Shadow* is simply perfect.[1] Long ago you would have said some beautiful thing, say about the sea or stars in this, which we would have forgiven for its beauty, but which would have destroyed the passionate intensity of the poem as a whole. Your art gets more perfect in these things. I suppose it is a necessity of your life that you must write these dreams in prose, but never forget that poetry is their proper language. They are there uncontested. When you put them into prose you invite opposition and argument, from which may the gods save us. I wish I could congratulate myself upon such a steady movement to mastery over my art as you. I write fitfully. Then one of your 'moods' comes and afflicts me and tells me it is only working in shadows I am, and it is all worth[less] and so I lose heart in it all and get no further. I have vague ideas of trying a long poem but I am afraid I must wait for happier days. My new book *The Earth Breath* will I suppose be out sometime this spring as it has been set up in America. I think sadly of it though I don't think there is anything really bad in it. It is too melancholy. This is a cursed disease Pryse[2] left me as a legacy when he went to America. It did not make me unhappy long ago to remember greater things but now it puts me in hell. I am afraid it would be a futile task to try consciously for the Celtic traditional feeling. A certain spirit of it I have but I am not Celt inside, not for many lives. I remember vividly old America and Chaldea, and sometimes as a mountain beyond lesser heights I get glimpses of the Dedanaan days[3] but they lie behind tradition and history; all we know of them have come strained through the Bardic mind of fourteen hundred years ago and it is very inferior to the truth. It is no use writing of these things for a vision of great mystical beauty is not necessarily an inspiration to write beautifully about it. This I know well. Indeed as my perceptions widen I find my inspirations, my genuine ones, narrow to a few emotions of earth. Interpret this for me. When I knew comparatively little of the invisible and my blood was hot I wrote

---

1 *The little song in the* Rose in Shadow...: 'The Rose of Shadow', in *The Secret Rose* (1897), contains a twelve-line poem, 'O, what to me the little room'.
2 *Pryse*: James M. Pryse (1859–1942), American Theosophist, and printer of the Theosophical Publishing House. He was AE's guru. Yeats referred to him as an American hypnotist. He returned to the United States in December 1895.
3 Dedanaan days: the Tuatha dé Danann, a mythical race of deified invaders, replaced the Fir Bolg, and were defeated by the Milesians.

most spiritually. Now as I perceive more and feel less I feel more drawn to write of the ordinary human emotions....

I think I would break any woman's heart whoever happened to love me. She would find me as elusive as the spirit itself. Perhaps it may be I am half a woman inside. My reviewers could never make out whether AE was he or she. Perhaps I am making ready for another life ....

My poems have come out of a sad heart, Willie, and a desperate endeavour to shake myself from it must be the excuse for the longer ones you do not care for. Adios, dear Brother. May the Rose flourish. AE.

JOHN EGLINTON (WILLIAM KIRKPATRICK MAGEE) (1868–1961)

Born in Dublin to Presbyterian parents, he was educated at the High School, where W.B. Yeats* was a contemporary, and at Trinity College, Dublin. He worked at the National Library of Ireland as an assistant librarian—and is eternalized in the library episode in Joyce's *Ulysses*. He became an influential critic (Yeats called him 'our one Irish critic'). In 1898, in the *Daily Express*, he engaged in a mild polemic with Yeats*, AE*, and William Larminie, about Irish legend as the subject matter of national drama. Their discussion appeared the following year as *Literary Ideals in Ireland*. He edited *Dana. An Irish Magazine of Independent Thought* (1904–05). In 'The De-Davisation of Irish Literature' he questions the literary value of cultural nationalism. He retired to England after the Treaty (George Moore* in *Hail and Farewell* depicts him as 'Contrairy John', 'a lonely thorn tree', who is pathologically opposed to Home Rule). His *Irish Literary Portraits* (1931) contains first-hand depictions of Yeats, AE, Moore, Joyce and Edward Dowden.

What Should be the Subjects of National Drama?

(1898)[1]

Supposing a writer of dramatic genius were to appear in Ireland, where would he look for the subject of a national drama? This question might serve as a test of what nationality really amounts to in Ireland—a somewhat trying one, perhaps, yet it is scarcely unfair to put the question to those who speak of our national literature with hardly less satisfaction in the present than confidence in the future. Would he look for it in the Irish legends, or in the life of the peasantry

---

1 First published in the *Daily Express* (1898), this essay appeared the following year in *Literary Ideals in Ireland*, edited by Eglinton.

and folk-lore, or in Irish history and patriotism, or in life at large as reflected in his own consciousness? There are several reasons for thinking that the growing hopes of something in store for national life in this country are likely to come to something. In the great countries of Europe, although literature is apparently as prosperous as ever and is maintained with a circumstance which would seem to ensure it eternal honour, yet the springs from which the modern literary movements have been fed are probably dried up—the springs of simplicity, hope, belief, and an absolute originality like that of Wordsworth. If also, as seems likely, the approaching ages on the Continent are to be filled with great social and political questions and events which can hardly have immediate expression in literature, it is quite conceivable that literature, as it did once before, would migrate to a quiet country like Ireland, where there is no great tradition to be upset or much social sediment to be stirred up, and where the spectacle of such changes might afford a purely intellectual impulse. More important, of course, and certain than any such chances from without is the positive feeling of encouragement which is now taking the place of the hatreds and despondencies of the past. We may think that the peasantry are outside the reach of culture, that the gentry exhaust their function in contributing able officers to the British army, and that, frankly, there is nothing going on in the political or ecclesiastical or social life of Ireland on which to rest any but the most sober hopes for the future, still no one can say that political feebleness or stagnation might not be actually favourable to some original manifestation in the world of ideas. What Renan[1] says, in speaking of the Jews, that 'a nation whose mission it is to resolve in its bosom spiritual truths is often weak politically,' may be used with regard to Ireland as an argument that at least nothing stands in its way in this direction.

The ancient legends of Ireland undoubtedly contain situations and characters as well suited for drama as most of those used in the Greek tragedies which have come down to us. It is, nevertheless, a question whether the mere fact of Ireland having been the scene of these stories is enough to give an Irish writer much advantage over anyone else who is attracted by them, or whether anything but belles lettres, as distinguished from a national literature, is likely to spring from a determined pre-occupation with them. Belles lettres seek a subject outside experience, while a national literature, or any literature of a genuine kind, is simply the outcome and expression of a strong interest in life itself. The truth is, these subjects, much as we may admire

---

1 *Renan*: Ernest Renan (1832–92), French philosopher and orientalist.

them and regret that we have nothing equivalent to them in the modern world, obstinately refuse to be taken up out of their old environment and be transplanted into the world of modern sympathies. The proper mode of treating them is a secret lost with the subjects themselves. It is clear that if Celtic traditions are to be an active influence in future Irish literature they must seem to us worthy of the same compliment as that paid by Europe to the Greeks; we must go to them rather than expect them to come to us, studying them as closely as possible, and allowing them to influence us as they may. The significance of that interest in folk-lore and antiquities, which is so strong in this country, can hardly be different from that of the writings of Herder[1] and others in German literature, and may lie in this, that some hint is caught in such studies of the forgotten mythopœic secret.

As to Irish history and the subjects which it offers—a well-known Scotch Professor once said that Ireland was not a nation because it had never had a Burns nor a Bannockburn. It is, however, as reasonable to think that these glorious memories of Scottish nationality will form a drag on its further evolution as that the want of a peasant poet, or of a recollection of having at least once given the Saxons a drubbing, will be fatal to an attempt to raise people above themselves in this country by giving expression to latent ideals. Ireland must exchange the patriotism which looks back for the patriotism which looks forward. The Jews had this kind of patriotism, and it came to something, and the Celtic peoples have been remarkable for it. The Saxon believes in the present, and, indeed, it belongs to him. The Romance nations, from whose hold the world has been slipping, can hardly be expected just yet to give up the consolations of history.

In short, we need to realise in Ireland that a national drama or literature must spring from a native interest in life and its problems and a strong capacity for life among the people. If these do not, or cannot exist, there cannot exist a national drama or literature. In London and Paris they seem to believe in theories and 'movements,' and to regard individuality as a noble but 'impossible' savage; and we are in some danger of being absorbed into their error. Some of our disadvantages are our safeguards. In all ages poets and thinkers have owed far less to their countries than their countries have owed to them.

---

1 *Herder*: Johann Gottfried von Herder (1744–1803), German poet and philosopher. He collected folk literature in *Stimmen der Völker in Lieder* (1778), and surveyed the stages of cultural development in *Ideen zur Philosophie der Geschichte der Menschheit* (1784–91).

D.P. MORAN (1869–1936)

Born in Manor, Co. Waterford, the son of a building contractor, he was educated at the Christian Brothers' School in Waterford and at Castleknock College, Dublin. He worked on *The Star* in London, where he studied extension economics. Secretary of the London branch of the Irish National League, he joined the Gaelic League in 1896. He returned to Ireland, and contributed, from 1898, polemical articles to the *New Ireland Review*, denouncing 'shoneens' and 'West-Britons' and propagating a Gaelic Catholic Ireland (collected in 1905 as *The Philosophy of Irish-Ireland*). He became proprietor and editor of *The Leader*, enlisting Padraic Pearse and Daniel Corkery. He condemned the Irish Literary Revival, and deprecated Arthur Griffith's *Sinn Féin*. In 1905 he published *Tom O'Kelly*, a political novel set in Ballytown. Conor Cruise O'Brien has called him 'the dark genius of Catholic nationalism'.

Is The Irish Nation Dying?

(1898)[1]

'We are a great race,' said a priest to me the first day I arrived in Ireland. As I had not been in my native land for a long period I was glad to hear that flattering statement. I readily assented to the view, the more so as it was so agreeable. Since then, however, I have spent a month in the South of Ireland, and if I met His Reverence this moment there would be a lively argument.

The resident native of a country is, perhaps, too familiar with everything to see anything. The foreigner is always prejudiced; everything that differs from his view is, so far, bad, for we know that each country would like to rule the destinies of the world for the greater good of the human race. I suggest that the native who has lived for years among a different people is usually the best equipped for the rôle of observer and critic.

I have no desire to add to the existing definitions of that which we call a nation. But if we regard countries as several collections of human energies, then one is differentiated from another by certain general characteristics affecting the manner in which these energies are put forth. A characteristic way of expressing thought, a distinct language, are usually the most prominent marks of a nation. Then there will be found a native colour in arts, industries, literature, social habits, points of view, music, amusements, and so on, throughout all the phases of human activity.

It is scarcely necessary to point out that of the things which go to

---

1 *The New Ireland Review* X (Sept. 1898–Feb. 1899).

the making of a nation, some, such as arts, practically do not exist in Ireland, others, such as the language we speak and the literature we read, are borrowed from another country. There are certainly some traits to be found in Ireland which stamp the people as a distinct race even yet; but they characterise her torpor and decay rather than her development. If one were asked to sum up the present condition of the country in one epigram, he might say that our activities spring from a foreign inspiration, and that we only preserve a national colour about the manner in which we don't do things.

The condition of a country might appear quite hopeless at the first glance, but if there were a real and virile national spirit left in it it would be too soon to say that the nation was dying. That reflection brings us to the question: Is there such a national spirit in Ireland at the present time?

One can never dare to find fault with one's countrymen but he will be instantly told that there are historical causes which explain all our defects. We are ever laying contribution on poor history to explain away our shortcomings. Was it not Fergus O'Connor,[1] of Chartist fame, something of a giant in physique, who told a gaping English mob that only for famines every Irishman would be as fine a specimen as he? And you will meet men every day who will ask you how in the world could Ireland be prosperous considering that England stole our woollen industry from us some hundreds of years ago. Heaven knows we have overdone that sort of nonsense. Those who don't see eye to eye with the 'national' politicians are held up as the enemies of their race—a state of public feeling which is responsible, I think, for the regrettable fact that in Ireland there is no criticism, only abuse.

Still, it were well to look at things as they are, apart from our boasting, our invincible spirit—of which we talk so much—and our '98 processions. There are after all no penal laws now, and we are getting little bits of freedom by degrees. Of course it is true that we cannot make our laws yet. That is a fact which we never forget, and, when we are playing at excuses, it is our trump card. There is an old saying about the making of a country's ballads,[2] the significance of which it would appear we have never rightly appreciated. Everything is to come straight when we can make those precious laws; in the meantime it would be futile to do anything. In other words, all the national life is to be left to bleed out of us, until we come by our right to make laws for the corpse.

---

1 *Feargus O'Connor* (1794–1855) MP for Co. Cork (1832–35); in England he became the foreman of Chartism, and proposed an alliance between the Irish peasant and the English labourer. Daniel O'Connell used to call him 'Balderdash'.
2 *an old saying about the making of a country's ballads*: 'Let me make the ballads, and who will make the laws'.

Throughout my visit a few unwelcome questions would keep troubling me for an answer. Has the relief, such as it is, come too late? Have we been crushed so thoroughly that we are unable to rise now that the weight has been somewhat lightened? I look in vain for that fiery hate of subjection we hear so much of from the political platforms. Contempt for England, and all things pertaining thereto, is not to be found outside the sunburstry songs.[1] The Irish Gael, when he does work himself into a passion of patriotism, generates no further energy than that which enables him to shout himself hoarse at the local political meeting. He then goes home, and looking out over his half-door, self-pitying, contemplates the weakness of his own, and the greatness of the English people. It never strikes him—how could it, as he was never told?—that, were he true to himself, he might, his rags notwithstanding, hold his head as proudly as any other man. I have no desire to direct contempt upon him. There he is, an honest, ignorant, spirit-broken man, swelling with a little national self-esteem whilst the brass bands and the banners of some political procession go by. After that his attitude may be summed up in an expression very frequently on his lips—'There's some "myaw" on poor ould Ireland.' The Land League, which seemed to make a spirited Irishman of him for a time, was—though a great and necessary agitation—in one sense an utter delusion; for, while it imposed itself upon the people as an outburst of patriotism, it was, in its essence, only a material movement. Whilst it bellowed and sent its echoes all over the world, the real national life was asleep or else gliding away.

The tendencies of the people, at the present time, are not altogether inspiring. The ignorant peasants are the most interesting portion of the population. In them are yet to be seen, undeveloped and clouded perhaps, the marks of the Gaelic race. An impassable gulf separates them from any type to be met with in England. They still possess the unspoiled raw material for the making of a vigorous and a real Irish character. The moment we mount up the social scale, the prospect is less pleasing. Teach the peasant to read and write in English, put a black coat on him and let him earn his living in some 'genteel' fashion, and what does he become? Well—they call him Irish.

If you go into a Kerry town in the centre of an Irish-speaking district at the fall of the day, you will probably meet the bank clerk in his knickers and brown boots stroking his moustachios with one hand and petting his dog with the other. He, of course, is above the inter-

---

1 *sunburstry songs*: the sunburst ('*Gal Gréine*' or '*Scal Ghréine*' in Irish) was an emblem which in the ballads of the Young Irelanders was associated with the Fianna.

ests of the common folk. He is not a bad looking specimen of a man, all the same, and he is a Gael if his name is any indication. The type will stand for thousands who are not in banks. A great world of interest and romance surrounds him. Not a stone nor a stream in the neighbourhood but has its history. Most of the interest is, however, inseparable from a knowledge of the Irish language, and of course he knows nothing so common as that; even if he did he would deny it. He might learn much about his country in the English tongue if he cared to, but he prefers to read *Tit Bits*, and discover how many times one issue if stretched out would go round the world and that sort of thing. He is a man of culture amongst the native savages. He may know an Irish phrase or two by rote which he will hurl now and again at the head of the servant-maid and laugh consumedly at the brilliant joke. But where are the distinctive marks of nationality about this man? Further up the street you will probably meet a young fellow who considers himself very clever, and who is credited, in a vague sort of a way, with being a classical scholar, and who certainly has written letters to the newspapers. Though about thirty years of age, he has never done anything for his living, as his father keeps him. The four or five others along with him by no means run any risk of sinking into any early grave by reason of the amount of work they have to do. This group are very 'patriotic.' The Irish language, it is well to remember, is spoken in their hearing every day. However, upon the language and upon the people who speak it, they look down with bragging contempt until they are challenged to justify their attitude. Then their superior airs desert them, and they begin to look sheepish. If you ask them why, as they are patriotic men and have leisure, they are not anxious to learn something of their native tongue and their native literature, they all have the one reply. If they said that the language was too difficult, it might pass as a kind of excuse, even though we knew that some of them stayed up of night learning a little bit of French or Latin. But nothing of the kind. The universal answer is—'Ah, sure, what use would it be to us?' The utilitarian point of view of these young men who during the greater part of the day have nothing useful to do is really exasperating. The busy man who can get profitable work for his every waking hour, may, with some reason, refuse work otherwise desirable, because it would be of no use to him; but when one hears men whose sentiments are hotly 'patriotic' and whose chief business is to kill time, talking in this way, it fills one with dismay. Has the iron gone in so far that even the sense of the ludicrous has been driven out? Of course the fact is, these men take no interest whatever in their country; they have ceased to be Irish, except in name and in what they call 'politics.' How they would chaff one of their friends if he told them that he loved one girl and despised another and showed his feelings by giving all his attention to the latter! For it is to England and her little tittle-tattle periodicals that they turn their eyes and open their hearts. On all sides one sees only too much evidence that the people are secretly content to be a conquered race, though they have not the honesty to admit it. Even the pride that frequently dignifies failure is not there. There is nothing masculine in the character; and when the men do fall into line, with green banners overhead, and shout themselves hoarse, is it not rather a feminine screech, a delirious burst of defiance on a background of sluggishness and despair?

I am being misunderstood if this is considered as a wholesale denunciation of the people; rather is it a denunciation of the false standards of Nationality that have grown up everywhere and are quickly driving everyone into the mire. The native charm of the Gaelic race takes a lot of killing, and good nature we have always with us. When this much has been admitted all that remains to be added is that the people have 'patriotic' opinions. It would be interesting to inquire into the development of that strange idea, that a set of professed political opinions, which may or may not be believed in, constitutes a man a patriot. Any person outside Ireland might, and many actually do, see eye to eye politically with Irishmen. I suggest that, looked at from any comprehensive standpoint, 'Ireland a Nation' is rapidly dissolving out of view.

Are there any causes, besides national degeneration, for this deplorable state of affairs? We must allow at once that an aristocracy and society, more or less alien in blood and almost exclusively alien in feeling, is a great stumbling-block to the growth and development of character racy of the soil. Irish fashionable society is, as we know, a satellite of Mayfair. It follows the English lead in everything. Under these circumstances, what is there for the Irish masses to follow? In Ireland the struggle between the path of least resistance and some other path that is vaguely felt to be national is always going on. The natural tendency is to follow our 'betters.' The people who drive in carriages, and hold authority in the land, form, under normal conditions, the social standards; in them is vested the right to confer social distinction and set the fashion for the manners and popular points of view of the country. In Ireland, where conditions are never normal, and where the right of the classes to influence the country is flouted, the temptation to follow their lead has, nevertheless, been apparently too great. A strong man may stand out against it; but the masses are

not composed of robust units. They must stand in a body with a clearly defined purpose, or drift straggling with the tide. I need not pause to point out what the Irish 'classes' think of anything Irish. In England they are glad enough to glory in the name of Ireland, on the principle, no doubt, that cows in Connaught have long horns. In Ireland they have been brought up to despise everything racy of their native land and of the Gaelic people. During all this century we notice these two contending forces at work—the sense of a separate nationality, with the duties it entails, warring against the natural tendency to imitate the rich and mighty, who happen to be a foreign race. Under the most favourable conditions the struggle would be a hard one. But there was no orderly struggle; every man was left to fight for himself if he chose; he generally didn't choose, and all along the line we have given our nationality away with our eyes open. We have given so much of it away that in recent years the word has lost all meaning for us except as an expression for a certain set of political opinions. We are now neither good English nor good Irish. While everyone has been quarrelling about political party cries, the essentials of national life have been overlooked. From whom can one get any rational expression of that nationality about which all talk so loudly? The '98 processions are a grand intoxication, and no more. What, after all, was the great Wolfe Tone demonstration significant of? Violent, undefined passions of love and hate probably filled most of the great mass who took I don't know how many hours to pass a given point. How many of them had any seriously considered views, reasonable or unreasonable, as to the building up of a national life? What was it all but a mere parade of men being dragged further and further after the British chariot, or rather not being dragged, but going open-eyed that way, the while they cried out to deceive themselves and the world:—
'We are not English!' If not, what are they? let me ask again. They have discarded their language, and they know nothing of their literature. The national character was not allowed to grow from its own roots, but was cut off from the parent tree and engrafted clumsily on the worst branches of the British oak. The prevailing manners at the present time are the resultant of good-nature, the influence of Lover's novels,[1] and a half-hearted attempt to copy the English lower-middle class, who, in the shape of cheap holiday trippers, are a dream of gentility to the Irish snob. Sulky West Britons is the only name by which the great majority of 'Nationalists' can be designated.

---

1 *the influence of Lover's novels*: Samuel Lover (1797–1868) is generally held responsible for introducing the stage-Irishman into Irish fiction.

Of course, everybody agrees to give up the well-to-do and 'respectable' natives—those who send, or would like to send, their children to English schools for good-breeding and the accent—as hopeless. Further, we are constantly told that the mainstay of 'nationality' are the working men in the towns; the people who preserve in some degree the traditions of the Gael are the ignorant peasants. This state of affairs points to a rather hopeless outlook. Improve the condition of the peasants and you wipe out the traditions and the language; advance the more intelligent of the working men, as a consequence of material prosperity, into a higher class, and you weaken the prop even of 'nationality,' and add to the already large contingent of the vulgar-genteel. Truly, there is something rotten in the state.

It is hard to put much blame on the masses. For what are they to do? They look for light and they get none. All the guidance they receive from those who would lead them is to join this political league or that political league, and cry—'Down with the English.' When they have done that they are taught that they have performed the whole duty of Irishmen. As for the language and such trifles as that, the politicians have taught them to ask,—What *use* are they? That material standard has been drummed into them with unwearied energy. It has one bright side. The people are now asking—What *use* are the politicians?

Has history ever presented such a sorry spectacle as an historic nation wiping herself out while her flags are flying and her big drums beating? Why not call ourselves British right away and have done with all this clatter and clap-trap about nothing, which we miscall nationality? It deceives no one but ourselves; and if we would only stop this self-deception for a while we might get a better perspective of things and a clearer view of what nationality means. If instead of talking pikes and blunderbusses and bragging about being a great people we learned in public, what so many have a suspicion of in private, that we are getting parlously near that time when we shan't be a distinctive people at all, we might then mend our ways and do something masculine.

ALICE FURLONG (1875–1948)

Born at Knocklaiguin Lodge, near Pelia, Co. Dublin, one of four daughters of John Furlong, a sporting journalist. Her elder sisters Mary and Katherine were also poets. Mary took care of the family after her parents' death. Alice trained as a nurse at Dr Stevens Hospital in Dublin she was a protégé of Father Mathew Russell; he published her in the *Irish Monthly* from the age of 16. He persuaded Elkin Mathews to publish her first collection of poetry, *Roses and Rue* (1899). It was followed in 1907 by *Tales of Fairy Folks, Queens and Heroes*. Her poetry also appeared in *The Shan Van Vocht*. Frequently anthologised in the early twentieth century (for instance in Quiller-Couch's *Oxford Book of Victorian Verse*), she has dwindled into relative obscurity.

The Bard to His Beloved

(1896)[1]

For love of you and hate of you
My very heart is torn in two;
As you please me or displease,
So I burn, and so I freeze.

I would build your wattled dun
With a gold roof like the sun;
I would stain the trellis bars
With the silver of the stars.

At my bitter heart's behoof
I would wreck your radiant roof,
Of your twinkling trellises
All my anger jealous is.

I would give you great-horned rams,
Fleecy sheep and milk-white lambs,
Fit for any king to own
By the turning of the stone.[2]

I would send your rams astray,
I would wile your sheep away;
Milk-white lambs should be my pelf
For the feeding of the wolf.

I would yoke the sleekest cows
To fine, sword-shaking, shining ploughs;
Turn your land and make it fit
For the sowing of the wheat.

---

1 Published in *The Shan Van Vocht*, 6 Nov. 1896.
2 *turning of stone*: On the 17th of March, St. Patrick turns the stone to change the weather. [*Furlong's note.*]

I would blight your cows with blain,
I would rust your ploughs with rain;
In your furrows, deep and brown,
I would scatter thistle-down.

Under your grey apple-trees
I would hive the heather bees,
Store away in each gold dome
A delicious honey-comb.

I would charm the heather bees
To forsake your apple trees;
Bitter bread might be your share
On the days of Lenten fare.

I would put twelve milking cows
On your pastures green, to browse;
I would stand twelve tubs of cream
On your diary's oaken beam.

Blasted by a curse of mine,
All your cows should ail and pine;
Off your fields I'd skim the dew,
Steal the cream away from you.

I would crown your head with gold,
Robe you, rich, in silken fold;
Win for you a magic wand
Won from Danaan fairy land.[1]

I would set you on a throne,
I would give you all to own—
All of me and all of mine;
I would make you half divine.

I would leave you in sore want,
I would have your hunger gaunt,
I would bring you to my feet
In subjection most complete.

---

1 *Danaan fairy land*: after being defeated by the Milesians, the Tuatha Dé Danann lived immortally underground.

I would lift you to the skies,
I would give you paradise;
I would suffer hell's worst dole
For the saving of your soul.

Wounding, coldness to reprove,
I would wound you in my love;
Suppliant still at your heart's gate
I do worship in my hate.

'Tradita'

(1897)[1]

While you were weary roaming the wide world over,
I gave my fickle heart to a new lover.
Now they tell me that you are lying dead:
O mountains, fall on me and hide my head!

When you lay burning in the throes of fever,
He vowed me love by the willow-margined river.
Death smote you there; here was your trust betrayed:
O darkness, cover me! I am afraid!

Yea, in the hour of your supremest trial
I laughed with him!—the shadow on the dial
Stayed not aghast at my dread ignorance,
Nor God, nor man, nor angel looked askance.

*   *   *

Under the mountains there is peace abiding,
Darkness shall be pavillion for my hiding.
On the grey wold is now a place of rest:
They who sleep lowliest sleep best.

JOSEPH HOLLOWAY (1861–1944)

Born in Dublin, the son of a baker who left him with independent means, he attended the School of Art in Kildare Street, and became an architect. In 1904, he redesigned the Mechanics' Hall and the adjacent morgue as the Abbey Theatre. An

---

1 Published in *The Shan Van Vocht*, 5 Feb. 1897.

avid theatre-goer, he contributed reviews to *The Irish Playgoer* in the early 1900s, and kept a diary for over forty years, which runs to about twenty-five million words, and is an invaluable source of information on Dublin theatre. It was edited by Robert Hogan and Michael J. O'Neill, and published as *Joseph Holloway's Irish Theatre* (3 vols, 1968–70), and *Joseph Holloway's Abbey Theatre: A Selection from his Unpublished Journal, 'Impressions of a Dublin Playgoer'* (1967).

From *A Dublin Playgoer's Impressions*

1899

[Jan.] 5 Thursday—Went to the Catholic Commercial Club where I heard Mr P. H. Pearse deliver a lecture on 'Irish Saga Literature.' The lecturer is quite a young man with a peculiar, jerky, pistol-shot-like delivery that becomes trying to listen to after a time as it makes him hack his sentences into single words & destroys the sense of his remarks on that account often. He was indiscriminantley eulogistic to absurdity over his subject & the adjectives he employed to discribe [*sic*] the extracts which he read from the Sagas were beyond the beyonds of reason when the stuff so praised became known to his listeners. Woeful exaggeration or absurd grotesqueness were the only merits they possessed as far as I could see, but then I am not a Gaelic speaking maniac (harmless but boresome) which makes all the difference in the world. With them art stopped short in the early ages & nothing outside the Irish language is worth a rag. Unfortunately I can see beauty & worth in many things written nowadays even outside our own country which a true Gael could never see or if they did would never acknowledge they did. Mr Pearse missed his mark in not being somewhat critical in his appreciation or if the extracts that he jerked out so inartistically were the best to be found in the saga's [*sic*] few would care to dip deeper into them. Had he been more discriminate in his prose one might be tempted to seek them out (in translation of course) & read them in their entirety but his overpraise of very ordinary exaggerated prose extracts killed the goose, if it had any golden eggs or not, as no one would be tempted to find out for themselves. It is this absurd, unmeaning, almost fanatical, praise that makes the few lovers of the Irish language left us so unbearable & impractical to all broadminded people.... I noticed that Mr Pearse used many words a-la Mrs Malaprop[1] in most inappropriate places & made use of such remarks as 'handed-down by word of mouth'—etc, which struck me as funny.

---

1. *Mrs Malaprop*: character in Richard Brinsley Sheridan's play *The Rivals* (1775), famed for her misuse of words (whence the term 'malapropism').

[*Jan.*] *9 Monday*—Amid most artistic surroundings the members of the National Literary Society held the first conversazione in the Leinster Lecture Hall.... Mr W. B. Yeats explained to us his scheme for a national theatre for the production of Celtic drama under the title of 'The Irish Literary Theatre,' & said it was the intention of the promoters to produce a medieval Celtic drama in verse, & a modern Celtic drama in prose in Dublin in May next. That the scheme may be successful is my ardent wish. If enthusiasm can command success, then it is assured as nothing could be more enthusiastic than the manner in which Mr Yeats has taken up the idea....

[*May*] *6 Saturday*—Attended Mr W. B. Yeats's rambling discourse on *'Dramatic Ideals and the Irish Literary Theatre,'* delivered at No. 6 Stephens Green, under the auspices of the National Literary Society before a fashionable and literary audience. Dr. Sigerson[1] presiding.

First of all, Mr Yeats answered effectively the attacks that had & are been [*sic*] made upon his play, *The Countess Cathleen*, by Frank Hugh O'Donnell[2] & 'The Daily Nation' & read a letter from an eminent divine re the correctness & inoffensiveness of its ideas from the Roman Catholic point of view, on which ground it had been bitterly assailed, for personal reasons it would seem. Then Mr. Yeats rambled off without notes to speak of the drama, & mistook the actor's calling for that of the orator or elocutionist in his ideas of how drama ought to be presented. He advocated that poetry should be rhymed or chanted, & that scenery & dress should be subordinated to the words spoken, in short, that good literary writing should appeal to the mind & not the eye, & that acting should not be acting but recitation of the old sing-song order. Certainly Mr Yeats in speaking acts up to his opinions, as he chants most of his remarks in a monotonous recitative most slumberful in result, only he is so erratic or overladen with ideas, that he continually breaks off at a tangent from a rhymed idea to a commonplace quite foreign to the previous sentence. This habit gives a discourse of his a most unsatisfying effect & leads to no finality of opinion; for at the best you can only guess what he is driving at in the vaguest fashion. He read a passage translated by Arthur Symons from Calderon's 'Life's A Dream'[3] in the way he advocates that all good

---

1 Dr Sigerson: George Sigerson 1836–1925), translator and physician (see Vol. II)
2 *Frank Hugh O'Donnell* (1848–1916), Parnellite politician, MP for Dungarvan, Co. Waterford (1877–85); in his pamphlet *Souls for Gold* (1899), he attacked *The Countess Kathleen* for being blasphemous.
3 Arthur Symons ... Calderon's Life's A Dream': Arthur Symons had written to Yeats on 11 Nov. 1898 that he had just translated 'a lovely song' from Calderón's *La vida es sueño*. It appeared in *The Dome*, June 1899.

dramatic poetry should be read but isn't (Thank God, say I) & I assure you that three gentlemen on the line of chairs with me were almost lulled to rest & peacefully closed their eyes as Mr Yeats's chanting fell on their ears My dear Mr Yeats should bear in mind that if he wants chanting he cannot have acting or *vice versa* & it is all bosh to talk of the acting drama if it is unnatural sing-song or actionless recitation you require. Acting is one thing, recitation another & monotonous rhyming is neither but a sort of effective sleeping draught nothing more or less. A Drama, literary or otherwise, to be effective must be acted—the mirror must be held up to nature—otherwise it is far better left alone. What could be more absurd than to listen to a number of persons monotonously droning out in a sort of rhythmic measure poetic lines supposed to be laden with human passions. Certainly to acquire a taste for such unnatural nonsense must require a deal of training. One would have to be a mystic (I beg pardon a Spiritual) Celtic poet at least!

Count Plunkett[1] proposed in his usual pause-between-each-word-dreamy-way the vote of thanks & Mr George Russell (AE) seconded it & went for Mr Yeats's spiteful detractors and castigated the poor spite of those who published & circulated attacks on his work out of pure malice. Dr Sigerson in putting the vote also had a 'go' at the 'geese' who will always screech, especially those of Celtic breed.

[*May*] 8 *Monday*—At last the Irish Literary Theatre is become an actuality—& the red letter occurrence in the annals of the Irish Literary movement took place in the Antient Concert Rooms where a large & most fashionable audience filled the hall. There a pretty little miniature stage, perfectly appointed, had been erected. W. B. Yeats's miracle play in 4 acts, 'The Countess Cathleen' was the work selected to inaugurate the Theatre & from one cause or another the event was looked forward to with considerable excitement and interest owing to the hostility exhibited in certain quarters to the author.[2] Expectation was satisfied, as an organised claque of about twenty brainless, beard-

---

1 *Count Plunkett*: George Noble, Count Plunkett (1851–1948), antiquarian and Sinn Fein politician. He was vice-president of the Irish National Literary society, and became director of the National Museum (1907–16). He was a papal Count. His son, the poet Joseph Mary Plunkett, was one of the leaders of the Easter Rising.

2 *The Countess Cathleen*...: the controversial nature of the play insured its publicity. Frank Hugh O'Donnell denounced it as blasphemous in the *Freeman's Journal* and in pamphlets; the *Daily Nation* urged the audience to demonstrate against its anti-Catholic sentiment; and, in a letter to the *Freeman's Journal*, thirty students from the National University attacked Yeats's representation of the peasant. Policemen were sent to the theatre to prevent rioting. 'I had', wrote Yeats, 'no reason to regret the result, for the stalls, containing almost all that was distinguished in Dublin, and a gallery of artisans alike insisted on the freedom of literature'.

less, idiotic-looking youths did all they knew to interfere with the progress of the play by their meaningless automatic hissing and senseless comments—& only succeeded in showing what poor things mortals can become when the seat of reason is knocked awry by animus, spite & bigotry.[1] Thomas Davis seemed to be the particular 'bee in their bonnets,' as they frequently made reference to the poet. That some disturbance should take place had been expected for weeks long back as a comment of W. B. Yeats on that vigorous poet's work had got Davis' admirers' backs up some time ago & evidently they had not had time to descend yet, so that the said admirers thought the production of one of Yeats' dramatic poems was a fitting opportunity to vent the venom of their spleen & thus gain a babble reputation. Their 'poor spite' was completely frustrated by enthusiastic applause which drowned their empty-headed expressions of dissension. But enough of this & let me record without further delay the gratifying success of the undertaking. Yeats' beautiful narrative poem in dramatic form, 'The Countess Cathleen' as the literary world knew for years past reads admirably but that it would make a good actable play as well its performance to-night incontestably proved. It was weirdly, fantastically, pathetically, or picturesquely effective by turns & as I followed its progress, Poe's words, 'All that we see or seem is but a dream within a dream'[2] floated in on my mind & a spiritual, half-mystic visionary sensation crept over my senses as I watched enraptured as if I were in fairy land the merchant-demons trafficking in the immortal souls of the poor starving peasants—until the benevolent, beautiful, self-sacrificing 'Countess Cathleen' barters her own to save the others & dies broken-hearted, to be awarded a crown of glory 'for so supreme a sacrifice.' As to the interpretation it was not acting in the ordinary sense but a laudable attempt 'to lend to the beauty of the poet's rhyme the music of the voice' in half chant-like tones & that the artists wholly succeeded in their 'object all sublime' I cannot truthfully say except in a few instances, as indistinctness was the result of their efforts, but then (the official journal of the Irish Literary Theatre '*Beltaine*' says) 'the speaking of (poetic) words, whether to music or not, is, however, so perfectly among the lost arts that it will take a long time before our actors, no matter how willing, will be able to forget the ordinary

---

1 *brainless, beardless, idiotic-looking youths...*: fellow students of James Joyce, who refused to join their protest. He recalls the event in Chapter V of *A Portrait of the Artist as a Young Man*. *The Daily Nation*, 9 May 1899, protested 'in the name of morality and religion and Irish nationality against the performance', and urged that 'the audience should hoot the impersonators of such grotesque impiety from the Irish stage'.
2 *All that we see ...*: Edgar Allan Poe, 'A Dream Within a Dream', 10–11.

methods of the stage or to perfect a new method;' therefore it will be seen that perfection was not to be hoped for, nor expected, even by those most interested in the movement. That this 'new method' of delivering dramatic poetry was even so effectively employed was a 'feather in the cap' of those who advocated its adoption....

Miss May Whitty[1] made an ideal 'Countess Cathleen,' sympathetic & lovable in manner & spoke her lines with a delicious, natural, sweet musical cadence expressively & most distinctly, looking the 'rare and radiant maiden' of the poet's dream to the life & always using simple yet graceful and picturesque gestures & posing artistically yet never artificially in every episode so as to create many memorable & beautiful stage pictures.... Miss Florence Farr[2] as 'Aleel' a bard declaimed all her lines in majestic beautiful rhythmic manner grand to listen to & most impressive if occasionally indistinct.... The awesome atmosphere of the opening act in Shemus's cottage ere the Demon-Merchants come on the scene to capture souls was capitally realized by all & struck the true key note of this legendary little drama with unerring correctness....

Much of the last act was spoiled by a creaky door & the too liberal use of palpable tin-tray-created thunder claps. The staging was good if unpretentious & the dresses excellent & the piece went without a hitch although the stage room was somewhat scanty)....

The twenty would-be immovable obstructions presented a sorry sight at the end as the thunders of applause which greeted the play, players & author simply wiped their ill-timed efforts out. By-the-way in taking his call Mr Yeats seemed most embarrassed & did not know what to do until prompted by the 'devil' in the person of Mr Trevor Lowe he took Miss Whitty's hand & shook it heartily & afterwards that of Miss Farr which he treated similarly. Mr Yeats must have felt very proud at the complete triumphing over his enemies! Note. Chanting is hard to follow until the ear grows accustomed to listening to measured rhythm. Many of the artists failed to allow those in front to clearly understand what they spoke. This should not be, of course, as the first essential of effective stage work is the clearness of articulation in the speech of the actors.

---

1 *Dame May Whitty* (1865–1948), English actress. She made her London debut in 1881, and had a long and distinguished career, starring in such films as *The Lady Vanishes* (1938) and *Mrs Miniver* (1942).

2 *Florence Farr* (1860–1917), an actress who acted in plays by Todhunter, Shaw* and Yeats*. She married an actor, Edward Emery, in 1884; they divorced in 1894. She became Principal of a girls' school in Ceylon, where she died of cancer. She had been a close friend of Yeats in England.

[*May*] *9 Tuesday*—To-night the second dramatic work prepared for our delight by the Irish Literary Theatre was presented & completely captured the listeners' attention at once & held them almost breathlessly mute to its tragic climax with the exception of well-timed oases of enthusiastic applause after almost every exit. A more absorbing play than Mr Edward Martyn's '*The Heather Field*' I have not witnessed for a long time. When I read the piece last week at the National Library I became deeply interested in its developement [*sic*] as the dialogue was so natural, yet full of beauty & keen observation & the action—ever culminating & well sustained, but my interest in the work was intensified considerably in following its working-out on the stage & the admirable manner in which it was acted & the grip it got on the highly cultured & fashionable gathering present proved it to be a work of real dramatic grit. The influence of the giant Norwegian dramatist, Ibsen, was distinctly traceable in Mr Martyn's clever & splendidly characterised play & the master's 'The Enemy of the People' was brought to my mind in watching Carden Tyrrell's anxiety about the success of his reclaimed 'Heather Field'. Evidently the unruly youths of last night had 'no crow to pluck' with Mr Martyn as they remained elsewhere & the audience were allowed to listen to the performance without any disturbance whatever. 'For which relief, much thanks.'...

One cannot give any idea of the amount of pathos & tenderness the dramatist has worked round the incidents leading up to the tragedy of this dreamer whose mind gives way on hearing that his dream has turned out nought but a dream, after all. His love for his brother, son, & friend were beautifully indicated & his utter hopelessness in trying to make his wife understand him one little bit was also admirably hit off. As a character study, the part of 'Carden Tyrrell' would be hard to better & his every phase of emotion was simply & clearly brought out with rare dramatic skill by Mr Thomas Kingston[1] who gained the complete sympathy of the house for the poor misunderstood visionary. There was no chanting in this play but the mirror was held up to nature rigidly & nature beheld herself reflected therein without flattery or exaggeration in speech action or manner....

The play was effectively staged & must be recorded a triumphant success as an acting drama. The applause was immense at the conclusion & the actors were called & recalled several times & finally Mr

---

1 *Thomas Kingston* (fl. 1890) played at the Adelphi and at the Comedy Theatre, Haymarket. He went to Australia and played Parsifal at the Majesty's Theatre in Sydney.

Edward Martyn appeared on the scene several times to receive the homage deservedly due to him ere the delighted spectators dispersed. Beyond a doubt the admirable performance of 'The Heather Field' has made the Irish Literary Theatre an unmistakably established fact, & an institution which all Irish people of culture & refinement ought to be justly proud of....

TIMOTHY MICHAEL HEALY (1855–1931)

Born at Bantry, the son of a clerk of the poor law union who could recite Homer, he was educated at the Christian Brothers School in Fermoy. In 1871 he emigrated and worked as a shorthand clerk for the North Eastern Railway Company in Newcastle-upon-Tyne, studying literature in his spare time (he had a prodigious memory, and was reputed to know most of Shakespeare by heart). In 1878 he moved to London, becoming parliamentary correspondent for *The Nation*, reporting on the rise of Parnell and his obstructionist policy. In 1880, Parnell cabled him from America to organize the Canadian end of his tour. In Montreal Healy referred to him as 'the uncrowned king of Ireland'. In 1882 he married Erina, the daughter of the politician T.D. Sullivan, who would be the first member of the Parliamentary party to repudiate Parnell. As MP for Wexford (1880–83), he secured an amendment to the Land Act which became known as the 'Healy Clause'. It protected tenants from charges on their improvements to the rented property. He was imprisoned in 1883 on charge of treason, and, after his release, was returned MP for Co. Monaghan. He was MP for South Londonderry (1885–86) and North Longford (1887–92). When, in the 1886 by-election, Parnell proposed Captain O'Shea as the 'unpledged' member for Galway, Healy, with Joseph Biggar, felt his leader's personal life was clouding his political acumen; they began to refer openly to Katharine O'Shea as Parnell's mistress. Yet initially he stood by Parnell at the time of the leadership crisis in 1890, until the publication of Gladstone's letter refusing any further cooperation with the Irish leader. It was Healy who asked if the collaboration with Gladstone was to end 'in the stench of the Divorce Court', and who retorted to the cry that Parnell was the party's master, 'Who is to be the mistress of the party?' The other anti-Parnellite leaders he accused of kow-towing to the Liberals; they expelled him from the Irish National Federation in 1895. From 1892 to 1910 he represented North Louth. After the reunion of the Irish Party he supported John Redmond, but was expelled in 1902. With his former foe William O'Brien he founded the All-for-Ireland League in 1910, and was returned for North-East Cork, a seat he lost to Sinn Féin in 1918. He represented William Martin Murphy and the employers in the inquiry into the Lock-Out strike of 1913. In 1922 he became the first Governor-General of the newly established Irish Free State.

On the Boer War: A Speech[1]

February 7, 1900

These are the people you want to put over the Dutch in South Africa. You want a settlement. You want the two races to mingle hand in hand waving the Union Jack and singing 'Rule Britannia,' and you would put in ascendency over the Dutch such men as have made their ascendency in Ireland hateful, and who call your own Irish soldiers 'rebels.' What wonder, then, if there is disaffection! I understand the principles of Pirate Smith who hoisted his black flag at Bristol and made war with all and sundry for the sake of booty. He had not a Bible on board. He swore by the Jolly Roger and not by the Ten Commandments. You want to syndicate Christianity, and take the Twelve Apostles into your limited liability company. Then you hold up your hands like the pharisee and invite other nations to rejoice that the English possess such virtues. The Irish people are a feeble folk, and the only advantage which the Irish have is that we are able to contemplate your virtues at close quarters. But the Dutch, you see, are 7,000 miles away. Therefore misunderstandings may crop up between you and the Dutch. They have not the advantage which the Irish have in this House of seeing the British constantly, of reading your newspapers, and chanting Rudyard Kipling. But I am told that Rudyard Kipling is an author whom it is extremely difficult to translate into Dutch. Therefore, I am inclined to doubt the theory that in the furnace of this war the Afrikander[2] and the Briton will be fused by the bloody flux of battle. No, we are here to-day to testify in the name and for the cause of race nationality. As I have already said, you may win. All your calculations are based upon that. If you win you will think that the results have justified your efforts. You will not think of the statesmanship of Gladstone, who held that there were bounds beyond which empire should not go, that there were limits even to British strength, and that by excessive effort, the extensor and contractor muscles of even the British right arm might tire. You disdain Gladstonian Councils, and you will go on and on and on in so far as time and circumstances permit you, and as long as you are successful you chant hosannas to the glories of your jingo statesmen. Is this wisdom? By what means do you hope to keep the Empire you have got? By what means do you hope to conciliate the races which you govern? Do you think the excuses on which you annex territory satisfy anyone but yourselves? I remember in 1879, when you were thinking of

---

1 From Hansard, Vol. 78 (1900).
2 *Afrikander*: obsolete form of 'Afrikaner'.

annexing Burma. The Tory Government was about to go out, but nobody knew that in India, where Reuter's telegrams are the great adjunct of civilisation, as anybody who turns up the history of that time will see. There came over suddenly one day a telegram from Rangoon, 'King Thebaw is drinking.'[1] I do not think the hon. Baronet the Member for Carlisle was much disturbed at that.[2] I had never heard of King Thebaw myself, and I was a little more surprised when I read the next day, 'The king is drinking still.' A week elapsed, and then came a telegram, 'King Thebaw has murdered his mother-in-law and three maiden aunts.' Nothing more was heard for two days, and then there arrived another telegram, 'Thebaw is drinking still.' Shortly after this there were troops on the frontier. This was something like the Uitlanders'[3] grievance. But before righteousness could invade Burma the Beaconsfield Ministry fell, and another five years elapsed in which Thebaw and his misfortunes, his want of temperance and the loss of his maiden aunts were entirely ignored by the British public. In June, 1885, a most appropriate circumstance occurred, for we put out the Gladstone Government over a dispute about the whisky tax, and within a week Baron Reuter telegraphed from Burma, 'Thebaw is drinking still,' and within a month or two after that you made war on Burma and King Thebaw was himself a Uitlander. Your pretext for taking Johannesburg is just the same. There, there is gold, and in Burma there were rubies, and commercial principles must triumph over backward native ways. Your policy is a policy of grab, and I do think it is pitiable that a nation whose qualities are great, whose courage is indomitable, whose resources are endless, should have, at this day, the canker of corruption eating at her heart. The principles which made you great are forgotten. The principles which make the British name a terror are represented by a statue of Cromwell outside Westminster Hall. You put up that statue to the memory of the author of the massacre of Drogheda after 'quarter' had been promised to its garrison,[4] at the very moment when your own forces are besieged in

---

1 *King Thebaw is drinking*: Thebaw's accession to the Burmese throne in 1878 was marked by a massacre of forty princes and princesses; he was exiled to Yadana Giri, India, after 1886. This episode of colonial justification was recalled by William Thomas Cosgrave, President of Dail Éireann, in a debate about the constitution on 21 September 1922.
2 *the hon. Baronet the Member for Carlisle was much disturbed at that*: Sir Wilfrid Lawson (1829–1906), MP for Carlisle, was a zealous advocate of Temperance; he was also an advocate of Home Rule, and an opponent of the Boer War.
3 *Uitlander*: Afrikaans for 'outlander'.
4 Cromwell ordered the massacre of Drogheda in September 1649; it was said that nearly 3,500 people died. It is not clear whether the order for 'no quarter' was given.

Ladysmith.[1] Where was your historic conscience? We represent a small country and a small fraction of the Queen's dominions, but we have memories and we have hopes, and here lift up the voice of that country in protest against your policy, and we declare that the men of Ireland will never join you in any composition of wrong or of injustice.

---

1 The siege of Ladysmith by Boer forces took place between 2 November 1899 and 28 February 1900.

Publishers' Acknowledgements

The editors and publisher gratefully acknowledge permission to reprint the following copyright material:

Augusta Gregory
Reproduced with permission of Colin Smythe:
'The Day Draws Near'
'What Have I Gained'
'Wild Words I Write'
Extracts from *Diaries 1892–1902*
in James Pethica, ed., *Lady Gregory's Diaries 1892–1902* (Gerrards Cross: Colin Smythe, 1995)
extract from *The Felons of Our Land*
in *Cornhill Magazine*, 47 (1900).

Joseph Holloway
Reproduced with permission of the Trustees of the National Library Ireland:
Extracts from Joseph Holloway's Journal, A Dublin Playgoer's Impressions (1899: Jan. 5 & 9; May 6, 8 & 9).

Douglas Hyde
Reproduced with permission of Douglas Sealy:
'I Shall Not Die for Thee'; 'The Red Man's Wife'; 'Young Breed of the Tresses' from *Love Songs of Connaught* (Dublin: Gill and Macmillan, 1893)
'Like a Star in the Night'
from *The Shan Van Vocht*, 4 September 1896
The Necessity for De-Anglicising Ireland
in *The Revival of Irish Literature: Addresses by Sir Charles Gavan Duffy, Dr George Sigerson, Dr Douglas* Hyde (London: Fisher Unwin, 1894).

Anna Margaret (Amanda) McKittrick Ros
Reproduced with permission of Belfast Central Library:
Extract from *Irene Iddesleigh* (chapter 18 and 19)

Index of First Lines

General Index

General Index

General Index

General Index